American Proverbs
and
Proverbial Phrases

A
DICTIONARY
of
AMERICAN PROVERBS
and
PROVERBIAL PHRASES
1820–1880

BY

ARCHER TAYLOR

AND

BARTLETT JERE WHITING

THE BELKNAP PRESS OF
HARVARD UNIVERSITY PRESS
Cambridge, Massachusetts

1958

FOR
HASSELTINE AND HELEN

Preface

The following collection contains the proverbs and proverbial phrases found in a variety of American authors whose works were published between 1820 and 1880. These authors have been chosen as representative of various regions and for their popularity. Although Thomas C. Haliburton was a Nova Scotian, his works have also been excerpted because they were very widely read in the United States and often contain early instances of locutions generally used there. It will be noted that very few proverbs or phrases used by Haliburton lack parallels in the United States. In order to make this collection more adequately representative of American traditional usage, Matthews' *Dictionary of Americanisms* has also been excerpted for the years covered.

That we begin with 1820 and end with 1880 is accidental to the degree that our earliest source was published in the one year and our latest in the other, but our choice of the general period was in no way fortuitous. Although the writings of no literature are at any time completely devoid of proverbs there are times in which the genres being written are peculiarly likely to be rich in proverbs and proverbial phrases. In the Middle Ages, for example, there was a belief in the validity of generalized wisdom, a belief given literary sanction by textbooks and the precepts of the rhetoricians. Mediaeval rhetorical practises lasted on into the Elizabethan period, and the use of proverbs was increased by the popularity of such collections of proverbs as John Heywood's, the example of such influential authors as George Pettie and John Lyly, and especially in the case of proverbial phrases, by the desire of novelists and dramatists to reproduce the vigorous homely idiom of contemporary speech.

The years with which we concerned ourselves saw the emergence and flowering in the United States of regional literature, extravagant, brash, exaggerated, humorous sketches, tales and novels whose purpose was to depict the life and language of non-urban areas in New England (Down East), the South and the Old Southwest. Description and dialogue are couched in local dialects, sometimes faithfully reproduced, sometimes heightened, and are studded with proverbs and proverbial phrases. There is no exaggeration in the statement that at no other time have so many American writers made proverbs so obvious an ingredient in their style. Along with the native urge to utilize the earthy phrases of the uneducated and semi-educated classes, there was a degree of literary influence on fiction coming from Sir Walter Scott, who made more use of proverbs than perhaps any other leading English novelist, both in his Scottish novels, where they serve to enrich the dialect, and elsewhere because he manifestly enjoyed them. Humorous writings and fiction have been our richest sources, but a glance at our Bibliography will show that we have not limited ourselves to them. We are the first to admit that we have been guilty of omissions and that our choice has been as often arbitrary as directed. Nevertheless we make no very serious apology for omissions, since experience toward the end of our accumulations showed that each added book gave few new sayings. The relatively infrequent items which we have taken over bodily from *The Dictionary of Americanisms* strengthen our belief that the law of diminishing returns was in effect. If we have any regret it is that we did not make greater use of periodicals, but some of the most important of these, such as *The Spirit of the Times,* are not readily accessible, they are bulky, and we did not intend this compilation to be the work of two lifetimes, even those which we may modestly expect. We have, however, been able to draw on a number of pieces which were originally published in *The Spirit of the Times* and subsequently collected by their authors or in miscellany volumes.

We must emphasize what is no doubt perfectly obvious, namely, that though we call our book a Dictionary of *American* Proverbs, its contents are no more American in a narrow sense of the word than the contents of dictionaries of *English, French,* or *German* proverbs are peculiar to the national stock or geographical limits of the countries in which they are found. Even if we disregard the international character of many proverbs, sayings are a standard commodity of export and import and the bulk of American proverbial material crossed the Atlantic with our ancestors.[1] Inevitably, however, there are many sayings, especially perhaps among the comparisons and proverbial phrases, which are clearly American.

In the choice of proverbs and phrases for inclusion we have been guided by such standard works as G. L. Apperson, *English Proverbs and Proverbial Phrases;* Janet E. Heseltine and W. G. Smith, *The Oxford Dictionary*

---

[1] For an attempt to analyze the origins of the sayings found in one American state, see the *Frank C. Brown Collection of North Carolina Folklore,* ed. N. I. White, Durham, N. C., I (1952) 332–342.

of English Proverbs; Burton E. Stevenson, *The Home Book of Proverbs, Maxims and Familiar Phrases;* and Morris P. Tilley, *A Dictionary of the Proverbs in England in the Sixteenth and Seventeenth Centuries* and by our own experience as students and collectors of proverbs. These authorities offer no definition of a proverb save the pragmatic one of inclusion. In other words, we find in them proverbial words like "aboveboard," "Every Tom, Dick and Harry"; proverbial phrases like "From A to Z"; proverbial verb phrases like "To cut off one's nose to spite one's face"; familiar quotations like "Absence makes the heart grow fonder" and "From out of the abundance of the heart the mouth speaketh"; clichés like "Age before beauty" and "In a coon's age"; aphorisms and sententious remarks like "Beauty is in the eye of the beholder"; platitudes and truisms like "Boys will be boys"; physiological observations, weather proverbs, and other statements of fact or supposed fact like "A full belly makes a strong back" and "Rain before seven, shine before eleven"; calendar rhymes like "Thirty days hath September," etc.; proverbial taunts or nicknames like "Big head, little wit," which might also be called a physiological or anatomical observation, and "John Bull" or "Barnburners"; proverbial comparisons like "As red as a beet"; and synonyms for "to die" or "to be drunk" like "to kick the bucket" and "to be over the bay." We have included the foregoing texts and have chosen also texts of similar quality. In two regards we have been somewhat more generous than our authorities. We have included a larger variety of synonyms for dying and being drunk and have made an especial effort to list proverbial comparisons. The selection of proverbial comparisons in our authorities seems somewhat haphazard. We would not insist upon the traditional nature of all the comparisons cited below, but until more material for comparison and study is available we have preferred to give a wide-ranging choice of texts.

In general, it is not unfair to say that we have allowed ourselves no more liberty of choice and decision than that which has been assumed by all conscientious compilers of dictionaries of proverbs from Erasmus on down. If new collections of proverbs contained only what was found in earlier compilations, their value would be limited to the evidence which they present for geographical and chronological spread. At no one time can it be safely concluded that all sayings have been identified, annotated and enshrined.

Defining a proverb in dictionary terms is no simple matter, and such definitions as we have found give no satisfactory standard for including and excluding tests. To define a proverb as "The wit of one, the wisdom of many" is instructive and throws light on its essential characteristics, but does not provide us with a test readily usable in deciding to accept or reject a particular item. W. C. Hazlitt's valuable discussion of these matters in the preface to a collection that has been superseded by our authorities shows where efforts in this direction lead.[2] He cites an old characterization of a proverb as short, plain, common, figurative, ancient, and true and then proceeds to give reasons for objecting to all six of these adjectives. Nor will he accept the definition in Worcester's Dictionary: "a common and pithy expression, which embodies some moral precept or admitted truth." After discarding these two definitions, he says that he "would rather set a proverb down as an expression or combination of words conveying a truth to the mind by a figure, periphrasis, antithesis, or hyperbole" (p. x). On the next page he accepts legal proverbs like "Forbearance is no acquittance" that have at best a very slight figurative element and "whimsical absurdities," which are not easily understood to be means of conveying a truth. The proof of the pudding is in the eating, and Hazlitt's choice of texts for inclusion varies widely from his definition and is virtually the same as that used by our authorities. One might go on and cite more definitions from such learned works as Friedrich Seiler, *Deutsche Sprichwörterkunde* (Munich, 1922), which is no doubt the best general treatise on proverbs, but they will not supply a convenient practical aid in identifying a particular saying as a proverb.

The old definition that Hazlitt rejects is perhaps as good as any formal inventory of the characteristics of a proverb can be. It is virtually the definition used by our authorities. Shortness is a relative term, and would in many instances call for interpretation. Plainness refers obviously to the speaker and hearer of the proverb and not to a later user, collector, or student. "By hook or crook" was, for example, once fully intelligible and can no longer be adequately explained. Commonness can be readily demonstrated by quoting parallels. Figurativeness is, on the other hand, a quality more difficult to define and must be taken with some elasticity. It is not an essential quality. "All's well that end's well" has been accepted for centuries as proverbial and can scarcely be called figurative. Age is also a quality to be interpreted with much generosity. As far as the record goes, "An apple a day keeps the doctor away" is less than a century old, but it

---

[2] *English Proverbs and Proverbial Phrases* (3d ed., London, 1907), pp. vii–xii. For a more extensive discussion of these problems see B. J. Whiting, "The Nature of the Proverb," *Harvard Studies and Notes in Philology and Literature*, XIV (1932), 273–307. Selwyn G. Champion's *Racial Proverbs* (N. Y., 1938) gives (pp. 3–9) an interesting, if not always instructive, group of "proverbs and sayings about proverbs."

and other proverbs with even shorter histories have been accepted by our authorities as proverbial. Truth is obviously a quality signifying the applicability of the saying to a particular situation and not its validity in the abstract. "Sing before breakfast and you'll cry before night" is no doubt an acceptable proverb, but few would probably care to maintain that it is a general truth. Were it so, singing in the shower would be rare indeed. Hazlitt's six characteristics imply some degree of stability in form, but he does not add this as a requirement (unless he implies it by mentioning such characteristics as commonness and age). Truth appears, moreover, in a very special and characteristic way. A proverb—and here we are including all the varieties such as comparisons, phrases, and Wellerisms—summarizes a situation and in its own inimitable way passes some sort of judgment on it or characterizes its essence. This is perhaps the true inwardness of the proverbial genre. All the examples quoted at the beginning of these remarks show this peculiar quality, whatever may be their form. It can be best illustrated by contrasting proverbial materials that we have included with traditional materials that we have rejected. Both "Once in a blue moon" and "Once upon a time" are traditional statements regarding time. The former we would regard as proverbial, while rejecting the latter. Both are short, plain, common, and old, but "Once upon a time" is neither figurative nor true (i. e., applicable to a present situation and summarizing it).

Efforts to set proverbs apart from such closely allied categories as clichés, aphorisms, sententious remarks, and familiar quotations meet with many difficulties. Clichés neatly illustrate these difficulties. "All my eye and Betty Martin" (cited below in a somewhat different form) is a cliché that our authorities accept as proverbial. It is, in its way, a summing up of a situation. Not all clichés, although they may be short, plain, and common, have been similarly accepted. On the other hand, "That's flat," a cliché that has the additional quality of figurativeness, seems to deserve inclusion. One might perhaps say that a cliché is a familiar quotation of anonymous origin and a familiar quotation is a cliché of known or supposedly known origin. The existence of variant versions implies the popular acceptance of a familiar quotation and justifies including it in a collection of traditional proverbs. Wordsworth said "The child is father of the man," but tradition has preferred the contrast of "boy" and "man" and gives us "The boy is father of the man." Rephrasings of the Shakespearean "Something is rotten in the state of Denmark" have become proverbial. Pope's verses lie behind "To forget is human, to forgive divine." But variation in form is not essential. Tradition and our authorities accept Bacon's "Knowledge is power" without making any ado over it.

The difficulties just described are in no way peculiar nor are they limited to proverbs. No one has set up a definition of a folktale that enables a student or collector to identify one as anything other than "a tale current among the folk." This leaves both "tale" and "folk" in the air. At least half a dozen kinds of tales can be easily pointed out in the Household Tales of the Brothers Grimm. Some of them have little or no narrative content; some of them have been excerpted from literature and adapted to popular idiom. The definition of a ballad has been the occasion of long dispute. Professor Louise Pound has called attention to many kinds of songs found in Francis James Child's *English and Scottish Popular Ballads.* Nor are difficulties of this kind limited to folklore or characteristic of it. A definition of the novel which will include Defoe's *Robinson Crusoe,* Beckford's *Vathek,* Conan Doyle's *Adventures of Sherlock Holmes,* Joyce's *Ulysses,* and Aldous Huxley's *Brave New World* will be as all-inclusive as the definition of a proverb that rests upon our authorities. And yet all the books *are* novels and all these sayings *are* proverbs.

The texts in the following collection have been arranged alphabetically according to the first noun or, when a noun is lacking, according to the first important word. The examples follow in chronological sequence after the first, which is dated (the digits 18 are omitted), except that a given author's works are not separated. After the examples of the proverb in American tradition the source in the Bible is cited, if there is one, and then the parallels in the reference works cited in the Bibliography in alphabetical order except that *Notes and Queries* stands at the end of the citations. Parallels from modern literature then follow in alphabetical arrangement according to authors. We have made no systematic effort to call attention to the appearance of a specific saying in languages other than English, although foreign sources or parallels are often quoted in many of the collections to which we refer.

Our obligations are many, and first of all to the collections and officials of the libraries of Harvard University and the University of California. Among the friends who have aided us with advice and counsel we mention particularly Professor C. Grant Loomis of the University of California. To our wives we owe thanks for assistance in ways proverbial and beyond.

A. T.

June 1958   B. J. W.

Bibliography

I

TEXTS

Alcott *Little Women:* Louisa M. Alcott, *Little Women* (1868–1869), New York, 1928. Pp. 1–258 in this edition were published in 1868, and pp. 259–535 in 1869.

Baldwin *Flush:* Joseph G. Baldwin, *The Flush Times of Alabama and Mississippi,* etc. (1853), 7th ed., New York, 1854.

Barnum *Struggles: Struggles and Triumphs; or, Forty Years' Recollections of P. T. Barnum,* etc. (1869), Buffalo, 1873.

Bennett *Border:* Emerson Bennett, *The Border Rover* (1857), Philadelphia, n. d.

Bennett *Kate:* Emerson Bennett, *Kate Clarendon: or, Necromancy in the Wilderness* (1854), Philadelphia, n. d.

Boker: George Henry Boker, *Bankrupt* (1853), *The World a Mask* (1850) in *Glaucus & Other Plays,* ed. Sculley Bradley, Princeton, 1940.

Boucicault: Dion Boucicault, *Dot* (1859), *Flying Scud* (1866), *Presumptive Evidence* (1869) in *Forbidden Fruit & Other Plays,* eds. Allardyce Nicoll and F. T. Cloak, Princeton, 1940.

Bowman *Bear-Hunters:* Anne Bowman, *The Bear-Hunters of the Rocky Mountains,* Boston, 1860.

Briggs *Harry:* [Charles F. Briggs], *The Adventures of Harry Franco,* *A Tale of the Great Panic,* 2 vols., New York, 1839.

Browne *Artemus:* [Charles F. Browne], *Artemus Ward His Book* (1864), New York, 1867.

Browne *Artemus Ward His Travels:* [Charles F. Browne], *Artemus Ward His Travels,* New York, 1865.

Browning *Forty-Four:* Meshach Browning, *Forty-Four Years of the Life of a Hunter* (1859), Philadelphia, 1864.

Burke *Polly:* Thomas A. Burke, ed., *Polly Peablossom's Wedding and Other Tales,* Philadelphia, 1851.

Butler *Nothing:* William A. Butler, *Nothing to Wear* (1857) *and Other Poems,* New York, 1899.

Cartwright *Autobiography: Autobiography of Peter Cartwright, the Backwoods Preacher,* ed. by W. P. Strickland, New York, n. d. (1856).

Cary *Clovernook:* Alice Cary [Carey], *Clovernook or Recollections of Our Neighborhood in the West.* First and Second Series, New York, 1852, 1853.

Cary *Married:* Alice Cary *Married, Not Mated* (1856), New York, 1859.

Chamberlain *Confession:* Samuel E. Chamberlain, *My Confession.* Introduction and Postscript by Roger Butterfield, New York, 1956. Apparently written before the outbreak of the Civil War.

BIBLIOGRAPHY

Clemens: Samuel Langhorne Clemens. With the exceptions noted below, the edition of Clemens' works used was the American Artists Edition, New York, n. d.

Clemens *Enterprise: Mark Twain of the Enterprise* (1862–1864) . . . ed. Henry N. Smith, Berkeley, 1957.

Clemens *Fairbanks: Mark Twain to Mrs. Fairbanks* (1867–   ), ed. Dixon Wecter, San Marino, 1949.

Clemens *Gilded:* S. L. Clemens and Charles D. Warner, *The Gilded Age* (1873), 2 vols.

Clemens *Innocents: The Innocents Abroad* (1869), 2 vols.

Clemens *Letters: Mark Twain's Letters,* (1853–   ) arranged . . . by A. B. Payne, 2 vols., New York, 1917.

Clemens *Love Letters: The Love Letters of Mark Twain* (1868–   ), ed. Dixon Wecter, New York, 1949.

Clemens *Roughing: Roughing It* (1872), 2 vols.

Clemens *Sandwich: Letters from the Sandwich Islands . . . By Mark Twain* (1866), Stanford, 1938.

Clemens *Sketches: Sketches Old and New* (1875), various dates.

Clemens *Tom: The Adventures of Tom Sawyer* (1876).

Clemens *Tramp: A Tramp Abroad* (1879), 2 vols.

Clemens *Washoe: The Washoe Giant in San Francisco, Being Hitherto Uncollected Sketches By Mark Twain* (1863–1866), ed. Franklin Walker, San Francisco, 1938.

Clift *Bunker:* [William Clift], *The Tim Bunker Papers, or Yankee Farming,* etc., New York, 1868.

Conant *Earnest Man:* H. C. Conant, *The Earnest Man; A Sketch of the Character and Labors of Adoniram Judson, First Missionary to Burmah,* Boston, 1856. Quotations from Judson's letters are inserted in the chronological sequence of references according to their respective dates.

Cooke, *Foresters:* John Esten Cooke, *The Last of the Foresters,* New York, 1856.

Cooper: James Fenimore Cooper. With the exception noted below, the edition of Cooper's novels used was the Mohawk, New York, 1895–1901.

Cooper *Chainbearer: The Chainbearer; or, the Littlepage Manuscripts* (1845).

Cooper *Pathfinder: The Pathfinder: or, The Inland Sea* (1840).

Cooper *Pilot: The Pilot; A Tale of the Sea* (1824).

Cooper *Pioneers: The Pioneers, or The Sources of the Susquehanna* (1823).

Cooper *Prairie: The Prairie* (1827).

Cooper *Redskins: The Redskins; or, Indian and Injin* (1846).

Cooper *Satanstoe* (1845), eds. Robert E. Spiller and J. D. Coppock, New York, 1937.

Cooper *Spy: The Spy: A Tale of the Neutral Ground* (1821).

Crockett *Account: An Account of Col. Crockett's Tour to the North and Down East, in the Year of Our Lord One Thousand Eight Hundred and Thirty-four,* etc., Philadelphia, 1835. Of uncertain authorship.

Crockett *Exploits: Col. Crockett's Exploits and Adventures in Texas . . . Written by Himself,* Philadelphia, 1836. Of uncertain authorship.

Crockett *Life: A Narrative of the Life of David Crockett . . . Written by Himself,* Philadelphia, 1834. Of uncertain authorship.

Curtis *Potiphar:* [George W. Curtis],

The Potiphar Papers (1853), New York, 1854.

Daly *Man:* Augustin Daly, *Man and Wife* (1870) *& Other Plays,* ed. Catherine Sturtevant, Princeton, 1942.

Dana *Two:* Richard H. Dana, Jr., *Two Years Before the Mast, A Personal Narrative* (1840), *With a Supplement by the Author and Introduction and Additional Chapter by His Son,* Boston, 1911.

Davis *Downing:* [Charles A. Davis], *Letters of J. Downing, Major, Downingville Militia, Second Brigade,* etc., New York, 1834.

Derby *Phœnixiana:* [George H. Derby], *Phœnixiana, or Sketches and Burlesques—by John Phœnix . . .* (1855), A New Edition . . . With an Introduction by John Kendrick Bangs, New York, 1903.

Derby *Squibob:* [George H. Derby], *The Squibob Papers,* New York, 1865.

Dorson *Jonathan:* Richard M. Dorson, *Jonathan Draws the Long Bow,* Cambridge, Mass., 1946. The references are only to Dorson's quotations of early newspapers and books that have been inaccessible to us. They are inserted in the chronological sequence of citations according to their respective dates.

Durivage *Three:* Francis A. Durivage, *The Three Brides, Love in a Cottage, and Other Tales,* Boston, 1856.

Eggleston *Circuit:* Edward Eggleston, *The Circuit Rider; A Tale of the Heroic Age,* New York, 1874.

Eggleston *School-Master:* Edward Eggleston, *The Hoosier School-Master,* New York, 1871.

Eliason: Norman E. Eliason, *Tarheel Talk: An Historical Study of the English Language in North Carolina to 1860,* Chapel Hill, N. C., 1956. Based on letters and diaries.

Emerson *Journals: Journals of Ralph Waldo Emerson, with Annotations,* eds. Edward Waldo Emerson & Waldo Emerson Forbes, 10 vols., Boston, 1909–1914.

Emerson *Letters: The Letters of Ralph Waldo Emerson,* ed. Ralph L. Rusk, 6 vols., New York, 1939.

Emerson *Works: The Works of Ralph Waldo Emerson,* ed. James Eliot Cabot. Standard Library Edition, 14 vols., Boston, n. d.

Fairfield *Letters: The Letters (1835–1847) of John Fairfield,* ed. Arthur G. Staples, Lewiston, Maine, 1922.

Field *Pokerville:* Joseph M. Field, *The Drama in Pokerville,* etc. (1847), published as 2d part of W. T. Porter, *Major Thorpe's Scenes in Arkansaw,* Philadelphia, 1858.

Haliburton *Attaché:* [Thomas C. Haliburton], *The Attaché; or Sam Slick in England* (1843), 2d ed., 4 vols., London, 1846.

Haliburton *Clockmaker* I: [Thomas C. Haliburton], *The Clockmaker; or The Sayings and Doings of Samuel Slick of Slickville,* [First Series, 1836], 4th ed., London, 1838.

Haliburton *Clockmaker* II: . . . Second Series (1838), 4th ed., London, 1839.

Haliburton *Clockmaker* III: . . . Third Series, London, 1840.

Haliburton *Letter:* [Thomas C. Haliburton], *The Letter-Bag of the Great Western; or Life in a Steamer,* London, 1840.

Haliburton *Nature:* [Thomas C. Haliburton], *Nature and Human Nature,* 2 vols., London, 1855.

Haliburton *Old Judge:* [Thomas C. Haliburton], *The Old Judge; or,*

BIBLIOGRAPHY

Life in a Colony, 2 vols., London, 1849.

Haliburton *Sam:* [Thomas C. Haliburton], *Sam Slick's Wise Saws and Modern Instances; or What He Said, Did, or Invented,* 2 vols., London, 1853.

Haliburton *Season-Ticket:* [Thomas C. Haliburton], *The Season-Ticket,* London, 1860.

Hall *Legends:* James Hall, *Legends of the West,* Philadelphia, 1832.

Hall *Purchase:* B. R. Hall [Robert Carlton, pseud.], *The New Purchase: or, Seven and a Half Years in the Far West,* 2 vols., New York, 1843.

Hall *Soldier's Bride:* James Hall, *The Soldier's Bride and Other Tales,* Philadelphia, 1833.

Hall *Wilderness:* James Hall, *The Wilderness and the War Path* (1846), New York, 1849.

Hammett *Piney:* [Samuel A. Hammett], *Piney Woods Tavern; or Sam Slick in Texas,* Philadelphia, 1858.

Hammett *Stray:* [Samuel A. Hammett], *A Stray Yankee in Texas,* by Philip Paxton, New York, 1853.

Hammett *Wonderful:* [Samuel A. Hammett], *The Wonderful Adventures of Captain Priest,* etc., New York, 1855.

Harris *Sut:* George W. Harris, *Sut Lovingood; Yarns Spun by a Nat'ral Born Durn'd Fool,* etc., New York, 1867.

Harris *Uncle Remus:* Joel Chandler Harris, *Uncle Remus His Songs and His Sayings,* New York, 1881. Although dated 1881, this book was published in 1880.

Hawthorne *House:* Nathaniel Hawthorne, *The House of Seven Gables and The Snow Image and Other Twice-Told Tales* (1851). Works,

Standard Library Edition, III, Boston, 1883.

Hawthorne *Mosses:* Nathaniel Hawthorne, *Mosses from an Old Manse* (written 1842–1846, collected 1854), Works, Standard Library Edition, II, Boston, 1882.

Hawthorne *Twice-Told:* Nathaniel Hawthorne, *Twice-Told Tales* (written c1830–1840, collected 1851), Works, Standard Library Edition, I, Boston, 1882.

Holmes *Autocrat:* Oliver Wendell Holmes, *The Autocrat of the Breakfast-Table* (1858), Works, I, Boston, 1892.

Holmes *Elsie:* Oliver Wendell Holmes, *Elsie Venner* (1859–1860), Works, V, Boston, 1892.

Holmes *Poet:* Oliver Wendell Holmes, *The Poet at the Breakfast-Table* (1872), Works, III, Boston, 1892.

Holmes *Professor:* Oliver Wendell Holmes, *The Professor at the Breakfast-Table* (1860), Works, II, Boston, 1892.

Hooper *Simon:* [Johnson J. Hooper], *Some Adventures of Captain Simon Suggs,* etc. (1845), Americus, Ga., 1928.

Irving *Attorney:* John T. Irving, *The Attorney: or, The Correspondence of John Quod,* New York, [1842].

Irving *Bracebridge:* Washington Irving, *Bracebridge Hall* (1820–1822), Works, VI, New York, 1860.

Irving *Tales:* Washington Irving, *Tales of a Traveller* (1823–1824), Works, VII, New York, 1860.

Irving *Wolfert:* Washington Irving, *Wolfert's Roost* (1855), Works, XVI, New York, 1861.

Jones *Batkins:* [Joseph S. Jones], *Life of Jefferson S. Batkins,* etc., Boston, 1871.

Jones Country: John B. Jones, Life and Adventures of a Country Merchant, etc. (1854), Philadelphia, 1857.

Jones Wild: John B. Jones, Wild Western Scenes, Second Series, etc. (1856), Philadelphia, 1863.

Jones Winkles: [John B. Jones], The Winkles; or The Merry Monomaniacs, etc., New York, 1855.

Judd Margaret: Sylvester Judd, Margaret. A Tale of the Real and the Ideal, Blight and Bloom (1845), rev. ed., Boston, 1857.

Judd Richard: Sylvester Judd, Richard Edney and the Governor's Family, Boston, 1850.

Kelly Humors: Jonathan F. Kelly, The Humors of Falconbridge, Philadelphia, [1856]. A posthumous publication of earlier writings.

Kennedy Horse-Shoe: John P. Kennedy, Horse-Shoe Robinson (1835, rev. ed., 1852), ed. Ernest E. Leisy, New York, 1937.

Kennedy Swallow: John P. Kennedy, Swallow Barn; or, A Sojourn in the Old Dominion (1832, rev. ed., 1851), ed. Jay B. Hubbell, New York, 1929.

Langdon Ida: Mary Langdon [Pike], Ida May (1854), Boston, 1855.

Lewis Odd: [Henry C. Lewis], Odd Leaves from the Life of a Louisiana "Swamp Doctor," by Madison Tensas, M. D. (1843), Philadelphia, n. d.

Lincoln: The Collected Works of Abraham Lincoln . . . eds. Roy P. Basler, M. D. Pratt and L. A. Dunlap, 8 vols., New Brunswick, N. J., 1953.

Locke (Nasby): David R. Locke, The Struggles (Social, Financial, and Political) of Petroleum V. Nasby, etc. (1872), Toledo, 1880. The "letters" were published from 1862 on.

Longstreet Georgia: [Augustus B. Longstreet], Georgia Scenes, etc. (1835), 2d ed., New York, 1840.

Loomis Farmer's Almanac: C. Grant Loomis, "Proverbs in The Farmer's Almanac(k)," Western Folklore, XV (1956), 172–178.

Lowell Biglow: James R. Lowell, The Biglow Papers (1848, 1867), Poems, II, Riverside Edition, VIII, Boston, 1893.

McCloskey Across: James J. McCloskey, Across the Continent (1870–73), in Davy Crockett & Other Plays, eds. Isaac Goldberg and Hubert Heffner, Princeton, 1940.

Mayo Kaloolah: W. S. Mayo, Kaloolah, or Journeyings to the Djébel Kumri, An Autobiography of Jonathan Romer (1849), 5th ed., New York, 1854.

Melville Works: The Works of Herman Melville, Standard Edition, London, 1922–1924.

Melville Confidence-Man: The Confidence-Man: His Masquerade (1857), Works, XII, 1923.

Melville Israel: Israel Potter: His Fifty Years of Exile (1855), Works, XI, 1923.

Melville Mardi: Mardi: and A Voyage Thither (1849), 2 vols., Works, III, IV, 1922.

Melville Moby-Dick: Moby-Dick; or, The Whale (1851), 2 vols., Works, VII, VIII, 1922.

Melville Omoo: Omoo: A Narrative of Adventures in the South Seas (1847), Works, II, 1922.

Melville Piazza: Piazza Tales (1856), Works, X, 1923.

Melville Pierre: Pierre; or, The Ambiguities (1852), Works, IX, 1923.

Melville Redburn: Redburn: His First Voyage, etc. (1849), Works, V, 1922.

Melville Typee: Typee: A Peep at

Polynesian Life, etc. (1846), Works, I, 1922.

Melville *White Jacket: White Jacket; or, The World in a Man-of-War* (1850), Works, VI, 1922.

Mitchell *Reveries:* [Donald G. Mitchell], *Reveries of a Bachelor,* etc. (1850), New York, 1851.

Nash *Century:* Willard G. Nash, *New England Life. A Century of Gossip or, The Real and the Seeming,* New York, 1876.

Neal *Brother J:* [John Neal], *Brother Jonathan: or, The New Englanders,* 3 vols., Edinburgh, 1825.

Neal *Charcoal:* Joseph C. Neal, *Charcoal Sketches,* etc. (1837), 5th ed., Philadelphia, 1840.

Neal *Down-Easters:* John Neal, *The Down-Easters &c., &c., &c.,* 2 vols., New York, 1833.

Neal *Rachel:* John Neal, *Rachel Dyer: A North American Story,* Portland, Maine, 1828.

New Hope; or, The Rescue. A Tale of the Great Kanawha, New York, 1855. Originally published as *Young Kate.* Cited as Anon., *New Hope.*

Paul *Courtship:* [G. Henry Howard Paul], *The Courtship and Adventures of Jonathan Homebred,* etc., New York, n. d. [c1860]. Authorship and date suggested to us, tentatively, by Lyle Wright of the Huntington Library.

Porter *Major:* W. T. Porter, ed., *Major Thorpe's Scenes in Arkansaw,* etc., Philadelphia, 1858.

Richardson *Beyond:* Albert D. Richardson, *Beyond the Mississippi; From the Great River to the Great Ocean . . . 1857–1867,* Hartford, Conn., 1867.

Richardson *Secret:* Albert D. Richardson, *The Secret Service, The Field, The Dungeon, and The Escape,* Hartford, Conn., 1865.

Riley *Puddleford:* Henry H. Riley, *The Puddleford Papers; or, Humors of the West,* New York, 1857. Three-quarters of this book had appeared in 1854 as *Puddleford and Its People.*

Robb *Squatter:* John S. Robb, *Streaks of Squatter Life,* etc. (1843), Philadelphia, n. d.

Saxe *Poems: The Poems of John Godfrey Saxe,* Boston, 1868.

Sedley *Marian:* Henry Sedley, *Marian Rooke; or, The Quest for Fortune,* New York, 1865.

Shillaber *Ike:* Benjamin P. Shillaber, *Ike Partington; or, The Adventures of a Human Boy and His Friends,* Boston, 1879.

Shillaber *Knitting-Work:* Benjamin P. Shillaber, *Knitting-Work,* etc., New York, 1859.

Shillaber *Mrs. Partington:* Benjamin P. Shillaber, *Life and Sayings of Mrs. Partington,* etc., New York, 1854.

Smith *Arp:* [Charles H. Smith], *Bill Arp, So Called. A Side Show of the Southern Side of the War,* New York, 1866.

Smith *Downing:* [Seba Smith], *The Life and Writings of Major Jack Downing,* etc. (1833), 2d ed., Boston, 1834.

Smith *Letters:* [Seba Smith], *John Smith's Letters, With 'Picters' to Match,* etc., New York, 1839.

Smith *My Thirty:* [Seba Smith], *My Thirty Years Out of the Senate. By Major Jack Downing* (1859), New York, 1860. The first 242 pages reprint Smith *Downing.*

Smith *'Way: 'Way Down East; or, Portraitures of Yankee Life,* Philadelphia, 1854.

Stephens *Fashion:* Ann S. Stephens, *Fashion and Famine,* New York, 1854.

Stephens *High Life:* [Ann S. Stephens], *High Life in New York,* by Jonathan Slick, Esq., 2 vols., London, 1844.

Stephens *Mary Derwent:* Ann S. Stephens, *The Old Homestead,* New York, 1855.

Stephens *Mary Derwent:* Ann S. Stephens, *Mary Derwent,* Philadelphia, [1858].

Stowe *Uncle:* Harriet B. Stowe, *Uncle Tom's Cabin* (1851), Novels and Stories, Fireside Edition, I, Boston, 1910.

Taliaferro *Carolina Humor:* David K. Jackson, ed., *Carolina Humor, Sketches by Harden E. Taliaferro* (1860–1863), Richmond, Va., 1938.

Taliaferro *Fisher's:* [Harden E. Taliaferro], *Fisher's River (North Carolina) Scenes and Characters. By "Skitt, Who Was Raised Thar,"* New York, 1859.

Thompson *Chronicles:* [William T. Thompson], *Chronicles of Pineville,* etc., (1843), Philadelphia, n. d.

Thompson *Major:* [William T. Thompson], *Major Jones's Courtship,* etc., 2d ed., Philadelphia, 1844.

Thomson *Doesticks:* Mortimer Thomson, *Doesticks' Letters,* etc. (1855), Philadelphia, n. d.

Thomson *Elephant:* Mortimer Thomson and E. W. Underhill, *The History and Records of the Elephant Club,* etc., New York, 1856.

Thomson *Plu-ri-bus-tah:* Mortimer Thomson, *Plu-ri-bus-tah,* etc., Philadelphia, 1856.

Wallack *Rosedale:* Lester Wallack, *Rosedale; or, The Rifle Ball* (1863) in Isaac Goldberg and Hubert Heffner, eds., *Davy Crockett & Other Plays,* Princeton, 1940.

Whitcher *Widow:* Frances M. Whitcher, *The Widow Bedott Papers,* New York, 1856.

Whitehead *Wild Sports:* Charles E. Whitehead, *Wild Sports in the South; or, The Camp-Fires of the Everglades,* New York, 1860.

Wiley *Billy:* Bell I. Wiley, *The Life of Billy Yank,* Indianapolis, 1952. Based in large part on letters and diaries.

Wiley *Johnny:* Bell I. Wiley, *The Life of Johnny Reb,* Indianapolis, 1943. Based in large part on letters and diaries.

Willis *Fun:* Nathaniel P. Willis, *Fun-Jottings,* etc., New York, 1853.

Willis *Life:* Nathaniel P. Willis, *Life, Here and There,* etc. (1850), New York, 1854.

Willis *Paul:* Nathaniel P. Willis, *Paul Fane,* etc., New York, 1857.

II

REFERENCE WORKS

Allan PADS XV (1951): Philip F. Allan, "A Sample of New Hampshire Dialect," pp. 65–68.

Apperson: George L. Apperson, *English Proverbs and Proverbial Phrases. A Historical Dictionary.* London, [1929].

Ayers PADS XIV (1950): Lucille Ayers and others, "Expressions from Rural Florida," pp. 74–80.

Babcock: C. Merton Babcock, "Melville's Proverbs of the Sea," *Western Folklore,* XI (1952), 254–265.

BIBLIOGRAPHY

Barrère and Leland: Albert Barrère and C. G. Leland, *A Dictionary of Slang, Jargon & Cant.* 2 vols. [London], 1889–1890.

Bartlett: John R. Bartlett, *Dictionary of Americanisms.* 4th ed., Boston, 1877, reprinted, 1896.

Bartlett *Familiar Quotations:* John Bartlett, *Familiar Quotations.* 11th ed., Boston, 1937.

Berrey: Lester V. Berrey and Melvin Van den Bark, *The American Thesaurus of Slang.* New York, 1947.

Bey PADS II (1944): Constance Bey and others, "A Word-List from Missouri," pp. 53–62.

Boshears: Frances Boshears, "Proverbial Comparisons from an East Tennessee County," *Bulletin of the Tennessee Folklore Society,* XX (1954), 27–41.

Bradley: F. W. Bradley, "South Carolina Proverbs," *Southern Folklore Quarterly,* I (1937), 57–101.

Bradley PADS XIV (1950): F. W. Bradley, "A Word-List from South Carolina," pp. 3–73.

Champion: Selwyn Gurney Champion, *Racial Proverbs. A Selection of the World's Proverbs Arranged Linguistically.* New York, 1938.

Combs PADS II (1944): Josiah Combs, "A Word-list from the Southern Highlands," pp. 17–23.

DA: *A Dictionary of Americanisms,* ed. M. M. Matthews, 2 vols., Chicago, [1951].

DAE: *A Dictionary of American English,* edr. Sir W. A. Craigie and J. R. Hulbert. 4 vols., Chicago, 1938–1944.

Dalton PADS XIII (1950): A. P. Dalton, "A Word-list from Southern Kentucky," pp. 22–23.

Faden: I. B. Faden, *How America Speaks and Writes. A Dictionary of American Idioms with a Swedish Vocabulary.* [Stockholm, 1949].

Farmer: John S. Farmer, *Americanisms—Old & New,* etc. London, 1889.

Farmer and Henley: John S. Farmer and W. E. Henley, *Slang and Its Analogues,* etc., 7 vols., [London], 1890–1904.

Fife: Austin E. Fife, "Folkways of a Mormon Missionary in Virginia," *Southern Folklore Quarterly,* XVI (1952), 92–123.

Figh PADS XIII (1950): Margaret G. Figh, "A Word-list from 'Bill Arp' and 'Rufus Sanders,'" pp. 3–15.

Funk: Charles Earle Funk, *A Hog on Ice and Other Curious Expressions.* New York, [1948].

Green: B. W. Green, *Word-book of Virginia Folk-Speech.* Richmond, Va., 1899.

Halpert: Herbert Halpert, "Proverbial Comparisons from West Tennessee," *Bulletin of the Tennessee Folklore Society,* XVII (1951), 49–61; "More Proverbial Comparisons from West Tennessee," *ibid.,* XVIII (1952), 15–21.

Hardie: Margaret Hardie, "Proverbs and Proverbial Expressions Current in the United States East of the Missouri and North of the Ohio Rivers," *American Speech,* IV (1929), 461–472. See the following.

Jente *American:* Richard Jente, "The American Proverb," *American Speech,* VII (1931–1932), 342–348. A commentary on the preceding.

Laughlin PADS II (1944): Hugh C. Laughlin, "A Word-list from Buncombe County, North Carolina," pp. 24–27.

Lean: *Lean's Collectanea.* Collections by Vincent Stuckey Lean. 4 vols. in 5, Bristol, Eng., 1902–1904.

Loomis *Thoreau:* C. Grant Loomis, "Henry David Thoreau as Folklorist," *Western Folklore* XVI (1957), 90–106 [esp. 101–104].

McAtee: W. L. McAtee, *Rural Dialect of Grant County, Indiana, in the 'Nineties,* privately printed, 1942.

McAtee: *Additional:* W. L. McAtee, *Additional Dialect of Grant County, Indiana,* privately printed, 1943.

McAtee *Grant County:* W. L. McAtee, *Grant County, Indiana, Speech and Song,* privately printed, 1946.

McAtee PADS XV (1951): W. L. McAtee, "Gleanings from the Dialect of Grant County, Indiana," pp. 51–64.

NC: B. J. Whiting, "Proverbs and Proverbial Sayings" in N. I. White and Paull F. Baum, eds., *The Frank C. Brown Collection of North Carolina Folklore,* Durham, N. C., I (1952), 331–501.

NED: *A New English Dictionary on Historical Principles.* 13 vols. (with *Supplement*), Oxford, 1884–1933.

Nixon PADS V (1946): Phyllis J. Nixon, "A Glossary of Virginia Words," pp. 9–43.

NQ: *Notes and Queries,* 1st Series, I (1850)–.

Oxford: W. G. Smith and Janet E. Heseltine, *The Oxford Dictionary of English Proverbs.* 2d ed. by Sir Paul Harvey, Oxford, 1948.

PADS: *Publications of the American Dialect Society,* I (1944)–.

Partridge: Eric Partridge, *A Dictionary of Slang and Unconventional English.* 4th ed., London, [1951].

Partridge *Clichés:* Eric Partridge, *A Dictionary of Clichés.* 3d ed., London, [1947].

Randolph and Wilson: Vance Randolph and George P. Wilson, *Down in the Holler. A Gallery of Ozark Folk Speech.* Norman, Okla., 1953.

Schele de Vere: Maximilian Schele de Vere, *Americanisms; The English of the New World.* New York, 1872.

Smith *Browning:* Cornelia M. Smith, "Proverb Lore in *The Ring and the Book,*" PMLA, LVI (1941), 219–229.

Snapp: Emma L. Snapp, "Proverbial Lore in Nebraska," *University of Nebraska Studies in Language, Literature and Criticism,* XIII (1933), 53–112.

Stevenson: Burton Stevenson, *The Home Book of Proverbs, Maxims and Familiar Phrases.* New York, 1948.

Stoett: F. A. Stoett, *Nederlandsche Spreekwoorden, Spreekwijzen, Uitdrukkingen en Gezegden.* 4th ed., 2 vols., Zutphen, 1923–1925.

Svartengren: T. Hilding Svartengren, *Intensifying Similes in English.* Lund, 1918.

Taylor *Comparisons:* Archer Taylor, *Proverbial Comparisons and Similes from California,* Folklore Studies 3, Berkeley, 1954.

Taylor *Index:* Archer Taylor, *An Index to "The Proverb,"* FF Communications, 113, Helsinki, 1934.

Taylor *Investigations:* Archer Taylor, "Investigations of English Proverbs, Proverbial and Conventional Phrases, Oaths, and Clichés," *Journal of American Folklore,* LXV (1952), 255–265.

Thornton I, II: Richard H. Thornton, *An American Glossary,* etc., 2 vols., paged continuously, London, 1912.

BIBLIOGRAPHY

Thornton III: Richard Thornton, *An American Glossary*, etc., Vol. III, edited by Louise Hanley, Madison, Wis., 1939. Originally published in *Dialect Notes,* 1931–1939, now issued with drop-folio pagination.

Tidwell PADS XI (1949): James N. Tidwell, "A Word-list from West Texas," pp. 3–15.

Tidwell PADS XIII (1950): James N. Tidwell, "Comments on Word-lists in PADS," pp. 16–21.

Tilley: Morris P. Tilley, *A Dictionary of the Proverbs in England in the Sixteenth and Seventeenth Centuries.* Ann Arbor, 1950.

Walker: Warren S. Walker, "Proverbs in the Novels of James Fenimore Cooper," *Midwest Folklore* III (1953), 99–107.

Whiting *American Wellerisms:* B. J. Whiting, "American Wellerisms of the Golden Age," *American Speech,* XX (1945), 1–11.

Whiting *Chaucer:* B. J. Whiting, *Chaucer's Use of Proverbs,* Harvard Studies in Comparative Literature, 11. Cambridge, Mass., 1934.

Whiting *Devil:* B. J. Whiting, "The Devil and Hell in Current English Literary Idiom," *Harvard Studies and Notes in Philology and Literature,* XX (1938), 201–247.

Whiting *Drama:* B. J. Whiting, *Proverbs in the Earlier English Drama,* etc., Harvard Studies in Comparative Literature, 14. Cambridge, Mass., 1938.

Whiting PADS XI (1949): B. J. Whiting, "A Maine Word-list," pp. 28–37.

Whiting *Scots* I, II: B. J. Whiting, "Proverbs and Proverbial Sayings from Scottish Writings before 1600," *Mediaeval Studies,* XI (1949), 123–205, XIII (1951), 87–164.

Williams PADS II (1944): Cratis D. Williams, "A Word-list from the Mountains of Kentucky and North Carolina," pp. 28–31.

Wilson: George P. Wilson, "Folk Speech" in *The Frank C. Brown Collection of North Carolina Folklore,* Durham, N. C., I (1952), 505–618.

Wilson PADS II (1944): George P. Wilson, "A Word-list from Virginia and North Carolina," pp. 38–52.

Woodard PADS VI (1946): C. M. Woodard, "A Word-list from Virginia and North Carolina," pp. 4–43.

Yamamoto *Dickens:* Tadao Yamamoto, *Growth and System of the Language of Dickens. An Introduction to a Dickens Lexicon.* Revised ed., [Osaka]: Kansai University Press, 1952.

American Proverbs
and
Proverbial Phrases

❦ A ❧

A, 1. She read the dictionary through from A to izzard (39 Briggs *Harry* I 4). DAE A 4; Green 201; NED Izzard; Stevenson 155–156:7; Tidwell PADS XI 3; C. B. Clason *Blind Drifts* (1937) 125; Charles King *Harper's Magazine* LXXVI (1888) 783 [He] knows "from a to izzard" every detail of a soldier's needs; E. M. Rhodes *West Is West* (1932) 61 [He] had him explain all about minin', from A to izzard.

2. We know several folks who have a way of beating round and boxing the compass, from A to Z, and back again (56 Kelly *Humors* 192). The pronunciation of Z in this quotation is uncertain. DAE A 4 I will teach you your alphabet from A to Zed; NED Z 3, commenting "The name Zee, now widespread in the United States of America, appears to have had some early currency in England," *Supplement* (A); Stoett 2, 78; NQ 13 i 468 Zed, CXLVI (1924) 17 Zed; Hugh Austin *Murder of a Matriarch* (1936) 98 Z.

3. If you say A, they'll make you say B (37 Neal *Charcoal* 190). Stoett 3.

A, B, C, 1. You are ignorant of the very ABC of meanness (72 Clemens *Roughing* II 288). P. G. Wodehouse *Laughing Gas* (1936) 196 The merest ABC of mothercraft.

2. Just as easy as a-b-c (79 Clemens *Tramp* I 262). Farmer and Henley I 5; Partridge 1; Svartengren 347. Cf. NC 360; Taylor *Comparisons* 73.

3. He has got their names as pat as A B C (c67 Clemens *Sketches* 351).

4. As plain as A. B. C. (34 Davis *Downing* 103; Smith *My Thirty* 431). NC 360; K. M. Livingston *The Dodd Cases* (1934) 258. Cf. Taylor *Comparisons* 73 simple.

A 1, 1. An A 1 kin' o' speech (61 Lowell *Biglow* 229, 279 The true fus-fem'ly A 1 plan; Holmes *Poet* 282 Where did he get those expressions "A 1" and "prime" and so on? They must have come from somebody who had been in the retail dry-goods business, or something of that nature, *Professor* 19 All right. A 1, 165 some "old Burbon," which he said was A 1, 169 producing . . . the bottle of whiskey described as A 1). Fannie Hurst *Humoresque* (1919) 248 That proves how you stand with me. A one! Ace high!

2. They [cigars] air A 1, and no discount (65 Sedley *Marian* 192).

3. We stand letter A. No. 1 abroad (40 Haliburton *Letter* 197, *Clockmaker* III 148, *Attaché* I 250, III 179; Thompson *Chronicles* 77 stood "A. No. 1"; Field *Pokerville* 94; Hammett *Piney* 59 A number one, first best, 118, 124, 140, 288; Barnum *Struggles* 166). Bartlett 1; DAE A No. 1; Farmer 1; Farmer and Henley I 1–2;

1

Schele de Vere 341–342; Stevenson 1778:5; W. S. Masterman *The Rose of Death* (1936) 151.

4. We claim him No. 1, letter A (36 Haliburton *Clockmaker* I 49, II 16, III 126). DA A No. 1.

Abraham. For her spirit has been conveyed by angels to Abraham's bosom (25 Conant *Earnest Man* 335; Cartwright *Autobiography* 514 He has long since fallen on sleep, and gone home to Abraham's bosom). Luke 16:22; NED Bosom 1 b; *Oxford* 1; Stevenson 224–225:14; Tilley A8; NQ 8 xi 67, 214, 494.

Abroad. The female boarder . . . looked so puzzled, and, in fact, "all abroad," . . . that I left her to recover her wits (60 Holmes *Professor* 5). NED Abroad 5.

Absence. Absence makes the heart grow fonder (54 Shillaber *Mrs. Partington* 271). Bradley 59 (the refrain of a popular song of the nineties); Fife 119; Lean III 411; *Oxford* 1; Snapp 80:6; Stevenson 4:6; Tilley A10; NQ CLXXXII (1942), 345, CLXXXIII (1943), 59; P. B. Kyne *Tide of Empire* (1932) 203 Too late he was experiencing the truth of the old adage; Robert Carson *The Revels Are Ended* (1936) 39, 318; D. B. Wyndham Lewis *Ronsard* (London 1944) 175.

Abundance. Out of the abundance of the heart, the mouth speaketh (53 Baldwin *Flush* 73). Matt. 12:34; Stevenson 1111:10, 2193:6; Stoett 848; Tilley A13; Whiting *Drama* 34, 98; J. G. Kunstmann "And Yet Again 'Wes das Herz voll ist, des gehet der Mund über" *Concordia Theological Quarterly* XXIII (1952) 509–527.

Accidents, 1. Never mind, Boss, you know accidents will happen (43 Thompson *Chronicles* 48; Clemens *Tom* 215 might). Stevenson 7:4; Bertram Atkey *Smiler Bunn* (1937) 224.

2. Accidents will happen in the best regulated places (38 Haliburton *Clockmaker* II 283–284; Melville *Pierre* 328 "It is a rather strange accident, I confess, my friend, but strange accidents will sometimes happen." "In the best of families," rejoined the other, a little ironically; Durivage *Three* 233 Mistakes will happen in the best regulated families). Apperson 1; Lean III 411; NC 360; *Oxford* 2; Stevenson 7:4; Yamamoto *Dickens* 400; NQ 11 x 271, 296, 351; W. W. Jacobs *Snug Harbour* (1931) 459; Vance Randolph *The Devil's Pretty Daughter* (1955) 23 Things like that do happen, even in the best families, but there ain't nothing to be gained by talking about it; R. S. Surtees *Plain or Ringlets?* (London [1860]) 350 Misfortunes [referring to accidents in the kitchen].

Account, 1. To hand in one's accounts [i. e., to die]. 73 DA Account.

2. We have a long account to settle (66 Boucicault *Flying Scud* 193). NED Settle vb. 35.

3. We intended to . . . squar our accounts with 'em [Indians]. (56 Kelly *Humors* 72). NED Square vb. 5 a.

Accounting. There is no accounting for tastes (45 Cooper *Satanstoe* 135; Haliburton *Old Judge* I 210 taste). *Oxford* 2; Stevenson 2282: 5; Tilley D385; Yamamoto *Dickens* 329; H. C. Bailey *Mr. Fortune Objects* (1935) 4, 207–209; Thomas Hughes *Tom Brown at Oxford* (1861) ch. 10, 12, 28.

Ace, 1. A piece of stiff paper about as big as the ace of spades (44 Stephens *High Life* II 22).

2. As black as the ace of spades (40 Haliburton *Letter* 140, *Nature* II 236, *Season-Ticket* 54; Kelly *Humors* 382 a gemman, whose complexion is four shades darker than the famed ace of spades; Wiley *Billy* 79; Locke [Nasby] *Struggles* 279; Richardson *Beyond* 532). Boshears 34:350; Farmer 337; NC 360; Taylor *Comparisons* 17; Francis Gibson *Unthinkable* (1933) 88.

3. I came within an ace of making my fortune (23–24 Irving *Tales* 262; Dana *Two* 316 If a man comes within an ace of breaking his neck; Kelly *Humors* 301 his life was within an ace of being wet out of his body; Jones *Wild* 103 I came within an ace of shooting, 137). Allan PADS XV (1951) 66; NED Ace 3; Partridge 3; Stevenson 8:8.

4. Good as four aces (45 Hooper *Simon* 31).

5. As sure as four aces (59 Hammett *Piney* 67).

6. I hilt four aces ontu the sheriff (67 Harris *Sut* 242).

Acorn, 1. Preachers of a sort are as plenty as acorns or beach nuts (43 Hall *Purchase* I 202).

2. As thick as acorns in the fall (44 Stephens *High Life* II 156).

3. He was cotch one day stealin' acorns from a blind hog (51 Burke *Polly* 50). Bartlett 808; Farmer 362; Farmer and Henley IV 295 mean enough; Schele de Vere 489.

4. To come to the acorns [i. e., to experience adversity]. 35 DA Acorn 1 b.

Act, vb. See Charm (1).

Action, 1. Action and reaction are equal (34 Emerson *Journals* III 247).

2. He had heard that 'actions speak louder than words,' and he acted (45 *The Knickerbocker* XXV 106; Lincoln II 352 "Actions speak louder than words" is the maxim; Taliaferro *Fisher's* 223). NC 360; *Oxford* 2; Snapp 108:126; Stevenson 2616:11; Francis Beeding, pseud. *Death in Four Letters* (1935) 68. Cf. Tilley A26 Neither praise nor dispraise thyself, thy actions serve the turn.

Active. See Cat (6), Dog (7), Panther (1), Weasel (1).

Adam, 1. The unadulterated ale of father Adam (51 Hawthorne *Twice-Told* 166; Melville *Pierre* 418 Adam's Ale; Haliburton *Nature* II 54 Adam's ale; Wiley *Billy* 241; Clift *Bunker* 153 Adam's ale). Farmer and Henley I 20; Fife 120; Green 38; NED Adam 2, Adam's Ale; Stevenson 51:9; Neil Bell, pseud. *The Lord of Life* (Boston 1933) 159.

2. Dead as old Adam (32 Kennedy *Swallow* 216). Stevenson 500:11; Svartengren 141.

3. He don't know me from Adam (44 Stephens *High Life* I 191; Haliburton *Sam* II 186, *Nature* II 123; Smith *'Way* 60; Kelly *Humors* 378). Funk 35; *Oxford* 344; Stevenson 14:5; J. T. Farrell *No Star Is Lost* (1938) 293.

4. The mischievous longing of the old Adam (25 Neal *Brother J* I 405; Haliburton *Clockmaker* II 238 keep old Adam down, III 49; Melville *Moby-Dick* II 239, *Piazza* 52, *Confidence-Man* 16; Smith *'Way* 7). McAtee 46; NC 360; Stevenson 14:2; Whiting *Scots* I 130; Gladys Mitchell *The Saltmarsh Murders* (Philadelphia 1933) 141.

5. When Adam delved and Eve span, Who was then the gentleman? (60 Holmes *Professor* 145). Apperson 2; *Oxford* 2–3; Taylor *Investigations* 255; Tilley A30.

Adamant, 1. Adams was as firm as adamant (69 Barnum *Struggles* 532). Stevenson 1115:4.

2. As hard as adamant (69 Clemens *Innocents* I 262). Svartengren 260; Frank L. Packard *Two Stolen Idols* (1927) 188.

Addition, division, and silence. 67 DA Addition 3.

Adjective. The pungent French proverb, that the adjective is the most deadly enemy of the substantive (65 Richardson *Secret* 85). Cf. Stevenson 2235:3.

Advice. Advice that ain't paid for ain't no good (53 Haliburton *Sam* II 3). Cf. Apperson 475 Ounce of wit, 699 Wit (12); *Oxford* 58 Bought, 480 Ounce; Stevenson 2546:3 Wit; Tilley W545, W567; Whiting *Scots* II 156 Wisdom.

Affectionate. See Pussycat.

Afterclap, 1. I'm for no rues and afterclaps [i. e., no complaining about a bargain once made]. (35 Longstreet *Georgia* 29; Haliburton *Attaché* II 227 There shall be no after claps, nor ruin bargains, nor recantin'). Farmer 7; NED Afterclap; Schele de Vere 577.

2. For fear of after-claps (51 Melville *Moby-Dick* I 113; Smith *My Thirty* 309 so that when the afterclap comes you may be a little prepared for it). Farmer 7; Green 38; Lean III 433; *Oxford* 43–44; Tilley A57; Whiting *Drama,* 222, 267, *Scots* I 131.

African. An allusion to "Nigger in the woodpile," q. v. 65 DA African 4.

Age (1), 1. Age gives good advice when it is no longer able to give a bad example (28 Emerson *Journals* II 228).

2. Old age, allays, afore beauty (43 Robb *Squatter* 94). Lean III 412; NC 360; E. S. Gardner *The Case of the Stuttering Bishop* (1936) ch. 7.

3. But with age comes wisdom (67 Richardson *Beyond* 554).

4. See Coon (1), Dog (3).

Age (2). To have an age [i. e., an advantage]. 44 DA Age, Edge, sb. 1.

Agile. See Deer (1), Goat (2).

Agony, 1. I wouldn't a minded ef he hadn't kept pilin on the agony 'bout my ears and smeller (58 Porter *Major* 45; Shillaber *Knitting-Work* 55 This was putting on the agony too thick; Locke [Nasby] *Struggles* 309 What in thunder . . . did they mean by pilin on the agony over the Yanks we killed?). DA Pile, vb.; Farmer 8; Farmer and Henley I 26; *Oxford* 500 pile up; Partridge 6; Stevenson 72:10; Thornton II 665–666.

2. How would you like to go it in uncle Billy Shakespeare and tip the natives the last hagony in the tragics? (37 Neal *Charcoal* 122).

Ahead. See Right, adj. (1).

Air, 1. As free as the air (36 Haliburton *Clockmaker* I 230, II 201 air of heaven; Cooper *Satanstoe* 220 and almost as swift; Boker *World* 40 the wide air which brushes the earth and yet takes not stain from it; Melville *Moby-Dick* II 240; Durivage *Three* 328; Jones *Country* 52). Apperson 234–235; NC 361; Stevenson 888:3; Svartengren 340; Taylor *Comparisons*

42 breeze; Tilley A88; P. G. Wode-house *The Code of the Woosters* (1938) 289 as the expression is.

2. Tim Crane was so tight he fairly begrudged the air he breathed (56 Whitcher *Widow* 90). Cf. Tilley A91.

Airs. If she didn't put on such airs (56 Whitcher *Widow* 363; Kelly *Humors* 416, 417, 419; Riley *Puddleford* 92 the drefulest sight of airs; Stephens *Mary Derwent* 249 I . . . don't thank any man to be putting on airs, as if he was the owner; Browne *Artemus* 105 a heap of airs, 130 as many airs as tho he was the Bully Boy with the glass eye; Smith *Arp* 179 He didn't run nobody down, nor put on airs; Richardson *Beyond* 444 the new-comer who puts on airs; Alcott *Little Women* 41 if I put on crushed airs, 75 assume the airs of a studious young peacock). DA Air 1 b (1); Green 40; Partridge 7; Stoett 66. Cf. NED Air 15 (give, take, take upon, show).

Alabaster. The top of his head . . . is . . . white as alabaster (35 Fairfield *Letters* 47; Clemens *Fairbanks* 162). Svartengren 232. Cf. NED Alabaster 1 fair; Whiting *Scots* I 131.

Ale. Staler than stale ale (49 Melville *Mardi* I 4).

Alike. See Bean (2), Drop, sb. (1) 2, Pea (3).

Alive, 1. I was still in the land of the living and a-kicking (34 Crockett *Life* 132; Haliburton *Attaché* IV 7 If poor Tom was alive and kickin'; Porter *Major* 51). Farmer and Henley I 31; McAtee PADS XV (1951) 51; Elsa Barker *The Redman Cave Murder* (1930) 60.

2. And as I am alive, if there aint

Delia (53 Cary *Clovernook* 2d Ser. 154).

3. She said she was as certain as she was alive (53 Cary *Clovernook* 2d Ser. 151).

4. As sure as I's 'live (60 Whitehead *Wild Sports* 115; Holmes *Elsie* 34, 371; Clemens *Gilded* I 56). NC 361; F. W. Crofts *Mystery in the English Channel* (1931) 4, 233.

5. As true as you are alive (33 Neal *Down-Easters* I 18; Smith *Downing* 78, 108, 232, *'Way* 336). Svartengren 358. Cf. Creature; Stevenson 2380:11 as I live.

6. Well, boys, said Haley, look alive now (51 Stowe *Uncle* 51). NED Alive 5.

All, 1. All at once makes light work (45 Cooper *Chainbearer* 140). Apperson 399; Bradley 78; Hardie 464:109; *Oxford* 405; Snapp 103:21; Stevenson 1060–1061:11; Stoett 789; Tilley H119; E. S. Gardner *The Case of the Negligent Nymph* (1950) ch. 20. The parallels usually have "Many hands . . ."

2. That round arm beat the gold all tu nothin (44 Stephens *High Life* II 238). Cf. NED All 12 (all to naught).

3. They allow that all's fair in war, I believe (35 Kennedy *Horse-Shoe* 135). Apperson 384; NC 439; *Oxford* 186; Snapp 80:7; Stevenson 1461–1462:13; Tilley A139; Yamamoto *Dickens* 331; NQ 11 xi 151, 198, xii 380, 446; 12 i 13, 58; Andy Adams *A Texas Matchmaker* (Boston 1904) 108; Austen Allen *The Loose Rib* (1933) 173 all fair in war; Bill Adams *Ships and Women* (Boston 1937) 169 All's fair in love; J. M. Cain *The Root of His Evil* (1951) ch. 15.

4. All fair in 'lection time (44 Stephens *High Life* I 37). Samuel Lover

5

Handy Andy (1842) ch. 3 (Everyman's Library 17) All's fair in war, and why not in electioneering?

5. All's well that ends well (22 Loomis *Farmer's Almanac* 178; Clemens *Fairbanks* 75, *Roughing* II 296). Apperson 6–7; NC 361; *Oxford* 701; Smith *Browning* 220; Stevenson 678–679:7; Stoett 542; Tilley A154.

Alley Croaker. Never, even in the days of Alley Croaker (23–24 Irving *Tales* 50).

Almanac. She's as good as an almanac at dates (54 Stephens *Fashion* 102).

Almond. Skin as white as a blanched almond (60 Holmes *Professor* 54).

Aloft. I leave fifty pounds to be spent in a good dinner within twelve months from the time I go up aloft (66 Boucicault *Flying Scud* 182, 222). Farmer and Henley I 42; NED Aloft 10 b, Go 28 b.

Alpha. I have been through it from Alpha to Omaha (c70 Clemens *Sketches* 287). Cf. NED Alpha 2.

American. Good Americans, when they die, go to Paris (58 Holmes *Autocrat* 125). *Oxford* 10. Cf. Bostonian.

Amiable. See Bear, sb. (1).

Amuck. Armed, with their keen mincing-knives . . . run amuck from the bowsprit to the taffrail (51 Melville *Moby-Dick* I 321). Babcock 262; NED Amuck 2; *Oxford* 552; Stevenson 2019:7; Tilley R209.

Amy Dardin. To hang on like Amy Dardin. 35 DA Amy Dardin.

Anchor, 1. The captain's anchor is pretty nigh atrip [i. e., he is near death]. (47 Melville *Omoo* 60). Cf. Tilley A241.

2. See Dutchman (6).

Ancient. See Hill (1).

Angel, 1. Beautiful as an angel (26 Conant *Earnest Man* 335; Thompson *Major* 36 All beautiful as angels; Durivage *Three* 33; Stephens *Mary Derwent* 148). NC 361. Cf. Svartengren 214 lovely, fair.

2. Gentle as an angel (50 Mitchell *Reveries* 265).

3. As harnsome as an angel (44 Stephens *High Life* I 118).

4. As pretty as an angel (40 Haliburton *Clockmaker* III 102, *Sam* I 201). H. C. Bailey *Shadow on the Wall* (1934) 8.

5. Pure as an angel (50 Mitchell *Reveries* 265; Bennett *Border* 491). Svartengren 4.

6. Radiant as an angel (55 Stephens *Homestead* 434).

7. As white as an angel (79 Clemens *Tramp* I 181).

8. Where a good dinner is looked upon as an angel's visit, and voted a miracle (36 Crockett *Exploits* 97; Joseph Reynolds *Peter Gott, the Cape Ann Fisherman* [Boston 1856] 137 "like angel visits, few and far between"). Fife 119; *Oxford* 10; Stevenson 66:2; NQ 4 iv 28, 164, xi 395, 7 x 346, 396.

9. I heard say as he was a going to splice with a gal that could pray like an angel afire (74 Eggleston *Circuit* 216).

10. See Best (1).

Animal. To go the whole animal. 33 DA Whole 2; Farmer and Henley I 55; Partridge 13. Cf. Hog (9), Whole.

Answer, 1. Give a civil answer to a civil question (53 Haliburton *Sam* II 48). Tilley Q10. Cf. Question.

2. Short answers save trouble (69

Alcott *Little Women* 440). Cf. Apperson 567; *Oxford* 585 The shortest answer is doing; Tilley A252.

Ant. "Ants live safely till they have gotten wings," says the old proverb (53 Willis *Fun* 274). Apperson 11; *Oxford* 11; Stevenson 74:12; Tilley A256.

Anything, 1. "Anything you like, Captane." "Anyting is nothin'" (53 Haliburton *Sam* I 167). See Time (1).

2. See Everything.

Apollo. By Sir John's account, the Indian was as handsome as a young Apollo (c58 Stephens *Mary Derwent* 224).

Apologies. Appolligies don't never make nothin' no better (56 Whitcher *Widow* 70). Cf. Stevenson 78:5.

Apostles. He will pyson you as sure as 'postles (55 Haliburton *Nature* II 156). Probably a reference to the Acts of the Apostles; cf. Genesis, Gospel (2), Holy Writ, Matthew, Scriptures.

Appearances, 1. Appearances ain't everything (44 Thompson *Major* 76). Cf. Look (3); W. B. M. Ferguson *The Murder of Christine Wilmerding* (1932) 18 outside appearances didn't matter a blast.

2. Appearances are often deceitful (23 Cooper *Pioneers* 289, 290; Melville *Typee* 235 But appearances all the world over are deceptive, *Confidence-Man* 62 No appearances can deceive me; Curtis *Potiphar* 166 Appearances are so deceitful; Kelly *Humors* 427). Apperson 13; NC 361; Snapp 87:9; Stevenson 83:2; Tilley A285; Andy Adams *A Texas Matchmaker* (Boston 1904) 54 Appearances are as deceitful on a cattle ranch as in the cut of a man's clothes; J. B. Cabell

Jurgen (1922) 115 are proverbially deceitful; Robert Carson *The Revels Are Ended* (1936) 349 deceptive; R. G. Dean *The Sutton Place Murders* (1936) 154 will deceive; E. S. Gardner *The Case of the Sleepwalker's Niece* (1936) ch. 10 So often appearances are deceitful, Sergeant; Natalie S. Lincoln *The Fifth Latchkey* (1929) 238 deceitful.

3. Appearances go a great ways (43 Thompson *Chronicles* 102).

4. You should not always judge from appearances (57 Jones *Country* 233). John 7:24; *Oxford* 328; Leslie Ford, pseud. *The Simple Way of Poison* (1937) 161.

5. Ne Crede Colori: Or, Trust Not to Appearances (68 Saxe *Poems* 177). Stevenson 82:4; Ellery Queen, pseud. *The Devil to Pay* (1938) 167 appearances weren't always to be trusted.

Appetite, 1. What a true saying it is that "appetite furnishes the best sauce" (46 Melville *Typee* 61). Apperson 318; *Oxford* 310; Stevenson 83:11; Tilley H819; Whiting *Scots* I 132.

2. The appetite grows by what it feeds on (67 Richardson *Beyond* 67). Cf. NC 361; *Oxford* 12; Stevenson 84:19; J. H. Neumann *Modern Language Quarterly* VII (1946) 474 n. 85; NQ 5 vii 327, viii 292–293.

Apple, 1. Hard as an apple (40 Haliburton *Clockmaker* III 284, *Old Judge* II 104 winter apple; Holmes *Elsie* 429 Hard and sour as a green cider-apple).

2. As naked as a peeled apple (60 Holmes *Professor* 43).

3. He . . . turned as red as a winter apple (44 Stephens *High Life* I 126, II 197 like a winter apple in the

fall time). Boshears 39:852 apple; Halpert 567; Svartengren 248 apple.

4. The airth is round . . . like a napple (54 Shillaber *Mrs. Partington* 280; Haliburton *Nature* I 141 as round as an apple). Boshears 39:879.

5. I felt as streaked [embarrassed] as a winter apple (44 Stephens *High Life* I 214; Baldwin *Flush* 172 her weathered [withered] old face streaked like a June apple). Cf. DA Streaked 2.

6. His face looked jest like a frost-bitten russet apple when its beginnin to thaw out (44 Stephens *High Life* II 208).

7. To avoid . . . these apples of discord (59 Lincoln III 391). NED Apple 5; *Oxford* 12; Stevenson 88:2.

8. See then, reader, "how we apples swim!" (43 Hall *Purchase* I 284; Lincoln II 450 How we national apples do swim!). Farmer 20; Farmer and Henley I 63–64; Lean IV 91; *Oxford* 13; Stevenson 86:2; Taylor *Investigations* 255; Tilley A302.

9. Rotten apples are the sweetest (45 Judd *Margaret* II 218).

10. And as men say *the apple never falls far from the stem,* I shall hope that another year will draw your eyes & steps to this old less odious haunt of the race (39 Emerson *Letters* II 243). Jente PMLA XLVIII (1933) 26–30; NC 362; Stevenson 1135:9; Stoett 55.

11. Whom . . . she loves as the apple of her eye (45 Cooper *Chainbearer* 38; Durivage *Three* 210; Melville *Confidence-Man* 209). Deut. 32:10; Prov. 7:2; Ps. 17:8; Funk 57; NED Apple 7; Stevenson 86:3; Stoett 101, 1697; Tilley A290 As dear as; Christopher Bush *The Body in the Bonfire* (1936) 68; F. P. Keyes *The River Road* (Boston 1945) 580. For discussion see M. B. Ogle *Transactions of the American Philological Association* LXXIII (1942) 181–191.

Apple-cart. Down with his apple-cart! (25 Neal *Brother J* II 388; Neal *Charcoal* 37 I'll upset your apple-cart, and spill your peaches). Apperson 14; Bartlett 16; DAE Apple-cart; Farmer and Henley I 62; NED *Supplement* Apple-cart; *Oxford* 13; Stevenson 88:5; Agatha Christie *Mr. Parker Pyne, Detective* (1934) 144.

Apple-pie. It [a piano] had evidently been . . . put in apple-pie order (68 Alcott *Little Women* 71). DAE Apple-pie; Barrère and Leland I 46; Farmer and Henley I 62–63; NED Apple-pie; Stevenson 1729:2; F. Marryat *Peter Simple* (1834) ch. 35 (London [1929] 303) Our fifteen sail of the line all in apple-pie order; R. S. Surtees *Mr. Sponge's Sporting Tour* ch. 41 (London [1853] 220); NQ 1 i 468, 485; 3 vii 133, 209; 4 iii 69–70; Valentine Williams *Death Answers the Bell* (Boston 1932) 227 as the saying goes.

Apple tree, 1. A head as round as an apple-tree (58 Holmes *Autocrat* 236).

2. A Vigilance Committee, which hangs the more vicious of the pestiferous crowd to a sour apple-tree (65 Browne *Artemus Ward His Travels* 151). Probably a reminiscence of the line "We'll hang Jeff Davis to a sour apple-tree" in a contemporary song, but allusions like the modern colloquial "I can't see him for sour apples" suggest a traditional background.

3. Within two rows of apple-trees [i.e., within a moderate distance]. 69 DA Apple 2 b.

April, 1. But this youth was an April man; the storm had departed; and now he shone in the sun, none braver than he (49 Melville *Redburn* 377).

Cf. Apperson 15 April 16; *Oxford* 13; Q. Patrick, pseud. *Murder at Cambridge* (1933) 128 [after tears] an April smile.

2. But his friends looked for it [publication of a book] . . . say on the 31st of April, when that should come round (72 Holmes *Poet* 15). Cf. Archer Taylor "Locutions for Never" *Romance Philology* II (1948) 125–126.

Apron-string. He is for everlastin'ly tied to his wife's apron-strings (38 Haliburton *Clockmaker* II 276, III 80 He is hardly cleverly growed up and cut his mother's apron-string afore he is spliced; Cooper *Redskins* 5 mother's; Lowell *Biglow* 90 Mr. Calhoun cannot let go the apron-string of the Past; Curtis *Potiphar* 51 of the Scarlet Woman; Durivage *Three* 261 She kept him as close to her apron strings as she did her Blenheim spaniel; Smith *My Thirty* 422 the Queen's; Boucicault *Flying Scud* 216 Tie him to her apron strings for safety; Alcott *Little Women* 358; Clemens *Letters* I 326). Apperson 15; Farmer and Henley I 64–65; Green 44; NED Apron-string; *Oxford* 13; Partridge 16; Stevenson 89:5; Alice Campbell *Keep Away from Water!* (1935) 14. Cf. Tilley A312.

Argue. It was not argued up, as the saying is, and cannot, therefore, be argued down (61 Lincoln IV 216).

Argus. Argus-eyed (43 Hall *Purchase* II 91; Melville *Mardi* I 115 Thus keeping Argus eyes on the sea). *Oxford* 184; Stevenson 2106:1; Tilley E254.

Arizona fever. 73 DA Arizona 2 a. See California fever.

Arm. Leases as long as my arm (46 Cooper *Redskins* 198; Willis *Fun* 344 a short cane; Melville *Confidence-Man* 36–37 a face). Boshears 38:723; NC 362; NED Arm (1) 2 b; Svartengren 283; Taylor *Comparisons* 54; Margery Allingham *The Fashion in Shrouds* (1938) 261.

Arms. Tha [they] is all up in arms about it (58 Porter *Major* 65). NED Arm (2) 4 b.

Arrow, 1. Sharp as an arrow (50 Mitchell *Reveries* 38). Svartengren 256 dart.

2. Straight as an arrow (25 Neal *Brother J* II 307; Haliburton *Sam* II 66; Melville "Jimmy Rose" in *Works* XIII 260; Bowman *Bear-Hunters* 87; Clemens *Innocents* I 154). Apperson 605; Boshears 40:968; NC 362; Taylor *Comparisons* 78; Tilley A321; H. S. Keeler *The Riddle of the Yellow Zuni* (1930) 211.

3. They are swift as an indian ar[row] (24–26 Lincoln I 1; Hammett *Stray* 67–68 as swift as an arrow from the bow, the water hurried me on). Taylor *Comparisons* 80; Tilley A322.

4(a). He would . . . dart off like an arrow (37 Neal *Charcoal* 45; Haliburton *Sam* I 234 darted off).

(b). The presiding elder's order . . . had gone after the zealous itinerant "like an arrow after a wild goose" (74 Eggleston *Circuit* 254).

(c). And shot forward like an arrow from a bow (32 Kennedy *Swallow* 263; Melville *Omoo* 318 They shot by us like an arrow; Derby *Phoenixiana* 329; Locke [Nasby] *Struggles* 65 they shot past me like an arrow).

(d). Sped like an arrow (35 Kennedy *Horse-Shoe* 210; Melville *Omoo* 84 The boat sped like an arrow through the water). Svartengren 375–376.

Ashamed. See Dog (8).

Ashes, 1. My heart all withered up and felt as dry as ashes (51 Stowe *Uncle* 212).
2. My cheek grew pale as ashes (35 Kennedy *Horse-Shoe* 345; Anon. *New Hope* 271; Lowell *Biglow* 214). Apperson 482; Lean II ii 860; NED Ash 6; Stevenson 1741:3; Svartengren 235–236; Tilley A339; George Bruce *Claim of the Fleshless Corpse* (1937) 104.
3. His cheeks grew as white as the ashes that cover a burning coal (59–60 Holmes *Elsie* 17).

Ash-hopper. You'll have to work your own ash-hopper (43 Hall *Purchase* I 63, II 10, 12). DA Ash 6.

Aspen, 1. She lifted one hand that shook like an aspen (54 Stephens *Fashion* 398). Walter B. Foster *From Six to Six* (1927) 62.
2. Trembling like an aspen (23 Cooper *Pioneers* 286, *Pilot* 413). NC 363; Whiting *Drama* 304:9; John G. Brandon *The One-Minute Murder* (1935) 268. Cf. NED Aspen 2; Whiting *Scots* I 133.

Aspen leaf. The major trembled like an aspen leaf (43 Thompson *Chronicles* 144; Cooper *Satanstoe* 254; Bennett *Kate* 140 his eyelid quivering like the leaf of the aspen; Derby *Phoenixiana* 213 quivered; Locke [Nasby] *Struggles* 508 shook; Barnum *Struggles* 467). Apperson 18; NC 363; *Oxford* 15; Stevenson 788:11; Svartengren 382; Tilley L140, cf. W677; Whiting *Drama* 304; Ring Lardner *The Big Town* (1921, publ. 1925) 70 shaking like an aspen leaf; Denis Mac-

kail *The Majestic Mystery* (1924) 97 shook; P. G. Wodehouse *Big Money* (1931) 84 quivering.

Ass, 1. He appeared in some danger of enacting again the fable of the Ass and the bundles of hay (53 Hammett *Stray* 269; Smith *My Thirty* 340 it would starve to death as sure as the ass between the two bundles of hay). *Oxford* 154 Donkey; Stevenson 1234: 5; William Gore, pseud. *The Mystery of the Painted Nude* (1938) 188 I am like Buridan's ass, between two piles of hay.
2. The ass knows in whose face he brays (67 Richardson *Beyond* 305). *Oxford* 16; Stevenson 106:11 (Spanish).

Aster. See China aster.

Attempt. I'll rescue Blore, or die in the attempt (55 Jones *Winkles* 405).

Attitude. Hattitudes don't prove nothing (66 Boucicault *Flying Scud* 197).

Augur hole, 1. Looked as small as if he was screwed into an auger hole (43 Haliburton *Attaché* III 99). Cf. Taylor *Comparisons* 53 To look like he'd been pulled through a knothole.
2. Can't bore an augur hole with a gimlet (45 Judd *Margaret* I 53).
3. Now this is precisely the way with two-thirds of the world—'making augur-holes with a gimlet' (53 "Editor's Drawer" *Harper's New Monthly Magazine* VII 712).

Awful. See Grave, sb. (1).

Awkward. See Boot (1), Get-out, Sheep (6).

Axe, 1. They had an axe to grind (43 Haliburton *Attaché* III 230; Locke [Nasby] *Struggles* 309; Clemens

Sandwich 198; Clift *Bunker* 61; Barnum *Struggles* 636). Farmer 27; Farmer and Henley I 84; DA Ax 2; NED Ax 5; *Oxford* 17–18; Schele de Vere 260; Stevenson 110:11; Thornton I 25, III 116; S. H. Adams *The Gorgeous Hussy* (Boston 1934) 325.

2. Long'z A. 'll turn tu an' grin' B's exe, ef B. 'll help him grin' hisn (67 Lowell *Biglow* 295).

3. I like to let every feller grind his own axe (53 Haliburton *Sam* I 321). Cf. Eel (10), Fox (10), Skunk (4); Vernon Loder *Death of an Editor* (1931) 50 people are always trying to get him to grind their axes for them.

B

B, 1. He don't know B from a broom-stick (56 Whitcher *Widow* 84, 308 He don't know B from a broomstick, nor bran when the bag's open). DAE B; Farmer and Henley I 85.

2. Persons who . . . had not suffi-cient discrimination to know the sec-ond letter of the alphabet from a buf-falo's foot (43 Hall *Purchase* II 80). Apperson 21; Lean III 310; McAtee *Additional* 9; NC 363; NED B 2 (bat-teldore, bull's foot); *Oxford* 346; Stev-enson 1329:10; Stoett 1 A from B; Tilley B1; NQ 6 viii 364, 476.

Babe, 1. Swearing and gambling, the latter of which I am as clear as the new born babe (63 Wiley *Johnny* 48).

2. Ignorant as the unborn babe! ig-norant as unborn *twins!* (72 Clemens *Roughing* II 288).

3. As harmless as the new born Babe (62 Browne *Artemus* 10, 63, 111). Boshears 37:648 baby; Halpert 435 baby.

4. The good old man, he is in pris-on, helpless as a babe (54 Stephens *Fashion* 359). NC 363; Paul and Ma-bel Thorne *The Sheridan Road Mys-tery* (1921) 231.

5. As innocent as a babe (43 Hall *Purchase* I 79; Baldwin *Flush* 272 I'm as innocent as yer Honor's sucking babe at the brist; Lowell *Biglow* 372 ez babes on knee; Stephens *Fashion* 308 creeping babe, 359 babe). Apper-son 327–328; Boshears 38:699, 700; NC 363; Taylor *Comparisons* 51; Til-

ley B4; Kathleen M. Knight *Acts of Black Night* (1938) babe; Brian Flynn *The Billiard Room Mystery* (Philadel-phia 1929) 144 new-born babe.

6. Uncompromised as a new-born babe (51 Melville *Moby-Dick* II 234).

7. I know no more of human affairs than the babe unborn (70 Daly *Man* 41). Jackson Gregory *The Emerald Murder Trap* (1934) 45. Cf. Svarten-gren 133.

Babes in the Wood. Arter wandering about like the Babes in the Wood (44 Stephens *High Life* II 68; Boucicault *Flying Scud* 219 We're like the poor little "Babes in the Wood"). Taylor *Comparisons* 14.

Baboon. A bowing and a grinning like a durned babboon (44 Stephens *High Life* I 241). Cf. NC 363 As ugly.

Baby, 1. As good-natured and harm-less as a chubby baby! (43 Hall *Pur-chase* I 189).

2. She looked as quiet as a baby (40 Haliburton *Clockmaker* III 36).

3. I am as sound as a new born ba-by (45 Judd *Margaret* II 50).

4. For all his grand looks, he's ten-der hearted as a baby (c58 Stephens *Mary Derwent* 280).

5. Bein' as weak as a baby (69 Boucicault *Presumptive* 233). NC 363; Svartengren 393. Cf. Child (9), Infant (4).

6. And ye [a panther] be a purty critter: yer eyes has babies in 'em (60

12

Whitehead *Wild Sports* 132). Apperson 21; NED Baby 3; *Oxford* 383; Whiting *Scots* I 143 Boys; NQ 9 ix 405, 516, x 56, 195, 299; T. F. Powys *The Left Leg* (London 1923) 280.

7. Folks that tend babies mustn't have pins about them (45 Judd *Margaret* II 121).

8. You can't wean babies in a day (45 Judd *Margaret* II 121).

9. He was innocent, and didn't know nothing about it no more than the little baby that never had subsistence (54 Shillaber *Mrs. Partington* 66). NC 364.

10. I . . . took tu crying like a sick baby (44 Stephens *High Life* II 6; Nash *Century* 51 You'll cry like a baby when you go away from there). Boshears 32:15; Halpert 95; McAtee 21; NC 364; Taylor *Comparisons* 14.

11. Goes to sleep like a nussin baby (44 Stephens *High Life* II 228). NC 364; Taylor *Comparisons* 14. Cf. Infant (5).

12. The old chap took to it like a nursin baby (44 Stephens *High Life* II 167).

13. As cosey as if she'd been acquainted with me when I was a nussing baby (44 Stephens *High Life* II 26).

14. It looks about as much like a team of horses, as I do like a nussing baby (44 Stephens *High Life* II 142–143).

15. See Cheek.

Bacchus, 1. As jolly as Bacchus (45 Hooper *Simon* 28).

2. The mare made her appearance, looking every inch a Bacchus, and fine as a star (58 Porter *Major* 117).

Bachelor. It [an old maid's lecture on matrimonial duties] partook largely of those peculiarities which are said to tincture the rules prescribed to govern bachelor's children (21 Cooper *Spy* 390). Cf. Apperson 21; *Oxford* 18; Stevenson 113:12; Tilley B10. See Maid (3).

Back, sb., 1. Our backs are fitted to our burdens (59 Shillaber *Knitting-Work* 167, 270 Every back). NC 364 shaped; *Oxford* 246. Cf. Stevenson 256:3.

2. You may scratch my back and I'll scratch your back (62 Browne *Artemus* 11). Apperson 554; *Oxford* 567; Stevenson 2045–2046:12; Tilley B643.

3. When her back once gits up (44 Stephens *High Life* I 224; Stowe *Uncle* 460 Mas'r's back's up high; Hammett *Piney* 84 They'd got their backs and tails both up, 284 it took a smart chaince of abuse to set his back up). Bartlett 244; Farmer 28–29; Farmer and Henley I 87; McAtee 28; NED Get vb. 72 p.

4. To be on one's back [i. e., at the end of one's resources]. 40 DA Back 2 c; Partridge 23.

5. She . . . turned her back on the house of Means forever (71 Eggleston *School-Master* 270). NED Back, sb. 24 g.

6. That the well of his good spirits had been "riled," or, in more familiar phrase, that he was "spotty on the back" (37 Neal *Charcoal* 34).

Back, adv. The captain used to boast that he could pack [drink] a gallon without its setting him back any (58 Porter *Major* 103).

Backbone, 1. It hez no more backbone than an eel (65 Locke [Nasby] *Struggles* 168).

2. He hasn't got backbone enough to handle those fellows (74 Eggleston

Circuit 255). NED Backbone 4, *Supplement* Backbone 4.

3. Their hearts so tarnally used up, that they have to lean agin their back bones to rest more than half the time (44 Stephens *High Life* II 193). See Dog (2), Sapling.

Back seat. I won't be after takin' a back seat for your sister (70–73 McCloskey *Across* 75). DA Back 1 c (13); Farmer 30; Farmer and Henley I 89; NED Seat 27 c; Partridge 24; Thornton I 29, III 15.

Back track. To make back tracks, take the back track. 37 DA Back (2) 14 b; NED *Supplement* Back track.

Bacon, 1. To cook one's bacon. 68 DA Bacon 1 c; Berrey 254. 2 (to hinder, thwart, balk).

2. You've saved your bacon (40 Cooper *Pathfinder* 169; Robb *Squatter* 155; Baldwin *Flush* 36; Willis *Fun* 121; Taliaferro *Fisher's* 133). Apperson 550–551; Farmer 31; Farmer and Henley I 91–92; McAtee 54; NED Bacon 5 a; *Oxford* 562; Partridge 25; Schele de Vere 630; Stevenson 114:4; Tilley B24; NQ 1 ii 424, 499, 2 iv 67, 132, 9 ii 407, iii 33, 472; Carter Dickson, pseud. *The Plague Court Murders* (1934) 182.

Bad, sb. We must take the bad with the good in every v'y'ge (40 Cooper *Pathfinder* 269). Cf. Apperson 539 Rough; *Oxford* 549; Stevenson 115:5; John Dos Passos *The Big Money* (1936) 543; Marco Page, pseud. *Fast Company* (1938) 80 So you have to take the good with the bad.

Bad, adj. See Itch.

Badger. As blind as a badger (69 Clemens *Sketches* 101).

Bag, 1. Don't lean against the gentleman as heavy as a bag of mush (53 Cary *Clovernook* 2d Ser. 152).

2. [She] had got ready bag and baggage, Ready for her homeward journey (c56 Thomson *Plu-ri-bus-tah* 152; Kelly *Humors* 173 Next morning, bag and baggage, the Triangles vamosed; Alcott *Little Women* 54 Here I am, bag and baggage). NED Bag 19; NQ 5 xii 229, 293, 457, 6 i 125, 11 vi 108; Claude S. Bowers *The Tragic Era* (1929) 383.

3. They say an empty bag can't stand straight (53 Haliburton *Sam* I 210). Apperson 181–182; Champion 26:287, 39:926; Hardie 461:6; NC 364 bag, 469 sack; *Oxford* 170–171; Stevenson 115:10; Tilley B30.

4. Someone has cut the bag open [i. e., there is an unusual number of game birds]. 74 DA Bag 3 b.

5. Some girl has given you the bag (25 Neal *Brother J* II 277). Apperson 23; Farmer and Henley I 96–97; NED Bag sb. 18; *Oxford* 19–20; Stevenson 116:2; Tilley B32. Cf. Sack (1); Whiting *Drama* 334:388.

6. Give me the bag to hold (55 Haliburton *Nature* II 70). Farmer and Henley I 97; NC 364; NED Bag sb. 18; *Oxford* 20; Stevenson 115:12; George C. Beston *Prelude to Murder* (1936) 96.

Baggage. To get away with the baggage [i. e., to escape detection in knavery]. 73 DA Baggage 1 b.

Bait, 1. Fish or cut bait. 76 DA Fish vb. 3; Taylor *Index* 33; Robert H. Fuller *Jubilee Jim* (1928) 70.

2. You can't shoot for sour owl bait (51 Burke *Polly* 175).

Baked. You never wuz half baked (66 Locke [Nasby] *Struggles* 259). Apperson 279; Farmer and Henley I 103; NED Bake vb. 6; Stevenson 1056:4.

Baker, 1. To spell Baker [i.e., to be up to the mark]. 68 DA Spell vb. 2 (2); Partridge 27.

2. Show 'em how to count baker's dozen (38 Haliburton *Clockmaker* II 24; Melville *White Jacket* 279; Clift *Bunker* 30; Saxe *Poems* 114; Barnum *Struggles* 713 What is thirteen but the traditional "baker's dozen," indicating good measure, pressed down, shaken together, and running over?). Farmer and Henley I 104–105; Green 49; Lean III 312; NED Baker 6; Stevenson 116:5; Edmund Gilligan *Boundary Against Night* (1937) 118.

Baking. Her face began to swell and puff up, like a baking of bread wet up with turnpike emptins (44 Stephens *High Life* II 78). DA Turnpike 1.

Bald. See Billiard-ball (1), Egg (1), Jug (1), Slate (1).

Baldheaded. I scent wich pays the best, an' then Go into it baldheaded (48 Lowell *Biglow* 102). Bartlett 27; Farmer 31; Farmer and Henley I 107; Partridge 28; Schele de Vere 581; E. J. Millward *The Copper Bottle* (1929) 145. Cf. DA Bald-headed 1 b (to snatch [jerk] bald-headed).

Ball, 1. Eyes like two balls uv fire (59 Taliaferro *Fisher's* 53, 161, 162 red like balls o' fire). NC 365.

2. Many a man would have " 'gi'n it up as a lost ball" (59 Taliaferro *Fisher's* 116).

3. Miss Hawkins, she kept the ball rollin' (56 Whitcher *Widow* 326). DA Ball 3 b; NED Ball 18; Partridge 28; David Fox, pseud. *The Doom Dealer* (1923) 181 start.

4. Spun round like a ball o' butter,

in a pewter plate (25 Neal *Brother J* II 85). Cf. Whiting *Scots* I 135.

Ball-hornet. Quick as a ball-hornet (59 Taliaferro *Fisher's* 196).

Balloon, 1. The North . . . Would go down like a busted balloon (48 Lowell *Biglow* 94). Cf. Anita Boutell *Death Brings a Storke* (1938) 197 collapse like a pricked balloon.

2. Banks are bustin every day, goin up higher nor any balloon of which we have any record (62 Browne *Artemus* 41).

Bamboo briar. Sin's ez sharp ez a bamboo-briar (80 Harris *Uncle Remus* 155). Svartengren 256 briar.

Banagher. That would bang Banaghar (55 Haliburton *Nature* II 226). *Oxford* 21–22; Stevenson 118:8 (beat, bang); NQ 5 i 255; Neil Bell, pseud. *Crocus* (1937) 208 he beats Banagher; Virgil Markham *The Black Door* (1930) 17 this beats banigar. Cf. Farmer and Henley I 114–115.

Bandbox. A maiden lady of fifty . . . as neat as if she had just stepped out of one of her own band boxes (33 Hall *Soldier's Bride* 190; Stephens *High Life* II 26 All dressed in white, as if she'd jest cum out of a band-box, 100 looked as if they'd just come out of a band-box; Burke *Polly* 25 as fresh and neat as if they [ruffles] had just come out of a band-box; Haliburton *Season-Ticket* 367 As neat and nice as if she was just taken out of a bandbox that was brought home from the milliner; Clemens *Tramp* I 3). Boshears 33:216; DA Bandbox; Green 50; Halpert 137; McAtee *Grant County* 2; NC 365; NED Bandbox, Bandbox thing; Partridge 554; Stevenson 626: 1; Charles J. Dutton *The Circle of*

Death (1933) 119 He looks as if he had just come out of a bandbox; Leslie Ford *By the Watchman's Clock* (1932) 12 fresh. . . . as if they'd just come out of the customary band box. Cf. Svartengren 218.

Bank, 1. I was as good as the city banks (44 Stephens *High Life* I 63). Svartengren 317.
2. As rich as a bank (36 Haliburton *Clockmaker* I 103).
3. It is a proverb that banks have no heart (53 Boker *Bankrupt* 83).

Bantam, 1. A feller stepped up to me as important as a bantam cock after he has crowed for the first time (c56 Thomson *Elephant Club* 158). Cf. James G. Edwards, pseud. *The Odor of Bitter Almonds* (1938) 183 No bantam half as cocky as an old bantam.
2. Struttin' like a bantam-hen (53 Haliburton *Sam* II 91; Barnum *Struggles* 588 bantam rooster). Cf. Boshears 35:422; NC 365; Svartengren 84 banty cock.

Bar. To let down the bars. 69 DA Let vb. 3 b.

Barber pole. A large, hollow cyprus . . . straight as a barber pole (56 Kelly *Humors* 115).

Bare. See Eel (1), Pumpkin (1).

Bargain, 1. A bargain is a bargain (54 Langdon *Ida* 163; Sedley *Marian* 277 I put it to ye now, ain't a bargain?). Apperson 26; *Oxford* 22; Stevenson 121–122:14; Tilley B76; Charles Reade *Jack of All Trades* (1858) ch. 11 (London 1932 p. 100).
2. My old father used to have a saying that "If you have made a bad bargain, *hug* it the tighter" (42 Lincoln I 280).
3. Yet it was soon seen . . . that it required more than one to make a bargain (51 Stowe *Uncle* 59; Smith *Arp* 120 it didn't take two to make that bargain—it took only one). Jente *American* 345; NC 491; Stevenson 120:15; Andy Adams *The Ranch on the Beaver* (Boston 1927) 158; J. G. Cozzens *The Just and the Unjust* (1942) 243; Tiffany Thayer *Three-Sheet* (1932) 279. Cf. "Two words to a bargain": Apperson 657; Lean IV 170–171; *Oxford* 681; Tilley W827 The second word makes the bargain; Samuel Lover *Handy Andy* (1842) ch. 14 (Everyman's Library 163) There's two words to that bargain.
4. See Best (4).

Bark (1), 1. Closer an' [than] buttonwood-bark (33 Neal *Down-Easters* I 81 [shrewd in a bargain], 106 [mean]; Stephens *High Life* I 135 Jase was as close as the bark of a tree; Burke *Polly* 50 that chap was closer than the bark on a hickory tree; Baldwin *Flush* 320 the closest man I ever saw,—as close as the bark is to a tree). Boshears 35:408; Brewster *Am. Speech* XIV 261; NC 365; Taylor *Comparisons* 82; Kenneth Roberts *Northwest Passage* (1937) 58.
2. She stuck as close to me as the bark on a hickory-log (53 Haliburton *Sam* II 286). Cf. NC 365; Tilley B83.
3. Mrs. Longbow was tighter than bark to a tree (57 Riley *Puddleford* 250; Eggleston *Circuit* 11 A man "as tight as the bark on a beech tree," and a Yankee besides, was next door to a horse-thief). Bartlett 807; DA Bark 2 c (5); McAtee PADS XV (1951) 61; NC 365; Taylor *Comparisons* 82; Woodard PADS VI (1946) 43.
4. To stick to (in) the bark [i. e., to deal superficially with a matter]. 22 DA Bark 2 c (1).

QUESTION: who said —
"barefoot in summer
pregnant in winter"
who? when? where?

SOURCES CHECKED: (SEE BACK ALSO)

ANSWER:

STATUS:

SPECIAL INSTRUCTIONS?

WHO? Mary Jo
(Assoc. Press)

PHONE: 374-5536

DATE:

BY:

052

SOURCES: _____
___ALMANACS
___ARK. DOCS
___CARD CATALOG
___DICTIONARIES
___ENCYCLOPEDIAS
___INFO FILE
___MAGAZINE INDEXES
___NEWSPAPER INDEXES
___U.S. DOCS
___VERTICAL FILE

OTHER:_____

_____

_____

_____

_____

_____

_____

5. The old man's going to take the bark off both of us (45 Hooper *Simon* 14). DA Bark 2 c (2); Farmer and Henley I 114–115.

6. That is the word with the bark on it (72 Clemens *Roughing* I 107). DA Bark 2 c (3); *Boston Herald* Nov. 25, 1957, p. 29 Nobody in the Administration . . . seems willing to give us the truth with the bark on.

Bark (2). 'Twill turn out that his bark is worse than his bite (45 Cooper *Chainbearer* 274, 278; Stephens *Homestead* 335). Apperson 26; NC 365; NED Bark sb. 2 b; *Oxford* 23; Stevenson 613:12; Tilley B86 Fearefull dogges do barke the sorer; NQ 4 iv 196; Frank Hamel *Lady Hester Lucy Stanhope* (London 1913) 244 Her bark was far worse; Kenneth Livingston *The Dodd Cases* (1934) 70.

Barking. There was another call as plain as barkin' (53 Haliburton *Sam* II 25).

Barn, 1. I'm as serious as an empty barn (37 Neal *Charcoal* 123).

2. Between you and I and the barn (54 DA Barn 4 b). See Gate-post (2). In a collection of modern phrases B. J. Whiting has examples of baby, beaver-dam, bed-post (see below), binnacle, door-post, gate-post (see below), lamp-post, post (see below), and well, but none of barn.

Barnacle. I clove to Queequeg like a barnacle (51 Melville *Moby-Dick* I 76). NED Barnacle 3.

Barnburners. Barnburners (48 Lincoln I 477, 493 Barnburnerism). Apperson 72; *Oxford* 69; Tilley H752; W. N. McCartney *Fifty Years a Country Doctor* (1938) 375 the man who burned his barn to destroy the rats.

Lincoln's term for a political faction involves an allusion to the proverb; see Bartlett 72; DA Barnburner; Farmer 39; Thornton I 44–45.

Barn door, 1. A dasher [of a stage-coach] as high as a barn-door (50 Judd *Richard* 116). Svartengren 289 as big as a barn-side.

2. I . . . put hir in a good humor by given hir about as many kisses as would cover a barn door (58 Porter *Major* 89).

3. You couldn't hit my barn-door, with a rest [for the gun] (57 Jones *Country* 181). NED Barn-door; Partridge 34. Cf. J. T. Farrell *No Star Is Lost* (1938) 10 [not able] to hit the blind side of a barn.

Barn-owl. We took to 'em ez nat'ral ez a barn-owl does to mice (67 Lowell *Biglow* 282).

Barrel. I'm empty as a bar'l (59 Taliaferro *Fisher's* 103). NC 366; Svartengren 48; Taylor *Comparisons* 38.

Base. To change one's base. 62 DA Base 2 d.

Bashan, 1. They'd hand a buff'lodrove a tract When they wuz madder than all Bashan (67 Lowell *Biglow* 348).

2. He bellered like all Bashan (67 Lowell *Biglow* 283). Ps. 22:12. Cf. Taylor *Comparisons* 21–22; Bull (9).

Bashful. See Girl (1).

Basket, 1. He was as perlite as a basket of chips (44 Stephens *High Life* II 54). NC 366; J. Frank Dobie *Coronado's Children* (Dallas 1930) 114. Cf. Ayers PADS XIV (1950) 80 pleasant; Thornton I 46, III 125. See Kitten (9).

2. Little Tom looks as smiling as a

basket of chips (34 Eliason 104; Stephens *High Life* II 232). Apperson 581; Bartlett 807; Svartengren 79; Thornton I 46. Cf. Phoebe A. Taylor *Death Lights a Candle* (Indianapolis 1932) 52 as happy an' cheerful.

3. He made more fuss . . . than eny mortal auctioneer cud tell ef he hed es meny tungs es a baskit full ove buckils (67 Harris *Sut* 71).

Bat (1), 1. As blind as a bat (33 Hall *Soldier's Bride* 108; Longstreet *Georgia* 28; Haliburton *Clockmaker* II 86, 262, 307, III 218, *Attaché* II 234, *Sam* II 56; Melville *Moby-Dick* II 199; Dorson *Jonathan* 82; Jones *Country* 89; Clemens *Sandwich* 38, *Innocents* II 202, *Roughing* II 194, *Gilded* II 195). Apperson 54; McAtee 15; NC 366; Taylor *Comparisons* 19; Tilley O92; Florence M. Pettee *The Palgrave Mummy* (1929) 240.

2. Then away I went like a leather-winged bat (35 Kennedy *Horse-Shoe* 261). Cf. NC 366; Taylor *Comparisons* 39.

Bat (2). To be on a bat. 48 DA Bat sb.[3]; Partridge 37.

Battery. This suggestion spiked his battery (79 Clemens *Tramp* II 27). NED Spike v.[1] 2. See Gun (8).

Bawbee. See Bobee.

Baxter. I shall travel like Baxter's hog—in a gang by myself (63 Clemens *Enterprise* 96).

Bay. Some on 'em were pretty well over the bay [i. e., drunk]. (44 Stephens *High Life* I 167; Hammett *Stray* 216, *Wonderful* 71; Thomson *Elephant Club* 50; Riley *Puddleford* 35; *Harper's New Monthly Magazine* XXIX [1864] 679 On one occasion, when about two-thirds over the bay,

he reeled into the tavern stable). DA Bay 5c; Farmer and Henley V 116.

Bayonet. Both'll be jest ez sot in their ways ez a bagnet (67 Lowell *Biglow* 319).

Bay State. And I've always heer'n say that the Bay State was provarbal for pronounsation (23 Cooper *Pioneers* 175). Cf. Bartlett 33; Thornton I 49.

Beagle. Noses as keen as that of a beagle (37 Neal *Charcoal* 142). Cf. NED Beagle 1.

Beam. There is no beam in an Englishman's eye; no not a smell of one; he has pulled it out long ago; that's the reason he can see the mote in other folks's so plain (43 Haliburton *Attaché* II 12). Luke 6:41; Apperson 430; *Oxford* 435; Stevenson 780:2; Tilley M1191; Whiting *Drama* 108, *Scots* I 134 (balk); G. Edinger and E. J. C. Neep *Pons Asinorum* (London 1929) 14 he set up a woodstore with the beams he took out of his own eye; Virgil Markham *Inspector Rusby's Finale* (1933) I can see . . . the mote in your eye; Reginald Davis *The Crowing Hen* (1936) 19 You are suggesting that I remove the beam from my own eye.

Bean, 1. Helpless ez spilled beans on a dresser (67 Lowell *Biglow* 350).

2. As much alike as if they'd been kidney beans shelled out of the same pod (44 Stephens *High Life* I 159). Whiting *Scots* I 135. See Pea (3).

3. For you know every tree . . . as well as you know beans (43 Haliburton *Attaché* III 17; Dorson *Jonathan* 76 but he 'knew' doughnuts as well as he "knew beans"; Nash *Century* 27 I told him he was a moon-

shiny calf . . . and didn't know beans, when the bag's open, 163). DA Bean sb. 4 (1); Farmer 45; Farmer and Henley I 152; McAtee PADS XV (1951) 56; Thornton I 50; Foxhall Daingerfield *The Linden Walk Tragedy* (1929) 188. Cf. Bran.

4. How I long to walk into some o' these chaps, and give 'em the beans (43 Haliburton *Attaché* I 108). DA Bean sb. 4 c; Farmer and Henley I 151; Archibald Marshall and H. A. Vachell *The Mote House Mystery* (1926) 160 give you beans [i. e., a scolding].

5. See Hill (6).

Bean-pole. As strait as a bean-pole (34 Davis *Downing* 324; Stephens *High Life* I 103 as straight as a bean pole stuck up on end). Halpert 674.

Bear, sb., 1. [Santa Anna's proclamation] made the inhabitants about as amiable and peaceably inclined as a she bear, who has just lost her cubs (58 Hammett *Piney* 181). Cf. Whiting *Drama* 119, 304:19.

2. They were about as civil . . . as tame bears (57 Bennett *Border* 467).

3. As crabbed as a wounded bear (59 Browning *Forty-Four* 114).

4. He was as crazy as a wild bear (44 Stephens *High Life* II 182).

5. And lookin' as cross . . . as a bear jist starved out in the spring (38 Haliburton *Clockmaker* II 57, III 243 as cross as a bear with a sore head, *Old Judge* II 118 as cross as a bear, *Sam* I 8 like a bear with a sore head, as cross as Old Scratch himself, *Nature* I 112 as cross as a bear that has cubs; Robb *Squatter* 61 He . . . was cross as a she bear with cubs; Burke *Polly* 63 then he was a bear with a sore head; Cary *Married* 281; Brown-

ing *Forty-Four* 41 wounded bear; Alcott *Little Women* 75 as cross as a bear; Clemens *Gilded* II 25 as cross as a bear). Apperson 123; Boshears 35:454; DA Bear 3; McAtee 21; NC 366; Oxford 26; Stevenson 129:7; Taylor *Comparisons* 30–31; A. T. Sheppard *Here Comes an Old Sailor* (1928) 307 with a sore head; Anita Boutell *Death Brings a Storke* (1938) 66 as cross as a bear.

6. I jumped through that winder as easy as a bar 'ud go through a cane brake (43 Robb *Squatter* 64).

7. As fat and heavy as a December bear (40 Haliburton *Clockmaker* III 128; Eliason 103 as fat as a bear). Boshears 36:537; Mary N. Murfree [Charles Egbert Craddock, pseud.] *The Mystery of Witch-Face Mountain* (Boston 1895) I'm getting fat as a bear.

8. He war naterally as good-humored as a she bar when her cubs is meddled with (58 Hammett *Piney* 69).

9. Doolittle looked as good-natured as a bear with a sore head (58 Hammett *Piney* 177).

10. I'm as hearty as a bear (40 Smith *Letters* 78, 135–136 eat as hearty as bears).

11. Hungry as a bear after his winter's nap (27 Cooper *Prairie* 138; Smith *Downing* 132 as a bear, 199, *My Thirty* 376; Haliburton *Clockmaker* II 57 lookin' . . . as hungry as a bear jist starved out in the spring; Fairfield *Letters* 368 as a bear; Judd *Margaret* I 263; Durivage *Three* 96 as a bear; Whitcher *Widow* 72 as a bear; Shillaber *Knitting-Work* 55 as bears and hypothenuses). Boshears 38:689; McAtee 35; Taylor *Comparisons* 51; Sloane Callaway *The Crime at the Conquistador* (1938) 213; Gerald

Fairlee *Scissors Cut Paper* (Boston 1928) 143 a starving bear.

12. As mad as a bear with his tail shot off (40 Haliburton *Clockmaker* III 53). Cf. S. H. Adams *The Gorgeous Hussy* (Boston 1934) 381 as a bear with a sore tail.

13. I stand about as much chance as a bar going to—the infernal regions (not to put too fine a point on it) without any claws (55 Derby *Phoenixiana* 286).

14. Ain't that as plain as a bar up a gum tree? (60 Whitehead *Wild Sports* 121).

15. It was all as plain as a bear's track (60 Whitehead *Wild Sports* 211). Cf. Wolf (10).

16. Albeit his manner was as rough as a Russian bear's (45 Hooper *Simon* 97). NC 366.

17. Safe as a bar in a hollow tree in the dead o' winter (59 Taliaferro *Fisher's* 48).

18. He's safe as a skin'd bar (43 Robb *Squatter* 75).

19. He was as savage as a white bear afore breakfast (38 Haliburton *Clockmaker* II 151, *Sam* II 96 they returned home as savage as bears). NC 366; Svartengren 92. Cf. Whiting *Drama* 304:18 curster.

20. He swallows them down slick as a bar swallerin' down a piece uv honey-comb (59 Taliaferro *Fisher's* 161, 163). Cf. Tilley B130.

21. Had your fist all skinned and beat as soft as a bear's foot (58 Porter *Major* 94).

22. Strong as a bear (25 Neal *Brother J* III 387; Robb *Squatter* 135). NC 366.

23. As sulky as a bear (43 Haliburton *Attaché* III 257). Apperson 123; *Oxford* 26. Cf. Svartengren 106 rude.

24. As wicked as a she-bear with a sore head (43 Haliburton *Attaché* II 256; Robb *Squatter* 143 wicked as a tree'd bar).

25. Lookin wilder nor a dyin bar (58 Porter *Major* 93).

26. Bring on your bears, I'm ready (68 Alcott *Little Women* 155). DA Bear, sb. 3; Lean III 334.

27. Bah! that's nothin! No more'n a bar to an elephant (59 Taliaferro *Fisher's* 86).

28. You are like a young bear, all your troubles are before you (39 Briggs *Harry* I 158). Apperson 365; *Oxford* 738.

29. The old gineral began to dance like a bear on red hot iron (40 Haliburton *Clockmaker* III 134). Cf. Whiting *Drama* 304:19.

30. I'll fight like a she-bear for her cubs (45 Cooper *Chainbearer* 337). Cf. Tilley S292.

31. Grumble and growl like a bear with a sore head (36 Haliburton *Clockmaker* I 322, *Attaché* IV 120). *Oxford* 26 sore ear. Cf. Whiting *Drama* 304:19 groan; Leslie McFarlane *The Murder Tree* (1931) 221 growl like a bear with a sore paw.

32. To skin the bear at once [i. e., to get down to essentials]. 44 DA Bear 3.

33. You've been a snorin' away like an old he-bar in a hard freeze, with his paws in his mouth (58 Hammett *Piney* 301).

34. Her new caliker swelled up round her like a bear with the dropsey (43 Lewis *Odd* 51).

Bear, vb., 1. We must bear and forbear (25 Neal *Brother J* I 206; Dana *Two* 317; Alcott *Little Women* 131). Lean III 426; *Oxford* 26; Stevenson 863:11; Tilley B135.

2. See Born.

Beard. I didn't think courage ought to be measured by the beard, for fear a goat would have preference over a man (36 Crockett *Life* 75). Cf. Apperson 250; NC 477 smell; *Oxford* 27; Tilley G169.

Beast, 1. All as drunk as beasts (40 Dana *Two* 294). Svartengren 207.
2. Better a beast than a miser (57 Melville *Confidence-Man* 138).

Beat, sb. Well, I never heard the beat on't (56 Whitcher *Widow* 318). DA Beat sb. 2; Thornton I 51.

Beat, vb., 1. This does beat all (36 Eliason 259; Whitcher *Widow* 153). DA Beat vb. 3 (1).
2. See Stick, sb. (6).

Beautiful. See Angel (1), Butterfly, (1), Day (1), Morning (1), Picture (1).

Beauty, 1. Beauty is a very fine thing, but you can't live on it (60 Haliburton *Season-Ticket* 38). Cf. NC 367.
2. See Justice.

Beaver, 1. As busy as a beaver. 79 DA Beaver 4; Taylor *Comparisons* 22.
2. As dull as a bachelor beaver. 77 DA Bachelor 1 a.
3. But it wouldn't hould, I were a gone beaver, bad all over, and no mistake (66 Bowman *Bear-Hunters* 382). DA Beaver 4 (5). See Coon (7).
4. Not to be up to beaver. 37 DA Beaver 4 (4).
5. And if I didn't *sweat like a beaver,* 'taint no matter (53 "Editor's Drawer" *Harper's New Monthly Magazine* VII 849).
6. Ingham worked honestly, like a beaver (35 Crockett *Account* 73; *Harper's New Monthly Magazine* XXXV [1867] 484; Clift *Bunker* 64; Clemens *Gilded* I 283). Boshears 34:303;

DA Beaver 4; Farmer 46; Fife 119; Halpert 857; McAtee 71; Schele de Vere 208; Svartengren 125; Thornton II 955, III 434; John Goodwin *When Dead Men Tell Tales* (1928) 216.

Bed, 1. Early to bed and early to rise (40 Cooper *Pathfinder* 235; Melville *Moby-Dick* I 21 he's an early bird—airley to bed and airley to rise; Porter *Major* 135 The old adage; Haliburton *Season-Ticket* 187 Poor Richard has given us his experience in rhyme, to impress it more easily on the memory: "Early to bed and early to rise Makes a man healthy, wealthy, and wise"; Clemens *Washoe* 83 Early to bed, and early to rise, Makes a man healthy, wealthy and wise—Benjamin Franklin, 88, *Sketches* 189, *Tramp* II 171 there is enough early rising in it to make a man far more "healthy and wealthy and wise" than any one man has any right to be). Apperson 173; Lean II ii 733; NC 368; *Oxford* 164; Snapp 93:15; Stevenson 1995:7; Taylor *Index* 14; Tilley B184; NQ 6 vii 438, viii 136, 8 xii 248, 336; H. C. Bailey *The Red Castle Mystery* (1932) 213; Sinclair Lewis *The Man Who Knew Coolidge* (1927) 51–52 I tell you there never was a truer saying than.
2. My long comrade was one of those, who from always thrusting forth the wrong foot foremost when they rise, or committing some other indiscretion of the limbs, are more or less crabbed or sullen before breakfast (47 Melville *Omoo* 269; Haliburton *Sam* I 257 I guess how he had got out of bed the wrong way that mornin'. Everything depends on how a man gets up. It's a great secret that. If it is done the wrong leg foremost, or wrong eend fust, you are wrong all day, cross

21

as old scratch; Taliaferro *Fisher's* 179 Lookin' fur all the world like a man that had got out'n his bed wrong eend foremost that mornin'). Apperson 715–716; Hardie 469:106; McAtee 28, PADS XV (1951) 54–55; *Oxford* 544 Rise; Stevenson 141:11; Stoett 173; Tidwell PADS XI (1949) 14; Tilley S426; Fulton Oursler *Joshua Todd* (1934) 133. Cf. Whiting *Drama* 360:800.

Bedbug, 1. As crazy as a bed bug (44 Stephens *High Life* II 157; Locke [Nasby] *Struggles* 103 drunken bedbug; Harris *Sut* 73, 104 in July). Bartlett 807; DA Bed sb. 2 (1); McAtee 21; NC 368; Stevenson 1497:1; Taylor *Comparisons* 29–30; Thornton I 221; Joel Y. Dane, pseud. *The Cabana Murders* (1937) 158.

2. Hamlick's as mad as a bed-bug (54 Shillaber *Mrs. Partington* 108).

3. Nabby run about from house to house like a crazy bed-bug (33 Smith *Downing* 176; Haliburton *Sam* II 21 a goin' round and round the room like a ravin' distracted bedbug, *Season-Ticket* 56 a racing all over the world like a).

4. Come back about the quickest to New York, and I guess with a bed-bug in his ear (33 Smith *Downing* 215–216). Cf. Ellery Queen, pseud. *The Devil to Pay* (1938) 222 if we can somehow plant the proverbial bug in her ear that little Anatol was lying all the time; Flea (7).

Bedpost. And between you and me and the bedpost (58 Hammett *Piney* 101). Apperson 47; Farmer and Henley I 161; NED, *Supplement* Bedpost; *Oxford* 43; Partridge 42; Stevenson 1838:1; Phoebe A. Taylor *The Mystery of the Cape Cod Players* (1933)

238. See Barn (2), Gate-post (2), Post, sb. (5), Pump (3).

Bed-quilt. Kivered the nation with glory, like a bed-quilt kivers a bed (59 Taliaferro *Fisher's* 252).

Bedrock. Down to bedrock. 69 DA Bedrock 2 c.

Bee, 1. As brisk as a bee (c61 Paul *Courtship* 111, 61 a hive of bees). Apperson 68; Green 2; Svartengren 161.

2. As busy as so many bees (33 Smith *Downing* 33, 74 as bees; Davis *Downing* 116; Haliburton *Clockmaker* II 144 a bee; Briggs *Harry* I 72 as busily employed as bees in a hive; Hall *Purchase* II 196; Cooper *Satanstoe* 15; Melville *Confidence-Man* 170 "Industrious?" "The busy bee"; Stephens *Fashion* 299, *Homestead* 213; Alcott *Little Women* 44 she was by nature a busy bee). Apperson 73–74; Bartlett 807; Boshears 35:388; McAtee *Grant County* 3; NC 368; *Oxford* 71; Taylor *Comparisons* 22; Tilley B202; Whiting *Scots* I 137; J. T. Farrell *Judgement Day* (1935) 341; Mary Plum *Murder at the Hunting Club* (1932) 260 as a whole hive of bees; Llewelyn Powys *Apples Be Ripe* (1930) 206 as a honey-bee.

3. As bisy as bees in a tar-barrel (44 Thompson *Major* 116; Eliason 103). DA Bee 2 d, Tar 1 b (2); NC 368.

4. Gettin' full as a bee on chamber-lye (59 Taliaferro *Fisher's* 255).

5. Wasn't I as happy as a bee on a red clover tip? (44 Stephens *High Life* II 75).

6. Industrious as a bee (55 Stephens *Homestead* 68).

7. Pouring in as thick as bees (33 Smith *Downing* 109, *Letters* 89; Baldwin *Flush* 173; Richardson *Secret* 285

they were so thick that they looked like swarming bees; Shillaber *Ike* 14). Svartengren 329; Tilley B210; Whiting *Drama* 305:21, *Scots* I 137; Vincent McHugh *Caleb Catlum's America* (1936) 298 in a honey-comb.

8. That *mout* be a bee, as the old woman said when she killed a wasp (35 Longstreet *Georgia* 197; Haliburton *Clockmaker* III 59 but it mought be a bee for all that, as the old woman said when she looked in the hornet's nest for honey).

9. [Crowds] like bees in hiving time (44 Stephens *High Life* II 154). Cf. Whiting *Scots* I 137 (5).

10. Running in and out of the great store-houses like swarms of bees around their hives (43 Robb *Squatter* 13).

11. The folks pouring out of their houses like bees out of a gum (35 Crockett *Account* 91).

12. Stick like a bee to my back (54 Melville "Rich Man's Crumbs" in *Works* XIII 209).

13. A party with gret aims like these Must stick jest ez close ez a hive full o' bees (48 Lowell *Biglow* 80).

14. Our creditors will swarm on us like bees on a treacle cask (66 Boucicault *Flying Scud* 219; Alcott *Little Women* 492 went to him like bees to a honey-pot). Cf. NC 368; Taylor *Comparisons* 22; Tilley B210; G. D. H. and M. Cole *The Sleeping Death* (1936) 175.

15. In this latter case the folks swarm like bees (43 Hall *Purchase* I 103; Lowell *Biglow* 228 An' they swarmed out like bees; Clemens *Innocents* II 382, *Roughing* II 13). NC 368. Cf. Tilley B210.

16. We'll work like bees (68 Alcott *Little Women* 131; Clemens *Roughing* I 100).

Beef, 1. My flesh would jerk like a dead beef's (59 Taliaferro *Fisher's* 55).

2. His mouf wer es red es a split beef (67 Harris *Sut* 199). Cf. Svartengren 246 beef, raw beef.

3. See Bull beef.

Bee line, 1. [A hurricane] just as straight as ye'd run a bee line (56 Kelly *Humors* 72). Elsie N. Wright *Strange Murders at Greystones* (Cleveland 1931) 198.

2. I maid a brake on a bee line for Urwinton (45 Hooper *Simon* 103; Melville *Redburn* 148 to make a bee-line from port to port; Anon., *New Hope* 219 he cum in a bee line to camp twenty miles; Hammett *Stray* 106, 131; Haliburton *Nature* II 12; Whitehead *Wild Sports* 77; Clemens *Roughing* I 220). Bartlett 37; DA Bee 1; Farmer 48–49; Farmer and Henley I 163–164; Green 54; NC 368; Schele de Vere 204; Stevenson 145:8 take; Thornton I 54, III 24; Eustace H. Ball *The Scarlet Fox* (1927) 75.

Bee-swarm. The crowd clustered together like a bee-swarm (58 Porter *Major* 21).

Beer, 1. They who drink beer think beer (67 Richardson *Beyond* 19). R. Austin Freeman *The Mystery of 31, New Inn* (1930) 84.

2. He thinks no small beer of himself (40 Haliburton *Clockmaker* III 164). Farmer 338; Farmer and Henley I 165; NED Beer 1 b; *Oxford* 650; Stevenson 147:4; A. T. Sheppard *Here Comes an Old Sailor* (1928) 305.

Beer barrel. To set a feller's patriotism to working like a beer barrel (44 Stephens *High Life* II 155).

Beet, 1. As crimson as a beet (68 Clift *Bunker* 98).

2. Lips . . . red as a blood beet (44 Stephens *High Life* II 195; Judd *Margaret* II 69 beet; Baldwin *Flush* 189 beet; Durivage *Three* 78 blood beets; Harris *Sut* 96 beet, 285 [nose] es taper, an' red an' sharp es a beet; Clift *Bunker* 79 as red in the face as a beet, 235). Boshears 39:854; McAtee 52; NC 368; Taylor *Comparisons* 68; S. L. Bradbury *Hiram Harding of Hardscrabble* (Rutland, Vt. 1936) 153 in the common expression of the neighborhood.

Beetle, 1. And he was as blind as a beetle in the New England Catechism (57 Riley *Puddleford* 35). Apperson 54 (12); NED Beetle sb.² 3; *Oxford* 50; Svartengren 171–172; Tilley B219.
2. [The birds] are dumb as beetles (56 Kelly *Humors* 316). NED Beetle sb.¹ 2; Whiting *Scots* I 137.

Beet leaf. [Ears] as long as beet leaves (44 Stephens *High Life* II 36).

Beetle-ring. I don't kear the valie of a beetle-ring which gets the better (23 Cooper *Pioneers* 448).

Beggar, 1. But "beggars must not be choosers" (53 Cary *Clovernook* 2d Ser. 325; Cartwright *Autobiography* 173 I will have you to know beggars are not to be choosers; Holmes *Poet* 56 beggars mustn't be choosers). Apperson 34; NC 368; *Oxford* 31; Snapp 90:5; Stevenson 149:2; Tilley B247; A. E. Fielding, pseud. *The Tall House* (1933) 231.
2. A mahogany patriot is a crittur that rides like a beggar ahorseback: you'll know him by his gait (40 Haliburton *Clockmaker* III 187; Hawthorne "Old News" in *House* 560 Now is the day when every beggar gets on horseback. And is not the whole land

like a beggar on horseback riding post to the Devil?; Richardson *Secret* 194 The mistake was discovered just in season to save the rider from the proverbial destiny of a beggar on horseback). Apperson 35; Hardie 464:124; *Oxford* 30–31; NED Beggar 1 c; Snapp 90:24; Stevenson 150:10; Tilley B239; Carolyn Wells *The Affair at Flower Acres* (1923) 29 there's an old proverb.

Beginning. A good beginning makes a good ending (43 Lewis *Odd* 109). Apperson 257; Lean III 390; NC 369 right ending; *Oxford* 250; Stevenson 156:3; Tilley B259; Whiting *Chaucer* 135, *Drama* 127, *Scots* I 137 A work weill begon hes the bettir end; George Weston *His First Million Women* (1934) 265.

Bell, 1. My head is as clear as a bell (37 Neal *Charcoal* 199; Haliburton *Sam* II 120 Your complexion is as clear as a bell; Porter *Major* 141 His voice as clear as a bell; "Editor's Drawer" *Harper's New Monthly Magazine* VII (1853) 849; Holmes *Poet* 175 [a liquid] as clear as a bell). Apperson 101; Boshears 35:404; Fife 118; NC 369; NED Clear 3 b; Taylor *Comparisons* 26; Tilley B271; Stuart Martin *The Fifteen Cells* (1928) 132.
2. His voice was low and deep-toned as a bell (55 Stephens *Homestead* 91).
3. All went "merry as a marriage bell" (43 Robb *Squatter* 84; Browne *Artemus* 30 Except this unpropishus circumstance all went as merry as a carriage bell, as Lord Byrun sez; Derby *Squibob* 125 all went berry as a marriage mell; Sedley *Marian* 326; Chamberlain *Confession* 210; Smith *Arp* 107; Clemens *Sketches* 111). Byron *Childe Harold's Pilgrimage* iii 21;

Hardie 468:59; Taylor *Comparisons* 57; M. J. Freeman *The Murder of a Midget* (1931) 267.

4. Prove it . . . by bell, book and candle, as it were (25 Neal *Brother J* I 9; Judd *Richard* 452 Without book, bell or prayer). Apperson 37; NED Bell 8; *Oxford* 32; Stevenson 474:4; Tilley B276; Whiting *Drama* 340:489, *Scots* I 138; C. B. Clason *The Death Angel* (1936) 8 I put on the whole show with bell, book and candle.

Bellow, vb. See Bashan (2).

Belly, 1. Hands as white as the belly of a flat fish (49 Haliburton *Old Judge* I 44). Svartengren 233 haddock.

2. Grandfather Slick used to say there was an old proverb in Yorkshire, "a full belly makes a strong back" (36 Haliburton *Clockmaker* I 158). Cf. Apperson 181 An empty belly makes a lazy back.

3. "Shall a man fill his belly with the east wind?" says the proverb (23–24 Irving *Tales* 161). Job 15:2.

Belly-full. Gut his belly-full (33 Neal *Down-Easters* I 70; Crockett *Exploits* 182 We have a prospect of soon getting our bellies full of fighting; Haliburton *Clockmaker* III 219). Farmer and Henley I 173; Green 56; NED Belly-ful; Stevenson 800:2; Tilley B306; Whiting *Drama* 335:396; Talbot Mundy *Tros of Samothrace* (1934) 53.

Bench, 1. Settin' on the anxious benches (38 Haliburton *Clockmaker* II 119). DA Anxious bench; Farmer 18; Green 43; NC 369. See Seat.

2. Mourner's bench. 45 DA Mourner 2.

Bend, sb. Above one's bend. 35 DA Bend sb. 1.

Bend, vb. I'll bend or break you (49 Melville *Mardi* II 216). Cf. Apperson 42 Beter bowe than brest; NC 369; *Oxford* 39; Stevenson 169:3; Tilley B566; Whiting *Chaucer* 69, *Scots* I 143; Samuel Lover *Handy Andy* (1842) ch. 1 (Everyman's Library 4) The boast, I may break, but I won't bend.

Bender. Crew all on a "bender" in the engine room (55 Thomson *Doesticks* 169; Kelly *Humors* 50 a rich man [in misery] applies to his banker, and tries on a "bender," 127 Peter Houp was on a "regular bender," a "big tare," a long spree; Lowell *Biglow* 238). Bartlett 39–40; DA Bender; Farmer 51; Farmer and Henley I 177; Green 56; Partridge 47; Schele de Vere 582; Stevenson 639:9; Thornton I 56. Cf. Fife 120.

Benefit. I'll give you the benefit of the doubt (69 Boucicault *Presumptive* 250). Stevenson 619:4.

Benjamin. On examination I found that mine [a letter of recommendation] contained a "Benjamin's mess" (c56 Cartwright *Autobiography* 59). Lean II ii 799; NED Benjamin 3.

Bermudas. The old couplet, which was quoted again and again by those who thought we should have one more touch of a storm before our long absence was up—"If the Bermudas let you pass, You must beware of Hatteras (40 Dana *Two* 444–445). *Oxford* 34; Stevenson 2047:1 (this passage only); A. H. Fauset *Folklore from Nova Scotia* (1931) 204:418 If Bermuda that you pass, Beware of Cape Hatteras. If Cape Hatteras chance to fail, In the Gulf [Stream] you'll get a gale. But if the Gulf should miss you first, On the coast you'll get it worse.

Berry. Oranges, tinged here and there, berry-brown (47 Melville *Omoo* 306, *Mardi* II 64). Boshears 35:384; NED Berry 4; NC 369; Taylor *Comparisons* 21; Whiting *Drama* 306:28, *Scots* I 138; Natalie S. Lincoln *Marked "Cancelled"* (1930) 241.

Berth. The monster was allowed a wide berth (45 Mayo *Kaloolah* 276; Melville *White Jacket* 233; Burke *Polly* 193; Bennett *Border* 59; Hammett *Piney* 271; Dorson *Jonathan* 48; Nash *Century* 113). Babcock 261; NED Berth 1.

Best, 1. I'll do my best. Angels can do no more, cried Pinckney (65 Sedley *Marian* 418). Edward Young *Night Thoughts* ii 91–92 Who does the best his circumstance allows, Does well, acts nobly; angels could do no more; A. E. Fielding *The Cluny Problem* (1926) 55 My grandmother used to say: Do your best and bury the rest. Angels can't do better.
2. Everything is best when it is ended (50 Judd *Richard* 188).
3. An old and favorite maxim of his, "that one way or other, all would turn out for the best" (20–22 Irving *Bracebridge* 403).
4. You must make the best of a bad bargain (38 Haliburton *Clockmaker* II 274–275; Melville *Typee* 193; Clemens *Gilded* II 114, *Tramp* II 23). Apperson 40; NC 370; *Oxford* 36; Tilley B326; O. R. Cohen *The May Day Mystery* (1929) 57.
5. An affair . . . in which I came off second best (72 Holmes *Poet* 118).

Bet. But a bet's a bet, you know—else what makes parsimmons pucker? (57 Bennett *Border* 288). Cf. Bargain (1).

Better, 1. Pete Hopkins aint no better nor he should be (43 Thompson *Chronicles* 74; Stephens *High Life* I 185 she was no better than she ought to be; Shillaber *Mrs. Partington* 105, 163, *Knitting-Work* 278; Riley *Puddleford* 29, 32, 37; Clemens *Sandwich* 196). *Oxford* 453; Stevenson 174:13; Tilley B335.
2. I couldn't have did it better myself (39 Briggs *Harry* II 88; Stephens *High Life* II 175).
3. Meriweather appeared to be getting no better fast (51 Burke *Polly* 116; Kelly *Humors* 189 However, things . . . grew no better fast, 418; Hammett *Piney* 109 the wind all the time getting no better very fast indeed).

Betty Martin. High Betty Martin—tip-top fine! (24 Neal *Brother J* II 365). Cf. Apperson 7; Farmer and Henley I 34–36; *Oxford* 8; Stevenson 732:9; NQ 3 xi 276, 346, 7 ix 216, 298, 8 xi 146, 512, xii 298, 11 iv 207, 254, 294, 313, 377; Charles Barry, pseud. *Murder on Monday?* (1932) 109.

Bib. Put on your best "bib and tucker" (57 Jones *Country* 205). Green 56; NED Bib 1 b, *Supplement* Bib 1 b; Partridge 49; Thornton I 57.

Bible. I'll jest swar on a stack of bibles (43 Robb *Squatter* 114; Hammett *Piney* 123–124 and I'll be qualified to that on a stack of bibles, as big as a meetin' house). McAtee 5.

Big. See Ace (1), Boot (9), Bull (1), Congressman, Drum (1), End (7), Football (1), Gooseberry, Haystack, Hen (2), Horse (6), Leviathan, Life (2), Meeting house, Mogul, Nebuchadnezzar (1), Outdoors, Pumpkin (2), Saucer, Side (1), Thunder (1), Walnut, World (1).

Bill. To fill the bill. 60 DA Bill sb. 3 b, Fill vb. 4 (1).

Billiard-ball, 1. As bald as a billiard-ball (53 Baldwin *Flush* 172; Locke [Nasby] *Struggles* 490). NC 370; Taylor *Comparisons* 15.

2. As smooth and as round as a billiard ball (34 Davis *Downing* 290; Clemens *Sketches* 13). Svartengren 270 smooth.

Bind. But fast bind, fast find, is a'most an excellent good rule for a traveller in the dark (35 Kennedy *Horse-Shoe* 288; Haliburton *Attaché* IV 57 Fast bind, sure find, is my way; Cary *Clovernook* 196). Apperson 204; *Oxford* 192; Stevenson 802:12; Tilley B352; Whiting *Drama* 100. Cf. J. A. Ferguson *The Man in the Dark* (1928) 27 safe bind, safe find.

Bird, 1. I'd rather have a bird in the hand than one in the bush (33 Smith *Downing* 192; Emerson *Works* IV 159 A world in the hand is worth two in the bush; Melville *Typee* 233 our old adage—"A bird in the hand is worth two in the bush"; Hall *Purchase* II 162; Judd *Margaret* II 211; Riley *Puddleford* 315 never again give "a bird in the hand for [none] in the bush"; Smith *My Thirty* 352; Stephens *Fashion* 161; Cary *Married* 92, 132; Boucicault *Flying Scud* 220 Yes, it's a hold saying, and a true one, That a bush in the hand is worth two in the bird; Jones *Batkins* 50). Apperson 48; McAtee *Grant County* 2; NC 370; NED Bird 6; *Oxford* 44–45; Snapp 70:270; Stevenson 181:3; Stoett 2464; Tilley B363; Whiting *Drama* 155, 172, 221, *Scots* I 139; S. and A. Seifert *Death Stops at the Old Stone Inn* (1935) 43. Cf. Edith Henrich *The Pacific Spectator* III (1949) 129 the poet does not grant that a fish in the hand is worth two in the sea.

2. Little bird sing sich song in my

ear—didn't like to hear it (46 Cooper *Redskins* 136; Hall *Wilderness* 108 The Indians say it was told him by a bad bird; Cary *Clovernook* 2d Ser. 236 Oh, a little bird told me). Eccles. 10:20; Apperson 48; NC 370; *Oxford* 45; Stevenson 176:9; Tilley B374; NQ i 232, 284, 394, 4 iv 292, 6 iv 366; C. Fraser-Simson *The Swinging Shutter* (1928) 48 "Who told you that?" "The proverbial bird"; Nancy B. Mavity *The Tule Marsh Murder* (1929) 222 the traditional and popular phrase would mention a little bird.

3. He had lived so much among the Indians, and was so accustomed to their way of biling things down to an essence, that he spoke in proverbs, or wise saws. Says he to me, with a shake of his head, *"a mocking bird has no voice of its own."* It warn't a bad sayin, was it? I wish I had noted more of them, for though I like 'em, I am so yarney, I can't make them as pithey as he did (35 Haliburton *Nature* I 317).

4. [Children] blithe as the birds (45 Judd *Margaret* II 250).

5. As bright as a bird (40 Dana *Two* 411; Stephens *Homestead* 313 as bright and spry).

6. As brisk as a bird (67 *Harper's New Monthly Magazine* XXXV 484).

7. As chipper as a flock of birds (44 Stephens *High Life* I 179, 249 as two birds on an apple-tree limb in springtime, II 137 as two birds, 234 as two birds teeterin on an appletree limb in springtime). Cf. Svartengren 160 peart.

8. As chirk as a bird (44 Stephens *High Life* II 62).

9. The glorious roving life they led, free as birds (23–24 Irving *Tales* 293; Stephens *Homestead* 434 thank God, we are as free as two wild birds).

10. There it [a guinea] is, harnsome as a yaller bird (c58 Stephens *Mary Derwent* 199).

11. Happy as a bird (54 Stephens *Fashion* 19, *Homestead* 199).

12. Isabel, light and graceful as the bird (55 Stephens *Homestead* 81).

13. Guide us, straight as the bird flies, to the Ravensnest (45 Cooper *Satanstoe* 332). See Crow (4). Cf. Taylor *Comparisons* 78 crow.

14. Two hundred miles as the bird flies (65 Richardson *Secret* 428, *Beyond* 313; Clemens *Roughing* II 230, *Tramp* II 185). See Crow (4).

15. Thick as birds arter a thunderstorm (45 Judd *Margaret* II 96).

16. I continued to walk on, . . . attracted thither, perhaps, by that secret sympathy which causes birds of the same feather to fly together (39 Briggs *Harry* II 49; Haliburton *Clockmaker* III 243 where there are birds of the same feather, *Attaché* I 148 "Birds of a feather flock together," as the old maxim goes, IV 156, *Sam* II 78; Boker *World* 19 Yes, we always go in flocks, on the birds-of-a-feather principle; Cary *Clovernook* 2d Ser. 41; Stephens *Mary Derwent* 186; Lincoln III 453 we know you are "all of a feather"; Boucicault *Flying Scud* 202 you know the old adage, "Birds of a feather flock together"; Saxe *Poems* 57 Birds of every feather, On a common level Travelling together; Nash *Century* 61 'Birds of a feather,' you know). Sirach 27:9 Birds dwell with their kind; Apperson 48; NC 370; NED Bird 5; *Oxford* 45; Snapp 70:272; Stevenson 1430:3; Tilley B393; Whiting *Drama* 161, 256; NQ 3 ix 176, 10 ii 8, 74; Miles Burton *The Clue of the Fourteen Keys* 269 the proverb; H. L. Ickes *Diary* (1953) I 539 He said that they were both birds of a feather;

Lynn Thorndike *History of Magic and Experimental Science* (8 v., New York 1923–1958) V 128.

17. There is some plaguy foul birds in Washington, and if some 'on em hain't siled their own neests, I'm mistaken (34 Davis *Downing* 87; Haliburton *Clockmaker* II 317). Apperson 323; NC 371; NED Bird 6; *Oxford* 314; Stevenson 179:5; Tilley B377; Whiting *Scots* I 139; Ralph C. Woodthorpe *The Public School Murder* (London 1932) 284.

18. Away she went, like a bird (25 Neal *Brother J* II 421; Smith *'Way* 57 sped, 239 was off; Porter *Major* 126 sped).

19. He's an early bird . . . the bird what catches the worm (51 Melville *Moby-Dick* I 21; Haliburton *Sam* I 146 It's the early bird that gets the worm; Clemens *Washoe* 35 the "early bird" whose specialty it hath been to work destruction, 56 Hope some early bird will catch this Grub, 84, 112 Wisdom teaches us that none but birds should go out early, and that not even birds should do it unless they are out of worms, *Enterprise* 182 It is the early bird that catches the worm, but I would not get up at that time in the morning for a thousand worms, if I were not obliged to; Saxe *Poems* 134 I like the lad who, when his father thought To clip his morning nap by hackneyed phrase Of vagrant worm by early songster caught, Cried "Served him right!—it's not at all surprising; The worm was punished, sir, for early rising!"). Apperson 173–174; NC 371; *Oxford* 163–164; Snapp 70:279; Stevenson 180–181:11; Tilley B368; Margery Allingham *Kingdom of Death* (1933) 56; Lovell Thompson *The Pacific Spectator* IV (1950) 208 or it may be that the mineral

minstrels and the cowboy and his catarrh [on the radio] believe that the early bird gets the worm.

20. On the morning of his intended execution, the cage was opened, but the bird had flown (21 Cooper *Spy* 125; Melville *Pierre* 504 Both birds were flown; Hammett *Stray* 336; Kelly *Humors* 95; Richardson *Secret* 252–253, 478 they found the birds flown). Apperson 49; *Oxford* 45; Stevenson 178:7; Tilley B364; Whiting *Drama* 291; E. D. Biggers *The Chinese Parrot* (Indianapolis 1926) 251; Kenneth Livingston *The Dodd Cases* (1934) 135.

21. We shall then verify the old proverb, by killing two birds with one stone (21 Emerson *Journals* I 45; Smith *Downing* 204 You can kill two birds with one stone; Hall *Soldier's Bride* 178; Haliburton *Clockmaker* I 327 unlike the stone that killed two birds, III 302; Thompson *Chronicles* 99 How to kill two birds with one stone [chapter heading]; Burke *Polly* 25; Melville *Moby-Dick* I 104 might as well kill both birds at once, *Pierre* 504 Kill 'em both with one stone; Cary *Clovernook* 2d Ser. 16; Willis *Paul* 178; Stephens *Mary Derwent* 200, 376; Clemens *Gilded* I 67). Apperson 340; NC 371; NED Stone 16 b; *Oxford* 334–335; Tilley B400; Nellise Child *The Diamond Ransom Murders* (1935) 173.

22. Catch old birds with chaff! (25 Neal *Brother J* II 101, 443, III 268, 303; Hall *Soldier's Bride* 20; Haliburton *Clockmaker* II 201 too old a bird to be caught by chaff; Stephens *Mary Derwent* 220 Catch an old bird with chaff, if you can!; Clift *Bunker* 13 that old proverb "old birds are not to be caught with chaff," 78 a kind of chaff that don't catch old birds but

once; Saxe *Poems* 155 For *that* sort of chaff he wasn't the bird; Barnum *Struggles* 693 But I had been too long in the business to be caught by such chaff; Clemens *Innocents* I 144 a snare to trap the unwary—chaff to catch fledglings with, *Gilded* I 288 Slum, who is too old a bird to be caught with chaff). Apperson 49; *Oxford* 85; Stevenson 180:7; Tilley B396. Cf. Green 36; NC 371:22; C. F. Gregg *Danger at Cliff House* (1936) 45.

23. Why, barber, are you reaching up to catch birds there with salt? (57 Melville *Confidence-Man* 299). Apperson 549; NC 470; *Oxford* 560; Tilley B401; Bertram Atkey *The Man with Yellow Eyes* (1927) 33. Cf. Salt (9).

24. Let a bird out o' your hand, and try to catch it ag'in, will you? (38 Haliburton *Clockmaker* II 80).

25. Her heart a swelling in her harnsome bosom, like a bird when it's first caught (44 Stephens *High Life* I 245).

26. It [dancing] was like a bird on an apple tree limb in spring time (44 Stephens *High Life* II 61–62).

Bird's egging. To go on with one's bird's egging. 54 DA Bird 4 d.

Bird's nest. See Nest (1).

Biscuit, 1. His flesh being hard as twice-baked biscuit (51 Melville *Moby-Dick* I 141). NC 371. Cf. Tilley B404.

2. They sot to my feet as slick as a biscuit (44 Stephens *High Life* I 198).

3. He . . . says he thinks you are rather hurrying up the biscuits (66 Kelly *Humors* 210). Cf. Cake (2).

Bishop, 1. A livin' Bishop is worth a hundred dead saints any time (53 Haliburton *Sam* II 292). Cf. Dog (5).

2. As calm as a bishop (59–60 Holmes *Elsie* 159).

3. As steady as a bishop (60 Haliburton *Season-Ticket* 170).

Bit, 1. Bit's in his teeth—never stop till his heart breaks (50 Boker *World* 46; Nash *Century* 100 Some of your pupils . . . will 'take the bit in their teeth'). *Oxford* 641; Stevenson 189:2, 1711:5; Stoett 610; Tidwell PADS XI (1945) 13; Tilley B424; David Fox, pseud. *Ethel Opens the Door* (1922) 258.

2. Your ministers there in Connecticut pull the bit on the church members a leetle too tight sometimes (44 Stephens *High Life* I 54).

Bitch. It will be like the old bitch and the rabbit, nip and tack every jump, and sometimes the bitch a leetle ahead (58 Porter *Major* 16).

Bite, sb. Never make two bites at a cherry (20 Loomis *Farmer's Almanac* 177). Apperson 653; NED Bite sb. 4; *Oxford* 678; Stevenson 190:1.

Bite, vb., 1. She looked pooty enough to tempt a feller to bite a piece out on her (43 Robb *Squatter* 145). Cf. Good (3).

2. To bite off more than one can chew. 77 DA Bite, vb. 2. NC 371; Stevenson 189–190:11.

Biter. The biters were bit (25 Neal *Brother J* II 441, *Down-Easters* I 23 the biter bit; Haliburton *Clockmaker* I 171 a biter bit, *Attaché* II 239; Barnum *Struggles* 168 the biter bitten, 703 the biters were bit). Apperson 50; NED Biter 2; *Oxford* 47; Stevenson 189:5; Tilley B429; Dana Scott *Five Fatal Letters* (1937) 162. Cf. Farmer and Henley I 205–206.

Bitter. See Gall (1), Sin (3), Wormwood.

Bitters, 1. The seal soon got his bitters [i. e., was killed]. (56 Porter *Major* 194). DA Bitters sb. pl. 2.

2. Mister, toe the mark and take yer bitters (55 Dorson *Jonathan* 57).

Black, 1. He cursed them black and blue (53 Baldwin *Flush* 288). NED Black 13; Stevenson 205:8 To pinch black and blue.

2. Declared by everything that's black and blue . . . they'd make the Jacksonites take a dose worth two of that (33 Smith *Downing* 118).

3. He kept on larfin till he was black in the face (62 Browne *Artemus* 140). NED Black 12.

4. All in my pocket in black and white (34 Davis *Downing* 161; Lincoln I 139; Melville *Redburn* 300, *Confidence-Man* 312, 324; Kelly *Humors* 191, 398; Riley *Puddleford* 38, 235; Smith *'Way* 183; Holmes *Autocrat* 300 And there was the will in black and white; Jones *Batkins* 397). Apperson 53; Farmer and Henley I 209; Green 59; NED Black 15; *Oxford* 47; Stevenson 194:1; Tilley B439.

5. If you had a black hat on, he could go to talking to you and in ten minutes he could make you think it was white (33 Smith *Downing* 195; Richardson *Beyond* 349 a few miserable, stinking lawyers . . . who for five dollars will prove that black is white [quoted from Brigham Young]). *Oxford* 48 prove; Stevenson 193:11; Tilley B440, 441; Whiting *Drama* 335:406, *Scots* I 140; Whitman Chambers *Murder for a Wanton* (1934) 243.

6. See Ace (2), Blaze (3), Coal (1), Coal-hole, Coat (1), Cow's horn, Crow (2), Death (1), Dirt (1), Ebony, Erebus, Face (3), Flea (1), Get out, Grave sb. (2), Hat (2), Hinge,

Ink (1), Jet, Midnight (1), Mine sb. (1), Mink (1), Nigger (1), Night (1), Pall, Pitch (1, 2), Pot sb. (1), Raven (1), Side (2), Soot, Spinning wheel, Tar (1, 2), Thunder (2), Thundercloud (1), Thunder-squall, Weasel (2), Wolf (2).

Blackberry, 1. Money is as plenty as blackberries (34 Davis *Downing* 102; Cooper *Redskins* 307 plentier than blackberries; Neal *Charcoal* 170; Mayo *Kaloolah* 55; Anon. *New Hope* 276; Jones *Winkles* 338; P. H. Myers *Thrilling Adventures of the Prisoner of the Border* (1857, ed. New York [1860] 320) Hunters here are plentier than blackberries in August; Smith *My Thirty* 413; Lincoln V 186 not as; Richardson *Beyond* 108 and quite as cheap). Apperson 53; *Oxford* 507; Stevenson 1815:10; Svartengren 395; Tilley B442; Rosamond Lehmann *The Weather in the Streets* (1936) 191 plentiful.

2. Constables are as thick as blackberries (37 Neal *Charcoal* 192; Haliburton *Sam* I 212 They aint quite as thick as blackberries, *Nature* I 7 as thick as blackberries in the Fall, after the robins have left to go to sleep for the winter). Stevenson 1815:10; Svartengren 395.

3. Blackberries don't grow on every bush (25 Neal *Brother J* II 220). Cf. Bush (1), Money (8).

Blackberrying. God goes 'mong the worlds blackberrying (51 Melville *Moby-Dick* II 195). Cf. Whiting *Chaucer* 185.

Blackbird, 1. As chipper as a blackbird (44 Stephens *High Life* II 170).

2. But the long and short is, you're free as a blackbird (54 Stephens *Fashion* 328).

3. [The young couple] as happy as a pair of blackbirds in a new furrow (32 Hall *Legends* 37).

4. Cousin Esther and Sally used to be about as thick as blackbirds in the pie (68 Clift *Bunker* 256). Cf. Taylor *Comparisons* 81.

5. We chatted away like blackbirds . . . with 'bout as much sense (59 Taliaferro *Fisher's* 183). Cf. Taylor *Comparisons* 19 jabber; Tilley P285.

6. They paid no more attention to my Lating [Latin] than to a blackbird a-chatterin' (59 Taliaferro *Fisher's* 195).

Black snake. Charmed me to the spot, like a black snake charms a catbird (59 Taliaferro *Fisher's* 126).

Bladder. He'd had his wind-pipe stopped as tight as a bladder (36 Haliburton *Clockmaker* I 35).

Blank, 1. Arter I'd drawed sech heaps o' blanks, Fortin at last hez sent a prize (67 Lowell *Biglow* 284). Partridge 240.

2. See Cartridge.

Blanket, 1. Yaller as a blanket (56 Durivage *Three* 116).

2. Puts a wet blanket on it (49 Haliburton *Old Judge* I 222; Willis *Life* 306; Smith *My Thirty* 311; Alcott *Little Women* 233 I know Meg would wet-blanket such a proposal, 527 Now don't be a wet-blanket). NED Wet blanket 2; Partridge 61; Tiffany Thayer *Thirteen Women* (1932) 134.

3. His "gift of gab," and unadulterated propensity to elongate the blanket (56 Kelly *Humors* 91). DA Blanket 5 stretch; Randolph and Wilson 289. See Stocking (1).

4. To wear the blanket [i. e., to be of Indian blood]. 39 DA Blanket 5.

Blanket Bay. Before we ride to anchor in Blanket Bay (51 Melville *Moby-Dick* I 215). Babcock 262. Cf. Tilley B198 Bedfordshire.

Blate. See Calf (3).

Blaze, 1. His face was red as a blaze (39 Smith *Letters* 29, 83, '*Way* 62; Whitcher *Widow* 316).

2. He would turn as red as a blaze of fire (33 Smith *Downing* 216). Cf. Whiting *Scots* I 140; Svartengren 249–250 (glede, fire).

3. His face as black as the very old blazes (43 Thompson *Chronicles* 49).

4. And every one on board ship looked as blue as blazes (58 Hammett *Piney* 136). Taylor *Comparisons* 19.

5. Cold as blue blazes (58 Hammett *Piney* 147). DA Blue a. 4; Taylor *Comparisons* 27; Howell Vines *This Green Thicket World* (Boston 1934) 149.

6. And the best thing I can think of, Is to cut her dead as blazes (c56 Thomson *Plu-ri-bus-tah* 242).

7. Hot as blue blazes (33 Neal *Down-Easters* I 99, 129 blazes). NC 372; Boshears 37:675; Taylor *Comparisons* 50.

8. As mad as blazes (33 Smith *Downing* 206). Boshears 38:734; Halpert 957.

9. All red as blazes (44 Stephens *High Life* II 236; Whitcher *Widow* 235).

10. He's . . . sassyer'n blazers (76 Nash *Century* 211).

11. Warm as blazes (44 Stephens *High Life* II 227).

12. Come out like all blazes agin one of your letters in the Express (44 Stephens *High Life* I 172; Burke *Polly* 83 I'll larrup you like blazes; Kelly *Humors* 190; Shillaber *Mrs. Partington* 85 lick you like blazes, 229 long

comes one of 'em, like blazes; Thomson *Plu-ri-bus-tah* 65 He would "wallop him like blazes"; Jones *Wild* 47 when the fire came like blazes; Taliaferro *Fisher's* 177 we went at it like blazes, 196 at it we went like blue blazes; Eggleston *School-Master* 37 licked the one [teacher] afore them like blazes). Farmer and Henley I 225; Schele de Vere 583–584; Whiting *Devil* 244 (3); Phoebe A. Taylor *Death Lights a Candle* (Indianapolis 1932) 72 lie; Arthur Gask *Murder in the Night* (1932) 96 ran.

13. That night it come on to blow like blazes (58 Hammett *Piney* 64).

14. Intimated that the department might go to blazes, for all he cared (39 Briggs *Harry* I 124). Whiting *Devil* 245 (3).

15. And the two Jacobs swore like blue blazes agin him (58 Hammett *Piney* 37).

16. He can whoop [whop] blue blazes out of ye (43 Thompson *Chronicles* 32).

Blessed. Swearin that he'd see em blest afore . . . (68 Locke [Nasby] *Struggles* 511). Farmer and Henley I 228–229; NED Bless vb. 11.

Blessedness. Remain in single blessedness (43 Lewis *Odd* 180; Willis *Paul* 330; Browne *Artemus* 22). NED Blessedness; Stevenson 307:9.

Blind, 1. None are so blind, I guess, as them that won't see (38 Haliburton *Clockmaker* II 3, *Sam* I 20, *Season-Ticket* 115 for none are so blind as them as won't see, so deaf as what won't hear, or so ignorant as won't know what ain't their business to know; Smith '*Way* 279). Apperson 55; NC 372; *Oxford* 50; Stevenson 198:10; Tilley S206; NQ CLIV (1928) 27;

Reginald Davis *The Crowing Hen* (1936) 72.

2. Political self government means the blind leading the blind (53 Haliburton *Sam* I 283; Jones *Country* 146 And he'll be like the man in Scripture —the blind leading the blind; Riley *Puddleford* 87 "When the blind lead the blind," as the newspapers say, "they all go head over heels into the ditch"). Matt. 15:14; Luke 6:39; Apperson 56; NC 372; *Oxford* 51; Stevenson 198–199:11; Tilley B452; Whiting *Drama* 98, *Scots* I 140; Natalie S. Lincoln *The Secret of Mohawk Pond* (1928) 189.

3. Yes, and you "went it blind" (57 Jones *Country* 273; Hammett *Piney* 67 I'll go it blind on your luck; Lowell *Biglow* 331 O little city gals, don't never go it Blind on the word o' noospaper or poet!). Bartlett 250; Farmer 63; Farmer and Henley I 231; Partridge 64; Schele de Vere 328; Stevenson 1224:5; Thornton I 367, III 164.

4. See Badger, Beetle (1), Owl (2).

Blister, 1. Fits it like a blister (79 Clemens *Tramp* I 128). John Goodwin, pseud., *When Dead Men Tell Tales* (1928) 257.

2. It will draw like a blister [i. e., the play will attract a large audience]. (37 Neal *Charcoal* 123).

Blithe. See Bird (4), Grasshopper (1), Lark (1).

Blood, 1. Blood red (25 Neal *Brother J* I 202, III 403; Kennedy *Swallow* 113; Dana *Two* 429; Judd *Margaret* I 161; Stephens *Fashion* 115, *Mary Derwent* 118 blood-red rubies; Melville *Mardi* I 145, 354, *Pierre* 129; Hawthorne *Twice-Told* 321; Holmes *Au-*

tocrat 122 blood-red wine, 123). Apperson 526; Boshears 39:856; NC 372; *Oxford* 535; Taylor *Comparisons* 68; Tilley B455; Whiting *Drama* 306: 31, *Scots* I 141; Dorothy Aldis *Murder in a Haystack* (1931) 198.

2. Blood for blood is the backwoodsman's rule (32 Hall *Legends* 31).

3. Blood is thicker than water (35 Crockett *Account* 36). Apperson 56; NC 372; *Oxford* 51–52; Stevenson 202:7; NQ 3 xi 34, 103, 163; 7 vi 50–51, xii 53, 78, 114, 487; 9 viii 238, 428; 12 iii 356; Vance Randolph *The Devil's Pretty Daughter* (1955) 143 They was all kin folks though, and blood's thicker than water, so finally they just let it [a deception] pass; M. K. Rawlings *The Yearling* (1938) 187; Stark Young *So Red the Rose* (1934) 60, 64.

4. He was the last man to boast of his relations, but blood was blood, whatever they might say (57 Riley *Puddleford* 234). William Faulkner *The Unvanquished* (1938) 303.

5. Game to the backbone—blood will tell (50 Boker *World* 38; Nash *Century* 74; *Harper's New Monthly Magazine* LIII [1876] 708). NC 372; Stevenson 201:17; Andy Adams *The Ranch on the Beaver* (Boston 1927) 113 Young blood; E. D. Biggers *Keeper of the Keys* (Indianapolis 1932) 153; Milla Logan *Bring Along Laughter* (1947) 203; W. G. French *Western Humanities Review* X (1955–1956) 52 An adherent of the "blood-will-tell" doctrine.

6. It has always been a rule among hunters that the first blood drawn takes the skin, be it bear or deer (59 Browning *Forty-Four* 58).

7. The blood of the martyrs is the seed of the church (53 Curtis *Poti-*

phar 52). Apperson 56; Lean IV 111–112, 251; *Oxford* 52; Stevenson 1544: 11; Tilley B457; NQ 6 ii 493; 10 x 487.

8. Your blood be upon your own heads, if you do not heed me (25 Neal *Brother J* II 117). Stevenson 203:1; Francis Beeding, pseud. *The House of Dr. Edwards* (1928) 62.

9. She was one of your real high sort, when her blood was up (51 Stowe *Uncle* 6; Kelly *Humors* 110; Eggleston *School-Master* 234 It was not wise to reject counsel, but all his blood was up). NED Blood 5; *Oxford* 702 Welsh blood; Stevenson 203:6; Tilley B462.

10. I'll be darned . . . if it didn't make my blood boil to hear how he went on (44 Stephens *High Life* I 40, 45 how it makes the blood bile and tingle in a feller's heart to see his writing printed, 85 I never felt my blood bile so in all my life, 217, II 183 three cheers that made the blood bile in my heart like maple sap in a sugar kettle; Mayo *Kaloolah* 192 My blood boiled at the outrage).

11. It kinder makes my blood run cold to think on't (51 Stowe *Uncle* 6, 128; Stephens *Fashion* 307 I can tell you it made my blood run cold to see her among those women).

12. You can't get blood out of a stump (53 Haliburton *Sam* I 89; Clemens *Enterprise* 39 I sent him that turnip . . . requesting him to extract from it a sufficient quantity of blood to restore his equilibrium—[which I regarded as a very excellent joke]). Apperson 56; McAtee 72; NC 372; Stevenson 203:8; Tilley B466; Neil Bell, pseud. *The Lord of Life* (Boston 1933) 57 a stone; Gertrude Beasley *My First Thirty Years* (Paris 1925) 278.

Bloodhound. The northwest breeze which had stuck to her like a bloodhound (53 Willis *Fun* 111).

Bloodthirsty. See Wolf (3).

Blooming. See Rose (1).

Blow, 1. When we blowed off, I judge he had the worst of it (45 Hooper *Simon* 37). DA Blow vb. 6 (4).

2. Instead of blowing the gals up [i. e., reprimanding them]. (44 Stephens *High Life* I 235). Cf. DA Blow vb. 6 (7); Farmer and Henley I 251; NED Blow vb. 25 b.

3. See Forge.

Blue, 1. Talk? Yes! till all is blue (54 Smith '*Way* 55, *My Thirty* 286 he'll fight agin us till all is blue!; Lowell *Biglow* 285). Farmer and Henley I 255; NED Blue, a. 10; Thornton I 79.

2. I cussed him blue (51 Burke *Polly* 153; Hammett *Piney* 158 I *hev* heard him cuss tell iv'ry thing turned blue).

3. All true blue, here (25 Neal *Brother J* II 393; Smith *Downing* 133, 196 true blue republican, *My Thirty* 405; Haliburton *Clockmaker* II 225 if they'd ahad the true blue in 'em; Melville *White Jacket* 13 He was a Briton, and a true-blue, *Israel* 42 a Yankee of the true blue stamp, 74–75, "Two Temples" in *Works* XIII 189; Clemens *Tom* 134). Apperson 648; Farmer and Henley I 256, VII 213–214; NC 372; NED Blue a. 6 b; *Oxford* 672; Partridge 69; Whiting *Chaucer* 179, *Scots* I 141; A. C. and C. B. Edington *The Monk's-hood Murders* (1931) 125; E. K. Gann *Soldier of Fortune* (1954) 169. Cf. Thornton II 909.

4. Until, by his frequent libations, he not only got *blue* (43 Robb *Squatter* 154; Thomson *Elephant Club* 157

I . . . hain't been blue since, unless I wos last night). Berrey 283:4; DA Blue a. 1; Partridge 69; Stevenson 1451:4.

5. The Rooshian black eagle looks blue in his eerie (48 Lowell *Biglow* 85; Alcott *Little Women* 173 My patience, how blue we are!, 364 I felt a trifle blue). NED Blue a. 3; C. L. Day, ed. *The Songs of Thomas D'Urfey* (Cambridge, Mass. 1938) 47 Nor any *Prig* here, Or Sneaking *Whig*, . . . That now looks blue.

6. But I didn't see no call to talk blue when we was doin' so well (65 Sedley *Marian* 162).

7. Ef ye ever see a chap turn blue around the gills, that saloon-chap did for sartin (58 Hammett *Piney* 71, 108). Cf. Stevenson 1451:4.

8. See Blaze (4), Brimstone, Eye (1), Heaven (1), Indigo bag, Larkspur, Maid (1), Razor (1), Sky, Squash, Steel (1), Violet (1).

Bluebird. As gay and cheerful as a blue bird in spring (38 Crockett *Exploits* 125).

Blue Flujin. Cold! It was cold as *Blue Flujin*, where sailors say fire freezes (50 Melville *White Jacket* 126). Babcock 256; Halpert 895. Cf. Flugence.

Bluejay. You are as spruce as a bluejay (45 Judd *Margaret* I 65).

Blues. You've got the blues, this morning (51 Stowe *Uncle* 167; Riley *Puddleford* 139; Saxe *Poems* 58 a fit of the blues; Nash *Century* 245 'Blues' is simply another name for mild insanity). DA Blues n. pl. Cf. Farmer and Henley I 262.

Blush. See Peony (2).

Board (1). Nearly as stiff as boards (40 Dana *Two* 72, 108; Melville *White Jacket* 102 My luckless hammock was stiff and straight as a board). Boshears 40:962; NC 373; Taylor *Comparisons* 77; Tilley B485; Henry Bellamann *The Gray Man Walks* (1936) 26.

Board (2), 1. Above board (44 Stephens *High Life* I 32). Apperson 1; *Oxford* 1; Green 37; Stevenson 3:1; Herbert Adams *Oddways* (Philadelphia 1929) 98.

2. Beautiful! . . . fine, inexpressible,—a high quotation! It carries the board (50 Judd *Richard* 391).

3. I should not be greatly surprised if, in a few years, this rule goes by the board (c56 Cartwright *Autobiography* 163). NED Board 12 b.

Boat, 1. The noomrous friends thet's in one boat with me (48 Lowell *Biglow* 137; Browne *Artemus Ward Ilis Travels* 30 We are all in the same boat; Clemens *Letters* I 168). Apperson 549; McAtee 12; NED Boat 1 d; *Oxford* 560; Partridge 72; Stevenson 209:8; Tilley B491; NQ 12 viii 432, ix 298, CLIV (1928) 407, 448, 465; Austen Allen *Menace to Mrs. Kershaw* (1930) 143.

2. I'll row my own boat against both wind and tide, if it be necessary (76 Nash *Century* 34).

3. Old Tomkins looked as if the boat had left him (58 Porter *Major* 19). Cf. Harriet W. Ponder *Cambodian Glory* (London 1936) 101 missed the bus.

Bob. Coming home and finding her "off, like Bob's horse, with nobody to pay the reckoning" (40 Dana *Two* 318).

Bobalink. As genteel as a bobalink in a wheat lot (44 Stephens *High Life* II 58).

Bobee. I don't care a bobee about his being free (66 Smith *Arp* 115). Randolph and Wilson 225 Bawbee.

Bobworm. What are you squirming at there, like a bobworm on a fish hook? (59 Boucicault *Dot* 140).

Body, 1. You don't go through this door to-night, without you pass over the dead body of Jack Downing (33 Smith *Downing* 137; Anon. *New Hope* 375 Those who attempt to violate the personal rights of any man by *Lynching him* will have to pass over my body). Faden 85; Elizabeth Enright in P. Engle and H. Martin, eds. *Prize Stories 1955: The O. Henry Awards* (1955) 141 No, Baby, over my dead body; Cornelia B. Gross *Harper's Magazine* CCX (April 1955) 40 over my dead body; F. P. Keyes *The River Road* (1945) 391; Stark Young *So Red the Rose* (1934) 366. See Corpse (2).
2. Body and breeches [i. e., entire, complete]. 78 DA Body 3 b.

Boil. As sore all over as a bile (44 Stephens *High Life* I 44). Boshears 40:955; McAtee 60; NC 373; Svartengren 96; Taylor *Comparisons* 76; Harriette Ashbrook *Murder Makes Murder* (1937) 186.

Boiler. Jest as if you was goin' to bust yer biler (55 Dorson *Jonathan* 57; Holmes *Professor* 78 Let him blow her off, or he'll bu'st his b'iler). DA Boiler 1 (b).

Bold. See Brass, Lion (1).

Bolt. [Sitting] bolt upright (25 Neal *Brother J* I 138, II 43, 162; Dorson *Jonathan* 91; Melville *Moby-Dick* I 94; Hawthorne *Twice-Told* 237; Holmes *Professor* 164). Lean III 300–301; NED Bolt adv. 1; Whiting *Chaucer* 157, *Drama* 306:35; John D. Carr *The Eight of Swords* (1934) 24.

Bombshell. This was a bombshell (43 Robb *Squatter* 80; Judd *Richard* 355 the other [i. e., blame] is like a bombshell in the midst of our activity, and arouses the impulse of flight). Arthur M. Chase *Twenty Minutes to Kill* (1936) 213 an explosion of the proverbial bombshell could scarcely have created a greater sensation.

Bone, 1. A bone of contention (53 Hammett *Stray* 241). NED Bone 7; *Oxford* 55; Stevenson 214:4; Lilian Bamburg *Beads of Silence* (1927) 48.
2. Cold as bones. 54 DA Cold 2 (4).
3. As dry as a bone (32 Kennedy *Swallow* 171; Haliburton *Clockmaker* II 83, *Sam* II 309; Mayo *Kaloolah* 54, 55; Melville *Mardi* I 51, *Redburn* 374 bone-dry, *White Jacket* 2 bone-dry; Bowman *Bear-Hunters* 56; Clift *Bunker* 308). Apperson 168; Boshears 36:504; Farmer and Henley I 284; McAtee 24; NC 373; Taylor *Comparisons* 36; Tilley B514; Victor Bridges *The Girl in Black* (1927) 221; John D. Carr *The Four False Weapons* (1937) 193 bone-dry.
4. They didn't seem tu make no bones of showing their legs (44 Stephens *High Life* I 179; Cooper *Redskins* 504 and makes no bones of saying so; Neal *Charcoal* 112; Burke *Polly* 147 he wouldn't make no bones; Kelly *Humors* 238; Bowman *Bear-Hunters* 378 I'd make no bones to leave two such useless dogs . . . to die and rot). Apperson 392:19; Farmer and Henley I 284; Green 64; NED Bone 8; *Oxford* 55; Schele de Vere 585; Stevenson 214:23; Tilley

B527; NQ 7 iii 408, 523, iv 137, 210, 8 xii 428; Anne Austin *The Black Pigeon* (1929) 291.

5. What is bred in the bone—you know the proverb (32 Kennedy *Swallow* 282; Haliburton *Nature* I 164 What's bred in the bone, you know, is hard to get out of the flesh; Judd *Margaret* II 223 What's bred in the bone will never be out of the flesh; Riley *Puddleford* 250 What's bred in the bone, stays there). Apperson 66; McAtee 16; NC 373; *Oxford* 63; Stevenson 238:7; Tilley F365; Whiting *Drama* 122, *Scots* I 142; Edward L. White *Lukundoo* (1927) 26 What's socked into the bone won't come out of the flesh, any more than what's bred there.

6. Hannah "felt in her bones" that it was going to be an unusually fine day (68 Alcott *Little Women* 239). NED *Supplement* Bone 3 b; *Oxford* 198; Brian Flynn *The Case of the Black Twenty-two* (Philadelphia 1929) 164.

7. I've got a bone to pick with you (40 Haliburton *Clockmaker* III 113). Farmer and Henley I 285; Green 64; NC 373; NED Bone 6 c; Stevenson 213:7; Woodard PADS VI (1946) 6; Herbert Adams *The Crime in the Dutch Garden* (Philadelphia 1930) 22.

8. As sailors say, "he hadn't a lazy bone in him" (40 Dana *Two* 113).

Boo, 1. And wouldn't let no man say boo to them for nothin' (40 Haliburton *Clockmaker* III 233; Robb *Squatter* 61 He could jest lick anythin' that said boo; Judd *Margaret* I 278 Hester might have thrashed the skin off his body, and he wouldn't have cried boo; Riley *Puddleford* 310 he couldn't say boo afore Mr. Howard Tinkham). Car-ter Dickson, pseud. *The White Priory Murders* (1934) 299.

2. As much as to say, "say boo *to a goose,* if you dare" (36 Haliburton *Clockmaker* I 136, *Season-Ticket* 276 He was an inoffensive kind of feller that wouldn't say boo to a goose). Apperson 58; Farmer and Henley III 182; NED Bo 1 b; *Oxford* 563; Tilley B481; NQ 4 vi 94, 164, 221, 372, 513; Charles Barry, pseud. *Murder on Monday?* (1932) 96.

Book, 1. You will read any man's heart, as plain as a book (43 Haliburton *Attaché* III 64, *Sam* I 67, II 65).

2. They took Their turns et watchin', reg'lar ez a book (67 Lowell *Biglow* 389).

3. True as a book (44 Stephens *High Life* I 189).

4. He knew the press "like a book" (43 Robb *Squatter* 25; Thompson *Chronicles* 74 the Curloos; Stephens *High Life* I 2 the critter; Boker *World* 32 him; Dorson *Jonathan* 82; Hammett *Stray* 130 the woods; Durivage *Three* 295 the firm; Riley *Puddleford* 149 'em; Haliburton *Season-Ticket* 332 her). Bartlett 355; Svartengren 131; Thornton I 541; J. Frank Dobie *Coronado's Children* (Dallas 1930) 182.

5. Life lies open like a book (50 Mitchell *Reveries* 180).

6. Read you off, like a book (25 Neal *Brother J* II 444; Haliburton *Attaché* IV 176; Boker *Bankrupt* 105 I read your black heart like an open book; Willis *Fun* 328 they are reading her at arm's length like a book; Taliaferro *Fisher's* 257; Clift *Bunker* 170 I could read his in'ards like a book). NC 373; *Oxford* 534; Stevenson 1939:7; Christopher Bush *The Body in the Bonfire* (1936) 72.

7. I remember it like a book (49 Dorson *Jonathan* 79).

8. Talking like a book (33 Davis *Downing* 25; Neal *Down-Easters* I 26; Kennedy *Horse-Shoe* 78 he talks as well as a book; Briggs *Harry* I 142; Haliburton *Attaché* I 148, *Season-Ticket* 48, 220, 226; Hammett *Piney* 301). *Oxford* 643; Partridge 79; Thornton I 541.

Book-learning. As old Jed'diah used to say, book-larnin spiles a man ef he's got mother-wit, and ef he aint got that, it don't do him no good (45 Hooper *Simon* 41). See Ounce (1).

Boot, 1. As awkward as a wrong boot (55 Haliburton *Nature* I 9, *Season-Ticket* 11).

2. The major's got his high-heeled boots on to-night [i. e., is riding high]. (43 Thompson *Chronicles* 137). Cf. Heel (2); Bartlett 286.

3. I felt a little, as the saying is, like sinking down in my boots (71 Jones *Batkins* 373).

4. I wouldn't be in your boots for a hogshead of niggers (53 Hammett *Stray* 411). Green 332 shoe. See Shoe (4).

5. The boot is decidedly on t'other leg (59 Smith *My Thirty* 360; Whitehead *Wild Sports* 81 I reckoned she [a panther] wouldn't be so much so [polite] when the boot got on t'other leg). NED Boot 1 b, *Supplement* Boot 1 b; *Oxford* 56; Agatha Christie *The Man in the Brown Suit* (1924) 190, *Murder in Three Acts* (1934) 272 Are you sure the boot is not on the other leg?

6. To bet your boots. 56 DA Boot 2 c (3); Partridge 49; Charles Barry *Murder on Monday?* (1932) 26.

7. To go it boots [i. e., quickly, vigorously]. 43 DA Boot 2 c (1).

8. To move (start) one's boots. 51 DA Boot 2 c (2).

9. To be big in one's boots. 79 DA Boot 2 c (4); Stevenson 221:6.

Boot-jack, 1. As clear as a boot-jack (38 Haliburton *Clockmaker* II 21).

2. It's as correct as a bootjack (43 Haliburton *Attaché* I 256).

3. He was a very clever man, and as fair as a bootjack (36 Haliburton *Clockmaker* I 305).

4. With a face as long as a boot-jack (56 Kelly *Humors* 189).

5. I see it as plain as a bootjack (38 Haliburton *Clockmaker* II 318, *Attaché* II 54, *Season-Ticket* 243).

6. I'll chalk it as straight as a boot-jack (38 Haliburton *Clockmaker* II 135, *Nature* II 19).

Born, 1. As naked as they were born (34 Crockett *Life* 92; Haliburton *Clockmaker* III 94 as when; Melville *Typee* 265 as when; Clemens *Sandwich* 83). Lean II ii 856; *Oxford* 442; Tilley B137; Whiting *Scots* I 143. Cf. NC 390 Day 7; Taylor *Comparisons* 58; C. C. Munz *Land without Moses* (1938) 21.

2. As sure as you are born (35 Kennedy *Horse-Shoe* 177; Longstreet *Georgia* 165; Haliburton *Clockmaker* I 132, 140, 148, II 74, 82, 131, 237, 296, 322, III 70, 208, *Attaché* II 175, 234, III 191, *Old Judge* II 74, *Sam* II 92, 94, *Nature* II 302; Hooper *Simon* 70, 116, 132; Cary *Clovernook* 2d Ser. 247; Paul *Courtship* 137; Browne *Artemus* 131; Smith *Arp* 28, 177; Harris *Sut* 219; Barnum *Struggles* 707; Nash *Century* 69, 129, 132, 149, 230, 269; Harris *Uncle Remus* 23 sho's you bawn). Brewster *Amer. Speech* XVI (1941) 21; McAtee 63; NC 373; Randolph and Wilson 180; Schele de Vere 639; Svartengren 358; Nard

Jones *The Case of the Hanging Lady* (1938) 196.

3. They say a man who is born to be hanged will never be drowned (21 Cooper *Spy* 98; Kennedy *Swallow* 400 a negro that is born to be hanged—you know the rest; Crockett *Life* 36 But this proved to me that if a fellow is born to be hung, he will never be drowned; Bennett *Border* 88 Them as is born to be hanged, needn't be skeered to Injins; Barnum *Struggles* 327 there is an old proverb about the impossibility of drowning those who are born to another fate). Apperson 60; *Oxford* 56–57; Stevenson 1066:2; Tilley B139; Whiting *Drama* 95, 190, 250, *Scots* I 184; Clifton Robbins *The Mystery of Mr. Cross* (1933) 343.

Borrower. The borrower runs in his own debt (38–39[?] Emerson *Works* II 112).

Boston. As Boston goes, so goes New England (71 Clemens *Love Letters* 162).

Bostonian. As good Bostonians when they die are said to go to Paris, all other Americans good and bad must go to California (67 Richardson *Beyond* 449). *Oxford* 10 Americans; A. D. H. Smith *The Treasure of the Bucoleon* (1923) 58 Americans; Van Wyck Brooks *New England Indian Summer* (1940) 164 It was [Appleton] who said, "Good Americans, when they die, go to Paris," and cf. p. 286. See American.

Bottle, 1. The midil [of the bull] wer green as a bottil (67 Harris *Sut* 130).

2. [Her hair] am es slick es this yere bottil (67 Harris *Sut* 76).

3. He has sealed up Elder's mouth as tight as a bottle (36 Haliburton *Clockmaker* I 226, III 23 corked it up

as; Dana *Two* 264 a ship . . . as tight; Shillaber *Ike* 38). Svartengren 263.

4. Let every man drink from his own bottle (58 Hammett *Piney* 73).

5. To use the words of young Jack, "he [a horse] shone like a bottle" (20–22 Irving *Bracebridge* 100; Hammett *Piney* 117 coat and breeches of store cloth, and shinin' like a glass-bottle, 131, 258).

6. [Horse's] skin shinin like a junk bottle (44 Stephens *High Life* II 195). Cf. Green 206.

Bottom. To look at the bottom of the glass. 42 DA Look vb. 1 b (1).

Bottom dollar. See Dollar (8).

Bough. As they say the bough of the tree has the character of the leaf, and the whole tree of the bough (38 Emerson *Works* I 180).

Bounce. To get the grand bounce. 77 DA Grand bounce.

Bow. Remarkable for drawing a long bow (40 Dana *Two* 229–230; Melville *Typee* 228 Jack, who has long been accustomed to the long-bow, and to spin tough yarns on a ship's forecastle, *Mardi* I 325 "But draw a long breath and begin." "A long bow," muttered Mohi; Dorson *Jonathan* 103 the chance of "drawing his bow"; Haliburton *Old Judge* I 150 He can draw any thing,—a long bow, a long cork, *Sam* II 84 draw as long a bow as any Indian or author, *Nature* I 247 I draw a thunderin long bow; Willis *Life* 267 lest you think I drew too long a bow; Smith *My Thirty* 322 there is such a thing as drawing too long a bow to hit the thing you shoot at; Richardson *Secret* 65). Farmer and Henley I 310, II 324, IV 225–

226; Green 122; NC 374; NED Bow sb. 4 c; *Oxford* 380; Stevenson 227:6; NQ 2 xi 349, 513, 3 xii 185; Lee Thayer, pseud. *Dead End Street* (1936) 125. Cf. Bowstring.

Bow-backed. See Ox yoke.

Bower. To christen the bower [i. e., to indulge in strong drink). c61 DA Bower 1 c.

Bowsprit. Tom's got a head as long as the bowsprit (40 Dana *Two* 244).

Bowstring. Not noticing the enormous length of the bow-string, the young fellow has just drawn (60 Holmes *Professor* 132). See Bow.

Bow-wows. Going to "the demnition bow-wows" (65 Richardson *Secret* 83). Farmer 197; Farmer and Henley II 269; Stevenson 607:5.

Box, 1. You are in a bad box whoever you are (37 Neal *Charcoal* 220). DA Bad 2 b (1). Cf. *Oxford* 735 wrong box; Partridge 87 box.
2. The rather incongruous acts of getting themselves in a box and into a pickle (42 Irving *Attorney* 244; Eliason 261; Sedley *Marian* 143 If I weren't in something like the same box as his'n). NED, *Supplement* Box sb. 21.

Boy, 1. As happy-hearted as a boy (69 Alcott *Little Women* 382).
2. Proud as a boy with a bran-new top (68 Saxe *Poems* 31).
3. Boys are little men, it is said (57 Melville *Confidence-Man* 272). Cf. Stevenson 228:6 Laddies will be men.
4. Boys is boys, and all boys is sassy (37 Neal *Charcoal* 214; Cary *Clovernook* 2d Ser. 189 Boys will be boys; Durivage *Three* 69 Boys will be boys; Alcott *Little Women* 461 Boys

will be boys). Lean III 435; *Oxford* 59; Tilley C337 Children will do like children; A. B. Caldwell *No Tears Shed* (1937) 132; J. P. Marquand *Melville Goodwin, USA* (Boston 1951) 524 gals had to be gals and boys, boys, within limits, *Sincerely, Willis Wayde* (Boston 1955) 325 Boys will be boys. See Child (14), Girl (6), People (4), Widow.
5. Little boys must not play with fire (48 Lowell *Biglow* 90). *Oxford* 505.
6. It shall be no boy's play to force my works (24 Cooper *Pilot* 180; Dana *Two* 357). See Child (19).
7. And there, as the boy said who was learning to spell, having reached m-u-d, we stuck (46 Fairfield *Letters* 401).
8. "It will come out right," said Mrs. Brandon. "As the boy remarked when he was gored by the cow's horn," observed Uncle Richard, philosophically (56 Durivage *Three* 170).
9. So here goes, as the boy said when he run by himself (34 Crockett *Life* 174).
10. Some . . . raised the very old boy (56 Kelly *Humors* 191). NED Raise 20b, *Supplement* Old 9 b. Cf. Whiting *Devil* 216:47.
11. He was a bully boy with a glass eye! (72 Clemens *Roughing* II 48, *Sketches* 64 You, Bully Boy with a Glass eye). Cf. Airs.

Brace. See Mainbrace.

Braddock. This supper was afterward alluded to as Braddock's deaf eat, and the simile "deaf as a Braddock," subsequently vulgarised into "deaf as a haddock," had its rise from that circumstance [i. e., firing guns in a sham fight]. (65 Derby *Squibob* 33). Apperson 138–139 haddock.

Brag. You remember your own adage,
—Brag was a good dog, but Holdfast
was better (35 Kennedy *Horse-Shoe*
111; Haliburton *Clockmaker* I 90,
206, *Attaché* III 54, IV 22, *Nature* II
177 Brag is a good dog, and holdfast
a better one, but what do you say to
a cross of the two?). Apperson 63;
Bradley 63; *Oxford* 60; Stevenson
229:6; Tilley B588; R. W. Winston
It's a Far Cry (1937) 276 a Southern
saying.

Bragging. Braggin saves advertisin
(55 Haliburton *Nature* I 206).

Brains, 1. I . . . sat down to pick his
brains of the little information I
wanted to fill out the story (50 Willis
Life 349). *Oxford* 498; Stevenson
229:7.

2. A sun hot enough to fry the
brains in his skull (50 Willis *Life*
216).

3. Turtle was a long-winded attorney, and what he lacked in brains he
made up in bottom (57 Riley *Puddleford* 258).

4. Our fishermen . . . haven't
brains enough to tell when their feet
are cold (76 Nash *Century* 165).

Bran. But sometimes it does seem as if
these gals couldn't tell bran when the
bag's open (44 Stephens *High Life* II
59; Whitcher *Widow* 308 He don't
know . . . bran when the bag's
open). Cf. Bean (3); McAtee 38
beans.

Brandy. [A man] hearty as brandy
. . . but not quite so spirited (60
Haliburton *Season-Ticket* 219).

Brass. But he came up to us as bold
as brass (54 Langdon *Ida* 88). Apperson 59; NC 374; Taylor *Comparisons* 20; Anne Austin *The Black Pigeon* (1929) 252.

Brave. See Bull-dog (1), Caesar (2),
Gamecock, Lion (2), Panther (2),
Rat (1), Steel (2).

Breach. The Deekin and I threw ourselves into the breech (68 Locke [Nas-
by] *Struggles* 508).

Bread, 1. [Began to wake him] a littil
faster nor light bread rises (67 Harris *Sut* 70).

2. If the gal means to git married,
her bread will be all dough agin (44
Stephens *High Life* I 86). See Cake
(3, 4).

3. And I scarce think I shall be
successful in explaining to you, even
now, why such "bread and butter" is
to be "quarrelled with" (57 Willis
Paul 396). Apperson 518; NC 374–
375; *Oxford* 528; Stevenson 1924:14;
Thornton I 100, III 151; Robin Forsyth *The Pleasure Cruise Mystery*
(1934) 201.

4. But *his* bread never fell on the
buttered side (67 Richardson *Beyond*
44). Stevenson 235:5. Cf. McAtee
Grant County 3; Anthony Gray *Dead
Nigger* (London 1929) 189 didn't her
bread and butter *always* fall butter
downwards?

5. He who loves not bread, dotes
not on dough (57 Melville *Confidence-Man* 163).

6. He will soon have his bread buttered on both sides (36 Haliburton
Clockmaker I 256, 299, III 305 eats
his bread buttered in both sides; Lowell *Biglow* 81 An' [they] butter their
bread on both sides with the Masses).
Apperson 64:8; *Oxford* 61; Stevenson
235:4; Tilley B623; David Frome,
pseud. *In At the Death* (1930) 222
he tried to butter his bread on both
sides.

7. He never had his bread so buttered in his life, as it would be then

[i. e., was beaten severely]. (35 Kennedy *Horse-Shoe* 110).

8. Only the bread was buttered on tother side (33 Smith *Downing* 57).

Break. See Crockery (2), Pipe-stem (2).

Breakers. He [a bear] would become furious, and I might look out for breakers (59 Browning *Forty-four* 176).

Breast. And, to use the common phrase, [he] "had made a clean breast of it" (20–22 Irving *Bracebridge* 247; Stowe *Uncle* 246 But if you will get me fairly at it, I'll make a clean breast of it); Hammett *Stray* 214; Willis *Fun* 214; Anon. *New Hope* 347; Cooke *Foresters* 348; Kelly *Humors* 407; Porter *Major* 49; Shillaber *Knitting-Work* 205; Holmes *Autocrat* 206; Boucicault *Flying Scud* 225; Locke [Nasby] *Struggles* 287; Eggleston *School-Master* 263, 264, *Circuit* 317–318; Nash *Century* 184). NED Breast 5 c; *Oxford* 96.

Breath, 1. As sure as you're a breathin' the breath o' life now (28 Neal *Rachel* 216).

2. Helps them to save their breath to cool their broth (36 Haliburton *Clockmaker* I 87, *Season-Ticket* 364, *Nature* I 371 or to groan with when you get home; Lowell *Biglow* 93). Apperson 65–66; *Oxford* 331; Stevenson 237:5; Tilley W422; Kathleen M. Knight *Death Blew Out the Match* (1935) 164. See Wind (22).

3. Smelt as sweet as a gal's breath (44 Stephens *High Life* II 178).

Breeches, 1. When a man gets too big for his breeches (35 Crockett *Account* 152; Haliburton *Letter* 19; Taliaferro *Fisher's* 47, 95; Holmes *Elsie* 31 a—

sight too big for his, etc.). McAtee 67; NC 375; Stevenson 221:16; Woodard PADS VI (1946) 34; Leighton Barret *Though Young* (1938) 78.

2. For when ladies wear the breeches, their petticoats ought to be long enough to hide 'em (36 Haliburton *Clockmaker* I 190, II 64 Measure that woman . . . for a pair of breeches; she's determined to wear 'em, III 32 Custom has given woman petticoats and man pantaloons, but it would be jist as nateral for woman to wear the breeches and men the apronstring, and there is a plaguy sight of them do it too; Hammett *Stray* 145 A number of the women, who for that purpose were inducted into the breeches, let us hope, for the first time; Melville *Israel* 107). Apperson 66; Farmer and Henley I 322–323; NC 375; NED Breech 2; *Oxford* 697; Stevenson 2506:4; Tilley B645; Wilson 523; Ed Bell *Fish on the Steeple* (1935) 107. See Pantaloons.

Breeze, 1. As impulsive as the breeze, and quite as refreshing (58 Field *Pokerville* 134). Cf. NC 375.

2. I think she would raise a breeze (i. e., cause trouble). (40 Eliason 144, 290). NED Breeze sb.² 4.

3. To strike a breeze of luck. 34 DA Luck 2.

Brevity. If the old saying be true that "brevity is the soul of wit" (44 Fairfield *Letters* 335, 408 "Brevity is the soul of"—short letters). Apperson 66; *Oxford* 64; Stevenson 240:4; Tilley B652.

Brick, 1. Flesh as hard as a brick (51 Stowe *Uncle* 142). Boshears 37:635; NC 375; Taylor *Comparisons* 46.

2. [A building] square as a brick (34 Davis *Downing* 79).

3. To feel like bricks [i. e., wretched]. 46 DA Brick 2 b (2).

4. To have a brick in one's hat [i. e., to be tipsy]. 46 DA Brick 2 b (3).

5. The bank suspended, and down like a pile of bricks went everyone of its congeners (58 Hammett *Piney* 300).

6. If I don't pitch into Ben Parson's ribs like a tousand of bricks (40 Haliburton *Clockmaker* III 50, *Attaché* II 264 walk into him like, *Nature* II 14 pitched into us . . . like; Robb *Squatter* 37 lit upon . . . ; Hooper *Simon* 85 fell; Shillaber *Mrs. Partington* 84 pitch into you; Hammett *Wonderful* 88 down on you; Riley *Puddleford* 28 am always on hand at the tap of the drum, like a thousand of bricks; Eliason 262 come down on them; Smith *My Thirty* 403 down upon you, 417, 421 sot down as hard as; Clemens *Washoe* 107 he was always on hand, like a thousand of brick; Saxe *Poems* 427 catch it some day). DA Brick 2 b; Farmer and Henley I 325; Schele de Vere 314, 642; Stevenson 243:3; Thornton III 48, 400. Cf. McAtee 19, *Additional* 14; Taylor *Comparisons* 83; Vincent Starrett *Murder on "B" Deck* (1929) 177.

Bridge, 1. I will put you across the swamp as clean as a bridge of gold (32 Kennedy *Swallow* 212). Cf. Apperson 67; *Oxford* 249; Tilley B665.

2. Don't cross the bridge before you get to it (66 Smith *Arp* 179). Apperson 123; *Oxford* 119; Stevenson 244:11, 2377:12. For discussion see Jente *American* 344; M. E. Schmidt and others *American Notes and Queries* I (1941–1942) 105, II (1942–1943) 79. Cf. Stevenson 2377:12 stile; Tilley S856 stile.

3. Now the bridge that has carried me so well over, shall I not praise it! (57 Melville *Confidence-Man* 211; Richardson *Beyond* 280 Praise the bridge which carries you safely over). Apperson 510; *Oxford* 515; Stevenson 244–245:13; Whiting *Scots* I 172 the ford.

4. We praise a bridge that carries us safe even if it is a poor one (45 Judd *Margaret* II 115).

Bridle. But as the proverb goes, "You may well walk if you hold the bridle of your horse in your hand" (45 Emerson *Journals* VII 27). Apperson 263 Good walking with a horse in one's hand; *Oxford* 690; Stevenson 2441:6; Tilley W10.

Brier. He's as keen as a brier (34 Davis *Downing* 24; Baldwin *Flush* 54). Cf. Boshears 40:895; Randolph and Wilson 175; Svartengren 256 sharp. See Bamboo briar.

Bright. See Bird (5), Button (1), Coffee (1), Corn-silk, Currants, Day (2), Diamond (2), Dollar (2), Flower (1), Gold (4), Guinea (1), Hawk (1), Heat, Lark (2), Moon (2), Morning (2), Peach (1), Plum (1), Rainbow (1), Rose (7), Sea (1), Silk (1), Star (1), Steel (3), Sun (1).

Brimstone. A light as blue as brimstone (55 Irving *Wolfert* 246).

Bringer. Then he 'gin pickin' up rocks an' slingin' um at the dogs like bringer! (51 Burke *Polly* 52). DA Bringer.

Brisk. See Bee (1), Bird (6), Buck (1), Pea (1).

Bristle. The har on my head standin stiff as bristles and rattlin like a raftman's bones (59 Porter *Major* 93).

Brittle. See Glass (1).

Broad. See Ocean.

Broadway. His mouth being as dry and dusty as Broadway in fly-time (51 Burke *Polly* 179).

Broker. Shaved as close as a Wall Street broker (44 Stephens *High Life* II 83).

Brood. See Hen (11).

Brook. [Speech] as soft as a brook over a bed of white pebble stones (44 Stephens *High Life* II 26).

Broom. A new broom sweeps clean, is a saying that finds its application every day (52 Cary *Clovernook* 251, *Married* 298; Richardson *Beyond* 220 One act was "for the relief of Betsey Broom," doubtless a good housewife—while she was new; Alcott *Little Women* 498 We are such very new brooms). Apperson 443; NC 376; NED Broom 3 b; *Oxford* 450; Snapp 93:3; Stevenson 246–247:12; Stoett 225; Tilley B682; Whiting *Drama* 221, 230.

Broomstick, 1. As straight as a broomstick (44 Stephens *High Life* II 46).

2. An honest woman is no better in his eyes than one of your broomstick jumpers (27 Cooper *Prairie* 354; Haliburton *Attaché* IV 160 We'll keep well, or hop the broomstick, or do anythin' we like, *Nature* I 81 and married, broomstick fashion, . . . a squaw; Kelly *Humors* 422 Let's make up a wedding party—let's jump the broomstick; Stephens *Mary Derwent* 215 No jumping the broomstick in this affair, 295 it's been a kind of Indian scrape—a jumping over the broomstick I spose). Green 70, 206, cf. 25; Laughlin PADS II (1944) 25; McAtee 37; NC 376; *Oxford* 66–67; Randolph and Wilson 257; Stevenson

1536:8; Tidwell PADS XIII (1950) 16; J. B. Cabell *Jurgen* (1919, ed. 1922) 274; Harnett T. Kane *The Bayous of Louisiana* (1943) 304.

Brother, 1. Lord Morpeth . . . begun to talk as if I'd been his twin brother (44 Stephens *High Life* II 100; Jones *Country* 282 you introduced yourself and seemed to be as familiar as a brother). Svartengren 328.

2. We got intimate as brothers (56 Kelly *Humors* 153). Cf. NC 376; P. B. Noyes *The Pallid Giant* (1927) 183 this man . . . stuck to me like a brother.

3. Watty loves you . . . like a brother (25 Neal *Brother J* II 124; Smith *Downing* 193 looked as loving as two brothers; Melville *Omoo* 13 the very men he flogged loved him as a brother; Clemens *Washoe* 136). Cf. Svartengren 136 dear.

Brown, 1. Her own representatives du her quite brown [i. e., deceive, cheat]. (48 Lowell *Biglow* 83; Hammett *Piney* 125; Boucicault *Flying Scud* 160). Bartlett 69–70; Farmer 90; Farmer and Henley I 338; NED Brown a. 5; Stevenson 250:2; Thornton I 256; Roger Scarlett *The Beacon Hill Murders* (1930) 136.

2. But Smith was bound to do the thing up brown (56 Kelly *Humors* 82). NED Brown 5; Partridge 96; Phoebe A. Taylor *The Annulet of Guilt* (1938) 117.

3. See Berry, Chestnut (1), Coffee (2), Mahogany (1, 2), Nut (1, 2), Saddle (1).

Brush. I wasn't born in the brush to be scared of garter snakes (44 Stephens *High Life* II 204). See Gartersnake, Marsh, Meadow, Woods (2).

Bubbles. [Dimples coming and going] like the bubbles on a glass of prime cider (44 Stephens *High Life* II 30).

Buck (1), 1. Brisk as a buck (57 Melville *Confidence-Man* 173).

2. I am as fat as a buck (31 Eliason 103).

3. Fresh as a mounting [mountain] buck jist scared up (59 Taliaferro *Fisher's* 54).

4. Gay as a buck (57 Melville *Confidence-Man* 230). Coombs PADS II (1944) 23 gaily. Cf. Svartengren 71 merry.

5. I'm haaty [hearty] as a puck (38 Crockett *Account* 8; Smith *Letters* 127 as hearty as bucks; Cary *Clovernook* 2d Ser. 125; Haliburton *Nature* I 2; Riley *Puddleford* 123). DA Buck 1 b (6); Bartlett 282; Farmer 92; Schele de Vere 208.

6. Ever since that event the Colonel has been like a buck shot in the eye (57 Jones *Country* 111).

Buck (2). To pass the buck. 65 DA Buck 1 b 6; Stevenson 250:8.

Bucket. He'd kicked the bucket (33 Smith *Downing* 203; Dorson *Jonathan* 104; Haliburton *Sam* II 176; Jones *Winkles* 387; Kelly *Humors* 119; Taliaferro *Carolina Humor* 17; Wallack *Rosedale* 13; Clemens *Roughing* II 47). Apperson 339; Farmer and Henley I 349; McAtee 38; NC 376; NED Bucket [2]; *Oxford* 334; Stevenson 506:4; Leighton Barrett *Though Young* (1938) 221.

Buckeye. Ole Bullin's eyes wer a-stickin out like ontu two buckeyes flung agin a mudwall (67 Harris *Sut* 55).

Buckle. All they cared for was "to make buckle and tongue meet" by raising stock, a few bales of cotton, and a little corn for bread (59 Taliaferro *Fisher's* 249). NC 376. Cf. Apperson 70–71 thong; *Oxford* 67; Stevenson 251:4; Tilley B696.

Bud, 1. I'll be as true to her as the bud to the blossom (c60 Paul *Courtship* 277).

2. But buds will be roses, and kittens, cats (68 Alcott *Little Women* 224).

3. [A headache] if not nipped in the bud (37 Neal *Charcoal* 17; Kelly *Humors* 137 his belligerent propositions were suddenly nipped in the bud; Alcott *Little Women* 270 He'd better nip his little passion in the bud). Apperson 446 Nip . . . briar; *Oxford* 453; Stevenson 245:10; Tilley B702.

Budget. You will be perfectly safe . . . in opening your budget [i. e., in telling what you know]. (53 Hammett *Stray* 214).

Buffalo, 1. For my old hide is as tough as bufflers is (57 Bennett *Border* 253).

2. Graminy! . . . if he didn't make brush crack and streak off like a herd of buffaloes (43 Hall *Purchase* I 268).

Bug, 1. As happy as a bug (75 Clemens *Sketches* 300).

2. Stowed away in ——'s Hotel, fine as a fiddle, snug as a bug, in a good room (56 Kelly *Humors* 285).

3. As snug as a bug in a rug (38 Haliburton *Clockmaker* II 25, *Letter* 215; Wiley *Billy* 187; Richardson *Beyond* 184). Apperson 585; McAtee *Grant County* 9; NC 376; *Oxford* 602; Taylor *Comparisons* 75–76; Kenneth P. Kempton *Monday Go to Meeting* (1937) 133.

4. [He was] warm, dry, and com-

fortable as a bug in a rug! (56 Kelly *Humors* 113). NC 376 warm. Cf. W. C. Wadsworth *Paul Bunyan and His Great Blue Ox* (1926) 45 as happy and contented as two bugs in a rug.

5. She's one of the big bugs here (56 Whitcher *Widow* 301; Hammett *Piney* 171). Bartlett 42; Farmer 53; Farmer and Henley I 188–189; Green 57; McAtee 14; Schele de Vere 392; Stevenson 251:7; Thornton I 60–61, III 129.

6. I might 'a' gone to the bugs [i. e., died]. (33 Neal *Down-Easters* I 124). DA Bug sb. 3 (3).

7. To put the bug on [i. e., to hoax]. 48 DA Bug sb. 3 (1).

8. I smell a bug (53 Hammett *Stray* 96, *Piney* 46, 71, 156). DA Bug sb. 3 (2). See Rat (10).

9. No more'n a bug moufful fur him (59 Taliaferro *Fisher's* 129, 191).

Bugle. [A call] es clar es a bugle (67 Harris *Sut* 82).

Bulge. To have the bulge on. 41 DA Bulge sb. 1.

Bull, 1. [A bear] big as a bull (43 Lewis *Odd* 173; Burke *Polly* 151).

2. It makes 'em as mad as a short-horned bull in fly time (56 Durivage *Three* 107). Cf. DA Bull 9 e; Svartengren 39–40 baiting bull; James T. Farrell *A World I Never Made* (1936) 229.

3. His eyes wer es roun an' es red es a bull's when he is a-jinin in battil wif anuther bull frum Bashan (67 Harris *Sut* 188).

4. Strong as von bull (43 Robb *Squatter* 146). McAtee 17; NC 377; Svartengren 392; Charles Kelly and H. Birney *Holy Murder* (1934) 113.

5. Like a bull in a chiny-shop, I see I have got into the wrong pew (55 Haliburton *Nature* II 41; Durivage *Three* 175 sorry to intrude, as the bull said when he rushed into the china shop; Locke [Nasby] *Struggles* 581 it's awkward to hev a man like him bustin thro em like a bull in a china-shop). Apperson 72; NC 377; *Oxford* 68; Taylor *Comparisons* 22; Claude G. Bowers *The Tragic Era* (1929) 380.

6. He tore thru that brush thicket like a bull wif honey-bees arter him (67 Harris *Sut* 112).

7. Mr. Calhoun would stand no more chance down east here, than a stump'd tail bull in fly time (34 Davis *Downing* 17; Lewis *Odd* 95 like a big bull in . . . a small pastur' in the worst of fly-time; Lowell *Biglow* 43 heern Him a thrashin round like a short-tailed Bull in fli-time; Burke *Polly* 72 cuttin up shines worse nor er bob-tail bull in fly time). Cf. Boshears 35:389; Bartlett 809; DA Bull 9 (3); Randolph and Wilson 174 busy as a stump-tailed cow; Thornton I 339, III 147.

8. He howled like a mad bull (55 Thomson *Doesticks* 235).

9. Roared again like a mad bull (53 Hammett *Stray* 35, *Piney* 206 I . . . roared out in a voice that a bull of Bashan might have envied; Cartwright *Autobiography* 143 like a bull in a net, and cried aloud for mercy; Paul *Courtship* 186 the fellow roared like a bull). Taylor *Comparisons* 21–22; Tilley B715; Richard Wormser *The Man with the Wax Face* (1934) 78 mad bull; C. F. Gregg *The Brazen Confession* (London c1940) 255 If the Bull starts bellowing like his ancestors from Bashan.

10. He rushed like a mad bull upon Sniger (74 Eggleston *Circuit* 119).

11. That's taking the bull by the

horns (25 Neal *Brother J* III 36; Dana
Two 9; Lincoln II 265 I rush in, I take
the bull by the horns, IV 4, 10). Ap-
person 72; NC 377; NED Bull 1 c;
Oxford 641; Stevenson 254:9; William
Gore, pseud. *The Mystery of the
Painted Nude* (1938) 46.

12. It happened now, however,
that it was "his bull that was goring
our ox" (45 Cooper *Chainbearer* 262).
See Ox (11).

13. See Tailor (1).

Bull beef. [He] knocked him as stiff
as a bull beef (56 Kelly *Humors* 381).

Bulldog, 1. He wast prave as a pull-
dog (45 Cooper *Chainbearer* 431).

2. Spunky as a bull dog (40 Haliburton *Letter* 196).

3. Hold on like a bull-dog (59
Smith *My Thirty* 264). E. C. R. Lorac,
pseud. *The Greenwell Mystery* (1934)
55.

Bullet, 1. They [eggs] will be as hard
as bullets (60 Whitehead *Wild Sports*
256). NC 377.

2. As like as two old bullets cast in
the same mould (51 Stowe *Uncle*
253).

3. Every bullet has its billet (40
Cooper *Pathfinder* 147; Wiley *Johnny*
35). Apperson 72; Lean III 455; *Oxford* 68–69; Stevenson 255:5; Tilley
B720; James Joyce *Ulysses* (Paris
1924) 356.

4. The words came out of his
mouth like hot bullets (44 Stephens
High Life I 251).

Bulletin. "As false as a bulletin" has
passed into a proverb (65 Richardson
Secret 258).

Bullfrog. Swellin' like a bullfrog (59
Taliaferro *Fisher's* 179). Cf. Apperson
614 Toad; Taylor *Comparisons* 65.

Bull-moose. I feel as strong as a bull-
moose a'most (40 Haliburton *Old
Judge* II 43).

Bullock. To nary one on 'em I'd trust
a secon'-handed rail No furder off 'an
I could sling a bullock by the tail (48
Lowell *Biglow* 140). Cf. Apperson 72
bull, 649 trust; DA Bull sb. 9 e; Halpert 778; NC 388 Cow (16); *Oxford*
673; Taylor *Comparisons* 39; Tilley
T556. See Cat (34), Tailor (1).

Bull-terrier. Commodores . . . looking as plucky as bull-terriers (59–60
Holmes *Elsie* 8).

Bulrush. They were as straight as bul-
rushes (49 Haliburton *Old Judge* II
83, *Sam* I 210, II 66).

Bumble-bee, 1. Gordon is buzzing
about like a Bumble-bee in a broken
lantern (58 Eliason 103).

2. Tories risin', all in a buzz; pocket full o' bumble bees. We'll have a
tussle soon (25 Neal *Brother J* I 107).

Bump. You have been sitting there
. . . like a bump on a log (63 Clemens *Enterprise* 103). NC 377; Taylor
Comparisons 22; Arthur M. Chase
Twenty Minutes to Kill (1936) 152.

Bung. I guess I'll whip out of the bung
while he's a lookin arter the spicket
(36 Haliburton *Clockmaker* I 301).
Cf. *Oxford* 609 Spare; Stevenson
2181:11, 2182:1. See Spigot.

Bungtown copper. See Copper (3).

Bunty hen. Ontil bunty hens sprouts
tails (67 Harris *Sut* 279).

Bur, 1. I follered arter as close as a
bur tu a chestnut (44 Stephens *High
Life* I 162). Svartengren 325.

2. She held fast to his cloak, like a
burr to a sheep's tail (43 Haliburton

Attaché II 258). Stevenson 258:4 cleave; Tilley B723.

3. And stick to our man like burrs to sheep's wool (40 Haliburton *Clockmaker* III 308, *Attaché* III 66 that stuck to you like a burr to a sheep's tail, *Nature* II 313 stickin to him like burr to a hosses tail; Richardson *Secret* 313 His stories began to stick like chestnut-burrs in the popular ear, *Beyond* 178 One of those happy alliterations which stick like burs in the public memory; Alcott *Little Women* 40 the kitten, which . . . stuck like a burr just out of reach). Apperson 601–602; Hardie 471:178; *Oxford* 97 cleave; Stevenson 258:5; Tilley B724; Whiting *Drama* 307:43, *Scots* I 144; H. Bedford-Jones *The Shadow* (1930) 266.

Burn. See Drummond light (1), Firecoals.

Bush, 1. As pig-tail "dooz'n't grow on every bush" (25 Neal *Brother J* II 81; Dorson *Jonathan* 129 but it is a fact that taller grows on the bushes; Lowell *Biglow* 129 For does not the old proverb, when it asserts that money does not grow on *every* bush, imply *a fortiori* that there were certain bushes which did produce it; Whitcher *Widow* 189 and then ministers don't grow on every bush). Anthony Pryde, pseud. and R. K. Weekes *The Emerald Necklace* (1931) 92 princes. Cf. Blackberries (3), Money (8).

2. If that don't bang the bush [i. e., surpass expectations]. (36 Haliburton *Clockmaker* I 95, 197, 233, II 184, 309, *Attaché* II 79, *Old Judge* I 223). DA Bush 5 (2); Stevenson 258:10; Anthony Abbot, pseud. *About the Murder of a Startled Lady* (1935) 87.

3. Arter a good deal of beating

about the bush (44 Stephens *High Life* I 124; Cooper *Chainbearer* 56; Taliaferro *Fisher's* 87; Daly *Man* 29; Jones *Batkins* 453). Apperson 31; *Oxford* 27; Stevenson 259:2; Tilley B742; Whiting *Scots* I 145; Henry Wade, pseud. *The Verdict of You All* (1927) 104.

4. Other men beat the bush, but you catch the bird (40 Haliburton *Clockmaker* III 175, *Sam* I 201 if I did beat round the bush, I always put up the birds). Apperson 31; *Oxford* 28; Tilley B740; Whiting *Scots* I 145. Cf. Stevenson 2178:7.

5. To drag the bush up [i. e., to surpass]. 45 DA Bush 5 (3).

Bushel. I have done nothing under a bushel [i. e., secretly]. (67 Richardson *Beyond* 130). Cf. Candle (6), Light (3).

Business, 1. Business fust and jokes arterwards (40 Haliburton *Clockmaker* III 175, 176; Melville *Israel* 55 Business before pleasure; Durivage *Three* 17; Sedley *Marian* 276 Business first and pleasure afterwards). Bradley 64; NC 377; *Oxford* 71; Stevenson 263:1; Whiting *American Wellerisms* 8; Yamamoto *Dickens* 209, 324; NQ CLXXXVII (1945) 283; Stephen Chalmers *The Affair of the Gallows Tree* (1930) 276; George Meredith *Evan Harrington* (1861) ch. 25 Pleasure first—duty after. Isn't that the proverb, Drummond?

2. Business is business (57 Melville *Confidence-Man* 271; Clemens *Roughing* II 147). Apperson 73; Bartlett *Familiar Quotations* 867; Bradley 64; Lean III 436; *Oxford* 71; Stevenson 261:8; Yamamoto *Dickens* 324; E. D. Biggers *The Chinese Parrot* (Indianapolis 1926) 12; J. B. Priestley *Angel*

Pavement ch. 9 pt. 4 (London 1931) 390 Business may be business, but give me a gentleman to deal with in it.

3. I jest told him to mind his own bisness (44 Stephens *High Life* I 45, 70 mind your own bisness; Cartwright *Autobiography* 218 I want you to take the negro's eleventh commandment: that is, Every man mind his own business; Jones *Country* 205; Richardson *Beyond* 289 The eleventh commandment: mind your own business). NC 378; NED Business 16 d; *Oxford* 425; Stevenson 263:8. Cf. 57 Emerson *Journals* IX 110 each minds his own part.

4. The best thing you can do with that chap is to send him eend foremost about his bisness (44 Stephens *High Life* I 1, *Mary Derwent* 249 I . . . sent him off about his business). NED Business 16 e.

5. What is everybody's business, is nobody's business (45 Cooper *Satanstoe* 4). Apperson 187; NC 378; *Oxford* 179; Stevenson 260–261:6; Tilley B746, W843; NQ 4 vii 453, 550; 7 viii 308, 413.

Bust. The goods had gone out on a bust long before I busted (37 Neal *Charcoal* 68; Lewis *Odd* 93 Till one day I got on a "bust" in town; Burke *Polly* 67 he would go on a "bust"). DA Bust 3; Farmer 108; Farmer and Henley I 393; NED Bust; Schele de Vere 216.

Buster. On a buster (burster). 48 DA Buster 1; Wilfred Partington *Forging Ahead* (1939) 169 but I am not in the habit of going busters.

Busy. See Beaver (1), Bee (2, 3), Devil (2), Flea (2), Humming-bird (1), Mother Cary's chicken, Pismire, Thief (2), Yellowjacket.

Butcher, 1. Commodores . . . looking as hearty as butchers (59–60 Holmes *Elsie* 8).

2. Cheated by butcher, baker, and candlestickmaker (53 Curtis *Potiphar* 225). Blanche C. Clough *More Down-East Yarns by Grandma* (Portland, Me., 1956) 140 the proverbial "butcher, baker and candlestick maker." Cf. NED Candlestick 3.

Butter, 1. As fat as butter (45 Cooper *Chainbearer* 199; Fairfield *Letters* 444 Aunt Augusta is as fat as one of Hepsey's lumps of butter; Anon. *New Hope* 73; Hammett *Piney* 131; Paul *Courtship* 33; Clemens *Fairbanks* 162). Apperson 205; NC 378; *Oxford* 193; Tilley B767. Cf. Taylor *Comparisons* 40; Whiting PADS XI (1949) 28 n. 5; Kay C. Strahan *Death Traps* (1930) 26.

2. "Very," sez she, a looking at the tall candlestick as soft as summer butter (44 Stephens *High Life* II 221). Svartengren 266 butter.

3. Looking as if butter wouldn't melt in her mouth (33 Neal *Down-Easters* I 10, 140 speak; Haliburton *Clockmaker* I 232 looking as meek as if, II 135 speakin' as soft as if, III 237 you'd think butter wouldn't melt in that feller's mouth, *Attaché* I 224 look as if, *Sam* I 118 Butter wouldn't melt in our mouth, if we had got any to put there, *Nature* I 285 Butter wouldn't melt in his mouth, II 171–172 You would have spoke as mealy-mouthed of it as if, *Season-Ticket* 283 look as calm and mild as if . . . and cheese wouldn't choke them; Stephens *High Life* I 120 as innocent as if, 180 looking as if, II 199 lookin straight ahead, jest as if butter wouldn't melt between them tanterlizing red lips of her'n, 238 as mealy mouthed as if;

Mayo *Kaloolah* 108; Baldwin *Flush* 171 Butter wouldn't melt in his mouth). Apperson 74–75; Farmer and Henley I 396; Lean III 368; McAtee *Additional* 7; NED Butter 1 c; *Oxford* 136; Stevenson 266–267:15; Tilley B774; Yamamoto *Dickens* 339–340; S. H. Adams *The Gorgeous Hussy* (Boston 1934) 378; T. H. White *The Sword in the Stone* (1939) 67 [a witch with] a general soft air of butter-wouldn't-melt-in-my-mouth.

Buttercup, 1. Miss Miles . . . as fresh and harnsome as a full blown buttercup (44 Stephens *High Life* I 98).

2. It's [a hickory] growing as yellow as a buttercup (56 Cooke *Foresters* 234).

Butterfly, 1. She's as beautiful as a butterfly (66 Boucicault *Flying Scud* 159). Cf. NC 378 gay.

2. A swarming round the President and I, like yaller butterflies round a mud hole (44 Stephens *High Life* II 159).

3. It was a pity to see such a gay butterfly broken on a wheel (73 Clemens *Gilded* II 89). *Oxford* 61–62; Kay C. Strahan *The Meriwether Mystery* (1933) 283.

Buttermilk. She is not . . . as sour as buttermilk (36 Fairfield *Letters* 70).

Butternut. I don't care the value of a butternut-shell (44 Stephens *High Life* I 101).

Button, 1. A fellow . . . as bright as a pewter button (36 Crockett *Exploits* 20; Haliburton *Clockmaker* II 303, *Nature* II 311 bran new; Hawthorne *Twice-Told* 135 a button). NC 378; Taylor *Comparisons* 20; E. D. Biggers *Behind That Curtain* (Indianapolis 1928) 45 buttons.

2. It was just as plain as the button on a man's coat (33 Hall *Soldier's Bride* 179).

3. She does not care a brass button for Singleton (32 Kennedy *Swallow* 94; Neal *Charcoal* 192; Davis *Downing* 76 a button; Haliburton *Attaché* I 238, *Old Judge* II 115 a button). Apperson 456; *Oxford* 78; Stevenson 1237:2; Tilley B782; Whiting *Scots* I 146; Christopher Bush *The Case of the Green Felt Hat* (1939) 200 button; G. D. H. Cole and M. Cole *Dr. Tancred Begins* (1935) 72 brass button.

4. Neither do I give a darn blew button (64 Wiley *Johnny* 138).

5. You may bet your last shirt button on it (66 Boucicault *Flying Scud* 159). Cf. the modern colloquial "You can bet your shirt on it."

6. Her eyes shine like new buttons (54 Smith '*Way* 344).

7. [A vest] sot like a button (44 Stephens *High Life* I 68).

8. For I can steel the buttons of[f] an old negroes coat when he is wide awake (63 Wiley *Johnny* 45).

9. Ballenger's life is not worth a button (55 Anon. *New Hope* 273; Lowell *Biglow* 390). Apperson 456; *Oxford* 72; Tilley B782; Whiting *Scots* I 146.

Button-hole. Ef ever I got er chance at Arch I'd let him down er button-hole er two (51 Burke *Polly* 147; Stowe *Uncle* 29 Better mind yourselves, or I'll take ye down a button-hole lower, when Mas'r George is gone). Apperson 618; NC 378; *Oxford* 640; Tidwell PADS XIII (1950) 21; Tilley P181.

Buzzards. As blind as buzzards (38 Haliburton *Clockmaker* II 88). Apperson 54–55; Tilley B792. Cf. Taylor *Comparisons* 19.

By and large. A man who . . . feels rather perplexed on the whole, take it by-and-large (33 Neal *Down-Easters* I 23; Judd *Margaret* II 62; Clemens *Innocents* I 31 Taking it "by and large," as the sailors say, *Tramp* II 247). DA By 2; NED *Supplement* By and large.

Bygones. Let byegones be byegones (53 Haliburton *Sam* I 79; Cary *Clover-nook* 2d Ser. 65; Jones *Country* 310; Lincoln IV 103; Daly *Man* 40; Nash *Century* 125). Apperson 76; NC 379; NED Bygone 1 c; *Oxford* 74; Stevenson 270:5; Tilley B793; Whiting *Scots* I 146; Herbert Adams *Caroline Ormesby's Crime* (Philadelphia 1929) 283; William McFee *The Harbourmaster* (London 1932) 61 But he was willing to let bygones be bygones.

❧ C ❧

Cabbage, 1. They prefer cabbages to roses (53 Curtis *Potiphar* 114).

2. As unlike true life as a cabbage is to a rose (54 Shillaber *Mrs. Partington* 23).

3. Wiltin' away, like a cabbage leaf, in the hot sun (25 Neal *Brother J* II 109; Stephens *High Life* II 60 I settled right down, like a cabbage sprout in a hot sun, II 224 I wilted right down agin, like a cabbage plant in the sun).

4. And the owner of the knife "that wouldn't stick a cabbage" (58 Porter *Major* 143).

Cable. The original Samuel must long ago have slipped his cable for the Great South Sea of the other world [i. e., died]. (51 Melville *Moby-Dick* II 206). Babcock 262; Farmer and Henley VI 251; NED Slip vb. 28 b.

Caesar, 1. B—— is as bald as Caesar (58 Field *Pokerville* 139).

2. Jim he knew to be as brave as Caesar (57 Jones *Country* 128).

3. He's as dead as Julius Caesar (39 Briggs *Harry* I 230; Haliburton *Old Judge* I 68; Dorson *Jonathan* 110; Mayo *Kaloolah* 45). Svartengren 141; Bon Gaultier, pseud. [Theodore Martin and W. E. Aytoun] *The Book of Ballads* (1845, 11th ed. Edinburgh 1870) 10; Eugene Thwing, ed. *The World's Best One Hundred Detective Stories* (1929) VII 139, 169.

4. In relation to these pledges, I must not only be chaste, but above suspicion (49 Lincoln II 41). Apperson 77; *Oxford* 75; Stevenson 271–272:7; *Life* XXXVIII (Mar. 28, 1955) p. 38, quoting F. D. Roosevelt at Yalta (1945) on the proposed election in Poland. He said it should be like Caesar's wife. "I didn't know her but they said she was pure." Stalin replied, "They said that about her, but in fact she had her sins."

Cahoot. I wouldn't swar he wasn't in cahoot with 'em (43 Thompson *Chronicles* 74; Hooper *Simon* 29 I'd make a cahoot business with old man Doublejoy; Field *Pokerville* 198 if he liked, he would "go in with him—in cahoot"). Bartlett 91; DA Cahoot; Farmer 114; Green 77; McAtee 17; Schele de Vere 106; Thornton I 136–137, III 60.

Cain, 1. As wicked as Cain (57 Riley *Puddleford* 90, 312).

2. In short, as Miss Ophelia phrased it, "raising Cain" generally (51 Stowe *Uncle* 277; Hammett *Piney* 303). Bartlett 513; DA Cain 2; Farmer 114, 364; Farmer and Henley II 17; McAtee 51; Schele de Vere 323, 627; Stevenson 273:3; Thornton II 720, III 314; J. T. Farrell *No Star Is Lost* (1938) 330.

Cake, 1. You cannot eat your cake and have it too (21 Loomis *Farmer's Almanac* 178; Haliburton *Clockmaker* I

52

256–257; Barnum *Struggles* 458 and keep it also). Apperson 178; Faden 139; NC 379; NED Cake 8; *Oxford* 167; Stevenson 274:2; Tilley C15; Thomas Hughes *Tom Brown at Oxford* (1861) ch. 31 [He] must be taught early that he can't have his cake and eat his cake; C. S. Lewis *The Screwtape Letters* (1943) 46 this ignoble idea is to eat the cake and have it, 155 The creatures are always accusing one another of wanting "to eat the cake and have it," but thanks to our labors they are more often in the predicament of paying for the cake and not eating it; J. P. Marquand *B. F.'s Daughter* (Boston 1946) 295 It was like having your cake and eating it too; Thorne Smith *Turnabout* (1933) 231.

2. Emeline, don't hurry up the cakes too fast (53 Cary *Cloveruuok* 2d Ser. 27). DA Cake 1 b (3); Stevenson 273:8. See Biscuit (3).

3. Wish his cake dough (33 Neal *Down-Easters* I 3; Smith *Downing* 140 she'll feel sorry enough, and wish her cake was dough again, *Letters* 96 if they wouldn't wish their cake was dough again, I'm mistaken). Stevenson 274:4, quot. 1886.

4. I hope our cake aint all turning to dough again (33 Smith *Downing* p. v, 66 their cake is all dough, *'Way* 334 So your short cake is all dough agin, 357 Charles felt that his cake was all dough again, and that he might as well give it up for a bad job; Crockett *Life* 48 I saw quick enough my cake was dough; Irving *Attorney* 164 I'm afraid your cake's dough; Burke *Polly* 19 the cake's all dough; Porter *Major* 15; Taliaferro *Fisher's* 117, *Carolina Humor* 63). Apperson 77; Brewster *Amer. Speech* XIV (1939) 265; NC 379; NED Cake 8,

Dough 1 b; *Oxford* 75; Stevenson 274:4; Tilley C12; Whiting *Drama* 336:430; Jeffrey Farnol *Winds of Chance* (Boston 1939) 31. Cf. Bread (2).

5. My cake was all *mud!* (43 Robb *Squatter* 66).

6. The winning horse takes the cakes—and no back out! (58 Porter *Major* 120). Farmer 115; Farmer and Henley II 18; McAtee 63; NED Cake 7; Stevenson 273:5; Thornton I 137, III 165; George Limnelius *The Medbury Fort Murder* (1929) 260.

7. To sell like hot cakes. 39 DA Hot cake 2. NC 428; Taylor *Comparisons* 23.

Calends. But his friends looked for it only in the Greek Calends (72 Holmes *Poet* 15). *Oxford* 266; Stevenson 1678:6; Tilley G441; Archer Taylor "Locutions for Never" *Romance Philology* II (1948) 112–113.

Calf, 1. He lay there as helpless as a calf in a butcher's cart (45 Mayo *Kaloolah* 107).

2. I ladles out my words at randum, like a calf kicken at yaller-jackids (67 Harris *Sut* 134).

3. He blated like a calf (59 Taliaferro *Fisher's* 205).

4. The way these . . . islanders opened their mugs and gaped was a caution to dying calves (55 Haliburton *Nature* I 6).

5. He'll turn up the whites of his eyes like a dying calf (49 Haliburton *Old Judge* II 172). Cf. Boshears 32:133; McAtee 53 roll; NC 379.

6. The English did sartainly deacon the calf here [Note: "to knock a thing on the head as soon as born or finished"]. (55 Haliburton *Nature* II 409). Bartlett 169; DA Deacon vb. 2; Farmer 193.

7. He stared at fust like a calf's

head jest dressed (44 Stephens *High Life* II 71).

8. A starin about like a stuck calf (44 Stephens *High Life* II 216). See Pig (22).

California bank-notes. Besides silver, they have no circulating medium but hides, which the sailors call "California bank-notes" (40 Dana *Two* 97).

California fever, 1. If the "California fever" [laziness] spares the first generation, it is likely to attack the second (40 Dana *Two* 216).

2. Mose Jenkins did not take the California fever when it first broke out (56 Durivage *Three* 58). DA California 2 (6). Cf. Arizona fever, Texas fever.

Calm, sb. If calms breed storms, so storm calms (49 Melville *Mardi* II 209, *Moby-Dick* II 264 a storm for every calm). Apperson 604; Babcock 258; Oxford 4; Tilley C24, S908. Cf. Stevenson 2222:2.

Calm, adj. See Bishop (2), Clock (1), Clockwork (1), Day (3), Death (2), Duck-pond, Infant (1), Mirror (1), Morning (3), Sea (2), Stalactite, Statue (1).

Cambric. Cain he turn white as bleach cambric (59 Taliaferro *Fisher's* 189).

Camel, 1. Draughts that would choke a camel (60 Haliburton *Season-Ticket* 374). Cf. NED Camel 1 c.

2. That order jest broke the camel's back (66 Smith *Arp* 141). NC 482. See Feather (6), Grain (1), Ounce (4).

3. No wonder the proverb has it, it is easier for a camel to pass through the eye of a needle than for a rich man to enter the place established for a different class of citizens (71 Jones *Batkins* 371). Matt. 19:24; Stevenson 278:9; Tilley C26; Whiting *Drama* 124, 157, 307:52. Cf. Clemence Dane and Helen Simpson *Enter St. John* (1928) 267 talk about looking for a camel in a needle's eye.

Camp. To take into camp. 66 DA Camp 7 b (3).

Canary, 1. As chipper es a canary bird (38 Haliburton *Clockmaker* II 125).

2. As purty as a hen canary (67 Harris *Sut* 260).

3. In June they'll strike the ledge and then "good-bye canary!" (62 Clemens *Letters* I 66).

Candle, 1. As straight as a candle (39 Smith *Letters* 99). Cf. Tilley C38.

2. Marm's face was as white as a taller candle (44 Stephens *High Life* II 134).

3. Large parties will range themselves [in bed] on opposite sides of the house as economically as candles in a box (58 Porter *Major* 56). Cf. Halpert 822.

4. Nothin can hold a candle to it (34 Davis *Downing* 233; Haliburton *Clockmaker* II 105, 181 not fit to, *Letter* 18 not fit to, *Attaché* II 94, III 208 not fit to, *Old Judge* II 134 warn't fit to, *Sam* I 29, II 123, *Nature* II 29; Stephens *High Life* II 9, 210; Judd *Richard* 45; Whitcher *Widow* 128; Smith *My Thirty* 382, 388, 417; Sedley *Marian* 278 and if even the Baubee grays kin hold a candle to that span, ye kin boot me, that's all!; McCloskey *Across* 75; Jones *Batkins* 392; Nash *Century* 154 A sewing circle can't hold a candle to you boys [in telling gossip]; Shillaber *Ike* 144). Lean III 350–351; NC 379; NED Can-

dle 5 c; *Oxford* 298; Stevenson 280–281:9; Tidwell PADS XI (1949) 13; Tilley C44; Ed Bell *Fish on the Steeple* (1935) 285.

5. My legs a stickin tight to my trousers like two tallow candles in a tin mould (44 Stephens *High Life* II 202). Cf. Moulds.

6. Knowledge is not to be concealed, like a candle under a bushel (23 Cooper *Pioneers* 332; Crockett *Exploits* 59 None but a fool would place his candle under a bushel on such an occasion). Matt. 5:15; Mark 4:21; Stevenson 281:3. See Light (3).

Candy, 1. She was as sweet as candy (43 Haliburton *Attaché* III 71). Boshears 40:977; Taylor *Comparisons* 80.

2. Jemima . . . looked a whole biling of 'lasses candy at Lord Morpeth (44 Stephens *High Life* II 96).

Cane brake, 1. And here he come like a cane brake afire (34 Crockett *Life* 19). Randolph and Wilson 181.

2. Pure patriotic principles, such as a person's having been "born in a canebrake and rocked in a sugar trough" (43 Hall *Purchase* II 13, 136).

Cannon. It was a-bawlin' louder than a cannon (59 Taliaferro *Fisher's* 161, 163). NC 379.

Cannon ball. Straight as a cannon ball (25 Neal *Brother J* II 307).

Canoe. Molly seems determined to . . . paddle her own canoe (40 Eliason 133, Judd *Margaret* II 182; Wiley *Billy* 312; Smith *Arp* 161; Clemens *Letters* I 156). Bartlett 447; DA Paddle; Farmer 121; Farmer and Henley II 26–27; Jente *American* 346; NC 379; *Oxford* 484; Stevenson 1235:14;

NQ 5 x 427, 457; H. L. Ickes *Diary* (1954) II 305; H. K. Webster *The Clock Strikes Two* (1928) 15.

Cap, 1. But you and I know who the cap fits (43 Haliburton *Attaché* I 215, *Nature* I 140 as much as to say, "Put that cap on, for it just fits you"). Apperson 81; NED Cap 9; *Oxford* 77–78; Stevenson 283:10; Woodard PADS VI (1946) 35; *Catalogue of Political and Personal Satires . . . 1811–1819* (London 1949) IX 171 No. 11951 If the cap fits, wear it; Georgette Heyer *Behold, Here's Poison* (1936) 149. Cf. Shoe (5).

2. I set my cap for the lieutenant (32 Hall *Legends* 242; Longstreet *Georgia* 124 I declare I must set my cap for him; Haliburton *Clockmaker* III 252; Stephens *High Life* I 47; Cooper *Redskins* 85 "setting a cap" is but a pitiful phrase to express the assault I had to withstand; Whitcher *Widow* 86, 87, 149; Willis *Paul* 81; Holmes *Professor* 98; Nash *Century* 155). Farmer and Henley II 32; NC 380; NED Cap 9; *Oxford* 576; Stevenson 283:7; NQ CLXIX (1935) 391, 427, CLXX (1936) 214, 268, 286, 305; Charles Barry, pseud. *Death in Darkness* (1933) 170.

Cape Forty. One of my own townswomen who has weathered cape forty without a husband (24 Cooper *Pilot* 80).

Cape Horn, 1. The longevity of Cape Horn whaling voyages is proverbial, frequently extending over a period of four or five years (46 Melville *Typee* 25).

2. What sailors call the *"Cape Horn Fever"* alarmingly prevailed [i.e., feigned illness to evade work]. (50 Melville *White Jacket* 416). Babcock

257; DA Cape sb. 2 (5) cape fever. See California fever.

Capers. My word of honor to Rolfe, that I would "cut no capers" (50 Willis *Life* 370; Cartwright *Autobiography* 202; Kelly *Humors* 147; Hammett *Piney* 306; Harris *Uncle Remus* 29–30 You bin cuttin' up yo' capers). Farmer 122; Farmer and Henley II 33, 237; McAtee 21; NED Caper [2] b; Partridge 201; Stevenson 284:3. Cf. Cat (11).

Cap-sheaf. Of all the scrapes that I ever see this beats the cap-sheaf (33 Smith *Downing* 107; Harris *Sut* 38 an' tu put a cap sheaf ontu his stack ove raskallity, [he] got religion, an' got tu Congress). Bartlett 98; Farmer 122; Thornton I 146, III 168.

Capstone. What put the capstone to all actions of the house, was the fortification bill (35 Crockett *Account* 232).

Captain Grand. You must every now and then play Captain Grand (37 Neal *Charcoal* 23; Judd *Margaret* I 51 As if every upstart of a lawyer was to Captain Grand it over all the girls here, II 48 Ra'aly, you look as if you Cappen Granded it over all creation, and the Hospital besides).

Carcass. Where the carcass is, there will the eagles be gathered (53 Baldwin *Flush* 84). Matthew 24:28; Apperson 81; NC 380; *Oxford* 78; Tilley C73; Christopher Bush *The Perfect Murder Case* (1929) 133 vultures.

Card, 1. Mrs. M. . . . will play her cards well (68 Alcott *Little Women* 98). Farmer and Henley V 227; NED Card 2 d; *Oxford* 505; Stevenson 286:5.

2. [He (a horse)] was a sure card (54 Dorson *Jonathan* 86). Farmer and Henley II 36; NED Card 2 c; Stevenson 285:3.

Carnation. Her lips are as red as carnations (56 Durivage *Three* 234).

Carnelian. The top of his head . . . becomes as red as a carnelian (35 Fairfield *Letters* 47).

Carpet. Cousin Fanny . . . stepped off the carpet [i. e., was married]. (43 Eliason 297). DA Carpet b (2).

Cart, 1. Another is an old farm saw we used to have to Slicksville. It aint the noisiest cart that's the easiest upsot always (53 Haliburton *Sam* II 283). Stevenson 290:7 (this quotation).

2. That's votin' the ticket backwards; putting the cart before the horse (65 Sedley *Marian* 338). Apperson 83; NC 380; NED Cart 5; *Oxford* 80; Stevenson 290–291:9; Tilley C103.

Cartload. As thirsty as a cart load of sand (37 Neal *Charcoal* 191). Cf. Desert (3).

Cartridge. His face was as blank as a sham cartridge (56 Kelly *Humors* 376).

Case, 1. And telling him to go away and that he was a case (51 Stowe *Uncle* 26; Porter *Major* 60 Now Cabe was as hard a "case" as you would meet on a fourth of July in Texas). DA Case 2, Hard case; Farmer and Henley II 45; Green 178; NED Case 8 c; Thornton I 418, III 182; Stevenson 291:4.

2. It was a desperate case, only as desperate a remedy could serve (55 Melville *Israel* 176; Stephens *Fashion* 376 A desperate case, to be cured on-

ly with desperate measures). Apperson 142; Stevenson 1951:6; Tilley D357 Stronge disease requyreth a stronge medicine; P. B. Kyne *Tide of Empire* (1928) 154 Desperate circumstances require desperate measures.

3. You can't get nothin special without a good price, pewter cases never hold good watches (36 Haliburton *Clockmaker* I 104).

4. It appeared to alter the case (33 Neal *Down-Easters* I 31; Smith *Downing* 230, *Letters* 92). Apperson 83; *Oxford* 80; Stevenson 291:3; Tilley C111; Whiting *Drama* 337:439; G. D. H. Cole and M. Cole *The Sleeping Death* (1936) 110. See Circumstance (1).

5. You're a gone case (43 Lewis *Odd* 38; Hooper *Simon* 14 It was evidently a "gone case" with Simon and Bell). Bartlett 252; DA Gone (1). See Coon (7).

6. To keep cases. 56 DA Case 3 (1).

Cash, 1. He . . . paid for every thing in cash down (20–22 Irving *Bracebridge* 58).

2. Cash down on the nail. 55 DA Cash 3 b 2; Apperson 435; *Oxford* 441; Taylor *Index* 50; Tilley N18; Dorothy L. Sayers *Lord Peter Views the Body* (1929) 234. See Nail (4).

Castle, 1. Building castles in the air (40 Haliburton *Letter* 288, *Sam* I 281, *Nature* II 283; Hawthorne *Twice-Told* 428, 453, *Mosses* 70, 81, 263, *House* 15, 288; Mayo *Kaloolah* 27 more than one glorious castle in the air, 134 built castles in the air as easily as in the moon; Irving *Wolfert* 86 this most delectable of air-castles; Anon. *New Hope* 233 the air-built castles of his imagination; Durivage *Three* 47

the agreeable occupation of castle building while supper was preparing, 188; Chamberlain *Confession* 192 But Fortune . . . kicked down all my airy castles of glory; Alcott *Little Women* 157, 159, 181; Clemens *Roughing* I 199 so toppled my airy castle to the earth, II 118 my fancy so rioted through its castles in the air, *Gilded* I 285 his air-castles crumbled to ruins about him). Apperson 84–85; NED Air 3 c (3), Castle 11; *Oxford* 82; Stevenson 292–293:13; Tilley C126; Whiting *Scots* I 147; R. M. Kennedy, pseud. *The Bleston Mystery* (1929) 269–270. Cf. Hall *Purchase* II 176 You lost sight of your own principles, and thought pyramids could be built on air!

2. A chateau in Spain (54 Hawthorne *Mosses* 263; Richardson *Beyond* 552 My own estates, being chiefly in Spain; Alcott *Little Women* 377 this delightful château en Espagne; Saxe *Poems* 9 a castle in Spain, . . . Spanish Chateau; Clemens *Fairbanks* 47 Some few castles in Spain going up; Holmes *Poet* 256 In this chest is a castle in Spain, a real one, and not only in Spain, but anywhere he will choose to have it). Apperson 84; *Oxford* 82; Stevenson 293:5; Taylor *Investigations* 257; Tilley C125; John Esteven *The Door of Death* (1928) 223.

3. It was not built for a long lease, as some English houses are said to be, which, at the expiration of ninety-nine years, will almost punctually rattle down of themselves, like so many castles of cards (65 Sedley *Marian* 464). NED Card 1 b; Stevenson 1191:6; A. L. Guérard *The Pacific Spectator* VIII (1954) 117 The empire of Charlemagne was short-lived, that of Napoleon proved a house of cards; Paul S.

Taylor *The Pacific Spectator* VIII
(1954) 352 [How does he arrive at] a
complete inversion of the intention of
the law? By building a house of cards,
with a joker in the deck; T. H. White
The Sword in the Stone (1939) 221
The scene changed as suddenly as a
house of cards falling down.

Cat, 1. Cat and monkey trick. 56 DA
Cat 9 g. See Chestnut (3).

2. A cat and a Yankee always come
on their feet, pitch them up in the air
as high, and as often as you please (55
Haliburton *Nature* I 316, Richardson
Secret 158 The banks, with their usual feline sagacity, alighted upon their
feet). Apperson 86; NC 381; *Oxford*
82; Stevenson 294:2; Tilley C153; C.
F. Gregg *The Murder in the Bus*
(1930) 282 he pitched the cat away
from him, relying on its proverbial
sense of balance.

3. A cat in the meal [i. e., something hidden]. 39 DA Cat 9 c.

4. Whose captain . . . has as many
lives as a cat (21 Cooper *Spy* 112;
Kennedy *Swallow* 216 they [musk-
rats] were swinging by their necks
long enough to strangle nine lives out
of them; Haliburton *Old Judge* I 68
Cat though it be, if it had fifty lives
instead of nine, it will never rise again,
Sam I 325 If a feller had nine lives
like a cat; Bennett *Border* 239 you
seem to hev the nine lives to the cat,
268; Smith *My Thirty* 275 as many
lives as a cat; Paul *Courtship* 248 as
many lives as a cat; Clemens *Roughing*
II 47 Do you reckon a man has got as
many lives as a cat?). Apperson 85;
Green 255; NC 381; NED Cat 13 b;
Oxford 83; Stevenson 294:1; Tilley
C154; Agatha Christie *The Big Four*
(1927) 265.

5. But a cat may look at a king, I

hope, as grandfather Slick used to say,
mayn't he? (43 Haliburton *Attaché*
III 190; Judd *Margaret* II 115; Jones
Country 180; Derby *Squibob* 168).
Apperson 85; Bradley 64; NED Cat
13 a; *Oxford* 83; Stevenson 296–297:
8; Taylor *Index* 20; Tilley C141;
Whiting *Drama* 112; NQ 7 xii 245; 8
xi 452–453; E. D. Biggers *Behind
That Curtain* (Indianapolis 1937) 37;
M. O. Collacott *Harper's Magazine*
CCXI (Sept. 1955) 8 The privilege
of a cat to look at a king existed long
before the freedom of the press.

6. Active as cats (40 Dana *Two*
271; Cooper *Satanstoe* 44; Haliburton *Season-Ticket* 180; Chamberlain
Confession 73 cat).

7. She . . . screamed as cross as
two cats (55 Haliburton *Nature* II
35). Svartengren 101; Shirley and
Adele Seifert *Death Stops at the Old
Stone Inn* (1938) 91 a cat.

8. All was as dark as a stack of
black cats (43 Robb *Squatter* 65; Kelly *Humors* 270 stack of black cats in
a coal cellar). Boshears 35:469; Fife
118; McAtee 22; Stevenson 192:13;
Thornton I 238; Eleanor A. Blake *The
Jade Green Cats* (1931) 114 seven
black cats.

9. Screams . . . more dreadful than
the war-squalls of an hundred cats in
fiercest battle (45 Hooper *Simon* 62).

10. As goodnatered as a pussy cat
(44 Stephens *High Life* II 173, 223).

11. Cutting up capers as high as a
cat's back (33 Smith *Downing* 200,
231 make you jump higher than a cat's
back). Boshears 37:659 As high as a
cat's back [i. e., expensive]; DA Cat
9 f; Figh PADS XIII (1950) 13, cf.
12.

12. The creature [Topsy] was as
lithe as a cat (51 Stowe *Uncle* 275).

13. As loving as two pussy cats (44

Stephens *High Life* I 85). Cf. *Oxford* 6 Agree; Tilley C185.

14. As meek as a gray cat with a dab of cream on her whiskers (44 Stephens *High Life* II 96). Cf. NC 381: 19.

15. Whatever may be said of the gravity of a monkey, or the melancholy of a gibed cat (23–24 Irving *Tales* 193). Apperson 412 gib cat; Lean II ii 852; *Oxford* 418; Stevenson 1560:9; Tilley C129.

16. Nimble as a cat (51 Melville *Moby-Dick* II 75). Apperson 85 Cat 10; NC 381 Cat 4; Svartengren 158; Taylor *Comparisons* 13; Tilley C130, C131.

17. Quick es a cat (67 Harris *Sut* 103, 118). Boshears 39:832; McAtee 51; NC 381; Taylor *Comparisons* 65; Hulbert Footner *Murder Runs in the Family* (1934) 7.

18. Quiet . . . es cats (67 Harris *Sut* 118). Taylor *Comparisons* 67.

19. He is jis' es redy . . . es a cat (67 Harris *Sut* 103).

20. Holler'd at him . . . savidge as a cat (67 Harris *Sut* 45).

21. You should be as silent as cats in a kitchen (35 Kennedy *Horse-Shoe* 183; Haliburton *Sam* II 290).

22. You must step as slow, and silent, and cautious as a cat (55 Irving *Wolfert* 262).

23. Steppen saft es a cat (67 Harris *Sut* 263).

24. Spry as a cat (25 Neal *Brother J* III 387; Smith *'Way* 49). DA Cat 9 a.

25. As still as a cat (59–60 Holmes *Elsie* 352).

26. A smile for all the world as sweet as a cat makes at a pan of new milk (36 Haliburton *Clockmaker* I 123). Cf. Taylor *Comparisons* 24.

27. Genius is as tender as a skinned cat (37 Neal *Charcoal* 55). Cf. Eel (5).

28. We had been chums together at Princeton, as thick as two cats in a bag (60 Whitehead *Wild Sports* 68).

29. I am just as weak as a cat (53 Cary *Clovernook* 2d Ser. 22). NC 381; Mari Sandoz *Slogum House* (Boston, 1937) 85. Cf. Kitten (12).

30. And then the old man and me stood facein' one another like two strange cats in a garret (40 Haliburton *Clockmaker* III 293). Cf. G. D. H. Cole and M. Cole *The Corpse in the Constable's Garden* (1930) 5 they got on about as well as two cats in a shoe-box.

31. Arter wandering around like a cat in a strange garret ever so long (44 Stephens *High Life* II 65). Cf. DA Cat 9 b; Stevenson 301:1; Taylor *Comparisons* 24; Thornton I 151; R. P. Tristram Coffin *Lost Paradise* (1934) 63.

32. Talking as soft and as mealy-mouthed as could be, like an old grey cat mewing round a bird cage (44 Stephens *High Life* I 96).

33. As easy as a cat could lick her ear (33 Smith *Downing* 130, *My Thirty* 350, 381, 416 as quick as; Longstreet *Georgia* 202 before a cat can lick her foot; Haliburton *Clockmaker* III 226 in less time than a cat takes to lick her paw; Taliaferro *Carolina Humor* 78 Quicker nor a cat can lick its paw). Cf. Apperson 85 Cat 13; Green 21; *Oxford* 30; Stevenson 298–299; Tilley C133.

34. I wouldn't believe him as far as you could swing a cat by the tail (57 Riley *Puddleford* 31). See Bullock, Tailor (1).

35. One might swing a cat in it, perhaps, but then it would be fatal to the cat to do it (66 Clemens *Sand-*

wich 139, *Innocents* I 13 there was still room to turn around in, but not to swing a cat in, at least with entire security to the cat, *Roughing* II 227 One might swing a cat in it, perhaps, but not a long cat). *Oxford* 548; Marcus Magill, pseud. *Death in the Box* (Philadelphia 1931) 56 in this house where there's not room enough to swing a cat.

36. That crittur is like a singed cat, better nor he seems (49 Haliburton *Old Judge* I 44; Clemens *Washoe* 61 The country looks something like a singed cat . . . and also resembles that animal in the respect that it has more merits than its personal appearance would seem to indicate, *Tom* 5 I reckon you're a kind of a singed cat, as the saying is—better'n you look). Bartlett 594–595; Green 337; *Oxford* 592; Stevenson 298:7; Tilley C178.

37. That cat wouldn't fight (69 Clemens *Innocents* I 26). DA Cat 9 h; Lee Thayer *Hell-Gate Tides* (1933) 11. Cf. Cock (4).

38. That cat wouldn't jump at all, would it? (38 Haliburton *Clockmaker* II 221, 236, *Attaché* II 224 to see whether that cat would jump or no, *Sam* I 98, 211, 217, 278). John D. Carr *The Four False Weapons* (1937) 127. Cf. Cat 47.

39. Dreads them . . . as a cat hates hot soap (44 Stephens *High Life* II 137). Cf. Apperson 85 Cat 11; *Oxford* 83; Tilley C150.

40. It's enough to make a cat sick to hear fellers talk (40 Haliburton *Clockmaker* III 26, *Letter* 193). Cf. Apperson 86 Cat 28 It would make a cat laugh; NED Cat 13 c; *Oxford* 83 speak; Henry Holt *The Sinister Shadow* (1934) 287 laugh.

41. But under these circumstances who is to bell the cat, and how is it to be done? (53 Hammett *Stray* 38). Apperson 88 Cat 65; NED Bell vb.[5] 1; *Oxford* 32–33; Stevenson 297–298:7; Tilley B277; Wyndham Martyn *The Recluse of Fifth Avenue* (1929) 231. Cf. P. F. Baum *Modern Language Notes* XXXV (1919) 462–470.

42. Eyeing each other like two tomcats (33 Neal *Down Easters* II 179). Cf. James E. Grant *The Green Shadow* (1935) 61 fought like a couple of tomcats on a fence.

43. It [hair] glistened like a black cat in the dark (44 Stephens *High Life* II 21).

44. She leaped from the bed like a cat (54 Smith *'Way* 384).

45. You know as much about a gentleman as a cat does of music (38 Haliburton *Clockmaker* II 268, *Old Judge* II 114 she can no more play her part on a farm than a cat can play a fiddle). Cf. Tilley J38, S679.

46. Things they knew as much of as a cat does of a punt (60 Haliburton *Season-Ticket* 85).

47. He knows how the cat jumps (33 Neal *Down-Easters* I 18; Smith *Downing* 38 there's never any telling which way the cat will jump, 39 But the cat jumped t'other way to both of 'em, 67 let the cat jump which way 'twill, *My Thirty* 414 When I found which way the cat was going to jump; Davis *Downing* 57 They tell us jest how the cat jumps, 208, 225; Haliburton *Clockmaker* I 85 I see how the cat jumps, II 171, *Attaché* I 125, *Letter* 26; Thompson *Major* 74; Sedley *Marian* 286 And the hull place is watchin' the thing to see how the cat'll jump; Jones *Batkins* 256 to see "which way the cat jumped," 318 I was getting information too, as to how the "cat was jumping," as the old saying is). Apperson 89 Cat 73; Farmer and Henley

II 51, IV 83, VII 300; NED Cat 13 e; *Oxford* 83; Randolph and Wilson 203–204; Stevenson 300:5; Agatha Christie *Death in the Air* (1935) 158 sitting on the fence watching which way the cat will jump.

48. The cat was out of the bag (34 Davis *Downing* 34; Haliburton *Clockmaker* I 194, III 245, *Attaché* II 90, *Sam* I 264 lettin' the cat, II 28, *Nature* I 320, II 191 tell you my secrets, let the cat out of the bag for you to catch by the tail, 192 you and the cat in the bag may run to Old Nick and see which will get to him first, and say tag; Stephens *High Life* II 79 let the cat; Thompson *Major* 93, 108 let the whole cat out of the wallit; Cooper *Satanstoe* 83; Melville "I and My Chimney" in *Works* XVII 307 Here . . . the cat leaps out of the bag; Kelly *Humors* 192, 227; Cary *Married* 135; Paul *Courtship* 269; Alcott *Little Women* 482 letting cats out of bags; Barnum *Struggles* 560 [a literal instance]; Eggleston *School-Master* 230 with a tone and a toss of the head that let the cat out; Jones *Batkins* 64; Clemens *Gilded* I 78). Apperson 89 Cat 68; *Catalogue of Political and Personal Satires . . . 1820–1827* X (London 1952) 57 No. 13739; Farmer and Henley II 51, IV 181; Hardie 470: 128; McAtee *Grant County* 3; NED Bag 18; *Oxford* 362; Stevenson 295:6; Eric B. Young *Dancing Beggars* (Philadelphia 1929) 222 my story had let the cat out of the bag, or the bee out of the bonnet; Ralph C. Woodthorpe *Death Wears a Purple Shirt* (1934) 202, 245 have done my best to keep the cat in the bag, but it has got out and spilled the milk, and there is no use crying over it.

49. The nigger showing his teeth, and rolling about his eyes, like a black cat in the dark (44 Stephens *High Life* I 19).

50. A singin like so many good natered pussy cats shut out o' doors (44 Stephens *High Life* II 190).

51. Springing like a cat up the slope of green sward (53 Willis *Fun* 263).

52. Watching me like a cat (33 Neal *Down-Easters* I 5). L. J. Vance *The Lone Wolf's Son* (Philadelphia 1931) 27.

53. You don't need 'em no more 'n a cat needs 2 tales (62 Browne *Artemus* 184; Clift *Bunker* 219). NC 381: 16. Cf. Hardie 468:56 dog. See Lizard (2); Toad (5).

54. As for politics, I don't believe wimmen have any right to meddle with them, more than a cat wants trousers (44 Stephens *High Life* II 122).

55. I only thought he might be pokin his dead cat at somebody what lives in this holler [i. e., seeking to exasperate]. (58 Porter *Major* 87). DA Cat 9 e (this quotation).

56. I'll play with you as a cat does with a mouse (53 Haliburton *Sam* I 30). Apperson 85 Cat 12; Tilley C127; Hugh Austin *Murder of a Matriarch* (1936) 178.

57. To watch him as narrowly as a cat would a mouse (54 Smith *'Way* 13). Apperson 85 Cat 12; *Oxford* 694; Tilley C128; Herbert Asbury *The Tick of the Clock* (1928) 144.

58. They got to quarrelling like cats and dogs (33 Smith *Downing* 77, *My Thirty* 340; Stephens *High Life* I 36 a mouth that twisted one way and his nose curling off on t'other side as if they hated each other like cats and dogs; Anon. *New Hope* 181 live a cat and dog life with her for one week; Whitcher *Widow* 332–333 She knows

just what couples live like cats and dogs; Browne *Artemus Ward His Travels* 210 and yet the Wilkenses may fight like cats and dogs in private). Apperson 87 Cat 40, 45; NC 381; *Oxford* 82, 568; Stevenson 48:9, 302:5; Taylor *Comparisons* 23–24; Tilley S165; Whiting *Scots* I 147; Will Scott *The Mask* (Philadelphia 1929) 138 hate; Carolyn Wells *Horror House* (Philadelphia 1931) 168 quarrel; A. W. Derleth *The Man on All Fours* (1934) 29 fight. See Dog (54).

59. No, said Mrs. Grey, she can't speak—the cat has got her tongue (52 Cary *Clovernook* 294). Brewster *Amer. Speech* XIV (1939) 264; Stevenson 2346:5; R. P. Warren *All the King's Men* (1946) 13 Huh? What's the matter? Cat got yore tongue?, 140 God damn it, has the cat got your tongue?

60. Rainin cats and dogs (36 Haliburton *Clockmaker* I 272, *Nature* II 270; Stephens *Homestead* 334). Apperson 523; Farmer and Henley II 57; NC 381–382; *Oxford* 531; Stevenson 1931: 2; Tilley C182; Clyde B. Clason *The Fifth Tumbler* (1936) 236.

61. He . . . made shoes, a trade which he prosecuted in an itinerating manner from house to house, "whipping the cat," as it was termed (45 Judd *Margaret* I 19, 42). Farmer and Henley II 50–51; NED Whip 16 a (c).

62. See Chestnut (3), Paw, Pussy cat, Way (12).

Catamount, 1. As fierce as a catamount (45 Cooper *Chainbearer* 95).

2. As lonely as a catamount. 77 DA Bachelor 1 a.

3. Indeed, although sixty years of age, he was, as he declared, "as spry as a catamount" (65 Sedley *Marian* 175).

4. If the President want [wasn't] tougher than a catamount (33 Smith *Downing* 203).

5. To drop like a catamount on a coon. 46 DA Coon 3 d (3).

6. He . . . jumped like a cattermount (25 Neal *Brother J* II 7; Robb *Squatter* 74).

Catching. Catchin' before spankin' is the rule (76 Nash *Century* 160).

Caterpillar. I wuz a-setten on the fence as harmless as a caterpiller (c60 Paul *Courtship* 55).

Cat-fish. If you don't have to fight, or get out of the way, then thar ain't no cat-fish in the Mississipp (58 Porter *Major* 136). See Snake (4, 6).

Cat fur. Now, I don't know much about this Laboo, but I don't think he is the clean cat fur, no how (51 Burke *Polly* 141).

Cat-head. Fellows that don't know a cat-head from a cat-harping (39 Briggs *Harry* I 270). Cf. NED Cathead, Harpings 2 (cat-harpings).

Catnip, 1. [A sailor] green as catnip (56 Kelly *Humors* 337).

2. A dear, pretty young man, smelling as sweet as catnip (54 Shillaber *Mrs. Partington* 113).

Cat's cradle. As quick as marm could undu a cat's cradle (44 Stephens *High Life* I 149).

Caucasus. I was cold as Caucasus (56 Kelly *Humors* 112).

Caulker. After bolting a caulker [i. e., taking a drink]. (51 Burke *Polly* 74). Cf. Farmer and Henley II 60 caulker; NED Caulk, sb.

Cause, 1. It is an ill cause the lawyer is ashamed of (34 Loomis *Farmer's Almanac* 178). Cf. Tilley C201.

2. Like causes are well known to produce like effects (27 Cooper *Prairie* 70; Barnum *Struggles* 480). Cf. Tilley C202; Whiting *Scots* I 147.

Caution. The way we cut water was a caution to small craft (44 Stephens *High Life* II 144; Haliburton *Sam* II 148 the way he pitched into that [fruit] was a caution to schoolboys, *Season-Ticket* 17 he was a caution to sinners to behold, 55, 276 the way it was beargreased . . . was a caution to a tar-brush; Judd *Richard* 210; Dorson *Jonathan* 108, 132; Mayo *Kaloolah* 107; Whitcher *Widow* 208 the way she squawked it out was a caution to old gates on a windy day; Bennett *Border* 468 and the way they [dollars] slides through these hyer old j'ints, is a caution to old Kaintuck; Porter *Major* 45 the way I pitched it in to him was a caution to mules, 88 and when I *did* get out of site the way I did sail was a caution to turtles and all the other slow varmints, 123 the way we went it was a caution to anything short of locomotive doin's, 138 and the way he walked at me with his two fore legs was a caution to slow dogs; Clift *Bunker* 111 The way the minister looked at her was a caution to all peacocks, dogs, and other vermin; Harris *Uncle Remus* 55). Bartlett 107; DA Caution sb. 1; Farmer 129–130; Farmer and Henley II 60–61; Stevenson 306:9; Thornton I 156–157. See Calf (4).

Cautious. See Cat (22).

Cavy. He'd be converted afore you could cry "cavy" (59 Taliaferro *Fisher's* 208). See Peccavi.

Cent, 1. As if she wanted to show me that she didn't care a cent for all I could do (44 Stephens *High Life* I

51; Lowell *Biglow* 28; Kelly *Humors* 235 not caring two cents; Clemens *Love Letters* 121 two cents). Farmer 131. Cf. NC 491.

2. And the late turnips were not worth a cent (53 Cary *Clovernook* 2d Ser. 303; Kelly *Humors* 96 Not a red cent's worth, 410 wasn't worth two cents; Clift *Bunker* 111 Tucker's father was never worth a red cent in the world; Eggleston *Circuit* 128 I cannot preach worth a cent). DA Cent 1 b; Farmer 131–132; McAtee 52; Schele de Vere 628; Thornton II 730, III 319; William Faulkner *The Sound and Fury* (1929) 237. Cf. Stevenson 2642: 1 (plack, a small Scottish coin), 2643: 2 (groat, farthing, etc.)

Center. To come to the center [i. e., to take a stand]. 73 DA Center 3 b (2).

Certain. See Alive (3), Fate (1), Live (1), Preaching (1), Turtle (1).

Chalk, 1. It is a long chalk ahead on us in others (36 Haliburton *Clockmaker* I 18, *Attaché* IV 208 a long chalk below our slaves). DA Chalk sb. 3 b (2) a chalk above; Farmer and Henley II 67; NED Chalk 6 b; *Oxford* 87.

2. As pale as chalk (36 Haliburton *Clockmaker* I 73). C. L. Day, ed. *The Songs of Thomas D'Urfey* (Cambridge, Mass. 1933) 108 Her Face is Pale as Chalk too; Hulbert Footner *The Ring of Eyes* (1933) 56.

3. [Music] as slick as a streak of chalk iled at both ends (44 Stephens *High Life* I 205).

4. She grew as white as chalk (36 Haliburton *Clockmaker* I 179, III 170, 185; Dana *Two* 420; Browne *Artemus* 20). Boshears 41:1016; Halpert 1038; NC 382; Svartengren 232;

Whiting *Scots* I 148; W. R. Bennett *Little Caesar* (1929) 42.

5. It whips English weather by a long chalk (36 Haliburton *Clockmaker* I 108, 121, 247, 279, 323, II 2, 29, 60, 75, 85, 93, 130, 220, 293, 319, III 38, 274, *Letter* 199, *Attaché* III 94, IV 242, *Old Judge* II 115, *Sam* I 27, 172, 289, 315, II 45, 257, *Nature* I 9, 280, II 53, 227, *Season-Ticket* 43, 59, 286, 341, 371; Lowell *Biglow* 142; Stowe *Uncle* 77). Bartlett 109–110; Farmer and Henley II 68; Green 81; NED Chalk 6 b; *Oxford* 87; Schele de Vere 318; Stevenson 310:7; Thornton I 160; Brian Flynn *Murder En Route* (Philadelphia 1932) 192; Evelyn Waugh *Brideshead Revisited* (1945) Bk. II ch. 1.

6. Not by two chalks! (33 Neal *Down-Easters* I 8, 124; Smith *Downing* 51).

7. As different from ourn in creed as chalk is from cheese (38 Haliburton *Clockmaker* II 65, 320 his writins ain't to be compared to the Clockmaker, no more than chalk is to cheese, *Season-Ticket* 321; Stephens *High Life* I 13 it's no more like them clocks . . . than chalk is to cheese, II 69 no more . . . than chalk's like a new milk cheese, 236 no more tu be sot up agin my gal, than chalk's like cheese). Apperson 90; Green 28; NC 382; NED Chalk 6 a; *Oxford* 87; Stevenson 310–311:9; Taylor *Comparisons* 34; Tilley C218; Whiting *Drama* 337:445; Miles Burton *The Clue of the Fourteen Keys* (1937) 127 as unlike; Robin Forsyth *The Pleasure Cruise Mystery* (1934) 208 as different. See Cheese (5).

8. They are neither chalk nor cheese (43 Haliburton *Attaché* IV 273, *Sam* II 270, *Nature* II 22).

9. He soon recovered himself and came up to the chalk again (36 Crock-ett *Exploits* 73; Stephens *High Life* I 215 right up to, II 227). Bartlett 135; DA Chalk 3 b; Thornton I 160.

10. I tell you what, it was the clear chalk, the ginuine thing (44 Stephens *High Life* II 202–203). DA Chalk 2.

11. Your drunken dad has run up a long chalk already (45 Judd *Margaret* I 53). NED Chalk 4.

12. That 'ere's most frequently the kin' o' talk Of critters can't be kicked to toe the chalk (62 Lowell *Biglow* 260). DA Chalk 3 b (4).

13. And jist walk the chalks exactly (43 Haliburton *Attaché* IV 137; Clemens *Sketches* 243). Bartlett 737; DA Chalk 3 b (5); Farmer and Henley II 68, VII 286; Schele de Vere 318; Stevenson 2441:10.

14. The old ladies always interfere, and make you walk right straight up to the chalk, whether or no (37 Neal *Charcoal* 190).

15. See Streak (2).

Chalk line, 1. He returns as straight as a chalk line (55 Haliburton *Nature* II 324). Cf. Apperson 604–605.

2. You can't swindle this boy; he's walked too many chalk-lines for that (59 Taliaferro *Fisher's* 246).

3. Walked a chalk-line [i. e., proved sober]. (c60 Paul *Courtship* 32). DA Chalk 3 b (5); Farmer and Henley II 68; Woodard PADS VI (1946) 32.

Chance. Mind the main chance (20 Loomis *Farmer's Almanac* 177). *Oxford* 398; Stevenson 312:2; Tilley E235; Whiting *Drama* 343:533. See Eye (13).

Chancery, 1. I would see it [a poem] in Chancery! cried the lawyer, in the height of his wrath (56 Cooke *Foresters* 33).

2. Then I feel as if I had old Time's

head in chancery (58 Holmes *Autocrat* 165).

Changeable. See Wind (13).

Charity, 1. The water is cool as Presbyterian charity (35 Crockett *Account* 145; Haliburton *Attaché* I 98 They are as cold as; Wiley *Johnny* 120 cold as the world's charity). Apperson 106; Bartlett 131; NC 382; NED Charity 9 a; *Oxford* 101; Stevenson 322:3; Taylor *Comparisons* 27; Tilley C249.
2. Charity begins at home, . . . I must take care of myself in these hard times (23–24 Irving *Tales* 405; Melville *Pierre* 35 Does not match-making, like charity, begin at home?; Holmes *Autocrat* 12 When was charity like a top? . . . When it begins to hum; Jones *Batkins* 260 charity begins at home; Nash *Century* 30 The Bible says). Apperson 91–92; NC 382; NED Charity 9 a; *Oxford* 88; Stevenson 322–323:7; Tilley C251; NQ 1 x 403, CLXXXV (1943) 108; T. L. Peacock *Headlong Hall* (1816) ch. 15 (*Works* [London] I 152), *Melincourt* (1817) ch. 5 (*Works* II 46).

Charity-sermon. As dry as so many charity-sermons (69 Clemens *Innocents* II 135).

Charlie. But when you came to any thing else, I was "Charlie on the spot" (35 Crockett *Account* 112). Thornton I 162, III 68.

Charm, 1. It acted like a charm (51 Burke *Polly* 40; Melville *Confidence-Man* 105; Browne *Artemus Ward His Travels* 102 works like; Clift *Bunker* 94 worked; Clemens *Gilded* I 278 works). Taylor *Comparisons* 25; F. N. Hart *The Crooked Lane* (1934) 104 work.
2. They had been my Sunday boots

and fitted me to a charm (49 Melville *Redburn* 94, *Confidence-Man* 180 To a charm, my little stratagem succeeded; Cary *Clovernook* 2d Ser. 133 the cake was just done to a charm; Riley *Puddleford* 193 it works to; Barnum *Struggles* 123 to give his imitations "to a charm").

Charming. See Morning (4).

Charon. As savage as Charon (57 Butler *Nothing* 16).

Chase, 1. A stern chase is a long chase (24 Cooper *Pilot* 416, *Pathfinder* 51 We seamen call a stern chase a long chase; Mayo *Kaloolah* 202). Apperson 601; NED Chase sb.[1] 1 d; *Oxford* 620; Stevenson 323:9.
2. A wild-goose chase (20–22 Irving *Bracebridge* 114; Kennedy *Swallow* 43 the most egregious fool that ever set out in quest of a wild goose, 155, 176 the quest of a wild-goose, 296; Crockett *Account* 115; Hammett *Stray* 43, *Piney* 202; Jones *Winkles* 262; Melville *Confidence-Man* 15, 332; Barnum *Struggles* 67; Clemens *Letters* I 245). Apperson 686; Farmer and Henley VII 352; NED Wild goose chase; *Oxford* 709; Stevenson 323–324:10; Tilley W390; Austen Allen *Menace to Mrs. Kershaw* (1930) 56, 73.

Chat. See Blackbird (5).

Chateau. See Castle (2).

Chatter. See Magpie.

Cheap, 1. A half price which led me to characterize his concern as "cheap and nasty" (69 Barnum *Struggles* 158). Farmer and Henley II 81–82; *Oxford* 89; Joseph Kirkland *Zury* (Boston 1887) 350.
2. See China aster (1), Dirt (2),

Dog (9), Flea (3), Herring (1), Sheeting.

Checker. That's the checker [i. e., that's the ticket]. (56 Whitcher *Widow* 324). DA Checker 1.

Checks. One of the boys has passed in his checks (72 Clemens *Roughing* II 46). DA Check 3 b; NED Check sb. 15; Alice Campbell *Juggernaut* (1928) 92 as your Yankee friends say.

Cheek. By-and-bye he got a noble, great apple . . . smooth as a baby's cheek (54 Stephens *Fashion* 336).

Cheerful. See Bluebird, Cricket (3), Day (8).

Cheery. See Lark (3).

Cheese, 1. As lively as Dutch cheese in the dog-days (36 Crockett *Exploits* 189).
2. They kept me as poor as a skim-milk cheese (62 Locke [Nasby] *Struggles* 60).
3. Cheese, which is proverbially not so easy of digestion as blanc-mange (53 Melville "Cock-a-doodle-do!" in *Works* XIII 159). Apperson 92; *Oxford* 90; Stevenson 331:1; Tilley C269; Whiting *Drama* 199.
4. Ef greenbacks ain't nut jest the cheese (68 Lowell *Biglow* 348). Farmer and Henley II 85; Stevenson 331:3.
5. Proud of "knowing cheese from chalk," On a very slight inspection (68 Saxe *Poems* 31). Stevenson 310:8; Whiting *Drama* 337:445. See Chalk (7).
6. He has to crumble like old cheese [i. e., give in]. (c60 Paul *Courtship* 51).
7. I know it as an old inhabitant of Cheshire knows his cheese (58 Holmes *Autocrat* 165).

Cherry, 1. As red as a cherry (23 Cooper *Pioneers* 161; Haliburton *Clockmaker* III 284 Lips like cherries; Stephens *Fashion* 81; Kelly *Humors* 398 Lips and cheeks like cherries). Apperson 526; NC 383; NED Cherry 8; Stevenson 1944:3; Svartengren 248; Tilley C277; Whiting *Drama* 307:59, *Scots* I 148; William Gore, pseud. *The Mystery of the Painted Nude* (1938) 13.
2. His cherry red lip (47 Melville *Omoo* 254; Holmes *Autocrat* 275). NED Cherry-red.

Cheshire cat. Grinnin like a chessy cat (36 Haliburton *Clockmaker* I 98, III 41 from ear to ear, *Nature* II 285; Neal *Charcoal* 162 chessy cat; Hammett *Stray* 275, *Piney* 140 cheese-cat). Apperson 94; Bartlett 112; Green 83; NC 383; *Oxford* 267–268; Taylor *Comparisons* 25; W. G. Cowen *Man with Four Lives* (1934) 67 the famous.

Chestnut, 1. [A turkey] brown as a chestnut (55 Stephens *Homestead* 76).
2. Dropped her hand . . . as if it had been a hot chestnut (44 Stephens *High Life* II 224). Cf. Hugh Lofting *The Twilight of Magic* (1930) 103 as hot as a chestnut.
3. As the good-natured pussy learnt when the monkey used her paw to draw chestnuts from the fire (37 Neal *Charcoal* 61; Lincoln II 384 He is in the cat's paw. By much dragging of chestnuts from the fire for others to eat, his claws are burnt off to the gristle). Apperson 94; *Oxford* 84, 90; Stevenson 296:4; Tilley C284; E. S. Gardner *The Case of the Caretaker's Cat* (1935) 253. See Paw.
4. But you know, Molly, you always find the chestnuts after a biting

frost and a hard wind (45 Judd *Margaret* II 181).

Chick. I've got . . . neither chick nor child in the world (56 Durivage *Three* 177; Kelly *Humors* 372 an old bachelor, without "chick or child"; Whitcher *Widow* 87). NED Chick 3; Partridge *Clichés* 44; Tilley C307 Neither child nor chicken; E. M. Rhodes *West Is West* (1917) 289 everyone in San Clemente, man, woman, chick and child; Christopher Bush *The Body in the Bonfire* (1936) 207. Cf. Stoett 1140, citing similar locutions meaning "child and illegitimate child."

Chicken, 1. They were as fat as chickens (43 Haliburton *Attaché* III 24).
2. As sociable as so many chickens in a coop (44 Stephens *High Life* II 106).
3. Reckon not your chickens before they are hatched (21 Loomis *Farmer's Almanac* 177; Neal *Brother J* III 269 Never count your chickens, before they're hatched; Thompson *Major* 196 But as the old sayin' is, we mustn't count our chickens fore they're hatcht; Melville *Piazza* 245; Sedley *Marian* 131 It seems like countin' our chickens afore they're hatched; Barnum *Struggles* 485 The plan of "Counting the chickens before they are hatched" is an error of ancient date; Jones *Batkins* 344 then is the time to count the chickens, not before they are hatched; Clemens *Letters* I 324 In my experience, previously counted chickens never *do* hatch). Apperson 95; Farmer and Henley II 91; NC 383; NED Chicken 6; *Oxford* 112; Stevenson 332:8–334:6; Tilley C292; F. D. Grierson *The Empty House* (1934) 134.
4. He'd got hold of the wrong sort of chicken for that sort of corn (44 Stephens *High Life* II 71).
5. The chickens might come home to roost (71 Jones *Batkins* 246). NC 383; NED Chicken 6; Snapp 70:246; Stevenson 332:7; Andy Adams *The Ranch on the Beaver* (Boston 1927) 275–276 Strange how chickens come home to roost; F. J. Anderson *Book of Murder* (1930) 207. See Curse (6).
6. Strike out, or you're gone chickens (37 Neal *Charcoal* 158; Jones *Wild* 108 No, he's a gone chicken). DA Gone (1) 3. See Coon (7).

Child, 1. But I am as frightened as a child to-day (42 Irving *Attorney* 293).
2. As gentle as a child (51 Stowe *Uncle* 260). Cf. Svartengren 63 babe.
3. Good and simple-hearted as a child (53 Cary *Clovernook* 2d Ser. 16).
4. She had lived as happily as a child (68 Alcott *Little Women* 98).
5. Helpless as a child (58 Hammett *Piney* 74). See Infant (2).
6. He was as innocent as a child (38 Haliburton *Clockmaker* II 151, *Attaché* IV 251, *Nature* I 140, 142, II 47; Hawthorne *Mosses* 85 that pattern and proverbial standard of innocence, the Child Unborn; Alcott *Little Women* 407 asked Beth as innocently as a child). Apperson 327–328; NC 383; *Oxford* 320; Taylor *Comparisons* 51.
7. There he stood as meek as a child (54 Stephens *Fashion* 273).
8. As playful as a child (50 Judd *Richard* 255).
9. I am as weak as a child (40 Haliburton *Clockmaker* III 201; Irving *Attorney* 176; Chamberlain *Confession* 149). Svartengren 393. See Baby (5), Infant (4).
10. I had no more idea of what a

play was . . . than a child unweaned (71 Jones *Batkins* 277).

11. You know no more what you are talking about than the child unborn (c78 Clemens *Sketches* 90). NED Child 20. See Babe (7).

12. It's an old saying, but a true one, "Bring up a child in the way he should go, and when he's old, he'll do what he likes" (66 Boucicault *Flying Scud* 179). Cf. Prov. 22:6; Stevenson 340:1.

13. "Children should be seen, not heard," was the motto in the good old days (76 Nash *Century* 178). Apperson 96; Lean III 410 maid; *Oxford* 92–93; Snapp 93:11; Stevenson 335:4; Tilley M45.

14. Children will be children, you know (73 Clemens *Gilded* I 106). See Boy (4).

15. It's a wise child that knows its own father (36 Haliburton *Clockmaker* I p. ix; Clemens *Sandwich* 84 They say it is easy to know who a man's mother was, but, etc., etc.; Harris *Sut* 67 I'se allers hearn that hit tuk a mons'us wise brat tu know hits daddy; *Puck* II [1877] No. 41 p. 13). Apperson 697; *Oxford* 717; Stevenson 770:8; Tilley C309; James Joyce *Ulysses* (Paris 1924) 85.

16. It's better never to wipe a child's nose at all . . . than to wring it off (36 Haliburton *Clockmaker* I 88). *Oxford* 37; Tilley C296. Cf. Stevenson 344:7.

17. It's only the child that burns its fingers that dreads the fire (55 Haliburton *Nature* II 237). Apperson 73; NED Burnt 3 b, Child 20; *Oxford* 70; Stevenson 727:2; Tilley C297; Whiting *Scots* I 133; T. L. Peacock *Melincourt* (1817) ch. 30 (*Works* [London 1924] II 324) twice the victim of paper-coinage, which seemed to contradict the old adage about a burnt child, *Nightmare Abbey* (1818) ch. 2 (*Works* III 13) He was a burnt child, and dreaded the fire of female eyes.

18. So true is the aphorism which the great Englishman announced, that the boy is father to the man (53 Baldwin *Flush* 123–124; Melville *Confidence-Man* 158 "the child is father of the man"). *Oxford* 91; Stevenson 339:9; J. P. Marquand *Point of No Return* (Boston 1949) 41.

19. Child's play (36 Crockett *Exploits* 39; Melville *Moby-Dick* II 120, 259; Lincoln III 375). NED Child 18; Tilley C324; Whiting *Drama* 338:452, *Scots* I 134 Bairn's; A. Muir *The Silent Partner* (Indianapolis 1930) 145. See Boy (6).

20. I sat down on a log and cried like a child (c61 Chamberlain *Confession* 25). Halpert 95 baby.

Childhood. A child of the second childhood, old boy (56 Melville *Piazza* 111, *Confidence-Man* 147). Cf. NC 441:28.

Chilly. See Death (3).

Chimney. Smoking like bad chimneys (69 Alcott *Little Women* 368).

Chin. Leaving the dock as clean as a chin new reaped (40 Dana *Two* 370).

China aster, 1. I thought thet gold mines could be gut cheaper than Chiny asters (48 Lowell *Biglow* 120).

2. As prim as a China-aster (68 Alcott *Little Women* 5).

Chinkapin. If that one . . . didn't have whiskers, I hope I may never see chinkapin time agin, dadfetch me! (43 Thompson *Chronicles* 65). DA Chinquapin.

Chip, 1. The pumpkin sarse will be bild dry as a chip (55 Stephens *Home-*

stead 347). Apperson 168; NC 384; Tilley C351.

2. That's a rale chip of the old block (34 Davis *Downing* 240; Crockett *Account* 66; Haliburton *Clockmaker* II 218, III 79, *Attaché* II 38, IV 93, *Sam* II 223, *Season-Ticket* 238 of the old American hickory block; Stephens *High Life* I 32; Burke *Polly* 30; Jones *Winkles* 4; Whitcher *Widow* 125; Smith *My Thirty* 307; Locke [Nasby] *Struggles* 494). Apperson 97; Farmer and Henley II 94; NC 384; NED Chip 6 b; *Oxford* 93; Stevenson 345:14; Tilley C352; Anne Austin *The Black Pigeon* (1929) 126; M. Thompson *Not As a Stranger* (1954) 224 I guess I'm a chip of the old block; R. P. Warren *All the King's Men* (1946) 217 Yeah, Boss, he's a chip of the old block [spoken of the Boss's baby].

3. Just knock that chip off my head (54 Shillaber *Mrs. Partington* 84; Kelly *Humors* 89 he don't wait for any body to "knock the chip off his hat"). Cf. Thornton I 169–170, III 177.

4. To knock the chip off one's shoulder. 30 DA Chip 4 b (1); Stevenson 346:3.

5. That chip made the pot bile over [i. e., brought matters to a head]. (67 Harris *Sut* 242).

6. For if it's too far back he stumbles, or too forward he can't "pick chips quick stick" (55 Haliburton *Nature* II 337).

Chipmunk. An' here I be ez lively ez a chipmunk on a wall (67 Lowell *Biglow* 234). Cf. NC 382 gay.

Chipper. See Bird (7), Blackbird (1), Canary (1), Grasshopper (2), Lark (4), Squirrel (1).

Chirk. See Bird (8), Grasshopper (3), Katydid, Skipper.

Chisel. Arter him full chisel (33 Smith *Downing* 87, 169, 198, 211, 241, *Letters* 121, 131; Haliburton *Clockmaker* II 16, 57, 80, 302, III 293, *Season-Ticket* 45, 286; Stephens *High Life* I 2, 26, 112, II 124, 144). Bartlett 116; DA Full 3 b; Farmer 141; Farmer and Henley II 96; NED Chisel sb. 3; Thornton I 349.

Chop, 1. At first chop boarding schools! (43 Hall *Purchase* II 13; Stowe *Uncle* 5 Capital, sir,—first chop!, 76). NED Chop sb. 4.

2. My boys aint men of the common chop (44 Stephens *High Life* I 48).

Chowder. All mingled, mixed, and conglomerated, like a Connecticut chowder (55 Thomson *Doesticks* 47).

Christmas, 1. This is a Christmas Eve, which comes, you know, but once a year (23 Cooper *Pioneers* 164; Thompson *Major* 89 Crismus don't come but once a year now-a-days; Haliburton *Nature* II 276 it don't come like Christmas, once a-year). Apperson 99; Bartlett *Familiar Quotations* 446; Bradley 65; *Oxford* 94; Stevenson 351:1; Tilley C369; Thomas Hood *Poems* (1843, ed. London 1911) 626.

2. In that case . . . we shall wait here till Christmas (57 Melville *Confidence-Man* 19; Harris *Uncle Remus* 42 I'm gwineter git 'im dis time ef it take twel Chris'mus). Cf. Allan PADS XV (1951) 65; Boshears 40:932; McAtee 18; NC 384; Taylor *Comparisons* 74.

3. During a green Christmas, inauspicious to the old (57 Melville *Confidence-Man* 179). Apperson 98; *Oxford* 266; Taylor *Index* 68; Tilley W508; K. P. Kempton *Monday Go to*

Meeting (1937) 145; Victoria Lincoln *February Hill* (1934) 330 an old-fashion saying; W. N. Macartney *Fifty Years a Country Doctor* (1938) 286 a popular belief . . . I know of no greater fallacy as applied to this section [Northern New York]; Fulton Oursler *Joshua Todd* (1934) 37 the hoary credo of all gravediggers. [The ordinary form is "A green Christmas makes a fat churchyard"].

Chronometer. He was as regular in his hours as a chronometer (40 Dana *Two* 200). Cf. Clock (4).

Chunk. To extinguish one's chunk [i. e., to kill]. 52 DA Chunk 4 b.

Church, 1. You're married . . . fast as a church (56 Kelly *Humors* 424).
   2. The mill had been as silent as a church (32 Kennedy *Swallow* 113). Cf. NC 384 quiet.
   3. He was planted as solid as a church (65 Clemens *Sketches* 21). Cf. Kenneth P. Kempton *Monday Go to Meeting* (1937) 14 steady.

Church-mouse. He was as poor as a church-mouse (45 Cooper *Satanstoe* 106; Haliburton *Sam* II 252 that has nothin' but hymn-books to feed on; Hammett *Piney* 73; Cary *Married* 302; Alcott *Little Women* 365). Apperson 505; Boshears 31:112, 39:806; Fife 119; Green 86; NC 447; NED Church-mouse; *Oxford* 510; Taylor *Comparisons* 63; Tilley C382; Helen Ashton *Doctor Serocold* (1930) 233.

Churchyard, 1. For it . . . smells as damp and close as a church-yard (42 Irving *Attorney* 74).
   2. About as gay as a churchyard (68 Alcott *Little Women* 120).

Cicero. The night was cold as Cicero (78 Shillaber *Ike* 132).

Cider, 1. "The sateful old kritter" went off crippling as if she was not fit to run for sour cider (58 Porter *Major* 13).
   2. See Talk (1).

Cider-press. Pat held him like a cider-press (56 Kelly *Humors* 92).

Cipher. The man who had never been there, was a cipher in the community (51 Burke *Polly* 28). Apperson 100; NED Cipher sb. 2; *Oxford* 95; Tilley C391.

Circumstance, 1. When they change the circumstance, they alter the case (32 Kennedy *Swallow* 19; Longstreet *Georgia* 162 Circumstances alter cases, as the fellow said; Cooper *Redskins* 253; Haliburton *Old Judge* II 136; Curtis *Potiphar* 132 Music does certainly alter cases; Durivage *Three* 91; Whitcher *Widow* 78, 79; Smith *My Thirty* 277, 294, 400; Eggleston *Circuit* 11; Shillaber *Ike* 177). Apperson 100; NC 384; *Oxford* 95; Snapp 103:7; Stevenson 356:8; Tilley C392.
   2. It warn't a circumstance to this (44 Stephens *High Life* I 86; Mayo *Kaloolah* 56; Field *Pokerville* 139 In short, a head of Washington . . . is "no circumstance" to the benign front of our friend B——; Dorson *Jonathan* 115 but it isn't a circumstance to what happened to me once; Lowell *Biglow* 226 Thinkin' he warn't a suckemstance, 233 For Jacob warn't a suckemstance to Jeff at financierin'). Bartlett 121; DA Circumstance (1); Farmer 148; Farmer and Henley II 116; Stevenson 356:6; Thornton I 168; Woodard PADS VI (1946) 9.

Civil. See Answer, Bear (2), Pill pedlar, Question (2).

Clam, 1. A small room, cold as a clam (51 Melville *Moby-Dick* I 23). Taylor *Comparisons* 28.

2. And prate of being "happy as a clam" (68 Saxe *Poems* 447). Taylor *Comparisons* 45–46.

3. Richard is as happy as a clam on Cape Cod beach (45 Fairfield *Letters* 369).

4. They seemed as happy as clams in high water (44 Stephens *High Life* I 179; Haliburton *Nature* II 411; Paul *Courtship* 53; Wiley *Billy* 43; Barnum *Struggles* 679). Bartlett 276, 807; DA Clam sb. 4 b (1); Farmer 151; Schele de Vere 345; Lee Thayer, pseud. *The Sinister Mark* (1928) 213.

5. As independent as a clam in high water (44 Stephens *High Life* II 88).

6. She was . . . as pale as a soft-shelled clam (56 Durivage *Three* 115).

7. As sober as a clam in high water (44 Stephens *High Life* II 26).

8. Shet your clam [i. e., mouth]. (25 Neal *Brother J* I 143, *Down-Easters* I 93 . . . hold your yop!). DA Clam sb. 3; Thornton I 180.

9. See Horn (14).

Clam-shell. He knows how to keep his clam-shell shut, when he don't think proper to let on (60 Haliburton *Season-Ticket* 15; Lowell *Biglow* 229 ef you let your clam-shells gape). Bartlett 124, 590; Farmer 151; Farmer and Henley II 118; NED Clam sb. 3; Schele de Vere 70. Cf. Thornton I 180.

Clay, 1. I'll kick more clay outen you in a minute, than you can eat again in a month (45 Hooper *Simon* 65).

2. Old Stub "moistened his clay," as he called it, with a little rye (57 Riley *Puddleford* 26). NED Clay 4 b.

Clean. See Bridge (1), Chin, Dinnerplate, Floor (1, 4), Pin (6), Whistle (1).

Cleanliness. You know the old saw, "Cleanliness is next to Godliness" (45 Judd *Margaret* II 246; Richardson *Beyond* 373 If cleanliness be next to godliness, they are the least divine of human creatures; Clift *Bunker* 178 Cleanliness is said to be next to godliness; Barnum *Struggles* 440 So far as cleanliness is concerned, in Holland it is evidently not next to, but far ahead of godliness). Apperson 101; NC 385; *Oxford* 96; Stevenson 361:9; J. T. Farrell *Studs Lonigan: Judgment Day* (1935) 395; NQ 1 iv 256, 491; 2 ix 446; 3 iv 419, vi 259, 337, vii 367; 5 vi 499, ix 6; 6 xi 400, 8 xii 260; CLXXIX (1940) 151, 232.

Clear, 1. Yet at times, as we say in the backwoods, when he swung clear, there were very few that could excel him in the pulpit (c56 Cartwright *Autobiography* 323–324). Schele de Vere 348.

2. See Babe (1), Bell (1), Bootjack (1), Bugle, Coon (2), Crystal (1, 2), Day (4), Daylight (1), Dollar (3), Figure (3), Gospel (1), Ice (1), Mirror (2), Morn, Morning (8), Mud (1), Noonday (1), One (1), Preaching (2), Spring, Sun (2), Sunshine (1), Tin horn, Whistle (2).

Cleave. See Barnacle.

Clever. See Day (5), Head (1).

Climax. To cap the climax (c56 Cartwright *Autobiography* 345). Thornton I 145–146, III 167; Percival Wilde *Design for Murder* (1941) 158.

Climb. See Squirrel (4).

Cling. See Shadow (4).

Clock, 1. Calm as a clock (25 Neal *Brother J* II 336; Smith *Downing* 192; Lowell *Biglow* 372). Apperson 78.

2. In punctuality, she was as inevitable as a clock (51 Stowe *Uncle* 176). Svartengren 372.

3. [He] appears on his beat punctual as a clock (55 Stephens *Homestead* 61).

4. Ez reg'lar as a clock (48 Lowell *Biglow* 140; Judd *Richard* 241 then the Stage-driver appears . . . just as regular and just as quiet as the old clock in the kitchen; Clemens *Love Letters* 190). Boshears 39:862; Halpert 980; NC 385; Svartengren 372; Charles Barry, pseud. *The Smaller Penny* (1928) 14, 93. Cf. Clock-work (2).

5. As sober as a meetin-house clock (44 Stephens *High Life* II 208).

6. Manages my farm like a clock (51 Stowe *Uncle* 2).

7. 'T would put the clock back all o' fifty years Ef they should fall together by the ears (67 Lowell *Biglow* 261). *Oxford* 525; Stevenson 365:11.

Clock-work, 1. Calm as clock-work (54 Smith *'Way* 121).

2. As regularly as clock-work (46 Cooper *Redskins* 83; Smith *My Thirty* 383 regular). Green 30; McAtee 52; NED Clockwork 1 e; Svartengren 372; Charles Dickens *Sketches by Boz,* (1836, Centenary ed. London 1910) I 257; John D. Carr *Poison in Jest* (1932) 41. See Clock (4).

3. The whole goes on like well-oiled clockwork, where there is no noise or jarring in its operations (20–22 Irving *Bracebridge* 30; Kennedy *Swallow* 32 All things go like clock-work; Barnum *Struggles* 470 conduct a hotel like; Clemens *Love Letters* 57). NED Clockwork 1 c; Douglas G. Browne

Plan XVI (1934) 59. Cf. Boshears 33: 240; Halpert 145.

Close. See Bark (1) 1, 2, Bur (1), Churchyard (1), Cow (1), Eel (2), Grave (3), Green (1), Mink (2), Nest (1), Nutshell (1), Oyster (1), Vise (2).

Closemouthed. See Freemason.

Cloth, 1. He was pale as a cloth (c56 Cartwright *Autobiography* 142; Browning *Forty-four* 50).

2. His face was as white as a cloth (39 Smith *Letters* 68, 107; Cary *Clovernook* 2d Ser. 103; Kelly *Humors* 119 bolt of cotton cloth).

3. Dat ain't all, honey, but 'twon't do fer ter give out too much cloff fer ter cut one pa'r pants (80 Harris *Uncle Remus* 39).

4. You must have made them out of whole cloth (38 Haliburton *Clockmaker* II 314–315, III 292, *Sam* I 5, II 212, *Season-Ticket* 25; Dorson *Jonathan* 104; Hammett *Piney* 150; Smith *My Thirty* 405; Richardson *Beyond* 84; Clemens *Fairbanks* 217). Bartlett 755–756; DA Whole 2 b; Farmer 558; Thornton II 943, III 428–429; Clyde B. Clason *The Death Angel* (1936) 40. See Color (2).

Clothes, 1. For clothes don't make a gentleman a bit more than boots make a farmer (49 Haliburton *Old Judge* II 102–103, *Nature* II 17 it tante fine clothes makes de gentleman; Jones *Country* 205 The clothes don't make the gentleman). NC 385 A man is not known by the clothes he wears; Stevenson 368:7; Tilley S451 It is not clothing can make a man be good; A. P. Herbert *The Water Gipsies* (1930) 116; F. Marryat *Peter Simple* (1834) ch. 49 (London [1929] 403) It is not the clothes which make the gentleman.

2. But the clothes, in this case, were to be the making of the man (54 Hawthorne *Mosses* 255). Apperson 13; NC 385; *Oxford* 12; Snapp 105:1; Stevenson 367:5; Tilley A283; Whiting *Drama* 50; Paul Thorne *Spiderweb Clues* (Philadelphia 1928) 226.

3. Fine clothes, they say, make fine birds (39 Briggs *Harry* II 31). Apperson 211–212; NC 406; *Oxford* 202; Snapp 70:275; Stevenson 791:7; Tilley F163; Dennis Wheatley *They Found Atlantis* (Philadelphia 1936) 12; H. F. M. Prescott *The Man on a Donkey* (1952) 57 Well, if fine feathers'll make a fine bird.

4. With his go-to-meetin clothes on (36 Haliburton *Clockmaker* I 64, 254, 272, II 137 dress, 304, III 101, *Attaché* II 124, 144, *Sam* II 293 bran new, go-to-meetin' coat, *Nature* I 73, 117; Neal *Brother J* I 148 coat, II 45 finery; Smith *Letters* 49; Stephens *High Life* I 150 Sunday-go-to-meeting, 236 Sunday-, II 123 their best go-to-meeting manners; Taliaferro *Fisher's* 171; Paul *Courtship* 96 Sunday-go-to-meeting outfit). Bartlett 257; DA Go-to-meeting; Green 165; McAtee *Grant County* 9; Thornton I 379, III 169; Woodard PADS VI (1946) 29; P. MacDonald *Warrant for X* (1938) 216 Sunday-go-to-meeting. See Sunday-go-to-meeting.

Cloud, 1. He that regardeth the clouds shall not reap (56 Durivage *Three* 50).

2. Ther is a silver linin to evry cloud (63 Locke [Nasby] *Struggles* 78; Barnum *Struggles* 406 "Every cloud," says the proverb, "has a silver lining"; Clemens *Gilded* II 207 Every silver lining has a cloud behind it, as the poet says). Cf. Alcott *Little Women* 182 There's always light behind the clouds. Apperson 572; NC 385; *Oxford* 98; Snapp 73:7; Stevenson 370:4; Tilley C439; NQ 4 ix 239, 289, 330; 7 vi 289, 375; Mignon G. Eberhart *The Patient in Room 18* (1929) 233; M. K. Rawlings *Cross Creek* (1942) 155 I am no great maker of silver linings.

3. I have shown the silver lining of this great social Cloud (65 Browne *Artemus Ward His Travels* 214). Andy Adams *The Log of a Cowboy* (1903) 79 I . . . Spent a month's wages showing her the cloud with a silver lining.

Clover. While I was in this way rollin' in clover (43 Robb *Squatter* 135; Hall *Purchase* II 57–58 It may be something to live in clover; Chamberlain *Confession* 147 I lived in clover; Lowell *Biglow* 30, 308; Melville *Typee* 75 we shall be in; Wiley *Johnny* 90; Barnum *Struggles* 60 we lived in). Apperson 104; NED Clover 3; *Oxford* 99; Stevenson 370:10 be, live, dwell, wade; John Dos Passos *The 42d Parallel* (1930) 49. Cf. Pig (16), Woodchuck (6).

Cluster. See Bee-swarm.

Coal, 1. Coal-black hair (33 Neal *Down-Easters* I 122; Dana *Two* 230; Cooper *Satanstoe* 144, *Chainbearer* 63 eyes . . . as black as coals; Melville *Omoo* 83, *Mardi* I 49, *Moby-Dick* I 148; Hawthorne *Mosses* 57; Clemens *Letters* I 118–119 black as, *Sandwich* 210). Apperson 51; Boshears 34:351; NC 385; NED Coal 10 as black, Coal-black; Taylor *Comparisons* 17; Tilley C458; Whiting *Drama* 308:65, *Scots* I 150; Peter Coffin *The Search for My Great-Uncle's Head* (1937) 157; Louis Golding *This Wanderer* (1935) 294 coal-black.

2. Have him over the coals (33 Smith *Downing* 158; Stephens *High Life* I 190 the way the gals du haul him over the coals is a sin to Crocket, 215 haul our Sam over the coals and sarmonize him, II 261 hauled; Haliburton *Sam* I 150 hauled; Whitcher *Widow* 348; Jones *Country* 204 haul; Nash *Century* 181 haul; Harris *Uncle Remus* 20 he sorter rake me over de coals). Apperson 478; NED Coal 12 haul, call, fetch, bring; *Oxford* 283; Stevenson 371:5; Tilley C467; Woodard PADS VI (1946) 25 rake; NQ 1 viii 125, 280; Agatha Christie *Thirteen at Dinner* (1933) 168 hauled.

3. It was like . . . carrying coals to Newcastle (40 Dana *Two* 175; Melville *Moby-Dick* II 87 The old proverb about carrying coals to Newcastle; Langdon *Ida* 65 Mercy! carry coals to Newcastle, but don't bring any young niggers here; Curtis *Potiphar* 188, 195). Apperson 104; Babcock 261; NED Coal 13; *Oxford* 80; Taylor *Comparisons* 27; Tilley C466; NQ 1 xi 281; 4 vi 90; 5 ix 486; 8 ii 484, iii 17, 136; 9 xi 495; 10 vii 105; 12 ii 250, 299; Norman Forrest *Death Took a Publisher* (1938) 230.

4. I will heap coals of fire on your head (55 Haliburton *Nature* II 157; Alcott *Little Women* 336 a final heaping of coals of fire on her enemy's head). Romans 12:20; *Oxford* 99; Stevenson 372:2; Tilley C468; E. A. Robertson *Four Frightened People* (1931) 121.

Coal-hole. The next house was as black as a coal-hole (69 Barnum *Struggles* 610).

Coal-kiln. He was sweatin' like a coal-kill (59 Taliaferro *Fisher's* 175–176).

Coal mine. All was dark as a coal mine (56 Kelly *Humors* 370). Cf. B. A. Botkin *Folk-Say* IV (1932) 17 as dark as a mine shaft.

Coast. The coast was clear (53 Haliburton *Sam* II 191, 212; Hammett *Wonderful* 72; Smith *'Way* 49 cleared the coast, 301 kept his coast clear; Chamberlain *Confession* 25 The Cub evidently wanted the coast clear for his own advancement; Richardson *Secret* 463, 473–474; Clemens *Roughing* I 195, 257). NED Clear, adj. 20, Coast 4 e, cf. Clear, vb. 10; *Oxford* 99; Stevenson 372:5; Tilley C469; Yamamoto *Dickens* 137; Moray Dalton *The Night of Fear* (1931) 60; Stark Young *So Red the Rose* (1934) 286.

Coat, 1. Black as a minister's coat (44 Stephens *High Life* II 84). Cf. C. G. Givens *The Jigg-Time Murders* (Indianapolis 1936) 108 a coat.

2. I am willing to change everything but my coat (35 Kennedy *Horse-Shoe* 29, 144 the day of the week when a man changes his coat, 192 and turn his coat whenever there is money in it). NED Coat 13 turn; *Oxford* 676; Stevenson 373:3; Tilley T353; Whiting *Scots* I 150; Alec Glanville, pseud. *The Body in the Trawl* (London 1938) 130 before I definitely turn my coat. Cf. Apperson 651–652 tippet.

3. If people choose to fit your coats to their own backs, 't ain't your fault (56 Whitcher *Widow* 342–343).

4. He seemed to have taken the measure of his own mind, and to have cut his coat according to his cloth (33 Hall *Soldier's Bride* 176; Hammett *Piney* 12–13 The traveller in Texas . . . must cut his "coat according to his cloth," arrange his day's journey according to his stopping places). Apperson 131; Lean III 445–446; NC

385; *Oxford* 126; Stevenson 373:4; Stoett 2250; Tilley C472; Whiting *Scots* I 150; Anthony Wynne, pseud. *The Cotswold Case* (Philadelphia 1933) 257.

Coat-tail. A boy saw him makin' a straight coat-tail for the brook (58 Hammett *Piney* 176; Smith *Arp* 144 Then they run back a-puffin and blow-in with a straight coat-tail). NC 385 Clothes (4). See Shirt-tail.

Cob, 1. As dry as a cob (34 Davis *Downing* 46; Lowell *Biglow* 293). See Corncob.

2. To confess the cob [i. e., to acknowledge the corn]. 53 DA Cob 2 b.

Cobbler. The familiar axiom of *Ne sutor ultra crepidam* (46 Cooper *Redskins* 53; Clift *Bunker* 73 that old saw about "sticking to the last," 203 that old saw "Let the cobbler stick to his last"; Saxe *Poems* 36 Who cut him off with a saw—and bade "The cobbler keep to his calling"). Apperson 104; *Oxford* 99–100; Stevenson 2098:4; Tilley C480; NQ 3 iii 302–303, x 169, 235, 323, 401–402; 4 iii 320, 396, 412, 441, 471; 8 xi 91, 292; 12 xii 293, 338–339; S. H. Adams *The Gorgeous Hussy* (Boston 1934) 305. See Shoemaker.

Cobweb, 1. I picked it up . . . for the handkerchief was fine as a cobweb (54 Stephens *Fashion* 39).

2. His head was full-er cobwebs or bumble-bees (57 Riley *Puddleford* 263). Apperson 33 Bee (13); NC 368 Bee (5); NED Cobweb 7; *Oxford* 29.

Cock, 1. Red es a cock's comb (67 Harris *Sut* 292). See Turkey (2) 6.

2. For as the old cock crows, the young one learns (57 Riley *Puddleford* 91). Apperson 719 Young (17);

Oxford 470; Stevenson 374:9; Tilley C491; Whiting *Scots* I 151. See Hog (6).

3. To pounce upon them, like a cock at a blackberry (36 Crockett *Exploits* 28). See Duck (11), Nighthawk.

4. But that cock wouldn't fight (36 Crockett *Exploits* 99; Lincoln III 392; Nash *Century* 61 That cock won't fight, father). Green 31; NC 385; NED Cock 2 c; *Oxford* 101; Stevenson 374:6; Anne Meredith *Portrait of a Murderer* (1934) 167. See Cat (37).

5. See Fighting-cock, Gamecock (1, 2).

Cock-a-hoop. I wish my friend, Mr. Jones here, to see this cock-a-hoop business tomorrow (50 Willis *Life* 323; Holmes *Autocrat* 300 And his mounted truckmen, all cock-a-hoop). Apperson 105; Lean III 327; NED Cock-a-hoop; *Oxford* 100; Stevenson 375:5; Tilley C493; Whiting *Drama* 338:460; NQ 2 v 426; 4 xi 211, 321, 474, xi 59, 316; Jeffrey Farnol *The Crooked Furrow* (1938) 40.

Cock-and-bull. A cock-and-bull story (32 Kennedy *Swallow* 144; Hall *Purchase* I 39; Melville *Typee* 354 proved to be literally a, *White Jacket* 121, *Moby-Dick* I 71, II 55; Lincoln III 181; Kelly *Humors* 169; Holmes *Autocrat* 107 That sounds like; Smith *My Thirty* 322). Apperson 105; NED Cock-and-bull; *Oxford* 100; Stevenson 2273:3; Tilley S910; NQ 6 x 260; 7 viii 447, ix 270, 452, 494; 10 iii 268, 334; Anthony Abbot, pseud. *About the Murder of the Night Club Lady* (1931) 88. Cf. Schele de Vere 380.

Cockle-bur. As thick all around me, as cuckle burrs in a colt's tail (45 Hooper

Simon 142). NC 386 as close. Cf. Svartengren 325 cockle, bur.

Cockles. Something that will warm the cockles of your heart better than quarts of wine (68 Alcott *Little Women* 204). Apperson 106; NED Cockle sb.² 5; *Oxford* 101; Stevenson 1108:7; Tilley C498.

Cockroach. Es restless es a cockroach in a hot skillit (67 Harris *Sut* 231, 55 he wer a-cuttin up more shines nor a cockroach in a hot skillet).

Cocoanut. Teeth like a fresh slice of cocoa-nut meat (53 Willis *Fun* 101).

Codex Vaticanus. [A calling card] as yellow as the Codex Vaticanus (60 Holmes *Professor* 151).

Codfish, 1. He's as deaf as a codfish (59 Boucicault *Dot* 122). Cf. Apperson 138–139 haddock; Svartengren 175.

2. You are as dumb as a cod-fish (24 Cooper *Pilot* 350).

3. I'll be mute as the codfish in the House of Representatives (56 Durivage *Three* 295). Cf. Apperson 434; *Oxford* 440; Tilley F300.

Coffee, 1. The landlady, who was all smiles again, as bright and sparkling as the coffee in his cup (54 Shillaber *Mrs. Partington* 369).

2. The water looked almost as brown as coffee flowing from its urn (59–60 Holmes *Elsie* 46).

3. Don't you call me names tho', or I'll settle your coffee for you without a fish skin, afore you are ready to swaller it (43 Haliburton *Attaché* II 238). DA Coffee 1 c.

Coffin, 1. You look as solemn as a coffin (51 Stowe *Uncle* 227).

2. See Mohammed.

Coin, 1. Well, I acknowledge the coin, you may take my hat (55 Haliburton *Nature* II 198). See Cob (2), Corn (1).

2. I will jist pay you off in your own coin (38 Haliburton *Clockmaker* II 111; Whitcher *Widow* 302; Barnum *Struggles* 70 they liked to see him paid in his own coin). Apperson 487; NED Coin 7 b; *Oxford* 491; Stevenson 1763: 2; Tilley C507; Harold W. Freeman *Hester and Her Family* (1935) 23.

Colander. It is as full of holes as a cullender (55 Haliburton *Nature* II 118). Dorothy L. Sayers *Have His Carcase* (1932) 337.

Cold, 1. To lay cold. c46 DA Cold 2 (2).

2. This . . . 'ud leave our vile plunderers out in the cold (67 Lowell *Biglow* 306, 319). Bartlett 347; Farmer and Henley II 150; NED Cold sb. 1 e; Partridge 169; Schele de Vere 261; Stevenson 377:5.

3. It was policy to "feed a cold and starve a fever" (c64 Clemens *Sketches* 364). NC 386; *Oxford* 627; S. H. Adams *The Gorgeous Hussy* (Boston 1934) 535; Archer Taylor, *Journal of American Folklore* LXXI (1958) 190.

4. See Blaze (5), Bone (2), Caucasus, Charity (1), Cicero, Clam (1), Death (4), Glacier, Greenland, Hair (6), Ice (1–3), Iceland, Icicle, (1, 3), Krout, Lookout Mountain, Marble (1), Rock (1), Sixty (1), Snake (2), Stone (3, 4), Tombstone (1), Wagontire, Wedge (1, 3).

Collapse. See Dish-cloth (2).

Color, 1. The young gentleman came out in due time in very bold colors (58 Porter *Major* 41).

2. A story, sir, may kinder git the color, as the diggers say, without be-

in' stuck together out of hull cloth (65 Sedley *Marian* 115). See Cloth (4).

3. To give color to the matter (51 Stowe *Uncle* 97).

4. We decided to stand by our colors (65 Richardson *Secret* 347; Alcott *Little Women* 385 stood to his colors like a man).

5. Let him show 'em [grey hairs], and not be a sailing under false cullers (58 Hammett *Piney* 124). NED Colour 7 d; *Oxford* 555; Stevenson 380:2 hang out.

Colt, 1. As much out of place as a colt in a flower-garden (68 Alcott *Little Women* 31).

2. Every one on 'em as ragged as year old colts (44 Stephens *High Life* I 36). Apperson 520; *Oxford* 530; Svartengren 230; Tilley C521; Whiting *Drama* 308:69.

3. As skeery es a year old colt (44 Stephens *High Life* II 186). Cf. NC 386.

4. She [a ship] steered as wild as a young colt (40 Dana *Two* 416).

5. You and marm cut about . . . like two spring colts jest let out to grass (44 Stephens *High Life* II 192).

6. She [a mare] danced about like a two year old colt jest off grass (44 Stephens *High Life* II 156).

7. He sits in the Ladies' Gallery, looking like a "motherless colt" (35 Fairfield *Letters* 40).

Comb (1). Which completely cut his comb [i. e., humiliated him]. (36 Crockett *Exploits* 119; Haliburton *Clockmaker* I 208, *Attaché* III 98–99, *Old Judge* II 127; Thompson *Chronicles* 141). Apperson 131 Comb (15); Green 109; NED Comb 5; *Oxford* 126; Stevenson 380:9; Tilley C526.

Comb (2). Had Tophet itself been raked with a fine-tooth comb (50 Mel-

ville *White Jacket* 237). DA Fine 3 (8); *Modern Language Forum* XXIV (1939) 80.

Come, 1. "Easy come, easy go," is an old and true proverb (69 Barnum *Struggles* 463, 482). Apperson 365 Lightly come, lightly go; Hardie 462:43; Jente *American* 365; NC 386; *Oxford* 165; Stevenson 660:5; Stoett 688; Taylor *Index* 29; Tilley C533 Lightly; Whiting *Scots* I 151 Lightly; A. M. Chase *Murder of a Missing Man* (1934) 220; P. B. Kyne *Tide of Empire* (1928) 211; T. H. White *The Sword in the Stone* (1939) 35 With owls, it is never easy-come and easy-go.

2. First come, says I, first sarved, you know's an old rule, and luck's the word now-a-days (38 Haliburton *Clockmaker* II 119, *Sam* I 147, II 306; Briggs *Harry* I 105 the strictly republican principle of "first come first served"; Cooper *Chainbearer* 326 that's my maxim; Melville *White Jacket* 441–442 is the motto; Boucicault *Flying Scud* 196). Apperson 214; NC 386; *Oxford* 204; Smith *Browning* 225; Snapp 87:22; Stevenson 815:4; Stoett 1452; Taylor *Index* 33; Tilley C530; Whiting *Drama* 271; Alice Campbell *Juggernaut* (1928) 320; F. P. Keyes *Dinner at Antoine's* (1948) 3; P. B. Kyne *Tide of Empire* (1928) 75.

3. Late come, late served (40 Cooper *Pathfinder* 338).

4. For light come is plaguy apt to turn out "light go" (40 Haliburton *Clockmaker* III 42). Stevenson 927–928:7; Tilley C533; Whiting *Scots* I 151; Georgette Heyer *They Found Him Dead* (1937) 66.

5. Suthin sot me to thinkin' of a chap I carried over to Orleans last

year, that come up with me a few—I tell you! (58 Hammett *Piney* 64). DA Come 1 l.

Comingo. It is as dark as Comingo (40 Haliburton *Clockmaker* III 183, *Attaché* I 233 comingo).

Command. As the only way to learn to command is to learn to obey (50 Melville *White Jacket* 31). Cf. *Oxford* 105; Stevenson 382:3; Tilley C552.

Commandments. I'll give you the ten commandments, says she (meaning her ten claws (36 Haliburton *Clockmaker* I 242, *Attaché* II 254 When a woman clapper claws her husband, we have a cant tarm with us boys of Slickville, sayin' she gave him her ten commandments, *Sam* I 308 they . . . have the ten commandments *at their fingers ends*). Apperson 622; Farmer and Henley VII 93–94; NED Commandment 3; *Oxford* 105; Stevenson 382–383:9; Tilley C553.

Common. See Water (1).

Communications. It is well known that evil communication corrupts good manners (35 Kennedy *Horse-Shoe* 206; Haliburton *Clockmaker* I 250 endamnify). I Cor. 15:23; Apperson 193; NC 386; NED Communication 4; *Oxford* 180; Stevenson 390:5; Tilley C558; John Rhode, pseud. *The Harvest Murder* (1937) 254 the principle that.

Company. One is known by the company he keeps (54 Melville "Rich Man's Crumbs" in *Works* XIII 208; Nash *Century* 61 and it is safe to judge men by the company they keep). Apperson 394; Bradley 66; Hardie 461:12; Snapp 107:101, 107:119; *Oxford* 106; Stevenson 386–387:12; Tilley M248; NQ 5 vii 445–446;

7 xi 208, 411; H. C. Bailey *A Clue for Mr. Fortune* (1936) 216 a man is judged by the company he keeps; E. M. Rhodes *Beyond the Desert* (Boston 1934) 121 J. H. Wallis *The Politician* (1935) 71 the old saying.

Comparison. I mean no odious comparison between the lion-hearted whigs and democrats who fought there (48 Lincoln I 515; Melville *White Jacket* 16 his comparisons were ever invidious; Baldwin *Flush* 2 I am aware that it is invidious to make comparisons; Riley *Puddleford* 346 comparisons are said to be odious; Richardson *Beyond* 191 The comparison is odious). Apperson 110; NC 386; *Oxford* 106; Snapp 108:133; Stevenson 390:9; Tilley C576; W. H. Mack *Mr. Birdsall Breezes Through* (1937) 50.

Conceited. See Peacock (1).

Confession. Some old stick-in-the-mud had said somewhere . . . that an honest confession was good for the soul (c56 Thomson *Elephant Club* 22). *Oxford* 478 Open confession; Snapp 87:7 honest; Stevenson 399:8 open; Tilley C591 open; NQ 6 iii 309, 495; Sinclair Lewis *The Man Who Knew Coolidge* (1928) 16; Mike Teagle *Murders in Silk* (1938) 236 they say an honest confession is good for the soul.

Congressman. And them fish [catfish] has mouths as big as Congressmen, and all but as foul (55 Anon. *New Hope* 248).

Conscience. Consequently, Americans and English, who intend to reside here, become Papists,—the current phrase among them being, "A man must leave his conscience at Cape Horn" (40 Dana *Two* 99).

Consistency. Consistency is a jewel rarely found in the casket of the Latter-day Saints (67 Richardson *Beyond* 352; Jones *Batkins* 73 I believed in consistency. I thought it was a jewel equal to diamonds). Bartlett *Familiar Quotations* 944; Bradley 66; Stevenson 410:9.

Constable. It's mighty mixed up, and there's no telling who's constable until the election is over (58 Porter *Major* 16).

Contented. See Dove (1), Get-out, Humming-bird (1), Tortoise.

Continental. He didn't give a continental (72 Clemens *Roughing* II 48). DA Continental 2 b; NED *Supplement* Continental 2 b; Partridge 177; Sidney Williams *The Drury Club Case* (1927) 137.

Contract-work. And cooked and eat, as fast as contract-work (49 Haliburton *Old Judge* II 41). See Day (19).

Contrary. See Mule (2).

Cook, 1. There are so many cooks, the broth most always comes out rather bad (33 Smith *Downing* 167; Haliburton *Letter* 25 too many cooks spoil de broth; Cary *Clovernook* 2d Ser. 38; Clemens *Innocents* I 20 If five cooks can spoil a broth, what may not five captains do with a pleasure excursion). Apperson 640; NC 386; NED Cook 2; *Oxford* 665; Snapp 93:41; Stevenson 419:5; Stoett 1224; Tilley C642; G. C. Bestor *Prelude to Murder* (1936) 229.

2. Chief cook and bottle-washer (59 Taliaferro *Fisher's* 256; Wiley *Billy* 187). Berrey 388:4, 446:15, 457:2; DA Chief 1 b (1); Vincent McHugh *Caleb Catlum's America* (1936) 53.

Cooky. I'll bet a cookey if . . . (44 Stephens *High Life* I 107, II 32, 37; Whitcher *Widow* 251). DA Cooky 1 c; Schele de Vere 83.

Cool. See Charity (1), Cucumber, December, Get-out, Icicle (2), January (1), Sherry, Snow (2), Snow bank, Statue (1).

Coon, 1. We won't hear the eend of this bis'ness for a coon's age (43 Thompson *Chronicles* 72, 128 in a, *Major* 145 in a; Eliason 266; Hooper *Simon* 111 in a; Burke *Polly* 74, 99; Hammett *Stray* 186, 201 this; Taliaferro *Fisher's* 201; Harris *Uncle Remus* 121). Barrère and Leland I 270; DA Coon 3 (12); Farmer 168; Farmer and Henley II 178; Green 96; NC 386; NED *Supplement* Coon; Partridge 179; Randolph and Wilson 212; Schele de Vere 52, 208; Thornton I 203; Wilson 529; George Milburn *Catalogue* (1936) 192; Damon Runyon *Money from Home* (1935) 113.

2. Got over [a river] clar as a pet coon (43 Robb *Squatter* 106).

3. You're cross as a coon when it's cornered (74 Eggleston *Circuit* 48).

4. Clay is as cunnin' as a coon (43 Haliburton *Attaché* II 206).

5. Happy as a . . . 'coon in a holler (59 Taliaferro *Fisher's* 240).

6. What did I want with the little cuss . . . that I should have got myself treed like a coon, as I am, this yer way (51 Stowe *Uncle* 70).

7. I'm a gone coon (43 Haliburton *Attaché* III 56, 70, 197; Dorson *Jonathan* 104; Hammett *Stray* 135, 309; Browne *Artemus* 137; Lowell *Biglow* 307; Browning *Forty-Four* 80; Bowman *Bear-Hunters* 385 But I'm gone under—a lost coon, 445; Clift *Bunker* 58). Bartlett 252; DA Gone 1 (4); Farmer 168; Farmer and Henley II

175, 177; Green 96; McAtee 29; NED Coon 3; Partridge 179; Schele de Vere 51–52, 208; Thornton I 373; Thorne Smith *Turnabout* (1933) 249. Cf. Bon Gaultier [i. e., Theodore Martin and W. E. Aytoun] *The Book of Ballads* (1845, 11th ed., Edinburgh 1870) 32 He's a finished 'coon. See Beaver (3), Case (5), Chicken (6), Fawn skin, Gander (1), Goose (2), Gosling (2), Horse (1), Nigger (13), Shoat, Sucker (2).

8. To be coon [i. e., wise, alert]. 52 DA Coon 3 d (5).

9. The perfection o' bliss Is in skinnin' thet same old coon, sez he (48 Lowell *Biglow* 93). DA Coon 3 d (2); Thornton I 201–202. Cf. NED Coon 3 (hunting).

10. And took through the huckleberry swamp like a 'coon (Taliaferro *Fisher's* 155).

11. See Catamount (5).

Coon-skin. Fifteen long miles—miles measured with a coon-skin, and the tail throwed in fur good measure, fur sure (59 Taliaferro *Fisher's* 73, 150).

Coot. Dey is as stupid and ignorant as coots (55 Haliburton *Nature* II 295). Cf. Farmer 168; NC 387; NED Coot 2 b; *Oxford* 720 Wit; Schele de Vere 209; Taylor *Comparisons* 30; Whiting *Drama* 308:71.

Cooter. As drunk as a cooter (51 Burke *Polly* 45). DA Cooter 1 c; Thornton I 204.

Copper, sb., 1. I didn't care a copper how much they walked together (44 Stephens *High Life* I 98; Shillaber *Ike* 11 Who . . . cared a continental copper what people said about him?).

2. Jess the way with ye all . . . aint a copper to choose (33 Neal *Down-Easters* I 108).

3. They wouldn't fetch a bungtown copper (45 Judd *Margaret* I 26; Kelly *Humors* 334 Beware of crossed sixpences, smooth shillings, and what are called Bungtown coppers; Hammett *Piney* 54 Well, he made every dollar of it; wasn't worth a Bungtown copper when he set up for himself). Bartlett 83; DA Bungtown, Copper 2 b; Farmer 106; Schele de Vere 587; Thornton I 123, III 160.

4. A string of old blue beads, that wasn't worth ten coppers (c58 Stephens *Mary Derwent* 372).

5. She would skin a copper the closest of any body she ever see'd (57 Riley *Puddleford* 250).

6. To steal the coppers off the eyes of a dead man. 56 DA Copper 5 b.

Copper, vb. To copper one's pocket [i. e., to embezzle]. 32 DA Copper, vb. 1.

Cork, 1. As dry as cork (43 Hall *Purchase* I 182).

2. As light as cork (53 Melville "Cock-a-doodle-doo!" in *Works* XIII 156). Cf. Stevenson 1490:2 like a cork.

Corkscrew, 1. [A name] as crooked as a corkscrew (44 Stephens *High Life* II 176; Clemens *Sandwich* 19, *Innocents* I 163, II 274; Richardson *Beyond* 518). NC 387; Taylor *Comparisons* 30.

2. I kept on reading as independent as a corkscrew (44 Stephens *High Life* I 8, II 40, 152, 237).

Corn, 1. I acknowledge the corn to that Miss Layton (55 Anon. *New Hope* 179; Haliburton *Season-Ticket* 276 He had a beard that wouldn't acknowledge the corn to no man's; Kelly *Humors* 227 If you don't own up the corn; Barnum *Struggles* 267).

Bartlett 3; DA Corn 8 (4); Farmer 171–172; Farmer and Henley II 185; NED Corn ² 2; Randolph and Wilson 222, 269; Stevenson 423:7; Thornton I 3–4, III 2. See Cob (2), Coin (1).

2. He replied that I need not try to feed him on *soft corn* that way [i. e., deceive, put off]. (58 Porter *Major* 22). Bartlett 624; DA Soft corn 2.

3. You measure other folks' corn with your own bushel, and judge your neighbors by yourself (49 Haliburton *Old Judge* II 144). Perhaps derived from II Cor. 10:12; see NQ 4 vi 494. Apperson 410; Green 36; *Oxford* 415–416; Stevenson 422:7, 1552:4; Tilley C663; Woodard PADS VI (1946) 40.

4. The gals began to hop about like parched corn on a hot shovel (44 Stephens *High Life* I 226). Bartlett 807.

Corncob, 1. Young men should continer to smoke their livers as dry as a corncob with Cuby cigars (65 Browne *Artemus Ward His Travels* 34). See Cob (1).

2. As rough as a corn-cob (43 Hall *Purchase* II 41).

Corned. Half corned (44 Stephens *High Life* I 1, 192; Thomson *Doesticks* 310 afraid he'd get corned; Whitcher *Widow* 353 gittin corned on cider). NED Corned 5; Partridge 181.

Corn shucking. Jest as easy as corn shucking (43 Robb *Squatter* p. vii).

Corn-sifter. But thar they stood with pistols 'nuff to make a corn-sifter ov my hide afore you could bat yer eye (59 Taliaferro *Fisher's* 127).

Corn-silk. Its tail looked like a handful of corn-silk, it was so yaller and bright (44 Stephens *High Life* I 156).

Corpse, 1. White as a corpse (25 Neal *Brother J* II 304). Svartengren 234 pale.

2. The skoolmaster, however, sed the Slave Oligarky must cower at the feet of the North . . . or pass over his dead corpse (63 Browne *Artemus* 186). See Body (1).

Correct. See Bootjack (2).

Cotton, 1. They made them small cotton [i. e., discomfited them]. (55 Haliburton *Nature* II 409). Cf. NC 387; Woodard PADS VI (1946) 20.

2. Spit a little cotton or so . . . and you'll see the fun (25 Neal *Brother J* II 391, 392 we'll see who spits cotton first; Burke *Polly* 179 He awoke spitting little wads of cotton). Neal refers to drinking, Burke to the after-effects of drinking, and the parallels to saliva filled with bubbles in a dry or thirsty mouth. Bey PADS II (1944) 55; Boshears 29:15; DA Cotton 7 (3); Green 354; Halpert 7, 43; McAtee 61; PADS III (1945) 11; Taylor *Comparisons* 82 thirsty; Tidwell PADS XIII (1950) 19; Wilson 593; Wilson PADS II (1944) 50; Ruth Darby *Death Conducts a Tour* (1940) 67 I'm so thirsty I could spit cotton. Cf. Stevenson 2200:3.

Cotton-gin. You hull out bones faster nur a cotting-gin can shell out cottingseed (59 Taliaferro *Fisher's* 219).

Cough. Churchyard cough (57 Melville *Confidence-Man* 137). Stevenson 429:7; Tilley C384 Choke up, the churchyard is nigh.

Coulter. I'm danged ef you hain't sot your coulter too deep to make a good crap (59 Taliaferro *Fisher's* 111).

Council. His remark applies equally to a council of war. According to the proverb it never fights; but it may do anything else under heaven (67 Richardson *Beyond* 40). *Oxford* 112; Stevenson 2446:9.

Country, 1. Every country has its ways (46 Cooper *Redskins* 198; Clemens *Tramp* II 19). Tilley C708. Cf. Stevenson 433:5 laws; Whiting *Drama* 229.

2. Free country, neighbor (33 Neal *Down-Easters* I 102; Hall *Purchase* I 236; Hooper *Simon* 27 It's a free country; Shillaber *Mrs. Partington* 84 This is a; Jones *Winkles* 261 It's a; Sedley *Marian* 132 Any how . . . it's a). Stevenson 433:10; F. P. Keyes *Dinner at Antoine's* (1948) 245; M. Thompson *Not As a Stranger* (1954) 184 It's a free country.

Couple. As pleased as a young couple at thar first christenin' (43 Robb *Squatter* 99).

Courage, 1. Poor Jerry could never get his courage to the sticking point (43 Lewis *Odd* 179; Hammett *Piney* 148 I screwed up my courage; Eggleston *School-Master* 222 But he screwed his courage to the sticking place). Shakespeare *Macbeth* I vii 60; Stevenson 437:6.

2. See Dutch (1).

Courageous. See Lion (3).

Course. For wisely has it been said, "that the current of true love never did run smooth" (32 Kennedy *Swallow* 363, *Horse-Shoe* 154, 333; Haliburton *Attaché* III 31 But then love never runs smooth; Hall *Wilderness* 23 But although the course of true love had, as usual, not run smooth; Cary *Clovernook* 24 aside from the ground that "the course of true love never did run smooth," 2d Ser. 320;

Barnum *Struggles* 48). Apperson 116; NC 439; *Oxford* 113; Snapp 80:41; Stevenson 1475:3; Yamamoto *Dickens* 215; P. B. Kyne *Tide of Empire* (1928) 123 But then, as the fellow says, the path o' true love never did run smooth; Armstrong Livingston *The Monk of Hambleton* (Indianapolis 1928) 76.

Course of sprouts. See Sprouts.

Courtesy. It is a proverb that 'courtesy costs nothing' (37–38 Emerson *Works* II 238). Apperson 264 Good words; *Oxford* 258; Stevenson 440:2; Tilley W808.

Coventry. [He] would undoubtedly have been put in Coventry (32 Hall *Legends* 70; Willis *Fun* 320 The men "sent him to Coventry" more unwillingly; Haliburton *Nature* II 288 a conspiracy to place her in Coventry; Kelly *Humors* 150 Captain V——'s Store was . . . "in coventry" [i. e., at a remote distance]; Sedley *Marian* 390). Apperson 117; Farmer and Henley II 193; NED Coventry 1; *Oxford* 114; Stevenson 441:15; NQ 1 vi 318, 589; 5 i 400, x 266; 9 iv 264, 335; 12 x 251; CXLIX (1925) 8, 33; Hans Duffy, pseud. *Seven by Seven* (1933) 190.

Cow, 1. Hit sot tu me es clost es a poor cow dus tu her hide in March (67 Harris *Sut* 33).

2. And had a licked 'um up like a cow a-lickin' salt (59 Taliaferro *Fisher's* 231).

3. Cursed cows have short horns (45 Judd *Margaret* II 253). Apperson 118; *Oxford* 125; Stevenson 446:5; Tilley C751; NQ 2 xii 394.

4. They didn't know what *tendon* meant, no more'n a cow knows about its grandmother (54 Shillaber *Mrs.*

Partington 244). Cf. Whiting *Scots*
I 153 Cow (1).

5. I went on the old saying, of salting the cow to catch the calf [i. e., to
court the mother to win the daughter].
(34 Crockett *Life* 60). DA Cow 9 c,
Salt vb.; Stevenson 445:6.

6. I'd a' stuck to a feller that done
that way, twell the cows come home
(45 Hooper *Simon* 38; Clemens *Letters*
I 74, *Gilded* II 312). Apperson 119;
Funk 42; Hardie 472:198; McAtee 20,
66; *Oxford* 116; 340; Partridge 186;
Stevenson 445:2; Thornton I 215–
216, III 95; Tilley C772; NQ 10 viii
507; CXLIX (1925) 315, 354, CLV
(1928) 466; John Donavan *The Case
of the Rusted Room* (1937) 43.

7. She has got the wrong cow by
the tail this time (43 Haliburton *Attaché* II 26). Cf. Apperson 715 Sow
(4) ear; *Oxford* 607; Stevenson 2175–
2176:13; Tilley S685. See Sow (2).

8. See Inside (1).

Cowardly. See Wolf (3).

Cowed. See Spaniel.

Cow-pea, 1. As thick as cow-peas in
thar hull (59 Taliaferro *Fisher's* 258).

2. More alike nor cow-peas (45
Hooper *Simon* 20). See Pea (3).

Cow's horn. [Teeth] as black as the
top of a cow's horn (59 Browning *Forty-four* 97).

Cow's tail, 1. They ain't right up-and-
down, like a cow's tail, in their deal-
in's (43 Haliburton *Attaché* II 204,
Nature I 100 I am like a cow's tail,
straight up and down in my dealins,
Season-Ticket 33). Cf. Tilley C770.

2. See Crack (1).

Cow tick. They aint worth a low country cow tick (64 Wiley *Johnny* 343).

Coy. See Dove (2).

Cozy. See Get out.

Crab-apples, 1. [Her face] looked as
if she'd been fed on crab-apples for a
hull month (44 Stephens *High Life* II
177; Kelly *Humors* 408 a countenance
indicative of having been tasting a
crab-apple). Cf. NC 388; Whiting
Drama 308:75; L. W. Meynell *On the
Night of the 18th* (1936) 79 as sour
as a crabapple.

2. Looking crab-apples at the poor
negro (56 Kelly *Humors* 395).

Crabbed. See Bear (3).

Crack, 1. I'll lick anybody here that
don't believe it, in two cracks of a
cow's thumb (37 Neal *Charcoal* 36;
Browning *Forty-four* 268 I . . . cut
his [a buck's] throat in the crack of a
thumb; Cary *Married* 307 he would
carry [accompany] me to old Throck's
in the crack of a cow's thumb). Cf.
Shake (1–3).

2. To walk (toe) a crack. 25 DA
Crack 1.

Cracked, 1. I have seen quite enough
of A Soldiers Life to satisfied me that
it is not what it is cracked up to be
(61 Wiley *Johnny* 129, 34). DA Crack
vb. 1; Vincent McHugh *Caleb Catlum's America* (1936) 291.

2. See Tea kettle.

Crackling. I should be cooked up to a
cracklin [i. e., punished]. (34 Crockett *Life* 31, 82).

Cradle. It [a pony] was as easy as a
cradle (51 Stowe *Uncle* 295).

Cranberry. I'll give 'em cranberry for
their goose (43 Haliburton *Attaché* I
87).

Cranberry tart. She was good as cranberry tart (56 Kelly *Humors* 232).

Crane, 1. A vicious mare as thin as a crane (60 Whitehead *Wild Sports* 88).

2. Swaller like a crane (53 Haliburton *Sam* II 81).

Crank. See Militia trainer (1), White man (1), Woodchuck (1).

Crassus. See Croesus.

Crazy. See Bear (4), Bed-bug (1), Fly (2), Hare (1), Loon (1), Rooster (1), Spirit-rapper.

Cream, 1. As different as this potted cream and a dancing cow (53 Willis *Fun* 25).

2. He said she was as rich as cream (55 Anon. *New Hope* 122). NC 388; Taylor *Comparisons* 68.

3. Cream is thicker than water (59–60 Holmes *Elsie* 302).

Creation. Wal now, if this don't beat all creation! (44 Stephens *High Life* I 71, *Mary Derwent* 297). DA Creation 3; Thornton I 9, 51, III 4.

Creature. As true as I'm a livin' critter (56 Whitcher *Widow* 255). Cf. Alive (5).

Creep. See Snail (1).

Crest. [A feather] as fresh as the crest of a fighting cock (60 Holmes *Professor* 136).

Cricket, 1. Gay as crickets (49 Melville *Redburn* 388; Harris *Uncle Remus* 82 ez gayly ez a June cricket). F. H. Shaw *Atlantic Murder* (1933) 31.

2. I'm as happy as a cricket here (68 Alcott *Little Women* 59).

3. Ez harmless an' cherfle ez crickets (67 Lowell *Biglow* 322). Eden Philpotts *Tales of the Tenements* (1910) 184 cheerful.

4. As lively as crickets (43 Haliburton *Attaché* III 24; Dorson *Jonathan* 97 a cricket; Mitchell *Reveries* 64 a cricket; Saxe *Poems* 321 or Kansas divorces; Harris *Uncle Remus* 31 cricket in de embers). McAtee 41; NC 388; NED Cricket 1 d; Svartengren 161; Eugene Thwing, ed. *The World's Best One Hundred Detective Stories* (1929) VII 124.

5. They are as merry as crickets (38 Haliburton *Clockmaker* II 212, 241, *Attaché* I 231 a cricket; Melville *Moby-Dick* I 312 a cricket; Barnum *Struggles* 317 a cricket). Apperson 413; NC 388; NED Cricket 1 d; Oxford 420; Svartengren 72, 76; Tilley C825; Whiting *Drama* 308:77; Agatha Christie *Mr. Parker Pyne, Detective* (1934) 210.

6. And now he's peart as a cricket (51 Stowe *Uncle* 438; Taliaferro *Fisher's* 121). Boshears 39:791; Halpert 529; NC 388.

7. Spry as a cricket (34 Davis *Downing* 242; Stephens *High Life* I 23, 52, 149, 188, II 213; Judd *Margaret* I 79). Halpert 1008; NC 389.

Criminal. But, mother, to change the subject, as the criminal said, when he found the judge was getting personal (56 Durivage *Three* 331).

Crimson. See Beet (1), Turkey 2 (1).

Crinkum-crankum. "I tell ye, men, them's Crinkum-crankum whales." "And what are them?," said a sailor. "Why, them is whales that can't be cotched" (49 Melville *Redburn* 127). NED Crinkum-crankum. Cf. Tilley C826a.

Cripple. A cripple in the right road beats a racer in the wrong road (34 Emerson *Journals* III 247, *Works* I 33).

Crisp. See Pie-crust (1).

Crockery, 1. My wind would a bin broke quick as crockery (59 Taliaferro *Fisher's* 135).

2. Don't break *all* the crockery, gentlemen, he shouted (45 Hooper *Simon* 56).

3. The Beaufins, I say, are rated rather crockery in Cheshire (50 Willis *Life* 283).

Crocodile. He shed some crokadile tears, I believe (53 Cary *Clovernook* 2d Ser. 222; Boucicault *Flying Scud* 220 Look at the crocodile's tears running down the end of your nose). NED Crocodile 5; *Oxford* 118; Stevenson 2288:8; Stoett 1283; Tilley C831; NQ 6 vi 92, 296, 496; 10 ii 23. Cf. Whiting *Drama* 309:79, *Scots* I 154; Frederica De Laguna *The Arrow Points to Murder* (1937) 42.

Croesus. I feel as rich as Croesus (31 Conant *Earnest Man* 389; Mayo *Kaloolah* 283 I was richer than Crassus or Croesus; Cary *Clovernook* 2d Ser. 18 Cresus; Shillaber *Mrs. Partington* 299 If I was as rich as Creosote; Haliburton *Season-Ticket* 9). Apperson 530; Boshears 39:863; NC 389; *Oxford* 540; Stevenson 1935; 10; Taylor *Comparisons* 68–69; Tilley C832; Whiting *Scots* I 154; A. W. Derleth *Sign of Fear* (1935) 103.

Crooked. See Corkscrew (1), Dog (10), Fishhook (1), Ram's horn (1), Sassafras root (2).

Crop. That sticks in some folks' crops (46 Cooper *Redskins* 150). Willoughby Sharp *Murder of the Honest Broker* (1934) 215.

Cross. See Bear (5), Cat (7), Coon (3), Gate-post (1), Sin (4), Thunder (3), Thundercloud (2), Tophet.

Cross-eyed. He was so cross-eyed he could *look at his own head!* (58 Porter *Major* 17).

Crow, sb., 1. A crow would shed tears if obliged by its errand to fly across the district (27 Cooper *Prairie* 82). Stevenson 461:10. See Killdeer.

2. As black as crows (44 Stephens *High Life* I 127, 163 as a crow's back, *Mary Derwent* 222 [hair] black and glossy as a crow's wing; Riley *Puddleford* 29 as a crow; Harris *Sut* 76 es a crow's wing et midnite; Locke [Nasby] *Struggles* 380 ez a crow, 398 only half ez black ez a crow). Apperson 51; Boshears 34:353; Halpert 226; McAtee 15; NC 389; *Oxford* 47; Stevenson 192:11; Svartengren 244; Tilley C844; Whiting *Drama* 309:80, *Scots* I 154; Dorothy Baker *Young Man with a Horn* (Boston 1938) 192.

3. As hoarse as a crow (38 Haliburton *Clockmaker* II 307). NC 389; Dorothy L. Sayers *Gaudy Night* (1936) 25.

4. Made a straight track of it for home as the crow flies (43 Haliburton *Attaché* II 30, *Sam* I 169 made tracks for the shore as straight as the crow flies, *Nature* II 324 He returns as straight as a chalk line or as we say, as the crow flies to his home; Cooper *Satanstoe* 195 sixteen miles as the crow flies). NED Crow 3; NQ 10 i 204, 296, 372, 432. Cf. Boshears 40:969; Taylor *Comparisons* 31. See Bird (13, 14).

5. She is as thin as a crow (53 Haliburton *Sam* I 270). Cf. NC 389 poor.

6. It's an old maxim, that "every crow thinks its own young ones the whitest" (44 Thompson *Major* 197; Clift *Bunker* 298). Apperson 124; Bradley 67; Hardie 462:58; NED Crow 3; *Oxford* 120; Stevenson 462:

4; Tilley C851; Whiting *Drama* 153, *Scots* I 154; Woodard PADS VI (1946) 36.

7. As usual, to use her own phrase, 'she was up before the crow put his shoes on' (55 Irving *Wolfert* 252).

8. To eat boiled crow. 77 DA Crow sb. 4 b.

9. The *rara avis*–the white crow–a good President (43 Hall *Purchase* II 235). Stevenson 462:1; Stoett 1907; Tilley C859.

10. Some long-remembered wrinkle or crow's foot (51 Hawthorne *Twice-Told* 266; Melville *Moby-Dick* I 90 concentrating all his crow's feet into one scowl, II 198 all crow's feet and wrinkles; Haliburton *Sam* II 137–138 The crow's feet at the corners of your eyes). Green 106; NED Crow's foot; Tilley C865; Whiting *Drama* 340:484.

11. You can't paint a crow green (60 Whitehead *Wild Sports* 174).

Crow, vb. See Game-rooster.

Crowbar, 1. I . . . sot right up, parpindicular as a cro-bar (44 Stephens *High Life* II 199).

2. Sticking my right arm out as stiff as a crowbar (44 Stephens *High Life* I 41, 98 iron crowbar, 201; Harris *Sut* 124).

Crumb. Your mother begun to pick up her crums immediately [i. e., improve in health and appetite]. (33 Smith *Downing* 176; Dana *Two* 295 The latter, however, had "picked up his crumbs"). Apperson 493; NED Crumb 4; *Oxford* 498; Stevenson 465: 11; Tilley C868.

Crumble. See Cheese (6).

Cry, sb. And the hogs to squeal as bad as the pig did, when the devil turned barber (34 Crockett *Life* 86, *Account* 135 it is like what the devil said when he was shearing the hog, "great cry, and little wool"; Haliburton *Clockmaker* I 190 Great cry and little wool, all talk and no cider, III 306 it's all cry and little wool with poets, as the devil said when he sheared his hogs. *Attaché* III 208 It's "great cry and little wool" with us, IV 283). Apperson 428, 432; NC 393; NED Cry 16; *Oxford* 263–264; Randolph and Wilson 188, 193; Stevenson 465–466:14; Tilley C871; Dornford Yates *Blind Corner* (1927) 199. Cf. Work sb. (5).

Cry, vb. See Baby (10).

Crystal, 1. Its waters were clear as crystal (33 Hall *Soldier's Bride* 45; Hawthorne *Mosses* 227 A heart as clear as crystal, "Snow Image" in *House* 406 faith . . . as pure and as clear as; Shillaber *Knitting-Work* 40 just as clear to me as; Paul *Courtship* 113, 268; Clemens *Sandwich* 27, *Tramp* I 181; Clift *Bunker* 152; Holmes *Poet* 176). Apperson 101; Boshears 35:405; Fife 118; NC 389; Randolph and Wilson 190; Stevenson 363: 5; Taylor *Comparisons* 26; Tilley C875; Whiting *Drama* 309:78, *Scots* I 155; George Dyer *The Catalyst Club* (1936) 5, 249.

2. Mary's lake, crystal-clear (58 Holmes *Autocrat* 39).

3. Transparent as crystal (20–22 Irving *Bracebridge* 189).

Cub. I'm as full as a young cub (35 Crockett *Account* 46).

Cucumber. Cool as a cowcumber (25 Neal *Brother J* I 371; Smith *Downing* 181, *Letters* 133; Crockett *Exploits* 117 such a cucumber blooded scoundrel; Fairfield *Letters* 170 Wise, who was as cool as a cucumber; Haliburton *Clockmaker* II 152 cucumbers, *Attaché* IV 92 cucumbers; Thompson *Chronicles* 143 cucumber; Stephens *High Life* I 252 cucumber, II 37 cucumber, 42 You'd a thought he'd swollered a basket of cowcumbers all of a sudden, he looked so frosty, 162, 260; Hooper *Simon* 15 cucumber; Melville *Moby-Dick* II 3 keep cool—cucumbers is the word; Cary *Clovernook* 2d Ser. 162 but I hate to see folks as cool as a cucumber about such things [matchmaking]; Whitcher *Widow* 98; Hammett *Piney* 48 cucumber, 93 cucumber; Porter *Major* 19 cucumber; Harris *Uncle Remus* 35 cowcumber, 184 cowcumber in de jew [dew]). Apperson 113; Boshears 35:440; Figh PADS XIII (1950) 12; McAtee 19; NC 389; NED Cucumber 2 b; Randolph and Wilson 179; Taylor *Comparisons* 29; Tilley C895; Anthony Abbot, pseud. *About the Murder of the Circus Queen* (1932) 45.

Cud. Chew your cud in silence (35 Kennedy *Horse-Shoe* 67). Apperson 94; NED Chew 4 b; *Oxford* 91; Stevenson 468–469:15; Tilley C896.

Cudgel. They were sort of delighted to see him beaten with his own cudgel (36 Crockett *Exploits* 81). Cf. Apperson 601 stick; NC 481 Stick (7); *Oxford* 617 staff; Stevenson 2213:10 stick; Tilley S802 staff, W26 wand.

Cuffee. [A Negro slave] all grand as Cuffee (51 Stowe *Uncle* 48; Mary N. Prescott *Harper's New Monthly Magazine* XXXII [1866] 62 Cuffy). Bradley PADS XIV (1950) 24; DA Cuffy; Farmer 186; Schele de Vere 152; W. M. Raine *On the Dodge* (Boston [1938]) 28 bold as Cuffey.

Cunning. See Coon (4), Fox (2), Wolf (4), Woodchuck (2).

Cup. 'Tis hard to carry a full cup even (36 Emerson *Works* I 33). Apperson 129, 241; *Oxford* 230; Stevenson 471: 3; Tilley C907.

Cupboard, 1. It ain't cupboard love (40 Haliburton *Clockmaker* III 141). Farmer and Henley II 230; NED Cupboard 4; *Oxford* 124; Stevenson 1462: 2; Tilley C912; Charles Barry, pseud. *The Shot from the Door* (1935) 222.

2. I could smell cupboard, as they say (33 Smith *Downing* 50). Cf. Apperson 37 Belly (5); NED Cupboard 3; *Oxford* 33; Stevenson 168:11 Belly cries cupboard; Tilley B301.

Curd, 1. Candles as white as curd (44 Stephens *High Life* I 73, 101 as a tub of curd, II 58 and thet looked eenamost as soft, 205 as any curd, 216 as if it had been cut out of a fust rate cheese curd, 260). Svartengren 230.

2. A curd-white grub (60 Whitehead *Wild Sports* 17). Hans Duffy, pseud. *Seven by Sevens* (1933) 256.

3. The finer the curd, the better the cheese (45 Judd *Margaret* II 115).

4. The words all run together like marm's curd when the cheese gets contrary and wont set (44 Stephens *High Life* I 39).

Cure, 1. I would cure 'em or kill 'em (66 Smith *Arp* 79). Stevenson 1952:1; Terry Shannon *The Catspaw* (1929) 11–12 kill or cure.

2. What can't be cured, must be endured, so, patience is the word (36 Fairfield *Letters* 67; Haliburton *Clockmaker* III 27, *Attaché* I 194, *Sam* I 79, *Nature* II 416; Thompson *Chronicles* 178 as the feller said when the monkey bit him; Francis Wayland *A Memoir of the Life and Labors of the Rev. Adoniram Judson, D. D.* (2 vols., Boston 1853) II 158; Durivage *Three*

128). Apperson 129; NC 390; *Oxford* 124; Stevenson 684:11; Tilley C922; Stella Gibbons *Miss Linsey and Pa* (1936) 178 as they say. Cf. Tilley A231.

Currants. As bright as a handful of ripe currants (44 Stephens *High Life* I 199).

Currant wine. The sunshine . . . looked as light and red as a hundred glasses of currant wine (44 Stephens *High Life* I 112).

Current. You can't swim long agin the current . . . without cuttin' your throat as a pig does (53 Haliburton *Sam* I 276). Cf. NC 482 Stream. See Pig (9).

Curse, 1. Air you well? Sound as a cuss! (62 Browne *Artemus* 193).

2. Not care a cuss for 'em (43 Robb *Squatter* 108; Nash *Century* 179 I don't care a continental cuss if they both git into the penitentiary). Apperson 456 Not (6); NED Curse 2; Stevenson 473:7; J. G. Brandon *The One-Minute Murder* (1935) 242.

3. I wouldn't care a tinker's cus (43 Thompson *Chronicles* 173; Kelly *Humors* 246 tinker's curse). Apperson 458 Not (34); NED Tinker 1 d; Stevenson 2641:9; NQ 8 xi 345, 452, 496. Cf. Apperson 456 Not (6) cobbler's curse.

4. He aint worth a cuss (43 Haliburton *Attaché* IV 119; Burke *Polly* 111; Cary *Clovernook* 2d Ser. 53; Lowell *Biglow* 311; Smith *Arp* 48–49 curse, 176 curse; Richardson *Beyond* 365). Apperson 456 Not (8); NED Curse 2; *Oxford* 124; Farmer and Henley II 232; Stevenson 2641:9; Christopher Bush *The Death of Cosmo Revere* (1930) 36 cuss.

5. A small sprinkling of the femi-nine gender, jest enough to take the cuss off and no more (44 Stephens *High Life* II 55). DA Cuss 1 b.

6. Lest, as the Persians say, these curses, like fowls, might return home to roost (55 Haliburton *Nature* II 379; Holmes *Elsie* 17 But once in a thousand times they act as curses are said to,—come home to roost). Cf. Ps. 109: 27 As he loveth cursing, so let it come to him. Apperson 130; NC 390; *Oxford* 124–125; Stevenson 473–474:11; A. E. Fielding, pseud. *The Mysterious Partner* (1929) 229. Cf. Tilley C924. See Chicken (5).

7. The curse av Cromwell on ye! (53 Hammett *Stray* 33). *Oxford* 124; Dorothy Bennett *Murder Unleashed* (1935) 214.

Curtain. A curtain lecture (57 Riley *Puddleford* 86). Apperson 130; *Oxford* 125; NED Curtain-lecture; Stevenson 474:2; Tilley C925; Carolyn Wells *Horror House* (Philadelphia 1931) 37.

Cuscaroarus, 1. As ugly and revengeful as a Cusccaroarus Injin, with 13 inches of corn whiskey in his stummick (62 Browne *Artemus* 44). Perhaps a reference to the Cuscarawaoc Indians, mentioned by Captain John Smith as living in Maryland and Delaware.

2. Yellin like Cuscororious Injins (64 Locke [Nasby] *Struggles* 149).

Cuss. See Curse.

Custom. Custom inures the most sensitive persons to that which is at first most repellent (73 Clemens *Gilded* I 151). Cf. Apperson 130; *Oxford* 125; Tilley C932, 933. See Habit.

Customer. Seeing that he [a panther] might become a bad customer, . . . I took a deliberate aim, and fired (59 Browning *Forty-four* 280). Farmer and Henley II 234; NED Customer 5; Stevenson 477:8 ugly.

Cut, sb., 1. I knew his voice and the cut of his jib (40 Haliburton *Clockmaker* III 199; Browne *Artemus* 132 I must say I like the cut of your gib). Babcock 259; Farmer and Henley IV 52; NED Cut 16 c, Jib 1 b; Stevenson 478:7, 1426:1.

2. To be on the cut and shoot [i. e., to be on the warpath]. 73 DA Shoot sb. 6 (3).

3. In two hours more he won't be able to step over the butt cut of a broom straw (45 Hooper *Simon* 30).

Cut, vb., 1. Git evry thing cut and dried for 'em (34 Davis *Downing* 236; Jones *Winkles* 387; Smith *My Thirty* 260, 441; Wallack *Rosedale* 51; Clemens *Sketches* 354). Bartlett 780; NED Cut, ppl. a. 10; Stevenson 447:11; Agatha Christie *Cards on the Table* (1937) 232.

2. And twenty sought her hand in vain, Were "cut," and didn't "come again," In the Ordinary fashion (68 Saxe *Poems* 92). Apperson 130; Farmer and Henley II 237; NED Cut, vb. 60; *Oxford* 125; Stevenson 478:9.

3. We all cut and run (33 Smith *Downing* 207, *My Thirty* 312; Stephens *High Life* I 210; Melville *Redburn* 159 [literal], *White Jacket* 19; Hammett *Piney* 37; Haliburton *Season-Ticket* 85). NED Cut 40; NQ 6 vi 246.

4. They didn't b-a-h at me for lettin' a *calf* cut me out of a gal's affections (43 Robb *Squatter* 100; Stephens *High Life* I 231; Jones *Country* 373; Eggleston *School-Master* 153, *Circuit* 332). Woodard PADS VI (1946) 11.

5. Do you think he has cut out, sure enough [i. e., run away]. (43 Thompson *Chronicles* 143).

6. See Razor (5), Stick (7).

Cute. See Nutmeg, Razor (2), Weasel (3).

Cut worm. Wickliff was as keen as a cut worm (35 Crockett *Account* 73).

D

Dagger, 1. While at daggers' points (59 Lincoln III 452). Apperson 133; NED Dagger 2; *Oxford* 127; Tilley D9. Cf. Stevenson 479:6 daggers drawing.

2. And you look daggers at him when you pass (50 Mitchell *Reveries* 113; Kelly *Humors* 94; Alcott *Little Women* 384 looked daggers at another Corinne). Berrey 284:3; NED Dagger 3 b; *Oxford* 383; Stevenson 479:3, 1451:5; Samuel Spewack *Murder in the Gilded Cage* (1929) 87.

Damage. Well, now, my good fellow, what's the damage, as they say in Kentucky? (51 Stowe *Uncle* 166). Farmer 191; NED *Supplement* Damage 5.

Damned. She's as sober "as be d—d" when she gets . . . the hearse behind her (58 Porter *Major* 49).

Damp. See Churchyard (1), Dishcloth (1).

Dan. Bein' dragged from Dan to Beersheba (53 Haliburton *Sam* II 43; Smith *My Thirty* 352 from Maine to Texas, nor from Dan to Beer Sheba, 416; Clemens *Innocents* II 206 Dan was the northern and Beersheba the southern limit of Palestine—hence the expression "from Dan to Beersheba." It is equivalent to our phrases "from Maine to Texas"—"from Baltimore to San Francisco." Our expression and that of the Israelites both mean the same—great distance). Judges 20:1; *Oxford* 128; Stevenson 479–480:11; Charles Dickens *Sketches by Boz* (1836, Centenary ed., London 1910) I 68 We were never able to agree with Sterne in pitying the man who could travel from Dan to Beersheba, and say that all was barren.

Dance. See Bear (29), Top 2 (1).

Dandelion. The rest wasn't no more to compare with her than a dandelion is to a cabbage rose (44 Stephens *High Life* II 58).

Dander, 1. My dander was up (34 Crockett *Life* 73, 81 to lay our dander, 89, 138; Stephens *High Life* I 11, 49, 84, II 204 my dander riz up so fast that it rolled together in chunks and stuck in my throat; Dorson *Jonathan* 57; Clemens *Letters* I 27, *Tom* 3, *Sketches* 245; Thomson *Plu-ri-bus-tah* 65 Plu-ri-bus-tah felt his dander rising, 152; Whitcher *Widow* 328; Porter *Major* 67; Whitehead *Wild Sports* 335 his dander was evidently riz; Sedley *Marian* 114, 116 my honorable friend here hists his dander at, 193; Eggleston *School-Master* 159). Bartlett 168, 513–514; Farmer 191; Farmer and Henley II 251; Green 110; McAtee 28; NED Dander [4]; Schele de Vere 461–462; Thornton I 236, III 105; NQ 11 iv 468, vii 15, 52, 153.

2. Pangborn's pride . . . bein' bound up in the issoo [issue], it riles

his dander to hev' it tech bottom (65 Sedley *Marian* 162).

3. Poverty . . . is equal to "martial law," in . . . keeping down the dander (56 Kelly *Humors* 50, 135 Choking down his dander, or disgust). Cf. Partridge 207.

Danger. There's danger in delay (76 Nash *Century* 310). See Delay.

Darby. Receiving a paternal benediction from old Darby and Joan (47 Melville *Omoo* 302, cf. 300, *Mardi* I 86 very often this husband and wife were no Darby and Joan). NED Darby 6; *Oxford* 129; Henry Wade, pseud. *No Friendly Drop* (1932) 72.

Dark, sb. I'm all in the dark (42 Irving *Attorney* 260; Sedley *Marian* 340). NED Dark sb. 5.

Dark, adj., 1. Keep dark! said one (43 Robb *Squatter* 113; Whitcher *Widow* 219; Hammett *Piney* 304; Boucicault *Flying Scud* 162 we kept it darker; Harris *Sut* 51; Lowell *Biglow* 328). NED Dark a. 7; Stevenson 487:4.

2. See Cat (8), Coal mine, Comingo, Death (5), Egypt, Fire sb. (1), Grave (4), Ink (2), Inside (1), Midnight (2), Night (2), Pitch (3, 4), Pocket, Raven (2), Wolf (5).

Darning-needle. Eyes . . . as sharp as darning-needles (44 Stephens *High Life* II 245). Cf. NC 450 Needle.

Dash, 1. I ruther guess I cut a dash (44 Stephens *High Life* I 68, 130 a considerable of a dash, 166, 213, II 13 so much of a dash, 61 Didn't they cut the dashes though!). Farmer and Henley II 237; NED Dash sb. 10.

2. The public like [likes] an actor that drinks. . . . You're the very man to make a dash with (23–24 Irving *Tales* 264).

Dashed. I feel sort of dashed (44 Stephens *High Life* I 217). NED Dash vb. 1 (7).

Davy Jones. If he has gone to Davy Jones' locker (23–24 Irving *Tales* 449; Neal *Charcoal* 31 Were all the passengers in a wherry to be of one mind, they would probably all sit upon the same side, and hence, naturally, pay a visit to the Davy Jones of the river, 158 them as can't tread water must go to Davy Jones; Dana *Two* 362 And pitch me over to Davy Jones, 372 What's the use in being always on the lookout for Davy Jones?; Melville *Omoo* 343 One boat's crew of 'em is gone to Davy Jones's locker, *White Jacket* 218 anything that smacks of life is better than to feel Davy Jones's chest-lid on your nose, *Moby-Dick* I 113 he got stove and went to Davy Jones, II 93; Hawthorne *Mosses* 80 Davy Jones, the distinguished nautical personage; Anon. *New Hope* 256 "There's no danger of shipping a sea, unless the devil that draws us tacks." "What do you think it is, captain?" "Don't know, unless it's Davy Jones himself"; Derby *Phoenixiana* 298; Durivage *Three* 347 go to Davy Jones, 349 I'll blow you all to Davy Jones; P. H. Myers *Thrilling Adventures of the Prisoner of the Border* [New York 1860] 92 More likely we should both be going downstairs to Davy Jones' cellar). Babcock 256, 261; Farmer and Henley II 258; NED Davy Jones; *Oxford* 130; Stevenson 2092:6; *Catalogue of Political and Personal Satires . . . 1811–1819* (London 1949) IX 216 No. 12018 Shiver my topsails—but if that damnable twenty decker were once fairly stowed in Davys Locker, we should have plenty of freight; Harry A. Franck *A Vagabond*

Journey Around the World (1910) 272 That lot [of memoirs] went to amuse Davy Jones when a tub I was playing second engineer on threw up the sponge in the Bay of Bengal; Ward Jones *The Case of the Hanging Lady* (1938) 8.

Day, 1. Beautiful as the day (25 Neal *Brother J* III 369, *Rachel* 186 a wife as beautiful; *Down-Easters* I 146; Boshears 34:330 spring day; Halpert 202.

2. As bright as day (40 Dana *Two* 274; Haliburton *Old Judge* II 77). Boshears 34:370; NC 390; Taylor *Comparisons* 21; Tilley D55; Whiting *Drama* 309:89.

3. His nerves were as calm as the summer day of that evening (59 Shillaber *Knitting-Work* 282–283).

4. Our motives . . . will stand forth clear as day (45 Mayo *Kaloolah* 464; Irving *Wolfert* 57 Everything was soon as clear to me as day; Clemens *Sketches* 74, *Gilded* II 308). Apperson 101; NC 390; Tilley D56.

5. She's as clever as the day is long (39 Smith *Letters* 17–18).

6. He is as frank as broad day (45 Cooper *Satanstoe* 262).

7. She was always good-natured as the day was long (52 Cary *Clovernook* 73).

8. Happy and cheerful as the day is long (35 Crockett *Account* 62; Haliburton *Clockmaker* II 212, *Letter* 303; Stephens *Mary Derwent* 270 and if his wife ain't as happy as the day is long). Apperson 283; Svartengren 78; Tilley D57; Anthony Berkeley, pseud. *The Silk Stocking Murders* (1926) 18.

9. They are as honest as the day (45 Cooper *Satanstoe* 48; Melville *Confidence-Man* 170 "Honest?" "As the day is long"; Clemens *Tom* 105 as the day was long). Boshears 37:672;

NC 390; Moray Dalton *One by One They Disappeared* (1929) 131; R. J. Casey *News Reel* (Indianapolis 1932) 16 as the day is long.

10. As industrious as the day is long (72 Clemens *Roughing* II 105).

11. It was as light as day (44 Stephens *High Life* I 186, II 168, 249; Willis *Life* 369). Boshears 38:715; NC 390; Svartengren 363; Taylor *Comparisons* 53.

12. She is lovely as the day (56 Durivage *Three* 34). NC 390.

13. No—a hallowed passion, my dear friend—open as the day (58 Field *Pokerville* 35). Svartengren 13; Lee Thayer, pseud. *Dead Man's Shoes* (1929) 196.

14. I heard it speak as plain as day (28 Neal *Rachel* 190; Crockett *Exploits* 18; Cooper *Pathfinder* 462; Stephens *High Life* I 94, II 3; Fairfield *Letters* 381 I can see her "as plain as day"; Anon. *New Hope* 108; Smith *My Thirty* 310; Clemens *Gilded* I 12). Boshears 39:794; NC 390; Taylor *Comparisons* 62; Whiting PADS XI (1949) 28 n. 5; J. C. Addams *The Secret Deed* (1926) 296. Cf. McAtee 49.

15. As sure as day (57 Jones *Country* 129). NC 390; Svartengren 360; Erskine Caldwell *Tobacco Road* (1932) 4 as day comes; J. T. Farrell *No Star Is Lost* (1938) 102 as the day is long.

16. He'll do it any day o' the week . . . let alone Saturdays—of course the speaker was a Marylander of Irish parentage (33 Neal *Down-Easters* I 134).

17. I've a great mind to knock off and call it half a day (37 Neal *Charcoal* 140). Partridge 121; H. C. Bailey *The Sullen Sky Mystery* (1935) 208.

18. Some rascally deed sent him

off "between two days" (40 Dana *Two* 313). DA Day 2 (1); NED *Supplement* Day 20; Stevenson 490:3; Joseph Kirkland *Zury* (Boston 1887) 246; Gerald W. Johnson, *The Lunatic Fringe* (Philadelphia 1957) 87. See Sun (10).

19. "Dat true," answered the Indian, smiling; for he seldom laughed; and he repeated a common saying of the country: "By de day; by de day— by de job, job job! Dat pale-face religion" (45 Cooper *Chainbearer* 114). See Contract-work.

20. A fine day is not a weather-breeder, but a fine day (32 Emerson *Journals* II 530). NED Weather-breeder.

21. If you begin the day with a laugh, you may, nevertheless end it with a sob and a sigh (50 Melville *White Jacket* 166). Lean IV 28; *Oxford* 352; Tilley D91.

22. One day a man is up, and then the laugh's on his side; next day he is down, and then the laugh's against him (38 Kennedy *Horse-Shoe* 206). Cf. Apperson 636.

23. Laying by something against a rainy day (56 Durivage *Three* 247; Melville *Confidence-Man* 280 put by a few dollars . . . against that rainy day he used to groan so much about; Barnum *Struggles* 461; Clemens *Fairbanks* 114). Apperson 523; Faden 232; Green 296; NC 391; NED Rainy 2 b; *Oxford* 532; Stevenson 491–492: 8; Tilley D89; Milward Kennedy *Death in a Deck-chair* (London 1930) 172.

24. Bill went into it like a day's work (54 Smith *'Way* 49; Hammett *Piney* 300 it's sot inter rainin' like a day's work).

25. The "Philadelphia Catechism" is "Six days shalt thou labor and do all thou art able, And on the seventh— holystone the decks and scrape the cable" (40 Dana *Two* 18). *Oxford* 593.

26. The better the day, the better the deed (46 Cooper *Redskins* 412). Apperson 45; Lean II ii 714–715; NC 391; *Oxford* 39; Stevenson 492:3; Tilley D60; NQ 4 v 147, 249–250, 548; 10 i 448, ii 16; Irvin S. Cobb *Murder Day by Day* (Indianapolis 1933) 215–216 they say.

27. The vulgar distich runs thus— "When the days begin to lengthen, The cold begins to strengthen" (50 Judd *Richard* 97). Apperson 136; *Oxford* 131; Stevenson 494:7.

28. It's all day with him now (40 Haliburton *Clockmaker* III 204; Whitcher *Widow* 328; Porter *Major* 49). DA All (4) 1.

29. But even ef they caird the day [i. e., won a political victory]. (48 Lowell *Biglow* 142). NED Carry 15 c.

30. For in that drive he meant to "name the day" and put his creditors at ease (53 Willis *Fun* 312).

31. We had put off the evil day as long as we could (58 Hammett *Piney* 269). *Oxford* 526 hour.

32. You'll excuse me . . . You are the day after the fair; it's too late now (28 Neal *Rachel* 91; Thomson *Elephant Club* 170). Apperson 136; Lean II ii 755; *Oxford* 130; Tilley D112; J. J. Connington, pseud. *Mystery at Lynden Sands* (1928) 191. Cf. Feast (1).

33. Next day after never (56 Cary *Married* 134).

34. See Summer's day.

Daylight, 1. It became as clear to him as daylight (32 Kennedy *Swallow* 110; Davis *Downing* 273; Whitehead *Wild Sports* 78; Barnum *Struggles* 336). Svartengren 363; Anthony Abbot, pseud. *About the Murder of the Circus Queen* (1932) 170. Cf. Day (4).

2. Could knock daylight out of a turkey's eye at two hundred yards (51 Burke *Polly* 162). McAtee 38.

3. I'll make daylight shine through on you (33 Smith *Downing* 176, 204, *Letters* 67; Lowell *Biglow* 48 Wen cold lead puts daylight thru ye, 60 They'd let daylight into me; Bennett *Border* 109 hyer's a nigger as'll let daylight through you again, 110 he'd get daylight clean through him, 237 afore I let daylight clean through ye). Berrey 342:6; Farmer and Henley II 259; Stevenson 492:2; Thornton I 239.

Deacon, 1. So off he steps, demure as a deacon (56 Whitcher *Widow* 259). Cf. Taylor *Comparisons* 56 mealymouthed.

2. As sober as a deacon (44 Stephens *High Life* I 147, II 97).

3. That's the reason deacons' sons seldom turn out well, and preachers' daughters are married through a window (55 Haliburton *Nature* II 52). Boshears 32:137; Halpert 786; B. B. Lindsey and W. Evans *The Revolt of Modern Youth* (1925) 95 the old saying about some ministers' sons and deacons' daughters.

Dead, sb., 1. Old Pompey'll keep dem ere silver platters . . . safe as de dead folks in em graves (c58 Stephens *Mary Derwent* 231).

2. She . . . was as still as the dead she mourned (c58 Stephens *Mary Derwent* 302).

3. Silk was not killed, and as for the rest I have nothing evil to say of the dead (71 Jones *Batkins* 495). Apperson 594; NC 491; *Oxford* 611; Schele de Vere 654–655; Stevenson 520:4–521:4; Tilley D124; Mary Rob-

erts Rinehart *Miss Pinkerton* (1932) 44.

4. After a rap "to wake the dead" (53 Willis *Fun* 40).

Dead, adj., 1. Who's dead, and what's to pay now? (38 Haliburton *Clockmaker* II 99, 129, 280, III 30–31, 130, *Attaché* I 92, II 24).

2. See Blaze (6), Caesar (3), Doornail, Frog (1), General Jackson, Herring (2), Mackerel, Mitten (1), Mutton (1), Nail (1), Pig (3), Raccoon (1), Rat (2), Saint Peter, Sausage (1), Skunk (1), Smelt, Stone (5, 6), Stump (1), Tecumseh, Timberhead, Wax figure, Wedge (2), Worm (1).

Dead-eye. You d—d lubberly monkey, with a blue-skin stuck in your mouth as big as a frigate's dead-eye (45 Mayo *Kaloolah* 105).

Deadwood. To get the deadwood on. 51 DA Deadwood 1 (b).

Deaf. See Braddock, Codfish (1), Door-post, Post (1), Shad (1).

Deal. That was a square deal, Miss Brown (76 Nash *Century* 30). DA Square 3.

Dear. See Deuce (1).

Death, 1. As black as death (33 Neal *Down-Easters* I 4). Svartengren 8; Edmund Snell *Kontrol* (Philadelphia 1928) 220.

2. The bay was as calm as death (47 Melville *Omoo* 26).

3. But I am chilly, chilly as death (54 Stephens *Fashion* 215).

4. As cold as death (33 Neal *Down-Easters* II 77; Stephens *Homestead* 141, *Mary Derwent* 160; Clemens *Gilded* II 260). Svartengren 312; Francis Beeding, pseud. *The Three Fishers* (Boston 1931) 216.

5. How dark as death the night! (49 Melville *Mardi* II 272).

6. Dumb as death! (50 Boker *World* 10; Melville *Pierre* 161). Apperson 571 silent. Cf. NC 391 mute; Svartengren 177, 386.

7. All were as hush as death (35 Longstreet *Georgia* 35; Stephens *Mary Derwent* 85).

8. As inevitable as death (65 Richardson *Secret* 314). NC 391.

9. A face as pale as death (21 Cooper *Spy* 43, 389, *Pathfinder* 489, *Chainbearer* 432; Neal *Brother J* I 132, II 109, 354, III 290, 304, *Rachel* 57, 182, *Down-Easters* I 35; Melville *Redburn* 332, *Israel* 37; Boker *World* 10 Dumb as death! As pale, too; Stowe *Uncle* 172; Haliburton *Sam* I 329; Hammett *Stray* 224; Bennett *Kate* 220; Anon. *New Hope* 295; Hawthorne *Mosses* 63, "My Kinsman" in *House* 639; Cartwright *Autobiography* 306; Jones *Wild* 251; Stephens *Fashion* 40 Then her cheek turned pale as death, *Homestead* 181, *Mary Derwent* 113, 323; Chamberlain *Confession* 207; Richardson *Beyond* 69, 545). Apperson 482; NC 392; NED Pale adj. 4 (pale-dead); Stevenson 1741: 5; Taylor *Comparisons* 61; Tilley D134; E. Best Black *The Ravenelle Riddle* (1933) 110.

10. It was pallid as death (54 Shillaber *Mrs. Partington* 362).

11. A stillness profound as death (25 Neal *Brother J* II 147).

12. [He snatched his gun] quicker than death (56 Kelly *Humors* 113).

13. He looks as sick as death in the primer (40 Haliburton *Clockmaker* III 278; Hammett *Piney* 115 as sick as death).

14. Silent as death (25 Neal *Brother J* III 30; Mayo *Kaloolah* 438; Stephens *Fashion* 404 all within the courtroom was silent as death). Apperson 571; NC 392; Svartengren 336; Tilley D135; I. T. Sanderson *Animal Treasure* (1937) 66.

15. Solemn as death (25 Neal *Brother J* I 355, III 315).

16. Steady as death (25 Neal *Brother J* II 336).

17. Everything is as still as death (24 Cooper *Pilot* 278; Neal *Brother J* I 193, 276, 402, III 166, *Down-Easters* II 71; Haliburton *Clockmaker* I 91; Thompson *Major* 120; Melville *Typee* 353; Hawthorne *Twice-Told* 230; Baldwin *Flush* 167; Stephens *Homestead* 323, *Mary Derwent* 301, 334; Willis *Fun* 302; Kelly *Humors* 148; Bowman *Bear-Hunters* 151). NC 392; F. J. Anderson *Book of Murder* (1930) 100.

18. Sure as death (25 Neal *Brother J* II 115; Kelly *Humors* 338; Bowman *Bear-Hunters* 156, 178). Apperson 611; NC 392; NED Sure B 4 a; Stevenson 2248:16; Taylor *Comparisons* 79–80; Tilley D136; Bon Gaultier [i. e., Theodore Martin and W. E. Aytoun] *The Book of Ballads* (1845, 11th ed. Edinburgh 1870) 42; Ridgwell Cullum *The Mystery of the Barren Lands* (1928) 106.

19. As tired as death (54 Smith 'Way 190).

20. I would have a woman as true as Death (58 Holmes *Autocrat* 270).

21. He did come forth at last, looking white as death (54 Stephens *Fashion* 421, *Homestead* 219, *Mary Derwent* 222; Holmes *Autocrat* 98). Elsa Barker *The Redman Cave Mystery* (1930) 68.

22. Dr. Slunk was "death on poker" (58 Field *Pokerville* 35, 131 Yes, said the challenger, you're death on teeth). DA Death 1 b; Farmer 195; Farmer and Henley II 266–267; NED Death

16; Schele de Vere 596; Thornton I 243–244, III 108.

23. But then he's death and the pale hoss on poker (56 Kelly *Humors* 78). Rev. 6:8 And I saw, and beheld, a pale horse; and he that sat on him, his name was Death. Cf. DA Death 1 b.

24. Them friends of your'n will be the death of you yit (44 Stephens *High Life* II 188). NED Death 7, 13.

25. And stick like death to the mane (53 Hammett *Stray* 270). NED Death 17.

26. He hung on like grim death (36 Crockett *Exploits* 151; Haliburton *Attaché* IV 249 hooks on to rich foreigners like; Melville *Moby-Dick* I 305 hold on like, "Happy Failure" in *Works* XIII 211; Hammett *Piney* 112). NED Death 17; *Oxford* 299; Stevenson 502:5; Thornton I 441; Gregory Baxter *The Ainceworth Mystery* (1930) 80.

27. A-hangin' on to it like grim death to a dead nigger (40 Haliburton *Clockmaker* III 173, *Attaché* II 254–255, III 43 hold on, *Sam* I 53 held on, II 207 our old sayin' "it sticks like," *Nature* II 313 hold on; Burke *Polly* 73 helt onto him; Riley *Puddleford* 161 it stuck to him like death; Sedley *Marian* 116 I stick to it like death to a dead nigger). Hardie 469:89; Taylor *Comparisons* 33.

28. Start her like grim death and grinning devils (51 Melville *Moby-Dick* II 23).

29. See Tickle (2).

Debt. The news came that his father had discharged the debt of nature (32 Hall *Legends* 113; Hammett *Wonderful* 39; Kelly *Humors* 399). Apperson 140; NED Debt 4 b; Stevenson 508:3; Stoett 2270; Whiting *Scots* I 157; NQ

4 x 430, 515, xi 44, 534; 7 xi 28, xii 158.

December. I am as cool [i. e., calm] as a December morning (37 Fairfield *Letters* 173).

Deck. Th' ole Constitooshun never'd git her decks for action cleared (67 Lowell *Biglow* 295). See Ship (4). Cf. The decks were cleared (49 Melville *Redburn* 374), which is used in a literal sense. Babcock 261.

Deed. Good deeds always have their reward (32 Hall *Legends* 78).

Deep. See Sea (3), Well, sb.

Deep-toned. See Bell (2).

Deer, 1. Agile as a deer (67 Richardson *Beyond* 47). Svartengren 158.

2. Swift as a deer (45 Judd *Margaret* II 151).

3. The deer that goes too often to the lick meets the hunter at last (40 Cooper *Pathfinder* 89). See Pitcher.

4. If . . . , then I allow I never killed no deer (43 Hall *Purchase* I 267, 269 If . . . , I never killed no deer).

5. He runs like a deer (25 Neal *Brother J* I 107, II 7, III 387; Haliburton *Clockmaker* II 44; Smith *'Way* 96 ran with the fleetness of a wild deer; Hammett *Piney* 280 runnin' like a scart deer in a perara a fire; Barnum *Struggles* 99). Boshears 33:242; McAtee 53; NC 392; *Oxford* 552; Taylor *Comparisons* 33, cf. 41; Tidwell PADS XI (1949) 13.

6. But bounding away with the fleetness of a deer (32 Hall *Soldier's Bride* 28). Taylor *Comparisons* 41 as fleet as.

Delay. Delays are dangerous (24 Fairfield *Letters* p. xxxi; Anon. *New Hope*

49 But delays are dangerous (Isaac felt the full force of the truism). Apperson 141–142; Lean III 447; NC 392; *Oxford* 136; Tilley D195; Brian Flynn *Murder En Route* (Philadelphia 1932) 262 delays are proverbially dangerous. See Danger.

Delicate. See Flower (2), Snowdrop (1).

Deluge. Our Parapets say, "after them the deluge." And so say their Southern prototypes. But like the prophet who said it before them, they may yet see and feel the storm (65 Sedley *Marian* 333). Lean IV 183; *Oxford* 5; Partridge *Clichés* 17; Stevenson 548: 14; NQ 1 iii 299, 397, v 619, xi 16; 3 ii 228, 279–280; 4 v 520, vii 188, 310; 9 vi 67, 276, 455; 10 i 340, vi 40; Åke Sandler *The Pacific Spectator* VII (1953) 162 But in all likelihood he [Stalin] believed with Louis XV: "Après moi le déluge"; R. Jungk *Tomorrow Is Already Here* (1954) 138 (a literal and a metaphorical instance).

Demon. The Campbellites, and especially their preacher, were as restless as fallen demons (c56 Cartwright *Autobiography* 400).

Demure. See Deacon (1), Harlot.

Desert, 1. Life as barren as the Dessert of Sarah (62 Browne *Artemus* 125). Boshears 34:329 a desert.

2. It's as dull here as the Desert of Sahara (68 Alcott *Little Women* 155).

3. As thirsty as the great desert of Sahara (39 Briggs *Harry* I 23). Cf. Sand (1).

4. See Sahara.

Desolate. See Sodom (1).

Desperation. Reflecting . . . that desperation will sometimes insure success

(58 Porter *Major* 31). Cf. Apperson 142 Despair; *Oxford* 137; Tilley D216; Whiting *Scots* I 157.

Deuce, 1. A war on tick's ez dear 'z the deuce (67 Lowell *Biglow* 348).

2. All in a terrible hurry to see what the deuce was to pay in the chamber of the bold dragoon (23–24 Irving *Tales* 55; Irving *Attorney* 204 there'll be the deuce to pay; Shillaber *Knitting-Work* 309 You'll find the deuce and all to pay). Farmer and Henley II 271 deuce to pay. See Devil (26).

3. I felt just ready to go to the deuce (68 Alcott *Little Women* 237).

Devil, 1. A nigger as black as . . . the devil's hind leg (60 Haliburton *Season-Ticket* 54). Cf. Apperson 52 Black (14, 15); NED Devil 22 c; Svartengren 239; Tilley D217; Whiting *Drama* 309:91.

2. Clark has been busy as the "- - - - in a gale of wind," as the sailors say (35 Fairfield *Letters* 37). Apperson 142 Devil (3); *Oxford* 140; Stevenson 558:5; Svartengren 122.

3. Obstinate as the devil (59 Boucicault *Dot* 130). Whiting *Devil* 212.

4. Proud as the devil (54 Langdon *Ida* 349). Whiting *Devil* 212. Cf. Taylor *Comparisons* 64 Beelzebub, Lucifer.

5. Scotch as the devil (43 Robb *Squatter* 167).

6. As sure as the devil is a hog (66 Smith *Arp* 136). Cf. Apperson 150 Devil (112); *Oxford* 139; Tilley D306.

7. I'm howldin' yeez tight as a divil (56 Kelly *Humors* 92).

8. I . . . lammed him wuss than the devil beatin tan-bark (55 Haliburton *Nature* II 60–61; Burke *Polly* 153 I'll larrup you worse nor; Harris *Sut*

82 a-thrashin his hide like, 263 [my heart] wud a been a-poundin like). Taylor *Comparisons* 34; Whiting *Devil* 211:34. See Hell (13), Tan-bark.

9. It was currently said, "that Mike Brown and the devil would one day be wearing each other's shirts" (32 Kennedy *Swallow* 223). Cf. NC 393: 17.

10. To beat the devil and carry a rail [i. e., to defeat decisively]. 72 DA Rail 2 (4).

11. Fight the devil with fire is my motto (66 Smith *Arp* 165). Cf. Apperson 213; Tilley F277; Whiting *Devil* 209:13; E. R. Burroughs *Swords of Mars* (Tarzana, Cal. 1936) 17.

12. What do they say in your country, "needs must," when the devil drives? (70 Daly *Man* 34). Apperson 440; *Oxford* 447; Stevenson 563:6; Tilley D278; Whiting *Devil* 209, *Drama* 135, 180; J. B. Cabell *The Line of Love* (1926) 49.

13. Once a devil, always a devil (60 Haliburton *Season-Ticket* 371). *Oxford* 474.

14. Take my advice, girl, own the truth and shame the—the old gentleman (54 Stephens *Fashion* 294). Apperson 649; Bradley 95; *Oxford* 646; Smith *Browning* 222; Stevenson 2389–2390:15; Tilley T566; Whiting *Devil* 209–210; NQ CLVIII (1930) 132; Anthony Abbot, pseud. *About the Murder of the Night Club Lady* (1931) 255; F. P. Keyes *Dinner at Antoine's* (1948) 332 Tell de troof an' shame de debbil, lak de preacher say.

15. The demagogues of this Province have raised the devil and can not lay him again (51 Hawthorne *Twice-Told* 301; Clemens *Letters* I 63 I have invoked a Spirit of some kind or other which I find some difficulty in laying). Apperson 146 Devil (58), 523; Oxford 532; Stevenson 562:7; Tilley D319.

16. Speak of old Saytin and he's sure to appear (36 Haliburton *Clockmaker* I 238, *Old Judge* II 36 Recollect the old proverb, "Talk of the Devil, and he will be sure to appear," *Sam* I 31 talk of the devil and he is sure to heave in sight directly; Boker *World* 8 Talk of the dev--; Whitcher *Widow* 348 the *Old One's* always at hand when you're talkin' about him). Apperson 145; Farmer and Henley II 274; McAtee 64; NC 393; NED Devil 22 l; *Oxford* 643–644; Snapp 108: 160; Stevenson 568:6; Stoett 520; Tilley D294; Whiting *Devil* 206; Yamamoto *Dickens* 328; H. S. Keeler *The Spectacles of Mr. Cagliostro* (1926) 51; Herman Landon *Murder Mansion* (1928) 220 talk.

17. You see the devil can quote Scripture (56 Durivage *Three* 289). Matt. 4:6; Apperson 145; NC 393; *Oxford* 138–139; Stevenson 566:2; Tilley D230; Whiting *Devil* 207; Carter Dickson, pseud. *The Peacock Feather Murders* (1937) 168.

18. Away goes the devil when he finds the door shut against him (32 Kennedy *Swallow* 216). Apperson 143 Devil (9); *Oxford* 17; Tilley D269.

19. A camp, through which the devil walks as openly as if he were a gentleman, and sure of his welcome (27 Cooper *Prairie* 354). Whiting *Devil* 210:22; Jeffrey Farnol *Over the Hills* (Boston 1930) 204 the devil is a gentleman.

20. Like the great bell of St. Paul's, which only sounds when the King or the Devil is dead (50 Melville *White Jacket* 42, *Moby-Dick* II 57 Who ever heard that the devil was dead?; Smith *Arp* 49 I begin to believe our old devil is dead). Apperson 146 Devil (57);

Oxford 140; Stevenson 563–564:8; Tilley D244, D293; Whiting *Drama* 19, 341:498, *Scots* I 158 (5); Lee Thayer, pseud. *Dead End Street* (1936) 247.

21. That the devil was good to his own (32 Kennedy *Swallow* 223). Apperson 146; NC 394; Stevenson 559–560:7; Tilley D245; Whiting *Devil* 207.

22. I find the Devil is not so black as he is painted (42 Irving *Attorney* 374; Willis *Fun* 204 But like the gentleman to whom he was attributed as a favorite protégé, he was "not so black as he was painted"; Haliburton *Nature* II 319 The devil we have painted black; Melville *Confidence-Man* 41 Exemplifying the old saying, not more just than charitable, that "the devil is never so black as he is painted"; Richardson *Secret* 103 He was daily declaring that the devil is not so black as he is painted, 382 as usual we found the devil not quite so black as he is painted). Apperson 147; Lean IV 116; NC 393 (28); NED Devil 22 c; *Oxford* 141; Stevenson 567–568:11; Tilley D255; Whiting *Devil* 207–208; Sidney Huddleston *Paris Salons, Cafés, Studios* (1928) 158.

23. As it is said the Prince of Darkness hates holy water (71 Jones *Batkins* 60). Apperson 143 Devil (7); *Oxford* 141; Stevenson 567:6; Taylor *Comparisons* 34; Tilley D220; Whiting *Devil* 203:1; R. J. Casey *The Third Owl* (Indianapolis 1934) 243.

24. My third proverb is as deficient in superficial melody as either of the others: "The Devil is an ass" (38 Emerson *Journals* V 55–56, *Works* II 109). Apperson 146 Devil (55); *Oxford* 139–140; Stevenson 562:6; Tilley D242.

25. I just determined to do the best I could, and the devil take the hindmost (34 Crockett *Life* 41; Haliburton *Letter* 35 it is "scabies occupet extremum," or the devil take the hindmost; Melville *Moby-Dick* I 288 here goes for a cool, collected dive at death and destruction, and the devil fetch the hindmost; Baldwin *Flush* 90 "Devil take the hindmost" was the tune to which the soldiers of fortune marched, 307 It was devil take the hindmost; Durivage *Three* 342 Besides, it's all fair play, life for life, and the gentleman with the single fluke tail take the loser). Apperson 148; *Oxford* 142; Stevenson 2058:10; Tilley D267; Whiting *Devil* 208; F. J. Anderson *Book of Murder* (1930) 72; M. K. Rawlings *The Yearling* (1938) 187 All a feller kin do, is fight for what he figgers is right, and the Devil take the hindmost; E. M. Rhodes *West Is West* (1917) 35 then may the Devil take the hindmost. See Man (14).

26. I sposed thar was gwine to be the devil to pay (51 Burke *Polly* 150; Baldwin *Flush* 170 the very devil, 308; Haliburton *Nature* II 257; Hammett *Piney* 112 the very old boy; Richardson *Secret* 187; Smith *Arp* 52 it is my duty to inform you that the Devil is to pay and he won't take Confederate money). Apperson 148 Devil (85); Farmer and Henley II 274; NED Devil 22 j; *Oxford* 142; Stevenson 561:2; Tilley D268; Whiting *Devil* 217–218:57; Elsa Barker *The Redman Cave Murder* (1930) 59. See Hell (10).

27. Here's the devil to pay and no pitch hot (28 Neal *Rachel* 70, *Down-Easters* I 91; Haliburton *Attaché* III 42, *Nature* I 114; Kelly *Humors* 170). Apperson 148; NC 394 Devil (33); NED Devil 22 j; *Oxford* 142; Steven-

son 561:2; Whiting *Devil* 217–218: 57; W. B. Foster *From Six to Six* (1927) 102.

28. There's no devil if I knowed what this meant (34 Crockett *Life* 139).

29. They say the d--l wouldn't make a sailor if he didn't look aloft (40 Cooper *Pathfinder* 438).

30. Ef raw-hide don't tar [tear], yu've got im till the devil freezes (67 Harris *Sut* 129). Cf. Whiting *Devil* 219:75, 221–222:4 Hell.

31. To give the devil his due (40 Cooper *Pathfinder* 53, *Chainbearer* 45 dat an ole sayin', 253; Haliburton *Clockmaker* III 244, *Attaché* IV 212; Hammett *Stray* 241; Porter *Major* 199; Clemens *Enterprise* 90; Locke [Nasby] *Struggles* 177). Apperson 143; NC 392; NED Due 2 b; *Oxford* 239; Snapp 87:23; Stevenson 568:1; Tilley D273; Whiting *Devil* 205; Hugh Austin *Murder of a Matriarch* (1936) 268; *Diary of Abraham de la Pryme* (1694) (Surtees Soc. 54 [London 1867]) 47.

32. Lost like the devil on the last Derby (63 Wallack *Rosedale* 7).

33. A quarrelsome toper . . . who, when half-seas over, plays the very devil (23–24 Irving *Tales* 379; Dana *Two* 47 If dey can't have dare own way, they'll play the devil with you; Irving *Attorney* 80; Thomson *Doesticks* 260 Spirits . . . began to play the devil with things generally; Boucicault *Flying Scud* 168; Daly *Man* 21). Partridge 216.

34. She [an old maid] had seen the devil, according to the common computation, three times, and had been so alarmed at his last visit that—the story goes—she swore an oath she would marry his cousin-german, rather than be importuned by his further atten-

tions (32 Kennedy *Swallow* 225). Cf. Tilley M105.

35. What is got over the devil's back, is sure to be spent under his bellie (35 Crockett *Account* 36; Haliburton *Clockmaker* II 227 I've observed that what's got over the devil's back is commonly lost under his belly; Jones *Batkins* 171 his fortune came in some way "over the devil's back," 172 I have referred to an old saying about "money got over the devil's back!" I will add that the proverb is continued by an allusion to the way in which such money is spent, and have also noted my opinion that there were exceptions. I suppose everybody has heard of the proverb, or saying; it was one Aunt Dolly used often to repeat). Apperson 150; NC 394; *Oxford* 260; Stevenson 564:6; Tilley D316; NQ 10 xii 489–490; 11 ix 427, 493; Jack Lindsay *1649* (London 1938) 551 sold under the belly.

36. Whipping the devil round the stump (73 Clemens *Gilded* I 116). DA Devil 5 (1); Partridge 952; Whiting *Devil* 211 (32) chasing, (33) meeting-house.

37. When the devil was sick, The devil a saint would be, But when the devil got well, The devil a saint was he (69 Barnum *Struggles* 403). Apperson 148–149; NC 394:36; *Oxford* 142; Stevenson 569:1; Whiting *Devil* 208–209; J. H. Wade *Rambles in Devon* (London 1930) 36.

38. He ran as though the very devil was in him and after him (c56 Cartwright *Autobiography* 323). Whiting *Devil* 218–219:63; Elsa Barker *The Redman Cave Mystery* (1930) 173 was after him.

39. Off Buggerry Island, or the Devil's-Tail Peak (46 Melville *Typee* 28). Cf. Tilley D317.

40. He lived an easy, devil-may-care life (46 Melville *Typee* 354; Chamberlain *Confession* 39 A . . . devil-may-care looking set; Richardson *Beyond* 299 expression). NED Devil-may-care; Whiting *Devil* 217: 52.

41. We drifted to leeward like the d--l in Lent (45 Mayo *Kaloolah* 183).

42. See Lots, Truth (2).

Dew, 1. They are evanescent as the dew (53 Curtis *Potiphar* 156).

2. Her thoughts were as pure as the morning dew (56 Jones *Wild* 140).

3. Then his kisses fell like dew (68 Saxe *Poems* 237). Cf. Whiting *Scots* I 158.

4. Evil rolls off Eva's mind like dew off a cabbage-leaf (51 Stowe *Uncle* 275). See Water (15).

5. It's the first time I shook the dew off my boots this morning [i. e., took a drink]. (58 Porter *Major* 157).

Dew-drop, 1. As fresh as dew-drops (53 Curtis *Potiphar* 112; Paul *Courtship* 88 a du-drap; Holmes *Elsie* 99 [diamonds] looking as fresh as morning dew-drops). Cf. NC 394.

2. Diamonds were as plentiful as dew-drops on a rose thicket (54 Stephens *Fashion* 169).

Diamond, 1. Rough diamonds, hey (25 Neal *Brother J* II 438; Boucicault *Dot* 133 Yes, so kind, yet with so rough a manner, you know, a rough diamond; Nash *Century* 104 She is a rough diamond). NED Diamond 7 b; *Oxford* 549; Partridge 708; Stevenson 570:9; Tilley D322; Phoebe A. Taylor *Death Lights a Candle* (Indianapolis 1932) 154.

2. Eyes as bright as diamonds (44 Stephens *High Life* II 101, *Fashion*

41, 337; Cooke *Foresters* 159 brook . . . as bright as diamonds; Kelly *Humors* 398 eyes brighter than Brazil diamonds). Whiting *Scots* I 158.

3. That peculiar light [in his eyes], diamond bright (59–60 Holmes *Elsie* 307).

4. Hard as the diamond (c60 Paul *Courtship* 18). NC 394; Svartengren 89.

5. Pebbles white as a queen's diamonds (59–60 Holmes *Elsie* 46).

6. 'Twill be diamond cut diamond (24 Cooper *Pilot* 65; Haliburton *Clockmaker* II 227; Boker *Bankrupt* 68; Hammett *Stray* 213, *Piney* 35; Boucicault *Flying Scud* 213 or a Roland for an Allover). Apperson 151; NC 394; NED Diamond 7 c; *Oxford* 144; Stevenson 570:12; Tilley D323; NQ 11 ix 227, CXCIV 126; [T. Gililand] *Diamond Cut Diamond, or, Observations on a Pamphlet entitled A Review of the Conduct of H. R. H. the Prince of Wales* (London 1806).

Dick. It's pull Dick, pull devil! (53 Boker *Bankrupt* 105; Smith *Arp* 91 I allow as it was pull Dick, pull devil, between 'em). Bartlett 502; Bradley 68; Farmer 442. Cf. Apperson 210, 516; *Oxford* 523; Stevenson 559:2; NQ 2 iii 228, 316; 7 i 16, 96.

Didoes. If you keep cutting didoes (37 Neal *Charcoal* 201; Hammett *Wonderful* 273 Apropos de Dido—a friend once asked us what in our free opinion might be the origin of that odd phrase "cutting didoes"; and we sagely and poetically answered in this wise: Aeneas was the father, we should say, Who "Cut a Dido" when he ran away; Kelly *Humors* 312, 316; Harris *Uncle Remus* 112). Bartlett 164; Farmer and Henley II 238; Funk 87; Green 115; McAtee 22; NED Dido; Partridge 201, 219; Randolph and Wilson 239; Schele de Vere 324; Thornton I 250; Williams PADS II (1944) 28–29; PADS III (1945) 10.

Die, sb., 1. Straight as a die (50 Melville *White Jacket* 198, "Cock-a-doodle-doo!" in *Works* XIII 163). McAtee 62; NC 394; NED Die 2 f; Taylor *Comparisons* 78; W. C. Brown *Laughing Death* (Philadelphia 1932) 98.
    2. Amos'll bring her up, as sure as a die (33 Neal *Down-Easters* I 117).
    3. The die is long since cast (35 Kennedy *Horse-Shoe* 101). NED Die 2 c; *Oxford* 144; Stevenson 572:6; Tilley D326; Claude G. Bowers *The Tragic Era* (1929) 230.

Die, vb., 1. If not [successful in the attempt] why we must all die (43 Hall *Purchase* I 221; Cooper *Redskins* 455 Ebberybody must die some time). *Oxford* 7–8; Stevenson 511:8, 512:5–7; Tilley B140, M505. Cf. Whiting *Drama* 262, *Scots* I 159.
    2. The misfortune is that a man can only die once (32 Hall *Legends* 30; Judd *Richard* 43 As has been justly observed, we cannot die but once). Lean III 395; NC 395; *Oxford* 400–401.
    3. Never say die (40 Dana *Two* 296; "Morus Multicaulis at Tinnecum" *The Knickerbocker* XXV [1845] 411; Mayo *Kaloolah* 65; Melville *Redburn* 308 is my motto, "Cock-a-doodle-doo!" in *Works* XIII 148, 160; Haliburton *Nature* II 98; Bowman *Bear-Hunters* 471; Alcott *Little Women* 199). Bartlett 424; Bradley 69; *Oxford* 449; Stevenson 500:6; Yamamoto *Dickens* 353; J. S. Fletcher *Murder of the Ninth Baronet* (1932) 98. See Drown, Fail.
    4. See Dog (35), Flower (4).

Different. See Cream (1), Hawk (3).

Dig. They hoped that the author'd write more, and give 'em another dig (56 Whitcher *Widow* 332). NED Dig 4 b; Partridge 220.

Digby chicken [i. e., smoked herring]. (53 Haliburton *Sam* II 155). NED *Supplement* Digby; Partridge 220 Digby duck.

Dike. To be out on a dike [i. e., to dress carefully for a party]. 71 DA Dike, sb.

Dime, 1. Let him get hold of a dime, and he griped it so hard you could hear the eagle squall (53 Baldwin *Flush* 171). NC 399 Dollar.
    2. Yu ken buy land thar fur a dime a acre, on tick at that (67 Harris *Sut* 226). Cf. the modern colloquial "a dime a dozen."

Dimity. It used to be a saying then, if a fellow was suitoring to the girls, he was after the dimity (71 Jones *Batkins* 52–53).

Dinner. If a man wants a good dinner he must pay for it (53 Curtis *Potiphar* 100).

Dinner-plate. The lam'-postez . . . warn't es clean as a dinner plate (67 Harris *Sut* 130).

Dip. Somebody in the crowd objected that there was no one present who could "hold a taller dip to Bill's shuckin'" (74 Eggleston *Circuit* 15). See Candle (4).

Dirt, 1. 'Twas as black as dirt (56 Whitcher *Widow* 126).
    2. As cheap as dirt (44 Stephens *High Life* II 228; Cooper *Redskins* 71; Anon. *New Hope* 213; Hammett *Piney* 262; Paul *Courtship* 70 dirt-cheap; Nash *Century* 72 dirt cheap).

Boshears 35:399; Farmer and Henley II 82; Halpert 263; NC 395; NED Cheap 6 (dirt-cheap); Stevenson 327: 6; Svartengren 346; David Frome, pseud. *The Strange Death of Martin Green* (1931) 145 dirt-cheap.

3. Mean as dirt, they is! (51 Stowe *Uncle* 108; Shillaber *Ike* 213). NC 395; Svartengren 9 viler than; Dorothy Bennett *Murder Unleashed* (1935) 117.

4. Eating away, as if money, to them, were "like dirt" (25 Neal *Brother J* II 146).

5. The dirt always goes before the broom (40 Haliburton *Clockmaker* III 73).

6. If you ever saw wax-works cut dirt, they cut it then (35 Longstreet *Georgia* 185; Haliburton *Clockmaker* III 104, 227, 240, *Attaché* II 30, III 170, 279; Stephens *High Life* II 34, 141; Cary *Married* 187; Jones *Wild* 134; Field *Pokerville* 132). DA Dirt 2 b (1); DAE Dirt 1 b; Bartlett 164–165; Farmer 203; Farmer and Henley II 238; NED Dirt 6 d; Schele de Vere 222; Stevenson 581:8; Thornton I 231–232. Cf. NC 401 Dust (2); Randolph and Wilson 238 mud.

7. Didn't I make dirt fly for the first ten miles betwixt me and them [Indians]! (60 Whitehead *Wild Sports* 318).

8. Makin' money like dirt [i. e., rapidly]. (56 Whitcher *Widow* 215; Wiley *Billy* 329).

9. Grant . . . played dirt on us here (66 Locke [Nasby] *Struggles* 314). Cf. DA Dirt 2 b (3) to do dirt.

Discretion. I will consult discretion, the better part of valor (40 Fairfield *Letters* 288; Richardson *Secret* 71 That discretion which is the better part of valor; Smith *Arp* 103; Barnum *Struggles* 588 agreeing with Falstaff as to what constituted the "better part of valor"). Apperson 153; Bradley 70; *Oxford* 147; Snapp 87:19; Stevenson 584:6; Tilley D354; Herbert Asbury *The French Quarter* (1936) 104; M. K. Rawlings *Cross Creek* (1942) 176 Discretion in both cases seemed the better part of valor; T. H. White *The Sword in the Stone* (1939) 54 direction is the better part of valor (used of a fish that swims boldly and awkwardly).

Disease. A desperate disease sometimes needs a desperate remedy (59 Smith *My Thirty* 456). Apperson 142; *Oxford* 137; Tilley D357; Anthony Wynne, pseud. *The Toll House Murder* (Philadelphia 1935) 131. See Case (2).

Dish, 1. If I only had him a day or two in Georgia, we'd pepper his dish (25 Neal *Brother J* II 299).

2. When it rains my dishes is alway Bottom upwards (54 Eliason 103). Apperson 522 If it should rain porridge. Cf. Mouth (8).

Dish-cloth, 1. Damp as a dishcloth (56 Kelly *Humors* 418).

2. Collapsed like a wet dish-cloth (55 Thomson *Doesticks* 157). Cf. NC 395; Taylor *Comparisons* 54.

Dishrag. As limber as a dishrag. 39 DA Dishrag 1.

Dismal. See Hearse.

Distance. Distance lends enchantment (65 Richardson *Secret* 189). Bradley 70; Stevenson 591:6; Yamamoto *Dickens* 225; NQ 1 vi 505; 4 iv 29; Thomas Hood *Poems* (1827, London 1911) 78 I fear the distance did not "lend enchantment to the view."

Divide. To go over the Divide [i. e., to die]. 72 DA Divide sb. 1 b.

Dizzy. See Fool (10).

Do, 1. It is a time to do, and not to talk (24 Cooper *Pilot* 34). Cf. Tilley D402; Whiting *Drama* 93.

2. We are commanded to do as we would be done by (33 Neal *Down-Easters* I 33, 106 do as you are done by—that my way; Crockett *Exploits* 128 I have always endeavored to act up to the golden rule of doing as I would be done by; Lincoln I 473 the precept "Whatsoever ye would that men should do to you, do ye even so to them"; Barnum *Struggles* 496 the golden rule, "As ye would that men should do to you, do ye also to them"; Clemens *Sketches* 9; Jones *Batkins* 358 a lack of "doing as you would be done by"; Nash *Century* 148 Our motto is: " 'Do as you are done by,' Deacon." "But it ain't accordin' to Scripter"). Luke 6:31; Matt. 7:12; Bradley 70; *Oxford* 148; Stevenson 2014:7–2016:6; Stoett 2581; Tilley D395; Whiting *Scots* I 159; J. J. Connington, pseud. *Mystery at Lynden Sands* (1928) 125 is my motto.

3. Do or die (60 Haliburton *Season-Ticket* 85, 101; Eggleston *Circuit* 193). NC 396; Stevenson 537:5; Whiting *Scots* I 159.

4. The old proverb is full of truth and meaning, "Whatever is worth doing at all, is worth doing well" (69 Barnum *Struggles* 476). Apperson 714; Bradley 71; Hardie 462:26 A thing worth doing is worth doing well; Lean IV 181; *Oxford* 734; Stevenson 563:3; H. Wouk *The Caine Mutiny* (1951) ch. 13 Anything worth doing at all is worth doing well.

5. Oncet done, done for ever (43 Haliburton *Attaché* III 35). Stevenson 538:6 That is once well done is done forever.

6. His motto, What has been done may still be done (56 Durivage *Three* 54). *Oxford* 401; C. F. Gregg *Tragedy at Wembley* (1936) 189 What man has done, man can do.

7. But what is done is done, and cannot be mended by words (27 Cooper *Prairie* 65, *Pathfinder* 417 it is now too late to remedy it, *Satanstoe* 357 and there is no use in regretting it, in words; Haliburton *Clockmaker* I 294 What's done . . . can't be helped, III 120 What's done is done, *Sam* I 276; Sedley *Marian* 351 But, my dear, since what's done cannot be undone; Clemens *Tramp* I 96 what was done could not be helped). Apperson 468 What's done already cannot be undone, 625 When dede is doun, hit ys to lat; NC 396; *Oxford* 154; Smith *Browning* 224; Snapp 103: 35; Stevenson 543–544:15; Taylor *Index* 28; Tilley T200; Whiting *Drama* 41, 50; NQ 4 x 135, 213; Charles Barry, pseud. *The Corpse on the Bridge* (1928) 214.

Docile. See Kitten (1), Lamb (8).

Doctor. Out with it, as the doctor said to the little boy that swallowed his sister's necklace (56 Durivage *Three* 129).

Dog, 1. Dogs that bark after a wagon . . . keep out of the way of the whip (45 Judd *Margaret* II 115).

2. Fourteen dogs, but all so poor, that when they would bark they would almost have to lean up against a tree and take a rest (34 Crockett *Life* 176). Apperson 355; Green 19; Lean II ii 846; *Oxford* 355; Tilley L587; NQ 1 i 382, 475, ii 42, iv 165; 4 ix 17,

187, 239, 317, 482; George Beaton *Jack Robinson* (London 1933) 125 as lazy as old Dick Mullet's dog, that leaned against the wall to bark. See Backbone (3), Sapling.

3. In a dog's age. 36 DA Dog 6 (6); Carter Dickson, pseud. *The Plague Court Murders* (1934) 8.

4. The second mate is proverbially a dog's berth (40 Dana *Two* 13, 138 he had had a dog's berth on board, 321 the change from a dog's berth to an officer's).

5. But a live dog is better than a dead lion (40 Dana *Two* 353; Lincoln II 467 But "a *living* dog is better than a dead lion"). Eccl. 9:4; Apperson 376; NC 396; *Oxford* 378; Stevenson 1418:3; Tilley D495; NQ 1 i 352, 370, 404, ii 62; Max Saltmarsh *The Clouded Moon* (1938) 168. See Bishop (1).

6. But an old dog, you know, . . . can't alter his way of barking (32 Kennedy *Swallow* 212; Baldwin *Flush* 243 the new dogs hadn't learned old tricks; Riley *Puddleford* 250 You can't learn old dogs new tricks; Clift *Bunker* 255 It is mighty hard for old dogs to learn new tricks; Clemens *Fairbanks* 104 teach, *Tom* 3 as the saying is; Jones *Batkins* 198 it was hard work "to teach old dogs new tricks"). Apperson 158; NC 399; *Oxford* 645; Stevenson 615:6; Tilley D500; Whiting *Scots* I 160; E. Balmer and P. Wylie *After Worlds Collide* (1934) 263; William McFee *The Harbourmaster* (London 1932) 369 But I tell her you can't make an old dog do new tricks.

7. As active as a tarrier dog (35 Crockett *Account* 54).

8. He'll . . . make us both as 'shamed of ourselves as dogs with tinkittles tied to their tails (71 Eggleston *School-Master* 145).

9. It's dog cheap (36 Haliburton *Clockmaker* I 102; Lowell *Biglow* 309; Saxe *Poems* 147; Barnum *Struggles* 151). Farmer and Henley II 82, 302; NED Cheap 6, Dog-cheap; Stevenson 327:6; Svartengren 346.

10. He is more crookeder in his ways nor a dog's hind leg (40 Haliburton *Clockmaker* III 49). Apperson 122; Coombs PADS II (1944) 22; McAtee 21; NC 396–397; Randolph and Wilson 179; Taylor *Comparisons* 30.

11. Dog drunk (59 Taliaferro *Fisher's* 254). NC 397 Dog (12).

12. Or else he'd a come up with Lizey as easy as a dog arter a coon (51 Stowe *Uncle* 82).

13. As faithful as a dog (35 Crockett *Account* 189). NC 397 Dog (13); Taylor *Comparisons* 38–39.

14. Ferocious as a mad dog (56 Kelly *Humors* 237).

15. They get as full of compliments as a dog is full of fleas (36 Haliburton *Clockmaker* I 123, III 150; Dorson *Jonathan* 96 and it's [a hat] just as chock full of piety now as a dog is full of fleas). Cf. NC 397 Dog (18).

16. Guilty as a dog (57 Riley *Puddleford* 272). Kay C. Strahan *Death Traps* (1930) 180 dog-guilty.

17. I'm as hungry as a dog (58 Hammett *Piney* 51). Apperson 318; Boshears 38:690; NC 397; Stevenson 1201:5; Svartengren 181; Whiting *Scots* I 192 hound.

18. As savidge as a mad-dorg (67 Harris *Sut* 73, 220 a dog).

19. As tired as a dog (39 Smith *Letters* 80; Riley *Puddleford* 162 he felt the awfullest tired any dog ever did; Clemens *Letters* I 297 dog-tired). NC 397; Sidney Horler The *Evil Château* (1931) 237. Cf. Green 394; Halpert 712; McAtee 66; NED Dog-tired; Svartengren 167; Tilley D441; Whit-

ing *Drama* 310:95, *Scots* II 147 Tyke (3); Wilson 533.

20. A mare . . . as yaller as a warter dorg wif the janders (67 Harris *Sut* 37).

21. To blow off one's dogs [i. e., to give up an enterprise]. 35 DA Dog 8 (4).

22. To cut open a dog [i. e., to make a blunder]. 67 DA Dog 8 (6).

23. To die dog for [i. e., to be loyal]. 37 DA Dog 8 (5).

24. The farce of "Dog eat dog" (58 Porter *Major* 118). Barrère and Leland I 317; DA Dog 8 (3); Snapp 64:4; Stevenson 611:1; Whitman Chambers *Dog Eat Dog* (1938); Jane Allen, pseud. *I Lost My Girlish Laughter* (1938) 162; William McFee *The Harbourmaster* (London 1932) 405 It's dog eat dog; Budd Schulberg *What Makes Sammy Run?* (1941) ch. 4 But when you come down to it, it's dog eat dog, ch. 9 I thought of him as a mangy little puppy in a dog-eat-dog world.

25. Dog won't eat dog (35 Kennedy *Horse-Shoe* 133; Haliburton *Nature* II 132). Apperson 158; Bradley 70; NED Dog 15 m; *Oxford* 151; Stevenson 511:1; Stoett 929; Tilley W606; F. D. Grierson *The Empty House* (1934) 133. See Wolf (11).

26. Not to be obliged to keep a dog and do your own barkin' (43 Haliburton *Attaché* IV 288). Apperson 162; NC 399 Dog (51); *Oxford* 329–330; Tilley D482; Richard Hull *Murder Isn't Easy* (1936) 164.

27. Every homely proverb covers a single and grand fact . . . Every dog his day, which covers this fact of otherism, or rotation of merits (38 Emerson *Journals* V 55–56; Dana *Two* 131 "Every dog must have his day, and mine will come by and by," and

the like proverbs, were occasionally quoted; Haliburton *Attaché* IV 26 For every dog has his day in this world; Shillaber *Mrs. Partington* 135; Smith *Arp* 66 Don Quixote says; Clift *Bunker* 8 they have had their day, like other dogs). Apperson 159; NC 397; NED Day 15; *Oxford* 151; Snapp 64: 5; Stevenson 609:8; Tilley D464; Whiting *Drama* 43, 131; W. B. M. Ferguson *The Murder of Christine Wilmerding* (1932) 156; Stark Young *So Red the Rose* (1934) 403; *Catalogue of Political and Personal Satires . . . 1811–1819* (London 1949) IX 818 No. 13013.

28. Jest like the dog-in-the manger (33 Smith *Downing* 56, *My Thirty* 445 No longer, dog-in-the-manger-like can you retain possession; Alcott *Little Women* 500). Apperson 160–161; Farmer and Henley II 303; NC 396; NED Dog-in-the-manger; *Oxford* 151; Stevenson 601:1; Tilley D513; Yamamoto *Dickens* 44–45; Christopher Bush *The Death of Cosmo Revere* (1930) 179.

29. "If you once give a dog a bad name," —as the sailor-phrase is,—"he may as well jump overboard" (40 Dana *Two* 121; Clemens *Roughing* I 69). Apperson 159; NC 398; NED Dog 15 h; *Oxford* 237; Snapp 64:6; Stevenson 605:8; Woodard PADS VI (1946) 36; J. J. Farjeon *The Mystery of Dead Man's Heath* (1934) 46.

30. Hungry dogs will eat dirty puddings (21 Loomis *Farmer's Almanac* 178). Apperson 319; *Oxford* 310–311 Hungry, 566 Scornful; Stevenson 607: 1; Tilley D538.

31. To "return, like the dog to his vomit, or the sow to her wallowing in the mire" (46 Cooper *Redskins* 304). Prov. 26:11; Fife 120; NC 398 Dog (48); *Oxford* 152; Stevenson 2438:2;

Tilley D458; Whiting *Scots* I 160; H. J. Forman *The Rembrandt Murder* (1931) 233.

32. The dog that trots about will find a bone (45 Judd *Margaret* I 127). *Oxford* 152; Stevenson 614:4.

33. The twenty-five per cent list was all dead dogs, wasn't it? [i. e., uncollectible bills]. (54 Smith *'Way* 233).

34. The reverend gentleman . . . who Simon was convinced was "the big dog of the tanyard" (45 Hooper *Simon* 88; Eliason 260 Dick . . . pretends to be the biggest dogg in the meat house; Field *Pokerville* 35 he was the "big dog" at Pokerville). Farmer 53; Schele de Vere 583.

35. I'd sooner die – die, like a dog (25 Neal *Brother J* I 195, III 158 Hale died, like a dog—on the tree bough, 425; Melville *Redburn* 74). NC 397 Dog (27); NED Dog 15 d; *Oxford* 144; Stevenson 499:5; Tilley D509; Whiting *Drama* 310:95, *Scots* I 159; Thorne Smith *Turnabout* (1933) 182, 294, 295.

36. He is made to fetch and carry like a dog (47 Melville *Omoo* 62).

37. Fled like a dog that had been stealing sheep (33 Smith *Downing* 197; Hammett *Piney* 138 The poor, mean feller looked jest like a dog ketched sheep-stealin'; Kelly *Humors* 376 Lev Smith sneaks off like a kill-sheep dog). Cf. Ayers PADS XIV (1950) 79 looks; Boshears 33:209; NC 398 Dog (43).

38. He sneaked away like a dog with his tail between his legs (55 Anon. *New Hope* 178–179). *The New Yorker* Feb. 18, 1956 p. 29 and then he'll be comin' back with his tail between his legs. See Tail (4).

39. Has gone to the dogs (36 Haliburton *Clockmaker* I 310, II 46; Judd *Richard* 184; Curtis *Potiphar* 177; Hammett *Stray* 142; Daly *Man* 49; Clemens *Tramp* II 36). Farmer and Henley III 161–162; Hardie 469:104; NED Dog 14; *Oxford* 242; Stevenson 601–602:4; Stoett 740; Tilley D543; James Aston *First Lesson* (1933) 146.

40. He went outen that shut [shirt] like a dorg outen a badger-barril (67 Harris *Sut* 215).

41. And be hanged like a dog (21 Cooper *Spy* 227; Neal *Brother J* I 234 He shall not go off, before a multitude —like a dog—with a halter about his throat, 285 Him hang . . . like dogue; Haliburton *Old Judge* II 293 and they will escape hanging like dogs). Apperson 161 Dog (82); *Oxford* 696; Tilley D497; Whiting *Drama* 310:95, *Scots* I 192 Hound (6).

42. Coots that hanker round sich foreign she critters like lean dogs a huntin around a bone (44 Stephens *High Life* II 23). Cf. NC 398 Dog (46).

43. Held on to 'em like a dog to a root (33 Smith *Downing* 118, *Letters* 85; Stephens *High Life* II 15 sassafras root; Riley *Puddleford* 103). Hardie 471:179; McAtee 62. See Dog (55).

44. They've hunted me like a dog (55 Melville *Israel* 121; Richardson *Secret* 173).

45. He dont no [know] enough to learn a dog to bark (63 Wiley *Billy* 185).

46. He leads the life of a dog (36 Haliburton *Clockmaker* I 237; Dana *Two* 256, 393; Melville *Redburn* 129; Irving *Wolfert* 240 dog's life; Chamberlain *Confession* 199 Davis . . . had a miserable dog's life; Whitcher *Widow* 91; Clemens *Letters* I 107 live like a dog, *Roughing* I 108 a perfect dog's life). McAtee *Grant County* 4; NC 397:34; NED Dog 15 g; *Oxford* 152;

Tilley D521; Whiting *Drama* 342:504; Thorne Smith *The Stray Lamb* (1931) 138.

47. To put on the dog. 71 DA Dog 5 b.

48. The English ministers are quarreling like "dog's delight" (54 Shillaber *Mrs. Partington* 367).

49. The mare runs like a scared dog (58 Porter *Major* 117). K. T. Knoblock *Take Up the Bodies* (1933) 35 yellow dog.

50. Excuse me, Mr. Quail, I can't stop. I've got to see a man about a dog. I forgot all about it until just now (66 Boucicault *Flying Scud* 221). DA See 5; Partridge 742; Stevenson 602: 4; Anthony Berkeley, pseud. *The Second Shot* (1930) 224.

51. My body shakin' like a dog with the ager (59 Taliaferro *Fisher's* 117).

52. Kill him like a dog! (72 Clemens *Roughing* I 59). Lilian Bamburg *Beads of Silence* (1927) 113.

53. We now shot them like dogs (34 Crockett *Life* 88; Fairfield *Letters* 172 We'll shoot you like von dog; Hammet *Stray* 343; Clemens *Roughing* I 102). S. H. Adams *The Gorgeous Hussy* (Boston 1934) 191.

54. Spitting fire at each other like dogs and cats (44 Stephens *High Life* I 127). See Cat (58).

55. My pussy she cousin stuck to him like a dog to a briar (44 Stephens *High Life* II 96). McAtee 62. See Dog (43).

56. Treated like a dog (40 Dana *Two* 247; Clemens *Tom* 74). McAtee *Additional* 10; NC 399 Dog (52); Hulbert Footner *Murder Runs in the Family* (1934) 25.

57. Don't turn me out like a dog (66 Boucicault *Flying Scud* 160; Daly *Man* 34 You wouldn't turn away a dog . . . on such a night as this). Thom-as Hood *Poems* (1844, London 1911) 366 a very bad night in which to turn out a dog; Charles Brackett *Entirely Surrounded* (1934) 223 You couldn't have turned a dog away in that storm; W. C. MacDonald *Destination Danger* (Philadelphia 1955) 111 At the same time, I'd hate to see even a dog go cold on a night like this.

58. You know I would work like a dog to do it (42 Irving *Attorney* 148; Stephens *High Life* I 216 Working like a dog to arn a decent living; Clift *Bunker* 301 I've worked like a dog; Eggleston *Circuit* 17 Work like dogs in a meat-pot). McAtee *Additional* 10; NC 399 Dog (53); Taylor *Comparisons* 35; Octavus R. Cohen *Scrambled Yeggs* (1930) 90.

59. Yellow dog under the wagon. 57 DA Yellow dog 3. See Team (2).

60. See Me, Way (13).

Dogiron. Clapshaw's ole mam wer es deaf es a dogiron (67 Harris *Sut* 92).

Dog-pie. I up and told him he was as mean as dog-pie (c60 Paul *Courtship* 36–37).

Dog-vane. Her tongue goes like a dog-vane in a calm, first one way and then another (24 Cooper *Pilot* 80). Cf. *Oxford* 698; Tilley V16, W223; Whiting *Drama* 331:346.

Dogwood. His eyes glared like two dogwood blossoms (51 Burke *Polly* 53).

Doll. She was painted up like a doll (53 Baldwin *Flush* 172). Cf. NC 399.

Dollar, 1. A dollar saved . . . is as good as a dollar earned (59 Shillaber *Knitting-Work* 313). Bradley 71. See Penny (3).

2. Bright as a "new dollar" (43 Robb *Squatter* 22; Stephens *High Life*

II 4, *Homestead* 273; Hammett *Stray* 219 as one of them half dollars; Shillaber *Mrs. Partington* 210 a dollar; Whitcher *Widow* 229 a dollar; Clemens *Fairbanks* 157 a dollar). Boshears 35:372; Fife 118; McAtee 16; NC 399; Taylor *Comparisons* 21; C. B. Clason *Blind Drifts* (1937) 59 new dollar; Dorothy Baker *Young Man with a Horn* (Boston 1938) 11.

3. Her voice had a tone clear as the ring of a silver dollar (53 Willis *Fun* 63).

4. As proud to see you as ef he'd found a silver dollar with a hole through it (45 Hooper *Simon* 120). Cf. Woodard PADS VI (1946) 37.

5. Sound as a dollar. 52 DA Dollar 2 b (1). NC 399; Taylor *Comparisons* 77.

6. Mixes up a dose that would float a dollar a'most, and made him drink it (40 Haliburton *Clockmaker* III 202). Cf. NC 494 Wedge.

7. Squire Longbow shone like a dollar (57 Riley *Puddleford* 293). Taylor *Comparisons* 72. Cf. NC 456 Penny 8.

8. I will invest my bottom dollar in this kind of money (66 Smith *Arp* 119; Clemens *Tramp* I 174 you bet your bottom dollar). Bartlett 61; DA Bottom 6 (2); Farmer 80; McAtee 15; Thornton I 93, III 43; NQ 12 vii 211, 318, 399; John G. Brandon *The One-Minute Murder* (1935) 24.

Doll rags. He . . . could "beat him into doll rags" whenever it came to a measurement (45 Hooper *Simon* 13; Burke *Polly* 83 I'll tear you into dollrags cornerways).

Donkey, 1. Lookin' as wise as a donkey (40 Haliburton *Clockmaker* III 84).

2. They know just as much about their business as a donkey does of music (55 Haliburton *Nature* I 169). Cf. Apperson 18–19; *Oxford* 16; Tilley A366; Whiting *Scots* I 133 Ass 3.

Doomsday. A new dress and bonnet, without which she would not go to church till Doomsday (52 Cary *Clovernook* 102; Whitcher *Widow* 297 I can't git 'em to listen to me if I try till Doomsday). Apperson 136; Whiting *Scots* I 160; Margery Allingham *Kingdom of Death* (1933) 108 come Doomsday.

Door, 1. She warn't behind the door when beauty was given out (53 Haliburton *Sam* II 273, *Season-Ticket* 11). Green 36, 55; Eudora Welty in *The New Yorker* Dec. 5, 1953 p. 56 When the brains were being handed around, my son Daniel was standing behind the door. Cf. Figh PADS XIII (1950) 14; Randolph and Wilson 192.

2. It is late shutting the door when the mare is stolen (45 Judd *Margaret* II 184). Apperson 598–599; NC 480; *Oxford* 587; Tilley S838; Philip MacDonald *Warrant for X* (1938) 47.

3. There was never a door shut up but what there was another one open (70–73 McCloskey *Across* 71). Apperson 469; Lean IV 184; *Oxford* 475–476; Stevenson 618:8; Tilley D563; R. S. Surtees *Mr. Sponge's Sporting Tour* (London [1853]) 198 When one door shuts, another opens, 261 When one door shuts, another opens, say the saucy servants.

4. I've got them in the door [i. e., in my power]. (63 Clemens *Enterprise* 63, *Sketches* 19 the other dog had him in the door, so to speak, *Sandwich* 178 as the missionaries say). DA Door c.

Doornail. Dead as a door nail (25 Neal *Brother J* III 277; Kennedy

Horse-Shoe 191; Briggs *Harry* I 207; Dorson *Jonathan* 100; Anon. *New Hope* 230; Smith *'Way* 21, 26, *My Thirty* 377; Jones *Country* 68, 154; Kelly *Humors* 104, 173; Riley *Puddleford* 162; Cary *Married* 120; Taliaferro *Fisher's* 58). Apperson 137; Boshears 36:475; Farmer and Henley II 260-261; NC 399; NED Dead 32 b; *Oxford* 131; Taylor *Comparisons* 33; Tilley D567; Colver Harris *Going to St. Ives* (Philadelphia 1936) 146; Anthony Wynne, pseud. *Door Nails Never Die* (Philadelphia 1939) 312 a proverb which has outlived its truth.

Door-post. He's as deaf as a door-post (59 Boucicault *Dot* 136). Cf. Apperson 138–139; *Oxford* 132; Taylor *Comparisons* 33.

Dose, 1. I'm glad he got his dose [i. e., got killed]. (56 Jones *Wild* 86; Harris *Uncle Remus* 190 I done got my dose [i. e., got enough], 192). Cf. DA Death 4.
2. To go through [it, one] like a dose of salts. 37 DA Dose 1.

Dough, 1. His heart . . . was now as heavy as dough (33 Hall *Soldier's Bride* 148; Haliburton *Old Judge* I 222 Pickinick stirs are as heavy as dough).
2. Looking as soft as dough, and as meechin as you please (36 Haliburton *Clockmaker* I 126, III 182, 252, *Attaché* III 106–107, 274, *Old Judge* II 138, *Nature* I 47, 142). Svartengren 266.

Doughnut. I wish I may be biled for a doughnut if . . . (58 Hammett *Piney* 58).

Dove, 1. As contented as a dove settin on its eggs (44 Stephens *High Life* II 233).

2. A charming creature to be sure; coy as a dove (50 Mitchell *Reveries* 76).
3. Babes that are innocent as the dove (28 Neal *Rachel* 143, 196).
4. In deportment, meek as the sucking dove (55 Thomson *Doesticks* 179). Bartlett 807. Cf. Hardie 468: 58; NC 400; Svartengren 65 mild.
5. Soft as doves . . . the ladies (47 Melville *Omoo* 287). Svartengren 267 dove's down.
6. He has . . . no more sense than a suckin' dove (76 Nash *Century* 27–28).

Down-east. Right away from down-east ain't ye, where a cow an' a caff an' a calico gown is a gals portion (33 Neal *Down-Easters* I 103).

Downstairs. It is better to walk down stairs voluntarily and quietly, than to be kicked down (57 Jones *Country* 112–113).

Dozen. See Baker (2).

Dragon, 1. As for Siar, he was as mad as the Dragon (56 Whitcher *Widow* 244). Whiting *Scots* I 161.
2. Heah's Santanner right across the San Jacinto, a raisin' the old dragon, and whose to help? (58 Hammett *Piney* 279).

Dragoon. Daughters, who dressed as fine as dragoons (23–24 Irving *Tales* 259).

Draw. See Blister (2).

Dream. Nothin' but a dream, and they allers go by contraries (57 Riley *Puddleford* 200; Haliburton *Season-Ticket* 30 Instead, the events of life, like dreams, appear in the words of the old proverb, "to go by contraries," 287 What onder the sun is the use of dreams, for in a general way they certainly do go by contraries?; Alcott *Little Women* 515 Women, like dreams, go by contraries). Apperson 164; Lean III 451; *Oxford* 157; Stevenson 621–622:15; Tilley D588; J. H. Wallis *The Capital City Mystery* (1932) 55.

Dress. Now Susan did not really think that dress made the man (43 Hall *Purchase* I 160). See Clothes (1).

Dried apple. I wouldn't care a dried-apple d—m for *"the boys"* to know it (45 Hooper *Simon* 100; Taliaferro *Fisher's* 117 let on like I didn't care a dried-apple durn, 204 Didn't care a dried-apple cuss whether I lived ur died, 260 durn).

Drill-sergeant, 1. I'll sit as straight as . . . a drill-sergeant (53 Haliburton *Sam* II 66).
2. He strutted up and down like a drill-sergeant (71 Eggleston *School-Master* 206).

Drink, vb., 1. We have an old sayin', "Only what I drink is mine" (53 Haliburton *Sam* II 169). A "German Polander" is speaking. Champion 242:110; Stevenson 630:11.
2. See Fish (12).

Drinks, sb. Nature seems to have intended him for President of the United States, but "left him two drinks behind" (56 Durivage *Three* 207–208).

Drive. See Jehu.

Drop, sb. (1), 1. No more than a drop in the bucket (33 Smith *Downing* 167; Haliburton *Clockmaker* II 294; Clemens *Sketches* 389 it was only a drop in the ocean). Cf. "The Betagat [a Burmese religious text]," says Malcom, "declares that the tears shed by any one soul, in its various changes from

eternity, are so numerous that the ocean is but a drop in comparison" (Conant *Earnest Man* 137). NED Drop 5 b.
2. Much alike, both on 'em, as two drops o' milk (25 Neal *Brother J* II 20).
3. Not much, but every drop helps (57 Melville *Confidence-Man* 44). Cf. Apperson 188; NC 400; *Oxford* 177; Tilley D617, W935.
4. The worthy old gentleman, who took a drop now and then (52 Dorson *Jonathan* 49).
5. Others . . . had taken a drop too much (53 Cary *Clovernook* 2d Ser. 50). Farmer and Henley II 330 (drop in the eye); Partridge 243.

Drop, sb. (2). To get the drop on. 69 DA Drop, sb. 3 b.

Drop, vb., 1. To drop on oneself [i. e., to become informed about]. 76 DA Drop, vb. 4 c.
2. See Chestnut (2), Potato (15), Ten-pins.

Dropping, 1. It was only the continual dropping that wore the stone at last (55 Haliburton *Nature* I 337; Jones *Country* 130 If the constant water-drop will wear away the rock; Shillaber *Knitting-Work* 29 little worriments, like the dropping that wears the stone, undermine our temper). Job 14:19 The waters wear away the stones; Apperson 112; NC 400; *Oxford* 107–108; Stevenson 2463:1; Tilley D618; Whiting *Drama* 249; Yamamoto *Dickens* 408; Edgar Wallace *The Flying Squad* (1929) 144 Water constantly dripping wears away stone; Carolyin Wells *Horror House* (Philadelphia 1931) 30 like the continual dropping that wears away a stone.
2. A man who would fight at the

dropping of a handkerchief (73 Clemens *Roughing* II 69, *Tramp* II 172). See Hat (5).

Drown. So courage! My Viking, and never say drown (49 Melville *Mardi* I 59). See Die, vb. (3).

Drug. Powders and pills were voted mere drugs in the market (47 Melville *Omoo* 158, "Cock-a-doodle-doo!" in *Works* XIII 147 a drug in the market; Clemens *Gilded* I 250–251). NED Drug, sb. 2; *Oxford* 159; H. S. Keeler *The Riddle of the Yellow Zuni* (1930) 161.

Drum, 1. His bump of vanity's big as a base drum (58 Hammett *Piney* 157).
2. As melancholy as an unbraced drum (37 Neal *Charcoal* 132).
3. The crew said she was as tight as a drum, and a fine sea boat (40 Dana *Two* 224; Sedley *Marian* 414 a sail). Louis Pendleton *Down East* (1937) 157 a ship's bottom.

Drum-head. I can testify't he was always as tight as a drum-head [i. e., miserly]. (56 Whitcher *Widow* 96). Cf. NC 400; Randolph and Wilson 176; Taylor *Comparisons* 82.

Drummond light, 1. A gilt-edged ile that burned like a Drummond light (c60 Paul *Courtship* 33). Cf. NED Drummond light (a limelight invented by Thomas Drummond, 1797–1840).
2. Bulliphant's face shone like a drummond-light (57 Riley *Puddleford* 144).

Drunk. See Cooter, Dog (11), Fiddler (1), Fool (11), Loon (2), Lord 2 (1), Owl (2, 3), Peep (1), Piper.

Dry. See Ashes (1), Bone (3), Broadway, Charity-sermon, Chip (1), Cob (1), Corncob (1), Herring (3), Image (1), Lime-kiln, Maid (2), Oven (1), Powder-horn, Powder-house, Powder-monkey, Sahara, Stick (1), Wheat-bin.

Dublin. See Head (23).

Duck, 1. We must now drink with the ducks (50 Melville *White Jacket* 67). Apperson 165; *Oxford* 157.
2. His heart, that was floundering away like a duck in a mud-puddle (44 Stephens *High Life* I 243, II 222).
3. My heart would begin to flutter like a duck in a puddle (34 Crockett *Life* 48).
4. A fellow that had no more watch in him . . . than a duck on a rainy day (35 Kennedy *Horse-Shoe* 25). Cf. Apperson 169:5; NED Duck 2 thunder-storm.
5. Catch a duck asleep! (43 Hall *Purchase* I 120, 254). Cf. Weasel (8).
6. And give them such cute teaching as makes them know how to make ducks and drakes of us out yonder when they comes among us (35 Crockett *Account* 58). Cf. Stevenson 1236:10 I esteem it all but ducks and drakes; NQ 12 vii 229.
7. "Making ducks and drakes" of the pretty little fortune left him by his defunct sire (56 Durivage *Three* 231, 292). Apperson 169; Farmer and Henley II 337–338; NED Duck and drake; *Oxford* 161; Stevenson 644:13; Tilley D632; H. C. Bailey *Black Land, White Land* (1937) 282.
8. I could swim like a duck (54 Smith *'Way* 64; Hammett *Piney* 253). Boshears 34:290; NC 401; *Oxford* 636; Taylor *Comparisons* 37; Tilley F328; Victor Bridges *Grasmere Island* (1922) 146.
9. He took to the water like a duck (40 Cooper *Pathfinder* 202; Richardson

Beyond 177 He takes to them as instinctively as a young duck to water). NED Duck 2; *Oxford* 642; Helen Burnham *The Telltale Telegram* (1932) 236.

10. Turnin up the whites of his eyes like a duck in thunder (36 Haliburton *Clockmaker* I 95, III 89, *Attaché* I 274, *Sam* I 305, *Nature* I 42, 223, II 14; Anon. *New Hope* 161). Apperson 169; Green 34; NED Duck 2; *Oxford* 163; Stevenson 645:6; NQ 7 vi 67.

11. You'll see me down upon him like a duck upon a June-bug (35 Longstreet *Georgia* 75; Haliburton *Clockmaker* III 40 He walked 'em into him as a duck does a June bug, 182, *Sam* I 291 snapped . . . up . . . as quick as, II 308 snap us up as, *Nature* II 313 pounces on him like; Judd *Margaret* I 116 running out of the store like a duck arter a tumble-bug; Porter *Major* 15 a Mr. Wash . . . snapped me up like a duck does a June-bug). Cox *Southern Folklore Quarterly* XI 264–265; Randolph and Wilson 181; Taylor *Comparisons* 36; Thornton I 505; Tidwell PADS XI (1949) 13. Cf. NC 420 Hawk (4). See Cock (3), Nighthawk.

Duck-pond. The water as smooth as a duck-pond (40 Dana *Two* 117, 363 calm). Cf. Mill-pond (2).

Duke Humphrey. A cadaverous figure who had been invited for no other reason than that he was pretty constantly in the habit of dining with Duke Humphrey (54 Hawthorne *Mosses* 85). Apperson 153; Farmer and Henley II 287–288; *Oxford* 145–146; Stevenson 578–579:11; Tilley D637; NQ 4 iv 313, 397, xii 439; 6 iv 166, 337, 475, v 58, 175; 10 xi 158.

Dull. See Beaver (2), Desert (2).

Dumb. See Beetle (2), Codfish (2), Death (6), Oyster (2), Stone (7).

Dun. See Hell (3).

Durn, 1. I tole him as how I didn't keer three continental derns for his whole band with Micajah Harp throw'd onto the top (74 Eggleston *Circuit* 148). DA Continental 2 b; Farmer 164–165; McAtee 19; Schele de Vere 276; Stevenson 1237:3; Thornton I 198.

2. I can't say that es a human shut [shirt] I'd gin a durn for a dozin ove em (67 Harris *Sut* 32).

3. Not wurf a durn (67 Harris *Sut* 25, 151).

Dust, sb., 1. Money was as plenty as dust (72 Clemens *Roughing* II 12).

2. Bello must bite the dust (49 Melville *Mardi* II 229; Shillaber *Mrs. Partington* 331 Thousands of the French . . . chivalry bit the mud (not dust) of Agincourt; Field *Pokerville* 86). NED Dust 4; *Oxford* 340 kiss; Stevenson 647:3; Tilley D651 lick. Cf. Farmer and Henley II 346; Taylor *Investigations* 258.

3. And you'll have to come down with that five-thousand dollar dust (76 Nash *Century* 68, 69).

4. If they go to kickin up a dust here, they'd better look out (33 Neal *Down-Easters* I 61; Stephens *High Life* I 127 since they got a kicking up a dust every other day at the Capitol, 143 Instid of kicking up a dust in your upper storey, it [cider] goes to the right spot at once, II 193 he seems to be kickin up an all fired dust). Farmer and Henley II 346; NED Dust 5 raise, kick up; Partridge 250; Stevenson 647:1.

5. Shook from my feet the dust

of New Orleans (65 Richardson *Secret* 94). Matt. 10:14; NED Dust 4; *Oxford* 578; Stevenson 647:5; Louis Cochran *Hallelujah, Mississippi* (1955) 212 he . . . would shake the dust of Hallelujah from his feet forever.

6. The opposition folks throw dust in your eyes (34 Davis *Downing* 212, 251; Crockett *Exploits* 22; Thompson *Major* 153; Shillaber *Mrs. Partington* 372; Durivage *Three* 130). Apperson 172; NED Dust 4; *Oxford* 162; Stevenson 647:6; Tilley D650; NQ 6 xi 166, 313; Carl Clausen *The Gloyne Murder* (1930) 60.

Dust, vb. To get up and dust. 60 DA Dust, vb. 1.

Dutch, 1. A little Dutch courage (35 Crockett *Account* 23; Hammett *Wonderful* 57). NED Courage 4 d; *Oxford* 162; Stevenson 437:10; John Donavan *The Case of the Rusted Room* (1937) 273. Cf. Farmer 219–220; Farmer and Henley II 348; NQ 6 iii 289, 458, 498; 8 ii 304, vii 88, 314, 375; 9 xi 47, 97, 237.

2. More'n half the words are all Dutch (54 Shillaber *Mrs. Partington* 293; Wiley *Billy* 41 it is Dutch to me). Green 128; NED Dutch B 2 b (High Dutch, double Dutch); Partridge 250; Schele de Vere 82–83. Cf. McAtee 64.

3. It beats the Dutch (68 Clift *Bunker* 77). Bartlett 196–197; DA Dutch 3 c; Farmer 219; Farmer and Henley II 347–348; NED Dutch B 3 c; Partridge 250; Schele de Vere 83; Stevenson 648:4; Thornton I 51, III 126; John Dos Passos *The Big Money* (1936) 293.

4. The recusant must either knock under, or be knocked down, which is . . . all the same in Dutch (37 Neal *Charcoal* 34).

5. I always sets old kit [his rifle] talkin' Dutch to them varmints (56 Kelly *Humors* 71, 216 The hostler having reappeared, and talked a little Dutch [i. e., emphatically] to the host, that worthy turned to the traveler).

Dutchman, 1. This was an immense sail, and held enough wind to last a Dutchman a week,—hove-to (40 Dana *Two* 417).

2. Which, as the Dutchman said, "is as fair a ding as eber was" (34 Crockett *Life* 208).

3. If they ain't, I'm a Dutchman! (57 Jones *Country* 134, 273). Farmer and Henley II 349; NED Dutchman 2 b; *Oxford* 162; Partridge 251; Stevenson 648:3; NQ 7 iv 25, 158, 256; Kenneth Livingston *The Dodd Cases* (1934) 199.

4. Slept as soundly as a Dutchman between two feather-beds (40 Dana *Two* 432).

5. Staggered about like a drunken Dutchman (55 Thomson *Doesticks* 157). Cf. Svartengren 193, 202; Tilley M399.

6. But it [a gift] is to him as the celebrated anchor was to the Dutchman; he can neither use nor exhibit it (37 Neal *Charcoal* 51). *Oxford* 162–163.

Dutch uncle. I must talk to you both like a Dutch uncle (37 Neal *Charcoal* 201). NC 401; *Oxford* 162; NQ 1 vii 65; 3 iii 471; 6 ii 309, 473; CXLVIII 28, 88; Neil Bell, pseud. *The Disturbing Affair of Noel Blake* (1932) 140.

Dwarf. You're like the dwarf with two heads, who is so old that nobody can tell his age (58 Porter *Major* 156).

E

Each. To each his own (48 Emerson *Letters* IV 9). Stevenson 1836:3; A. Otto *Die Sprichwörter und sprichwörtlichen Redensarten der Römer* (Leipzig 1890) pp. 337–338.

Eagle, 1. My heart is as free as the eagle (49 Haliburton *Old Judge* I 146).

2. Have you never tried to capture the eagle-bird by chance? [i. e., to gamble]. (65 Sedley *Marian* 180). Cf. NED Eagle 8.

3. [He had] ne'er a red cent, bein' played out chasin' the eagle 'board the boat (65 Sedley *Marian* 193).

4. To fly the eagle [i. e., to indulge in high-flown oratory]. 72 DA Eagle 1 b (2).

5. To make the eagle scream. 47 DA Eagle 1 b (1).

6. An eye like an eagle (42 Irving *Attorney* 74). Stevenson 730:4 eagle-eyed.

Ear, sb. (1), 1. You got up on your ear (72 Clemens *Roughing* II 286). DA Ear sb. 1 (1 b 1); NED *Supplement* Ear sb. 1 (1 h); Sinclair Gluck *Shadow in the House* (1929) 200. Cf. Stevenson 653:4 on his ear.

2. I know of many a fine feller that would give his ears to git sich a card (44 Stephens *High Life* II 36). NED Ear 1 c.

3. Grinning from ear tu ear (44 Stephens *High Life* II 6; Harris *Uncle Remus* 27). NED Grin vb. 1 b.

4. To hop off on one's ear [i. e., with a flea in one's ear]. 73 DA Ear sb. 1 (1 b 1).

5. Set those Siouxes and the brood of squatters by the ears (27 Cooper *Prairie* 239; Neal *Down-Easters* I 66 fall together by, 132 set us altogether by; Smith *Downing* 86, 120; Haliburton *Clockmaker* I 162 take any two men that are by the ears, *Old Judge* I 237; Derby *Phoenixiana* 233 we all get together by the ears, and a pretty state of affairs ensues; Riley *Puddleford* 32; Lowell *Biglow* 261). Apperson 76; NED Ear 1 d; *Oxford* 576; Stevenson 654:5; Tilley E23; Whiting *Drama* 343:518, *Scots* I 162; NQ 6 iii 185, 331, 476; Anthony Abbot, pseud. *About the Murder of the Nightclub Lady* (1931) 43.

6. I'll pull down the whole Longbow nest around her ears (57 Riley *Puddleford* 249). NED Ear 1 c.

7. If the feller's ears don't burn then ther ain't no truth in old sayins (44 Thompson *Major* 79; Whitcher *Widow* 299 If her ears didn't burn that afternoon, I'm mistaken). Apperson 173; Green 25; McAtee 24; *Oxford* 164; Stevenson 651–652:12; Tilley E14.

Ear, sb. (2). Dang it, Uncle Moss, ef your bones don't fall as hard on the floor as ears o' corn on the floor of an empty corn-crib at a corn-shuckin', and nearly as fast (59 Taliaferro *Fisher's* 220).

Early, 1. Guess wen he ketches 'em at thet he'll hev to git up airly (48 Lowell *Biglow* 59; Clemens *Roughing* II 99 a man had to get up ruther early to get the start of old Thankful Yates). Farmer and Henley II 351; NED Early 1 a; Partridge 252; Whiting *Drama* 333:380; NQ 4 x 163; Kenneth Whipple *The Fires at Fitch's Folly* (1935) 14. Cf. Morning (9).

2. The earlier the better (55 Anon. *New Hope* 363). Cf. Sooner.

Earth. That arr true as the yearth (43 Robb *Squatter* 96).

Earthquake, 1. As savage as a young arthquake (44 Stephens *High Life* II 87).

2. A litill slower then a yearthquake wakes weasels (67 Harris *Sut* 70).

Easily. See Hand (2), Shingle (1).

East, 1. He was born *too far east* to be overreached by a specious pretender (32 Hall *Legends* 79).

2. If ther's any body that *won't* knuckle tew her, I tell ye they have to take it about east (56 Whitcher *Widow* 303; Lowell *Biglow* 289 They'll take 'em out on him 'bout east). Bartlett 198; DA East 2; NED East 2 b.

Easy. See A, B, C. (2), Bear (6), Cat (33), Corn shucking, Cradle, Get out, Glove (1), Hand (1, 2), Jack (4), Lion (8), Log (1), Lying, Mocking bird, Nature (1), Nothing (1), One (2), Outdoors (2), Potato (1), Print (1), Radish (1), Rocking chair, Shoe (1), Shooting (1), Trigger (1), Turtle (2), Water (2).

Eat. I had some idea, in imitation of Sardanapalus, "all in one day to see the race, then go home, eat, drink, and be merry, for all the rest was not worth a fillip" (Porter *Major* 14). Is. 22:13 let us eat and drink, for tomorrow we die; Eccl. 8:15; Luke 12:19; I Cor. 15:32; I Esdras 9:54; Stevenson 666:3; Earl D. Biggers *Seven Keys to Baldpate* (1913) 225 Eat, drink, and be merry, for tomorrow the cook leaves, as the fellow says; F. P. Keyes *Dinner at Antoine's* (1948) "Isn't there something in the Bible itself about eating and drinking and making merry? . . . "And forget about the rest of the quotation," Aldridge requested.

Eavesdropper. Eave-drappers don't hear no good er deyse'f (80 Harris *Uncle Remus* 54–55). See Listeners.

Ebenezer, 1. When an amateur hunter gets his Ebenezer set on a real deer (56 Kelly *Humors* 110). DA Ebenezer 2.

2. Puts my Ebenezer up (36 Haliburton *Clockmaker* II 203, 305, III 62, *Attaché* I 26, II 207, 271, *Old Judge* II 21, 166, *Nature* I 114, *Season-Ticket* 247; Stephens *High Life* I 16, 38, 50, II 115; Smith *My Thirty* 286; Paul *Courtship* 196). 1 Sam. 7:12; DA Ebenezer 1; Farmer 222; NED Ebenezer, *Supplement* Ebenezer 1 b; Thornton I 281.

Ebony. As black as ebony (49 Haliburton *Old Judge* II 199; Hawthorne *Twice-Told* 260, 293; Irving *Wolfert* 41). Taylor *Comparisons* 17; Tilley E56a; W. B. Seabrook *Jungle Ways* (London 1931) 131.

Edge, 1. Ef a feller don't make every aidge cut, he's in the background directly (45 Hooper *Simon* 59). Green 28.

2. The edge not being worn off, they [first appearances] were sure to be gratifying, either in one way or the

other (37 Neal *Charcoal* 122). NED
Edge 2 a.

3. See Age (2).

Edom. You'll see 'em in Edom 'fore
they ventur' to go where their doc-
trines 'ud lead 'em (67 Lowell *Biglow*
323). Cf. Ps. 60:8, 108:9; Jer. 49:17;
Joel 3:19.

Eel, 1. As bare as a skinned eel (59
Browning *Forty-four* 379).

2. As close as the skin to an eel (44
Stephens *High Life* II 100).

3. Grog makes me feel as good-
natured as a sooped eel (40 Haliburton *Clockmaker* III 155).

4. He is a perfect vegetable, as limber as an eel (59 Shillaber *Knitting-
Work* 181). Whiting PADS XI (1949)
28 n. 5.

5. He is as sensitive as a skinned
eel (43 Haliburton *Attaché* I 244).

6. As slippery as a soaped eel (43
Haliburton *Attaché* II 59, *Old Judge*
II 66 a tongue as slippery as an eel,
Nature II 60 an eel; Stowe *Uncle* 62
eels; Hammett *Stray* 147 an eel; Smith
My Thirty 276 an eel). Apperson 579;
Boshears 40:929; Fife 119; McAtee
58; NC 402; *Oxford* 597; Taylor *Comparisons* 74; Tilley E60; Carter Dickson, pseud. *The White Priory Murders*
(1934) 205. Cf. Whiting *Drama* 311:
108, *Scots* I 162.

7. I begun to feel as subtle and
slimpsey as an eel (44 Stephens *High
Life* I 198).

8. Supple as an eel (36 Haliburton *Clockmaker* I 136, II 44, III 76,
Old Judge II 82).

9. If there warnt a hullaballo there
then there aint no eels in Tusket (53
Haliburton *Sam* II 300). See Snake
(6).

10. I just let folks be, and suffer
them to skin their own eels (55 Haliburton *Nature* II 145). DA Eel 2 b;
Stevenson 669:9. See Axe (3), Fox
(10), Skunk (4).

11. It seemed to him as if [it] was
a sliding out of his grip like a wet eel
(44 Stephens *High Life* I 249). Cf.
Apperson 179; DA Eel 2 b (greased
eel); *Oxford* 298; Tilley E61; Whiting
Drama 311:108.

12. Made the old feller squirm like
a speared eel (62 Browne *Artemus*
22).

13. Mrs. Slick, a twisting round like
an eel (44 Stephens *High Life* I 154).
See Apperson 715 wriggle.

14. You might jist as well try to
hold an eel by the tail (37 Neal *Charcoal* 133).

Egg, 1. Leaving his aunt's head as
bald . . . as an egg (55 Jones *Winkles* 179, *Wild* 197, *Country* 373).
Hardie 466:17; NED Egg 6 c (egg-
bald); Stevenson 117:4; H. K. Webster *Who Is the Next?* (Indianapolis
1931) 227.

2. Wat wer es plum blind es if his
eyes wer two tuckil aigs (67 Harris
Sut 243).

3. As full of flattery as an egg is
full of white & yolk both (38 Fairfield
Letters 245; Stephens *High Life* II
101 chuck full of brains as an egg is
full of meat; Shillaber *Mrs. Partington*
265 as full of mischief "as an egg is
full of meat," to use an expressive
modernism; Melville *Confidence-Man*
241 full of fun as an egg of meat;
Cary *Married* 400 as full of news;
Clift *Bunker* 39 as full of good reading as an egg is of meat). Fife 118;
NC 402; NED Egg 4 b; Stevenson
672:1; Svartengren 294; Whiting
Drama 311:109.

4. Leaving his aunt's head . . . al-

most as smooth . . . as an egg (55 Jones *Winkles* 179).

5. As sure as aiggs (c60 Paul *Courtship* 44). Gladys Mitchell *The Saltmarsh Murders* (Philadelphia 1933) 75.

6. As sure as eggs is eggs (35 Haliburton *Clockmaker* I 290, II 224, 303). Apperson 179–180; Farmer and Henley II 354, VII 30; NED Egg 4 b; *Oxford* 632; Stevenson 2249:14; Tilley E84. Cf. Taylor *Comparisons* 79; Gladys Mitchell *Death in the Wet* (Philadelphia 1934) 246.

7. In spite of the saw that "eggs is eggs" (68 Saxe *Poems* 162).

8. Leaving his aunt's head . . . almost as . . . white as an egg (55 Jones *Winkles* 179). Whiting *Scots* I 162.

9. No blartin'—no cacklin' afore layin' the egg (43 Haliburton *Attaché* IV 186). Cf. Apperson 77; *Oxford* 74; Tilley C5.

10. In the language of his class, the Perfect Bird generally turns out to be "a bad egg" (55 Hammett *Wonderful* 319). Bartlett 776; Farmer 31; NED Egg 4 a; Partridge 25; Stevenson 670: 7; Thornton I 32; John Dos Passos *The 42d Parallel* (1930) 394.

11. We crept along as careful as if we was going on eggs (39 Smith *Letters* 100; Judd *Richard* 383 Richard found he had eggs to walk on). McAtee *Grant County* 10; NC 403; NED Egg 4 a (tread); Stevenson 670:11; Tilley E91; C. G. Givens *The Jigg-Time Murders* (Indianapolis 1936) 193 those guys are walking on eggs.

12. He'll put them down as if they were eggs (51 Stowe *Uncle* 180).

13. She looked dreadful womble-cropped, as if she'd jest made the discovery of a new mare's egg in the Bible, and was waiting to see what sort of critter it would hatch out (44 Stephens *High Life* II 127). Apperson 402; *Oxford* 408; Tilley M658. See Mare (2).

14. Ef hit hedn't, I'd a dun been busted intu more scraps nur thar's aigs in a big catfish (67 Harris *Sut* 84).

15. I've felt like sucking eggs ever since I got on the durned staff, and may be a little more fighting will make me feel better (66 Smith *Arp* 45; Clemens *Tom* 8 anybody that'll take a dare will suck eggs). McAtee 42; NC 398 Dog (44).

16. I lost one half of a Dollar [at gambling] . . . and that Broke me from sucking Eggs that is one thing s[h]ore (62 Wiley *Johnny* 38).

17. I had too many eggs in that basket, as your father used to say (38 Fairfield *Letters* 207; Holmes *Poet* 40 A man should not put all his eggs in one basket). Apperson 180–181; Faden 228; NC 403; *Oxford* 169; Snapp 93:14; Stevenson 672:2; Stoett 1044; Tilley E89; Charles Barry, pseud. *Death in Darkness* (1933) 156.

18. Broken eggs can never be mended (Lincoln V 389 n. 2, 350, VI 48 Still, to use a coarse but an expressive figure, "broken eggs can not be mended"). Cf. Stevenson 671:7 The omelette will not be made without the breaking of eggs; A. E. Apple *Mr. Chang's Crime Ray* (1928) Eggs cannot be unscrambled.

19. All eatables, from "the egg to the apple" (43 Hall *Purchase* I 181). Apperson 180; *Oxford* 169; Stevenson 154–155:5; Tilley E85.

20. See Grandmother (2).

Eggshell, 1. His face's as smooth as an eggshell (43 Lewis *Odd* 145).

2. You are in the palm of the hand of your Great Father at Washington,

who can crush you like an egg-shell! (55 Irving *Wolfert* 302).

Egypt. It looked as dark as Egypt (36 Haliburton *Clockmaker* I 249, 272, III 174, *Attaché* II 117, *Old Judge* II 44; Hawthorne *Mosses* 548 some Egyptian darkness in a blacking jug; Smith 'Way 72, 326; Alcott *Little Women* 35). Exod. 10:22; NC 403; Stella Gibbons *Miss Linsey and Pa* (1936) 24.

Elbow, 1. The fiddlers began to put on elbow grease (44 Stephens *High Life* I 186; Clift *Bunker* 72 using wind power instead of elbow grease, 268 In farming, there is no ile like elbow grease). Farmer and Henley II 355–356; Green 131; NC 403; NED Elbow-grease. Cf. Apperson 181; *Oxford* 170; Stevenson 674:7.

2. So as we two wanted a little more elbow room (43 Hall *Purchase* I 172; Irving *Wolfert* 273 That's too close neighborhood; I want elbow-room; Willis *Paul* 189 We see that we shall require the elbow-room of another chapter; Barnum *Struggles* 471 You will find plenty of elbow room in America). Green 131; NED Elbow-room; Stevenson 674:4; Thornton I 283; Tilley E104.

Elder stalk. [The tree] was as hollow as an elder stalk (55 Anon. *New Hope* 64).

Element. He was in his element (45 Hooper *Simon* 63; Lowell *Biglow* 283). NED Element 12; Stevenson 821:3; Stoett 548; Tilley E108.

Elephant, 1. To draw the elephant [i. e., to succeed in a difficult enterprise]. 72 DA Elephant 3.

2. "They had seen the elephant." . . . It is a cant term we have, and signifies "going out for wool and com-

ing back shorn" (55 Haliburton *Nature* II 402; Thomson *Doesticks* 170 had invited me to be present and see "the elephant"; Kelly *Humors* 81, 189, 261, 322, 336, 386; Porter *Major* 87 I axed him if he'd ever seed the Elephant; Wiley *Billy* 36 since I seen you last I hav seen the elephant [i.e., unusual sights], 69 The Twenty-fourth Ohio Volunteer Infantry had seen the elephant [i. e., been in battle] several times, and did not care about seeing him again unless necessary; Sedley *Marian* 180 I've seed the elephant, and I know his way, 196, 216; Richardson *Beyond* 202 Among thousands of returning emigrants we passed one jovial party with a huge charcoal sketch of an elephant on their wagon cover, labeled, "What we saw at Pike's Peak"; Clift *Bunker* 89 I've been on a journey of five thousand miles, and got home alive. I've seen the elephant from trunk to tail; Barnum *Struggles* 360 So I went with him to "see the elephant" [there *was* an elephant in this instance]; Jones *Batkins* 238 You won't go without seeing the elephant?, 288 I had seen a real elephant at the "Saint's Rest"). Bartlett 199–200, 568–569; DA Elephant 3; Farmer 224; Farmer and Henley II 356–357; Partridge 256; Schele de Vere 600; Stevenson 675:6; Thornton I 286–287; Constance Rourke *Troupers of the Gold Coast* (1928) 29; Elisabeth Margo *Taming the 49er* (c1955) 3, 95 the first smash of the California stage, *Seeing the Elephant.* Cf. Lion (16), Tom Haynes.

Emerald. Green spots, green as emerald (25 Neal *Brother J* III 382; Stephens *Mary Derwent* 188 the grass was green as emeralds). NED Emerald 5 c (emerald-green).

Empty. See Barrel, Irishman (2), Nut-shell (2).

End, 1. It was a sharp sort of *practice,* but the *ends* seemed to justify the *means* (56 Kelly *Humors* 314). *Oxford* 171; Taylor *Index* 30; Tilley E112; A. R. Clark *High Wall* (1936) 190 copybook maxim.

2. The rest on 'em took it up, till the poor feller he didn't know which eend his head was on (44 Stephens *High Life* I 81, 151, 171, 186, 203, II 28).

3. Old Miss Stallins was flying about like she didn't know which eend she stood on (44 Thompson *Major* 119).

4. But as everything good is sure to have an end (37 Neal *Charcoal* 167; Haliburton *Clockmaker* III 138 Rejoicin', like everything else in the world, must have an eend at last; Stephens *High Life* II 233 But there must al'ers be an eend tu every thing that's sweeter than common; Hammett *Wonderful* 251 But there is an end to all things—except, perhaps, a ring; Whitcher *Widow* 311 Well, every thing arthly comes to an eend; Porter *Major* 14 The race, like all things, had an end). Apperson 8; *Oxford* 180; Tilley E120; Whiting *Drama* 223; Albert Halper *The Foundry* (1934) 333 everything must come to an end sometime.

5. When a rascal in either the States or Texas had fairly arrived at the end of his rope (58 Hammett *Piney* 210, 292, 309; Clemens *Tramp* I 53 string). NC 403; Stevenson 2007:6; Tilley E133; Anne Austin *The Black Pigeon* (1929) 75. Cf. Tether.

6. Affairs were all wrong-end-foremost at the Longbows (57 Riley *Puddleford* 249).

7. Not bigger . . . than the leetle eend—o' nothin'—sharpened, as the Irishman said (25 Neal *Brother J* I 145; Haliburton *Clockmaker* III 70 He actilly looked as small as the little eend of nothin' whittled down; Stephens *High Life* II 2 if I don't use her up til she aint bigger than the tip eend of a pine stick whittled down to nothing; Taliaferro *Fisher's* 258 We'd look like the peaked eend uv nothin'; Paul *Courtship* 47 I felt like the little end of nothin' whittled down tew a pint). Bartlett 807; Randolph and Wilson 192. Cf. NC 484.

8. He nebber come out o' de little eend o' de horn yit (33 Neal *Down-Easters* II 40; Neal *Charcoal* 95 I'm always crawling out of the little end of the horn; Smith *Downing* 123, *My Thirty* 395; Haliburton *Clockmaker* I 68, 222 They'll find the, III 75 pass out of the, *Nature* I 243 slip out of the; Willis *Fun* 203 that "tight place" in life, commonly understood in New England as "the going in at the little end of the horn"; Porter *Major* 24; Taliaferro *Fisher's* 128 Whether I got out'n the big eend or the little eend o' the horn; Wiley *Johnny* 273 thrust through; Clift *Bunker* 262). Apperson 370–371; Bartlett 359; Bey PADS II (1944) 57; Coombs PADS II (1944) 23; Farmer 160, 305; Farmer and Henley III 355; Hardie 471:188; McAtee 40; Stevenson 1172:3; Thornton I 282, 544; Tilley E131; NQ 7 iv 323, vii 257, 376; S. L. Bradbury *Hiram Harding of Hardscrabble* (Rutland, Vt., 1936) 174.

9. Everything goes to loose ends where there ain't no woman (57 Riley *Puddleford* 256). Cf. Farmer 225; Whiting *Drama* 20; R. M. Kennedy *The Bleston Mystery* (1929) 145.

10. We have got hold of the right

eend of the rope (55 Haliburton *Nature* I 25). Cf. NED Stick 14 e; *Oxford* 39, 171; Tilley E132; Whiting *Drama* 343:528, *Scots* I 163; F. D. Grierson *The Empty House* (1934) 246.

11. If the York folks don't know how to hold up their eend of the yoke at that trade, I'm a coot (44 Stephens *High Life* I 190). Stevenson 680:11; Joseph Kirkland *Zury* (Boston 1887) 453 Zury he 'llaowed he c'd keep up his eend of the double-tree 'n' pay his debts.

12. The mystery of "bringing two ends of the year together" (35 Kennedy *Horse-Shoe* 15; Haliburton *Clockmaker* III 88 so as to make two eends cleverly meet together when the year is out, *Sam* I 130 to make two ends meet; Stephens *High Life* I 5 It's as much as we can du to make both eends meet afore the banks shut up days; Smith *'Way* 217 in order to make both ends meet; Irving *Wolfert* 244 had resorted to smuggling to make both ends meet; Durivage *Three* 155 contrived . . . to make both ends meet at the expiration of each year). Apperson 392; NC 403; NED End 24; *Oxford* 58; Stevenson 678:9; Stoett 546; Tilley E135; Anthony Gilbert, pseud. *The Body on the Beam* (1932) 196.

13. Who'd expect to see a tater All on eend at bein' biled (46 Lowell *Biglow* 45).

14. I can see which end of the stick is up (71 Jones *Batkins* 281). Stevenson 680:5 to know which end is up.

Enemy. The surest way to make enemies was to have too many friends (71 Jones *Batkins* 45).

Engine. In punctuality, she was . . . as inexorable as a railroad engine (51 Stowe *Uncle* 176).

Enough, 1. Enough is as good as a feast, you know (54 Melville "Poor Man's Pudding" in *Works* XIII 192; Holmes *Professor* 280 The Koh-i-noor had got enough, which in such cases is more than as good as a feast; Barnum *Struggles* 522). Apperson 184–185; Bradley 73; NC 403; *Oxford* 174; Smith *Browning* 225; Stevenson 699: 3; Tilley E158; Whiting *Drama* 192, 241, *Scots* I 163; NQ 4 v 137; A. B. Cox *The Amateur Crime* (1928) 42; T. H. White *The Sword in the Stone* (1939) 77 with the proper whisper of Enough-Is-As-Good-As-A-Feast.

2. Enough's enough (33 Neal *Down-Easters* I 16; Anon. *New Hope* 163; Whitehead *Wild Sports* 142; Clemens *Innocents* I 63 Enough of a thing's enough). Apperson 185; NC 404 Enough of anything's enough; *Oxford* 174; Snapp 103:9; Stevenson 699:8; Tilley E159; Whiting *Drama* 139; Jesse Lilienthal *Gambler's Wife* (Boston 1933) 255; F. P. Keyes *The River Road* (1945) 226.

3. And I says, Well, ef God sends me to hell He can't make me holler 'nough nohow (71 Eggleston *School-Master* 159).

Enticing. See Jay-bird (1).

Erebus. It was as black as Erebus (40 Dana *Two* 433; Willis *Fun* 140; Hammett *Wonderful* 16; Paul *Courtship* 27; Richardson *Beyond* 245). Inglis Fletcher *Roanoke Hundred* (1948) 461. Cf. NED Erebus (dark); Svartengren 237.

Error. One error always leads to another (40 Haliburton *Clockmaker* III 54).

Ethiopian. Can the leopard, or the Ethiopian, or the liar change at will? (25 Neal *Brother J* III 303; Haliburton

Clockmaker II 215 though you cannot make the Ethiopian change his skin, you can make the Frenchman change his language, Sam I 128; Hawthorne Twice-Told 132 On hearing this sudden question, the Ethiopian appeared to change his skin [literal]). Jer. 13: 23; Apperson 53; Oxford 693; Stevenson 1673:6; Tilley E186, L206; Whiting Drama 41; Dorothy L. Sayers Busman's Honeymoon (1937) 123 the Ethiopian shall stay black and leave the leopard her spots.

Evanescent. See Dew (1).

Even, 1. I'll be even with him, and one to carry, see if I ain't (74 Eggleston Circuit 48). Stevenson 710:2. See Two (3).

2. To get even. 45 DA Even 1 b.

Evening. The evening red, the morning gray, Is a sure sign of a fair day (52 Cary Clovernook 264). Matt. 16: 2–3; Apperson 186; Oxford 176–177; Stevenson 2474–2475:11; Taylor Index 30–31; Tilley E191; Charles Reade Hard Cash (1863, London [1913]) 156.

Event, 1. Coming events cast their shadows before (45 Cooper Chainbearer 302, Redskins 314; Hawthorne Twice-Told 142; Thomson Doesticks 272; Smith My Thirty 272 and poetry says). Bradley 73; Oxford 104–105; Snapp 108:132; Stevenson 711:5; C. J. Daly The Man in the Shadows (1928) 45; J. P. Marquand Melville Goodwin, USA (Boston 1951) 418, 420. Cf. NQ 1 v 418, vi 506, xi 238, 435.

2. Great events hinge upon small causes (53 Hammett Stray 349). Cf. Apperson 271.

Everyone. Everyone for himself (44 Stephens High Life II 56). Apperson 189; Oxford 178; Tilley M112; Whiting Drama 343:531; Christopher Hale, pseud. Ghost River (1937) 109.

Everything. Everything has its price (29 Emerson Journals II 275, Works II 115 it is impossible to get anything without its price; Cooper Redskins 42). Cf. NC 441.

Evil, 1. Of two evils . . . choose the least (43 Haliburton Attaché I 190; Hall Purchase I 19 "of two evils to bear the least"; Melville Pierre 78 lesser; Richardson Beyond 316). Apperson 654; NC 404; Oxford 181; Snapp 83:45; Stevenson 715:11–716: 5; Stoett 1304; Tilley E207; Whiting Drama 155, Scots I 164; Alice Campbell The Murder of Caroline Bundy (1932) 256.

2. I have heard the proverb that there is no evil but can speak (33 Emerson Journals III 202).

Example. Example, it is said, is better than precept (71 Jones Batkins 475). Apperson 194; Oxford 181; Stevenson 718:3; Tilley E213.

Exception, 1. But exceptions only prove the rule (50 Melville White Jacket 60; Hammett Wonderful 38 It is said; Sedley Marian 65 You know exceptions are admitted to prove general rules; Nash Century 19 The idea that the 'exception proves the rule' won't do, 48). Apperson 194; NC 404; Oxford 181–182; Stevenson 2014:1; Tilley E213a; NQ 2 xii 347, 463; 3 i 177; 4 xi 153, 197–198, 258, 433–434; F. P. Keyes The River Road (1945) 223 Merry's [a proper name] the exception that proves the rule; Rufus King Murder by the Clock (1929) 45.

2. There are exceptions to every rule, you know (54 Langdon Ida 195;

Baldwin *Flush* 2 The axiom, that there is some exception to all general rules; Barnum *Struggles* 493; Nash *Century* 18 Of course there are exceptions to all rules, 19 No fact is better established than that 'there are exceptions to all general rules'; Clemens *Tramp* I 263 there are exceptions to the rule). Apperson 540; *Oxford* 552; Stevenson 2014:1; Tilley R205; Raymond Robins *Murder at Bayside* (1933) 8 Thomas Evans was the proverbial exception to the rule; R. S. Surtees *Mr. Sponge's Sporting Tour* (London [1853]) 67 there is no rule without exception. See Rule (2).

Exchange. A fair exchange is no robbery, all the world over (38 Haliburton *Clockmaker* II 34, *Attaché* IV 252; Thompson *Major* 92 Exchange is no robbery). Apperson 199; Green 23; Hardie 463:65; *Oxford* 182; Stevenson 719:6; Tilley C228; Christopher Bush *The Perfect Murder Case* (1929) 36 Exchange; W. Y. Darling *The Bankrupt Bookseller* (Edinburgh 1947) 34 and older teaching announced to a sceptic world before Genovesi [an Italian economist], that fair exchange is no robbery; M. C. Keator *The Eyes through the Trees* (1930) 7.

Experience, 1. Experience is the best teacher, after all (56 Whitcher *Widow* 375; Melville *Confidence-Man* 65 "Experience, sir," originally observed the sophomore, "is the only teacher"; Alcott *Little Women* 283 Mrs. March knew that "experience was an excellent teacher"). Apperson 195 Experience is the mother of al things; Bradley 73; *Oxford* 182 Experience is mother of prudence; Snapp 87: 21b; Stevenson 724:5; Stoett 1675; Tilley E221 Great experience . . . is the very mother and maistres of wisedome; Whiting *Scots* I 164; NQ 7 viii 369, ix 59; Virginia Rath *Murder with a Theme Song* (1939) 138. See Charles Knapp "Experientia docet" *Classical Weekly* XXIX (1935) 1.

2. Experience is said to be a hard schoolmaster (69 Barnum *Struggles* 523). Apperson 195; NC 404; *Oxford* 182; Snapp 87:21a; Tilley E220.

Extremes, 1. All extremes meet (38 Haliburton *Clockmaker* II 165, I 93 don't extremes meet?, II 255, III 190, *Attaché* I 275, II 107, IV 160, 277 in proverbial philosophy, extremes are said to meet, *Old Judge* I 191 the maxim, *Season-Ticket* 364; Cooper *Redskins* 67; Barnum *Struggles* 573 illustrate the old proverb sufficiently to show how extremes occasionally met in my Museum). Apperson 195; *Oxford* 183; Stevenson 658:16, 729:11; J. B. Cabell *The Line of Love* (1926) 181.

2. Extremes nary way are none o' the best (36 Haliburton *Clockmaker* I 131). Cf. *Oxford* 183, 628; Tilley E222, E224.

Eye, 1. The violets blue as a baby's eyes (c58 Stephens *Mary Derwent* 188).

2. It's all in my eye (36 Haliburton *Clockmaker* I 117, *Old Judge* I 148, *Nature* II 63; Dana *Two* 402 "Land in your eye!" said the mate . . . "they are ice islands"; Mayo *Kaloolah* 97 Mrs. Smith's tears are all in my eye; Melville *Omoo* 59 the whales he had in his eye (though Flash Jack said they were all in his); Hammett *Wonderful* 252 what is vulgarly termed "all in their eye"; Durivage *Three* 48). NED Eye 2; Arthur Train *The Adventures of Ephraim Tutt* (1930) 680.

3. And old laws are "all my eye" (34 Davis *Downing* 141). Farmer and Henley I 34–36; NED Eye 2 h; Stevenson 732:9; Herbert Adams *The Golf House Murder* (Philadelphia 1933) 198.

4. Tender es a sore eye (67 Harris *Sut* 294). Cf. NC 404 Eye (3).

5. It's a lucky thing as heyes ain't got tooth, or you'd eat him (66 Boucicault *Flying Scud* 196).

6. The old adage, "the eye of the master does more work than both his hands" (54 Smith *'Way* 29). Apperson 196 Eye (13); *Oxford* 183. Cf. NC 404.

7. We are all eyes and ears (49 Haliburton *Old Judge* II 15).

8. The very sight of Yankee galls is good for sore eyes (36 Haliburton *Clockmaker* I 324, II 199, *Attaché* III 111, *Old Judge* I 316; Robb *Squatter* 61 she *was* a critter good for weak eyes; Stephens *High Life* I 228). Apperson 589; McAtee 57; NC 474–475; R. M. Baker *Death Stops the Bells* (1938) 142.

9. My boots blacked up till they glistened like a gal's eye (44 Stephens *High Life* II 84).

10. To cut an eye. 27 DA Eye 1 b (1).

11. To be cut in the eye [i. e., intoxicated]. 57 DA Eye 1 b (4).

12. I didn't let on, but kep a top eye on him (43 Robb *Squatter* 99; Lowell *Biglow* 82 You must keep a sharp eye on a dog that hez bit you once; Shillaber *Mrs. Partington* 365 he always carries it before him so he can have an eye on it; Jones *Winkles* 42 I shall keep my eye on you).

13. He keeps his eye on the main chance (55 Melville *Israel* 18, *Confidence-Man* 264 With one eye on the invisible, did he not keep the other on the main chance?). Apperson 391; *Oxford* 398; Stevenson 312:2; Tilley 235; Whiting *Drama* 343:533. See Chance.

14. Joe laughed at me, and said he'd keep his eyes wide open (58 Hammett *Piney* 257; Harris *Uncle Remus* 60 he'd sorter keep one eye open). Stevenson 735:3.

15. But keep an eye out for Farnes (57 Jones *Country* 123). DA Eye 2 b (8).

16. To keep one's eyes peeled. 53 DA Eye 1 b (3); Farmer and Henley IV 89.

17. Keep your eyes skinned (51 Burke *Polly* 75; Hammett *Stray* 40; Jones *Wild* 63, *Country* 233; Bennett *Border* 121; Harris *Sut* 126; Lowell *Biglow* 325). Bartlett 204; DA Eye 1 b (2); Farmer 230–231; Farmer and Henley II 361, IV 89; Partridge 450; Randolph and Wilson 284; Schele de Vere 199; Stevenson 735:6; Thornton I 297. Cf. McAtee 37.

18. I could almost pipe my eye to think on't (50 Melville *White Jacket* 113). Babcock 262; *Oxford* 501.

19. And yet he never . . . shipped as much water as you could put in your eye (45 Mayo *Kaloolah* 418). Lean III 359.

20. To skin the eyes off [i. e., to beat completely]. 73 DA Eye 1 b (6).

21. If his eyes don't stick out tomorrow, I'll lose my guess (Stephens *High Life* I 29).

22. I see it all with half an eye (49 Haliburton *Old Judge* II 86; Kelly *Humors* 82 a man with half an eye might see Smith would be as blind as owl [i. e., drunk] in the course of the evening). Apperson 279; Tilley H47; NQ 6 iv 28, 136.

23. If he don't sleep with one eye open (33 Neal *Down-Easters* I 7;

Mayo *Kaloolah* 59 tell general to sleep with one eye). Apperson 577; *Oxford* 596; Tilley E250.

24. Two eyes ain't much better than one, if they are both blind (36 Haliburton *Clockmaker* I 86). Cf. Apperson 654; *Oxford* 679; Stevenson 730:3; Tilley E268.

25. Afore you could bat yer eye (59 Taliaferro *Fisher's* 127).

26. See Pig (8), Weather-eye.

Eyelid. Here you have to "hang on with your eyelids" and tar with your hands (40 Dana *Two* 60, 228 and nothing left for Jack to hold on by but his "eyelids"; Smith *My Thirty* 454 Lettin' the whole country hang by the eye-lids—war and all; Haliburton *Season-Ticket* 31 Hold on by your eyelids and belay where you be). Christopher Bush *The Case of the Chinese Gong* (1935) 82 eyebrows.

Eye-teeth, 1. He ought to have cut his eye-teeth (32 Kennedy *Swallow* 212; Neal *Down-Easters* I 3; Davis *Downing* 47, 53–54, 236, 298, 310; Haliburton *Clockmaker* I 302, II 29, 90 Whenever a feller is considerable 'cute with us, we say he has cut his eye teeth, he's tolerable smart, 176, 244

they'll larn you how to cut your eye-teeth, them galls, 319, III 210, *Attaché* II 142, III 283–284 I had my eye-teeth sharpened before your'n were through the gums, IV 252 and sharpened my eye-teeth a few, *Sam* I 53, *Season-Ticket* 101, 240; Robb *Squatter* 175; Stephens *High Life* I 27, 45, 62–63, 81, 213 A feller that's got his eye teeth in his head can al'ers see enough to larf at in his sleeve; Burke *Polly* 30; Willis *Paul* 36; Taliaferro *Fisher's* 111; Sedley *Marian* 219 A few thousand 'cute chaps with their eye teeth cut same as his'n; Jones *Batkins* 129). DA Eye 1 b (2); Farmer and Henley II 362; NC 488; NED Cut vb. 38, Eye-tooth 1 (b); Stevenson 2352:7; Thornton III 133; Hulbert Footner *A Self-made Thief* (1929) 142. Cf. Irving *Attorney* 216 If you've cut your wisdom-grinders.

2. They talk about the Yankees having a nack of cheating people out of their eye teeth (44 Stephens *High Life* I 190; Durivage *Three* 195 You'd hev' a fellur's eye teeth afore he knowed it, ef you wanted 'em). McAtee 58.

3. The whole operation was like . . . jerking out eye-teeth (56 Kelly *Humors* 132).

❧ F ❧

Face, 1. All painted and varnished up as neat and shining as one of your New York gal's faces on a Sunday (44 Stephens *High Life* I 46). Cf. Face (11).

2. It's all as plain as the face of the bull yonder (55 Jones *Winkles* 417). Cf. Boshears 39:795; Peter Hunt, pseud. *Murder at Scandal House* (1933) 18 your face.

3. Cussed himself black in the face (79 Clemens *Tramp* I 20). *Oxford* 635 swear; Tilley F15; Dorothy L. Sayers *Suspicious Characters* (1931) 336 swear.

4. Quoting the old proverb— "Strike me in the face, but refuse not my yams" (49 Melville *Mardi* II 296). A manufactured proverb.

5. We would have supposed that the results of flying directly in the face and eyes of all authority would have satisfied him for a while (58 Hammett *Piney* 183; Clemens *Innocents* I 30 That . . . was simply flying in the face of Providence). NED Face 4 b; *Oxford* 211 Providence; Stevenson 741:7.

6. How can you have the face to talk to me? (51 Burke *Polly* 149). Farmer and Henley II 363; NED Face 7 a.

7. Taters, I daren't look 'em in the face (66 Boucicault *Flying Scud* 158). Cf. NED Face 2 b.

8. This movement puts a new face upon affairs (64 Locke [Nasby] *Struggles* 123). NED Face 10; Stevenson 741:5; Tilley F17.

9. It was, therefore, time to "run his face" (45 Hooper *Simon* 47; Lowell *Biglow* 286 Men thet can run their face for drinks). Bartlett 543; DA Face 1 b (1); McAtee 53; NED Face 7 b; Schele de Vere 303, 325; Thornton I 299. Cf. Farmer and Henley II 363.

10. Sir Harry . . . set his face against the acquaintance (50 Willis *Life* 284). Leviticus 20:3; Stevenson 740:2. Cf. *Oxford* 576; Tilley F18.

11. Shinin' like a gal's face when she's a fixin' to be married (44 Stephens *High Life* II 194–195). Cf. Face (1).

12. 'T aint by no means agreeable to have dead folks throw'd in yer face from mornin to night (56 Whitcher *Widow* 225). Apperson 683–684; NED Face 2 f; *Oxford* 410; Tilley W336.

13. To travel on one's face [i. e., on credit]. 56 DA Face 1 b (2).

14. She is not the first . . . that wears two faces in this business (46 Cooper *Redskins* 66; Jones *Batkins* 458 your own friend . . . carries two faces). Apperson 654; NED Face 2 a; *Oxford* 679; Tilley F20; Whiting *Drama* 368:920, *Scots* I 165. Cf. Stevenson 741–742:8.

Facts, 1. All the world over, facts are more eloquent than words (47 Melville *Omoo* 223). Stevenson 742:3 more powerful than arguments.

2. Facts are stranger than fiction (53 Haliburton *Sam* I 5, 34 There are stranger things . . . in rael life than in fiction). Bradley 74; E. J. Millward *The Copper Bottle* (1929) 64. See Truth (5).

3. Facts is waterproof (66 Boucicault *Flying Scud* 197). Cf. Apperson 198; *Oxford* 185.

4. Always twittin a feller upon facts (68 Clift *Bunker* 72, 104 twitting on facts, riles up people dreddfully). Cf. Tilley J43.

Fade. See Flower (5).

Fail. One resolve uppermost in their minds, "never to say fail" (58 Field *Pokerville* 110). See Die, vb. (3).

Fair, 1. Softly, softly . . . fair and softly (25 Neal *Brother J* I 158, II 362). Whiting *Drama* 242, 364:858. Cf. Apperson 585; NED Fair adv. 7; *Oxford* 185–186; Stevenson 1083:1, 1372:5; Tilley S601.

2. Make things all fair and square (47 Melville *Omoo* 60). Bartlett 205.

3. See All (3, 4), Bootjack (3), Peach (2).

Fair-weather. Your fair-weather speeches to Squire Dickens to his face (23 Cooper *Pioneers* 392, *Pilot* 350 a little fair-weather talk; Kennedy *Swallow* 303 a fair-weather friend). NED Fair-weather 2; W. B. M. Ferguson *The Murder of Christine Wilmerding* (1932) 19.

Faithful. See Dog (13).

Fall. See Hailstones (2).

False. See Bulletin, Hell (5).

Familiar. See Brother (1).

Familiarity. The old adage holds true, about familiarity breeding contempt (49 Melville *Mardi* I 36; Richardson *Secret* 101, *Beyond* 256, 518 No familiarity, however long, makes it prosaic). Apperson 203; NC 405; NED Familiarity 6; *Oxford* 190; Snapp 107: 106; Stevenson 756:6; Tilley F47; Whiting *Drama* 156, *Scots* I 166; NQ CLXXI (1936) 46, 124; Raoul Whitfield *Death in a Bowl* (1931) 64.

Family. Never mind—it's all one, all in the family too (51 Melville *Moby-Dick* I 123).

Far, 1. So far so good (33 Neal *Down-Easters* II 142; Haliburton *Clockmaker* II 78; Melville *Typee* 79 So far so well; Clemens *Sandwich* 171). *Oxford* 602; Stevenson 993:1; Colver Harris *Murder in Amber* (Philadelphia 1938) 242.

2. See Humming bird (3).

Farm. My farm troubles me, for a farm and a wife soon run wild if left alone long (43 Haliburton *Attaché* IV 56).

Fast, 1. The game of fast and loose (40 Haliburton *Letter* 191; Eggleston *Circuit* 32 He only meant to play fast and loose a while). Apperson 500; Farmer and Henley II 376; *Oxford* 504; Stevenson 1807:7; Tilley P401; Whiting *Drama* 344:541, *Scots* I 166; R. G. Anderson *The Tavern Rogue* (1934) 188.

2. See Bread (1), Church (1), Contract-work, Fence (6), Hail (1), Horse (7), Lightning(1), Pine stump (1), Rifle gun, Star (2), Wolf (6).

Fat, sb. 1. I reckon I was about the last one to get on—no chance to holler "fat and go last" (66 Smith *Arp* 41).

2. The fat was all in the fire (33 Smith *Downing* 216, *Letters* 35, 44,

My Thirty 251; Haliburton *Clockmaker* I 282, *Letter* 192; Langdon *Ida* 31; Whitcher *Widow* 194; Hammett *Piney* 67, 177; Porter *Major* 126; Lincoln III 411; Taliaferro *Fisher's* 120; Nash *Century* 37 Then you'll have the fat in the fire, father, 63). Apperson 205; Farmer and Henley II 377; NED Fat sb. 3 c; *Oxford* 193; Snapp 93:34; Stevenson 764:5; Tilley F79; E. S. Gardner *The Case of the Curious Bride* (1934) 199; M. McCarthy *The Groves of Academe* (1952) 71, 96.

Fat, adj., 1. If that ain't cutting it fat, I'll be darned [i. e., making excessive demands on one's forbearance]. (37 Neal *Charcoal* 65, 66 That's considerable fatter—it's as fat as show beef; Curtis *Potiphar* 131 is cutting it rather too fat; Kelly *Humors* 88 [He] got married, and cut it very "fat"). NED Cut vb. 8 b, Fat adj. 4.

2. See Bear (7), Buck (2), Butter (1), Chicken (1), Fool (12), Hog (1, 2), Horse (9), Nebuchadnezzar (2), Pig (1, 2), Porpoise (1), Seal (1, 2).

Fate, 1. As certain as fate (60 Whitehead *Wild Sports* 71; Saxe *Poems* 209).

2. I held him fixed as fate (43 Hall *Purchase* I 32).

3. As sure as fate (34 Crockett *Life* 183; Haliburton *Clockmaker* I 300, *Old Judge* I 28, 316, II 99, *Sam* II 289, 312, *Nature* II 11; Alcott *Little Women* 311). NC 405; Stevenson 2249:7; Svartengren 355; Tilley F81; Mrs. Wilson Woodrow *The Moonhill Mystery* (1930) 37.

4. True as fate (49 Haliburton *Old Judge* II 294; Riley *Puddleford* 350).

Father, 1. Gathered to his fathers (45 Hooper *Simon* 10). Gen. 25:8.

2. As sure as I'm your father (60 Whitehead *Wild Sports* 73).

3. Like father like child (45 Judd *Margaret* II 119). Cf. Apperson 366; NC 406 son; *Oxford* 194 son; Snapp 107:113; Stevenson 770–771:12; Tilley F92; George Meredith *Evan Harrington* (1860) ch. 1, 26.

Favor, 1. The smallest favours in that way were thankfully received (50 Melville *White Jacket* 40; Haliburton *Sam* I 285 you seem thankful for small favours). Lean IV 138 donations, mercies; McAtee 59; Whitman Chambers *13 Steps* (1935) 172; R. S. Surtees *Plain or Ringlets?* (London [1860]) 205 Rabbit, cried Ranger, smallest donation thankfully received; H. Wouk *The Caine Mutiny* (1951) ch. 56 Well, thank heaven for small favors.

2. He . . . has a great dislike to currying favor—as he calls it (32 Kennedy *Swallow* 26; Davis *Downing* 106 to curry favor). Green 108; NED Curry vb. 5 b; Stevenson 782:7; Tilley C724; Whiting *Scots* I 166; Edward Rathbone *The Brass Knocker* (1934) 167.

Fawn, 1. Graceful as a fawn (50 Willis *Life* 122). Taylor *Comparisons* 44.

2. His wife was as handsome as a pet fawn (33 Hall *Soldier's Bride* 107).

3. She . . . became shy as a fawn (c58 Stephens *Mary Derwent* 245).

4. Timid as a fawn (32 Hall *Legends* 92; Stephens *Fashion* 88 young fawn).

Fawn skin. A gone fawn skin. 33 DA Gone 1 (5). See Coon (7).

Feast, 1. Our arrival was hailed with great applause, though we were a little after the feast (34 Crockett *Life* 102–103). Stevenson 70:9 To come after the feast. See Day (32).

2. See Enough (1).

Feather, 1. It was as light as feathers (21 Cooper *Spy* 132, *Pioneers* 263; Hall *Legends* 114, *Purchase* I 189; Smith *Letters* 54; Thompson *Major* 191 as a handfull of chicken feathers; Stowe *Uncle* 25; Cary *Clovernook* 24; Shillaber *Knitting-Work* 179; Boucicault *Flying Scud* 170). Apperson 364; Boshears 38:716; McAtee 40; NC 406; *Oxford* 366; Taylor *Comparisons* 53; Tilley F150; Whiting *Drama* 311:111, 112, *Scots* I 166.

2. Soft as a feather (35 Kennedy *Horse-Shoe* 465). Cf. Svartengren 267 down.

3. The sound and well established principle that, as fine feathers make fine birds (37 Neal *Charcoal* 115; Melville *Pierre* 463 Fine feathers make fine birds, so I have heard . . . but do fine sayings always make fine deeds?; Stephens *Mary Derwent* 253 Well, fine feathers do make fine birds, and no mistake). Apperson 211–212; NC 406; *Oxford* 202; Snapp 70:275; Stevenson 791:7; Tilley F163; H. F. M. Prescott *The Man on a Donkey* (1952) 57 Well, if fine feathers'll make a fine bird; Dennis Wheatley *They Found Atlantis* (Philadelphia 1936) 12.

4. Toucan fowl. Fine feathers on foul meat (57 Melville *Confidence-Man* 175).

5. A feather in the author's cap (40 Haliburton *Letter* 137, *Attaché* IV 215, *Sam* I 40; Stephens *High Life* I 127; Cooper *Satanstoe* 33). William Hone *The Year Book of Daily Recreation and Information* (London 1832) July 28; NC 406; *Oxford* 197; Steven-son 791–792:8; Stoett 1843; NQ 1 ix 220, 378, x 315; 2 iv 331; Frances Noyes Hart *The Crooked Lane* (1934) 150.

6. I felt that it was indeed "the last feather that breaks the camel's back" (69 Barnum *Struggles* 284; Clemens *Sketches* 327 This was the feather that broke the clerical camel's back, *Tom* 97 This final feather broke the camel's back; Locke [Nasby] *Struggles* 592 This wuz the feather that broke the camel's back). Apperson 351; NC 482; *Oxford* 351; Smith *Browning* 223; Stevenson 791:2; Tilley F158. See Camel (2), Grain 1 (1), Ounce (4).

7. All their malice and slander had never "ruffled a feather," as he used to say (57 Riley *Puddleford* 125). Green 310.

8. And he didn't like me, for I could take the feather out of his hair any day (60 Whitehead *Wild Sports* 84).

9. Time or tide did not weigh a feather (32 Kennedy *Swallow* 228). Whiting *Drama* 344:546.

10. Alit like a feather upon the rock (50 Willis *Life* 194).

11. Put the screw on while Goodge is in feather [i. e., in funds]. (66 Boucicault *Flying Scud* 165).

12. But in 1850 all those choice and eccentric spirits . . . were in high feather (65 Sedley *Marian* 186; Clemens *Tom* 10). Farmer and Henley II 379; C. G. Bowers *The Tragic Era* (1929) 320. Cf. Stevenson 791:4.

13. And I moseyed fur home with my feathers cut [i. e., discomfited]. (59 Taliaferro *Fisher's* 73–74). Cf. Apperson 131; NED Feather 2 b; Tilley F160.

14. Challenge him right here, now? Yes, and you'll see how he'll drop his feathers (43 Thompson *Chronicles*

141; Jones *Winkles* 103 our haughty neighbors . . . must lower their feathers).

15. You might knock me down vith a fedder (66 Boucicault *Flying Scud* 183). *Oxford* 342–343; Stevenson 791:3; Georgette Heyer *Behold, Here's Poison* (1936) 289.

16. He'd make the feathers fly (25 Neal *Brother J* I 94, II 339, *Down-Easters* I 66, II 179). DA Feather 1 e (2); Stevenson 792:8. See Fur.

17. Showin' the white-feather (33 Neal *Down-Easters* I 132; Crockett *Exploits* 27; Melville *Omoo* 93 the cooper had sported many feathers in his cap; he was now showing the white one; Kelly *Humors* 49 They, Jenks felt satisfied, would not show the "white feather"; Browne *Artemus Ward His Travels* 63; Bowman *Bear-Hunters* 395; Barnum *Struggles* 471). Farmer and Henley II 380; NED Feather 1 b; *Oxford* 705; Stevenson 791:6; G. B. Means and M. D. Thacker *The Strange Death of President Harding* (1930) 222.

Feed. I'm not in the best sorts today; little off my feed (50 Boker *World* 3; Porter *Major* 51 His horse was off his feed for a week; Holmes *Poet* 64 A little "off my feed," as Hiram Woodruff would say). Farmer and Henley II 381; NED Feed 1 b.

Fellow, 1. He . . . was hail fellow well met (55 Irving *Wolfert* 239; Taliaferro *Fisher's* 194; Richardson *Secret* 100). Apperson 277; Farmer and Henley III 246; Green 174; NED Fellow 3 c; *Oxford* 270; Stevenson 794:1; Tilley H15; James Aston *First Lesson* (1933) 35.

2. Pulled away like a good feller (44 Stephens *High Life* II 187, 191).

Fence, 1. A man represents Not the fellers thet sent him, but them on the fence (48 Lowell *Biglow* 88, 110, 287, 392). DA Fence 2 c; Farmer 236; Farmer and Henley II 384; NED Fence 5 c; Partridge 271; Schele de Vere 193; Stevenson 794:2; Thornton I 310–311; R. C. Woodthorpe *Death in a Little Town* (1937) 71 sitting on the fence.

2. Fences last the longest when the logs are peeled (45 Judd *Margaret* I 278).

3. How the young chaps begun tu make fence along the stun-side walks towards night (44 Stephens *High Life* I 167).

4. To ride the fence. 34 DA Fence 2 b (3, 4).

5. It's allers best to stand Missis' side the fence, now I tell yer (51 Stowe *Uncle* 49). DA Fence 1 b (2); Kay C. Strahan *Death Traps* (1930) 288 it's always a good thing to know which side of the fence a person is on.

6. We went so fast that the posts and rails looked like a log fence (58 Porter *Major* 50).

Ferocious. See Dog (14).

Festus. As rich as Festus (59 Taliaferro *Fisher's* 176).

Fetch. See Dog (36).

Fid. He . . . had got just about one fid too much aboard [i. e., was drunk]. (66 Clemens *Sandwich* 63). Cf. p. 68 "a fid is an instrument which the sailor uses when he splices the main brace on board ship."

Fiddle, 1. She was . . . as fine as a fiddle (34 Davis *Downing* 30; Haliburton *Clockmaker* I 139; Stephens *High Life* I 148; Anon. *New Hope* 145; Kelly *Humors* 285; Alcott *Little*

Women 489). Apperson 211; NED Fiddle 1 b (fit); *Oxford* 201; Stevenson 804:3; Tilley F202; Thornton I 316, III 141; Whiting PADS XI (1949) 28 n. 5; Lee Thayer, pseud. *The Last Shot* (1931) 40.

2. She was as spruce as a fiddle (34 Davis *Downing* 30).

3. A kind of general suspension for want of capital—the fiddle's on hand, but the bow is gone (57 Riley *Puddleford* 150). Cf. Apperson 209; Bradley 74; *Oxford* 199; Stevenson 796:17; Tilley F203; Marjorie K. Rawlings *The Yearling* (1938) 226 The fiddle can't play without the bow.

4. If this don't carry it, you'll have to hang up your fiddle till another year (33 Smith *Downing* 84; Whitcher *Widow* 155 Well, if I couldn't make out better'n she does, I'd hang up my fiddle—that's all; Hammett *Piney* 268 I guess we've all on us about . . . stock cattle, and old red-backs, enough to afford to hang up our fiddles, and wait for high tide). Bartlett 275; DA Hang 3 c (1); Farmer 238; NED Fiddle 1 (b); Stevenson 796:9.

5. To play secont fittle (45 Cooper *Chainbearer* 184; Willis *Life* 232 In everything she played a; Melville *Confidence-Man* 250; Langdon *Ida* 357; Locke [Nasby] *Struggles* 176; Richardson *Secret* 56; Clemens *Sandwich* 9 does not even play third fiddle to this European element). DA Third 2 b; Farmer and Henley II 388–389; NED Fiddle 1 (b); *Oxford* 504; Stevenson 796:11; D. Q. Burleigh *The Kristiana Killers* (1937) 244.

Fiddler, 1. As drunk as a fiddler. 48 DA Fiddler 3 (2). Apperson 166; *Oxford* 159 common fiddeler.

2. It is an old maxim and a very sound one, that he that dances should always pay the fiddler (37 Lincoln I 64; Clift *Bunker* 93 If the young chaps want to cut up, and have music, it is fair they should pay the fiddler). Apperson 133; McAtee *Grant County* 8; *Oxford* 128 music; Stevenson 1798:9 music. See Piper (2).

Fiddle-strings. I'll just appeal, and blow this Court into fiddle-strings (57 Riley *Puddleford* 31, 86). Cf. *Oxford* 226.

Field, 1. A clear field and no favor (40 Cooper *Pathfinder* 201; Durivage *Three* 14 A fair field; Richardson *Beyond* 556 a fair field). Apperson 198–199; *Oxford* 186 fair field and a clear course; Stevenson 1390:9 free field; L. W. Meynell *Mystery at Newton Ferry* (Philadelphia 1930) 206–207 fair field.

2. A long introduction . . . is like a green field to a starving horse when the fence is sorry (59 Taliaferro *Fisher's* 19).

Fierce. See Catamount (1), Hawk (4), Lion (4), Panther (3), Texas Norther, Tiger (1, 4), Turkey 2 (2), Wildcat (1).

Fiery. See Flint (1).

Fifty-six, 1. My boots feel heavier than fifty-sixes (37 Neal *Charcoal* 199).

2. For it seems to me that it would be like loading a fifty-six to kill a fly (c56 Cartwright *Autobiography* 401).

Fig, 1. A fig for your dreams (35 Kennedy *Horse-Shoe* 374; Crockett *Exploits* 59 for the dirty children; Hawthorne *House* 322 for medical advice; Saxe *Poems* 205 for your song). NED Fig 4; Stevenson 797:6; Whiting *Drama* 344:553, *Scots* I 167; Ellery Queen, pseud. *Halfway House* (1936) 103.

2. You would not care a fig for distinction (23 Cooper *Pioneers* 180; Neal *Brother J* I 90, 411, III 10, 256, *Down-Easters* I 14, 46, 127, 151, II 33; Smith *Downing* 191; Fairfield *Letters* 142 He didn't care a fig; Briggs *Harry* I 64; Hall *Purchase* I 98; Cartwright *Autobiography* 188, 321; Lincoln II 363, VI 139; Melville *Omoo* 197, *Redburn* 141 one fig, "I and My Chimney" in *Works* XIII 309; Lowell *Biglow* 111, 268; Haliburton *Nature* I 17, II 212, *Season-Ticket* 363; Willis *Paul* 45; Clemens *Roughing* II 18). Farmer and Henley II 392; *Oxford* 200 not worth; Stevenson 797:6; Whiting *Drama* 345:554; Anthony Abbot, pseud. *About the Murder of the Night Club Lady* (1931) 122.

3. I wouldn't give a fig for all your politics (51 Stowe *Uncle* 88). David Frome, pseud. *The Black Envelope* (1937) 232.

4. He was a gallant six-footer of a Highlander *in full fig* (49 Melville *Redburn* 147). Babcock 260; Farmer and Henley II 392; NED Fig. sb.[3] 1.

5. Office ain't worth a fig (34 Davis *Downing* 160; Saxe *Poems* 69). Apperson 456; NC 407; *Oxford* 200; Stevenson 2642:7; Tilley F211.

Figg. Then he'd up and tell the whole story, till it got to be a by-word. Whenever any one sees a feller now a-doin' big, or a-talkin' big, they always say, "Don't I look pale?" as ready-made Figg said (43 Haliburton *Attaché* IV 39).

Fight, sb. To be spoiling for a fight. 61 DA Spoil vb.

Fight, vb., 1. "Oft he that doth abide, Is cause of his own paine, But he that flieth in good tide Perhaps may fight again." Old Proverb (35 Kennedy *Horse-Shoe* 201 [chapter motto]; Hammett *Stray* 23 the old proverb touching "fighting and running away," in the hope of "living to fight another day"). Apperson 211; NC 407; *Oxford* 200–201; Stevenson 800–801:9; Tilley D79; NQ 3 iv 61–63, 134, viii 444–445; 4 xi 33; CXLVIII (1925) 63, 144, 161, 195; Nellise Child *Murder Comes Home* (1933) 111 one of those discrete [*sic*] persons who love to fight another day.

2. See Bear (30), Cat (58), Lion (13), Tiger (6, 7), Turk (3).

Fighting-cock. We lived like fighting-cocks for a week or two (40 Dana *Two* 202; Kelly *Humors* 114, 322). Green 140; *Oxford* 200; Stevenson 1414:4.

Figure, 1. I meant to . . . cut the hull figger when I once begun (44 Stephens *High Life* II 13, 140–141 if we didn't cut a figger, you never saw one in the multiplication table). Farmer 239; Farmer and Henley II 394; NED Figure 7. Cf. Bartlett 256; DA Figure 2 b, 3 b; Stevenson 802:2; Stoett 565.

2. Mitchell and Olmstead have missed the figure as we say in the "West Countree" in their speculations on the gold mines (29 Eliason 135). DA Figure 3(1).

3. It's jest ez clear ez figgers (48 Lowell *Biglow* 47).

4. They say figures can't lie (45 Cooper *Chainbearer* 156; Derby *Phoenixiana* 39 figures won't lie; Jones *Batkins* 51 I had often heard that "figures will not lie," 412). NC 407; Stevenson 802:1; Willoughby Sharp *Murder of an Honest Broker* (1934) 13.

Fillip. For all the rest was not worth a fillip (58 Porter *Major* 14). NED Fillip 1 b.

Finder. "Finders, keepers," you know (74 Eggleston *Circuit* 139). Bradley 74 Findings is keepings; *Oxford* 201, 386; Stevenson 803:5; David Frome, pseud. *The Eel Pie Murders* (1933) 207 Finders, keepers; M. K. Rawlings *Cross Creek* (1942) 253 For finders seem to be keepers.

Fine. See Cobweb (1), Dragoon, Fiddle (1), Mincemeat, Silk (2), Star (3), Web.

Finger, 1. Fingers were made afore knives and forks (55 Haliburton *Nature* II 249; Porter *Major* 87 Nives is scase, let the balance use their paws —they was invented afore nives, eney how). Apperson 212; Lean III 464; McAtee *Additional* 8; NC 407; *Oxford* 202; Stevenson 805:4; Tilley F235; Woodard PADS VI (1946) 38; Agatha Christie *The Boomerang Club* (1935) 236.

2. My fingers is got stiff with Rhumatiz and cold, and is all Thums (33 Smith *Downing* [Appendix] 242; Neal *Charcoal* 117 he could do almost anything—if by a singular fatality all his fingers were not thumbs; Haliburton *Attaché* III 60 for women's fingers aint all thumbs like men's, 188 My fingers is all thumbs; Melville *White Jacket* 45 Clumsy seamen, whose fingers are all thumbs). Apperson 212; Hardie 466:7; NC 407; NED Finger 3 b; *Oxford* 202; Stevenson 805:1, 2314:10; Tilley F233; R. H. Fuller *Jubilee Jim* (1928) 211.

3. A finger in the pie (33 Smith *Downing* 104, 166, 190, *My Thirty* 284, 416; Irving *Attorney* 320; Stephens *High Life* I 54 poking their fingers into everybody's pie as well as their own, 192 in my dish; Mayo *Kaloolah* 135; Melville *Redburn* 102 for everyone had a finger, or a thumb, and sometimes both hands, in my unfortunate pie, *Moby-Dick* II 49 such a ravenous finger; Baldwin *Flush* 10; Hammett *Piney* 16; Paul *Courtship* 219 in the pastry; Barnum *Struggles* 399 I must have a finger [or at least a "thumb"] in that pie [from a letter by General Tom Thumb]). Apperson 212–213; NED Finger 3 c, Pie 1 c; *Oxford* 202; Stevenson 805:5; Tilley F228; Whiting *Drama* 357:767.

4. For he lets them make him all sorts of trouble, and never lifts a finger (51 Stowe *Uncle* 193). NED Finger 3 a (stir).

5. We lost a fine creature when we let her slip through our fingers (50 Willis *Life* 375; Jones *Country* 205 if you don't want that trump of a girl to slip through your fingers; Anon. *New Hope* 212; Boucicault *Presumptive* 256 I expected to get the money, but I saw it slip between my fingers). Tilley F242.

6. I could put my finger on them (71 Eggleston *School-Master* 245). NED Finger 3 a.

7. I can turn him round with my little finger (56 Whitcher *Widow* 328). NED Finger 3 a; *Oxford* 677.

8. And I'll twist him round my little finger (52 Cary *Clovernook* 278). Stevenson 805:7; Stoett 2409; Winifred Greenleaves *The Trout Inn Mystery* (1929) 217.

9. I can wind her round my finger in every one of 'em (39 Smith *Letters* 48; Alcott *Little Women* 487). Tilley F232; Gail Stockwell *The Embarrassed Murderer* (1938) 227.

10. It is said that when a woman wets her finger fleas had better flee

(54 Shillaber *Mrs. Partington* 305–306). Cf. Stevenson 805:3.

Fire, sb., 1. Dark as fire (25 Neal *Brother J* III 87).

2. They [feverish fingers] are as hot as fire (42 Irving *Attorney* 314; Haliburton *Old Judge* II 53; Cary *Married* 208). Apperson 315; Boshears 37:677; Halpert 447; NC 408; Stevenson 1185:12; Svartengren 312; Tilley F247; Whiting *Drama* 312:115, *Scots* I 168; J. D. Carr *The Burning Court* (1937) 198.

3. As little alike at bottom as fire and water (46 Cooper *Redskins* 187). Tilley F246.

4. Mad as fire, you are, this minnet (25 Neal *Brother J* III 14; Smith *Letters* 51; Anon. *New Hope* 166, 179). Green 229; NC 408; Whiting *Scots* I 168 Fire (13) and cf. 167–168 Fire (3, 5, 6, 12).

5. Bran-fire noo (25 Neal *Brother J* I 151, *Down-Easters* I 18; Crockett *Life* 139 a bran-fire new business, 145, 168). Dalton PADS XIII (1950) 22; Green 351.

6. Debby coloured as red as fire (39 Smith *Letters* 19, *My Thirty* 331; Thompson *Major* 35, 113; Jones *Winkles* 81). Apperson 526; Boshears 39:858; NC 408; Stevenson 1944:3; Taylor *Comparisons* 68; Tilley F248; Whiting *Drama* 312:115, *Scots* I 168; Carl von Hoffman *Jungle Gods* (London 1929) 53 coals of fire.

7. A bunch of fire-red trees (45 Judd *Margaret* II 61).

8. The famous copy-book sentence . . . 'Fire is a bad master, but *a good servant*' (Hall *Purchase* I 241; Cooper *Redskins* 355 Fire is a good servant, but a hard master; Barnum *Struggles* 473–474). Apperson 213; Bradley 75; Oxford 203; Stevenson 809–810:10;

Tilley F253. Cf. Whiting *Drama* 272.

9. Fire will fight fire (46 Cooper *Redskins* 356; Emerson *Journals* VII 192 Fire fights fire, the larger fire the less; Barnum *Struggles* 661 Do you intend to fight fire with fire?). Bradley 74; Stevenson 808:5; Thorne Smith *The Bishop's Jaegers* (1932) 200. See Devil (11).

10. All fire and tow (38 Haliburton *Clockmaker* II 152, III 175). Apperson 213; *Oxford* 202; Stevenson 807:6; Tilley F268.

11. But the hotter the fire the whiter the oven (45 Judd *Margaret* II 182).

12. The nigger driv like fire and smoke (44 Stephens *High Life* I 149).

13. Sooner 'n thet, I'd go thru fire an' water (48 Lowell *Biglow* 148). Apperson 214; NED Fire 5 d; *Oxford* 202; Stevenson 813:6; Tilley F285; David Fox, pseud. *The Doom Dealer* (1923) 257.

14. She looked wrathy enough to spit fire (44 Stephens *High Life* I 223). Boshears 30:42; Halpert 761.

15. Nap now supposed the girl would "hang fire" [i. e., refuse to proceed with a proposal]. (57 Jones *Country* 29). Stevenson 811:2.

16. A simpleton; with hardly wit enough to keep herself out of the fire (25 Neal *Brother J* I 26).

17. A man who was so monstrous smart that they do say he never missed fire, ner had the wind took out of his sails in his life (58 Hammett *Piney* 54).

18. See Smoke (1, 4).

Fire, vb. Fire away! (45 Hooper *Simon* 22; Jones *Country* 287; Shillaber *Knitting-Work* 266). *Oxford* 203 Fire away, Flanagan!; Stevenson 967:9. Cf. DA Fire vb. 3 (4).

Fire-coals. My face burns like fire-coals (54 Shillaber *Mrs. Partington* 310). Cf. NC 408:6; Whiting *Drama* 312:115.

Fire cracker. Till at last she let herself off like a fire cracker on the fourth of July (44 Stephens *High Life* II 62).

Fire stick. Des [just] ez stiff en stuck up ez a fire-stick (80 Harris *Uncle Remus* 36).

Firm. See Adamant (1), Flint (1), Granite (1), Iron (1), Liberty-pole, Rock (2), Stone (8).

Fish, 1. All is fish that comes into the Dutchman's net (35 Kennedy *Horse-Shoe* 194; Hammett *Stray* 356). Apperson 6; *Oxford* 207; Stevenson 820: 8; Tilley A136; Yamamoto *Dickens* 325; Carolyn Wells *Where's Emily?* (1927) 258.

2. And the boat floated up noiselessly as a fish (60 Whitehead *Wild Sports* 218). Cf. Apperson 434 mute; *Oxford* 440; Partridge 545; Charlotte M. Russell *Murder at the Old Stone House* (1935) 122 mute. See Fish (4).

3. As uneasy as a fish out of water (33 Smith *Downing* 28, 159, 227, *Letters* 32, *My Thirty* 305; Willis *Fun* 347 a fish out of water is happy in comparison with Snooks; Shillaber *Mrs. Partington* 245 a minister preaching politics is like a fish out of water; Whitcher *Widow* 298; Clift *Bunker* 281). Apperson 216; Boshears 38:703; NC 409:6; NED Fish 1 c; *Oxford* 206–207; Stevenson 821:1; Taylor *Comparisons* 41; Tilley F318. Cf. Halpert 473; A. E. Fielding, pseud. *The Case of the Two Pearl Necklaces* (1936) 10 such a fish out of water; John S. Strange, pseud. *For the Hangman* (1934) 140 like a.

4. I makes them as whist as fishes (51 Stowe *Uncle* 74). Cf. Fish (2).

5. Big fish were never found in small ponds (60 Haliburton *Season-Ticket* 231). *Oxford* 265 Great rivers; Stevenson 817:6.

6. Away they go; every fish for itself, and any fish for Samoa (49 Melville *Mardi* I 173). Babcock 263.

7. That "there were as good fish in the sea as had ever been caught out of it" (34 Crockett *Life* 57, 60 when she said there were still good fish in the sea; Emerson *Journals* V 55–56 Every homely proverb covers a single and grand fact . . . "There are as many good fish in the sea as ever came out of it," which was Nelson's adage of merit, and all men's of marriage; Haliburton *Old Judge* II 99 Do you just bait your hook and try your luck agin, for there is as good fish in the sea as was ever hauled out of it, *Nature* I 186 the consolation that is always offered, "of the sea having better fish than ever was pulled out of it"; Whitcher *Widow* 241 ther's as good fishes in the sea as any 't ever was ketcht yit; Jones *Batkins* 475 Aunt Dolly used to say "There are as good fish in the sea as ever were caught"; Holmes *Poet* 40–41 there are as good fish in the sea as ever came out of it; Clemens *Gilded* II 207 There's been as good fish in the sea as there are now; Nash *Century* 43 My doctrine is that there air better fish in the sea than has ever been ketched). Apperson 216; Hardie 465:148; Lean II ii 733; NC 409; NED Fish 1 d; *Oxford* 206; Stevenson 816:9; R. S. Surtees *Mr. Sponge's Sporting Tour* (London [1853]) 16, *Plain or Ringlets?* (London [1860]) 19 declaring that there were as good fish in the sea as ever came out of it, he resolved to make up

to her; J. P. Marquand *Wickford Point* (Boston 1939) 388 Just remember that there are a lot of fish in the sea.

8. Being, as it were, neither fish nor flesh—neither white man nor savage (23 Cooper *Pioneers* 473, *Satanstoe* 60 neither fish, flesh, nor redherring, as we say of a nondescript; Kennedy *Horse-Shoe* 23 rice, which I consider neither fish, flesh, nor good salt herring; Haliburton Old *Judge* II 102 a cretter that was neither fish nor flesh, nor chalk nor cheese, as a body might say; Clemens *Innocents* I 240 neither fish, flesh, nor fowl). Apperson 219–220; Farmer and Henley III 305; Hardie 470:122; *Oxford* 206; Stevenson 820:12; Tilley F319; NQ 9 v 125, 290, 437–438, vi 15; Walter Scott *Redgauntlet* (1824) II ch. 5 neither fish, nor flesh, nor salt herring of mine; Hulbert Footner *The Velvet Hand* (1928) fish, flesh, nor good red herring.

9. Old fish and young uns don't git along in double harniss (76 Nash *Century* 43).

10. People don't cry stinking fish, in a giniral way, in any market I was ever in yet, because folks have noses, and can smell for themselves (49 Haliburton *Old Judge* II 145). Apperson 603; *Oxford* 455; Stevenson 818:8; Tilley M325; Robert Graves *Claudius the God* (1935) 257 You know the proverb.

11. We only know there's big fish 'cause we see the little ones (76 Nash *Century* 238).

12. He drank like a fish (49 Haliburton *Old Judge* II 151), Boshears 32:159; Green 33; McAtee 23; NC 409; NED Fish 1 c; *Oxford* 157; Taylor *Comparisons* 41; Tilley F325; Thorne Smith *Rain in the Doorway* (1933) 268. Cf. NC 408:3.

13. He had "other fish to fry" (25 Neal *Brother J* III 138, 262 I'd fish o' my own to fry; Crockett *Account* 119 What a pretty kittle of fish we shall have to fry [See Kettle (1)]; Stephens *Mary Derwent* 291 the captain's got better fish to fry; Smith *My Thirty* 437 so many other fish to fry; Saxe *Poems* 124 Don't tell me about "other fish," *Your* duty is done when you buy 'em, And you never will relish the dish, Unless you've a woman to fry 'em!; Harris *Uncle Remus* 70). Apperson 216; Farmer and Henley II 401; NC 409:5; NED Fish 4 c; *Oxford* 207; Stevenson 818:2; Tilley F313; R. J. Casey *The Secret of 37 Harley Street* (Indianapolis 1929) 72.

14. Swom like a fish (25 Neal *Brother J* III 387, *Down-Easters* I 118). Boshears 34:291; NC 409:7; *Oxford* 636; Taylor *Comparisons* 41; Tilley F328; Charles Barry, pseud. *Death of a First Mate* (1935) 234.

15. A sailor has no more business with a horse than a fish has with a balloon (40 Dana *Two* 294).

Fisherman. I perceived the force of that sailor saying, intended to illustrate restricted quarters, or being *on the limits*. It is *like a fisherman's* walk, say they, *three steps and overboard* (49 Melville *Redburn* 124). Apperson 217; Babcock 256; NED Fisherman 4.

Fish-hook, 1. Jest as crooked as a fish-hook [literal]. (43 Thompson *Chronicles* 167). Cf. Boshears 35:447; NC 409; Woodard PADS VI (1946) 36.

2. Every thing's jest as strait as a fish-hook [i. e., in good shape]. (44 Thompson *Major* 81).

Fist. To make a blue fist of [i. e., to fail in an undertaking]. 34 DA Blue a. 5 (2). Cf. NED Fist 1 c.

Fit, sb., 1. Have chicken fits, a dozen at a time (45 Hooper *Simon* 25). Cf. Green 126 Duck-fit.

2. Arter she'd larfed herself into a caniption fit, and out on it agin (44 Stephens *High Life* I 226, 242, II 34, 181 conniption-fit, 210 conniption-fit). Bartlett 139; DA Conniption; Farmer 164; Green 95; Thornton I 197.

3. Give 'em fits! (54 Shillaber *Mrs. Partington* 332; Durivage *Three* 350; Hammett *Piney* 63, 84; Whitehead *Wild Sports* 92; Browne *Artemus* 97). Bartlett 220; DA Fit sb. 1 (1); Farmer 242; McAtee 28; Schele de Vere 602; Stevenson 825:6; Thornton I 324.

4. To have forty fits. 77 DA Fit sb. 2 (2).

Fit, vb. See Blister (1), Charm (2).

Five. He that would thrive must rise at five; He has that thriven may lie till seven (52 Cary *Clovernook* 190). Apperson 631; *Oxford* 656; Stevenson 2313:11; Tilley T265.

Fix. Now I *am* in a fix (51 Burke *Polly* 179; Porter *Major* 23 he had never in his life been in such a fix). DA Fix; Farmer 243; NED Fix sb. 1.

Fixed. See Fate (2), Knot-hole (1).

Flag-staff, 1. Stiff as a flag-staff . . . was Wilson (47 Melville *Omoo* 187).

2. I'll sit as straight as . . . a flag-staff (53 Haliburton *Sam* II 66).

3. Thin as a flag staff (c60 Paul *Courtship* 29).

Flail. Arms like a pair of flails hung up arter threshing (44 Stephens *High Life* I 129).

Flame. But sometimes the largest flame is soonest extinguished (57 Jones *Country* 175–176).

Flannel. Your face is as red as flannel (57 Jones *Country* 41).

Flap jack. Flat enough . . . like a flap jack in a fryin' pan (25 Neal *Brother J* I 272). Halpert 387; Irvin S. Cobb *Judge Priest Turns Detective* (Indianapolis 1936) 132. Cf. NC 409 Flitter. See Hoe-cake; Pancake.

Flash, 1. Quick's a flash (33 Neal *Down-Easters* I 106; Davis *Downing* 44; Thompson *Chronicles* 50, *Major* 44 quicker than; Melville *Israel* 20, *Confidence-Man* 156; Riley *Puddleford* 200; Smith *My Thirty* 325; Chamberlain *Confession* 25; Lowell *Biglow* 227 quicker 'n). Allan PADS XV (1951) 67; Boshears 39:833; NC 409; Taylor *Comparisons* 66; Dorothy Baker *Young Man with a Horn* (Boston 1936) 119.

2. Swift as the flash (37 Neal *Charcoal* 187; Saxe *Poems* 423 On, on they sped as swift as a flash). Gladys Mitchell *Speedy Death* (1929) 137.

3. Gone like a flash (25 Neal *Brother J* II 377; Kelly *Humors* 180 [fear] passed like a flash). E. B. Quinn *One Man's Muddle* (1937) 156.

Flat, 1. We're going a fishing—that's flat (37 Neal *Charcoal* 27; Stowe *Uncle* 372 I buy him, that's flat!; Porter *Major* 86). Farmer and Henley III 14; NED Flat 6 b; *Oxford* 209; Stevenson 826:3; Tilley F345; Thomas Hood *Poems* (1825, London 1911) 22 I'm Certain sure Enuff your Ann sisters had no stream Ingins, that's Flat; Thomas Hughes *Tom Brown at Oxford* (London 1861) ch. 3 Well, I won't order any now, that's flat.

2. See Flap jack, Flounder (1), Hand (3), Hoecake, Pancake, Poetry, Shad (2), Table (1).

Flatfooted. To come out flatfooted. 46 DA Flatfooted 1 (b).

Flattery. In some sermon or play I have read, I remembered this line: "A little flattery does well sometimes" (71 Jones *Batkins* 409). Cf. Tilley F349.

Flax. As white as flax (40 Dana *Two* 222).

Flax seed. [People] jammed up so close that you couldn't a hung up a flax seed edgeways between 'em (44 Stephens *High Life* II 55–56, 194).

Flea, 1. Hit wer es black inter that durn'd ole hanted loft, es hit wud be tu a bline flea on a black catskin, onder the fur, an' hit onder forty bushil ove wet charcoal dust (67 Harris *Sut* 117).

2. And while old Capt. Figgles was as busy as "a flea in a tar bucket"—to use the old gentleman's simile (56 Kelly *Humors* 422; Harris *Uncle Remus* 20 I'm monstus full er fleas dis mawnin'). Cf. Bee (3), Fly sb. (1).

3. Whiskey's cheap ez fleas (67 Lowell *Biglow* 234). Cf. Apperson 456 (Not worth 12); Tilley F353; Whiting *Scots* I 170 Flea 7.

4. Dar Jonah he lie snug in de ship as a flea under a nigger's shirt collar (59 Taliaferro *Fisher's* 190). NC 409; Magdalene King-Hall *Gay Crusader* (1934) 328 in a quilt.

5. Strong argimunts ez thick as fleas (48 Lowell *Biglow* 136; Bennett *Border* 188 I've seed 'em here as thick as fleas to a dog's back). Brewster *Am. Speech* XIV 287; Taylor *Comparisons* 81.

6. The way they'd a-foxed him and a-larned him fleas ain't lobsters (40 Haliburton *Clockmaker* III 204).

7. If you'd taken a friend's advice, you'd never have come away from Doncaster races with a flea in your ear! (20–22 Irving *Bracebridge* 141; Neal *Brother J* II 277 Sent away with a flea in your ear, 364 pack you off, III 144; Kennedy *Horse-Shoe* 110 He'd a got a flea in his ear, if he had stay'd; Crockett *Exploits* 191; Neal *Charcoal* 54 dismissed with something more substantial than a flea in his ear; Dana *Two* 218, 263; Lowell *Biglow* 125; Whitcher *Widow* 84). Apperson 219; Farmer and Henley II 350, III 18; NED Flea 4; *Oxford* 209; Stevenson 831:1; Tilley F354; Whiting *Drama* 345:558, *Scots* I 169; NQ 1 ix 322; 7 ii 265, 332; 9 xii 67, 138, 196; 10 i 34; Irvin S. Cobb *Murder Day by Day* (Indianapolis 1933) 213 put; Georgette Heyer *They Found Him Dead* (1937) 27 send. See Bedbug (4).

8. The old school gentlemen who split a knife that cost a fourpence, in skinning a flea for his hide and tallow (56 Kelly *Humors* 213, 219 It's not your cute folks who . . . skin a flea for its hide and tallow, and spoil a knife that cost a shilling,—that come out first best in the long run). Apperson 383 louse; NC 409; *Oxford* 209, 595. See Flint (7).

9. The silence was so immense you could have heard a flea jump in the saw-dust on the floor (66 Smith *Arp* 61). Cf. NC 458 Pin (8).

10. But soon found the critters [turkeys] had been too quick and, like Paddy's flea, wasn't there (43 Hall *Purchase* I 174).

Flea-bite. It aint a flee-bite to what I want (44 Stephens *High Life* II 51). NED Flea-bite 2.

Flecker. See Flicker.

Fleetness. See Deer (6).

Flesh, 1. All flesh is grass, we are told (36 Haliburton *Clockmaker* I 157).

I Pet. 1:24; Stevenson 832:2; Tilley F359; J. B. Priestley and G. Bullett *I'll Tell You Everything* (1933) 159.

2. I do wish I could jist slip off my flesh and sit in my bones for a space, to cool myself (38 Haliburton *Clockmaker* II 118).

Fliance. We'll plump him off of baste before he can say fliance (37 Neal *Charcoal* 96). Cf. Flugence.

Flicker. You shine like a flecker on a sunny day (35 Kennedy *Horse-Shoe* 372).

Flinders. Shoutin' like flinders (51 Burke *Polly* 72). Cf. Green 145.

Flint, 1. He was as firm and fiery as a flint (57 Riley *Puddleford* 42). Cf. Whiting *Scots* I 170 Flint (1).

2. They [hearts] was as hard as flints (53 Haliburton *Sam* I 240). Apperson 284; NC 409; *Oxford* 278; Tilley S878; Whiting *Drama* 312:120, *Scots* I 170; C. G. Bowers *The Tragic Era* (1929) 336.

3. If I didn't fix his flint for him [i. e., discomfit, defeat]. (36 Haliburton *Clockmaker* I 171, 216, 296, 299–300, II 16, 20, 48, 244, 295, III 41, 78, 122, 169, 244, 278, *Attaché* I 32, II 257, III 173, 205, IV 8, 166, *Old Judge* II 278, *Sam* I 35, *Nature* II 140, 156, 329, *Season-Ticket* 300; Hammett *Stray* 122, 223; Kelly *Humors* 110; Shillaber *Mrs. Partington* 252; Barnum *Struggles* 541; Jones *Batkins* 438). Bartlett 221; Farmer 243; Farmer and Henley II 404–405; Thornton I 326.

4. It takes two flints to make a fire (68 Alcott *Little Women* 444). Cf. Tilley F374.

5. We shall find out whether his flint will strike fire (40 Cooper *Pathfinder* 29).

6. I shall set my face against the East wind "like a flint" (46 Fairfield *Letters* 399; Melville *Moby-Dick* I 276 His face set like a flint, II 204). NED Flint 4; *Oxford* 576; Schele de Vere 241; Stevenson 739:1; Tilley F18; Mrs. Baillie Reynolds *The Stranglehold* (1930) 306.

7. They are so mean that they would skin flints to make money (68 Clift *Bunker* 200). Apperson 576; Farmer and Henley III 17; Green 339; NED Flint 4; *Oxford* 209; Stevenson 2125:9; Tilley F373. See Flea (8).

Flock. To fire into the wrong flock. 35 DA Fire vb. 3 (2).

Floor, 1. Hard and clean as a puncheon floor (43 Hall *Purchase* I 168).

2. Level as a floor (66 Clemens *Sandwich* 19, *Innocents* II 355; Richardson *Beyond* 203).

3. As smooth as a floor (69 Clemens *Innocents* I 262). NC 409.

4. You might eat off the floor a'most, all's so clean (43 Haliburton *Attaché* I 201). *Oxford* 168; Stevenson 362:2; A. R. Martin *The Death of the Claimant* (1929) 121 You could eat your dinner off the floor, as the saying is.

Floor-board. I see it all now, as plain as a new floor-board (53 Haliburton *Sam* II 110).

Flounder, sb., 1. As flat as a flounder (36 Haliburton *Clockmaker* I 60, II 183, *Attaché* II 258; Hooper *Simon* 47 in half an hour Suggs was "as flat as a flounder" [i. e., bankrupt]; Melville *Mardi* II 85 Flat as the foot of a man with his mind made up . . . did you sup on flounders last night?, *Redburn* 94–95; Jones *Country* 219 I've got him down as flat as a flounder [i. e., made him retract completely]). Ap-

FLOUNDER

person 218; NC 409; NED Flounder 1; *Oxford* 209; Stevenson 826:5; Taylor *Comparisons* 41; Tilley F382; Jeffrey Farnol *The Crooked Furrow* (1938) 66. Cf. Whiting *Scots* I 171 Fluke.

2. As motionless as a dead flounder (45 Mayo *Kaloolah* 107).

Flounder, vb. See Duck (2), Pullet (2).

Flower, 1. She looked as bright and sweet as one of the flowers (44 Stephens *High Life* I 170).

2. Her cheek delicate as a flower (50 Mitchell *Reveries* 41; Stephens *Fashion* 88).

3. Her breath sweet as a prairie flower (43 Robb *Squatter* 133). NC 409 flower; Stevenson 2259:1 bramble-flour; Svartengren 308.

4. Then Katey will break her heart and die off like a flower (66 Boucicault *Flying Scud* 222).

5. He never held up his head after the Proclamashen, but faded away like a frostd flower (66 Locke [Nasby] *Struggles* 368). Tilley F386; Whiting *Drama* 313:123, *Scots* I 171 Flower (6). Cf. Stevenson 1374:2 leaf.

Flue. There is one thing Sure, the war cant go on always I will either go up the flew [i. e., die] or come home before a graitwhile (62 Wiley *Johnny* 130). NED Flue sb.[3] 4; Partridge 289.

Flugence, 1. It was as hot as flugence (c60 Taliaferro *Carolina Humor* 62). Bradley PADS XXI (1954) 27 flugins; DA Flugens; Tidwell PADS XI (1949) 13 cold. See Blue Flujin. Cf. Fliance.

2. I were mad as flugence (59 Taliaferro *Fisher's* 204).

3. Yes, and you're a nice chap, ain't you, to run like flugins from a dead

man that you killed yourself (56 Jones *Wild* 86).

Flume. One of the boys has gone up the flume [i. e., died]. (72 Clemens *Roughing* II 47). DA Flume 3; NED Flume 3 c.

Flute, 1. I was . . . hollow as a flute (56 Kelly *Humors* 112, 135, 146).

2. The name of it wouldn't a-fixed his flute for him (40 Haliburton *Clockmaker* III 106).

Flutter. See Duck (3), Hen (13).

Fly, sb., 1. He is as much bothered as a fly in a tar pot to get out of the mess (36 Crockett *Exploits* 15). Apperson 220 Fly (10); *Oxford* 78 Capers; Tilley F395.

2. Till I was as crazy as a fly in a drum (53 Willis *Fun* 352). NC 410.

3. As thick as flies in August (33 Smith *Downing* 208; Thompson *Major* 27 thick as flies round a fat gourd; Clift *Bunker* 28–29 Thick as flies in Hooker town in fish time). NC 410; Svartengren 397; Madeleine Johnston *Comets Have Long Tails* (1938) 206 around a stable.

4. It is an old and true maxim, that "a drop of honey catches more flies than a gallon of gall" (42 Lincoln I 273; Jones *Batkins* 256 I am still of opinion . . . that, as in case of the flies, "it is easier to catch them with molasses than with vinegar"). Apperson 220; Hardie 464:110; Jente *American* 345; Lean IV 206 spoonful of honey . . . gallon of vinegar; McAtee 72; NC 410; Stevenson 1158–1159:14; Tilley F403; C. J. Daly *The Third Murderer* (1931) 85 molasses; W. C. MacDonald *Destination Danger* (Philadelphia 1955) 120 I also know the old saying relative to honey catching more flies than vinegar; Mrs. Wil-

son Woodrow *The Moonhill Mystery* (1930) 306 there's an old saying that it's easier to catch flies with honey than with vinegar.

5. I take to him like flies du to a 'lasses cup (44 Stephens *High Life* II 178).

6. A sister so ugly the flies won't light on her face (45 Hooper *Simon* 136).

Fly, vb., 1. I couldn't get a hull hand in, no more than I could fly (44 Stephens *High Life* I 95).

2. A nervous, fussy old lady, who . . . worries you till you're ready to fly out of the window or cry (68 Alcott *Little Women* 4).

3. See Hailstone (3).

Fly trap, 1. My head went round like a fly trap (44 Stephens *High Life* II 19).

2. If I wasn't a preacher . . . I'd keep my fly-trap shot 'tell the day of judgment (52 Burke *Polly* 49, 71 I shut up my fly trap). Cf. NC 410; NED Fly-trap 3.

Foam. White as foam (50 Melville *White Jacket* 244). Svartengren 234; Whiting *Scots* I 171; Abraham Merritt *Creep, Shadow, Creep!* (1934) 295.

Fodder, 1. Feller cant cut his own fodder, if he dont shave tarnation close (33 Neal *Down-Easters* I 84; Lincoln I 175 it not only, to use a homely phrase, cut its own fodder, but actually threw a surplus into the Treasury, V 375 to "cut their own fodder," so to speak; Stephens *High Life* I 32 in a free country every feller ought to cut his own fodder, 141, 212, II 173, 184; Riley *Puddleford* 123 all old residents—came in when the country was new, and have cut their own fodder

ever since). DA Fodder 2 b; Stevenson 1236:7.

2. The act was constitutional, . . . and it must be lived up to, fodder or no fodder (57 Riley *Puddleford* 233).

3. I'm a man that always stands up to my fodder, rack or no rack (58 Porter *Major* 24). DA Fodder 2 b. See Rack.

Fog, 1. He was completely in the fog [i. e., confused]. (58 Hammett *Piney* 161). Farmer and Henley III 48; NED Fog 2 b.

2. [She] wasn't to be grinned at in a fog [i. e., was handsome]. (44 Stephens *High Life* I 255).

Folks, 1. Mr. Doubleday is queer as anybody's folks, has a sober face, a sly eye and much humor (35 Fairfield *Letters* 37). Lawrence W. Meynell *On the Night of the 18th* (1936) 230 the old, old truth that queer though nature might be in parts, there's "nout as queer as folks."

2. Folks that tend babies mustn't have pins about them (45 Judd *Margaret* II 121). See Nurse.

3. It takes a great many different kinds of folks to make a world (60 Haliburton *Season-Ticket* 39; Nash *Century* 238 It takes all kinds of people to make a world, you know). Apperson 7–8 sorts; Bradley 98; *Oxford* 8; Stevenson 2628:8; Tilley S666; NQ 11 ii 534; Andy Adams *The Ranch on the Beaver* (Boston 1927) 238; T. W. Duncan *O, Chatauqua* (1935) 120; M. Zolotow *It Takes All Kinds to Make a World* (London 1953). See People (2).

4. Some folks are born to be lucky (52 Cary *Clovernook* 75). See People (3).

5. The littler folks be, the bigger

they talk (36 Haliburton *Clockmaker* I 223).

6. Here we shall be safe from the long ears of little folks (45 Cooper *Chainbearer* 337; Cary *Clovernook* 295 Hush, hush! . . . little folks have big ears, 2d Ser. 236 Little folks must not have big ears). Cf. NC 459 pitchers.

7. If he behaves himself like folks (44 Stephens *High Life* II 109).

8. Young folks will be young folks (55 Anon. *New Hope* 66; Holmes *Elsie* 109). Cf. J. S. Fletcher *The Ebony Box* (1934) 29 The young will be young; Esther Forbes *Paradise* (1937) 294 Young people; P. G. Wodehouse *Thank You, Jeeves* (Boston 1934) 115 Young gents. See Boy (4), People (4).

Food. The rest of them were certainly only food for powder (58 Hammett *Piney* 255). Stevenson 842:1; Georg Büchmann *Geflügelte Worte* (27th ed., Berlin 1925) 317.

Fool, 1. They attribute your good fortune to the old hackneyed adage, "A fool for luck" (57 Jones *Country* 232). DA Fool 1 b; McAtee 26; NC 410; Nell Martin *The Mosaic Earring* (1927) 199. Cf. Apperson 224; Tilley F517; Whiting *Drama* 117.

2. The old saying—"A fool for luck, and a poor man for children" (34 Crockett *Life* 170). Bradley 88 A poor man for chillun, a nigger for gourds, and a fool for luck; NC 410.

3. But then a fool *is* a fool all the world over (40 Haliburton *Clockmaker* III 110). Tilley F547.

4. A fool's counsel is sometimes worth the weighing (32 Kennedy *Swallow* 212). Apperson 223; *Oxford* 214; Tilley F469; Whiting *Drama* 155.

5. On the same fool's errand (54 Hawthorne *Mosses* 188; Clift *Bunker* 89). Stevenson 706:2; Glen Trevor *Was It Murder?* (1933) 97.

6. You know all the fools never die (56 Cary *Married* 395).

7. Fools ask questions that wise men cannot answer (71 Jones *Batkins* 408). Apperson 224; Bradley 76; *Oxford* 214; Stevenson 858:12; Stoett 625; Tilley F468.

8. Old fools is the biggest fools there is (76 Clemens *Tom* 3). Apperson 228; Bradley 75; NC 410; *Oxford* 216; Taylor *Index* 34; Tilley F506; Francis Beeding, pseud. *Death Walks in Eastrepps* (1931) 10.

9. One fool makes many (40 Haliburton *Clockmaker* III 84). Apperson 228; *Oxford* 214; Tilley F501.

10. I . . . talked to the Briggses till I got as dizzy as a fool (56 Whitcher *Widow* 201).

11. Drunk as a fool, and forty times as stupid (51 Burke *Polly* 134; Wiley *Billy* 187). Green 19; McAtee 24; Svartengren 201.

12. He'll get as fat as a fool (36 Haliburton *Clockmaker* I 170). Apperson 204–205; *Oxford* 193; Svartengren 182; Tilley F443; Whiting *Drama* 313:126.

13. Jest as thick with him as two fools could be (44 Thompson *Major* 67).

14. Miss Warren is nobody's fool (69 Barnum *Struggles* 587). Arthur Train *The Adventures of Ephraim Tutt* (1930) 129.

15. I woodunt be a fool if I had common cents (62 Browne *Artemus* 140).

16. You've hove your money away like a fool (40 Dana *Two* 319).

Foot, 1. Even supposin' we come down feet first (34 Davis *Downing* 261). See Cat (2).

2. Ef *I'd* expected sech a trick, I wouldn't ha' cut my foot By goin' an' votin' for myself like a consumed coot (48 Lowell *Biglow* 138).

3. When not only one foot, put pot' feet an haf my poty in t'e pargain, may well pe sait to pe in t'e grave (45 Cooper *Chainbearer* 430, *Redskins* 403 a woman . . . who had one foot in the grave; Melville *Redburn* 113 an old man with one foot in the grave; Shillaber *Knitting-Work* 388; Daly *Man* 12). Apperson 470; Farmer and Henley III 54; NC 411; NED Foot 26 a; *Oxford* 476; Stevenson 1027:13; NQ 3 iii 251; Marcus Magill, pseud. *Murder Out of Tune* (Philadelphia 1931) 11. Cf. Tilley F569, M346.

4. How they pulled foot, when they seed us commin' (25 Neal *Brother J* I 107; Smith *Downing* 27 and pulled foot for home, 170, *Letters* 69; Stephens *High Life* I 70, 108). Bartlett 502; Farmer 249; Farmer and Henley III 54; Schele de Vere 625; Thornton II 708, III 307.

5. The military rule is to put the best foot foremost (33 Hall *Soldier's Bride* 16; Thompson *Chronicles* 102 He resolved to put the "best foot foremost"; Stephens *High Life* I 149, II 46; Haliburton *Sam* I 29 put my best foot out). Apperson 40; Hardie 471: 157; *Oxford* 35; Stevenson 862:12 better foot; Stoett 176; Tilley F570; F. W. Crofts *The Strange Case of Dr. Earle* (1933) 184; H. R. Patch *On Re-reading Chaucer* (Cambridge, Mass., 1939) 89 And here we find the reason for his [Troilus's] habitual trick of not putting his best foot forward. See Leg (7).

6. They've put their foot in it (36 Haliburton *Clockmaker* I 147; Lowell *Biglow* 55; Shillaber *Mrs. Partington* 315, *Knitting-Work* 306; Hammett

Wonderful 58, *Piney* 13). Berrey 156: 3, 170:6, 188:17, 256:7, 258:5; Farmer and Henley III 53; Partridge 295; Stevenson 863:3; Milward Kennedy *Death in a Deck-chair* (London 1930) 147.

7. And so he put down his foot, like a rock (51 Stowe *Uncle* 250; Sedley *Marian* 286 [He] went so far as to tell me it was my duty to put my foot down). Stevenson 863:1.

8. I jest sot down my foot (44 Stephens *High Life* I 101, 199; Stowe *Uncle* 193).

9. I . . . tuck my foot in my hand and walked all the way back to Old Bucksmasher (59 Taliaferro *Fisher's* 73). Coombs PADS II (1944) 23; NC 411; NED Foot 29; Stevenson 862:13; Wilson 542; Caroline Gordon *The Garden of Adonis* (1937) 57–58.

Football, 1. As big as a football (60 Holmes *Professor* 42).

2. I rose early . . . and like a football, bounded up the hill (53 Melville "Cock-a-doodle-doo!" in *Works* XIII 153).

3. The flying-jib was swept into the air, rolled together for a few minutes, and tossed about in the squalls like a football (50 Melville *White Jacket* 131; Irving *Wolfert* 240 they . . . kicked him [a dog] about like a football).

4. I'll let you use my head for a foot-ball (33 Smith *Downing* 217; Haliburton *Clockmaker* II 243 If you don't succeed I will give you my head for a foot-ball, 274 She amused . . . herself by using his hat for a football; Judd *Margaret* II 89 King George and old Johnny Trumbull playing football with the head of the people). Francis P. Magoun Jr. *History of Football from the Beginnings to 1871*, Kölner

Anglistische Arbeiten 31 (Bochum-Langendreer 1938) 45. See Gourd (4).

Foresight. You know a man's foresight ain't as good as his hind sights (66 Smith *Arp* 130; Locke [Nasby] *Struggles* 435 Our foresite isn't alluz ez good ez our hind-site). NC 425. Cf. Stevenson 865:7.

Fore-topsail. Or else—in the Navy phrase—preparing to pay their creditors *with a flying fore-topsail* [i. e., run away]. (50 Melville *White Jacket* 4).

Forever. Why it runs forever and ever, and a few days over (66 Smith *Arp* 50).

Forewarned. Fore-warned, fore-armed (33 Neal *Down-Easters* I 72; Emerson *Journals* VI 274 Forewarned, thought Arthur once more; Judd *Richard* 102; Richardson *Secret* 106; Sedley *Marian* 50). Apperson 230; NC 411; *Oxford* 220; Stevenson 2455:7; Tilley H54; Helen Reilly *Mr. Smith's Hat* (1936) 219.

Forge. He begun to blow like an iron forge (59 Taliaferro *Fisher's* 130).

Forgive. Forgive and forget (23 Cooper *Pioneers* 175; Neal *Brother J* II 35 Forgit an' forgive, 375 I forgive you! —I cannot—shall not forget you; but I forgive you, *Down-Easters* I 18 Forgit and forgive; Haliburton *Clockmaker* II 24 We must forget and forgive, *Attaché* IV 122 We can forgive or forget; Melville *Mardi* I 133; Alcott *Little Women* 92 everything was forgiven and forgotten, 336; Daly *Man* 40 not a bad motto; McCloskey *Across* 82 You should seek consolation in the old adage . . . which says "forget and forgive"; Clemens *Roughing* I 227

Let us forget and forgive bygones, *Tramp* I 89 able to forgive and forget). Apperson 230; Lean IV 13; NC 411; NED Forget 3 b; *Oxford* 220; Stevenson 869:1; Tilley F597; Yamamoto *Dickens* 333; A. E. Fielding, pseud. *Murder at the Nook* (1930) 104.

Fortune, 1. But by a turn of Fortune's wheel they became suddenly rich (69 Barnum *Struggles* 247). Cf. Irving *Wolfert* 168 there were exclamations of impatience and despair, as if the wheel of fortune had suddenly been stopped when about to make its luckiest evolution. Apperson 231; *Oxford* 221; Stevenson 877:3; Tilley F617; Whiting *Drama* 35, 84, 243, 252, 253, 287, 288, 289, *Scots* I 173; R. Austin Freeman *The Penrose Mystery* (1936) 8.

2. It must be true that "fortuna favet fortibus," and I'll een risk a little upon the strength of the maxim (35 Longstreet *Georgia* 175; Judd *Margaret* II 191; Cooke *Foresters* 372 fortune favors the brave, recollect; Barnum *Struggles* 476 Fortune always favors the brave, and never helps a man who does not help himself). Virgil *Aen.* 10. 284 Audentes fortuna iuvat; Apperson 231; Bradley 76; *Oxford* 221; Stevenson 878:9; Tilley F601; Whiting *Scots* I 172–173; Marquis James *Andrew Jackson, Portrait of a President* (Indianapolis 1937) 431.

3. Likewise Fortin' allers helps them as helps theirselves (65 Sedley *Marian* 163). See God (3).

4. That's the fortune of war, as Peppercorn calls it (35 Kennedy *Horse-Shoe* 196; Barnum *Struggles* 699 he will take this heavier loss as simply the fortune of war). Stevenson 2447:2; Whiting *Drama* 271; Hulbert

Footner *The Mystery of the Folded Paper* (1930) 333.

Forty. I has principles and I sticks to 'em like forty (51 Stowe *Uncle* 86; Porter *Major* 66 all going like forty). DA Forty 2 b; NC 411; NED Forty 1 (b); Schele de Vere 313. Cf. Farmer and Henley III 68 forty to the dozen.

Forward. A remaining bottle of whiskey . . . "wouldn't set one forward" much [i. e., would not be very intoxicating]. (58 Porter *Major* 91).

Fox, 1. For a fox that is hunted and runs away, May live to be hunted another day (32 Kennedy *Swallow* 177). See Fight, vb. (1).

2. I was as cunning as a . . . fox (34 Crockett *Life* 203; Haliburton *Clockmaker* II 136, III 192, *Attaché* IV 223–224, *Nature* II 135; Hammett *Stray* 147; Holmes *Elsie* 201 red fox; McCloskey *Across* 109; Jones *Batkins* 250). Apperson 232; NC 411; Taylor *Comparisons* 31; Q. Patrick, pseud. *The Grindle Nightmare* (1935) 98. Cf. Tilley F629.

3. Look at the top of my head— gray as a fox (35 Kennedy *Horse-Shoe* 59).

4. He all the time looked as knowing as a fox (33 Smith *Downing* 147; Paul *Courtship* 133). Hardie 468:53.

5. Light on the foot as a fox (40 Haliburton *Clockmaker* III 284).

6. Quick es a fox kin cum outen a bag (67 Harris *Sut* 277). Stanley H. Page *The Resurrection Murder Case* (1932) 87.

7. I was as sly as a fox when he is going to rob a hen-roost (34 Crockett *Life* 127). McAtee 59; NC 411; Taylor *Comparisons* 74.

8. Spry as a fox (36 Haliburton *Clockmaker* I 136).

9. I could read and spell like a fox (33 Smith *Downing* 27).

10. My rule is to let every man skin his own foxes (40 Haliburton *Clockmaker* III 137, *Attaché* II 217 I skin my own foxes, and let other folks skin their'n, *Sam* I 8, *Season-Ticket* 31). See Axe (3), Eel (10), Skunk (4).

11. If a lawyer takes to cantin, its like the fox preachin to the geese, he'll eat up his whole congregation (36 Haliburton *Clockmaker* I 122–123, *Sam* II 252 When the fox turns preacher, the geese had better not go to night meetins). Apperson 234; NED Fox 1 c; *Oxford* 223; Stevenson 2063:3; Tilley F656; Whiting *Drama* 16, 69, 245, 272; Archer Taylor *Problems in German Literature of the Fourteenth and Fifteenth Centuries* (1939) 82.

Fox-trap, 1. Gretchen was as quick as a foxtrap (53 Haliburton *Sam* I 47).

2. She was as smart as a fox-trap (38 Haliburton *Clockmaker* II 127). See Taylor *Comparisons* 74 steel-trap.

3. He grinned like a fox-trap (40 Haliburton *Clockmaker* III 70–71).

Fraction. To a fraction [i. e., exactly]. 58 DA Fraction 1 b.

Fracture. Fractures well cured make us more strong (34 Emerson *Journals* III 247).

Frank. See Day (6).

Fray. We mustn't quarrel with the chances of war. There is not often a fray without a broken head (35 Kennedy *Horse-Shoe* 191).

Free, 1. Free gratis for nothing (44 Stephens *High Life* I 56; Hammett *Stray* 122; Durivage *Three* 116).

Farmer and Henley III 67; Stevenson 887:9.

2. See Air (1), Bird (9), Blackbird (2), Eagle (1), Glove (1), Hail (2), Thought (1), Wind (1).

Freemason. As closemouthed as a freemason (40 Cooper *Pathfinder* 186).

French. Excuse my French [i. e., unconventional language]. (65 Sedley *Marian* 342). See Frenchman (2).

Frenchified. See Sunflower (1).

French leave. If I did take French leave of him (49 Melville *Redburn* 290; Durivage *Three* 176; Richardson *Secret* 379; Mary N. Prescott *Harper's New Monthly Magazine* XXXIII [1866] 777). Apperson 235; Farmer and Henley III 70; NED French leave; *Oxford* 225; Stevenson 1380:2; NQ 1 i 246; 5 xii 87; 6 v 347, 496, viii 514, ix 133, 213, 279; 7 iii 5, 109, 518; R. C. Ashby *He Arrived at Dusk* (1933) 97. Cf. DA French (4).

Frenchman, 1. He was jest as polite as a Frenchman (58 Hammett *Piney* 34).

2. Well then you-go-to-hell! as the Frenchman said (33 Neal *Down-Easters* I 97). Cf. French.

Fresh. See Buck (1) 3, Buttercup (1), Crest, Dewdrop (1), Hawk (2), Lark (4), Lip (1), Morning (5), Pansy, Rose (3), Springwater, Venison.

Fried. But what's all that when it's fried? [i. e., what does it mean?]. (40 Haliburton *Clockmaker* III 244, *Nature* I 73, *Season-Ticket* 37). Farmer and Henley III 79.

Friend, 1. No doubt of it, now that we have a friend at court (55 Stephens *Homestead* 62; Lincoln III 518 We consider you our peculiar friend at court; Jones *Batkins* 221 I should not have fared so well but for this friend at court). Apperson 237; NED Friend 5 c; *Oxford* 227; Stevenson 901:10–902:1; Tilley F687; C. F. Gregg *Inspector Higgins Sees It Through* (1934) 146.

2. I have with me . . . a friend good at need (35 Kennedy *Horse-Shoe* 49, 414 A friend in need . . . is the greatest of God's blessings; Crockett *Exploits* 18 my rifle . . . my best friend in time of need; Haliburton *Letter* 86 A friend in need is a friend indeed; Smith *'Way* 263 a friend in need was a friend indeed; Stephens *Fashion* 301; Durivage *Three* 176–177 What's the use of a friend, unless he's a friend in need; Barnum *Struggles* 522 Mr. Johnson had been a "friend indeed," for he has been truly a "friend in need"). Apperson 237; NC 412; NED Friend 1 b; *Oxford* 227; Stevenson 902:5; Stoett 1645; Tilley F693; Whiting *Drama* 148, 233, *Scots* I 175; Herbert Adams *Oddways* (Philadelphia 1929) 52; Ed Bell *Fish on the Steeple* (1935) 87.

3. For "friends are better than money" (53 Haliburton *Sam* I 242). Cf. Apperson 237; *Oxford* 227; Tilley F687; Whiting *Drama* 71, 83.

4. The best friends in the world must part (59 Smith *My Thirty* 247). Apperson 238; *Oxford* 228; Stevenson 897–898:12; Q. Patrick, pseud. *Death for Dear Clara* (1937) 275. Cf. Whiting *Scots* I 175 Friend (4).

5. Too menny fr'en's spiles de dinner (80 Harris *Uncle Remus* 59).

Friendship, 1. "No friendship in trade" (71 Jones *Batkins* 45, 54). W. M. Thackeray *The Newcomes* (1855, London 1926) 704 In business, begad, there are no friends and no enemies, at all.

2. Friendship can't stand on one leg long, and, if it does, it's plain it can't go ahead much at any rate (49 Haliburton *Old Judge* II 147). Cf. *Oxford* 229; Tilley F760.

Frightened, 1. He was not much hurt, but a good deal frightened (40 Dana *Two* 154; Hammett *Stray* 31–32 Although more frightened than hurt; Mayo *Kaloolah* 341; Lincoln II 523 I do hope you are worse scared than hurt). Apperson 426–427; *Oxford* 432; Stevenson 785:7; Tilley A55; Louis Tracy *The Manning-Burke Murder* (1930) 271.

2. See Child (1).

Frink. " 'Coming to Frink,' you mean," said Stephen. "Coming to the point is old-fashioned, and has no fun in it; but 'Come to Frink,' is all the go now. I'll tell you how that sayin' was raised. Oncest upon a time, in the House of Assembly in New Brunswick, there was a committee a-sitting on a petition of a harbour-master called Frink, and the lawyers talked about everything, as they always do, but the petition; and an old member, who got tired out, and a'most wearied to death with their long yarns, used to stop them every minnit, and say 'Come to Frink'; and when they wandered off he'd fetch them back agin with a voice of thunder, 'Why don't you come to Frink?' His manner and accent was so droll, for he talked broad Scotch (which is a sort of howl, growl, and bark, all in one it made every body laugh a'most; and now it's a by-word all over that province, in the legislatur, and courts, and story-telling, and everywhere, 'Come to Frink' " (49 Haliburton *Old Judge* II 67–68).

Frisco. We did in Frisco as the Friscans did (67 Richardson *Beyond* 445). See Rome (2), Turkey (1).

Frisky. See Steer (1).

Frog, 1. There he lays as dead as a frog (55 Jones *Winkles* 130).

2. Bullies . . . that are as thick over this country as the frogs in the kneading troughs, that they tell of (35 Kennedy *Horse-Shoe* 244).

3. He swum like a frog (25 Neal *Brother J* II 7).

4. See Fun (2).

Frogstool. Her skin wer es white es the inside ove a frogstool (67 Harris *Sut* 76).

Frost, 1. Frost-white (49 Melville *Mardi* I 286).

2. Ontil thar's enuf white fros' in hell tu kill snapbeans (67 Harris *Sut* 242).

Frosty. See Methuselah (1).

Froth. Her forehead and neck . . . were as white as the froth on a pail of new milk afore it is strained (44 Stephens *High Life* I 181). Cf. Foam.

Fruit, 1. Fine fruit will have flies about it (50 Willis *Life* 217).

2. It is a proverb, "He that would eat the fruit must first climb the tree and get it" (43 Hall *Purchase* I 225). Apperson 240; *Oxford* 166; Stevenson 918–919:18.

Frying-pan. Don't jump out of the frying-pan into the fire (21 Loomis *Farmer's Almanac* 177; Hall *Purchase* I 59 Such know . . . where they are likely to fulfil the proverb "out of the frying pan into the fire"; Haliburton *Old Judge* II 108–109 It was like going out of the frying-pan into the fire; Taliaferro *Fisher's* 129 I'd "jump'd out'n the fryin'-pan smack inter the fire, "as the parrabal runs, 161; Whitehead *Wild Sports* 183; Richardson *Secret* 26 It would be jumping out of the frying-pan into the fire; Eggleston *Circuit* 250 Out of the frying-pan into the fire). Apperson 240; NC 413; NED Frying-pan; *Oxford* 230; Stevenson 814:1; Tilley F784; *Catalogue of Political and Personal Satires* . . . 1811–1819 (London 1949) IX 42 No. 11758 I have jump'd out of the fry-pan into the fire; Aldo Sand *Señor Bum in the Jungle* (1932) 63 jumping from.

Fuel. Added fresh fuel to the fire (54 Smith *'Way* 249; Paul *Courtship* 302 The incident added fuel to the fire). Apperson 240–241; Stevenson 807:1; Tilley F785. Cf. Whiting *Scots* I 175–176.

Full. See Bee (4), Colander, Cub, Dog (15), Egg (3), Kitten (2), Nut (3), Tick (1).

Fun, 1. Fun is fun, but furling one yard-arm of a course at a time, off Cape Horn, is no better than man-killing (40 Dana *Two* 410; Haliburton *Nature* I 176 Fun is fun, and we may carry our fun too far). Cf. Joke (1); Stevenson 960:10; Tilley J46, J47.

2. Yes, it may be fun for you, but, as the boy said to the frogs, it's death to me (c56 Thomson *Elephant Club* 96–97). The speaker is drunk and has reversed the proverb. Stevenson 916:15; Lean IV 20, 159 What's sport to you is death to us poor straddybreeks [frogs]; R. S. Surtees *Plain or Ringlets?* (London [1860]) 350 Fun to her [a drunken cook] but death to us; *Aesop's Fables,* with . . . Drawings by Louis Rhead (1927) 28.

3. See wut they've done Jest simply by stickin' together like fun (48 Lowell *Biglow* 81). Berrey 227:3,

229:5; NED Fun 2 b; Svartengren 406.

Funeral. This is *our* funeral (69 Clemens *Love Letters* 66). DA Funeral 3; NED *Supplement* Funeral 1 c; Mike Teagle *Murders in Silk* (1938) 144.

Fur. To make the fur fly (34 Crockett *Life* 30; Thompson *Chronicles* 178; Hooper *Simon* 116 and the furr a flyin' every time she jumped, like you'd busted a feather bed open!; Riley *Puddleford* 177, 269; Haliburton *Season-Ticket* 177; Anon. *New Hope* 86; Browne *Artemus* 198; Clemens *Sketches* 241). Bartlett 380; DA Fur 1 b; Farmer 256; Farmer and Henley III 43; McAtee 42; NED Fur 2 b; Stevenson 921:3; Thornton I 350, III 155; Agatha Christie *The Mysterious Mr. Quin* (1930) 22. See Feather (16).

Fury, 1. The proverb, "Beware the fury of a patient man" (65 Richardson *Secret* 112). Dryden *Absalom and Achitophel* i 1005; Stevenson 1756–1757:12.

2. She turned and run like fury (47 Dorson *Jonathan* 92; Jones *Wild* 250 They hurt like fury; Whitcher *Widow* 289 a churnin' away like fury). Bartlett 807; NED Fury 3 b; Kathleen M. Knight *The Clue of the Poor Man's Shilling* (1936) 195 itches.

Fuss, 1. He was all fuss and feathers (56 Kelly *Humors* 142, 159 no fuss, no feathers, 167; Alcott *Little Women* 103 I don't like fuss and feathers, 106). DA Fuss 3; NED Fuss 1 b; Mary Plum *The Killing of Judge MacFarlane* (1930) 257 no fuss or feathers about him; Nard Jones *The Case of the Hanging Lady* (1938) 86 without fuss or feathers.

2. See Hen (14, 19).

G

Gabriel, 1. Gabriel, a sort of local Farquhar Tupper, seemed to be blowing his horn, after taking several horns too many (67 Richardson *Beyond* 539). Apperson 242; Lean III 345, IV 183; *Oxford* 231; Stevenson 1679:7; Tilley G1.

2. Secession will be in the hands of the undertaker, sheeted for so deep a grave that nothin short of Gabriel's trombone will ever awaken it (62 Browne *Artemus* 198; Lowell *Biglow* 320 For who'd thought the North wuz agoin' to rise . . . 'thout 't wuz sumthin' ez pressin' ez Gabr'el's las' trump?). Mary Roberts Rinehart *Miss Pinkerton* (1932) 5 nothing but Gabriel's horn would ever waken me again; Abraham Merritt *The Ship of Ishtar* (1926) 19 I don't want to be disturbed for anything less than Gabriel's trumpet.

Gains, 1. Great gains cover many losses (40 Haliburton *Clockmaker* III 180).

2. There are no gains, without pains (55 Melville *Israel* 69 [from Poor Richard]). Apperson 242; NC 413; NED Gain sb. 2 b; *Oxford* 457–458; Stevenson 924:6; Tilley P24.

Gall, 1. Grow as bitter as gaul (36 Haliburton *Clockmaker* I 93; "Editor's Drawer" *Harper's New Monthly Magazine* VII [1853] 849 tansy-tea, *bitter as gall*). Apperson 50; Boshears 31: 88, 34:348; Fife 117; NC 413; Taylor

Comparisons 17; Tilley G11; Whiting *Drama* 314:135, *Scots* I 176; Kathleen M. Knight *Seven Were Killed* (1937) 15.

2. I'm goin' if it busts yeour gall (c60 Paul *Courtship* 50). NED Gall 3 c.

Galley-west. Your verdict . . . has knocked what little I *did* have galleywest (75 Clemens *Letters* I 249–250, *Tramp* I 22 that knocked the mystery galley-west). DA Galley-west; Farmer and Henley III 103; NED *Supplement* Galley-west; Stevenson 929:7; Carolyn Wells *The Crime in the Crypt* (Philadelphia 1928) 54.

Gallop. Don't gallup when you're goin' down hill (76 Nash *Century* 145).

Gallows (1). "The gallows and the sea refuse nothing," is a very old sea saying (50 Melville *White Jacket* 475 [Melville finds a reference to the proverb in the last print of Hogarth's Idle Apprentice]). Apperson 555 Sea refuses; Babcock 259; *Oxford* 568; Stevenson 2049–2050:14; Tilley S178.

Gallows (2). It kinder seems to me as if Boz Dickens had stretched his galluses a trifle, in writing out sich an all fired varmint [Quilp]. (44 Stephens *High Life* I 232). Cf. Farmer and Henley III 105 bust my boots and gallowses. See Blanket (3), Stocking (1).

Gamble. You kin gamble on that thar [i. e., you may be certain of it]. (57

149

Bennett *Border* 68). NED Gamble 1 b.

Gamboge. He was as yellow as gamboge (49 Melville *Redburn* 71).

Game, sb., 1. Better play at small game than stand out (45 Judd *Margaret* I 318). Apperson 500; *Oxford* 505; Stevenson 934:4; Tilley G21.

2. For my part, I could never believe the game paid for the candle (65 Sedley *Marian* 420, 473 The game is not worth the candle, but the fact is only discovered when it is burnt out). Apperson 242; Lean IV 123; NC 413; NED Candle 5 f; *Oxford* 232; Stevenson 933:11; Taylor *Investigations* 259; *Tilley* S776.

3. Our game is played out (67 Lowell *Biglow* 306).

4. The game was up (25 Neal *Brother J* III 94; Robb *Squatter* 130; Mayo *Kaloolah* 89 all up, 243 up; Melville *Redburn* 303; Boker *World* 12; Curtis *Potiphar* 112; Shillaber *Mrs. Partington* 334; Durivage *Three* 176; Harris *Uncle Remus* 99 Brer Fox, he seed his game wuz up). NC 413; NED Game 6 b; Stevenson 934:5; A. C. Brown *Dr. Glazebrook's Revenge* (1928) 267. See Jig (2).

5. All of the dozen young babies in attendance silently dilated their astonished eyes—struck utterly dumb at being so signally beaten at their own peculiar game [i. e., screaming]. (45 Hooper *Simon* 62; Haliburton *Nature* I 249 They'd beat you at your own game; Porter *Major* 88; Taliaferro *Fisher's* 237 It is difficult to beat an experienced man at his own game; it sometimes happens, however; Richardson *Beyond* 86, 153). Bradley 76; NC 413. Cf. Tilley W204.

6. To block one's game. 44 DA Block vb. 1.

7. You don't come no gum games over me with your soft sodder and all that (71 Eggleston *School-Master* 153). Cf. DA Gum 5 d, Gum game.

8. I wish I could spoil her game this time (74 Eggleston *Circuit* 305). Stevenson 934:6.

9. See Name (4), Two (6).

Game, adj. See Hawk (5).

Game-cock, 1. As brave as a game-cock (45 Cooper *Satanstoe* 43).

2. Went at it like two game-cocks (40 Dana *Two* 295).

Game-rooster. Crowed like a game-rooster (59 Taliaferro *Fisher's* 205).

Gammon. [You] mus'n't come no gammon over me (56 Kelly *Humors* 162). Cf. Game (7).

Gander, 1. A gone gander. 48 DA Gone 1 (6). See Coon (7).

2. To see how the gander hops. c45 DA Gander 1 b.

Garret. I don't know of anything that proves a feller a leetle soft in the garret, so much as keeping up a quarrel (44 Stephens *High Life* I 109). Cf. NED Garret 3 wrong in one's garret.

Garter-snake. I recollect now, wunst when you and I went through the long grass to the cherry-tree, your mother said, "Liddy, beware you are not bit by a garter-snake," and I never knew her meanin' until now (55 Haliburton *Nature* II 64). See Brush.

Gas. Though, to be honest about this last idea, it was my French maid that turned the gas on to that [i. e., made it clear, threw light on it]. (57 Willis *Paul* 79).

Gate-post, 1. Makes me feel as cross as two crooked gate-posts (55 Hali-

burton *Nature* II 338). Cf. NC 481
Stick (2).

2. But *I* say, a-twix you and me
and the gate-post, don't you never believe nothing that Mirandy Means
says (71 Eggleston *School-Master*
155). DA Gate 4 b (1); John Donavan *The Case of the Rusted Room*
(1937) 23. Cf. Apperson 47; Brewster
Am. Speech XVI (1944) 21; *Oxford*
43. See Barn (2), Bed-post, Post (5),
Pump (3).

Gaudy. See Sunflower (2).

Gaunt. See Greyhound (1).

Gauntlet (1). Oh, I run the same
gauntlet, said Blevins (57 Willis *Paul*
76). NED Gauntlet sb.² 2 b; *Oxford*
553; Stevenson 937:3.

Gauntlet(2). He should never be suf-
fered to depart hence, without your
throwing him the gauntlet (55 Irving
Wolfert 148). NED Gauntlet sb.¹ 1 c;
Stevenson 937:4.

Gay. See Blue bird, Buck (1) 4,
Churchyard (2), Cricket (1), Hymn,
Lark (5), Morning (6), Oriole.

General. It has been said that one bad
general is better than two good ones;
and the saying is true (61 Lincoln V
51). *Oxford* 475; Stevenson 938:1;
Holger Cahill *Look South to the Polar
Star* (1947) 147 One bad leader is
better than two good leaders . . . I
was just quoting Napoleon.

General Jackson. And the next morning he was dead as General Jackson
(59 Shillaber *Knitting-Work* 175). Cf.
Caesar (3).

Generation. The old proverb says that
"It takes three generations to make a
gentleman" (23 Cooper *Pioneers* 206;
Richardson *Secret* 444 Someone has

said that it needs). *Oxford* 234; Stevenson 945:6; Louis Tracy *The Manning-Burke Murder* 1930) 170 It
takes three centuries to make a gentleman.

Generous. See Lord 2 (2).

Genesis. It's all as true as the book of
Genesis (54 Smith *'Way* 183; Porter
Major 163). Svartengren 371. See
Apostles.

Genteel. See Bobalink.

Gentle. See Angel (2), Child (2), Kitten (3), Lamb (1, 2), Sheep (7),
Woman (10).

Geranium. Her eyes as red as geran-
nums (c60 Paul *Courtship* 50).

Get out. Hum-sick as git out (44 Stephens *High Life* II 9, 60 as easy as,
109 as mean as, 118 as impudent as,
149 as contented as, 170 as lonesome
as, 200 as nat'ral as, 222 as black as,
233 as awk'ard as, 245 jest as cozey as,
263 as cool as). Boshears 38:708; Mc-
Atee 11, *Additional* 10, *Grant County*
5; NC 413; Taylor *Comparisons* 43.

Ghost, 1. Pale as a ghost (40 Dana
Two 83, 313; Melville *White Jacket*
9; Hawthorne *House* 60 at cock-
crow; Haliburton *Sam* II 21; Durivage
Three 226; Whitcher *Widow* 238;
Mary N. Prescott *Harper's New
Monthly Magazine* XXXIII [1866]
776; Locke [Nasby] *Struggles* 206,
515). Boshears 39:788; McAtee 47;
NC 413; Taylor *Comparisons* 61;
Andy Adams *The Outlet* (Boston
1905) 133; Adam Bliss *Four Times a
Widower* (Philadelphia 1936) 197.

2. She turned as white as a ghost
(44 Stephens *High Life* I 183). Boshears 41:1017; NC 414; Taylor *Comparisons* 87; W. S. Masterman, *The
Perjured Alibi* (1935) 125.

3. We all began to get ready to give up the ghost, and lie down and die (34 Crockett *Life* 118; Melville *Mardi* I 135; Thomson *Doesticks* 157; Taliaferro *Fisher's* 20 In the expressive language of that section, "to give up the ghost"; Locke [Nasby] *Struggles* 170). Job 14:10; John 19:30; NED Ghost 1; Stevenson 948:10.

Gilderoy. She got it knocked higher than Gilderoy's kite—to use the language of the Pilgrims (69 Clemens *Innocents* I 263). DA Kite; Partridge 328; Taylor *Comparisons* 48; Herbert Corey *Crime at Cobb's House* (1934) 35. See Kite 2 (1).

Gills. Bill turned powerful white about the gills (53 Hammett *Stray* 133). J. J. Connington, pseud. *Tragedy at Raventhorpe* (Boston 1928) 33. Cf. Farmer and Henley III 143 blue, green, rosy; McAtee *Additional* 11 pale; NED Gill 3 b blue, red, rosy, white, yellow.

Giraffe. To come the giraffe over [i. e., to cheat]. 44 DA Giraffe 2.

Girl, 1. He was as bashful as a girl (33 Hall *Soldier's Bride* 63). Svartengren 67 mayden.

2. But now he is as pale and spoony as a milliner's girl (66 Bowman *Bear-Hunters* 123).

3. You must come and see it, if you have to come afoot and alone as the gal went to be married (33 Smith *Downing* 233, *'Way* 172 afoot and alone, as the gal went to be married).

4. Nice putty stars, but lord love you, as the gal said to her feller, if you could only see the bunch thats right over our front door (33 Neal *Down-Easters* I 135).

5. They [girls] say No when they

mean yes (69 Alcott *Little Women* 395). Apperson 704; *Oxford* 397; Stevenson 2576–2577:10, 2577:7; Tilley W660.

6. Girls will be girls, you know (70–73 McCloskey *Across* 98). John S. Strange, pseud. *Silent Witnesses* (1938) 216. See Boy (4).

7. Little girls have little wit (66 Bowman *Bear-Hunters* 412).

8. Little girls shouldn't ask questions (68 Alcott *Little Women* 81). Cf. Apperson 391 Maid (12); *Oxford* 92–93 Children (Maidens) should be seen and not heard; Tilley M45.

9. There is a good deal of truth in the old saying, "if the girls won't run after the men, the men will run after them" (55 Haliburton *Nature* II 88).

10. There is somethin' wus than galls in the bushes (40 Haliburton *Clockmaker* III 130).

Give, 1. That's what I call giving as good as they saunt (35 Kennedy *Horse-Shoe* 24; Thompson *Chronicles* 113 However, his tongue was free, and with it he gave Mr. Harley as good as he sent; Stephens *High Life* II 94, 156 gin the mayor back as good as he sent, with a pint cup full over; Cooper *Redskins* 179; Haliburton *Sam* I 165; Paul *Courtship* 44). Apperson 247; Stevenson 955:4; bring; Tilley G122.

2. Never seeking a fight even then, he had, nevertheless, when any ambitious champion came from afar for the purpose of testing his strength, felt himself bound to "Give him what he came after" (74 Eggleston *Circuit* 119).

3. Those who give so freely should know how to take a little in return (45 Cooper *Chainbearer* p. v; Clemens *Gilded* II 29 She thought that

"give and take was fair play"). *Oxford* 238; Tilley G121.

Gizzard, 1. Woman, fret not thy gizzard! (53 Cary *Clovernook* 2d Ser. 186; Whitcher *Widow* 133 Don't fret your gizzard, Melissy, 241; Riley *Puddleford* 143). Farmer and Henley III 151; NED Gizzard 2; Partridge 331; Stevenson 961:9.

2. Why, that chap over thar couldn't make sich a picture as that to save his gizzard (51 Burke *Polly* 161; Eggleston *School-Master* 71, *Circuit* 144).

Glacier. Cold as the glacier of an unsunned cavern! (60 Holmes *Professor* 141).

Glaive. He is said to be a double-edged glaive, cutting both friend and foe (65 Sedley *Marian* 326). Cf. Sword (3).

Glass, 1. The bread . . . was . . . brittle as glass (47 Melville *Omoo* 343). Apperson 68; Halpert 883; NC 414; Stevenson 246:5; Svartengren 265; Tilley G134; Whiting *Drama* 314:140, *Scots* I 177.

2. Slippery as glass (39 Briggs *Harry* II 135; Bennett *Kate* 164). Boshears 40:930; Taylor *Comparisons* 74; Whiting *Drama* 314:140.

3. Smooth as glass (25 Neal *Brother J* III 419; Smith *Downing* 24; Thompson *Major* 132–133; Stephens *High Life* II 13, *Mary Derwent* 235–236; Shillaber *Mrs. Partington* 258; Paul *Courtship* 31; Browne *Artemus* 20; Clemens *Innocents* II 377). Apperson 582; Boshears 40:941; NC 414; Taylor *Comparisons* 75; Tilley G136; Stanley F. Bartlett *Beyond the Sowdyhunk* (Portland, Me., 1937) 16.

4. An eye that when he looked at you made you feel as transparent as a piece of flint glass (45 Mayo *Kaloolah* 106). Svartengren 362.

5. See Bottom.

Glisten. See Cat (43), Eye (9), Gold (1), Hailstorm.

Gloomy. See Grave (4).

Glossy. See Crow, sb. (2), Raven (2).

Glove, 1. I'm as easy as an old glove, but a glove aint an old shoe to be trod on (36 Haliburton *Clockmaker* I p. xi, *Attaché* IV 34 as free and easy as). Svartengren 346.

2. Uniforms fitting like a glove (c61 Chamberlain *Confession* 186; Clemens *Roughing* I 95 and fitted like a glove, *Gilded* II 279, *Tramp* II 206). NC 414; Svartengren 319; Taylor *Comparisons* 44; The Aresbys, pseud. *Murder at Red Pass* (1931) 150.

3. I'll give you a touch of natur' without no gloves on (37 Neal *Charcoal* 217).

4. I'll handle it [a poem] without gloves (56 Cooke *Foresters* 34). DA Handle vb. 1; NED Glove 1 f; Stevenson 963–964:13; Isabel Ostrander *The Crimson Blotter* (1921) 126. See Mitten (3).

5. To handle with kid gloves. 64 DA Kid sb. 4.

Gnat. You are just the chap to strain at a gnat, and swaller a camel, tank, shank, and flank, all at a gulp (36 Haliburton *Clockmaker* I 156; Cooper *Pathfinder* 293 one is not to strain at a gnat lest they swallow a camel, *Redskins* 205–206 This is straining at the gnat and swallowing the camel, 244 Well has it been said, that man often strains at a gnat and swallows a camel; Jones *Batkins* 260). Matt. 23:24; Bradley 77; *Oxford* 624; Stevenson

153

966:6; Tilley G150; Edison Marshall *Dian of the Lost Land* (1935) 126 he had swallowed a camel to choke on a gnat.

Go, 1. She may go farther and fare worse, afore she'll meet his equal (45 Cooper *Chainbearer* 382; Cary *Clovernook* 2d Ser. 356; Stephens *Mary Derwent* 309 A feller might go farther and fare worse [in choosing a wife]). Apperson 250; NC 405; *Oxford* 241; Stevenson 967:1; Tilley G160; Kay C. Strahan *The Hobgoblin Murder* (Indianapolis 1934) 193.

2. I like the idee, and said I'd go in for it (56 Whitcher *Widow* 274; Boucicault *Flying Scud* 197 Sometimes, sez he, my heart goes in for her). DA Go 6 d. See Farmer and Henley III 162 (expressing doubt of its quality as an Americanism).

3. See Aloft, Bat 1 (2), Bird (18), Mill 1 (3), Streak (2), Wind (10).

Goat, 1. It is about as easy to find a good inn in Halifax, as it is to find wool on a goat's back (36 Haliburton *Clockmaker* I 17, *Sam* I 118 I might as well go to a goat's house to look for wool, *Nature* II 412). Apperson 709; *Oxford* 242; Tilley G170; Woodard PADS VI (1946) 38; Liam O'Flaherty *The Tent* (London 1926) 136 You can't get wool off a goat. See Pigsty.

2. Almost as swift and agile as goats (54 Langdon *Ida* 156).

Go-by. I give them the go-by for the Dimitys (53 Willis *Fun* 54, 112, *Paul* 57; Butler *Nothing to Wear* 5 Gave . . . go by to the duties [i. e., ignored them]). Farmer and Henley III 169; Green 163; NED Go-by; Partridge 335; Tilley G171.

God, 1. Surely, as there is a God above (25 Neal *Brother J* II 115). NC 415; Tilley G175; Whiting *Drama* 314:145. Cf. Stevenson 2249:6 God in Gloucestershire; Neil Bell, pseud. *The Disturbing Affair of Noel Blake* (1932) 14 as sure as God.

2. God comes to see us without a bell (32 Emerson *Journals* II 480 a Spanish proverb, IV 127, *Works* II 271). Apperson 250; *Oxford* 243; Stevenson 972:5; Tilley G181.

3. What's this Poor Richard says, "God helps them that help themselves" (55 Melville *Israel* 70, 79, 153, 156). Apperson 251; NC 415; *Oxford* 244; Snapp 87:25; Stevenson 979:11; NQ 2 iv 292, 317; 3 vi 339; H. C. Kittredge *Mooncussers of Cape Cod* (Boston 1937) 152; R. P. Warren *All the King's Men* (1946) 102. Cf. Fortune (3); NC 422 Heaven.

4. Well says the German proverb "God is patient because he is eternal" (65 Richardson *Secret* 21).

5. God never sends mouths . . . but he sends meat (32 Kennedy *Swallow* 216). Apperson 252; *Oxford* 245; Stevenson 971:10; Tilley G207.

6. How true it is that "God tempers the wind to the shorn lamb" (41 Lincoln I 260). Apperson 253; NC 415; *Oxford* 246; Stevenson 980–981: 15; Tilley S315; E. C. Bentley and H. W. Allen *Trent's Own Case* (1936) 4.

7. There's nothin' impossible—with God (25 Neal *Brother J* II 35). Stevenson 971:9; Whiting *Drama* 17, 30.

Gods. The saying is wise . . . That "the gods don't allow us to be in their debt" (68 Saxe *Poems* 11).

Gold, 1. It ain't all gold that glitters (38 Haliburton *Clockmaker* II 179, III 38; Thompson *Major* 75; Cooper *Chainbearer* 148; Kelly *Humors* 188; Hammett *Wonderful* 243 glistens, *Pin-*

ey 151 shiney; Whitcher *Widow* 247; Clemens *Roughing* I 199). Apperson 6; NC 416; *Oxford* 249; Snapp 90:4; Stevenson 990:13; Tilley A146; Whiting *Drama* 122, 134, 215, *Scots* I 179; E. B. Black *The Ravenelle Riddle* (1933) 36; J. P. Marquand *Sports* II (1955) 29 and here as elsewhere, all that glitters is not gold; NQ 11 xi 393, xii 10, 59.

2. Those who have a little old corn are as chary of it as if it were gold (58 Hammett *Piney* 207).

3. I didn't like to touch it, for they say another's gold is apt to stick (21 Cooper *Spy* 138).

4. Bright as gold (56 Cary *Married* 193). NC 416; Taylor *Comparisons* 21.

5. The offer . . . was as good as gold (35 Longstreet *Georgia* 160; Shillaber *Knitting-Work* 253; Bowman *Bear-Hunters* 37; Lowell *Biglow* 232; Alcott *Little Women* 186–187 The girls are all as good as gold). Apperson 256; Boshears 37:601; NC 416; Taylor *Comparisons* 44; V. R. *American Notes and Queries* IV (1944–1945) 59; K. P. Kempton *Monday Go to Meeting* (1937) 228.

6. Yellow as gold (49 Melville *Mardi* II 227; Stephens *Fashion* 336; Clift *Bunker* 184). Apperson 717; Boshears 41:1044; NC 416; Svartengren 252; Taylor *Comparisons* 89; Tilley G280.

Gold mine. See Silver mine (3).

Goober, 1. If the armys of the West were worth a goober (63 Wiley *Johnny* 340).

2. To hull the goobers for [i. e., to defeat]. 67 DA Goober 2 b.

Good, 1. It is good to be shifty in a new country (45 Hooper *Simon* 12).

2. The often repeated verse which followed, that The good die young (52 Cary *Clovernook* 39; Nash *Century* 225). Apperson 254; NC 416; *Oxford* 247; Snapp 88:61; Stevenson 510:3, 525:3, 526:5; Tilley G251; NQ 1 iii 377; 3 viii 171, 216, 342, 483; 4 x 439; 12 iv 78, 118; Margaret M. Bryant *Southern Folklore Quarterly* XII (1948) 284; E. S. McCartney *Papers of the Michigan Academy of Science, Arts and Letters* XIII (1931) 126 We say the good die young.

3. You look good enough tu eat (44 Stephens *High Life* II 233; Clemens *Washoe* 37).

4. Too good to be true (57 Melville *Confidence-Man* 322; Clemens *Roughing* I 274, *Gilded* I 44). Stevenson 994:3; Tilley N156; Charles Reade *Hard Cash* (1863, ed. London 1913) 484; Anthony Boucher, pseud. *The Case of the Seven of Calvary* (1937) 167.

5. See Ace (4), Almanac, Bank (1), Child (3), Cranberry tart, Gold (5), Honey (2), Meeting (1), New (1), Nut (4), Nutcake (1), Oracle, Pie (1), Play (2), Show (1), Thrip, Wheat (1), Word (4, 7).

Good-humored. See Bear (8).

Good-natured. See Baby (1), Bear (9), Cat (10), Day (7), Eel (3), Kitten (4), Lamb (3), Pig (4), Robin (1).

Goods, 1. His face before was as white as his bleached goods (39 Briggs *Harry* I 151). See Cambric.

2. To deliver the goods. 79 DA Goods 6 (1).

Good will. It is a proverb of the world that good will makes intelligence, that goodness itself is an eye (c54 Emerson *Works* VIII 342).

Goodwin Sands. The snow and water had formed a delusive compound as unstable as the Goodwin Sands (37 Neal *Charcoal* 179).

Goose, 1. As much like real snow, as wild geese are like wooden legs (55 Thomson *Doesticks* 182–183).

2. It's a gone goose with him (47 Dorson *Jonathan* 100; Smith *Downing* 71 It'll be gone goose with us, 115, '*Way* 21 it's a gone goose with him, 70, 102, 248 he was a "gone goose," 329, *My Thirty* 307, 320, 342 we are a gone-goose people, 381, 449 a gone goose; Haliburton *Clockmaker* I 151, 244, 311, 325, II 16, 210, III 103, 278, *Letter* 192, *Attaché* II 29, 252, *Sam* II 193, *Season-Ticket* 46). Bartlett 252; DA Gone 1 (7); Farmer and Henley III 176; Stevenson 1009:5; Thornton I 373; Kathleen M. Knight *Death Blew Out the Candle* (1935) 142. See Coon (7).

3. Sound upon the goose (67 Lowell *Biglow* 280, 311). Bartlett 254, 630; DA Goose 4 a; Farmer 272; Farmer and Henley III 182; Partridge 343; NED Goose 1 d; Schele de Vere 267; Stevenson 1008:3; Thornton II 740, III 368.

4. Every man thinks his own geese swans (21 Loomis *Farmer's Almanac* 178; Neal *Down-Easters* I 26 Every goose a swan; Haliburton *Nature* II 396 It seems English geese are all swans; Judd *Margaret* I 278 Some people's geese are always swans; Holmes *Autocrat* 273). Apperson 265; NED Goose 1 d; *Oxford* 234; Stevenson 1010:11; Tilley G369; Whiting *Drama* 86; Alice Campbell *Keep Away from Water!* (1935) 18.

5. The goose hangs high. 63 DA Goose 4 b; Stevenson 1010:4.

6. You will wish that you hadn't turned up your nose at the goose that lays the golden aig (76 Nash *Century* 34, 126 Keep mum, and stick to the goose that lays the golden aig). Apperson 266; NC 416; NED *Supplement* Goose 1; *Oxford* 334; Stevenson 1007–1008:9; Tilley G363.

7. She was a salin' along like a goose in a mud puddle, with her great eyes a starin' at nothin' (56 Whitcher *Widow* 154).

8. I love to talk—he said—as a goose loves to swim (72 Holmes *Poet* 89).

9. You have . . . the head of a goose (56 Boucicault *Flying Scud* 188).

10. A man ought to know a goose from a gridiron (55 Haliburton *Nature* II 249). *Oxford* 343; Stevenson 1328:15; Tilley H226.

11. We will live to eat the goose that will fatten on the grass that grows on yer own grave (c61 Chamberlain *Confession* 227). Apperson 266; *Oxford* 166; Tilley G353.

12. He seemed to be a man of fine feelings, altogether above his station; a most inglorious one, indeed; worse than driving geese to water (49 Melville *Redburn* 174).

13. But I never interfere with nobody's business, not I indeed; as we say in the north [of England]—"Who mells with what another does, Had best go home and shoe his gooze" (60 Haliburton *Season-Ticket* 202–203). Apperson 565–566; Lean II ii 700; *Oxford* 582; Tilley G354; Whiting *Drama* 347:587.

14. See Noddy.

Gooseberry. Ef thar was a chance for you arter that, as big as a gooseberry, Old One-Eyed couldn't diskiver it (57 Bennett *Border* 436). Cf. Farmer and

Henley III 183; Stevenson 2643:8 not worth a gooseberry.

Goose grease, 1. Talk as iley as goose-grease (43 Robb *Squatter* 94).

2. I'll take you through as slick as goose grease (51 Burke *Polly* 192). DA Goose grease; NC 416; Svartengren 348; Thornton II 810. See Grease (1).

Goose's foot. And he was as red as a goose's foot during a cold day in winter (59 Browning *Forty-Four* 144).

Gosling, 1. I know just about as much of the law as a spring gosling (54 Stephens *Fashion* 307).

2. Me and the whole on 'em is little better nor a flock of gone goslings (37 Neal *Charcoal* 179). NC 416. See Coon (7).

Gospel, 1. Thar were her [a panther's] tracks as clare as Gospel (60 Whitehead *Wild Sports* 80).

2 (a). True as gospel (35 Kennedy *Horse-Shoe* 235; Haliburton *Clockmaker* III 237, *Attaché* I 237, II 128 gospel truth, *Old Judge* I 319, *Sam* I 231 I don't suppose his stories are all just Gospel, 336; Cooper *Chainbearer* 220, *Redskins* 147, 148; Durivage *Three* 59; Thomson *Plu-ri-bus-tah* 208 and her words proved true as Gospel; Jones *Wild* 87; Clift *Bunker* 18). Farmer and Henley III 186–187; Stevenson 2381:1; Svartengren 371; Alice Campbell *The Murder of Caroline Bundy* (1932) 153.

(b). To be true as the gospel (27 Cooper *Prairie* 132, *Satanstoe* 41, 254 The gospel is not more certain, *Redskins* 501; Stephens *Mary Derwent* 214). Apperson 647; NC 417; NED Gospel 4; *Oxford* 672; Stevenson 1011:9, 2381:1; Tilley G378; Whiting *Drama* 315:148; Magdalene King-

Hall *Gay Crusader* (1934) 139. See Apostles.

Goss. Giving "particular goss" to the lower town editor and his abettors (43 Robb *Squatter* 33, 75 gin him goss without sweeten'; Burke *Polly* 99, 170; Field *Pokerville* 80 but de debbil gin Massa Slunk goss night 'fore las', I reckon, 114 Old Sol was going to get goss; Thomson *Plu-ri-bus-tah* 58 Give the red men Goss; Porter *Major* 86, 115). DA Goss; Farmer and Henley III 188; Thornton I 377; NQ CLVIII (1930) 406.

Gossamer. Thin as gossamer (49 Melville *Mardi* I 141). Cf. NC 417.

Gourd, 1. They'll never make gourds out o' me [i. e., deceive me]. (51 Burke *Polly* 31). DA Gourd 1 c (this example).

2. Till his skull rattled like ontu a ole gourd (67 Harris *Sut* 71).

3. To saw gourds [i. e., to snore]. 70 DA Saw vb. 1.

4. If it a'n't the next place to no whar, you can take my head for er drinkin' gourd (51 Burke *Polly* 67). Cf. Football (4).

Government. I concur in the old maxim, that that government is best which governs least (45 Judd *Margaret* II 104). Stevenson 1015:5.

Gowdy. Give 'em gowdy (76 Nash *Century* 76). DA Gowdy.

Grace. There is no grace in giving that which sticks to the fingers (34 Loomis *Farmer's Almanac* 178).

Graceful. See Bird (12), Fawn (1).

Grain (1), 1. It was the grain that broke the back of the camel (59 Shillaber *Knitting-Work* 55; Richardson *Secret* 324 that was the last grain of sand which broke the camel's back, *Beyond* 265 My negative was the last grain of sand, and he turned despairingly away). See Camel (2), Feather (6).

2. 'Tis time to reap when the grain is shrunk and yellow (45 Judd *Margaret* II 121).

3. When the grain is weedy, we must reap high (45 Judd *Margaret* II 115).

Grain (2). Slyly rubbing the old man against the grain (20–22 Irving *Bracebridge* 104; Smith *Downing* 25 to go rather against my grain; Davis *Downing* 182; Stephens *High Life* II 17 it goes agin the grain, 258; Judd *Margaret* II 182 It's no use talking agin the grain; Jones *Country* 101 it goes mightily agin the grain, 219; Melville *Confidence-Man* 179 much against; Lowell *Biglow* 279 my grain; Clemens *Washoe* 115, 134; Saxe *Poems* 152). Apperson 4; NC 417; NED Grain 16 b; *Oxford* 5; Stevenson 1019:10; Tilley G404.

Grampus. Sighing like a grampus (49 Melville *Mardi* I 337, *Moby-Dick* I 174 this fish, whose loud sonorous breathing, or rather blowing, has furnished a proverb to landsmen). Babcock 262; NED Grampus 1 c; *Oxford* 261.

Grand. See Cuffee, Play, sb. (3), Turk (1).

Grandmother, 1. So she . . . looked as if she'd jest lost her granny (44 Stephens *High Life* I 243).

2. Larn your granny how to suck eggs—will ye? (25 Neal *Brother J* II 50). Apperson 620–621; Farmer and Henley III 193, VII 23; NC 417; NED Egg 4 b; *Oxford* 645; Stevenson 1020–1021:11; Tilley G406–409; Mar-

gery Allingham *Dancers in Mourning* (1937) 156.

3. You showed her how she had shot her grandmother (55 Haliburton *Nature* II 297 [Note: "means fancying you have discovered what was well known before"]; Hammett *Piney* 40 "*barking up the wrong tree,*" leastways that's how *we* baptize it. "Nutmegs" [a nickname] thar, he'd call it "shooting yer granny," and it's pretty much knowed in the white settlements as "finding a mar's nest"). Bartlett 587; DA Shoot vb. 7 (2); Farmer 274; Farmer and Henley III 193; Stevenson 1020:8.

4. Don't teach your grandmother to clap ashes (53 Haliburton *Sam* I 78). Ayers PADS XIV (1950) 80 Teach . . . lap.

5. I couldn't . . . no more than I would strike my granny (44 Stephens *High Life* II 89). See Quaker (2).

Granite, 1. He is as firm as granit (34 Davis *Downing* 66, 240). Svartengren 261; Van Wyck Mason *Seeds of Murder* (1930) 92.

2. As hard as granit (34 Davis *Downing* 74). Svartengren 89.

Granny. See Grandmother.

Grape, 1. Mellow as a grape [i. e., drunk]. (47 Melville *Omoo* 172).

2. An unlucky miss . . . uttered something in a loud whisper about "sour grapes" (33 Hall *Soldier's Bride* 213; Thompson *Major* 43 They's sour grapes to them as can't git 'em; Willis *Fun* 53 I felt that I must remove "sour grapes" from my escutcheon). Apperson 268; NC 417; *Oxford* 262; Stevenson 1021:2; Stoett 501; Tilley F642; Yamamoto *Dickens* 45; Bruce Graeme, pseud. *A Murder of Some Importance* (Philadelphia 1931) 213; R. P. War-

ren *All the King's Men* (1946) 128 Or perhaps it was because I had . . . the case of sour grapes that a wallflower has.

Grape vine. As loving as a young grape vine round a black elder bush (44 Stephens *High Life* II 151, 235 as lovin as a grape vine round an oak limb).

Grass, 1. Green as grass! a regular cabbage-head! (49 Melville *Redburn* 37; Whitcher *Widow* 308; Harris *Uncle Remus* 49 dem 'simmons wuz green ez grass). Apperson 273–274; Boshears 37:620; McAtee 31; NC 417; Randolph and Wilson 177; Stevenson 1039:10; Taylor *Comparisons* 45; Tilley G412; Whiting *Scots* I 181; Charlotte M. Russell *Murder at the Old Stone House* (1933) 78.

2. As long as grass grows. 71 DA Grass 4 d; Stevenson 1024:1.

3. Between grass and hay. 48 DA Grass 4 c; Stevenson 1023:6, 1092:3.

4. She may go to grass for what I keer (33 Smith *Downing* 140, 180 I'd sooner let nullification go to grass and eat mullen, 'Way 291, *My Thirty* 259; Thompson *Major* 195; Stephens *High Life* I 40, 55 tell him to go to grass and eat bog hay, 110, 122, 132, 141, II 10, 154, 215; Riley *Puddleford* 186, 199). Bartlett 256; Brewster *Am. Speech* XIV 266; DA Grass 4 a; Farmer and Henley III 196; NC 417; NED Grass 9 c; McAtee *Additional* 9; Stevenson 1023:10; Thornton I 370; Tidwell PADS XIII (1950) 17; Wilson 547; Woodard PADS VI (1946) 15; Vincent Starrett *Murder on "B" Deck* (1929) 42.

5. He tripped and "went to grass," so far as the back-yard of our boarding-house was provided with that vegetable (60 Holmes *Professor* 279).

6. We mustn't have the grass growing to our horse's heels, when we have a whole pack of King George's hounds on our trail (35 Kennedy *Horse-Shoe* 427; Stephens *High Life* I 29 I didn't let the grass grow under my feet, 70, II 11; Cary *Married* 88 s'pose we walk faster and keep the grass from growing under our trotters; Irving *Wolfert* 251; Whitehead *Wild Sports* 83; Browne *Artemus* 140). Apperson 269; McAtee 31; NED Grass 1 c; *Oxford* 262; Stevenson 1024:2; Stoett 727; Tilley G421; S. L. Bradbury *Hiram Harding of Hardscrabble* (Rutland, Vt. 1936) 206.

7. There an't no two spears of grass alike (45 Judd *Margaret* II 182).

Grasshopper, 1. He was singing blithe as a grasshopper (20–22 Irving *Bracebridge* 247).

2. Chipper as a grasshopper on a high rock in a sunshiny day (44 Stephens *High Life* II 192).

3. As chirk as a grass-hopper (44 Stephens *High Life* I 196).

4. As quick as a grasshopper (44 Stephens *High Life* II 62). Cf. Svartengren 161 nimble, lively, pert.

5. They hadn't grit enough tu hist a grasshopper out of a bog of swampgrass (44 Stephens *High Life* II 155).

6. Desarves tu be kicked tu death by grasshoppers (44 Stephens *High Life* I 133, II 185 I hope I may be kicked to death with grasshoppers, if . . . , 208 ought tu be kicked tu death by grasshoppers, and have his buryin hymn sung by tree-toads; Durivage *Three* 396 I hope I may be kicked to death by grasshoppers if I ever take charge of a lady again). Bartlett 811.

7. He ought to be sung to death by screech owls, and knocked into the

middle of next week by crippled grass-hoppers (44 Stephens *High Life* II 130).

Grave, 1. A stillness . . . awful as the grave (25 Neal *Brother J* II 147).
2. Black as the grave (25 Neal *Brother J* III 30–31). Svartengren 241.
3. But your mouth must be as close as the grave (42 Irving *Attorney* 63).
4. The struggle was dark as the grave (44 Stephens *High Life* II 107, *Mary Derwent* 141 The night came on, dark and gloomy as the grave). Svartengren 237 dark.
5. Mute as the grave (25 Neal *Brother J* III 165).
6. All quiet as the grave (23 Cooper *Pioneers* 324, *Pilot* 405; Neal *Brother J* III 210, 406, *Rachel* 144, 234). Halpert 562 graveyard; Taylor *Comparisons* 67; Barnaby Ross, pseud. *The Tragedy of Y* (1932) 244.
7. I will be as secret as the grave (42 Irving *Attorney* 270; Haliburton *Nature* I 177, 361; Durivage *Three* 215). NED Grave 1 d; Svartengren 129; Nicholas Blake, pseud. *Shell of Death* (1936) 32.
8. Silent . . . as the grave (24 Cooper *Pilot* 65, 273, *Pathfinder* 432; Haliburton *Clockmaker* I 91, *Attaché* IV 186; Jones *Country* 39; Clemens *Washoe* 87 the man . . . was as cold, and as silent, and as solemn as the grave itself). Apperson 571; Boshears 40:912; Halpert 609 tomb; NC 417; *Oxford* 589; Stevenson 2111:11; Taylor *Comparisons* 73; Anthony Gilbert, pseud. *The Murder of Mrs. Davenport* (1928) 253.
9. Still as the grave (33 Neal *Down-Easters* II 121; Dana *Two* 366; Melville *Omoo* 29, *Mardi* I 157, *White Jacket* 85; Stephens *Fashion* 415, *Homestead* 124). *Oxford* 589; Taylor *Comparisons* 78; Gordon Gardiner *At the House of Dree* (1928) 140.
10. I am not one of them who dig their graves with their teeth (27 Cooper *Prairie* 16). Apperson 152; Bradley 77; *Oxford* 145; Stevenson 965:9; Tilley E53; Helen Ashton *Doctor Serocold* (1930) 58.

Grave, adj. See Lion (5), Willow (1).

Gravel. He looked all about him for a moment . . . and then 'scratched gravel' like a new one (51 Dorson *Jonathan* 74; Sedley *Marian* 234 but ye'd best scratch gravel if ye don't want your har frizzled). DA Scratch vb. 3 (2).

Graveyard, 1. And then says she, as solum as a grave-yard (54 Shillaber *Mrs. Partington* 52).
2. The town is still as a graveyard (65 Browne *Artemus Ward His Travels* 192). Cf. NC 417 quiet.

Grease, 1. Slick as grease, we say (33 Neal *Down-Easters* I 62; Smith *Downing* 184; Haliburton *Clockmaker* III 190, *Attaché* II 211; Stephens *High Life* I 64, 149, II 12; Lowell *Biglow* 45; Dorson *Jonathan* 77 He done me out of that ere cent as slick as grease upon a cartwheel; Hammett *Piney* 114, 172, 259). Bartlett 607; DA Slick 6 (1); Halpert 995; NC 418; Thornton II 809; Maurice C. Johnson *Damning Trifles* (1932) 215. See Goose-grease (2).
2. A feas'ble plan, thet 'ud work smooth ez grease (67 Lowell *Biglow* 288, 339).
3. She . . . began to pour the grease on without mercy [i. e. to beat]. (59 Browning *Forty-Four* 42).

Grease spot. There was scarce enough left of him, after the canvass was over, to make a small grease spot (36 Crockett *Exploits* 22; Fairfield *Letters* 308 I heard three sermons upon Millerism . . . they left nothing but a grease spot [of it]; Smith *My Thirty* 302 This . . . investigation . . . is likely to use General Scott all up to nothing; there won't be so much as a grease spot left of him). Bartlett 262; McAtee 31; Thornton I 387.

Greasy. See New Zealander.

Greedily. See Pike sb. (2).

Greek, 1. Fetchin' home nasty puckery apples to eat, as sour as Greek, that stealin' made sweet (43 Haliburton *Attaché* IV 113–114).
2. [Terms of falconry] all heathen Greek to old Christy (20–22 Irving *Bracebridge* 23; Melville *Redburn* 36 This was all Greek to me, *Israel* 47 a long string of French, which of course was all Greek to poor Israel; Kelly *Humors* 192; Anon. *New Hope* 217 As all this is Greek to us; Locke [Nasby] *Struggles* 211 their talk is all Greek to our voters; Clemens *Innocents* I 145 This was all Greek to him, *Gilded* II 257). Apperson 273; NED Greek sb. 8; *Oxford* 266; Stevenson 1037–1038:8; Tilley G439; Whiting *Drama* 347:594; H. K. Webster *The Man with the Scarred Hand* (1930) 264. See Hebrew.
3. When "Greek meets Greek" (37 Neal *Charcoal* 37; Haliburton *Nature* II 86 then comes the tug of war; Kelly *Humors* 220; Saxe *Poems* 454; Jones *Batkins* 199, 344). Bradley 77; NED Greek sb. 1 b; *Oxford* 266; Stevenson 1038:4; Tilley G440; Aldous Huxley *Two or Three Graces* (London 1926) 175 in this case, an exchange of anecdotes; Arthur Train *The Adventures of Ephraim Tutt* (1930) 660 When Tutt meets Tutt.

Green, 1. The closest man I ever saw, —as close . . . as green is to a leaf (53 Baldwin *Flush* 320). Cf. Bark (1) 1.
2. Do you see anything that looks green in there? he said, pulling down his eyelid with his forefinger (39 Briggs *Harry* I 75; Baldwin *Flush* 244 looking him . . . in the eye, and seeming to say by the expression of his own, "Squire, do you see anything green here?"). Farmer and Henley III 205; NED Green 1 h; *Oxford* 266; Stevenson 1039:13; William Gerhardi *Pretty Creatures* (London 1927) 85.
3. I ain't as green as you Gusty [Augusta] folks thinks (51 Burke *Polly* 33; Stowe *Uncle* 48; Kelly *Humors* 89 You was so green you could hardly tell a crossed quarter from a bogus pistareen; Whitcher *Widow* 219 Jaby Clark, don't you feel green?; Riley *Puddleford* 205 You're green, . . . you'll sprout if you get catched in a shower; Nash *Century* 41 Yes, father, he orter be planted somewhere; he's green enough to sprout). Stevenson 1039–1040:15; C. F. Gregg *The Brazen Confession* (London [c1940]) 25 The man was not so green as he looked. Cf. Cary *Clovernook* 2d Ser. 87 Zeb, my dear boy, how very verdant you are!; Farmer and Henley III 205.
4. See Bottle (1), Catnip (1), Emerald, Grass (1), Jimson weed, Leek, Potato (2), Pumpkin (3), Sap (1), Sea (4).

Greenland. Found it cold as Greenland (36 Fairfield *Letters* 130, 401). Taylor *Comparisons* 28.

Green River. To send one up Green River [i. e., to kill]. 71 DA Green River.

Grenadier, 1. Stiff as a grenadier with his stock on, and marching in time, as if t' band were playing (66 Bowman *Bear-Hunters* 87).

2. A . . . girl . . . almost as tall as a grenadier (55 Irving *Wolfert* 195).

Grey. See Fox (3), Opossum (1), Rat (3), Steel (4).

Greyhound, 1. As gaunt as greyhounds (45 Mayo *Kaloolah* 329). Apperson 243; Svartengren 187–188; Tilley G444.

2. As lank as a greyhound (60 Haliburton *Season-Ticket* 24). Cf. Svartengren 188 lean.

3. I looked as trim as a grayhound (59 Taliaferro *Fisher's* 87).

4. Some of the girls ran like greyhounds (40 Dana *Two* 147).

Grief. There's no grief that hasn't its relief (46 Cooper *Redskins* 419).

Grig. The whole . . . party were getting as merry as grigs [i. e., drunk]. (56 Kelly *Humors* 35). Apperson 413; *Oxford* 420; Svartengren 72–75; Tilley G454; David Frome, pseud. *The Black Envelope* (1937) 219.

Grin, 1. I shall try to "tough it out," i. e., "Grin and bear it" (35 Fairfield *Letters* 38; Stephens *High Life* I 109 So I may as well grin and bear it, II 242; Melville *Moby-Dick* I 5; Hammett *Piney* 101; Thomson *Plu-ri-bus-tah* 151 If you're murdered 'grin and bear it'; Clemens *Washoe* 84; Barnum *Struggles* 218). McAtee 31; NED Grin vb. 3; *Oxford* 267; Snapp 87:27; Stevenson 682:2; Algo Sand *Señor Bum in the Jungle* (1932) 216 but I had to bear it—and I didn't even dare the proverbial grin.

2. See Cheshire cat, Foxtrap (3), Hyena (1), Monkey (2), Opossum (4), Whippoorwill, Wolf (14).

Grindstone, 1. They are as hard as the two sides of a grindstone (40 Haliburton *Clockmaker* III 154; Paul *Courtship* 51 a man may be as hard as a grindstone).

2. The proverb teaches that "there is a pound of grindstone to a pound of cheese," but I always think there are always many pounds of grindstone to an ounce of cheese (46 Emerson *Journals* VII 153).

3. My father . . . could "see as far into a grindstone" as anybody else (Jones *Batkins* 262). Van Tassel Sutphen *In Jeopardy* (1922) 160 he can see through a grindstone with a hole in it as quickly as the next man. See Millstone (3).

4. If he don't shave putty nigh the grinstun [i. e., be careful]. (33 Neal *Down-Easters* I 3).

5. If he ain't, I'll eat a grin-stone (33 Neal *Down-Easters* I 64).

Grip. To lose one's grip. 76 DA Grip 7 (1).

Grist. Some of that grist has gone to your mill (24 Cooper *Pilot* 414; Thompson *Chronicles* 104 But what of that, if it did not "bring grist to his mill?"; Jones *Batkins* 49 All was grist to his mill). Apperson 275; NC 418; NED Grist 1 c; *Oxford* 268; Stevenson 1042:11; Tilley A122; Bertram Atkey *The Man with Yellow Eyes* (1927) 81 bring; Anthony Gilbert, pseud. *The Mystery of the Open Window* (1930) 247 All is.

Gristle. Tough as grissle (59 Taliaferro *Fisher's* 168).

Grit, 1. The business folks and men of gumption were generally on the grit

[meaning perhaps "well-informed"].
(58 Porter *Major* 13).

2. To cut grit [i. e., to depart]. 59
DA Grit sb. 3.

3. I got up a leetle grit (44 Stephens *High Life* I 28, 47, 184 it made
my grit rise; Stowe *Uncle* 141 gal's got
grit; Whitcher *Widow* 149 Thinks me
she's got grit; Eggleston *School-Master*
39 it takes grit to apply for this
school). Farmer and Henley III 219.
Cf. NC 418; NED Grit 5.

Groat. Remember what Franklin has
said, my son—"A groat a day's a penny
a year" (c70 Clemens *Sketches* 189).
Hardly Franklin, but cf. Apperson 496
A pin a day is a groat a year; *Oxford*
500.

Ground, 1. The season was so completely "run into the ground" (58
Field *Pokerville* 122, 143 for even
pleasantry may, occasionally, be "run
into the ground"; Porter *Major* 16 it's
no use to run the thing into the
ground). Bartlett 542; DA Run vb.
20 (1); Schele de Vere 629; Thornton II 755; Wilson 586–587; Woodard
PADS VI (1946) 25.

2. He . . . stood his ground like a
man (55 Thomson *Doesticks* 255–
256). Cf. Tilley G467.

Grow, 1. I [Topsy] spect I grow'd.
Don't think nobody never made me
(51 Stowe *Uncle* 268). Taylor *Comparisons* 83; I. J. Gelb in American
Philosophical Society *Year Book 1955*
(Philadelphia 1956) 354 It seems that
the Egyptian dictionary just grew,
like Topsy.

2. See Jonah, Pumpkin (7), Weed,
sb.

Growl. See Bear (31).

Growth. Mother has frightened you
out of one year's growth (59 Browning
Forty-Four 50).

Gruel. Like Ehud, who . . . got what
English bullies call his gruel (43 Hall
Purchase II 199; Kelly *Humors* 271
Vowing they'd give Heeltap his gruel
next night). NED Gruel 4; Partridge
358.

Grumble. See Bear (31).

Grundy. The fear of what Mrs. Grundy may say (69 Barnum *Struggles*
460, 527). Farmer and Henley IV
369; NC 418; NED Grundy; *Oxford*
427; Snapp 81:45; Stevenson 1043:5;
J. S. Fletcher *The Burma Ruby* (1933)
111; Thomas Hood *Poems* (1840,
London 1911) 560 But what is your
opinion, Mrs. Grundy?; *Catalogue of
Political and Personal Satires . . .
1811–1819* (London 1949) IX 170
No. 11950.

Guards. Loaded to the guards. 76 DA
Guard 1 b.

Guileless. See Infancy.

Guilty. See Dog (16).

Guinea (1). Varnished over, bright
as a guinea (56 Melville "Apple-tree
Table" in *Works* XIII 316; Stephens
Mary Derwent 304 the orange in the
warp is as bright as a guinea). Van
Wyck Mason *The Budapest Parade
Murders* (1935) 133 new guinea. Cf.
Svartengren 223 farthing, penny.

Guinea (2). I'd a seen him in Guinea,
and further yet, afore he'd a got one
speck of a bow more than he give me
(44 Stephens *High Life* II 94). Samuel Pepys *Diary* June 29, 1665 Saying
truly that it had been better he had
gone to Guinny; DAE Guinea 3 I've
wished the Bark to Guinea more than

fifty times; Wilson 518; Stark Young *So Red the Rose* (1934) 62 Get up, I tell you. And go to Guinea. The explanation of "Guinea" as "synonymous with any unknown distant country" that is offered in DAE does not seem wholly convincing. Is it not rather a corruption of "Gehenna"? A confusion with Guinea may no doubt be present in the minds of speakers and hearers.

Gums. Hain't I cut my gums? (51 Burke *Polly* 33).

Gun, 1. He walked home as straight as a gun (57 Riley *Puddleford* 144). Svartengren 274 gunstick; Whiting PADS XI (1949) 28 n. 5.

2. As sure as a gun (37 Neal *Charcoal* 191; Haliburton *Clockmaker* III 306, *Letter* 192, *Attaché* II 91, III 122; Stephens *High Life* I 199, 210, II 64, 86, 135; Jones *Wild* 21; Field *Pokerville* 44–45; Shillaber *Knitting-Work* 179, 290; Anon. *New Hope* 65; Whitehead *Wild Sports* 98; Bowman *Bear-Hunters* 75). Apperson 611; Farmer and Henley III 235–236, VII 30; Green 20; NED Gun 6 a, Sure 4 a; *Oxford* 632; Schele de Vere 639; Stevenson 2249:11; Svartengren 357–358; Tilley G480; *Catalogue of Political and Personal Satires . . . 1820–1827* (London 1952) X 718 No. 15458 Oh! this is pretty fun As sure as a gun; Charles Barry, pseud. *The Corpse on the Bridge* (1928) 17.

3. Sure as gun's iron (59 Taliaferro *Fisher's* 45, 53, 93 But as sure as old Bucksmasher is made uv iron). Randolph and Wilson 180.

4. Old Bony'll beat as true as guns (45 Judd *Margaret* I 233). Svartengren II gun.

5. *"Born under a gun, and educated in the bowsprit,"* according to a phrase of his own, the man-of-war's man rolls round the world like a billow (50 Melville *White Jacket* 479). Babcock 259. Cf. NED Gun 6 c; Stevenson 2162:6.

6. Shoot, Luke, or give up the gun (60–63 Taliaferro *Carolina Humor* 17). Andy Adams *The Ranch on the Beaver* (Boston 1927) 116 It's shoot, Luke; Joseph Kirkland *Zury* (Boston 1887) 385 Shoot, Luke, er give up the gun, said one, using a slang phrase well known as a common filip to a hesitating speaker.

7. Let all Republicans stand fast by their guns (58 Lincoln III 341, 453; Holmes *Autocrat* 101 so she must stand by the guns and be ready to repel boarders). NED Gun 6 b; *Oxford* 618; Stevenson 1047:1 stand to, stick to.

8. That will spike their guns (76 Nash *Century* 209; Clemens *Tramp* I 232 That spiked my gun). William E. Hayes *Black Chronicle* (1938) 198. See Battery.

9. It blows like great guns (38 Haliburton *Clockmaker* II 163, *Sam* I 90, *Nature* I 57; Kelly *Humors* 337; Clemens *Sandwich* 62). Farmer and Henley III 202; *Oxford* 52; Stevenson 2513:4; Anthony Wynne, pseud. *The White Arrow* (Philadelphia 1932) 301–302.

Gun-barrel. Straight as a gun-bar'l (59 Taliaferro *Fisher's* 24). NC 418; Randolph and Wilson 197; Gregory Baxter, pseud. *The Ainceworth Mystery* (1930) 182.

Gunner. He [a sailor] had better have hugged the *gunner's daughter* (53 Hammett *Stray* 168; Melville *Billy Budd* (1890–1891) in *Works* XIII 54 "Such sneaks I should like to marry to the gunner's daughter!" by that expression meaning that he would like to subject them to disciplinary castigation over a gun). Babcock 262; Farmer and Henley III 236; NED Gunner 2; *Oxford* 410; Stevenson 1916:12.

Gunpowder. Quick es gunpowder (67 Harris *Sut* 53).

Gunter. Ben—bin—bean—I wonder which is accordin' to Gunter? (33 Neal *Down-Easters* I 101; Neal *Charcoal* 216; Stephens *High Life* I 145 and if I don't du everything according to gunter, 246 gunter, II 23 gunter, 80 Gunter, 101 gunter; Taliaferro *Fisher's* 232 Should these lines ever fall under his eye, he will see that they are "according to Gunter"). Bartlett 2; DA Gunter 2; Farmer 281–282; NED Gunter; Schele de Vere 309.

Guts. Them that's good enough to carry guts to a bear, they'll go with me (28 Neal *Rachel* 161, *Down-Easters* I 81 Aint fit to; Hall *Purchase* I 238 Was *he* the man to go to the legislature and carry skins [Footnote: Sausage sort] to a bear?; Haliburton *Nature* II 315 Why dat cook aint fit to tend a bear trap, and bait it wid sheep's innerds; Wiley *Johnny* 237 Our major is a fine man, the rest are not fit to tote guts to a Bear). Apperson 276; Farmer and Henley III 238; NED Gut 4; *Oxford* 80; Stevenson 2640:8; Tilley G486.

Gutter. And a drinking like so many house gutters (44 Stephens *High Life* II 152).

H

Habit. Habit they say is second natur (36 Crockett *Exploits* 29; Barnum *Struggles* 465 There is an old proverb which says that "habit is second nature," but an artificial habit is stronger than nature, 606). Apperson 130; NC 418; *Oxford* 125; Stoett 689; Stevenson 475–476:8; Tilley C932 custom. Cf. Kay C. Strahan *Death Traps* (1930) 102 Habit is a cable; A. C. and C. B. Edington *The Monk's Head Murders* 67 Habit is a mighty thing. See Custom.

Hack. To bring to a hack [i. e., to show one up]. 35 DA Hack sb. 2 b (1).

Haddock. See Braddock.

Hail, 1. Flora talked Gaelic as fast as hail (55 Haliburton *Nature* I 152). Svartengren 101.
   2. They bestow their money on the poor as free as hail (60 Haliburton *Season-Ticket* 33).
   3. Cannon balls was flying around me as thick as hail (62 Wiley *Johnny* 33). Apperson 623; NC 418; Svartengren 398; Tilley H11; Whiting *Chaucer* 164, *Drama* 315:157, *Scots* I 182.

Hail Columbia. His monkey wer a-dancin Hail Columby all over the road (67 Harris *Sut* 46; Lowell *Biglow* 228 An' kin' o' go it 'ith a resh in raisin' Hail Columby). Brewster *Am. Speech* XIV 267; DA Hail Columbia 1 b;

Thornton I 408, III 180; M. C. Keator *The Eyes through the Trees* (1930) 26 get Hail Columbia.

Hailstones, 1. Showers of balls as thick as hailstones (59 Smith *My Thirty* 272). Whiting *Scots* I 183. Cf. NC 418; Stevenson 2295–2296:9 hail; Svartengren 398; Whiting *Drama* 315: 157.
   2. The oaths fell like hailstones (47 Melville *Omoo* 94). Whiting *Drama* 315:157. Cf. Tilley H11.
   3. The bullets were flying about our heads like hail-stones (40 Cooper *Pathfinder* 74). Whiting *Scots* I 183.

Hail storm. They [girls] glistened like a hail storm (44 Stephens *High Life* I 202).

Hair, 1. It's all "hair of the same dog" (34 Davis *Downing* 40). Apperson 278; Farmer and Henley III 247; NC 418 Hair 5; *Oxford* 271; Stevenson 1051:4; Tilley H23; Stuart Palmer *The Puzzle of the Pepper Tree* (1933) 14. Cf. Taylor *Investigations* 260.
   2. It will come to me straight as a hair (39 Smith *Letters* 29, 111–112 walk as straight as a hair).
   3. Thick, according to Joe, as "the hairs on a dog" (53 Hammett *Stray* 58). Boshears 40:984. Cf. Halpert 1024; McAtee *Additional* 13; Svartengren 395; Tilley H30; Whiting *Scots* I 183; Woodard PADS VI (1946) 43.
   4. True as a hair (38 Haliburton

Clockmaker II 314; Smith *'Way* 67). F. H. Shaw *Atlantic Murder* (1933) 195.

5. 'Twont do to spile property [i. e., injure a kidnapped child] this way or Kelly'll be in my hair (54 Langdon *Ida* 45). Stevenson 1053:11. Cf. W. E. Hayes *Black Chronicle* (1938) 194 she got in Neil's hair. See Wool (3).

6. Cold enough a'most to freeze the hair off a dog's back (53 Haliburton *Sam* I 213).

7. Right to a hair (33 Neal *Down-Easters* II 127; Davis *Downing* 33; Briggs *Harry* I 63; Melville *Moby-Dick* II 239). NED Hair 8 c; Stevenson 1053:7; Stoett 754; Tilley H26; Eden Phillpotts *Found Drowned* (London c1931) 272.

8. The devil a hair I care (40 Haliburton *Clockmaker* III 151). Cf. *Oxford* 270 not worth; Stevenson 2640–2641:12; Tilley I119; Whiting *Drama* 347:599.

9. The conviction I have just stated was "getting through my hair" (53 Willis *Fun* 318). Cf. Clifford Knight *The Affair of the Scarlet Crab* (1937) 43 this fellow . . . is beginning to get in my hair.

10. We shan't give back a hair (59 Smith *My Thirty* 454). Cf. Whiting *Drama* 347:599, *Scots* I 183.

11. To have in one's hair. 51 DA Hair 5 (3). See Hair (5), above.

12. I've got it where the hair's short (79 Clemens *Tramp* I 173). DA Hair 5 (4); Dashiell Hammett *Red Harvest* (1929) 191. Cf. NED *Supplement* Hair 8 p; Stevenson 1053:9.

13. So that story has more hair than head (53 Haliburton *Sam* II 162). Cf. Apperson 278 More hair than wit; *Oxford* 70–71; Stevenson 1081:5; Tilley B736.

14. To make the hair fly. 55 DA Hair 5 (2). See Fur.

15. A noise that made my hair stand on eend (44 Stephens *High Life* I 36, 42 my hair stood up on an eend I felt so dandery, II 135 it made my hair stand on eend to look at her; Eggleston *School-Master* 109 It's pleasant to have one's hair stand on end, you know, when one is safe from danger to one's self). Farmer and Henley III 247; McAtee 32; Randolph and Wilson 109; Stevenson 788:3, 1050:11; Stoett 760; Thornton I 282.

16. I won't hurt a hair of your beautiful head, Miss Crum (53 Boker *Bankrupt* 91). J. J. Connington, pseud. *A Minor Operation* (Boston 1937) 91.

17. To split no hairs on this point (49 Melville *Mardi* I 7; Smith *My Thirty* 286 he always splits everything in two—even to a hair, 361 you can't split a hair). Apperson 597; Farmer and Henley III 246; Hardie 471:174; NED Hair 8; *Oxford* 127 cut; Stevenson 1053:5; Tilley H32; Hulbert Footner *Murder Runs in the Family* (1934) 76.

Hair's breadth. Exact . . . to a hair's breadth (54 Smith *'Way* 203; Lincoln III 380 I am against letting down the republican standard a hair's breadth, IV 58 I do not wish the sense changed, or modified, to a hair's breadth, V 191 the writer's word is good to the utmost hair's-breadth, VI 350 Do not lean a hair's breadth against your own feelings; Clemens *Sketches* 66, *Fairbanks* 151). NED Hair-breadth; Stevenson 236:8; Tilley H29. Cf. Farmer and Henley III 246 to a hair; Whiting *Scots* I 183 Hair 1.

Half, 1. Half a loaf is better than no bread (33 Hall *Soldier's Bride* 146, *Purchase* I 142 The proverb, "half a loaf better than no bread," applies here; Lewis *Odd* 39; Haliburton *Nature* II 226 for colonists won't take half a loaf; Smith *My Thirty* 297; Paul *Courtship* 222 but half a loaf is better than none). Apperson 278; Green 23; Hardie 463:73; McAtee *Grant County* 6; *Oxford* 271; Stevenson 235:12; Stoett 534; Tilley H36; Whiting *Drama* 265, 295; *Catalogue of Political and Personal Satires . . . 1811–1819* (London 1949) IX No. 11946; Georgette Heyer *Why Shoot a Butler?* (1936) 192, 203, 252.

2. As simple as puttin' two halves together to make a unit (74 Eggleston *Circuit* 268).

Half-cocked. Goes off half-cocked (53 Hammett *Stray* 226; Dorson *Jonathan* 57 at half cock, 86 Half-cocked; Lowell *Biglow* 257 Now don't go off half-cock; Nash *Century* 155 half-cocked). Bartlett 273; Farmer 284; DA Half 4 (2); McAtee 29; NC 419; NED Half-cock; Schele de Vere 197.

Half-seas. In that state which by marine imagery is called "half-seas-over" (23 Cooper *Pioneers* 399; Irving *Tales* 379; Neal *Down-Easters* II 179 half-seas over; Stephens *High Life* II 112; Melville *Moby-Dick* II 201; Haliburton *Nature* I 48; Kelly *Humors* 423 [He] was half-seas over in infatuation with Miss Betsy; Hammett *Piney* 77 By this time the bottle was half gone, and Fred's friends half seas over; Saxe *Poems* 96 Was on the seas, and "half-seas-over"). Babcock 259; DA Half 4 (2); Isaac D'Israeli *Curiosities of Literature* (4 v., New York 1862) III 26; Farmer and Henley III 250–251; NED Half-seas-over; *Oxford* 271; Partridge 368; Stevenson 639:13; Stoett 907; Taylor *Investigations* 258, 263; Tilley H53; NQ 2 iii 30, 136; 3 viii

454, ix 188; 7 iv 526, v 56; 8 ix 125; CLII (1927) 423; P. R. Shore *The Bolt* (1929) 25.

Half sled. Like a half sled on ice. 73 DA Half 4 (5).

Halt. To call a halt. 75 DA Halt sb.

Halter. If I wasn't as tough as a halter (33 Smith *Downing* 203).

Haman. The dead arm swinging high as Haman (49 Melville *Mardi* I 89; Thomson *Plu-ri-bus-tah* 226–227 a temple out of shingles, Higher, far, than Haman's gallows; Hammett *Piney* 167 I'm going to have you hung, sir—higher than Haman, sir; Stephens *Mary Derwent* 292, *Fashion* 380; Wiley *Billy* 280; Smith *Arp* 161 They built a fence around the institution as high as Haman's gallows; Clemens *Roughing* I 107). Hardie 469:108; Svartengren 280; Christopher Reeve *The Ginger Cat* (1929) 295.

Hammer, 1. As dead as a hammer (42 Irving *Attorney* 373). DA Hammer 2 b; Svartengren 142.

2. And at it I went, hammer and file (34 Davis *Downing* 47).

3. They've been at it again all day, hammer and tongs (33 Smith *Downing* 117). Farmer and Henley III 254; NED Hammer 6; Stevenson 1058:6; Anne Austin *Murder Backstairs* (1930) 270. See Shovel (2).

Hand, 1. As easy as kiss my hand (38 Haliburton *Clockmaker* II 23, 314, III 109, *Attaché* IV 250, *Sam* I 341, *Nature* II 22). Apperson 175; Stevenson 659:15; Svartengren 348; Tilley H64; Dorothy L. Sayers *Busman's Honeymoon* (1937) 148.

2. And he says that my daughter can get a divorce as easy as to turn her hand over (52 Cary *Clovernook*

241; Paul *Courtship* 153 as easily as "turn his hand over").

3. It was as flat as your hand (c60 Paul *Courtship* 59; Lowell *Biglow* 307). Boshears 36:561; NC 419; Svartengren 271 back of your hand.

4. "Witness, Simon Varney," as plain as your hand (59 Shillaber *Knitting-Work* 92). Boshears 39:796; Christopher Bush *The Kitchen Cake Murder* (1934) 137 as the back of; Paul McGuire *Death Tolls the Bell* (1933) 304 as the palm of. Cf. Svartengren 364.

5. Then help hands, for I have no lands, as Poor Richard says (55 Melville *Israel* 69). Apperson 297; *Oxford* 291; Stevenson 1060:4; Tilley H116.

6. Quarrel not being one of his habits, he manages it roughly and with great energy,—or, as Mike would say,—"like a new hand at the bellows" (32 Kennedy *Swallow* 240).

7. Many hands make light work (21 Loomis *Farmer's Almanac* 177). See All (1).

8. The maxim which says, "One hand for the owner, and t'other for yourself" (24 Cooper *Pilot* 68).

9. I haint much behind with him [i. e., am not inferior]. (44 Stephens *High Life* I 32).

10. Aint he hand and glove with all the judges and lawyers (44 Stephens *High Life* I 48; Melville *Omoo* 144, *Redburn* 287; Hawthorne *Twice-Told* 283, *Mosses* 73 hand-and-glove associate). Apperson 281; NED Hand 60 b, Hand and glove; *Oxford* 273; Smith *Browning* 221; Stevenson 1063:6; Tilley H92; Elizabeth Daly *Murder in Volume 2* (1941) 257.

11. But the iron hand is not less irresistible because it wears the velvet glove (58 Holmes *Autocrat* 153, 258 Look out for "la main de fer sous le gant de velours" (which I printed in English the other day without quotation marks, thinking whether any *scarabæus criticus* would add this to his globe and roll in glory with it to the newspapers,—which he didn't do it, in the charming pleonasm of the London language, and therefore I claim the sole merit of exposing the same). *Oxford* 321; Stevenson 1058:11; F. P. Keyes *The River Road* (1945) 386 And now you figure it will be the straight iron fist with no velvet glove.

12. The Gin'ral hez n't gut tied hand an' foot with pledges (48 Lowell *Biglow* 138). See Hog (15).

13. This was carrying it with a high hand (47 Melville *Omoo* 13). NED High 17 b.

14. At length the hawk got the upper hand (20–22 Irving *Bracebridge* 121; Kennedy *Swallow* 227, 400, *Horse-Shoe* 30, 159; Smith *Downing* 102, *My Thirty* 270, 298, 397, 414, 423, 455; Haliburton *Clockmaker* I 244; Stephens *High Life* I 109; Hooper *Simon* 34; Melville *Omoo* 243, *Mardi* II 216, *Moby-Dick* I 1; Judd *Margaret* II 121 till nater got the upper hands once more; Holmes *Elsie* 273; Clemens *Washoe* 113, *Roughing* II 5, *Tramp* I 20). Farmer and Henley III 256; Green 409; Stevenson 1058:8; Stoett 336; Tilley H95; Whiting *Drama* 369:926, cf. 356:745, *Scots* I 184 (6), cf. (5); Darwin L. Teilhet *The Ticking Terror Murders* (1935) 6.

15. Pru . . . will get the whip-hand of her (32 Kennedy *Swallow* 266; Crockett *Exploits* 21 get the whip hand of Job Snelling; Stephens *Mary Derwent* 401 she has given me the whip-hand to-night). *Oxford* 705;

Stevenson 2484:5; Tidwell PADS XI (1949) 13; Tilley W307; J. H. Wallis *The Capitol City Mystery* (1932) 305.

16. And of course he had his "hands full" (57 Jones *Country* 131; Porter *Major* 50). NED Hand 60 d; Stevenson 1060:8; Tilley H114.

17. I'll have neither hand nor foot in hanging to an awning-post [i. e., no share in]. (37 Neal *Charcoal* 200).

18. Lived from hand to mouth (61 Clemens *Letters* I 50; Boucicault *Presumptive* 238). Apperson 280; Green 176; McAtee *Grant County* 6; NED Hand to mouth; *Oxford* 376; Stevenson 1408:8; Stoett 791; Tilley H98; Lynn Brock, pseud. *The Stoke Silver Case* (1929) 124.

19. I always make a hand when about [i. e., join in]. (58 Porter *Major* 14). Cf. Tilley H99.

20. He thought that perhaps it was not best to "show his hand," as he expressed it, too soon (71 Eggleston *School-Master* 165). NED Hand 23 d, Show vb. 2 k.

21. The new-comers "took a hand" in all the sports (74 Eggleston *Circuit* 69). DA Take 2 b (4); Stevenson 1059:3.

22. Well, I wash my hands of the whole affair! (68 Alcott *Little Women* 254). Tilley H122.

23. See Satan (1).

Handle, 1. Such judges I should take it are like the handle of a jug, all on one side (36 Crockett *Exploits* 24–25). NC 432 Jug-handle.

2. Most off the handle, some o' the tribe, I guess [i. e., out of their senses]. (25 Neal *Brother J* I 107). DA Handle 1 a.

3. Fly off the handle (33 Smith *Downing* 207, 224, 'Way 40; Halibur-

ton *Clockmaker* III 216 that are old boy would have flowed right off the handle, 261, *Sam* II 177, *Nature* I 337, II 415, *Season-Ticket* 374 at the handle, 375; Lowell *Biglow* 261). Bartlett 229, 435, 784; Brewster *Am. Speech* XIV 262; DA Handle 1 a; Farmer 285; Farmer and Henley III 42, 259; McAtee 26; NED Handle 1 b; PADS III (1945) 10; Partridge 292; Schele de Vere 195–196; Stevenson 1065:1; Thornton I 338, III 146; Woodard PADS VI (1946) 13; J. D. Carr *Poison in Jest* (1932) 181.

4. Captain, siz I, ye must be mighty keerful not to give the inimy any handle onto ye (74 Eggleston *Circuit* 84).

5. I thought the tarnal critter would a gone off the handle (44 Stephens *High Life* I 33, 184 She looked as if she would go off the handle at that, 199 Here John went off the handle agin, like a broken coffee mill, 205 I thought Mary would a gone off the handle, she was so tickled, II 10 the old woman would go off the handle if I should come back without you, 36 haw-hawed till it seemed as if he'd go right off the handle, 170 it seemed as if I should go off the handle, all I could du; Judd *Richard* 86 O, I shall go off the handle!). DA Handle 1 a; NED Handle 1 b; Stevenson 1065:1; Wyndham Martyn *Murder Island* (1932) 228.

6. So he at last went off the handle—Lev buried him (56 Kelly *Humors* 374). DA Handle 1 a; NED Handle 1 b.

7. If Old Cran. was to slip off the handle, I think I should make up to her (43 Haliburton *Attaché* II 248; Kelly *Humors* 392 Old Job Carson will soon slip off the handle). Bartlett 784; Stevenson 1065:2.

8. Munk took things by the smooth

handle; but sometimes the handle was rough, and sometimes there was no handle at all; then he seized the vessel bodily (50 Judd *Richard* 133; Kelly *Humors* 114 They were all the better prepared to take things as they came, and by the smooth handle). Stevenson 1065:3. Cf. NED Handle 3 to take a thing by the best handle.

Handsome, 1. She aint no Wenus, Sir, . . . but handsome is as handsome does (58 Porter *Major* 48). Apperson 281–282; Bartlett *Familiar Quotations* 253; Farmer and Henley III 260; NC 420; NED Handsome 6; *Oxford* 274–275; Stevenson 639:2; Tilley D410; NQ 4 xi 197; 9 i 389; Melville "Billy Budd" in *Works* XIII 41 "Handsomely done, my lad! And handsome is as handsome did it, too," 48 the proverb *"Handsome is as handsome does"*; R. S. Surtees *Mr. Sponge's Sporting Tour* (London [1853]) 308 Handsome is that handsome does; J. G. Brandon *The One-Minute Murder* (1935) 165. See Pretty (1).
2. See Angel (3), Bird (10), Buttercup (1), Fawn (2), Heifer, Moon (1), Picture (2), Rose (4).

Hang, sb., 1. He "hadn't got the hang of the game" (45 Hooper *Simon* 34; Mayo *Kaloolah* 106 Some green hands couldn't at first get the hang of him; Field *Pokerville* 87 Suffice that all Pokerville "got the hang" of the Miss Wilkins's mystery at last; Shillaber *Ike* 20 "hang of the schoolhouse"). Bartlett 274–275; DA Hang 2 (1); Farmer 286; Farmer and Henley III 260–261; NED Hang 3; Stevenson 1065:12.
2. To lose the hang of. 57 DA Hang sb. 2 (2).

Hang, vb. See Dog (41), Mohammed.

Hanging. Hangin's too good for 'em (44 Stephens *High Life* I 218, II 208; Mayo *Kaloolah* 207; Haliburton *Season-Ticket* 55). McAtee *Additional* 9; Stevenson 1065:6; Sidney Williams *The Drury Club Case* (1927) 110. Cf. Smith *Downing* 174 Shooting.

Hang on. See Death (26, 27), Lamprey-eel, Leech (2), Nature (3), Toothache, Turtle (8, 9).

Happily. See Child (4), Turtle-dove.

Happy, 1. "Happy go lucky" with Jack! (40 Dana *Two* 260). NED Happy-go-lucky.
2. See Bee (5), Bird (11), Blackbird (3), Bug (1), Clam (2–4), Coon (5), Cricket (2), Day (8), King (1), Lark (6), Lord 2 (3), Opossum (2), Pig (5, 6), Queen (1).

Happy-hearted. See Boy (1).

Hard. See Adamant (2), Apple (1), Biscuit (1), Brick (1), Bullet (1), Diamond (4), Flint (2), Floor (1), Granite (2), Grindstone (1), Horn (1), Iron (2), Marble (2), Millstone (1), Pineknot, Racer, Rock (3), Sinner (1), Sole-leather (1), Stone (9).

Hardest. But if the nullifiers begin it, then the hardest must fend off (33 Smith *Downing* 186; Cooper *Chainbearer* 316 if it comes to that, 't will be "hardest fend off." We are a strong party of stout men, and aren't to be frightened by the crier of a court; Shillaber *Ike* 111). Bartlett 784.

Hare, 1. As crazy as March hares (57 Riley *Puddleford* 233). Taylor *Comparisons* 30.
2. Mad as a march hare [insane] (25 Neal *Brother J* II 333; Smith *Downing* 115 [angry], 136 [angry], 186 [angry], 195 [angry]; Stephens

High Life I 259 [angry]; Melville *Israel* 185 [insane]; Boucicault *Dot* 134 Not a gleam of reason left—mad as a March hare!; Clift *Bunker* 79 [angry]; Shillaber *Ike* 147 [angry]). Apperson 389; Farmer and Henley IV 264; Green 231; NC 442; *Oxford* 396; Taylor *Comparisons* 55; Tilley H148; Whiting *Drama* 316:159, 320:218; Nora and G. E. Jorgenson *The Circle of Vengeance* (1930) 112. Cf. Boshears 41:1029; Whiting *Scots* I 185.

3. But Bell bounced up like a hare from under a cabbage leaf (55 Jones *Winkles* 103). Cf. Apperson 286 Hare (8).

Harlot. He looked as demure as a harlot at a christenin' (38 Haliburton *Clockmaker* II 137). Svartengren 67. Cf. Halpert 872; Taylor *Comparisons* 29 bastard cousin.

Harm, 1. Harm watch, harm catch (c38 Emerson *Works* II 109). Apperson 287; *Oxford* 280; Stevenson 1077–1078:11; Tilley H167.

2. No harm in trying (57 Melville *Confidence-Man* 131). Lean IV 66 in asking; Thomas Hood *Poems* (1841, London 1911) 604 Try it again! no harm in trying; F. S. Fitzgerald *The Great Gatsby* (1925, New Classics ed., New York 1945) 68; E. S. Gardner *The Case of the Dangerous Dowager* (1937) ch. 9 Well, Drake said, there's no harm in asking.

Harmless. See Babe (3), Baby (1), Caterpillar, Cricket (3), Kitten (13), Lamb (4).

Harness, 1. The selection of the mate with whom he was to go in double harness so long as they both should live (59–60 Holmes *Elsie* 288). NED *Supplement* Harness 4.

2. There's nothing like pulling together in the harness (76 Nash *Century* 207).

3. To trot in double harness. 38 DA Harness 1 b (1).

4. To work in harness [i. e., to get along well together]. 73 DA Harness 1 b (2).

Hash. See if they couldn't settle the hash [i. e., arrange the matter]. (39 Smith *Letters* 133; Stephens *High Life* II 9, 205 your hash for you, *Mary Derwent* 253 You won't have any difficulty about settling his hash, 298; Dorson *Jonathan* 79; Jones *Wild* 133 your hash, *Country* 100; Butler *Nothing* 11 to use an expression More striking than classic, it "settled my hash"; Nash *Century* 71; Harris *Uncle Remus* 46). Bartlett 572–573; DA Hash 2 b 2 (fix); Farmer and Henley III 276; Green 179; NED Hash 3 b; Partridge 377; Schele de Vere 631; Stevenson 1080:6; Thornton I 423–424; E. S. Gardner *The Case of the Stuttering Bishop* (1936) 159.

Haste, 1. Make haste slowly (62 Lincoln V 166; Clift *Bunker* 31 the delay was only a wise way of making haste slowly). Apperson 288; Bradley 78; *Oxford* 398; Stevenson 1081:2; Tilley H192; Mike Teagle *Murders in Silk* (1938) 42.

2. Marry in haste and repent at leisure (43 Haliburton *Attaché* IV 102, *Sam* I 293; Kelly *Humors* 420 a time-honored idea; Riley *Puddleford* 137 My uncle Joe, who married in a hurry, and repented arterwards; Richardson *Beyond* 440 An overland trip is a sort of limited matrimony. One is bound to his companions for better or worse; if he select them in haste he will repent at leisure). Apperson 404; NC 443; NED Haste 6; *Oxford* 411; Stevenson 1539:1; Tilley H196; R. H. Barham

Ingoldsby Legends (1842, London 1903) 373 They 'repent at leisure who marry at random'; K. P. Kempton *Monday Go to Meeting* (1937) 143.

3. No haste and no want (57 Emerson *Journals* IX 110).

4. The more haste the worse speed (23 Cooper *Pioneers* 95; Mayo *Kaloolah* 204 the old saying, "the more haste the less speed"). Apperson 427; Hardie 465; NC 420 Great haste is not always great speed; *Oxford* 281; Stevenson 1085:1; Stoett 2134; Tilley H197; Whiting *Drama* 139, 217; Leo Bruce *Case for Three Detectives* (1937) 153 remember the English proverb, the more you haste, the less you speed.

Hasty pudding. Red stuff [dentifrice], about as thick as hasty pudding, and sweet as honey (44 Stephens *High Life* I 69). Taylor *Comparisons* 81. Cf. NC 463 Pudding; Svartengren 293 porridge.

Hat, 1. Shocking bad hat [literal]. (43 Robb *Squatter* 68; Field *Pokerville* 20 Everybody has heard of a "shocking bad hat," without being able to fix in their minds what the peculiarity expressed). Farmer and Henley III 278; NED Hat 5 c; Partridge 25; Stevenson 1068:2; Virginia Swain *The Hollow Skin* (1938) 217.

2. It was Tomally, an Egyptian as black as your hat (59 Shillaber *Knitting-Work* 113, 299 a cloud as black and opaque as my hat; Cary *Married* 402). Boshears 34:355; McAtee 15; NC 420; NED Hat 5 c; Taylor *Comparisons* 17; Richard Blaker *The Jefferson Secret* (1929) 215.

3. Quick es a 'oman kin hide a strange hat (67 Harris *Sut* 239).

4. Slick and shiny as a bran new hat (49 Dorson *Jonathan* 79).

5. You said you'd marry me at the drop of a hat (57 Jones *Country* 175). DA Drop sb. 4; Stevenson 1086:3; C. G. Givens *All Cats Are Gray* (Indianapolis 1937) 26. See Dropping (2).

6. To bet one's hat. 79 DA Hat 1 b (2).

7. Knocked into a cocked hat (34 Crockett *Life* 36; Longstreet *Georgia* 54; Neal *Charcoal* 66, 181; Hall *Purchase* II 62; Stephens *High Life* I 85, 228; Thompson *Major* 54; Cooper *Redskins* 16 cocked-hat; Lowell *Biglow* 109 Formaly to knock a man into a cocked hat wus to use him up, but now it ony gives him a chance fur the cheef madgustracy; Field *Pokerville* 62 cocked-hat; Smith *My Thirty* 306, 438; Browne *Artemus* 63 She's knockt trade into a cockt up hat). Bartlett 339; Partridge 166; Schele de Vere 591–592; Stevenson 1087:4; Thornton I 188, III 79; NQ 5 x 128, 236; 6 x 440; Anne Austin *The Black Pigeon* (1929) 250.

Hat cover. I wer on han' es solemn es a old hat kivver on collection day (67 Harris *Sut* 51).

Hatchet. I'm as ready to bury the hatchet with the Mingos as with the French (40 Cooper *Pathfinder* 185, *Chainbearer* 107 Hatchet buried berry deep . . . all, bury 'e hatchet; Jones *Country* 108 Bury the hatchet with Nap Wax; Melville *Confidence-Man* 197 engaging to bury the hatchet, smoke the pipe, and be friends forever; Lincoln II 455 Douglas and the President have probably burned [*sic*] the hatchet; Smith *Arp* 162 we would have made friends and buried the hatchet; Alcott *Little Woman* 74; Clemens *Gilded* II 111). Apperson 289; Bartlett 279–280; DA Hatchet 4 a; Farmer 290; Farmer and Henley I

389; *Oxford* 70; Partridge 112; Schele de Vere 35–36; Stevenson 1087:6; Thornton I 424, III 184; Molly Thynne *The Draycott Murder Mystery* (1928) 227.

Hate. See Cat (39), Poison (3), Sin (10), Snake (8).

Hateful. See Henbane, Serpent (1).

Hatred. Hatred begets hatred (25 Neal *Brother J* III 119).

Hatter. Looking as mad as a hatter [i. e., angry, and so in the quoted passages from American literature, but not necessarily in the comparative references]. (36 Haliburton *Clockmaker* I 58, 221, III 51, 70, *Attaché* II 271, III 161, IV 178, *Nature* II 40, 335, *Season-Ticket* 160; Shillaber *Ike* 163). Apperson 389; NC 420; NED Mad a. 8; *Oxford* 396; Taylor *Comparisons* 55–56; J. S. Fletcher *The Ebony Box* (1934) 107; Charlotte M. Russell *Murder at the Old Stone House* (1935) 84; Phoebe A. Taylor *Deathblow Hill* (Indianapolis 1935) 84; James Aston *First Lesson* (1933) 197 (insane). Cf. *The New Yorker* Feb. 26, 1955, p. 40 The saying "mad as a hatter" and the Mad Hatter of "Alice in Wonderland" both derive from the lurching gait, the tangled tongue, and the addled wits of mercurialism [caused by the mercury used in the processing of felt hats].

Have. Have it now, or wait till you can git it? (33 Neal *Down-Easters* I 82).

Haw haw. There is some critturs here, I guess, that have found a haw haw's nest, with a tee hee's egg in it (43 Haliburton *Attaché* II 89). See Mare (2).

Hawk, 1. Eyes as bright as a hawk's (44 Stephens *High Life* I 204, *Mary Derwent* 215 she is . . . bright as a hawk.

2. Paul looked . . . fresh as a daybreak hawk (55 Melville *Israel* 82).

3. About as much like the original letters, as a hawk is like a hand-saw (33 Smith *Downing* 241; Haliburton *Clockmaker* I 146 I never see one of your folks yet that could understand a hawk from a handsaw, III 187 as different from each other as . . . a hawk from a handsaw, 213 How innocent we are not to know a hawk from a handsaw). Apperson 290–291; *Oxford* 343; Stevenson 1091:13, 1329:4; Taylor *Investigations* 260; Tilley H226; Jesse Lilienthal *Gambler's Wife* (Boston 1933) 12.

4. He was as fierce as a welk hawk (53 Willis *Fun* 257).

5. Cousin Elsie was . . . game as a hawk (59–60 Holmes *Elsie* 199).

6. Hungry as hawks (38 Haliburton *Clockmaker* II 287, 320; Eliason 103). Apperson 318; Svartengren 182; Tilley H222; Gordon Gardiner *At the House of Dree* (1928) 207.

7. As sharp as hawk's claws (59 Taliaferro *Fisher's* 198).

8. As wide awake as a night hawk (44 Stephens *High Life* I 123, II 6).

9. Look at one another as wild as hawks (33 Smith *Downing* 209; Haliburton *Clockmaker* I 192 he looked as wild as a hawk, III 293). Apperson 686; NC 420; Svartengren 111 haggard [a kind of wild hawk]; Frances Pitt *Woodland Creatures* (London 1922) 141 has passed into a proverb, and when that saying was framed there can be no question that it was the sparrow-hawk that was meant.

10. I entered Richmond between hawk and buzzard—the very best hour,

I maintain, out of the twenty-four, for a picturesque tourist (32 Kennedy *Swallow* 14, 97 about twilight, between hawk and buzzard). NED Hawk 1 c; Stevenson 1091:1. Cf. NQ 5 ix 46, 134.

11. I declare, a body who has young ones, has no peace of her life. She's just between hawk and buzzard, as a body may say (56 Cary *Married* 226; Smith *Arp* 48 What satisfaction is there in living between hawk and buzzard). Apperson 290; *Oxford* 283; Stevenson 1091:1; Tilley H223.

12. With an eye like a hawk (33 Smith *Downing* 46; Stephens *Homestead* 175 She has got the eye of a hawk). NC 420; Taylor *Comparisons* 47; Lynn Brock, pseud. *Murder on the Bridge* (1930) 93.

13. Come full drive at me, like a fishin' hawk dartin' at a fish (59 Taliaferro *Fisher's* 205).

14. I knowed 'Gius had his eye on her like a blue-tailed hawk watchin' a chicken (59 Taliaferro *Fisher's* 117; Clemens *Gilded* II 84 she watches me like a hawk). Boshears 34:301; Halpert 187; McAtee *Additional* 14; Stevenson 1091:10; Taylor *Comparisons* 47; Tiffany Thayer *The Greek* (1931) to watch like the proverbial hawk.

15. He jest tuk to her from the word go, like a hawk does to a chicken (57 Bennett *Border* 436). NC 420.

Hawse-holes. In sea parlance, "they come in at the hawse-holes" [i. e., up from the ranks—not as gentlemen officers]. (50 Melville *White Jacket* 30). Babcock 261; Farmer and Henley III 283; NED Hawse-hole; *Oxford* 284; Stevenson 2026:5. See Window.

Hay, 1. Flowers . . . smelt as sweet as new hay (44 Stephens *High Life* I 73; Boucicault *Flying Scud* 163 His character is as sweet as new mown hay). Cf. Taylor *Comparisons* 42 fresh.

2. I'll thump him, Monty, I will—feed me on hay, if I don't (37 Neal *Charcoal* 45). Beaumont and Fletcher *The Humourous Lieutenant* (1619) II ii (*Works*, ed. Waller and Glover, Cambridge, Eng. 1906, II 300) If ye catch me then Fighting again, I'le eat hay with a horse.

3. Make hay while the sun shines (36 Emerson *Works* I 33; "Morus Multicaulis at Tinnecum" *The Knickerbocker* XXV [1845] 409; Melville "Jimmy Rose" in *Works* XIII 261 as if now, while Jimmy's bounteous sun was at meridian was the time to make his selfish hay; Richardson *Secret* 397). Apperson 291; Farmer and Henley VII 27; Richard Jente *Southern Folklore Quarterly* I No. 4 (1937) 63–67; Lean IV 40; NC 421; *Oxford* 398–399; Tilley H235; Tobias Smollett *The Adventures of Ferdinand Count Fathom* (1753) ch. 9; Brian Flynn *The Case of the Black Twenty-Two* (Philadelphia 1929) 189; Thomas Hood *Poems* (1839, London 1911) 247 They say while we have sun we ought to make our hay.

Hayseed, 1. And said there must be hayseed in my hair (49 Melville *Redburn* 29). Babcock 262.

2. His boat's crew were a pretty raw set, just out of the bush, and, as the sailor's phrase is, "hadn't got the hayseed out of their hair" (40 Dana *Two* 39, 264; Judd *Richard* 194 A pleasant party; it takes some of our young men from the country a good while to get the hay-seed out of their hair; but no one would imagine, Edney, you had ever seen a barn). Stevenson 1002:2.

Hay stack. My ideas are all as big as hay stacks (33 Smith *Downing* 214). Whiting *Scots* I 186.

Hazlenut. [Forehead] sort a brown and slick, alike a hazlenut jest afore it rattles from the shuck (44 Stephens *High Life* II 196). Svartengren 253 brown.

Head, 1. As clever a feller as ever toted an ugly head (45 Hooper *Simon* 98). Cf. J. A. Gade *Christian IV* (1928) 127 a wise head is better than a pretty face.
  2. So quick 'twould make your head swim (76 Nash *Century* 51). NED Swim 7.
  3. Now it's all heds and pints [i. e., in a mess]. (34 Davis *Downing* 155). NED Head 46.
  4. An old head on young shoulders is plaguy apt to find afore long the shoulders too old and weak for the head (38 Haliburton *Clockmaker* II 201; Cary *Married* 299 it seemed like as if she had an old head on young shoulders). Apperson 464; NC 421; NED Shoulder 2 c; *Oxford* 470–471; Stevenson 1093:2; Tilley M500; F. S. Fitzgerald *Tales of the Jazz Age* (1922) 17 You got—you got old head on—[the dash is Fitzgerald's]; Helen Reilly *McKee of Centre Street* (1934) 151; C. S. Lewis *The Screwtape Letters* (1943) 29 I do not expect old heads on young shoulders.
  5. Heads I win, tails you lose (60 Holmes *Professor* 200; Lowell *Biglow* 267 Who made the law thet hurts, John, *Heads I win,—ditto tails*). Apperson 293; Farmer and Henley III 286; *Oxford* 285; Stevenson 329:4; Tilley C834; Bonamy Dobree, ed. *The Letters of Philip Dormer Stanhope, 4th Earl of Chesterfield* (London

1932) p. 2900 (Letter 2576 [1769]) Heads you win, tails I lose; C. F. Gregg *Inspector Higgins Sees It Through* (1934) 124 tails you lose; Bill Adams *Ships and Women* (Boston 1937) 159.
  6. Harris will be with you, head up and tail up (54 Lincoln II 227). Cf. NC 421:5; NED Tail (1).
  7. He didn't know whether he was standin' on his head or his heels (38 Haliburton *Clockmaker* II 306, *Old Judge* I 138). NED Stand, vb. 8; H. C. Bailey *The Twittering Bird Mystery* (1937) 222.
  8. It is amusing to observe what a "Raw Head and Bloody Bones" Seward is to universal Locofocoism (52 Lincoln II 156; Clemens *Roughing* I 71 the raw-head-and-bloody-bones the nursing mothers of the mountains terrified their children with). Green 300; *Oxford* 533; Archer Taylor "Raw Head and Bloody Bones" *Journal of American Folklore* LXIX (1956), 114, 175, D. C. Simmons LXX (1957) 358; Tilley R35; S. H. Adams *The Gorgeous Hussy* (Boston 1934) 202.
  9. Couldn't find head nur tail uv 'um (59 Taliaferro *Fisher's* 52; Cary *Married* 186 I haven't seen head nor heels of him for the last three days). NED Head 48; Whiting *Drama* 348: 614 foot. Cf. Tilley H258.
  10. I couldn't make head nor tail on't (34 Davis *Downing* 106; Smith *Letters* 33 There's no head nor tail to it; Cooper *Chainbearer* 176; Melville *Omoo* 45; Whitcher *Widow* 174; Hammett *Piney* 177, 289; Clemens *Innocents* I 302, *Sketches* 4). Stevenson 1099:5; Stoett 1242; John Rhode, pseud. *Body Unidentified* (1938) 60.
  11. Came along to look at her winder, as fellers will when they are over head and ears in love (44 Stephens

High Life I 185, 236 over head and ears in debt; Irving *Wolfert* 205 John . . . has run himself over head and ears in debt; Durivage *Three* 295 over head and ears in love; Whitcher *Widow* 333 over head and ears in debt). Apperson 477–478; Farmer and Henley III 287; Hardie 469:110; NED Head 39 b; *Oxford* 481; Stevenson 1093:8; Tilley H268; E. J. Millward *The Copper Bottle* (1929) 75 in love.

12. Head over heels in love (34 Crockett *Life* 47, 131 debt; Clemens *Sandwich* 66 in debt). Stevenson 1099:5, 1123:9 heels over head; C. G. Givens *All Cats Are Gray* (Indianapolis 1937) 227 in love. See Heel (7).

13. I'm afeard you'll find the cider . . . rather apt to get into your head (44 Stephens *High Life* I 23, II 76 She seems to get into a critter's head like a glass of Cousin Beebe's cider).

14. You've got your head in the bear's mouth now;—git it out, as well as you can (25 Neal *Brother J* II 112; Stowe *Uncle* 451 until he would sooner have put his head into a lion's mouth than to have explored that garret). Apperson 369:8; *Oxford* 273, 370; Stevenson 1437:5; Tilley H82. Cf. NC 421; Anthony Gilbert, pseud. *The Dover Train Mystery* (1936) 190 lion's.

15. Purty gals—them that . . . hold up their heads as if they were queens too (44 Stephens *High Life* I 97; Whitcher *Widow* 206 I hild my head; Shillaber *Knitting-Work* 274 I can hold; Sedley *Marian* 362 I heard . . . that you were . . . holding your head as high as the best; Boucicault *Presumptive* 254 We'll go to America —over there we can afford to hold our heads high). Stevenson 1097:1.

16. My head was in the clouds (23–24 Irving *Tales* 141).

17. We are just, therefore, keeping our heads above water (31 Conant *Earnest Man* 385; Kelly *Humors* 89 I gave you a chance to keep your head above water, 403 the necessary labors of his craft, to enable him to keep his head above water; Sedley *Marian* 101 But it's gittin' on [i. e., prospering], and keepin' our head above water). NED Head 50 b; *Oxford* 330; Stevenson 1094:5.

18. He and the Squire, to use his own words, "might lay their heads together" (20–22 Irving *Bracebridge* 250; Hammett *Piney* 120 When he and Cousin Sam lay their heads together agin; Lowell *Biglow* 121 An' jest ez th' officers 'ould be a layin' heads together). NED Head 59; Stevenson 1093:10; Tilley H280.

19. But you don't open yer head about it to no other indiwiddiwal (56 Whitcher *Widow* 184, 211; Hammett *Piney* 293, 294). DA Head 7 d (4); Stevenson 1095:13.

20. To put a head on someone [i. e., to beat him severely]. 68 DA Head 7 d (3); Stevenson 1095:4.

21. To shut one's head. 56 DA Head 7 d (2); Stevenson 1095:13 Shut up your head.

22. Two heads are better than one (53 Baldwin *Flush* 311). Eccl. 4:9; Apperson 655; NED Head 62; *Oxford* 680; Stevenson 1096:1; Tilley H281; Whiting *Drama* 132; T. L. Peacock *Crotchet Castle* (1831, *Works* IV [London 1924] 176); Will Scott *The Mask* (Philadelphia 1929) 92 the old saying.

23. The old bull . . . let after 'em head-bent for Dublin (51 Dorson *Jonathan* 107). Cf. Whiting *Devil* 225:18 hell-bent [for Kittery, Sunday, Texas].

24. See Nail (10).

Headstrong. See Mule (3), Ram (1).

Heap. He felt all struck up of a heap (44 Stephens *High Life* I 250). Farmer and Henley III 289; NC 422; NED Heap 5 e; *Oxford* 626; Stevenson 1104:13; W. S. Masterman *The Bloodhounds Bay* (1936) as the saying goes.

Hear. [A noise] till a feller couldn't hear himself think, and wouldn't have known what he was thinking about if he did hear (44 Stephens *High Life* I 38).

Hearse. The boy remained as dismal as a hearse (76 Clemens *Tom* 105).

Heart, 1. Cushions . . . as soft as a young gal's heart (44 Stephens *High Life* II 168).

2. Faint heart never won fair lady (32 Kennedy *Swallow* 362; Emerson *Journals* IV 57; Haliburton *Clockmaker* III 287, *Sam* II 20; Dorson *Jonathan* 98 a fair girl; Eggleston *SchoolMaster* 222 the adage). Apperson 198; NC 422; *Oxford* 185; Stevenson 1108:9; Tilley H302; Whiting *Drama* 256; NQ 9 vii 263, 278, 358–359, vii 119, 394, CLXXIV (1938) 46; J. Fletcher *The Faithful Shepherdess* (c1608, Beaumont and Fletcher *Works* [Cambridge, Eng. 1906] II 398) Let men that hope to be belov'd be bold; Reginald Davis *The Crowing Hens* (1936) 127 fair Elinor; Vincent McHugh *Caleb Catlum's America* (1936) fair donkey, as the old sayin' goes.

3. Does his heart say one thing, and his tongue another? (27 Cooper *Prairie* 220). Cf. Apperson 295:12; *Oxford* 288; Tilley H333; Whiting *Drama* 45, 96, *Scots* I 187:7.

4. Large heart never loved little cream-pot (59–60 Holmes *Elsie* 302).

5. As the old song says "A light heart and thin pair of breeches goes thro' the world cheerily" (39 Eliason 100). Apperson 364.

6. Light hearts and heavy purses; short prayers and long rent-rolls (49 Melville *Mardi* II 344). Apperson 296; *Oxford* 289; Stevenson 1921:6; Tilley P655; Whiting *Drama* 232.

7. No more heart, as the Nigger said, than stick your head in the fire; and pull 'um out, agin (25 Neal *Brother J* I 144).

8. Crying enough to break the heart of a loco foco (39 Briggs *Harry* I 128; Dorson *Jonathan* 127 an' cryin' as if his heart would break).

9. A heart of stone (65 Browne *Artemus Ward His Travels* 136). Stevenson 1115:6; Whiting *Scots* I 187. Cf. Stevenson 1115:13 (flint); Taylor *Comparisons* 46; Tilley H311.

10. Turning their good natured eyes at a feller every string [of onions], till his heart is a cuttin pigeon wings agin his ribs to the music of their larf (44 Stephens *High Life* II 193).

11. With his coward heart in his boots (69 Clemens *Innocents* I 235). Apperson 294–295; NC 422; *Oxford* 287; Partridge 383; Hulbert Footner *The Velvet Hand* (1928) 174.

12. My heart is in my mouth (38 Haliburton *Clockmaker* II 127; Dana *Two* 332 would make an English peasant's heart leap into his mouth; Stephens *High Life* II 130 didn't it make my heart jump right up into my mouth; Smith *'Way* 371; Boucicault *Flying Scud* 198). Apperson 295; NC 422; NED Heart 54 b; *Oxford* 288; Stevenson 1109:11; Tilley H331.

13. I thought my heart would a jumped out of my mouth (39 Smith *Letters* 52; Thompson *Major* 155 My

heart seemed like it was gwine to jump rite out of my mouth). NED Heart 54 b; Stevenson 1109:11 jumped up amongst my lungs.

14. It comes tough to keep a feller's heart in the right place [i. e., to avoid temptation]. (44 Stephens *High Life* I 192; Stowe *Uncle* 211 but we all think that his heart is in the right place, after all; Boucicault *Flying Scud* 225 Some of these high and mighty people have got their hearts in the right places after all). NED Heart 54 d; Stevenson 1111:7.

15. She wasn't a gal to let her heart run away with her head (44 Stephens *High Life* I 239).

16. A lookin as if his heart would bust (44 Stephens *High Life* II 205).

17. His heart must be as hard as iron, or my tears would have melted him (66 Boucicault *Flying Scud* 197). Svartengren 260. Cf. Stevenson 1115:5.

18. It was enough to melt the very heart of a stone (33 Smith *Downing* 18; Haliburton *Attaché* II 256 move). Whiting *Drama* 348:617, *Scots* I 187; W. W. Jacobs *Snug Harbour* (1931) 71 a man must 'ave a 'art of stone if that doesn't touch it. Cf. Stevenson 1115:6.

19. Plucking up heart of grace (49 Melville *Mardi* I 193). Apperson 295; Lean III 293–294, 333; *Oxford* 288; Tilley H332; Whiting *Drama* 348: 617; L. W. Meynell *Mystery at Newton Ferry* (Philadelphia 1930) 192.

20. If, indeed, it is true that the main road to the heart passes through the stomach (55 Anon. *New Hope* 217). *Oxford* 696; Stevenson 165:7, 2217:8 The way to many an honest heart lies through the belly; M. Spillane *Kiss Me, Deadly* (1952) ch. 11 One line, "The way to a man's heart

—," and under it the initials "B. T." [The solution of the mystery is the key in Berga Torn's stomach]. Cf. Whiting "Some Current Meanings of 'Proverbial,'" *Harvard Studies and Notes in Philology and Literature* XVI (1934) 237.

Hearty. See Bear (10), Buck (5), Butcher (1), Horse (8).

Heat. Lightning . . . es bright es a weldin heat (67 Harris *Sut* 77).

Heaven, 1. Her eyes were blue as heaven's cerulean deeps (59 Shillaber *Knitting-Work* 296). Svartengren 251 sky.

2. Heaven and earth, and the waters under the earth, had been moved to furnish it [a supper]. (23–24 Irving *Tales* 282). E. S. Gardner *The Case of the Howling Dog* (1934) 123 move heaven and earth.

3. Heaven is Heaven (76 Nash *Century* 310).

4. He will raise heaven and earth after us (51 Stowe *Uncle* 452).

Heavy. See Bear (7), Dough (1), Fifty-six (1), Lead (1).

Hebrew. I think English is Hebrew to her (53 Willis *Fun* 169). Farmer and Henley III 293; NED Hebrew 2b; Stevenson 1037:8; A. T. Sheppard *Here Comes an Old Sailor* (1928) 89. See Greek (2).

Heel, 1. I always found my heels my best weapons (67 Richardson *Beyond* 246). Cf. *Oxford* 485; Tilley P34; Whiting *Drama* 96.

2. They got their heels too high for their boots [i. e., were conceited]. (36 Haliburton *Clockmaker* I 208). See Boot (2); Instep; Farmer and Henley III 311 shoes.

3. Well, when the Sewin' Society

muss come up, she was on her high heels (Whitcher *Widow* 333). DA High 6 c (high-heeled shoes).

4. The days o' light heels and light hearts (38 Haliburton *Clockmaker* II 13).

5. I did feel a little down at the heel (71 Jones *Batkins* 197). Farmer and Henley III 297; McAtee *Grant County* 4; NED Heel 11; Stevenson 1123:6.

6. Meredith, I have you under my heel (66 Boucicault *Flying Scud* 208).

7. Turning heels-over-head (42 Irving *Attorney* 233; Holmes *Professor* 53 knocked him heels over head). See Head (12).

8. See Pair (1).

Heifer. Miss Jones was as handsome as a prize heifer (53 Willis *Fun* 62).

Hell, 1. Jest as much fit fur guvnur as h-ll is fur a icehouse (58 Porter *Major* 43).

2. So I told him I'd see him as deep in h-ll as a pigeon could fly in a fortnight (45 Hooper *Simon* 36). See NED Hell 11 d (hell-deep).

3. Night . . . grow dun as hell (50 Boker *World* 26).

4. Quicker than hell could scorch a feather. 40 DA Hell 2 d (1).

5. 'Tis false—false as hell! (42 Irving *Attorney* 332). Svartengren 20.

6. All the dead and damned John Smiths between hell and San Francisco (66 Clemens *Washoe* 123).

7. Scattered from Hell to Breakfast (62 Wiley *Billy* 78). DA Hell 2 d (7); Whiting *Devil* 227:31.

8. Here's hell broke loose (67 Lowell *Biglow* 347). Apperson 297; Farmer and Henley III 299–300; NED Hell 10; *Oxford* 290; Tilley H403; Whiting *Devil* 221:3.

9. But when they get Hell in their

Neck [i. e., obstinate] I cant do any thing with them (63 Wiley *Johnny* 140).

10. Hell to pay (51 Burke *Polly* 74). McAtee 33; Whiting *Devil* 240: 73; Anthony Berkeley, pseud. *Mr. Pidgeon's Island* (1934) 176. Cf. Devil (26).

11. Play hell and Tommy with them (38 Haliburton *Clockmaker* II 213). Farmer and Henley III 300; NED Hell 10; Whiting *Devil* 224– 225:12 play hell; NQ 2 xii 167.

12. There are many of them who would willingly send you to Hell to pump thunder at 3 cts a clap (39 Eliason 104; Wiley *Billy* 186 I . . . heard a great many speaches made about him [a dead general] such as he was in hell pumping thunder at 3 cents a clap).

13. And the noise increased, until he said "it sounded as if all h-ll was pounding bark" (58 Porter *Major* 140; Wiley *Johnny* 323; Walter Lord, ed. *The Fremantle Diary* (London [1956]) 36 We descended the hills at a terrific pace—or, as Mr. Sargent ["a Northerner by birth"] expressed it, "going like h-ll a-beating tan bark"). See Devil (8), Tan bark. Cf. Farmer 293–294.

14. You may see Boston, but you've got to "smell hell" before that good day (40 Dana *Two* 359).

15. See Lots.

Hellespont. One more, and the others may go to the Hellespont (43 Lewis *Odd* 129).

Help, 1. Well, there's always plenty of help when it's not wanted (32 Hall *Legends* 37).

2. You can't get any more talk out of these specialists away from their

own subjects than you can get help from a policeman outside of his own beat (72 Holmes *Poet* 79).

Helpless. See Babe (4), Bean (1), Calf (1), Child (5), Infant (2), Rag baby.

Hemlock. But hemlock is hemlock, now-a-days (76 Nash *Century* 148).

Hemp, 1. All right on the hemp [i. e., holding sound political views]. 57 DA Hemp.

2. Getting ready to go down the river . . . to see a notorious desperado "stretch hemp" (56 Kelly *Humors* 149). NED Hemp 3. Cf. Farmer and Henley III 301–302, VII 11.

Hen, 1. A hen is on [i. e., something important is in preparation]. 78 DA Hen 2 b (2).

2. [Berries] big as hen's eggs (59 Taliaferro *Fisher's* 59).

3. He was jealous as a hen with young chickens (43 Robb *Squatter* 133).

4. As mad as a wet hen. 23 DA Hen 2 b (3), Mad 1 (b); NC 423; Taylor *Comparisons* 56; Kay C. Strahan *Death Traps* (1930) 103.

5. As popler as a hen with 1 chicking (48 Lowell *Biglow* 43, 282). Bartlett 807; Schele de Vere 522.

6. As proud as a hen with one chick (60 Haliburton *Season-Ticket* 54). NC 423. Cf. McAtee 17; Svartengren 84; Taylor *Comparisons* 70.

7. I believe arter all that the true ginuine lords and counts that come out here are as scarce as hen's teeth (44 Stephens *High Life* I 102; Melville *Moby-Dick* I 198 Whales are scarce as hen's teeth; Eliason 276; Wiley *Billy* 187; Cary *Married* 131). Bartlett 809; Boshears 39:890; DA

Hen 2 b (1); NC 423; Randolph and Wilson 177; Taylor *Comparisons* 70; Thornton III 187–188; Lewis Pendleton *Down East* (1937) 10.

8. You are as spiteful as a hen with a fresh brood (35 Kennedy *Horse-Shoe* 144).

9. A hen frightened from her nest is hard to get back (45 Judd *Margaret* II 121).

10. When hens are shedding their feathers they don't lay eggs (45 Judd *Margaret* II 182).

11. Brooding over his thoughts, like a hen at midnight (54 Shillaber *Mrs. Partington* 277).

12. She brustled up like a settin' hen (Whitcher *Widow* 260).

13. All three cum a flutterin like a flock of hens at seeing a handful of corn (44 Stephens *High Life* I 210).

14. Fussing about like an old hen that's got ducks for chickens (44 Stephens *High Life* I 145). Cf. Emmett Gowen *Old Hell* (1937) 90 he's as busy as a hen with one chick and it a duck.

15. Like a hen with her head cut off (56 Cary *Married* 101, 394; Barnum *Struggles* 250 The fool jumped around like a). Cf. Boshears 33:239; McAtee 53 run; NC 383 chicken; Taylor *Comparisons* 48.

16. These greasers don't know as much as a farrer hen (56 Durivage *Three* 349).

17. She had no more use for one, nor er sittin' hen had for a midwife (51 Burke *Polly* 71).

18. It [emotion] made me . . . ketch my breath like a dying hen (44 Stephens *High Life* I 177).

19. She made more fuss nor er settin' hen with one chicken (51 Burke *Polly* 71). NC 424. Cf. Hulbert Footner *A Self-Made Thief* (1929) 130

watches over her like a hen with one chicken.

20. See House (7).

Henbane. Hateful as henbane (44 Stephens *High Life* II 50).

Here, 1. Here to-day, and gone tomorrow (43 Haliburton *Attaché* IV 137, *Old Judge* I 163, *Sam* I 293; Hammett *Stray* 285). *Oxford* 293; Stevenson 1133:6, 2336:4; Tilley T368; Thomas Middleton *The Old Law* (c1600) V i (*Works* [London 1885] II 239) Alas! you are here to-day, and gone to sea to-morrow; J. V. Turner *Homicide Haven* (1936) 149; M. Thompson *Not As a Stranger* (1954) 890.

2. That is neither here nor there (32 Hall *Legends* 113; Smith *Downing* 148, *Letters* 44, *My Thirty* 294; Longstreet *Georgia* 163 as the fellow said; Burke *Polly* 150; Cary *Clovernook* 240; Riley *Puddleford* 270; Sedley *Marian* 285, 339). Green 27; NED Here 12; *Oxford* 448; Stevenson 1133–1134:8; Tilley H438; NQ 10 x 282; R. S. Surtees *Mr. Sponge's Sporting Tour* (London [1853]) 39, *Plain or Ringlets?* (London [1860]) 5; Edmund Gilligan *Boundary Against Night* (1938) 194 but it's neither here nor there, as the broad said when she got into the wrong bed.

Herod. He could out-Herod Herod if he'd a been there (60 Haliburton *Season-Ticket* 349). *Oxford* 481; Stevenson 1138:16.

Herring, 1. They are . . . as cheap as Potomac herrings (55 Jones *Winkles* 338).

2. The fellow was as dead as a . . . herring (35 Kennedy *Horse-Shoe* 196 pickled; Haliburton *Clockmaker* II 130, III 171, 279, *Attaché* IV 262, *Old Judge* II 61, *Sam* I 341, *Nature* II 57, 239; Jones *Country* 154 smoked herring; Browning *Forty-Four* 245; Smith *My Thirty* 322, 344; Taliaferro *Fisher's* 57, 161; Clift *Bunker* 186; Saxe *Poems* 417; Barnum *Struggles* 114). Apperson 137; Farmer and Henley III 305; NC 424; NED Dead 32 b; *Oxford* 131; Svartengren 146; Tilley H446. Cf. Taylor *Comparisons* 32–33; D. Q. Burleigh *The Kristiana Killers* (1937) 295; W. Dickinson *Dead Man Talks Too Much* (Philadelphia 1937) 284 kippered herring.

3. I'm as dry as a herrin' (54 Smith 'Way 205). Cf. Apperson 168; Svartengren 190 fish.

4. And went to smokin' [a pipe] like ketchin' herrin' (59 Taliaferro *Fisher's* 130).

Herring pond. If they were like you Yankees with a land of promise within reach—a Mississippi valley with no herring pond rolling between—there might have been more migration (65 Sedley *Marian* 441). Farmer and Henley III 305–306; Lean III 359; NED Herring-pond; Stevenson 225:5, 1139:3; Sir Walter Scott *Guy Mannering* (1815) II ch. 5 he'll plague you, now he's come over the herring-pond.

Hickory, 1. It takes a feller as tough as Old Hickory [General Jackson] to stand that (36 Haliburton *Clockmaker* I 219; Mayo *Kaloolah* 93 as tough and withy as a young hickory). Bartlett 437, 809; NC 424; Schele de Vere 58; Thornton II 624–625.

2. But one of the nominees for the ermine was a hickory over any body's persimmon in the way of ugliness (58 Porter *Major* 16). See Huckleberry (2).

Hide, 1. He couldn't find hide nor hair of one of 'em (33 Smith *Downing* 66, *Letters* 116, *'Way* 60; Shillaber *Mrs. Partington* 220; Taliaferro *Fisher's* 143 har nur hide; Sedley *Marian* 51 We hain't seen ne'er a hide nor a hair). NED Hair 8 e (hair and hide), Hide 1 b; McAtee *Grant County* 6; Stevenson 1140:3; Stoett 977; Woodard PADS VI (1946) 38; Andy Adams *The Outlet* (Boston 1905) 152 neither hide, hair, nor hoof could we find; John Metcalfe *Sally* (1936) 549; M. Thompson *Not As a Stranger* (1954) 268 the next morning there wasn't hide nor hair of him, 310 We haven't seen hide nor hair, 901; T. Williamson *The Woods Colt* (1933) ch. 9 pt. 2 I hain't seen hide nor ha'r of you since I disremember when.

2. I fired . . . without ever touching either hide or hair of him (59 Browning *Forty-Four* 172).

3. An outburst of laughter, so sudden and so violent that Bunch almost jumped out of his hide in a paroxysm of fright (45 Hooper *Simon* 25). See Skin (6).

4. Couldn't I just take it out of his hide? (42 Irving *Attorney* 218).

High, 1. How is hallucination "for high"? (70 Clemens *Fairbanks* 132, *Roughing* II 48 How's that for high?). DA High 6 c 2; NED *Supplement* High sb. 3 b.

2. See Balloon (2), Barn door (1), Cat (11), Haman, House (3), Meeting-house (2), Sky-high.

Hill, 1. If she don't look as ancient as the hills (44 Stephens *High Life* I 117).

2. The generations were cold and holy as the hills (51 Melville *Moby-Dick* I 317).

3. He was as old as the hills (36 Haliburton *Clockmaker* I 328; Stephens *High Life* II 69; Melville *Mardi* I 151 as the elderly hills; Alcott *Little Women* 421; Clemens *Roughing* I 22). Boshears 38:780; NC 425; Taylor *Comparisons* 60; E. D. Biggers *The Chinese Parrot* (Indianapolis 1926) 103.

4. It is hard swimming up hill (25 Neal *Brother J* II 246). Cf. Apperson 309; *Oxford* 303; Tilley H469.

5. They're sure to curse you up hill and down dale (35 Crockett *Account* 200; Stowe *Uncle* 248 You can't begin to curse up hill and down as we can, 372 I'll reform him, up hill and down—you'll see; Eggleston *Circuit* 114 this chasin' afther me sins up hill and down dale all the toime). Stevenson 1142:5.

6. Not worth a hill of beans. 63 DA Hill 2 b.

Hindsights. We could knock the hindsights off 'em, if we was only a mind to (56 Durivage *Three* 43; Porter *Major* 18 tear the hind sights off him; Eggleston *School-Master* 121, 268). Bradley PADS XIV (1950) 37; DA Hindsight 1 b; McAtee 38; Thornton I 436, III 190.

Hinge. As black as "de hinges of hell" (39 DA Hinge 1 b). Cf. Svartengren 7–8, 241 hell; Whiting *Devil* 222:5, 230:65.

Hint, 1. A hint's about as good as a kick, to some people (25 Neal *Brother J* II 220).

2. I can take a hint as soon as another (36 Crockett *Exploits* 92).

Hip. He was sure to have you on the hip (40 Dana *Two* 244; Lowell *Biglow* 145 seein' 'z I've gut ye on the hip). Farmer and Henley III 316; Green 261; NED Hip 2 b; *Oxford*

296; Stevenson 1142:11; Tilley H474; Whiting *Drama* 349:624, *Scots* I 189.

History. History, it is said, repeats itself (65 Sedley *Marian* 432; Barnum *Struggles* 484; Clemens *Sketches* 330). NC 425; *Oxford* 296; Stevenson 1145:8; NQ 4 ix 139, x 319; 9 iii 407. Cf. J. Delevsky "L'Idée du cycle éternel dans l'histoire du monde" *Studies and Essays in the History of Science and Learning Offered . . . to George Sarton* (1947) 375–401; Mircea Eliade *The Myth of the Eternal Return* (1954).

Hit. Hit or miss (42 Emerson *Letters* II 103; Stephens *High Life* I 151). Apperson 302; NED Hit vb. 22; *Oxford* 296; Stevenson 1146:9; Tilley H475.

Hitch. Well, then, friend, 'once mounted,' . . . I guess that's the hitch [i. e., the difficulty]. (66 Bowman *Bear-Hunters* 454).

Hoarse. See Crow (3).

Hob. To play hob with. 38 DA Hob 1. NED Hob 2 b.

Hobson. It's "Hobson's Choice" (57 Jones *Country* 198; Sedley *Marian* 441). Apperson 303; Farmer and Henley III 323; *Modern Language Forum* XXIV (1939) 69–70; *Oxford* 297; Stevenson 347:7; Tilley H481; Edmund Snell *Kontrol* (Philadelphia 1928) 197.

Hoe. As dull as a hoe (49 Haliburton *Old Judge* II 61). McAtee 24; NC 425; Taylor *Comparisons* 37 grub hoe.

Hoe cake. Knocking him down flat as a hoe-cake (56 Kelly *Humors* 434). See Pancake.

Hog, 1. The colt was fat as a hog (56 Durivage *Three* 193). Apperson 205;

NC 425; Taylor *Comparisons* 40; Tilley H483; Whiting *Drama* 316:171.

2. Fat as a nigger's hog. 58 DA Hog 10 (2).

3. As independent as a hog on ice. 57 DA Hog 10 (1). Taylor *Comparisons* 51.

4. Muddy as a hog (59 Taliaferro *Fisher's* 156). Cf. NC 425 dirty; Taylor *Comparisons* 34 dirty.

5. Es nakid es a well-scraped hog (67 Harris *Sut* 121.)

6. As the old hog squeals the young ones learn, you know (54 Shillaber *Mrs. Partington* 327). See Cock (2).

7. I keered no more for 'um than a hog does fur holiday (59 Taliaferro *Fisher's* 117). Cf. Hog (12), NC 389 Crow (7), 458 Pig (13); McAtee 38; Thornton III 191.

8. The old saying, root hog or die (34 Crockett *Life* 117–118; Richardson *Beyond* 166; Clemens *Roughing* I 205). Bartlett 537; DA Root 3; McAtee 53; NC 425; Stevenson 1147:9; Thornton II 750, III 330; Fulton Oursler *Joshua Todd* (1934) 154. See Pig (11).

9. We never fairly knew what goin the whole hog was till then (36 Haliburton *Clockmaker* I 41, II 35, 98, 227, III 190 *Whole hogs,* who won't hear of no change, *Letter* 133 not satisfied with less than the whole hog, *Attaché* I 195, *Nature* I 218 almost the whole hog, II 160; Crockett *Exploits* 41 a whole hog Jackson man; Neal *Charcoal* 180 I never see a pig go the whole hog in my life, 'sept upon rum cherries; Jones *Country* 223; Riley *Puddleford* 104; Willis *Paul* 77; Smith *My Thirty* 372; Sedley *Marian* 117 fortin' [fortune] on a big scale, the hull hog and no discount). Bartlett 256; DA Whole hog; McAtee 71, PADS XV (1951) 62; NC 425; NED

Hog 11 b; Schele de Vere 606; Stevenson 1148:3; Taylor *Investigations* 261; Thornton I 368–370, III 164, 429; NQ 1 iii 224, 250, iv 240; 2 v 49, 113; E. Greenwood *The Deadly Dowager* (1935) 226. See Animal.

10. Went sailing along up the side walk like a prize hog jest afore killing time (44 Stephens *High Life* I 137).

11. Knowed no more about um nor a hog does about Baker in the Spelling Book (60–63 Taliaferro *Carolina Humor* 61). Cf. Thornton III 370 spell Baker; Randolph and Wilson 187.

12. To know no more than a hog does about a holiday. 78 DA Hog 10 (3). Cf. Hog (7); J. Frank Dobie *Coronado's Children* (Dallas, Tex. 1930) 65 he knew as little about mining as a hog does about Sunday.

13. Roared out his words like a hog that had been larned to talk (44 Stephens *High Life* I 39).

14. Sleep like a hog (53 Haliburton *Sam* II 81). Apperson 577 pig; Svartengren 168; Whiting *Drama* 316:171; J. G. Strange, pseud. *For the Hangman* (1934) 227. Cf. Tilley H497.

15. Tied me hand and foot like a hog (59 Taliaferro *Fisher's* 126). See Hand (12).

16. I'd give as much agin for ye—with the bristles off (33 Neal *Down-Easters* I 8; Stephens *High Life* I 79 there are some men that would be hogs if only they had brustles, as we say in Connecticut). Cf. Apperson 304; *Oxford* 182; Tilley T484.

Hold, sb. I knowed tail holt were better than no holt (59 Taliaferro *Fisher's* 138). Cf. DA Tail 3 (8).

Hold, vb. 1. We held our own (40 Dana *Two* 351; Hooper *Simon* 41 I've never seed many but what I could hold me own with).

2. See Bulldog (3), Bur (2), Death (26, 27), Dog (43), Turtle (10), Wax (4).

Hole, 1. We're in a hole (66 Boucicault *Flying Scud* 179, 196, 209, 225). DA Hole 6; Farmer and Henley III 332; NED Hole 3.

2. And then put them in the hole they intended for us (66 Boucicault *Flying Scud* 211). Cf. Ps. 7:15; Eccl. 10:8; Stevenson 1799:10 pit; Stoett 1299; Tilley P356.

3. Lookin as though they had jest ben snaked through a gimblet hole (34 Davis *Downing* 273).

4. His eyes . . . looked like two burnt holes in a blanket, they was so deep (40 Haliburton *Clockmaker* III 172, *Attaché* I 191). Halpert 132; Hardie 469:94; W. B. M. Ferguson *The Black Company* (1924) 23.

5. A cross-grained, ugly critter, that was allers a pickin' a hole in the boys' coats [i. e., finding fault with]. (58 Hammett *Piney* 175; Shillaber *Knitting-Work* 191 The picking of holes in each other's coats May end at last with knives at your throats; Lowell *Biglow* 296 [They] hain't no record, ez it's called, for folks to pick a hole in). Apperson 492; NED Hole 9; *Oxford* 498; Partridge 624; Stevenson 457:19, 1149:2; Tilley H522.

6. For Brown was a man of excellent sense; Could see very well through a hole in a fence (68 Saxe *Poems* 154). See Ladder.

Hollo. She never hollers unless she's hurt (40 Haliburton *Clockmaker* III 153, 226 I am a narvous man, and sometimes sing out afore I am hit). Apperson 125–126; DA Holler; *Oxford* 121; Stevenson 466:1; Tilley

C873; Hugh Baker *Cartwright Is Dead, Sir!* (Boston 1934) 45 cry. Cf. Whiting *Drama* 247. See Kick, vb. (1).

Hollow, 1. She preferred me all holler (34 Crockett *Life* 62, 169 I could beat him electioneering all hollow, *Account* 37 the number of the ships beat me all hollow; Fairfield *Letters* 218 They beat all hollow, everything of the kind that I have seen before; Hall *Purchase* II 289 although to-day the drum *beat* the other instruments *hollow;* Stephens *High Life* I 4; Dorson *Jonathan* 103; Riley *Puddleford* 198 he'd had one that beat it all holler; Saxe *Poems* 48 *Racine* beat all the others hollow). Bartlett 8, 35; Farmer and Henley III 334; McAtee 34; NED Hollow adv. 2; Schele de Vere 609–610.
2. See Elder stalk, Flute (1), Nut (5), Nutshell (2).

Hollyhock. She shows amung wimen like . . . a hollyhawk in a patch ove smartweed (67 Harris *Sut* 75).

Holy. See Hill (2).

Holy Writ. True as Holy Writ (46 Cooper *Redskins* 67; Hammett *Stray* 316 as if it were as true as the Holy Writ). See Apostles.

Home, 1. Well, home, they say, is where the heart is (70–73 McCloskey *Across* 79). NC 426; Stevenson 1152: 8; J. C. Addams *The Secret Dead* (1926) 116; H. M. Gay *The Pacific Spectator* IV (1950) 91.
2. Home is home, however homely (32 Haliburton *Attaché* III 17, *Nature* I 164; Stephens *High Life* II 4 there is no place like hum, if it's ever so humly; Durivage *Three* 96 he warbled, "Though never so humble, there's

no place like home"). Apperson 305; *Oxford* 300, 503; Tilley H534; W. B. M. Ferguson *The Black Company* (1924) 154.
3. To our long home (25 Neal *Brother J* II 404; Cartwright *Autobiography* 335; Wiley *Johnny* 140). Apperson 379; NED Home 4; *Oxford* 381; Tilley H533; Whiting *Scots* I 190; Geraint Goodwin *The White Farm* (London 1937) 272.

Homely. See Log fence, Sassafras root (1), Stump fence.

Hone. As smooth as a hone (43 Haliburton *Attaché* II 213).

Honest. See Day (9), House dog, Light, sb. (1), Noonday (2), Steel (5).

Honesty, 1. Honesty is the best policy (38 Haliburton *Clockmaker* II 167, *Attaché* I 255, IV 89, *Sam* II 305; Hall *Purchase* II 23; Hooper *Simon* 32; Jones *Country* 347 until they have grown rich, when they preach honesty as the best policy; Richardson *Beyond* 510 The man in the play must have lived in a mining region before he learned the profound truth, that "Honesty is the root of all evil, and money is the best policy"; Alcott *Little Women* 507 honesty is the best policy in love as in law; Saxe *Poems* 155 Not only that honesty's likely to "pay"; Barnum *Struggles* 499 the maxim of Dr. Franklin . . . that "honesty is the best policy," 636). Apperson 306; NC 426; *Oxford* 301; Stevenson 1155:2; Stoett 530; Tilley H543; NQ 5 x 187, 254–255; 6 iii 278; Leo Markus *Mrs. Grundy* (1930) 413 *Poor Richard's Almanac* . . . proves that honesty is the best policy.
2. Honesty pays large dividends (76 Nash *Century* 295). Vance Ran-

dolph *The Devil's Pretty Daughter* (1955) 141 It just goes to show that honesty pays off in the long run, like the old man says.

Honey, 1. All honey an' hug a minnit ago (33 Neal *Down-Easters* I 82). DA Honey b.

2. She will pretend to be as good as honey (56 Cary *Married* 281).

3. As sweet agin as all the honey he ever stole from a clover top (44 Stephens *High Life* II 195; Haliburton *Season-Ticket* 371 talk as sweet as honey; Alcott *Little Women* 144). Apperson 614; Boshears 31:115, 40: 978; McAtee 63; NC 426; *Oxford* 635; Taylor *Comparisons* 80; Tilley H544; Whiting *Drama* 316:173, *Scots* I 190; Francis Gérard *The Concrete Castle Murders* (1936) 69.

4. They have honey on their lips, but pyson in their tongues (60 Haliburton *Season-Ticket* 60). Cf. *Oxford* 301; Stevenson 146–147:10; Tilley H561; Whiting *Drama* 237.

Honey-locust. [A preacher], one of the kind that's as thorny as a honey-locust (74 Eggleston *Circuit* 114).

Honor. They say that there is honour among thieves (50 Melville *White Jacket* 224; Judd *Margaret* II 25; Baldwin *Flush* 296 "Honor among, &c." —you know the proverb; Sedley *Marian* 326 unmindful of the old-time axiom, which attributes honor to thieves who deal with each other). Apperson 308; NC 426; *Oxford* 302; Stevenson 2296–2297:13; NQ CXLVIII (1925) 443, CXLIX (1925) 13, 68, 175.

Hook, 1. By hook or by crook, as they term it (33 Neal *Down-Easters* I 87; Crockett *Account* 216 by hook and by crook; Fairfield *Letters* 112 by hook or by crook; Haliburton *Attaché* III

56, *Sam* II 125; Stephens *High Life* I 32; Cooper *Chainbearer* 82, 184, 354; Melville *Omoo* 72, *Pierre* 467 by hook or crook; Curtis *Potiphar* 157; Irving *Wolfert* 253; Smith *My Thirty* 428, 456). Apperson 308–309; Farmer and Henley III 343; Figh PADS XIII (1950) 7; Lean III 351; NED Hook 14, commenting "As to the origin of the phrase there is no evidence; although invention has been prolific of explanatory stories, most of them at variance with chronology"; *Oxford* 303; Smith *Browning* 220; Stevenson 1165:1; Tilley H588; Whiting *Drama* 349:631, *Scots* I 190; NQ 1 i 168, 205, 222, 237, 281–282, 405–406, ii 78, 204–205, iii 116, 212; 2 i 522; 4 viii 64, 133, 196, 464, ix 77–78; 7 viii 306; 8 i 185; 10 iii 409; 11 xi 66–67, 215; 12 xii 473; 13 i 15, 60; F. Marryat *Peter Simple* (1834, London 1929) 428 if you can't gain it by *hook,* you must by crook, 619 I saved up five guineas, by hook or by crook.

2. Look sharp, or you're gone, hook and line (34 Davis *Downing* 214; Lincoln II 113 she has already let you take that, hook and line, 342 his nomination will save every whig, except such as have already gone over hook and line). DA Hook 2 (4). Cf. DA Hook 2 (6) hook, line, and sinker; McAtee *Grant County* 6; Stevenson 1248:10; Tilley H589; Glen Burne *Murder to Music* (1934) 263 We've got him hook, line and sinker.

3. Has the bloody agent slipped off the hooks? [i. e., in grave trouble, such as insanity or death]. (40 Dana *Two* 315). Apperson 463; NED Hook 15; *Oxford* 468; Stevenson 1164:8; Tilley H592. Cf. Farmer and Henley III 342 drop, go, pop.

4. We was all on our own hook (34 Davis *Downing* 35; Neal *Charcoal*

141; Lincoln I 284 candidates for the legislature on their own hooks, 315; Robb *Squatter* 23, 65 made every hair stand "on its own hook"; Stephens *High Life* I 38 every man went on his own hook, 56, 152, II 110; Eliason 277; Burke *Polly* 132; Stowe *Uncle* 168 I'm a thinkin' that every man'll have to hang on his own hook in them ar quarters; Smith *'Way* 216, *My Thirty* 266, 345, 414; Whitcher *Widow* 194; Bennett *Border* 93 set off, in colloquial phrase, "on our own hook," 445; Hammett *Piney* 141). Bartlett 294; DA Hook 2 b; Farmer and Henley III 342; NED Hook 16; *Oxford* 303; Stevenson 1165:2; Thornton I 445–446, III 194; Woodard PADS VI (1946) 18; Vincent McHugh *Caleb Catlum's America* (1936) 56.

5. I hear you have got young Goodwin on your hooks, now, and that you mean to marry him against his will (74 Eggleston *Circuit* 323–324).

6. Some station or settlement where I can . . . start off on a new hook (66 Bowman *Bear-Hunters* 33).

Hooky. To play hooky. 48 DA Hooky.

Hooter. Not to budge one hooter, not to care a hooter. 39 DA Hooter.

Hop. See Corn (4), Pea (4).

Hope, 1. As a man volunteers upon a "forlorn hope" (50 Willis *Life* 171; Shillaber *Mrs. Partington* 39 He was always selected to lead the forlorn hope in an attack; Cartwright *Autobiography* 476 and, said he, you are the forlorn hope). Isaac D'Israeli *Curiosities of Literature* (4 vols., Boston 1860) II 341; NED Forlorn hope; Taylor *Investigations* 261; NQ 5 ix 266, 375, 415.

2. You can't live on hope (53 Haliburton *Sam* I 245; Judd *Margaret* II 107; Melville *Israel* 69 he that lives upon hope will die fasting, as Poor Richard says). Apperson 309; *Oxford* 377. Cf. Stevenson 1166:11; Tilley H597, H598.

3. Hope deferred makes the heart sick (53 Haliburton *Sam* I 245; Clemens *Letters* I 38; Richardson *Secret* 424 maketh). Prov. 13:12; Apperson 309; *Oxford* 303; Stevenson 1168:3; Tilley H600; Whiting *Drama* 185.

Hops, 1. As thick as hops (33 Smith *Downing* 22, 96; Haliburton *Clockmaker* III 91; Stephens *High Life* II 67; Riley *Puddleford* 118). Apperson 623–624; NC 426; NED Hop 3; Taylor *Comparisons* 49, 81; Tilley H595.

2. His sermon was as . . . sleepy as a pillow of hops (44 Fairfield *Letters* 341). Cf. *Encyclopædia Britannica* 11th ed. XIII 678 b.

Hop-toads. The injuns were as humble as hop-toads (c60 Paul *Courtship* 85).

Horn, 1. His heart's harder 'n the devil's off horn (76 Nash *Century* 237).

2. When her deluded lord charged upon the scandalmongers with the very horns she had bestowed upon him (49 Melville *Mardi* I 134). Apperson 310–311; Farmer and Henley III 351–354; NED Horn 7; *Oxford* 304; Tilley H622–H626; Whiting *Drama* 349: 633, *Scots* I 191; Gene Fowler *Timber Line* (1933) 121 he was wearing horns as big as any bull moose.

3. I tell you I helt nothin' but trumps, and could 'a' beat the horns off a billygoat (45 Hooper *Simon* 14).

4. "Borin' them fur the holler horn" to their hearts' content (59 Taliaferro *Fisher's* 31–32). Bradley PADS XIV (1950) 38; DA Hollow 1 b; Thornton I 441. Cf. Randolph and Wilson 253.

5. "Here and there a *horn?*" asked

the mate, in the dryest manner [i. e., suggesting that the previous statement had been false]. (40 Dana *Two* 443; Cary *Married* 300; Smith *Arp* 56 Methinks I see them as in a horn, crowding the road, 100). Bartlett 296 A low phrase, now common, used to qualify a falsehood, equivalent to the English "over the left"; Farmer 305; Farmer and Henley III 354; Green 191; Thornton I 451; B. J. Whiting "William Johnson of Natchez: Free Negro" *Southern Folklore Quarterly* XVI (1952) 151.

6. He thinks he has a soft horn to deal with [i. e., an easy mark]. (40 Haliburton *Clockmaker* III 58, *Season-Ticket* 52 while he thought *how soft their horns was*). Bartlett 796.

7. Then we shall have John Bull by the horns (59 Smith *My Thirty* 417). Apperson 72; *Oxford* 641; Stevenson 254:9.

8. The old man hauled in his horns (33 Smith *Downing* 176, 192, *My Thirty* 112; Haliburton *Attaché* III 99; Stephens *High Life* I 11–12, 34, 131, 224; Thompson *Major* 79; Whitcher *Widow* 334 draw). Apperson 164; DA Horn 3 c (2); Green 33, 180; NED Horn 5 b (draw, shrink, pluck, pull in); *Oxford* 156; Stevenson 1173:5; Tilley H620; Leslie Ford, pseud. *The Strangled Witness* (1934) 38 draws in; David Frome, pseud. *The Strange Death of Martin Green* (1931) 62 pull in.

9. So we locked horns without a word, thar all alone, and I do think we fit an hour (58 Porter *Major* 89; Locke [Nasby] *Struggles* 247). DA Horn 3 c (3); Stevenson 1173:2.

10. One of them 'ere folks . . . who would spile a horn, or make a spoon (34 Davis *Downing* 83–84). Apperson 597; Hardie 464:108; *Ox-*ford 398; Randolph and Wilson 194; Stevenson 2201:9.

11. Permit me to "blow my horn" (59 Clemens *Letters* I 43; Lincoln VIII 98 n. He declined to "blow his own horn," as he expressed it). Apperson 57; NC 426; *Oxford* 52; Tilley T546; Wilson 521; Tiffany Thayer *Thirteen Women* (1932) 65.

12. The Mormon precept: "Sound your own horn, for behold if you sound not your own horn, your horn shall not be sounded" (58 Lincoln II 525; Locke [Nasby] *Struggles* 79 Whoso bloweth not his own horn, the same shall not be blown, but whoso bloweth his own horn, the same shall be blown with a muchness). Bradley 79; Helen Pearce "Folk Sayings in a Pioneer Family of Oregon" *Western Folklore* V (1946) 234; Stevenson 2382:1.

13. In this hard dilemma, some have chosen one horn and some the other (64 Lincoln VII 535). *Oxford* 304–305; Stevenson 576:2; J. J. Connington, pseud. *Grim Vengeance* (Boston 1929) 203 the choice between the two horns of the original dilemma.

14. Just go in and toot your horn, if you don't sell a clam (72 Clemens *Roughing* II 49). DA Clam 4 b (2).

15. See Cow's horn, End (8), Ram's horn, Tin horn.

Hornbug. Oh Lor! Mas'r George, if ye wouldn't make a hornbug laugh! (51 Stowe *Uncle* 27). Thornton I 452.

Hornet, 1. He got as mad as a hornet (44 Thompson *Major* 115; Cary *Clovernook* 2d Ser. 148; Hammett *Piney* 54, 102; Chamberlain *Confession* 272; Harris *Sut* 105; Clemens *Gilded* II 237). Boshears 38:740; DA Hornet 1; NC 427; Taylor *Comparisons* 56; Cornelia Penfield *After the Deacon Was Murdered* (1933) 163.

2. Ugly as a she ho'net (67 Harris *Sut* 278).

3. I don't choose a hornet's nest about my ears (21 Cooper *Spy* 136). NED Hornet 2; Stevenson 1773:7 get, stir up; Brian Flynn *The Ladder of Death* (Philadelphia 1935) 250.

Hornety. See Nature (1).

Horrors. Oh, Judge, you'll give me the double-breasted horrors (51 Burke *Polly* 64; Shillaber *Mrs. Partington* 288 There is enough in one such spectacle to give any man the "double-breasted horrors" for a whole day). Cf. NED Horror 3 b (the horrors).

Horse, 1. She's a gone horse (42 Irving *Attorney* 112). DA Gone 1 (9). See Coon (7).

2. The Spanish proverb: "A running horse is an open sepulcher" (67 Richardson *Beyond* 257). *Oxford* 553; Stevenson 1178:6; Tilley H687.

3. It is a hoss of another colour (43 Haliburton *Attaché* II 265, *Nature* II 110; Hammett *Piney* 31 an accident, but that ain't nothin' on earth to do with smart men—it's a chestnut horse of another color, I guess, 282; Paul *Courtship* 261; Nash *Century* 26 That's a hoss of another color). Apperson 311; Bradley 80 That's a gray horse of another color; Hardie 466: 11; NED Horse 25 a; *Oxford* 305; Stevenson 1180–1181:9 cattle of this color; Tilley H665; S. H. Adams *The Gorgeous Hussy* (Boston 1934) 63; Stark Young *So Red the Rose* (1934) 61. Cf. Thornton I 453.

4. The old saying, "A short horse is soon curried" (34 Crockett *Life* 204; Hooper *Simon* 88 it don't take long

to curry a short horse, accordin' to the old sayin'; Smith *My Thirty* 374 old Sam Houston's horse can be curried in short order; Clift *Bunker* 117; Barnum *Struggles* 95). Apperson 567; Bradley 79; NC 427; *Oxford* 584; Randolph and Wilson 192–193; Stevenson 1175:7; Tilley H691; Whiting *Drama* 232; Irvin S. Cobb *Murder Day by Day* (Indianapolis 1933) 125; F. P. Keyes *Dinner at Antoine's* (1948) 324 However, that's a short horse and soon curried.

5. I'm jest like a skeery horse that al'rs backs up hill when you want to lead him down (44 Stephens *High Life* II 82). Cf. NC 427 Horse (9).

6. A fat 'oman, es big es a skin'd hoss, an' ni ontu es ugly (67 Harris *Sut* 55, 198 [a man] big es a hoss). Randolph and Wilson 174; Taylor *Comparisons* 16; Whiting *Drama* 317: 176. Cf. Horse (13).

7. He lied as fast as a horse could trot (53 Haliburton *Sam* I 170; Cary *Married* 301 lightning was going faster than). McAtee 40; NC 427; Svartengren 377 my hand can trot; Tilley H660.

8. The very best negro woman in the town . . . is as hearty as a horse (67 *Harper's New Monthly Magazine* XXXV 484).

9. Ez plump, en ez fat, en ez sassy ez a Moggin [Morgan] hoss in a barley-patch (80 Harris *Uncle Remus* 20).

10. As steady as a mill horse (54 Smith *'Way* 271).

11. As strong as a horse (40 Haliburton *Clockmaker* III 76; Hooper *Simon* 87 it's a workin' in him as strong as a Dick horse; Mayo *Kaloolah* 85; Stowe *Uncle* 166). Apperson 312; NC 427; NED Horse 25; Taylor *Comparisons* 78; Whiting *Scots* I 191:6

wicht; Vernon Loder *The Death Pool* (1931) 80.

12. Es tetchy . . . es a soreback horse is 'bout green flies (67 Harris *Sut* 277).

13. [A woman] ugly es a skin'd hoss (67 Harris *Sut* 36). Cf. Horse (6).

14. But the old Captain and the young Captain didn't exactly "hitch horses" (56 Kelly *Humors* 421). DA Hitch 5 (1).

15. One man may lead a horse to water, but ten canna gar him drink (31 Emerson *Journals* II 375). Apperson 314; NC 428; *Oxford* 356; Snapp 65:77; Stevenson 1179–1180:9; Tilley M262; Tiffany Thayer *Three-Sheet* (1932) 134.

16. And aint above lookin' a gift horse in the mouth (53 Haliburton *Sam* II 89; Whitcher *Widow* 56 Mustent find fault in a gift hosses mouth, you know; Stephens *Mary Derwent* 309 Besides, 'tain't manners, dad used to say, to look a gift horse in the mouth; Locke [Nasby] *Struggles* 385 Liberty is a gift hoss, wich, ef dis niggah had it to do over agin, he wood look in de mouth, shoah). Apperson 245–246; Green 159; NC 427; *Oxford* 236; Stevenson 1182:2–4; Stoett 1753; Tilley H678; NQ 4 xi 473, xii 18; Kay C. Strahan *Death Traps* (1930) 76; H. L. Ickes *Diary* (1953) I 437.

17. It's a good horse that never stumbles (21 Loomis *Farmer's Almanac* 178). Apperson 312–313; *Oxford* 253; Stevenson 1179:6; Tilley H670.

18. I am reminded, in this connection, of a story of an old Dutch farmer, who remarked to a companion once that "it was best not to swap horses when crossing streams" (64 Lincoln VII 384; Smith *Arp* 178 'Twasn't no time to be swappin

hosses). Lean IV 9 It is a bad time to swop horses when you're crossing a stream; NC 427; *Oxford* 634; Stevenson 1178:10; NQ 11 iii 269, 358, 433–434; Robert Graves *Good-bye to All That* (London 1929) 311 We have a proverb in England. See Time (4).

19. He who is carried by horses must deal with rogues (58 Holmes *Autocrat* 278).

20. Horse and horse [i. e., equally matched]. c46 DA Horse 8 (3); Stevenson 1181:9.

21. Has drunk more yarb tea than enough to kill a horse (44 Thompson *Major* 185).

22. It was enough to make a hoss larf, if he could understand it (43 Haliburton *Attaché* I 187). McAtee 24; Stevenson 611–612:12 dog; Ruth P. Thompson *The Great Horse of Oz* (Chicago 1928) 142.

23. If there be any inferior denomination of the horse laugh, known as the horse chuckle (53 Hammett *Stray* 73; Taliaferro *Fisher's* 127 They gin me no answer but a great big hoss laugh; Paul *Courtship* 36 a hoss-laugh). NC 427; NED Horse-laugh; Stevenson 1355:8.

24. The pithy proverb, that "it is easy to walk when one leads a horse by the bridle," was hardly true in my case (65 Richardson *Secret* 493). Apperson 263; *Oxford* 690; Tilley W10.

25. She was well described in the equine language of the late lamented Colonel, as "an off horse" (55 Hammett *Wonderful* 43). DA Off 1.

26. Jest hold your horses, boys (43 Robb *Squatter* 24, 95 hold your hoss for a minit; Hammett *Piney* 259). DA Horse 8 (2); McAtee 34; NC 427; Stevenson 1180:5; Wilson 552; Woodard PADS VI (1946) 38; Harriette

Ashbrook *Murder of Sigurd Sharon* (1933) 96.

27. A good deal of "hard common sense like a hoss" (59 Taliaferro *Fisher's* 44). Farmer 306; Green 192; Hardie 469:105; Thornton I 454, III 196–197; Anon. *The Great American Ass* (1926) 158 horse sense.

28. College life might be well for slow folks, but it was a one-horse affair, and he was a whole team (57 Willis *Paul* 36; Sedley *Marian* 227 Nuthin' but a one-horse fight; Richardson *Beyond* 384 If it kills every one-horse judge in the State of California; Jones *Batkins* 206 Some one-horse-power town; Clemens *Sketches* 38, 300 town). Bartlett 439–440; Farmer 306, 402; Green 260; Schele de Vere 221; Thornton II 631, III 272; Anthony Berkeley, pseud. *Top Story Murder* (1931) 171 one-horse place.

29. When the old woman's mad, she is a horse to whip! [i. e., is formidable]. (32 Kennedy *Swallow* 35).

30. Didn't appear to care no more about Democracy than a horse does about his grandfather (59 Smith *My Thirty* 422).

31. And broke [ran] like a quarter horse after my bear (34 Crockett *Life* 163; Hammett *Stray* 161 a-coming like a quarter-horse, *Piney* 66 a humpin' it like a quarter horse; Durivage *Three* 157 streakin' it like a quarter hoss). Thornton II 714.

32. We all ate like horses (40 Dana *Two* 407). McAtee 24; Leane Zugsmith *Home Is Where You Hang Your Childhood* (1937) 52.

33. Wild horses shan't drag it out of me (68 Alcott *Little Women* 230). George A. Birmingham *Gold, Gore and Gehenna* (1927) 51.

34. His imagination flew on like a horse without a rider (50 Willis *Life* 228).

35. Kick with their feet like a horse (59 Taliaferro *Fisher's* 198).

36. Whereupon Wise got on his tall horse and rode off, splashing the mud all over the House (36 Fairfield *Letters* 105; Haliburton *Attaché* II 176 You hante rode the high horse; Cary *Married* 189). Apperson 531; Farmer and Henley III 311; NED Horse 22 b; *Oxford* 542; Partridge 406; Stevenson 1173–1174:8; Tidwell PADS XIII (1950) 20; Woodard PADS VI (1946) 38; NQ 11 iv 490, v 15, 54, 114; L. W. Meynell *Mystery at Newton Ferry* (Philadelphia 1930) 47. Cf. Allan PADS XIV (1951) 66.

37. Uncle John were swelled out like a hoss with the colic (59 Taliaferro *Fisher's* 87).

38. Whirling the foreign girls around like so many horses grinding cider (44 Stephens *High Life* I 205).

39. Worked like a horse (40 Dana *Two* 247; Clemens *Washoe* 97). NC 428; *Oxford* 730; Taylor *Comparisons* 49–50; Brian Flynn *The Crime at the Crossways* (Philadelphia 1932) 259.

40. Working out a debt is often called "working a dead horse" (54 Shillaber *Mrs. Partington* 291; Barnum *Struggles* 472 this is properly termed "working for a dead horse"). Apperson 138; Bartlett 171; NED Horse 18; *Oxford* 730; Stevenson 1174:1; Thornton I 242; Tilley H699; Herbert Childs *El Jimmy* (Philadelphia 1936) 142 pay for a dead horse; Gordon Young *The Devil's Passport* (1933) 101 behind at poker.

41. See Bob, Door (2), Trooper's horse.

Horse-apple [a large summer apple]. He got snapt on egnog when he heard of my ingagement, and he's been as meller as hos-apple ever since (44 Thompson *Major* 102).

Horseback. One of those men recognized as a class in the West, and defined as "born a-horseback" (57 Willis *Paul* 74).

Horse block. Is little Anna's head as square as a horse block yet? (46 Fairfield *Letters* 406).

Horse-radish. He was . . . as *hot* as hoss-radish (58 Porter *Major* 88).

Hose. Those unmentionable articles, which are used, in fireman's phraseology, to "light up the hose" [i. e., feminine underclothing]. (55 Thomson *Doesticks* 175).

Host. You reckon without your host (32 Kennedy *Swallow* 185). Apperson 525–526; Farmer and Henley III 361; NC 428; NED Host 2 b; *Oxford* 535; Stevenson 1184:4; Tilley H728; Whiting *Drama* 222, *Scots* I 191–192; Anthony Pryde, pseud. and R. K. Weekes *The Emerald Necklace* (1931) 163.

Hot, 1. I begun to think York was a going to be rather too hot to hold me (44 Stephens *High Life* II 1). Cf. Farmer 307; Farmer and Henley III 362; NED Hot 11 e; *Oxford* 665; Stevenson 1185:7.

2. A person that could blow hot and cold with the same breath (43 Hall *Purchase* II 270; Lowell *Biglow* 83 Warn't we gittin' on prime with our hot an' cold blowin'?). Apperson 57; NC 428; NED Blow 2 b; *Oxford* 52; Stevenson 1186:2; Tilley M1258; Wyndham Martyn *Murder Island* (1932) 216.

3. See Blaze (7), Cake (7), Fire (2), Flugence (1), Horse-radish,

Mustard (1), Oven (2), Pepper, Pepper-box (2), Pepper-corn.

Hound. A hound don't yowl much when he's hard hurt (60 Whitehead *Wild Sports* 289). Cf. NC 398 Dog (49).

Hour. The darkest hour is just before the day, and that's a comfortable old saying (35 Kennedy *Horse-Shoe* 316; Haliburton *Nature* II 359 the darkest hour is always just afore day). Apperson 135; Bradley 68; Green 32; *Oxford* 129; Stevenson 489–490:16; Tilley D84; E. B. Young *The Murder at Fleet* (Philadelphia 1928) 173. Cf. Craig Rice *The Lucky Stiff* (1945) ch. 25 It is always darkest just before it rains.

House, 1. Your dwelling . . . which is a castle (23 Cooper *Pioneers* 289; Smith *Downing* 137 A man's house is his castle; Emerson *Works* VII 132 The language of a ruder age has given to common law the maxim that every man's house is his castle; Stephens *Fashion* 296–297 My home's my castle; Richardson *Beyond* 80 the ancient legal fiction that every man's house is his castle, 171, 495; Saxe *Poems* 250 your cottage is your castle). Apperson 316; NC 429; NED Castle 3 e; *Oxford* 308; Stevenson 1191:15–1192:1; Tilley M473; NQ 12 i 509, ii 17, 59, 218, 277, iii 274; R. S. Surtees *Plain or Ringlets?* (London [1860]) 18 and, as the judges lay it down in every assizes, that a man's house is his castle; Hulbert Footner *The Velvet Hand* (1928) 319.

2. A small house . . . well filled is better than an empty palace (53 Haliburton *Sam* I 26). Cf. Apperson 371; *Oxford* 373; Tilley H779.

3. It was high as a house (59 Talia-

ferro *Fisher's* 163). NC 429; Svarten-gren 283; Whiting *Drama* 317:178. Cf. Meeting house (2).

4. Don't throw stones till you put your window-shutters to, or you may stand a smart chance of gettin' your own glass broke (43 Haliburton *Attaché* II 39–40; Stowe *Uncle* 204 I am one of the sort that lives by throwing stones at other people's glass houses; Hammett *Piney* 285 so don't ye go to throwin' stuns, not tell your own glass house is insured; Clift *Bunker* 104 folks as lives in glass houses should not throw stuns, 113 talking of throwing stones because I live in a glass house; Eggleston *School-Master* 164 People who lives in glass house have a horror of people who throw stones). Apperson 248; *Oxford* 285; Stevenson 1193:2; Stoett 322; Taylor *Investigations* 261; Tilley H789; NQ 8 iv 366, 535, v 416, x 192; B. S. Keirstead and D. F. Campbell *The Brownsville Murders* (1933) 262; F. P. Keyes *Dinner at Antoine's* (1948) 223.

5. He got on like a house a fire (Haliburton *Clockmaker* I 253, II 74 go like, 306, III 137 went on like, 201, *Attaché* II 94 they crack on like; Neal *Charcoal* 215–216; Smith *Letters* 128 hoorah'd like; Stephens *High Life* I 29 went . . . like, 112 went right up the steps agin like, 127 glistened and shone in the sun like, 252 [talking] like, II 105 up he jumped like, 112 called out "Whoa!" like; Hammett *Piney* 144 blew out like; Clemens *Roughing* II 14 go down again like). Brewster *Am. Speech* XVI (1941) 25; NC 429; Stevenson 1192:6; Taylor *Comparisons* 51; Valentine Williams and D. R. Sims *Fog* (Boston 1933) 47 get on; J. S. Fletcher *The House in Tuesday Market* (1929) 243 going ahead.

6. They are fairly eat up by them out of house and home (36 Haliburton *Clockmaker* I 64, *Old Judge* I 90, *Nature* II 293). Apperson 177; McAtee 24; NED Eat 4 a, House 12; *Oxford* 166; Stevenson 1191:4; Tilley H784; John Dos Passos *The Big Money* (1936) 216.

7. It was as bad . . . as to hear a hen crow at night from the roost (32 Kennedy *Swallow* 128; Haliburton *Nature* I 283 the old proverb, "woe to the house where the hen crows," *Season-Ticket* 327 *He* soon larned what it was to live in a house where the hen crows). Apperson 298; *Oxford* 291; Tilley H778. Cf. Stevenson 2505:2–5.

8. And [he] finally "brought down the house" by a suddenly drawn picture of the good Henrich appearing in their midst (50 P. H. Myers *The King of the Hurons* [1850] 114; Dorson *Jonathan* 93 Waggery, which was always sure to "bring down the house with 'Bravo!'"). NED Bring 15 f.

House dog. Honest as a house dog (54 Stephens *Fashion* 305).

How de do. Wal, that is a purty how de do, I must say (c58 Stephens *Mary Derwent* 371). R. P. Warren *All the King's Men* (1946) 197 It is a fine how-de-do to have a sick man for president. NED How-do-you-do 3.

Howl. See Bull (8), Wolf (13, 15).

Huckleberry, 1. As thick as huckleberries (34 Davis *Downing* 116; Haliburton *Attaché* II 36, IV 250). DA Huckleberry 3 c. Cf. Taylor *Comparisons* 81.

2. To do this . . . was at least a huckleberry over my persimmon (34 Crockett *Life* 135, *Exploits* 13 it is a huckleberry above my persimmon;

Hammett *Piney* 45 Stranger, says I, ye'r just one huckle-berry above my persimmon, 158 and ef it wer cussin', which I recon's about a huckleberry above swearin's pesimmon—I niver want to [hear it] agin; Taliaferro *Fisher's* 47 But I'll show him I'm a huckleberry over his 'simmon, 88 I'm danged . . . ef that don't take the huckleberry off of my 'simmon). Bartlett 301; DA Persimmon 2 c (1, 2); Farmer 308, 416–417; Farmer and Henley III 370; Randolph and Wilson 220; Schele de Vere 50; Stevenson 1194:9; Thornton I 458–459; NQ 8 x 295; J. C. Harris *Uncle Remus and His Friends* (Boston 1892) 147 Den I'm a punkin ahead er yo' 'simmon, is I? See Hickory (2); Woodard PADS VI (1946) 38.

3. All ye've got in that there cake-basket is no more—than a minner to a whale, nor a huckleberry to a pumkin! (65 Sedley *Marian* 132).

4. Why, this thing [a dead she-bear] laying here ain't a circumstance —hardly a huckleberry to him [a he-bear]. (55 Anon. *New Hope* 227).

Humble. See Hop-toad, Nigger (2), Rabbit (1).

Humble-pie. Humble-pie before proud-cake for me (57 Melville *Confidence-Man* 180; Alcott *Little Women* 238 he went to partake of humble-pie dutifully; Lowell *Biglow* 261 eatin' umble-pie). Farmer and Henley III 378; NED Humble pie; Stevenson 1196:12; Theda Kenyon *Witches Still Live* (1929) 169.

Humbug. It has been asserted, that no humbug can be invented which is so improbable that it will find no believers (55 Thomson *Doesticks* 64). Lean IV 152 There is none so great a lie but

some will hold therewith; Stevenson 1395:8. Cf. E. S. Morby *Romance Philology* VIII (1955) 271, citing Lope de Vega: Las truchas y las mentiras, cuanto mayores, tanto mejores.

Humming bird, 1. Busy as a humming-bird (55 Stephens *Homestead* 278).

2. [Her hand] lay as contented as a humming bird gone tu sleep under a seed onion top (44 Stephens *High Life* II 199).

3. I shall wish you as far in the sea as a humming-bird can fly in a month (59 Browning *Forty-Four* 203).

4. I gits right inter it, like a homminny-bird inter a tech-me-not flower (59 Taliaferro *Fisher's* 102).

5. She had not been of much more use in the world than a humming-bird, she said (74 Eggleston *Circuit* 314).

6. They both came with a humbird's eye of it [i. e., very close]. (33 Smith *Downing* 38).

Humor. No wonder it is almost a proverb, that a man of humour, a man capable of a good loud laugh—seem how he may in other things—can hardly be a heartless scamp (57 Melville *Confidence-Man* 218).

Hunger, 1. The most potent of sauces —a genuine woodsman's unaffected hunger (53 Hammett *Stray* 74). Apperson 318; Bradley 80; *Oxford* 310; Stevenson 1201:13; Tilley H819; Whiting *Scots* I 132; Henry Fielding *Joseph Andrews* (1742) Bk. III ch. 8 hunger is better than a French cook; Victoria Lincoln *February Hill* (1934) 43.

2. Hunger will break through a stone wall (54 Smith *'Way* 166, 228 Hunger will drive a man through a

stone wall). Apperson 317–318; NED Hunger 1 c; *Oxford* 310; Stevenson 1199:16; Tilley H811.

Hungry. See Bear (11), Dog (17), Hawk (6), Hunter, Poorbox, Shark (1), Turkey (2) 3, Wolf (7).

Hunt. See Dog (44).

Hunter. We're both as hungry as hunters (69 Alcott *Little Women* 303). Apperson 318; *Oxford* 310; Partridge 415; Svartengren 180; Hulbert Footner *The Mystery of the Folded Paper* (1930) 23.

Hurrah. There was a complete "hurrah's nest," as the sailors say, "every thing on top and nothing at hand" (40 Dana *Two* 6; Melville *White Jacket* 295 What's this hurrah's nest here aloft?; Haliburton *Season-Ticket* 323 and be no better than a hurrah's nest). Bartlett 305 A woman's word; Bradley PADS XIV (1950) 40; DA Hurrah's nest; Farmer 309; Farmer and Henley III 385; Green 196; Lean II ii 755; NED Hurrah 3; Thornton I 464.

Hurricane, 1. Out of the room she went like a she-hurricane (44 Stephens *High Life* I 49).

2. His horse's tail switchin' in every direction like a young hurricane (51 Burke *Polly* 27).

Husband. For, as Hannah says, a poor husband is better than none (49 Haliburton *Old Judge* I 211, *Season-Ticket* 327 he ain't the tallest and richest husband in the world, but he is a *peowerful sight better than none*). Tilley H833.

Hush. See Death (7).

Hydrant. My heart was as prodigal as a Croton hydrant (53 Willis *Fun* 55).

Hyena, 1. I . . . walked right straight up to them a grinning like a hyena (44 Stephens *High Life* I 98). Bartlett 809; Halpert 123; Svartengren 319. Cf. NED Hyena 6 Hyena-like grin.

2. He laughed like a hyena over a dead nigger (55 Haliburton *Nature* I 26). Boshears 33:203; NC 429; *Oxford* 352; Svartengren 319; Tilley H844; Whiting *Drama* 316:170. Cf. NED Hyena 6 hyena-laughter.

3. And the second mate, yelling like a hyena (40 Dana *Two* 439).

Hymn. I feel as gay as a hymn (73 Clemens *Love Letters* 183).

I

I, 1. This kinder law . . . you'll find all along in this ere book, from I to Izzard (57 Riley *Puddleford* 184). See A (1, 2).

2. The "firm" who save a hogshead of ink, annually, by not allowing their clerks and book-keepers to dot their i's or cross their t's (56 Kelly *Humors* 213). NED Dot 1 b; *Oxford* 155; Stevenson 728:11; Helen Reilly *Mr. Smith's Hat* (1936) 265 a passion for the dotting of i's and the crossing of t's.

Ice, 1. [Eyes] clear and cold as ice (55 Stephens *Homestead* 257; Holmes *Professor* 72 clear as Wenham ice).

2. [Brethren in Christ at home] just as cold and repulsive as the mountains of ice in the polar seas (31 Conant *Earnest Man* 390; Hawthorne *House* 117 cold as ice; Durivage *Three* 56; Kelly *Humors* 111 My thin garments . . . were cold as cakes of ice to my flesh, 271; Stephens *Mary Derwent* 164 It [her hand] was cold as ice; Chamberlain *Confession* 125 The rain was cold as ice). Apperson 106; Boshears 35:426; NC 429; Taylor *Comparisons* 28; Tilley 12; Whiting *Scots* I 192; Octavus Roy Cohen *Star of Earth* (1932) 100.

3. An ice-cold length of body (54 Hawthorne *Mosses* 313; Holmes *Autocrat* 275 ice-cold stream, *Elsie* 334 this ice-cold beauty). NED Ice-cold.

4. White as ice (44 Stephens *High Life* II 103).

5. A noise every time I moved, like the loose ice rattling off a tree arter a freezing rain (44 Stephens *High Life* I 197).

6. Didn't my pussy cousin look as if he'd fell through a thin place in the ice! (44 Stephens *High Life* II 93).

7. The ice once broken (21 Cooper *Spy* 198, *Pioneers* 64, *Satanstoe* 373; Kennedy *Swallow* 99; Haliburton *Attaché* II 73, *Old Judge* II 83; Robb *Squatter* 14; Melville *Confidence-Man* 179; Riley *Puddleford* 123; Smith *Arp* 126; Alcott *Little Women* 137; Barnum *Struggles* 506; Daly *Man* 14). Apperson 65; NED Ice 2 b; *Oxford* 62; Stevenson 1211:9; Stoett 992; Tilley 13; Robert H. Fuller *Jubilee Jim* (1928) 453.

Iceland. It was cold as Iceland—no fire at all (51 Melville *Moby-Dick* I 16).

Ice-pitcher. Sweating like an ice-pitcher (79 Clemens *Tramp* I 20). DA Ice 5 (6).

Icicle, 1. The bishop seemed as cold as an icicle (c56 Cartwright *Autobiography* 298). Boshears 35:428; Halpert 282.

2. As cool as an icicle (51 Melville *Moby-Dick* I 38).

3. He stood bolt upright, as cold and as straight as an icicle (37 Neal *Charcoal* 67).

Idiot. The greater idiot ever scolds the lesser (51 Melville *Moby-Dick* II 301).

Idle. See Wind (2).

Idleness. Idleness, everywhere, is the parent of vice (47 Melville *Omoo* 226). Apperson 322; *Oxford* 313; Stevenson 1214:3; Tilley I13; Whiting *Drama* 104, 119, 146, 183, 212, *Scots* I 192–193.

Ignorance. I could not help saying what all the world should know, if it be true, from its having been pretty frequently repeated, "When ignorance is bliss, 'tis folly to be wise" (53 Cary *Clovernook* 2d Ser. 25; Haliburton *Nature* II 32 There is some truth in the old saw "Where [etc.]"). T. Gray "Ode on a Distant Prospect of Eton College" (1747 [1742]) lines 99–100; *Oxford* 313; Stevenson 1222:3; Thomas Hood *Poems* (1837, London 1911) 490 I'm sure my ignorance is bliss; Gerald Fairlie *The Man Who Laughed* (1928) 100 how true the old saying is; R. P. Warren *All the King's Men* (1946) 80.

Ignorant. See Babe (2), Coot, Owl (4).

Image, 1. For I've spoke till I'm dry ez a real graven image (67 Lowell *Biglow* 328). Exod. 20:4.
2. Slept like a graven image (76 Clemens *Tom* 134, *Sketches* 88).
3. En dey wuz all de ve'y spit en image er de ole man (80 Harris *Uncle Remus* 82, 91, 177). NED Spit sb.² 3; Stevenson 1426:8.

Imagined. As the saying is, "they may be better imagined than described" (43 Thompson *Chronicles* 94).

Immovable. See Rock (4), Stone (10).

Impudent. See Get out.

In, 1. But once in, fast in, with me (45 Cooper *Satanstoe* 41).
2. Captain Job is "in for it" at last (55 Hammett *Wonderful* 52). Farmer and Henley IV 4–5; NED In adv. 8 b.

Inch, 1. "A true gentleman, every inch of him" (20–22 Irving *Bracebridge* 61; Mayo *Kaloolah* 106 every inch a sailor; Holmes *Autocrat* 91 A gentleman, every inch of him; Eggleston *Circuit* 35 She's every inch a lady). NED Inch 3 c.
2. In these particulars, "yielding an inch would be giving an ell" (45 Cooper *Chainbearer* 376). Apperson 327; NC 430; NED Ell 1 b; *Oxford* 238; Stevenson 1232:3; Tilley I49; Whiting *Scots* I 193; J. J. Connington, pseud. *Gold Brick Island* (Boston 1933) 92 people who took an ell when you gave them an inch.
3. Give them an inch, and they take a mile (37 Emerson *Journals* IV 313).
4. I'll be tempered to whip you within an inch of your skin (54 Shillaber *Mrs. Partington* 81; Eggleston *School-Master* 47 I 'low I could whip you in an inch of your life with my left hand; Nash *Century* 266 I'll lick you within an inch of your life). McAtee *Additional* 2; NED Inch 2; *Oxford* 211 flog; Stevenson 1232:5; David Frome, pseud. *The Strange Death of Martin Green* (1931) 263 thrash.

Income-tax. For hanged she'll be, as sure as income-tax (60 Haliburton *Season-Ticket* 361). See Rates (1), Taxes.

Independent. See Clam (5), Corkscrew (2), Hog (3), Militia trainer (2), Swallow (1), Woodsawyer.

India ink. The hide growed over it, and the larnin' couldn't get out, like

Ingey ink in a sailor's arm (37 Neal *Charcoal* 33).

Indian, 1. They have an old proverb here, and I like proverbs, there is so much truth in 'em, in a small compass. An Indian, a partridge, and a spruce tree can't be tamed (53 Haliburton *Sam* II 86). Stevenson 2507:8 (this passage).

2. You're meaner than an Ingin (43 Robb *Squatter* 108; Haliburton *Sam* II 81 It's a common phrase with us white folks, that a feller is as mean as an Indgin, or begs like an Indgin; Chamberlain *Confession* 24 Uncle committed an act of meanness that would have shamed an Indian).

3. He is as . . . superstitious as an Indian (58 Porter *Major* 132).

4. Almost as wild and untamable as Indians (55 Irving *Wolfert* 266). Taylor *Comparisons* 88 wild.

5. And don't lub Injin fashion of gibbin' t'ings; and dat is gib him and den take away ag'in (46 Cooper *Redskins* 451). Bartlett 312; DA Indian 9 b; Farmer 314; NC 430; Stevenson 958:8; Thornton III 202; J. T. Farrell *A World I Never Made* (1936) 340 an Indian giver.

6. Ah! Sir! that critter [a mare] knows as much as an Injun, and more than a Nigger (58 Porter *Major* 49).

7. To play Indian [i. e., to be stoic]. 40 DA Indian 6 (3 a).

8. To play the sober Indian [i. e., not to join in drinking]. 32 DA Indian 6 (2).

9. To see Indians [i. e., to be in a delirium]. 50 DA Indian 6 (4).

10. To sing Indian [i. e., to defy death]. 29 DA Indian 6 (1).

11. To turn Indian. 62 DA Indian 6 (5).

12. They hollered and yelled . . . like so many Injuns jest broke loose (44 Stephens *High Life* I 42, II 63 The folks stomped and yelled like a pack of Injuns).

13. She run like a wild Injun (60 Whitehead *Wild Sports* 337).

14. I've worked hard as an Injun on my land (68 Clift *Bunker* 149).

Indigo bag. Turned as blue as an indigo bag (34 Davis *Downing* 86; Baldwin *Flush* 291 She was as blue as an indigo bag [i. e., highly moral]; Hammett *Piney* 260 He was a hardshell baptist, and the deacon an old-fashioned presbyterian, blue as an indigo bag; Nash *Century* 87 nose). Cf. Boshears 34:366; NC 430; Taylor *Comparisons* 19.

Industrious. See Bee (6), Day (10).

Inevitable. See Clock (2), Death (8).

Infancy. [A wife] guileless as infancy (50 Mitchell *Reveries* 37).

Infant, 1. You'll feel as calm as an infant (57 Riley *Puddleford* 62; Holmes *Professor* 13 His countenance was as calm as that of a reposing infant).

2. As helpless as an infant (53 Hammett *Stray* 223; Stephens *Homestead* 161 more helpless than infants; Bennett *Border* 343). See Child (5).

3. The eyes . . . were as blue and as mild as an infant's (39 Briggs *Harry* I 173).

4. I was as weak as an infant (40 Dana *Two* 393; Melville *White Jacket* 324; Clemens *Enterprise* 74). See Baby (5), Child (9).

5. I'll sleep as calmly as an infant (57 Jones *Country* 40). Svartengren 167; Keble Howard *The Peculiar Major* (1919) 50 sleep like. See Baby (11).

Inflammable. See Tow (1).

Ink, 1. As black as ink (40 Haliburton *Letter* 43, *Attaché* I 192, 230, II 220, *Sam* II 244, *Season-Ticket* 165, 372; Irving *Attorney* 340, *Wolfert* 264; Clemens *Sandwich* 209; Alcott *Little Women* 143). Apperson 51; Boshears 34:356; NC 430; Taylor *Comparisons* 17; Tilley I73; W. B. Seabrook *Jungle Ways* (London 1931) 178.
2. It was as dark as ink in the room (43 Haliburton *Attaché* I 20, *Old Judge* II 44).
3. To sling ink. 67 DA Sling 1 b (1). Cf. Farmer and Henley IV 9.
4. See India ink.

[Inn-keepers]. Prepared as he was for exorbitancy—the proverbial exorbitancy of such people (25 Neal *Brother J* II 137).

Innocent. See Babe (5), Baby (9), Child (6), Dove (3), Kitten (5), Lamb (6), Pansy, Rabbit (2), Sheep (8), Snowdrop (2).

Inside, 1. As dark as the inside of a cow (63 Clemens *Enterprise* 64, *Roughing* I 20). Taylor *Comparisons* 31.
2. To be inside [i. e., to have confidential information]. 70 DA Inside 3 b (1).
3. See Track (4).

Instep. They are too high in the instep [i. e., conceited]. (36 Haliburton *Clockmaker* I 254). Apperson 301; NED Instep 1 b; *Oxford* 294; Tilley I84.

Insult. They add insult to injury (47 Melville *Omoo* 212, *White Jacket* 171 he felt the insult more than the injury, *Moby-Dick* II 23; Alcott *Little Women* 255; Barnum *Struggles* 710; Clemens *Sketches* 65). Apperson 328; *Ox-*

ford 320; Stevenson 1251:1; Margery Allingham *Kingdom of Death* (1933) 68.

Intention. Intention is half the battle (40 Cooper *Pathfinder* 469).

Intimate. See Brother (2).

Irish, 1. The barbarian incursions of the *"wild Irish"* emigrants (49 Melville *Redburn* 314). NED Irish B 1.
2. We feared to eat much at a time, till, like the Irish by hanging, we got used to it again (34 Crockett *Life* 120). Cf. *Oxford* 465 Nothing when.
3. But her Irish was up too high to do anything with her (34 Crockett *Life* 65). Bartlett 317; Farmer and Henley IV 13; McAtee 36; Stevenson 1253:13. See Blood (9), North Carolina.
4. Many companies after immense expenditures reap only assessments, which in this region are termed "Irish dividends" (67 Richardson *Beyond* 375).
5. No fag-ends of ropes and "Irish pendants" aloft (40 Dana *Two* 222).

Irishman, 1. We had, for the most part, what the sailors call "an Irishman's hurricane,—right up and down" (40 Dana *Two* 364).
2. Almost as large and as empty as an Irishman's pocket at the present time (23–24 Irving *Tales* 46).

Iron, 1. Firm as iron (42 Irving *Attorney* 369). Svartengren 261.
2. His hands and fingers were nearly as hard as iron (43 Hall *Purchase* II 33; Stowe *Uncle* 379 Well, I tell ye this yer fist has got as hard as cast-iron *knocking* down niggers; Boucicault *Flying Scud* 197 His heart must be as hard as iron; Clemens *Innocents* II 40, 236). NC 430; Svartengren 260; Hen-

ry Holt *The Midnight Mail* (1931) 232. See Heart (17).

3. Hold your arm stiff—stiff as iron (25 Neal *Brother J* III 282). Svartengren 263 rigid.

4. His well-seasoned arms were like iron (71 Eggleston *School-Master* 166).

5. Willing to strike while the iron was hot (23 Cooper *Pioneers* 112; Kennedy *Horse-Shoe* 365; Emerson *Works* II 235; Haliburton *Clockmaker* III 20 strike while the iron was hot and hissin'; Judd *Richard* 216; Smith *My Thirty* 417; Lowell *Biglow* 292 While, 'long o' Congress, you can't strike, 'f you git an iron het; Alcott *Little Women* 403). Apperson 605–606; NC 430; *Oxford* 626; Stevenson 1256:11; Stoett 999; Tilley I94; Whiting *Drama* 230, 244, *Scots* I 193; Tobias Smollett *The Expedition of Humphrey Clinker* (1771, Letter of Winifred Jackson, Oct. 14); Samuel Lover *Handy Andy* (1842) ch. 29 (Everyman's Library p. 320); A. C. Brown *Dr. Glazebrook's Revenge* (1928) 238; William McFee *The Harbourmaster* (London 1932) 404.

6. He had but sixteen irons in the fire at this time (32 Kennedy *Swallow* 110; Haliburton *Clockmaker* I 308 Too Many Irons in the Fire [chapter-heading], 309 There's a plaguy sight of truth in them are old proverbs. They are distilled facts steamed down to an essence. They are like portable soup, an amazin deal of matter in a small compass. They are what I valy most, experience . . . That's the beauty of old proverbs; they are as true as a plum line, and as short and sweet as sugar candy. Now when you come to see all about the country you'll find the truth of that are one— "*a man that has too many irons in the*

fire, is plaguy apt to get some on 'em burnt," 311 Too many irons agin, 312, 316 too many irons in the fire not to get some on 'em burnt, 317, 318 the old sayin' about "too many irons," 320 *You have too many irons in the fire, some on 'em will get stone cold,* and tother ones will get burnt so, they'll never be no good in natur; Shillaber *Mrs. Partington* 335 Sir Hildebrand had "too many irons in the fire"; Barnum *Struggles* 485 There is good sense in the old caution against having too many irons in the fire at once). Apperson 328; Farmer and Henley IV 15; NC 430; NED Iron 9 b; *Oxford* 405–406; Stevenson 1255:4; Tilley I99; Whiting *Scots* I 193; Kathleen M. Knight *Seven Were Veiled* (1937) 186 too many.

7. This is what is called "hazing" a crew, and "working their old iron up" (40 Dana *Two* 114).

8. See Smoothing iron.

Irreconcilable. See Wolf (9).

Irresistible. See Thunder (4).

Israel. I'll just give my nigger Jake perfect Israel when I git home (51 Burke *Polly* 109).

Itch. Hit pester'd 'em ni ontu es bad es the eatch (67 Harris *Sut* 116). George H. Coxe *Murder with Pictures* (1935) 136.

Ivory, 1. Limbs . . . smooth . . . as ivory (56 Jones *Wild* 219). Svartengren 270.

2. Her teeth were as white as ivory (55 Haliburton *Nature* II 137, *Sam* I 296 teeth like ivory; Jones *Wild* 219 limbs . . . white as ivory). Apperson 680; NC 430; Stevenson 2487:6; Svartengren 232; Taylor *Comparisons* 86; Tilley I109; Whiting *Scots* I 193–194.

❦ J ❦

Jack (1), 1. You be von Jack All-trade (23 Cooper *Pioneers* 229; Dana *Two* 355 our forecastle looked like the workshop of what a sailor is—a Jack-at-all-trades; Melville *Redburn* 152 A Sailor A Jack of All trades [chapter heading], 154 in short, he must be a Jack of all trades, in order to master his own, *Moby-Dick* II 309 a jack-of-all-trades, *Israel* 62 Jack of all trades, master of each and mastered by none; Hammett *Stray* 284 and a thorough jack he was at almost all trades; Paul *Courtship* 24 a jack-of-all-trades). Apperson 330; Farmer and Henley IV 25; Oxford 323; Stevenson 1259:1; Tilley J19; Anne Meredith *Portrait of a Murderer* (1934) 52.

2. I'm a sort of Jack of all trades, and master of none (53 Haliburton *Sam* I 147). Farmer and Henley IV 25; NC 430; Oxford 323; Stevenson 1259:1; F. Marryat *Frank Mildmay* (1829, ed. London 1929) Ch. 24, p. 342; W. M. McCartney *Fifty Years a Country Doctor* (1938) 120.

3. Afore you can say Jack Robberson (25 Neal *Brother J* I 244, II 293 afore you can say—[presumably "J. R."]; Davis *Downing* 32 afore we could say Jack Robinson, 275 before; Haliburton *Clockmaker* I 198, II 162; Hall *Purchase* I 190 Jack Robison; Stephens *High Life* I 204 Before; Thompson *Major* 36 As quick as; Hooper *Simon* 106; Kelly *Humors* 301; Riley *Puddleford* 236 quicker'n; Hammett *Piney* 33, 52, 70, 113, 145; Paul

Courtship 57 in less than you could say John Robinson backwards; Eggleston *School-Master* 148; Nash *Century* 63 quicker'n you can say Jack Roberson; Shillaber *Ike* 127). Apperson 330; Boshears 39:839; Farmer and Henley IV 31–32; McAtee 51; NC 430; NED Jack 34 b; Oxford 29–30; Taylor *Comparisons* 66; Christopher Bush *The Case of the Chinese Gong* (1935) 164 before; Charlotte M. Russell *Murder at the Old Stone House* (1935) 272 quicker than. See Nick Biddle, Tony.

4. Just as easy as for me to say Jack Robinson (51 Dorson *Jonathan* 107). Svartengren 347.

5. The old sailor, far from a drunkard, nevertheless held firmly to the maxim that every Jack should have his gill and have it too at regular intervals (55 Hammett *Wonderful* 71). Apperson 329; NC 430; NED Jack 2 c; Oxford 322–323; Stevenson 1262:1; Pierce Egan *Life in London* (1821, ed. London 1869) 120 and as the proverb informs us, every Jack has his Jill.

6. I felt very much about it as Jack did when he saw the skunk & hedgehog fighting, he said he didn't care a fig which licked (36 Fairfield *Letters* 142).

Jack (2), 1. To be full of jack [i. e., animal spirits, mischief]. 72 DA Jack 12 d.

2. His first experiment at "hooking

jack" (56 Durivage *Three* 208; Sedley *Marian* 121 And although what he called "hooking Jack" caused him to grow up awfully deficient in even the simpler branches). Bartlett 294; DA Hook 2.

3. I seen that were my time to make my Jack [i. e., make a supreme effort to escape]. (59 Taliaferro *Fisher's* 137). Bartlett 378; Farmer 320; Stevenson 1259:4. Cf. DA Jack 12 d.

4. To raise jack [i. e., a disturbance]. 67 DA Jack 12 d.

5. To tear up jack. 45 DA Jack 12 d.

6. To turn up jack. 28 DA Turn 11 (1).

Jackass, 1. Es solemn es a jasack in a snow storm, when the fodder gin out (67 Harris *Sut* 80).

2. He knows the old proverb that if a feller gets a rap from a jackass, he hadn't ought to tell of it (43 Haliburton *Attaché* III 200). *Oxford* 16.

Jackdaw. Jackdaw birds, that borrow feathers to strut in (40 Haliburton *Clockmaker* III 190). Apperson 48–49; *Oxford* 45; Stevenson 180:9; Tilley B375.

Jackknife, 1. I drew up agin easy, like a jack-knife with a tough spring (44 Stephens *High Life* II 29).

2. A sneaking critter with a face like a jack-knife (44 Stephens *High Life* II 57).

3. He was said to be the undisputed possessor of the celebrated jackknife [a prize for ugliness]. (58 Porter *Major* 17). Cf. DA Jackknife 1 b.

January, 1. Cool as January [i. e., unexcited]. (53 Boker *Bankrupt* 107). Svartengren 315 cold.

2. Let January be January, and let May be May (43 Haliburton *Attaché*

IV 160; Saxe *Poems* 188 Does January wed with May?). Apperson 332; *Oxford* 413; Tilley M768; Whiting *Scots* I 194.

Jaw. All jaw like a sheep's head [i. e., talkative]. (33 Neal *Down-Easters* I 79, 104; Haliburton *Clockmaker* III 175).

Jay bird, 1. As enticin as a jay bird (32 Robb *Squatter* 98).

2. Dez [Just] ez sassy ez a jay-bird (80 Harris *Uncle Remus* 24, 47 jaybird at a sparrer's nest). Svartengren 160 pert.

Jealous. See Hen (3), Nature (1), Pointer.

Jehu. Driving like Jehu as we did flee for life (66 Smith *Arp* 126). II Kings 9:20; Stevenson 1265:4; Val Gielgud *The Ruse of the Vanished Woman* (1934) 176. Cf. Farmer and Henley IV 43.

Jelly. But he contrives to laugh lustily, and his flabby dimensions shake like a bowl of jelly (45 Judd *Margaret* I 249; Baldwin *Flush* 313 muscles twitching and shaking like a bowl of jelly; Shillaber *Knitting-Work* 397). NC 431; Taylor *Comparisons* 52.

Jericho. Or else I would see you at Jericho before you should have my Kate (47 Jones *Country* 317). 2 Sam. 10:5; Apperson 332–333; Green 203; McAtee 36; NED Jericho; *Oxford* 325; Stevenson 1265:6; Tilley J39; Eden Phillpotts *Found Drowned* (London c1931) 210 wished him at Jericho.

Jessy. That's the way to give him jessy (43 Robb *Squatter* 33, 59 the afarr [affair] raised jessy in Nettle Bottom, 81 Allen was giving him "particular jesse"; Kelly *Humors* 212 jessy; Thomson *Plu-ri-bus-tah* 91 was always slyly watching For a chance to "give him Jesse," 140, 237; Shillaber *Mrs. Partington* 334; Jones *Country* 234 Jesse; Cary *Married* 226 jessie). Bartlett 322; DA Jesse 1, Particular; Farmer 324; Farmer and Henley IV 50; Green 203; NC 431; Schele de Vere 612; Thornton I 493–494, III 221; Tidwell PADS XI (1949) 14. Cf. Louise Pound *Am. Speech* XXI (1946) 151–153.

Jet, 1. A mustache as black as jet (56 Durivage *Three* 33; Taliaferro *Fisher's* 191; Browning *Forty-Four* 49 eyes; Richardson *Beyond* 498). Apperson 51; Boshears 34:357; NC 431; Taylor *Comparisons* 18; Tilley J49; Whiting *Scots* I 194; Peter Coffin *The Search for my Great-Uncle's Head* (1937) 145.

2. Eyes of jet-black (24 Cooper *Pilot* 102, *Prairie* 122, *Satanstoe* 35; Neal *Brother J* I 16; Kennedy *Swallow* 225, *Horse-Shoe* 33; Melville *Omoo* 251, *Mardi* I 182, 338, II 393, *Redburn* 2, 324, *Moby-Dick* II 175; Holmes *Elsie* 201 the jet-black Africans, *Poet* 38 jet-black horses; Durivage *Three* 373). NED Jet-black; Elsa Barker *The Redman Cave Murder* (1930) 85.

Jew, 1. As mean as a Jew (60 Haliburton *Season-Ticket* 9). Cf. NC 431.

2. As rich as a Jew (34 Crockett *Life* 179; Stephens *High Life* I 166, 254; Haliburton *Sam* II 145; Kelly *Humors* 129; Whitcher *Widow* 80; Shillaber *Knitting-Work* 85, 179, 289). Apperson 529; Fife 119; Stevenson 1985:6; Svartengren 341.

Jew's eye. Tho' they are no good to you, they are worth a Jew's eye to us (38 Haliburton *Clockmaker* II 292).

Apperson 333; Farmer and Henley IV 51; *Oxford* 734; Stevenson 2642:8; Svartengren 127; Tilley J53.

Jib, 1. To fly off one's jib [i. e., to be in poor health]. 48 DA Fly 3.

2. See Cut, sb. (1).

Jiffy. In less than half a jiffy (44 Stephens *High Life* II 28; Kelly *Humors* 113 A piece of his fawn was . . . roasted in a jiffy; Clemens *Letters* I 66 in a jiffy). Farmer and Henley IV 53; NED Jiffy.

Jig, 1. My opponent might as well have whistled jigs to a milestone as attempt to beat up for votes in that district (36 Crockett *Exploits* 22).

2. The jig is up with me (33 Smith *Downing* 103, 164, 'Way 206, *My Thirty* 288, 310, 343, 367; Crockett *Life* 130 I thought now the jig was mighty nigh up with me; Haliburton *Clockmaker* I 244, III 202; Hooper *Simon* 90, 135; Kelly *Humors* 263; Jones *Wild* 194; Clemens *Love Letters* 138; Nash *Century* 68). Bartlett 323; Farmer and Henley IV 54; McAtee 36; NED Jig 5; Thornton I 494, III 211; Madeleine Johnston *Comets Have Long Tails* (1938) 190. See Game (4).

Jimson weed. Green [ignorant] as a jinson weed (58 Porter *Major* 135). Thornton I 489.

Job (1), 1. He is as mean as Job's turkey (53 Haliburton *Sam* II 252).

2. We are as poor as Job (66 Smith *Arp* 142). Apperson 505; NC 432; NED Job 1 a; *Oxford* 510; Stevenson 1856:11; Svartengren 342; Tilley J60; Whiting *Drama* 318:187 bare, *Scots* I 194.

3. As poor as Job's cat (54 Smith 'Way 184). DA Job (1) 1; Taylor *Comparisons* 63; Thornton I 496.

4. Captain Jack looks as poor as Job's turkey (38 Haliburton *Clockmaker* II 21, *Attaché* II 269; Hall *Purchase* II 85; Riley *Puddleford* 91, 255; Taliaferro *Fisher's* 175; Eggleston *School-Master* 70). Boshears 39: 805; DA Job (1) 4; McAtee 50, PADS XV (1951) 58; NC 432; Schele de Vere 645; Taylor *Comparisons* 63; Thornton I 495–496; C. G. Givens *All Cats Are Gray* (Indianapolis 1937) 157.

5. Enough to wear the patience of Job out (33 Smith *Downing* 167; Haliburton *Old Judge* II 161 enough to try the patience of Job; Melville *Redburn* 106; Harris *Sut* 76 She kerried enuf devil about her tu run crazy a big settlement ove Job's Children; Clemens *Love Letters* 85). NC 432; NED Job 1 b; *Oxford* 490; Stevenson 1271:5; Thornton I 495; Tilley J59; Todd Downing *The Case of the Unconquered Sisters* (1936) 109 try Job's patience.

Job (2). So at last I giv it up for a bad job (44 Stephens *High Life* I 69; Dorson *Jonathan* 119). Cf. NED Job 5.

Joe. En ef we don't git 'im for supper, Joe's dead en Sal's a widder (80 Harris *Uncle Remus* 58, 73–74).

John O'Groat. He's as far awa' frae the truth as John O'Groat's house is frae Jericho (70 Daly *Man* 48). *Oxford* 349–350; Stevenson 1344:8 from Land's End to John o'Groat's house.

Johnson. He becomes fond of the meat, and considers other game as "not worth a notice, "as old Johnson said of the devil (34 Crockett *Life* 182).

Joke, 1. A joke is a joke, but that's no joke (38 Haliburton *Clockmaker* II 231, 322, *Season-Ticket* 32; Emerson Bennett *Viola* [Philadelphia n. d. (1852)] 38 A joke is a joke, and so let it end; P. H. Myers *The King of the Hurons* [1850] 79 Well, well, he said, a joke's a joke, and you are welcome to yours). Charles Dickens *Sketches by Boz* (1836), Centenary ed., London 1910) 51; R. G. Browne *By Way of Confession* (1930) 52. See Fun (1).

2. But this is carrying a joke a little too far (45 Mayo *Kaloolah* 304; Sedley *Marian* 287 But there is sech a thing as kerryin' a joke too far; Richardson *Beyond* 186 Such a thing as carrying a joke too far). Cf. Tilley J47.

Jolly. See Bacchus (1).

Jonah. It growed an' growed like Jonah's gourd (67 Lowell *Biglow* 283; Richardson *Beyond* 77 the locust grows like Jonah's gourd, 372 Here has sprung up, like Jonah's gourd, a city upon a hill). Jonah 4:6.

Josey. Don't make a josey of yourself [i. e., don't be over-conscientious]. (39 Briggs *Harry* I 164). Perhaps from Joseph's behavior in Gen. 39:7–11.

Jousley. A man must be mean as jousely, and meaner yet, who could do a small action (44 Stephens *High Life* I 108).

Joyous. See Lark (7).

Juba. The niggers were patting Juba on every corner (58 Field *Pokerville* 14). Bartlett 325; Bradley PADS XIV (1950) 51; DA Juba 1; Green 206, 267; NED Juba; Thornton I 501, III 214.

Judge, 1. As serious as a judge (44 Thompson *Major* 76). David Frome, pseud. *The Man from Scotland Yard* (1932) 281.

2. As sober as a judge (35 Longstreet *Georgia* 17; Haliburton *Attaché*

I 111, *Old Judge* II 281 though they ain't always the soberest neither, *Season-Ticket* 109 that old saying; Hammett *Stray* 132 as sober as a judge—ought to be; Kelly *Humors* 83; Barnum *Struggles* 122). Apperson 585; Boshears 40:944; NC 432; Taylor *Comparisons* 76; Tilley J93; Vincent Starrett *The Blue Door* (1930) 4.

3. Es solemn ez a judge (67 Locke [Nasby] *Struggles* 484). Boshears 40:954; NC 432; Taylor *Comparisons* 76; K. S. Cole *I'm Afraid I'll Live* (Boston 1936) 24.

4. As steady as a judge (44 Stephens *High Life* II 112).

Judgment. There's judgment in all things (23 Cooper *Pioneers* 229).

Judy. They made chairmin and secketaries, and passed resolutions, and made pretickelar Judies of theyselves ginerally (58 Hammett *Piney* 68). Bartlett 326; Farmer 327; Farmer and Henley IV 79.

Jug, 1. She was as bald as a jug (72 Clemens *Roughing* II 101).

2. Right dar's whar he broke his merlasses jug (80 Harris *Uncle Remus* 25).

Jug-full. Not by a jug-full (33 Neal *Down-Easters* I 126; Smith *Letters* 92, *My Thirty* 429; Stephens *High Life* II 208; Lowell *Biglow* 148; Baldwin *Flush* 149; Riley *Puddleford* 162; Hammett *Piney* 123, 171, 294; Smith *Arp* 115 Not by three or four jug fulls; Clift *Bunker* 278). Bartlett 326; DA Jugful; Farmer 327; Farmer and Henley IV 80; Green 206; McAtee 37; NED Jugful; Stevenson 551:7; Thornton II 615, III 215; Tidwell PADS XI (1949) 14; M. D. Post *Walker of the Secret Service* (1924) 208.

Juggernaut. The changes of the times, which roll onward like a Juggernaut (37 Neal *Charcoal* 95).

Jug-handle. If not, say so, and I'm orf like a jug-handle (62 Browne *Artemus* 154).

Juicy. See Peach (3).

Jujube. Nonsense, as sweet as the jujube paste (44 Stephens *High Life* I 240).

Julius Caesar. See Caesar.

July. They never alleviate talking about them from July to eternity (36 Haliburton *Clockmaker* I 190, 220, III 297, *Attaché* I 277; Smith *My Thirty* 451 it might take 'em pretty near from July to eternity).

Jump, sb. 1. To be a jump above one's persimmon. 45 DA Persimmon 3 c (3). See Huckleberry (2).

2. See Squirrel (6).

Jump, vb., 1. He's an old fox, and always knows where to jump (33 Smith *Downing* 190).

2. I raly felt as if I could a'most have jumped over the housen, eend foremost, I was so glad to git ashore (44 Stephens *High Life* II 12).

3. Why do you jump afore you're spurred? (55 Dorson *Jonathan* 57).

4. See Catamount (6), Hen (15), Pea (8), Rabbit (5), Wildcat (5).

Jumping-off place. See Place (3).

Justice. One man's justice is another man's injustice; one man's beauty another man's ugliness; one man's wisdom another's folly (c40 Emerson *Works* II 315). Cf. Apperson 410–411 meat; NC 444; *Oxford* 416; Tilley M483.

Kangaroo. Sammy went leaping, like a kangaroo with a split stick on his tail (43 Thompson *Chronicles* 67).

Katy-did. A queer-looking chap, as chirk as a caty-did (44 Stephens *High Life* II 63). Cf. Grasshopper (3).

Keel. But as I was not in the habit of using spirits at all, I knew that a very little would keel me up (c56 Cartwright *Autobiography* 204).

Keen. See Beagle, Brier, Cutworm, Knife, Lizard (1), Weasel (2).

Keep, sb. He wun't be wuth his keep (67 Lowell *Biglow* 280; Eggleston *Circuit* 82 and many a backwoods housewife, perishing of *ennui*, has declared that genial Brady's "company wus worth his keep"). NED Keep 6 c.

Keep, vb. Keep yourself to yourself (73 Clemens *Gilded* I 13, *Tom* 170). Partridge 450; Austen Allen *The Loose Rib* (1933) 133.

Kettle, 1. What a pretty kittle of fish we shall have to fry (35 Crockett *Account* 119; Neal *Charcoal* 29; Haliburton *Clockmaker* I p. viii and a pretty kettle of fish I've made on it, II 52, 125; Cooper *Redskins* 27 we should soon have a pretty kettle of fish between landlord and tenant; Stowe *Uncle* 96 a pretty kettle of fish it would be for me, too, to be caught with them both here; Boucicault *Flying Scud* 165). Apperson 338–339; Farmer and Henley IV 94; NED Kettle 2; *Oxford* 333; Stevenson 817:1; NQ 4 viii 549, ix 102, 521; 7 viii 63; Thomas Hood *Poems* (1825, ed. London 1911) 23 Youl make a fine Kittle of fish of your Close [clothes] some Day; William McFee *The Harbourmaster* (London 1932) 148 Ah! but this is another kettle of fish, 272 I thought: here's a kettle of fish; R. G. Anderson *The Tavern Rogue* (1934) 152; E. M. Rhodes *Beyond the Desert* (Boston 1934) 143. Sir Walter Scott describes a "kettle of fish" as a "fête-champêtre of a particular kind" and tells at length the proper way of cooking and eating a salmon on such an occasion; see *St. Ronan's Well* (1824) ch. 12.

2. Likely to upset our whole kettle of fish (59 Smith *My Thirty* 287, 385). Kathleen M. Knight *Death Blew Out the Match* (1935) 238.

Key. But it worked jest ez smooth ez the key of a safe (67 Lowell *Biglow* 322).

Kick, sb. 1. If a man is only determined to go ahead, the more kicks he receives in his breech the faster he will get on his journey (36 Crockett *Exploits* 14). The modern colloquial "Every kick is a boost" does not seem to have been recorded by collectors.

2. When a man is going down, every body lends him a kick (55 Derby *Phoenixiana* 222). Cf. NC 441:27; Stevenson 1292:8.

3. How many fellers get more kicks than coppers in their life (55 Haliburton *Nature* II 339). Green 33; *Oxford* 431 Monkey's; Stevenson 1294:2 than half-pence; Arthur Gask *Murder in the Night* (1932) 124 halfpence.

4. To have no kick coming. 63 DA Kick 1.

Kick, vb., 1. You needn't kick before you're spurred (36 Longstreet *Georgia* 11; Haliburton *Clockmaker* III 155 So don't kick afore you are spurred, *Attaché* I 87, IV 262). Green 22. Cf. *Oxford* 121 cry. See Hollo, Jump, vb. (3).

2. See Horse (35).

Kill, 1. A young gal, finified off to kill (44 Stephens *High Life* I 155, 159 dressed up, 176, 254). Bartlett 192; Bey PADS II (1944) 56; DA Kill 1; Farmer 332; McAtee 26; Schele de Vere 596; Stevenson 626:8; Thornton I 324; Charles Barry, pseud. *Death in Darkness* (1933) 168 dressed up.

2. Pshaw! you might as well kill me as scare me (56 Cary *Married* 186).

3. See Way (12, 13).

Killdeer. Please goodness!, but that's a poor country down yander; it makes the tears come into the kildear's eyes when they fly over the old fields (35 Crockett *Account* 90). See Crow (1).

Killoch. Afore you up killoch and off (36 Haliburton *Clockmaker* I 203; Dana *Two* 319 she was "up keeleg and off" before you were outside of Cape Cod; Hammett *Piney* 256 killick, 267 killeck; Lowell *Biglow* 137 So I edvise the noomrous friends . . . To jest up killick, jam right down their hellum hard alee). Bartlett 332–333. Cf. NED Killick, killock (a heavy stone used as an anchor), Keeleg. See Line (3).

Kind, sb., 1. Kind must cling to kind, and country to country (40 Cooper *Pathfinder* 283).

2. See Folks (3).

Kind, adj. See Kitten (6), Robin (1).

Kindness. These people will actually kill me with kindness (43 Haliburton *Attaché* III 93; Barnum *Struggles* 483 almost "killed with kindness"). Apperson 340; Green 33; *Oxford* 335; Stevenson 1297:7; Tilley K51; Whiting *Drama* 351:660; Jennings Rice *The Man Who Insulted Somersville* (1938) 294.

King, 1. He was as happy as a king (50 Mitchell *Reveries* 76; Cary *Married* 96; Saxe *Poems* 25; Barnum *Struggles* 678). Apperson 283; NC 433; *Oxford* 277; Stevenson 1074:6; Svartengren 77; Tilley K54; NQ 2 x 350. Cf. Whiting *Drama* 318:192; Arthur Gask *Murder in the Night* (1932) 80.

2. He jest went anywhere as nateral as a king (66 Smith *Arp* 130).

3. Looking proud as a king (50 Melville *White Jacket* 31; Shillaber *Knitting-Work* 179). Boshears 39:817; Halpert 547; NC 433. Cf. Svartengren 81 duchess, peer, princess, queen.

4. As rich as kings (55 Stephens *Homestead* 360). NC 433; Svartengren 341; Tilley C832.

5. Think you . . . to how long a period the mighty arm of the British king may extend (24 Cooper *Pilot* 139). Apperson 341; Lean IV 25; *Oxford* 339; Stevenson 1307–1308:10; Tilley K87; Whiting *Drama* 235, *Scots* I 195. Cf. P. B. Noyes *The Pallid Giant* (1927) 37 Governments proverbially have long arms.

6. Feasted like kings (60 Whitehead *Wild Sports* 21; Clemens *Roughing* II 152). Cf. NC 433 live.

7. Treat yer like a king (59 Taliaferro *Fisher's* 268).

Kingdom. Some body once said—"That in the kingdom of the blind, the one-eyed are monarchs" (57 Riley *Puddleford* 81). Apperson 342; *Oxford* 338; Stevenson 197–198:8; Woodard PADS VI (1946) 34.

Kingdom Come. Other pitiful nobodies between Kingdom Come and Baalbec (69 Clemens *Innocents* II 171). Cf. *Oxford* 338.

Kink, 1. To come the kink [i. e., to steal a Negro in the country and sell him in town]. 63 DA Kink 2 c.
2. He got another kink into his head that did beat all (44 Stephens *High Life* I 139, 147 suppose you jest go over the manœuvre about the wine, so that I can git the kink on it). DA Kink 1; NED Kink 2; Stevenson 1310: 1. Cf. Hang, sb. (1, 2).

Kiss. These violets "kiss and tell," Mr. Tyrell (53 Willis *Fun* 288). Apperson 343; Lean IV 179; Stevenson 1312:2; Tilley K106; K. Whipple *The Killings in Carter Cave* (1934) 175 a girl who kissed and told.

Kissing. Kissing goes by favors (21 Loomis *Farmer's Almanac* 178; Haliburton *Clockmaker* III 305 When kissin' goes by favour; Nash *Century* 47 the homely adage). Apperson 344; Green 27; *Oxford* 341; Stevenson 1311:1; Tilley K108; Lee Thayer, pseud. *Dead Man's Shoes* (1929) 3.

Kit. The hull kit and cargo on 'em had conspired together (56 Whitcher *Widow* 257; Eggleston *School-Master* 85 He'll beat the whole kit and tuck 'em afore he's through). NC 433; Randolph and Wilson 258. Cf. DA Kit; McAtee 38; NED Kit 3.

Kite (1), 1. She looks as yaller as a kite's foot (49 Haliburton *Old Judge* I 223). Apperson 717; *Oxford* 737; Svartengren 252; Tilley K115.
2. Hoisted his tail like a kite (59 Taliaferro *Fisher's* 67).

Kite (2), 1. This doctrin . . . knocks Dimokracy higher than a kite (64 Locke [Nasby] *Struggles* 125; Clemens *Enterprise* 156; Barnum *Struggles* 628 the White Mountains were "knocked higher than a kite" by Mont Blanc). DA Kite; NC 433; Randolph and Wilson 179; Taylor *Comparisons* 48. See Gilderoy.
2. To fly one's own kite. 65 DA Fly vb. 3.

Kitten, 1. He is docile as a kitten (45 Judd *Margaret* II 117).
2. As full of fun as a kitten (43 Haliburton *Attaché* II 92, *Old Judge* II 82).
3. He is as gentle as a kitten when I am present (50 Willis *Life* 67). NC 433; Taylor *Comparisons* 43.
4. As good-natured as a kitten (44 Stephens *High Life* I 147).
5. As innocent as a kitten (44 Stephens *High Life* I 251).
6. Kind as kittens (52 Melville *Pierre* 27).
7. The damsels were . . . more playful than kittens (49 Melville *Mardi* I 283; Judd *Richard* 161 jocose, lively, playful as a kitten). Boshears 39:800; NC 433; Taylor *Comparisons* 62.
8. As quiet as a kitten (44 Stephens *High Life* I 168; Chamberlain *Confession* 152 he lay as quiet as a choked kitten).
9. Des [Just] ez soshubble ez a baskit er kittens (80 Harris *Uncle Remus* 26). See Basket (1).

10. As spry as a kitten (44 Stephens *High Life* II 167; Lowell *Biglow* 44; Hammett *Piney* 122). McAtee 61; NC 433; C. W. Tyler *Blue Jean Billy* (1926) 140.

11. She sot as still as a kitten (44 Stephens *High Life* I 180).

12. I was weaker than a kitten (52 Melville *Pierre* 464; Clemens *Roughing* I 270 weak as). McAtee 70; NC 381 cat 13; Stevenson 2470:1; Taylor *Comparisons* 85; C. F. Gregg *Inspector Higgins Sees It Through* (1934) 137. See Cat (29).

13. Wild as a kitten she was, but as harmless too (55 Stephens *Homestead* 430).

14. Him got no harm in him no more'n a little kitten (43 Thompson *Chronicles* 97).

15. The leetle chap a holding on as you've seen a kitten to an old cat's tail (44 Stephens *High Life* I 209).

16. Then they [girls] would lean to me like a sore eyd kitten to a Basin of Milk (62 Wiley *Johnny* 275). Cf. NC 433 Kitten (8).

17. Her hand took tu mine as a kitten does tu warm milk (44 Stephens *High Life* II 199). Cf. Apperson 87; *Oxford* 83.

18. But buds will be roses, and kittens, cats (68 Alcott *Little Women* 224). Helen Burnham *The Telltale Telegram* (1932) 41 Kittens will be cats.

Knee, 1. They are bowin the knee to Linkin (64 Locke [Nasby] *Struggles* 159). NED Knee 3 a.

2. I was gettin' sorter weak in the knees (51 Burke *Polly* 74; Paul *Courtship* 32 The men all got so weak in the knee-pans; Browne *Artemus* 168 We should indeed be weak in the knees, unsound in the heart, milk-white in the liver, and soft in the head). Ezek. 7:17 all knees shall be as weak as water; Schele de Vere 267.

Knee-high. When he want [wasn't] more 'n knee high to a bumbly-bee (33 Neal *Down-Easters* I 78; Haliburton *Clockmaker* II 179 goose, III 98 chaw of tobacco, 232 goose, *Attaché* II 169 goose, IV 164 goose, *Season-Ticket* 49 goose; Stephens *High Life* I 59 toad, 203 toad, II 67 toad, 225 toad; Judd *Margaret* I 192 toad; Hammett *Piney* 30 injin puddin'; Cary *Married* 291 bull-frog; *Puck* II [1877] No. 33 p. 5 grasshopper). Apperson 33 as big as a bee's knee; Ayers PADS XIV 79 jack-rabbit; S. T. Byington *Am. Speech* XV (1940) 219; DA Knee 3 b (toad, mosquito, grasshopper, bumbly-bee, duck, nothing); Farmer 334, assigning versions with "toad" to New England and "grasshopper" to Maryland; McAtee 38, *Additional* 9; NC 433 duck, duck's tail, grasshopper; Partridge 459; Stevenson 1316:7 splinter, woodchuck; Taylor *Investigations* 260; Thornton I 519; Tidwell PADS XI (1949) 8 duck; E. M. Rhodes *West Is West* (1917) 204 hoppergrass; John Russell *Cops n' Robbers* (1930) 169 pup; Vernon Loder *Red Stain* (1932) 165 since he was no higher than a bee's knee; T. Williamson *The Woods Colt* (1933) ch. 1 pt. 2 away back thar when the devil warn't no more than knee-high to a toad-frog; C. J. Daly *Murder from the East* (1935) 29 pint of gin; Vernon Patterson *All Giants Wear Yellow Breeches* (1935) 259 grasshopper; F. P. Keyes *Dinner at Antoine's* (1948) 9 paddle duck.

Knife. Then with appetites keen as a knife (68 Saxe *Poems* 142). Whiting *Drama* 318:194.

Knitting. I went over and onraveled all 'Gius's knittin' [i. e., foiled him]. (59 Taliaferro *Fisher's* 118).

Knock. Mike Hooter'll knock under [i. e., yield, confess defeat]. (51 Burke *Polly* 74; Willis *Fun* 355). Apperson 345; NED Knock vb. 15; *Oxford* 342; NQ 2 iii 369, 433, ix 225.

Knot, 1. The fellow sat there like a knot on a log (c66 Clemens *Sketches* 361). Boshears 33:259. Cf. NC 434 As still.

2. Cut the Gordian knot (53 Hammett *Stray* 34, 46; Conant *Earnest Man* 94 This [treatment of the children and domestics of converted heathen] . . . was the "Gordian knot," whose "gripe" he heartily wished his brethren at home . . . could feel as he did; Richardson *Secret* 233; Locke [Nasby] *Struggles* 347 Androo Johnson had cut the Gorjan knot with someboddy's soard). *Oxford* 260; Stevenson 1318:11; Tilley G375; C. B. Clason *The Fifth Tumbler* (1936) 179. Cf. Taylor *Comparisons* 83.

3. I can never consent to tie a knot with my tongue which I cannot untie with my teeth (33 Hall *Soldier's Bride* 212; Haliburton *Old Judge* I 297 I'll tie the knot to-night with my tongue, that I can't undo with my teeth). Apperson 345–346; Lean III 398; NED Knot 11 b; *Oxford* 658; Stevenson 1318:9; Tilley K167.

4. I might make you faithful, if the knot were once tied (57 Jones *Country* 304).

Knot-hole, 1. The critter was fixed as a knot-hole (c60 Paul *Courtship* 57).

2. I could have skulked through a knot hole, I felt so dreadful mean (44 Stephens *High Life* I 226, II 205 I could a crept through a knot hole;

Whitcher *Widow* 263 she looked as if she'd like to crawl into some knot-hole). McAtee 20; Thornton I 521.

3. It's worse than being dragged through forty knot holes (33 Smith *Downing* 203, *My Thirty* 350 looking as tired as a rat that had been dragged through forty knot-holes). Hardie 470: 134; McAtee 23; Taylor *Comparisons* 53. Cf. Hole (3); Green 33 keyhole.

Know, 1. Certes, he didn't know Colonel Benson from the great chief of the Pawnees (45 Hooper *Simon* 32). See Man in the Moon.

2. A . . . majority . . . that knew just about enough to come in when it rained (66 Clemens *Sandwich* 84, *Letters* I 145 I don't suppose you know more than enough to come in when it rains). DA Rain vb. 1; NED *Supplement* Rain vb. 1; Anthony Gilbert, pseud. *The Body on the Beam* (1932) 23; Ralph C. Woodthorpe *The Shadow on the Downs* (1935) 246 The Americans have a proverb, "He's too big a fool to come in out of the rain."

3. He don't know enough to warm his feet when they're cold (76 Nash *Century* 312).

4. See Book (4), Cat (45, 46), Dog (45), Hen (16), Hog (11).

Knowing, 1. When that will be, "not knowin', can't say" (46 Fairfield *Letters* 399; Durivage *Three* 340).

2. See Fox (4).

Knowledge. Knowledge and timber shouldn't be much used until they are seasoned (58 Holmes *Autocrat* 134).

Knuckles. Afor you've time to chalk your knuckles (37 Neal *Charcoal* 96).

Krout. Thar a-lying . . . es cold es krout (67 Harris *Sut* 73). Boshears 35:430; Halpert 283; Randolph and Wilson 172.

ℒ

Labor, 1. Which with her was a labor of love (51 Hawthorne *Twice-Told* 333; Melville *Moby-Dick* I 196; Smith *Arp* 151). I Thess. 1:3; Heb. 6:10; Helen McCloy *Dance of Death* (1938) 169. Cf. Apperson 348; *Oxford* 347; Stevenson 1322:2. See Love (10).

2. And she'd treat me cool, and I'd have my labor for my pains (56 Whitcher *Widow* 340). Apperson 348; *Oxford* 347; Stevenson 1330:9; Tilley L1; W. N. McCartney *Fifty Years a Country Doctor* (1938) 97–98 When I hear the old phrase . . . , I feel it must have originated in reference to a still-birth.

Laborer. The laborer is worthy of his hire (71 Jones *Batkins* 45). Luke 10: 7; NC 434; *Oxford* 347; Tilley L12.

Lackey. Who was your lackey last year? (40 Haliburton *Letter* 60; Cary *Married* 101 Who was your negro waiter last year?). Cf. the modern colloquial "Who was your nigger last year?" See NQ 11 ii 286.

Ladder. If I can't see thro' a ladder, I reckon I'm not fit for that mission (38 Haliburton *Clockmaker* II 147; Stowe *Uncle* 49 but can't ye see through a ladder, ye black nigger?). Cf. Apperson 55; DA Ladder 1 c; NED Ladder 1 c; Stevenson 2107:3. See Hole (6).

Ladder Lane. When a man is hung at sea, which is always done from one of the lower yard-arms, they say he *"takes a walk up Ladder Lane, and down Hemp Street"* (49 Melville *Redburn* 106). Babcock 263.

Lady-bug. [Smiles on mouth] like lady bugs round a full blown rose (44 Stephens *High Life* II 70).

Lamb, 1. The horses are gentle as lambs (23 Cooper *Pioneers* 39; Neal *Brother J* III 372; Haliburton *Season-Ticket* 371; Browne *Artemus Ward His Travels* 16 with mint sauce). Boshears 37:597; NC 434; *Oxford* 234; Taylor *Comparisons* 43; Tilley L34.

2. He is as gentle as the lamb by nature, though the lion is not his equal when roused (21 Cooper *Spy* 275). Cf. Apperson 348–349; Halpert 405; McAtee 28; Whiting *Scots* I 196; David Frome, pseud. *The Strange Death of Martin Green* (1931) 37.

3. I am as good-natured as a lamb (56 Kelly *Humors* 86).

4. He turned out harmless as a lamb (56 Kelly *Humors* 153).

5. A southern wolf is as harmless to man as a cosset lamb (58 Hammett *Piney* 204). Cf. Svartengren 317.

6. As innocent as a lamb (35 Crockett *Account* 172; Longstreet *Georgia* 37; Stephens *High Life* II 160, 199 I never see a cosset lamb cropping white clover look half so innocent; Melville *Mardi* I 132; Burke *Polly* 38; Baldwin *Flush* 150; Boker *Bankrupt* 110 a lamb unborn; Durivage *Three*

76, 77; Hammett *Piney* 107 a nussin'
lamb; Clift *Bunker* 227; Harris *Sut*
258; Nash *Century* 185 We're as innersent as a lamb; Shillaber *Ike* 76).
NC 434; Taylor *Comparisons* 51; Roger Delancey *Murder Below Wall
Street* (1934) 227.

7. As meek as a cosset lamb (44
Stephens *High Life* II 157, *Fashion*
250–251 lamb; Melville *Typee* 362
lamb; Haliburton *Sam* I 184 lamb;
Jones *Country* 396 lamb). Boshears
38:753; McAtee 42; NC 434; *Oxford*
234; Taylor *Comparisons* 57; Tilley
L34; Whiting *Drama* 318:197, *Scots*
I 196; Vincent McHugh *Caleb Catlum's America* (1936) 272 lamb.

8. You were mild and docile as a
lamb (23 Cooper *Pioneers* 394). Apperson 416; *Oxford* 234; Tilley L34.

9. And live as peaceable as lambs
(59 Smith *My Thirty* 340). Lee Thayer, pseud. *Mystery of the Thirteenth
Floor* (1919) 64 peaceably.

10. As peaked and wamble-cropped
as a sick lamb (44 Stephens *High Life*
I 183).

11. But they [roisterers] are as quiet as lambs when they fall singly into
the clutches of a fine woman (20–22
Irving *Bracebridge* 64; Haliburton
Clockmaker III 181 and go as quiet as
a lamb; Anon. *New Hope* 212; Cartwright *Autobiography* 307; Hammett
Piney 126; Locke [Nasby] *Struggles*
405). Apperson 519; Stevenson 1928:
12; Svartengren 62; Tilley L34; Lili-
am Bamburg *Beads of Silence* (1927)
178.

12. As sportive as lambs in a pasture (54 Shillaber *Mrs. Partington*
106). Cf. Svartengren 71 frisky.

13. But when he came to himself
he was as tame as a lamb (c56 Cartwright *Autobiography* 323).

14. Now Uncle John's countenance

was as tender as a lamb's (43 Hall
Purchase II 41).

15. Humour it like a cosset lamb
(44 Stephens *High Life* II 66).

16. She will sleep like a lamb (59–
60 Holmes *Elsie* 341).

Lamp. The most oddly-paired and
happiest couple that ever "smelt the
lamps" (58 Field *Pokerville* 92).

Lamplighter, 1. Make me spry and
jump about like a lamplighter (37
Neal *Charcoal* 193). NED Lamplighter 1; Partridge 468.

2. The little bodies [children] did
climb up and down like lamplighters
(43 Hall *Purchase* I 81).

Lamp-post, 1. I mite ez well hev
talked to a lamp-post (67 Locke [Nas-
by] *Struggles* 478). Cf. Tilley P491.

2. To chalk the lamp-post [i. e., to
bribe]. 57 Farmer and Henley II 68.

Lamprey-eel. Mr. Van Buren hung on
like a lamper-eel (34 Davis *Downing*
23, 54 He stuck to him like a lamper-
eel).

Land, 1. A Missouri proverb asserts
that land which will raise hemp will
produce any other crop (67 Richardson *Beyond* 144).

2. Each proboscis sounds the
charge into the land of Nod (37 Neal
Charcoal 186; Dana *Two* 272 the
land of Nod; Burke *Polly* 168 was
soon in the land of dreams; Melville
Moby-Dick I 25 made a good offing
toward the land of Nod; Hammett
Stray 153, *Piney* 231; Whitcher *Wid-
ow* 91 Miss Jinkins herself! land o'
Nod! [an interjection]; Haliburton
Season-Ticket 277). Apperson 447;
Farmer and Henley IV 152, V 58;
Green 214; NED Nod 2 b; *Oxford*
349; Stevenson 1691:3.

3. See how the land lays (59 Smith

My Thirty 450; Harris *Uncle Remus* 179, 200). A. W. Derleth *The Man on All Fours* (1934) 174.

4. Mr. Wetherbe had, the previous autumn, "missed a land" in the sowing of his wheat field, and that, she had always heard say, was a sure sign of death (53 Cary *Clovernook* 2d Ser. 49).

Lane. That is a long lane which has no turning (40 Dana *Two* 131; Haliburton *Letter* 147 It's a long lane that has no turn in it, as the chap sed to console himself in the tredmill, *Sam* II 305 it's a long lane that has no turn in it; Hall *Purchase* II 59 Uncle John's old saw—"'tis a long lane that has no turn"; Clemens *Gilded* II 305 It's a long turn that has no lane at the end of it, as the proverb says). Apperson 379; NC 434; NED Lane 1 b; *Oxford* 381; Stevenson 1345:1; Tilley R207; F. Marryat *Peter Simple* (1834, London 1929) 407 so good-bye; Benjamin D'Israeli *Sybil* (1845, London 1929) 410 the longest lane has a turning, they say; Smith *Browning* 219; Stephen Chalmers *The House of the Two Green Eyes* (1928) 349; F. P. Keyes *The River Road* (1945) 409.

Lank. See Greyhound (2), Shad (3), Weasel (4).

Large, See Irishman (2), Life (3, 4), Oven (3).

Lark, 1. The damsels were as blithe as larks (49 Melville *Mardi* I 283). NC 434; Whiting *Scots* I 197; E. R. Burroughs *The Mucker* (1921) 288.
2. She's as bright . . . as a lark (44 Thompson *Major* 133).
3. As cheery as larks (68 Alcott *Little Women* 85).
4. I was as chipper and fresh as a lark (78 Clemens *Letters* I 336). Rus-

sell Thorndike *The Slype* (1928) 75 fresh.
5. Gay as a lark (42 Irving *Attorney* 116; Melville *Confidence-Man* 280). Taylor *Comparisons* 43; Means Davis *The Chess Murders* (1937) 256.
6. As happy as a lark (44 Thompson *Major* 133, 184). Boshears 37: 633; NC 434; Taylor *Comparisons* 46; C. H. Towne *This New York of Mine* (1931) 151.
7. Joyous as a lark (56 Cooke *Foresters* 263).
8. A lark is better than a kite (25 Loomis *Farmer's Almanac* 178).
9. Have not both these cautious people expressed a determination to take an interest in the Ilium mine when they catch their larks? (73 Clemens *Gilded* II 190). DA Lark 1 b. Cf. Apperson 576 Sky; *Oxford* 595; Tilley S517.
10. She rises with the lark (32 Kennedy *Swallow* 32; Durivage *Three* 238; Browne *Artemus* 189; Clemens *Washoe* 18, *Tramp* I 278; Saxe *Poems* 133 Rise with the lark, and with the lark to bed, Observes some solemn, sentimental owl; Maxims like these are very cheaply said; But, ere you make yourself a fool or fowl, Pray just inquire about his rise and fall, And whether larks have any beds at all). Apperson 533; NED Lark 1 b; *Oxford* 28; Stevenson 1996:7; Tilley B186; Virgil Markham *Inspector Rusby's Finale* (1933) 142.
11. Phoebe . . . is carolling from morning to night like a lark (20–22 Irving *Bracebridge* 456).
12. Singing like a lark (68 Alcott *Little Women* 14, 45 a little lark, 456). NC 434; Tilley L70.

Larkspur. Her eyes as blue as larkspurs (56 Durivage *Three* 234).

Lashorn [the Fraser balsam fir]. See Laushong.

Latch-string. To say that "the latch-string was out" was to open your door to a friend (74 Eggleston *Circuit* 228, 289 When I joined the church Father pulled the latch-string in). DA Latch 2; Green 36, 215; NC 434; NED Latch-string.

Late, 1. Better late than never (44 Stephens *High Life* I 9; Haliburton *Old Judge* II 285; Holmes *Elsie* 90; Jones *Batkins* 475). Apperson 44; NC 434; Oxford 40; Stevenson 1348:5; Tilley L85; Whiting *Drama* 197; Anthony Berkeley, pseud. *Mr. Pidgeon's Island* (1934) 21.

2. Never Too Late To Mend (68 Saxe *Poems* 453 [a title]). Apperson 443; Hardie 463:92; *Oxford* 450; Stevenson 1563:7; Tilley M875; *Catalogue of Political and Personal Satires . . . 1811–1819* IX (London 1949) 829 No. 13037; Sidney Williams *The Drury Lane Case* (1927) 57.

Lath. He was as thin as a lath (25 Neal *Brother J* I 373). Apperson 625; NC 435; NED Lath 2 b; Svartengren 187; E. R. Punshon *Genius in Murder* (Boston 1933) 288.

Lather. You are as white as if you were all in a lather (66 Boucicault *Flying Scud* 178). Tilley L87. Cf. Foam.

Laugh, 1. Such as you can afford to laugh and get fat, but I can't (37 Neal *Charcoal* 112; Eliason 281 they pretty near laughed me fat; Barnum *Struggles* 146 I always believe we must laugh and grow fat). Apperson 351–352; NC 435; *Oxford* 352; Stevenson 1352–1353:8; Tilley L91; W. B. Seabrook *The Magic Island* (1929) 145.

2. Let them laugh that lose (33 Smith *Downing* 46; Saxe *Poems* 465 Let those laugh who—lose!).

3. Let those laugh who win (c60 Paul *Courtship* 9). Apperson 352; *Oxford* 352; Stevenson 1353:4; Tilley L93; Whiting *Drama* 237, 257, 264; *The Diary of Abraham de la Pryme* (1692, Surtees Soc. 54 [London 1869]) 26; Claude G. Bowers *Jefferson and Hamilton* (1925) 406 for the converse of the maxim the consolation of railing ought to be allowed to those who lose.

Laughing. Boys, ses Joe, . . . laugh-in's ketchin' (58 Hammett *Piney* 264). NC 435.

Laurels, 1. Look to your laurels (71 Jones *Batkins* 298). NED Laurel 2 c.

2. By this decision our hero won new laurels (43 Thompson *Chronicles* 133).

Laurence. Lazy Laurence (69 Alcott *Little Women* 437 [chapter title]). Apperson 355; Lean III 344; NC 435; *Oxford* 355–356; Stevenson 2140:9.

Laushong. For I call it as tuf as lau-shong, and that will bear chawin all day (36 Haliburton *Clockmaker* I 157). Probably "lashorn," the Fraser balsam fir, is intended, for which see DA.

Law, 1. But even in the eye of the law it is said all men are equal (40 Haliburton *Letter* 104). Stevenson 705:1, 7.

2. The law is all for the rich and none for the poor (45 Hooper *Simon* 114). NQ 7 ix 288, 453, x 72, 291, 372. Cf. *Oxford* 353; Stevenson 1364:4; Whiting *Drama* 77, *Scots* I 197.

3. Gabriel says: "The law rules the poor man, and the rich man rules the

law" (67 Richardson *Beyond* 539). Cf. Stevenson 1364:4.

4. The notorious lawlessness of the commander has passed into a proverb, familiar to man-of-war's men, *The law was not made for the captain* (50 Melville *White Jacket* 377). Babcock 264.

5. Pick-up law is the cheapest law for a poor man (32 Kennedy *Swallow* 217).

Lawyer, 1. Copying law-papers being proverbially a dry, husky sort of busivous (56 Melville *Piazza* 27).

2. I [a lawyer] belong to a profession proverbially energetic and nervous (56 Melville *Piazza* 20).

3. See Man (7), Philadelphia (2).

Lay, sb., 1. He "put the boss on the lay" [i. e., informed him about the plan]. (51 Burke *Polly* 90; Boucicault *Flying Scud* 195 She's on a lay, *Presumptive* 237 you are on a lay [i. e., have plans for committing a theft]). Farmer and Henley IV 162–163; NED Lay sb.[7] 6.

2. An old hunter . . . giving us the lay of the land (56 Kelly *Humors* 108). NED Land 3, Lay sb.[7] 7; Harriette Ashbrook *Murder of Sigurd Sharon* (1933) 113. See Land (3).

Lay, vb. [The courthouse] is "bound" to lay every thing in the way of architecture . . . west of the Alleghanies "out cold" (58 Field *Pokerville* 93; Eggleston *Circuit* 15). DA Cold 2 (2), citing only the meaning "to knock unconscious."

Lazy. See Laurence, Ox (1), Shinglemaker, Turtle (3, 11).

Lead, 1. His heart grew heavy as lead (25 Neal *Brother J* III 150). Apperson 296; Boshears 37:658; McAtee 33; NC 435; Taylor *Comparisons* 47; Tilley L134; Whiting *Drama* 319:201, *Scots* I 198 Lead (5); Edwin Greenwood *The Fair Devil* (1935) 219.

2. My heart . . . sunk agin like a chunk of lead (44 Stephens *High Life* II 9).

Leaf (1), 1. I shall be as nervous as a leaf (c60 Paul *Courtship* 156).

2. They are as numerous as the leaves on the trees (46 Hall *Wilderness* 94).

3. And yet, although "signs were plenty as leaves," not a bear was started (58 Porter *Major* 139). Cf. NC 435; Whiting *Scots* I 198; Jackson Gregory *Ru the Conqueror* (1933) 88 as many as the leaves on the trees.

4. If the Tories were as thick as the leaves of the trees (35 Kennedy *Horse-Shoe* 162). Philips Russell *Red Tiger* (1929) 12 as leaves.

5. Leaves have their time to fall (65 Browne *Artemus Ward His Travels* 145).

6. She shook like a leaf (51 Hawthorne *Twice-Told* 122; Smith *My Thirty* 433 But now he quivers and shakes one way and t'other, like a leaf in the wind; Stephens *Fashion* 263). Boshears 33:248; Halpert 840; McAtee 55; NC 435; Stuart Palmer *The Puzzle of the Pepper Tree* (1933) 295 quiver; Herbert Asbury *The Tick of the Clock* (1928) 135 shake. Cf. Taylor *Comparisons* 71.

7. Our ship trembled like a leaf (39 Briggs *Harry* I 188; Melville *White Jacket* 52; Stephens *Homestead* 96). NC 435; Svartengren 383; Tilley L140; Whiting *Scots* I 198; George Goodchild *The Monster of Grammont* (1930) 179.

Leaf (2), 1. I'll take a leaf out of her book (58 Alcott *Little Women* 338).

Apperson 617; *Oxford* 639; Partridge 79; Taylor *Index* 44; Mignon G. Eberhart *Hasty Wedding* (1938) 219.

2. I'm goin to turn over a new leaf (34 Davis *Downing* 155; Alcott *Little Women* 237 turn over a new leaf and begin again, 362 accused of turning over a new leaf). Apperson 652; NC 435; NED Leaf 7 b; *Oxford* 676; Stevenson 1374:1; Tilley L146; Tobias Smollett *The Expedition of Humphrey Clinker* (1771, Letter of Tabitha Bramble, Sept. 18) If the house were mine I would turn over a new leaf; E. R. Punshon *Genius in Murder* (1933) 291.

Leak. See Sieve (1).

Lean. See Leg (2).

Learning, 1. " 'A little science [i. e., skill in boxing] is a dangerous thing,' as well as a little 'learning'," he said to himself, "only it's dangerous to the fellow you try it on" (59–60 Holmes *Elsie* 67). *Oxford* 374; Stevenson 1377: 1; Yamamoto *Dickens* 220.

2. Learnin', they say, is better than houses and lands (37 Neal *Charcoal* 69; Jones *Batkins* 376 I began to have faith in the saying, "Learning is better than house and land"). Apperson 316; *Oxford* 308; Stevenson 1376:1.

Leap. See Cat (44), Kangaroo.

Least. The maxim applies, "Where the least is said it is soonest mended" (32 Kennedy *Swallow* 147; Haliburton *Attaché* II 227 the least said, is the soonest mended; Stephens *High Life* II 38 the least said, the soonest mended; Hall *Purchase* I 213 less; Lincoln V 65 I thought the maxim "least said, soonest mended" applied to the case; Holmes *Elsie* 109; Clift *Bunker* 79–80 The least said is soonest mended;

Clemens *Gilded* I 291). Apperson 357; McAtee PADS XV (1951) 56; NC 469; *Oxford* 359; Stevenson 2190: 10; Tilley L358; Woodard PADS VI (1946) 39; Herbert Adams *The Body in the Bunker* (Philadelphia 1935) 144; H. F. M. Prescott *The Man on a Donkey* (1952) 224; Vance Randolph *The Devil's Pretty Daughter* (1955) 98 Next morning everybody seen they had made a fool out of theirself, and the least said the soonest mended; *Time* LXVI No. 13 (Sept. 28, 1955) 52 a society which still hopes to survive by the peasant adage, "least said, soonest mended."

Leech, 1. I sot my 'fections on her right smack like a leech on to a fish (59 Taliaferro *Fisher's* 117).

2. The three O'Regans hung on to him like leeches (49 Melville *Redburn* 347). Molly Thynne *The Draycott Murder Mystery* (1928) 50.

3. Stick to him like a leach (43 Haliburton *Attaché* II 31; Boucicault *Flying Scud* 164). Boshears 33:281; NC 436; Stevenson 1380:4; Taylor *Comparisons* 53; F. W. Crofts *Double Death* (1932) 252.

Leek. As green as a leek (69 Clift *Bunker* 23, 209). Apperson 273; Green 23; *Oxford* 266; Stevenson 1039:10; Svartengren 250; Tilley L176.

Leeward. Here he went dead to leeward among the pulperias, gambling-rooms &c [i. e., to the dogs]. (40 Dana *Two* 312). Joanna C. Colcord *Sea Language Comes Ashore* (1945) 116.

Left-handed. And so, to be hated cordially, is only a left-handed compliment (47 Melville *Omoo* 230; Clemens *Roughing* II 184 blessing; Jones *Batkins* 100 some kind of left-handed blessing). Whiting *Drama* 335:409; Weed Dickinson *Dead Man Talks Too Much* (Philadelphia 1937) 189. Cf. Apperson 359; NED Left-handed 3.

Leg, 1. I would sooner have my leg taken off with a wood-saw (58 Porter *Major* 53).

2. As lean as a gander's leg (45 Judd *Margaret* I 95).

3. You are right . . . right as this leg (50 Melville *White Jacket* 239). Apperson 531; *Oxford* 543; Svartengren 368; Tilley L180.

4. His joints are as stiff as wooden legs in the last war (59 Shillaber *Knitting-Work* 181).

5. And stop lending him money, for he is on his last legs (60 Holmes *Professor* 281; Lowell *Biglow* 327 They're mos' gin'lly argymunt on its las' legs). Apperson 350–351; Farmer and Henley IV 176; NED Leg 2 d; *Oxford* 351; Stevenson 28:2, 1382:7; Tilley L193.

6. He . . . was just getting on his legs again, from a "big drunk" (67 Harris *Sut* 29).

7. Now, put my best leg foremost (37 Neal *Charcoal* 140). Apperson 40; NED Leg 2 b; *Oxford* 35; Stevenson 862:12; Charles Barry, pseud. *Death of a First Mate* (1935) 105. See Foot (5).

8. To leave the poor, talkative old brigadier, without a leg to stand upon, as a lawyer would say (25 Neal *Brother J* I 8). Bartlett 348; Hardie 470: 145; NED Leg 2 c, Stand 2; Vincent McHugh *Caleb Catlum's America* (1936) 66.

9. See Loon (7).

Leg bail. To give them leg bail when Judge Lynch made his appearance (36 Crockett *Exploits* 97). Apperson 359; Farmer and Henley IV 177; NED Leg-bail; *Oxford* 360; Stevenson 1381:7; J. C. Harris *Nights with Uncle Remus* (c81 Boston [1883]) 97 he watch he chance, he did, en he gin 'im leg bail.

Lemon. A looking as if he'd jest eat a sour lemon, without any sweetening (44 Stephens *High Life* I 248).

Leopard. Can the leopard, or the Ethiopian, or the liar change at will? (25 Neal *Brother J* III 303). Jer. 13:23; NED Leopard 2; Stevenson 1673:6; Tilley L206.

Less. Less said the better (57 Riley *Puddleford* 249). NC 470; Stevenson 2184:10; F. Marryat *Peter Simple* (1834, London 1929) 66 the less we say about that the better; Charlotte Brontë *Jane Eyre* (1847) ch. 4 Perhaps the less said on that score the better; Andy Adams *A Texas Matchmaker* (Boston 1904) 255; D. Q. Burleigh *The Kristiana Killers* (1937) 95.

Letter, 1. That something white, which is fluttering in the breeze from his midships, is . . . merely a bit of linen which under such circumstances is known to our *gamins* as "a letter in the post-office" (55 Hammett *Wonderful* 28).

2. Now, contrary to all precedents, luck was a dead letter [i. e., in a gambling game]. (58 Porter *Major* 200).

Level, 1. On the level. 75 DA Level sb. 1.

2. See Floor (2), Ocean, Sea (5).

Leviathan. As big as the Leviathan (60 Haliburton *Season-Ticket* 12).

Liar. Once a liar, allers a liar, is my motto (76 Nash *Century* 193).

Liberty-pole. My mind wuz as firm as a liberty-pole (c60 Paul *Courtship* 37).

Lick, sb. 1. We have had the first lick at him, and that, the Gineral says, is the best part of the battle (34 Davis *Downing* 103). Cf. Apperson 214 First blow; *Oxford* 204; Stevenson 204:13; Tilley B472.
2. He kept up his lick for seven long years (64 Clemens *Washoe* 108, 103 they still "keep up their lick").
3. You mean, then that I'm to begin now to put in my best licks for Jesus Christ, and that he'll help me? (71 Eggleston *School-Master* 161). Bartlett 506; DA Lick 5; Schele de Vere 499; Stevenson 1391:4; Thornton III 230.

Lick, vb. See Sack (2).

Lick-log. I was determined to stand up to my lick-log, salt or no salt (34 Crockett *Life* 170; Haliburton *Season-Ticket* 237 I like to see a feller stand up to his lick-log like a man, and tell the truth). DA Lick vb. 2. Cf. Rack (1, 2); Figh PADS XIII (1950) 8; Randolph and Wilson 260; Thornton III 230.

Lie, sb. Loose bait ain't bad . . . look a lie and find the truth (57 Melville *Confidence-Man* 329). Cf. Apperson 362; *Oxford* 646; Stevenson 2394:5; Tilley L237.

Lie, vb. Who has a better right to lie than them that pays taxes? (40 Haliburton *Clockmaker* III 228).

Life, 1. For they say an unquiet life makes an uneasy grave (21 Cooper *Spy* 129).
2. There they was as big as life (38 Haliburton *Clockmaker* II 100; Harris *Uncle Remus* 59). Boshears 34:338; McAtee 14; NC 436; Taylor *Comparisons* 16; E. S. Gardner *The D. A. Calls It Murder* (1937) 164.
3. Printed it in the Courier as large as life (33 Smith *Downing* 33, 225, *Letters* 18; Crockett *Life* 62, *Account* 82; Neal *Charcoal* 138; Hall *Purchase* II 59; Haliburton *Attaché* II 194; Stephens *High Life* I 12, 18, 29, 79, 191 [name], II 192, 203, 215; Judd *Margaret* I 223; Hammett *Wonderful* 74; Whitcher *Widow* 317; Riley *Puddleford* 260; Field *Pokerville* 127; Sedley *Marian* 286). Hardie 466:18; *Oxford* 350; Colin Ward *House Party Murder* (1934) 261.
4. As large as life and twice as nateral (36 Haliburton *Clockmaker* I 143, *Attaché* I 233, *Season-Ticket* 373; Stephens *High Life* I 33 a picter of my own self as large as life and twice as nat'ral, II 138, 194 gals as large as life, and eenamost as nat'ral [on a theatre curtain]; Jones *Country* 63 they had Napoleon, Josephine, Wellington, &c., as large as life, and twice as natural, as they told me). McAtee 14; NC 436; *Oxford* 350; Taylor *Comparisons* 16 big; Diplomat [i. e., John F. Carter] *Death in the Senate* (1933) 204.
5. It's as nateral as life (38 Haliburton *Clockmaker* II 243, *Old Judge* I 312; Stephens *High Life* I 13, 22, 118, 119, II 167, *Fashion* 132; Burke *Polly* 161; Whitcher *Widow* 206, 209, 224; Jones *Country* 355; Hammett *Piney* 291 [wooden doughnuts]; Holmes *Professor* 191; Clift *Bunker* 30). NC 436.
6. Life has its ups and downs (71 Jones *Batkins* 64).
7. Life is a merry-go-round (53 Curtis *Potiphar* 141). Cf. Apperson 363 shuttle; *Oxford* 366; Stevenson 1399:6 tumble-about, 1400:10 shuttle.
8. We occasionally meet with one

possessing sufficient philosophy to look upon life as a pilgrimage (36 Crockett *Exploits* 42). *Oxford* 365–366; Stevenson 1400:6; Tilley L249.

9. This life ain't all beer and skittles (55 Haliburton *Nature* I 60). Barrère and Leland I 26; Bradley 83; Farmer and Henley I 165–166, VI 234; *Oxford* 366; Partridge *Clichés* 24; Stevenson 1403:4 porter and skittles; NQ 9 vii 88; 12 iii 230).

10. Life is short (53 Curtis *Potiphar* 141). Cf. Apperson 16 Art; *Oxford* 14; Stevenson 97:10 Life is short, art is long, 1404:4 Life is short but sweet, 1407:10 short in itself.

11. A short life and a merry one (79 Clemens *Letters* I 355). Apperson 567; *Oxford* 585; Tilley L261; Marcus Magill, pseud. *Murder Out of Tune* (Philadelphia 1931) 132.

12. Sleep is sweet . . . but life is sweeter still (40 Cooper *Pathfinder* 257–258, 456 Life is sweet; Melville *Mardi* I 30 But life is sweet to all, death comes as hard). Apperson 363; *Oxford* 366; Stevenson 1404:4; Tilley L254; Whiting *Drama* 8, 37, 257; Robert Hare, pseud. *The Doctor's First Murder* (1933) 299.

13. He . . . was climbin for dear life (43 Thompson *Chronicles* 93; Stephens *High Life* II 152 eating away for; Eggleston *School-Master* 103 spelling for). NED Life 3 c.

14. "Sich is life" (56 Durivage *Three* 265; Kelly *Humors* 327; Clemens *Sketches* 194, *Innocents* II 257, 365; Locke [Nasby] *Struggles* 552). Stevenson 1402:4; J. P. Marquand *So Little Time* (Boston 1949) 534 It's life; *The* [London] *Times Literary Supplement* LIV No. 2790 (Aug. 19, 1955) 482 When the Australian bushranger Ned Kelly stood on the scaffold in Melbourne gaol on November 11,

1880, he murmured three words, "Such is life"; Neil Gordon *The Silent Murders* (1930) 30.

15. While there is life, you know, there is hope (21 Cooper *Spy* 94, 100; Melville "Happy Failure" in *Works* XIII 217; Smith *'Way* 51 As long as there's life there's hope, *My Thirty* 419; Cary *Married* 137, 232). Apperson 364; NC 436; *Oxford* 366; Stevenson 1170:3; Stoett 1373; Tilley L269; Dennis Wheatley *They Found Atlantis* (Philadelphia 1936) 95; T. H. White *The Sword in the Stone* (1939) 265.

Lifeless. See Log (2).

Light, sb., 1. As honest as noon-day light (45 Cooper *Satanstoe* 43, *Chainbearer* 109 as honest as light). See Noonday (2).

2. Quick as light (51 Burke *Polly* 170; Sedley *Marian* 457). Svartengren 380; Taylor *Comparisons* 66; Audrey Newell *Who Killed Cavelotti?* (1930) 100 a light.

3. I do not wish to hide my light under a bushel (40 Cooper *Pathfinder* 164, *Satanstoe* 121 our fellow subjects of the eastern provinces are not addicted to hiding their lights under bushels; Melville *Confidence-Man* 178 forced to hide his light under the bushel of an inferior coat; Clift *Bunker* 272 a promise which we kept by taking his light from out under his bushel, and putting it upon your candlestick; Barnum *Struggles* 564 I had no idea of hiding my light under a bushel; Nash *Century* 25). Matt. 5:15; *Oxford* 294; Stevenson 281:3, 1423:5; Tilley L275; Herbert Asbury *The French Quarter* (1936) 128 the proverbial bushel. See Candle (6).

4. I'm a tarnal goose to be willin'

to stand in my own light jest for the sake of accomodatin' the wimmen folks (56 Whitcher *Widow* 117; Sedley *Marian* 118 But if he is cunning enough to teach us . . . , we needn't stand in our own light). Apperson 599–600; Bradley 83; NED Light 1 g; *Oxford* 618; Stevenson 1421:10; Tilley L276; Whiting *Scots* I 200 sit.

5. There is always light behind the clouds (68 Alcott *Little Women* 182).

Light, adj. See Bird (12), Cork (2), Day (11), Feather (1), Fox (5), Panther (4), Snow (3), Zephyr.

Lightning, 1. Faster nur . . . lightnin' (59 Taliaferro *Fisher's* 64). Boshears 31:98, 36:534; NC 436; Taylor *Comparisons* 39; R. S. Allen and Drew Pearson *Washington Merry-Go-Round* (1931) 243.

2. As quick as lightning (39 Smith *Letters* 116 a stream of; Stephens *High Life* II 258; *Mary Derwent* 235; Cooper *Satanstoe* 333, 340; Lowell *Biglow* 139; Dorson *Jonathan* 84 quicker; Hammett *Wonderful* 242 Quick as the lightning flash; Browning *Forty-Four* 305–306; Melville *Israel* 117; Porter *Major* 69 quick as ze lightnin'; Taliaferro *Fisher's* 151; Clemens *Innocents* I 215 quicker than the lightning's flash, *Roughing* I 48 Quicker than lightning, *Tom* 227). Apperson 518; Boshears 39:834; McAtee 51; Randolph and Wilson 173; Taylor *Comparisons* 66; W. S. Masterman *The Yellow Mistletoe* (1930) 61.

3. Quicker 'n greased lightnin' (65 Sedley *Marian* 94; Whitehead *Wild Sports* 339). NC 436; Constance Rourke *Davy Crockett* (1934) 234. See Lightning (14, 15).

4. Red as chain lightnin' (59 Taliaferro *Fisher's* 53, 56 Eyes red as forked lightnin').

5. He'd hev had to make tracks, he would; and them tracks would hev had to be as spry and ily [oily] as greased lightnin' (Sedley *Marian* 179).

6. Jis' a small scrimpshun slower nur chain litenin (67 Harris *Sut* 46). See Lightning (12).

7. He's smarter on 'em [cards] than greased lightnin' (65 Sedley *Marian* 216).

8. He's as smart as litenin (57 Riley *Puddleford* 118). R. H. Fuller *Jubilee Jim* (1928) 395 chain lightning.

9. My gun is as sure as a streak of lightning run into a barrel of gunpowder (56 Jones *Wild* 21).

10. As swift as lightning (44 Stephens *High Life* II 66). Hardie 467: 41; Taylor *Comparisons* 80; Tilley L279; Kenneth Roberts *Northwest Passage* (1937) 378.

11. Lightning never strikes twice in the same place (57 P. H. Myers *Thrilling Adventures of the Prisoner of the Border* [1860] 91). Bradley 83; NC 437.

12. I'm goin there like a streek of chain-lightning (34 Davis *Downing* 37). D. L. and H. Teilhet *The Crimson Hair Murders* (1936) 220 go like chain lightning.

13. I went right slap into him, like a flash of lightnin into a gooseberry bush (36 Haliburton *Clockmaker* I 175; Whitcher *Widow* 237 Then it all come thro' my head like a flash o' lightnin'). Clifton Robbins *The Mystery of Mr. Cross* (1933) 151 off like.

14. Like a streak of greased lightning (44 Stephens *High Life* II 88, 203; Hammett *Piney* 260 I went by the hull bilin', all but Joe, jest like greased lightnin'; Paul *Courtship* 196 in less than a flash of greased lightnin'; Whitehead *Wild Sports* 83).

Farmer and Henley III 201. Cf. NC 436; Randolph and Wilson 173; Svartengren 379–380 thunderbolt; Thornton I 387–388, III 173; R. A. J. Walling *In Time for Murder* (1933) 38 taken it away from me like a streak of greased lightning; Patrick Wynnton *The Ten Jewels* (Philadelphia 1931) 241 up you go . . . like greased lightning.

15. Streak it off like iled lightning (43 Haliburton *Attaché* IV 217, *Sam* I 120 off with you like, *Nature* I 314 away we went like, *Season-Ticket* 130; Hall *Purchase* I 85 [a snake] darted . . . at us . . . like "greased lightning"; Stephens *High Life* II 141 we went cutting dirt down Chatham Street like a streak of iled lightning). Cf. Tilley L279.

16. Up went Bullet's tail like lightning (35 Longstreet *Georgia* 25; Neal *Charcoal* 75; Haliburton *Letter* 198 streak it off for Maine like, *Old Judge* II 282 off like, *Nature* I 292 away we flew like; Stephens *High Life* II 250 a handin em round like; Melville *Typee* 135 wheeled round his weapon like; Shillaber *Mrs. Partington* 71 darted like; Derby *Phoenixiana* 329 like lightning from the cloud; Jones *Wild* 47 gained on me like; Riley *Puddleford* 140 flew through the seams like). Christopher Bush *Dead Man Twice* (1930) 10 move, *The Death of Cosmo Revere* (1930) 122 turn.

17. Pulled foot for home, like a streak of lightning (39 Smith *Letters* 69; Stephens *High Life* I 69 went agin to the office like, 84 put it down right and left like, 150 away they went like; Haliburton *Old Judge* II 130 off they started like two streaks, *Season-Ticket* 31 going like; Burke *Polly* 26 was off like; Anon. *New Hope* 83 and if I didn't leave a streak of light behind me, lightning never did, 190; Fairfield *Letters* 394 I shall start for home like a). Newton Gayle *Death in the Glass* (1937) 140 vanished; Jim Tully *Blood on the Moon* (1931) 110 moved.

18. Started off like a stream of lightning (34 Smith *Downing* 102).

19. To catch particular lightning. 71 DA Particular.

Like, sb., 1. Everybody to thar likes (57 Bennett *Border* 69, 116 Every one to his liking, 248). Cf. Apperson 191; *Oxford* 178–179; Stevenson 1426:2.

2. It is the principle of moral, as well as of physical nature, that like should produce like (45 Cooper *Chainbearer* 231; Haliburton *Old Judge* I 252 Like begets like — unlike begets unlike; Barnum *Struggles* 496 Like begets like). Stevenson 1428:6; Tilley L282 breeds; Whiting *Drama* 225 breeds; David Frome, pseud. *The Strange Death of Martin Green* (1931) 155 breeds. Cf. *Oxford* 389 Love begets.

3. Like loves like (40 Cooper *Pathfinder* 137, 289 it is nat'ral for like to seek like, 295; Haliburton *Sam* II 78 for like seeks like, the brave like the brave, *Nature* I 349–350 like takes to like). *Oxford* 368. Cf. Apperson 367–368, 368 Likeness; NC 437; Stevenson 1428:7, 1431:2; Tilley L286; Whiting *Drama* 122, 127, 128, 273.

4. The grand maxim of Mr. Similia Similibus Curantur Hahneman does not hold true, since, with them, *like cures* not *like,* but only aggravates *like* (50 Melville *White Jacket* 284–285, *Moby-Dick* II 317 methinks like-cures-like applies to him). *Oxford* 368; Stevenson 1557:15.

Like, vb., 1. If you dont like it, you may lump it (28 Neal *Rachel* 70, *Down-Easters* I 104 Let 'em lump it if they dont like it; Haliburton *Clockmaker* I p. viii if you don't like it you may lump it, II 254, III 200, *Attaché* I 24, *Old Judge* I 221; Clemens *Tom* 8 You can lump that hat if you don't like it). Apperson 366; Bartlett 375; DA Lump; McAtee 41; NC 437; *Oxford* 368; Partridge 483, 499, 1010; Randolph and Wilson 216; Stevenson 1425:5; Thornton III 238; NQ CLXXXIV (1943) 286; James Aston *First Lesson* (1933) 245; Dana Scott *Five Fatal Letters* (1937) 106.

2. I liked it, and what you like aint hard (53 Haliburton *Sam* I 153). Cf. Whiting *Scots* II 95:14.

Like, adj. See Bullets (2), Cow-pea (2), Goose (1), Pea (3), Purse (3).

Lily, 1. [A girl] as pale as a lily (32 Hall *Legends* 92). Svartengren 236.

2. Lily-white (55 Haliburton *Nature* II 42; Paul *Courtship* 94). NED Lily-white; Whiting *Drama* 320:210, *Scots* I 200; R. J. Casey *The Secret of 37 Hardy Street* (Indianapolis 1929) 136.

3. Made her neck and face look as white as a lily (44 Stephens *High Life* I 227). Apperson 680; Boshears 41: 1018; NC 437; Svartengren 233; Taylor *Comparisons* 87; Tilley L296; Whiting *Drama* 320:210, *Scots* I 200.

Lima. You know the proverb all along this coast — "Corrupt as Lima" (51 Melville *Moby-Dick* I 316). For the corruption of Lima, see *Moby-Dick*, ed. Luther S. Mansfield and H. P. Vincent (1952) 743–746.

Limber. See Dishrag, Eel (4), Rag (1), Steer (1), String (1), Withe.

Lime kiln. His eyes . . . wich I notist wuz ez dry ez a lime kiln (66 Locke [Nasby] *Struggles* 258, 576 throats like lime kilns). Partridge 484; Svartengren 190; J. Frank Dobie *Coronado's Children* (Dallas 1930) 214 as dry as a limeburner's hat.

Limpsey. See Rag (2).

Line, 1. Straight as a line (66 Clemens *Sandwich* 19, *Innocents* I 262). Apperson 604–605; NC 437; *Oxford* 624; Stevenson 2223:10; Svartengren 275; Tilley L303; Whiting *Scots* I 201.

2. Let me tell the tale,—straightforward like a line (49 Melville *Mardi* II 202).

3. I might as well haul up line and be off (54 Smith *'Way* 171). See Killoch.

4. But if too large and too frequent libations carried him over the line (55 Hammett *Wonderful* 71, *Piney* 77 as for himself, he had crossed the line long ago [i. e., was drunk]).

5. It ain't half sech hard lines to be an honest man (69 Boucicault *Presumptive* 238). Farmer and Henley III 269; NED Line 6; Stevenson 1433: 11; NQ 4 xii 67, 174; 5 iv 407, v 34. Cf. Ps. 16:6 The lines are fallen to me in a pleasant place.

6. Croquet is not in my line (70 Daly *Man* 9). NED Line 28 b; Stevenson 1433:5.

Links. To let out the links [i. e., to travel at high speed]. 68 DA Let 2 c.

Lion, 1. He is as bold as a lion (32 Kennedy *Swallow* 90; Dana *Two* 295; Stephens *High Life* I 42, *Mary Derwent* 295, *Fashion* 38; Cooper *Chainbearer* 3; Melville *Mardi* I 76; Mitchell *Reveries* 111; Stowe *Uncle* 99; Hammett *Stray* 408, *Piney* 178; Smith

'Way 113; Jones *Winkles* 77; Porter *Major* 132). Apperson 59; NC 437; Taylor *Comparisons* 20; Whiting *Scots* I 201.

2. Catherine, my mother, who was once brave as a lion (c58 Stephens *Mary Derwent* 275, 337; Haliburton *Season-Ticket* 321 lions; Paul *Courtship* 124). Halpert 245; NC 437; Svartengren 113.

3. He is said to be as courageous as a lion (36 Fairfield *Letters* 74). Cf. NC 437.

4. Looked as fierce as a lion (38 Haliburton *Clockmaker* II 182; Alcott *Little Women* 348). NC 437; Taylor *Comparisons* 40; Tilley L308; Whiting *Drama* 320:214, *Scots* I 201.

5. A physiognomy as grave as a lion's (20–22 Irving *Bracebridge* 57, 59 the same grave, lion-like demeanor).

6. Adams was . . . as resolute as a lion (69 Barnum *Struggles* 532).

7. Strong as a lion (25 Neal *Brother J* III 369; Haliburton *Clockmaker* II 74; Mayo *Kaloolah* 327; Stephens *Fashion* 305, *Homestead* 362). Svartengren 392; Whiting *Scots* I 202:14 wight.

8. It's easy to kick a dead lion, any ass can do that (49 Haliburton *Old Judge* II 275). Cf. Apperson 369; *Oxford* 279, 370; Stevenson 1435:1; Tilley H165.

9. They saw many lions in the way (65 Richardson *Secret* 459; Alcott *Little Women* 235 and he stood at the foot, a lion in the path). Prov. 26:13; *Oxford* 370; Stevenson 1437:6; Tilley L312; Whiting *Scots* I 201.

10. Lions are never caught with cobwebs (25 Neal *Brother J* I 309, II 35, 97).

11. But like the lion in the fable the Mexicans had no painter (67 Richardson *Beyond* 259). Stevenson 1435:2; Whiting *Chaucer* 189; Joseph Jacobs *The Fables of Aesop* (London 1899) I 251, II 121.

12. We will beard the lion in his den (56 Durivage *Three* 216; Smith *My Thirty* 303; Jones *Batkins* 367 you would beard this lion clique of city influence in its den). McAtee *Grant County* 2; NC 437; *Oxford* 27; Stevenson 1437:7; J. G. Edwards, pseud. *The Odor of Bitter Almonds* (1938) 86.

13. Fought like a lion (44 Stephens *High Life* II 107; Sedley *Marian* 100). Whiting *Scots* I 202; John Collier *Full Circle* (1932) 106.

14. Her lion-like heart (c58 Stephens *Mary Derwent* 259; Boucicault *Flying Scud* 188). Bombardier "X" *So This Was War!* (London c1930) 155.

15. As mishap had in some sort made a little lion of me (39 Briggs *Harry* II 170; Hooper *Simon* 90 Captain Suggs was now the "lion of the day"; Curtis *Potiphar* 17 and are a small species of lion to very young ladies). NED Lion 4 b.

16. Mr. Warhoss repeated his kindnesses to me so often in showing me the lions, as he called it (39 Briggs *Harry* I 141; Stephens *High Life* II 4 you raly ought to go to Washington, to see the President and the lions; Jones *Country* 258 yet he had ample leisure to run about the city and see the lions and the elephants; Kelly *Humors* 141 these fellers . . . want me to ride hout . . . and see some of their Yankee lions, 247 I spent much of my time in surveying "the lions"; Paul *Courtship* 45 you have been around to see the "lions," I suppose; Richardson *Beyond* 297). Apperson 369; Farmer and Henley IV 205;

NED Lion 4; *Oxford* 371; Stevenson 1436:8; Tilley L322. See Elephant (2).

Lip, 1. Looking fresh as a gal's lip (44 Stephens *High Life* II 126).

2. Red as a gal's lip (44 Stephens *High Life* II 103). Cf. Stevenson 1440:6.

3. I kept a close lip (44 Stephens *High Life* I 149).

4. Keepin' a good stiff upper lip . . . like a nigger lookin' 't a gingerbread; ever seed him, any of ye, on a trainin' day? (25 Neal *Brother J* I 157, *Down-Easters* I 15; Kennedy *Swallow* 241; Smith *Downing* 16, 93, 195, *My Thirty* 287, 297, 401, 402, 404, 419, 429; Briggs *Harry* I 269; Thompson *Chronicles* 150; Stephens *High Life* I 51, 85, 103, 202, II 7, 236, 237; Eliason 297; Stowe *Uncle* 114, 136; Jones *Country* 219; Riley *Puddleford* 275; Taliaferro *Fisher's* 117; Locke [Nasby] *Struggles* 167). Bartlett 330; DA Keep 2 (1); Farmer and Henley IV 207, VII 262; NC 437; NED Lip 2, Stiff 11; *Oxford* 620; Partridge 831 carry; Thornton I 509; Tidwell PADS XI (1949) 15; Kirke Mechem *A Frame for Murder* (1936) 137.

5. He said it was the perfection of scientific lip labor (71 Jones *Batkins* 375). NED Lip-labour.

6. Lip-Service (68 Saxe *Poems* 237 [a title]). NED Lip-service.

Listeners. The old saw, "listeners never hear any good of themselves" (33 Hall *Soldier's Bride* 217; Jones *Country* 177 I say, listeners rarely hear any good of themselves). Apperson 370; NC 437; *Oxford* 371–372; Stevenson 1441:7; Tilley L336; S. L. Bradbury *Hiram Harding of Hardscrabble* (Rut-land, Vt. 1936) 100 the common saying of his locality; Sir Walter Scott *Rob Roy* (1818) II ch. 4 A hearkener always hears a bad tale of himself. See Eavesdropper.

Lithe. See Cat (12).

Little, 1. A little of theyre sa-as goes a great way with me (c60 Paul *Courtship* 41). Mary Plum *Dead Man's Secret* (1931) 40.

2. Every little helps, you know (73 Clemens *Gilded* I 242). Apperson 188; Bradley 82; NC 437; *Oxford* 177; Partridge 635; Taylor *Index* 45; Henry C. Bailey *The Red Castle Mystery* (1932) 234.

Live, 1. Jest as sartin as you live (44 Stephens *High Life* II 149).

2. As sure as you live (59 Browning *Forty-Four* 105; Clemens *Washoe* 102). Svartengren 358; Tilley L374.

3. True as you live (42 Irving *Attorney* 272; Stephens *High Life* I 18, 59, 99, 118, 189, II 205, 240, 255, *Fashion* 34 Why, as true as I live; Cary *Clovernook* 2d Ser. 194 as true as I live and breathe, *Married* 63 live and breathe, 130; Whitcher *Widow* 272). Svartengren 372.

4. They that come after us must live and learn (32 Kennedy *Swallow* 185; Haliburton *Clockmaker* III 67 We must live and larn; Anon. *New Hope* 112 'tis live and larn, sure enuf, out here in de woods, 249; Stephens *Mary Derwent* 191 But 'live and learn' is a good saying; Lowell *Biglow* 287 but folks must live an' larn). Apperson 375; NC 437; *Oxford* 375–376; Stevenson 1378:1; Tilley L379 We live to learne; Whiting *Drama* 246 We live to learne, for so Sainct Paul doth teach; Yamamoto *Dickens* 334; Andy Adams *The Outlet* (Bos-

ton 1905) 248 Oh well, it's live and learn, die and forget it; M. J. Freeman *The Case of the Blind Mouse* (1935) 94; F. Marryat *Peter Simple* (1834, London 1929) 73 Live and larn, boy.

5. But the longer we live, the more we learn of commodores (50 Melville *White Jacket* 27). Babcock 264; NC 438.

6. The longer I live, I believe the more that there is a great deal in that saying, "The more you live, the more you see; the more you see, the more you know" (71 Jones *Batkins* 262). Cf. Stevenson 1411:6; Tilley L393; J. J. Connington, pseud. *The Sweepstake Murders* (Boston 1932) 194 them that lives longest'll see most.

7. He wants to live and let live (43 Haliburton *Attaché* II 115, *Sam* II 300 Give and take, live and let live, that's the word, *Season-Ticket* 112; Hooper *Simon* 93 Live and let live is a good old mottear; Lincoln I 364, II 416). Apperson 375; NC 438; NED Live 3 b; *Oxford* 376; Snapp 88:43; Stevenson 1408:7; Tilley L380; H. Bennett *We Never Called Him Henry* (1951) 169; Christopher Bush *The Body in the Bonfire* (1936) 185 his motto; H. L. Ickes *Diary* (1954) II 400 she . . . is willing to live and let live; M. McCarthy *The Groves of Academe* (1952) 15 Live and let live, he finally opined, was the most politic motto for the occasion.

8. Eternally—my soul, (his favorite oath), gentlemen, if I don't think we have lived long enough (he threw a keg marked "Dupont" in the fire). (58 Porter *Major* 105). Cf. the cry inspiring the attack of the Marines at Belleau Wood; J. F. Dobie in *Folk Travelers* Publications of the Texas Folklore Society 25 (Dallas, Tex. 1952) 4.

9. Where one lives [i. e., at a vital spot]. 60 DA Live 2 (3).

10. See Fighting-cock.

Lively. See Cheese (1), Chipmunk, Cricket (4), Rocket (1), Skipper, Thrasher.

Living. It looked like living, I can tell you (44 Stephens *High Life* I 3, II 163 this is what I call livin').

Lizard, 1. My eye was as keen as a lizard (36 Crockett *Exploits* 51, 80).

2. As proud as er hee lizzard with two tails (51 Burke *Polly* 71). Cf. Cat (53); Stevenson 1883:7 dog, 11 pig.

Load. If a man goes in for betting, I say let him go his load (58 Porter *Major* 16).

Loaf. See Half (1).

Lobster. A tongue into your head as red as a biled lobster (57 Bennett *Border* 293; Locke [Nasby] *Struggles* 262, 484 a lobster; Clemens *Love Letters* 157). NC 438; Taylor *Comparisons* 68; Tilley L405.

Lock. All moved, lock, stock, and barrel (44 Thompson *Major* 66; Hammett *Wonderful* 76 He sold off his feathered stock, "lock, stock, and barrel," *Piney* 134 he . . . cal'lated to sell off lock, stock and barrel). Apperson 377; Bartlett 366; McAtee *Grant County* 7; *Oxford* 622; Schele de Vere 196; Stevenson 1446:9; Joseph Gollomb *The Portrait Invisible* (1928) 53 moved out. See Shot (9), Stock (4).

Locomotive. The litenin wudn't mine [mind] him no more nur a locomotum wud mine a tumble-bug (67 Harris *Sut* 124).

Locust. Silk . . . as thin as a locust's wing (44 Stephens *High Life* II 217).

Log, 1. As easy as rolling off a log (43 Robb *Squatter* 83, 162; Richardson *Secret* 335; Sedley *Marian* 148). Allan PADS XV (1951) 66; Bartlett 810; Boshears 36:524, 525; Brewster *Am. Speech* XVI (1941) 22; DA Log 5 (1); Figh PADS XIII (1950) 13; McAtee 24; NC 438; Taylor *Comparisons* 38; Thornton II 747; Phoebe A. Taylor *Deathblow Hill* (1935) 36.

2. Apparently as lifeless as a log (45 Mayo *Kaloolah* 153).

3. As shure as fallin' off a log (53 Hammett *Stray* 226; Cary *Married* 305).

4. And the business is settled jist like fallin' off a log (51 Burke *Polly* 26).

5. To keep the log rolling. 50 DA Log 5 (3).

6. I have . . . no logs to roll (69 Barnum *Struggles* 636). Farmer 350; NED Log-rolling; Schele de Vere 260–261; Thornton I 556–557, III 235–236.

7. Sleep like log (40 Cooper *Pathfinder* 381; Clemens *Love Letters* 170). Boshears 33:263; Halpert 155; McAtee 58; NC 438; Svartengren 169; Tilley L410; Anne Austin *Murder Backstairs* (1930) 145 as the old sayin' is.

8. To split the log [i. e., to explain]. 32 DA Log 5 (2).

Log fence. She is not as homely as a log fence (36 Fairfield *Letters* 70). See Mud fence, Stump fence.

Logger-heads. He never fights; never goes to logger-heads (25 Neal *Brother J* I 257, II 337). Farmer and Henley IV 221; Green 224; NED Loggerhead 8; Victor MacClure *The Clue of the Dead Goldfish* (Philadelphia 1934) 127.

London. You have heerd tell of a man who couldn't see London for the houses (36 Haliburton *Clockmaker* I 19). Cf. *Oxford* 570 city; Schele de Vere 561.

Lonely. See Catamount (2).

Lonesome. See Get out, Staddle.

Long, sb. What he calls the "upshot of the business," or, in other words, "the long and short of the matter" (20–22 Irving *Bracebridge* 60; Hall *Legends* 163 Then the long and short of the matter is . . . that I am to be cheated out of my money; Briggs *Harry* II 75 The long and the short of it is . . . I have been very misfortunate; Stephens *High Life* I 51, 94 the long and short of it, II 99, *Homestead* 288; Dorson *Jonathan* 99; Hooper *Simon* 52 The "long and short" of all this was; Stowe *Uncle* 78 the long and short is, 203 that's the long and short of it; Cary *Clovernook* 2d Ser. 18; Smith *'Way* 20; Lincoln IV 242; Sedley *Marian* 118). Apperson 378; Bartlett 370; Hardie 471:191; McAtee *Grant County* 7; NED Long, adj. 3; *Oxford* 380; Stevenson 1449:5; Thornton III 236; Tilley L419; NQ 8 xii 388, 452–453, 497; 9 i 91; F. D. Grierson *The Smiling Death* (1927) 155; Stark Young *So Red the Rose* (1934) 304.

Long, adj., 1. It's ez long ez it's broad (48 Lowell *Biglow* 46). Apperson 68–69; NC 376; Stevenson 236:6; Stoett 348, 1360; Tilley B677; H. K. Webster *Who Is the Next?* (Indianapolis 1931) 162. The order of the adjectives is often reversed.

2. See Arm, Beet leaf, Bootjack (4), Bowsprit, Grass (2), Maypole (1), Middle (1), Nail (2), Outdoors (3), Railroad, Rope-walk, Sassafras

root (2), Sermon, Sunday (1), Sword (1), Topmast (1), Turnpike, Weasel (5).

Longest. Hence our backwoods axiom —"the longest is the shortest" (43 Hall *Purchase* I 89).

Look, sb., 1. As quick as a look (33 Smith *Downing* 160, *My Thirty* 395).

2. Looks are one thing, and facts are another (57 Melville *Confidence-Man* 16). Cf. J. D. Carr *The Arabian Nights Murder* (1936) 199 looks are often deceptive.

3. Who cares for looks? looks is nothin'—behaviour's all (39 Smith *Letters* 134). Edwin Greenwood *The Fair Devil* (1935) 151; Gladys Mitchell *Speedy Death* (1929) 273; Edgar Wallace *The Dark Eyes of London* (1929) 10.

Look, vb., 1. Look before you leap (26 Loomis *Farmer's Almanac* 178; Kennedy *Horse-Shoe* 158 Always look before you leap, that's common sense). Apperson 380; NC 438; *Oxford* 383; Stevenson 1452:11; Tilley L429; Whiting *Drama* 129, *Scots* I 203; Yamamoto *Dickens* 327–328; NQ 5 xii 509; Will Scott *The Mask* (Philadelphia 1929) 253; R. S. Surtees *Mr. Sponge's Sporting Tour* (London [1853]) 289.

2. See Dagger (2), Picture (7, 8), Pitchfork.

Looking glass. Why, the old feller [a horse] shines like a looking-glass (c58 Stephens *Mary Derwent* 306).

Look out, 1. Well, that's *my* look out, says I (56 Whitcher *Widow* 251; Porter *Major* 24 it is his own look out). NED Look-out 4 b.

2. We'd kept a sharp look out for a chance to pay him off (58 Hammett *Piney* 175).

Lookout Mountain. Es cold es the no'th side ove Lookout Mountin in January (67 Harris *Sut* 175).

Loon, 1. As crazy as a loon (57 Riley *Puddleford* 140; Clemens *Enterprise* 46, *Sandwich* 60, *Roughing* I 199; Browne *Artemus* 70; Nash *Century* 150). Allan PADS XV (1951) 66; Boshears 35:443; DA Loon 1 b; NC 438; Stevenson 1497:10; Taylor *Comparisons* 30; Thornton I 221; John Chancellor *The Dark God* (1928) 30; William Faulkner *Sanctuary* (1931) 57.

2. As drunk as loons (c68 Clemens *Sketches* 253). DA Loon 1 a; James T. Farrell *The Young Manhood of Studs Lonigan* (1934) 398.

3. Mad as a loon! (57 Bennett *Border* 518). DA Loon 1 a; John Chancellor *The Dark God* (1928) 30.

4. He fights as shy as a loon (40 Haliburton *Clockmaker* III 58).

5. As simple [i. e., crazy] as a loon (55 Jones *Winkles* 90).

6. They marched right by us straight as loons (39 Smith *Letters* 129).

7. As strait as a loon's leg (34 Davis *Downing* 42; Neal *Charcoal* 189 the law is as straight as a loon's leg on that pint; Stephens *High Life* I 257; Haliburton *Nature* II 12). Bartlett 668, 807; DA Loon 1 a; Farmer 351; Schele de Vere 209, 381.

8. As wild as loons (57 Riley *Puddleford* 233). DA Loon 1 a.

9. To hunt the loon with a handnet. 80 DA Loon 1 a.

Lord (1), 1. As sure as the Lord made Moses (36 Haliburton *Clockmaker* I 156, 220, 295). Cf. NC 415; Svartengren 354.

2. The Lord sends provisions, but the devil sends cooks (53 Haliburton

Sam II 184). Apperson 253; *Oxford* 246; Stevenson 419:2; Tilley G222; James Joyce *Ulysses* (Paris 1924) 164 God made food, the devil the cooks; John C. Powys *Wolf Solent* (1929) 129 the Lord gives us beef, but we must go to the Devil for sauce, as my granddad used to murmur.

Lord (2), 1. They were as drunk as lords (39 Briggs *Harry* I 186, II 79; Hammett *Stray* 131; Haliburton *Season-Ticket* 109; Clemens *Sketches* 252, *Roughing* II 119). Apperson 166; Boshears 36:499; DA Bang-up 1; Farmer and Henley IV 237; NC 438; Taylor *Comparisons* 36; John Taine, pseud. *Quayle's Invention* (1927) 414.
2. He is as generous as a lord (27 Cooper *Prairie* 135). Whiting *Scots* I 204.
3. I was just as happy as a lord (70 Clemens *Love Letters* 140).
4. But new lords, new laws (23 Cooper *Pioneers* 170, *Satanstoe* 263 they say, *Redskins* 36 So far as "new laws and new lords" would permit). Apperson 444; *Oxford* 451; Stevenson 1299:2; Tilley L446.
5. Have they not treated you very kindly? Like a lord (57 Jones *Country* 274). NED Lord 8 b.

Loss, 1. However, "there is no great loss but what there is some small gain" (68 Clift *Bunker* 134). *Oxford* 264; Stevenson 928:8; Tilley L463; Van Wyck Mason *The Washington Legation Murders* (1935) 229.
2. Jimmy said that he was sorry for them, but what was one man's loss was another man's gain (55 Anon. *New Hope* 203). Sir Walter Scott *The Pirate* (1822) I ch. 6 But doubtless one man's loss is another man's gain. Cf. Stevenson 928:6.

Lots. Across lots. 48 DA Lot 4 b (2) to go (send) to Hell (the Devil) across lots.

Lotus. A creature . . . as white as the lotus (53 Willis *Fun* 260).

Loud. See Cannon, Pistol, Thunder (5), Tin horn.

Lousy. To be lousy with. 50 DA Lousy 2.

Love, 1. It is best to be off wi' the old love Before ye be on wi' the new (41 Emerson *Journals* VI 62). Apperson 467; Hardie 465:153; Lean IV 20; *Oxford* 468; Stevenson 1480:5; Sir Walter Scott *The Bride of Lammermoor* (1819) ch. 29 an old song; R. S. Surtees *Mr. Sponge's Sporting Tour* (London [1853]) 201, *Plain or Ringlets?* (London [1860]) 7, 72 It had been generally thought by the household, that our fair friend had cried off with the old love before she began with the new.
2. You can't get them for love or money (49 Haliburton *Old Judge* II 40; Hawthorne *Mosses* 449; Clemens *Letters* I 66, *Innocents* II 322; Riley *Puddleford* 118; Richardson *Beyond* 185; Jones *Batkins* 104). Apperson 386; NED Love 7 c; *Oxford* 392; Stevenson 1469:1; Tilley L484; H. W. Sandberg *The Crazy Quilt Murders* (1938) 130.
3. In love, as in war, each man must gain his own victories (40 Cooper *Pathfinder* 201).
4. It was a clear case of love at first sight on both sides (56 Durivage *Three* 93; Barnum *Struggles* 585 a case of "love at first sight"; Jones *Batkins* 444 mine was not a love at first sight). *Oxford* 388–389; Stevenson 1462:5; Tilley L426; Brian Flynn *The*

Billiard Room Mystery (Philadelphia 1929) 103.

5. Love covers a multitude of sins (69 Alcott *Little Women* 428). Cf. Tilley L503. See *Oxford* 88 Charity.

6. Love is fabled to be blind (37–38 Emerson *Works* II 238; Saxe *Poems* 100 The man who wrote that "Love is blind" Could ne'er have known a genuine lover; Nash *Century* 314). Apperson 384; NC 439; *Oxford* 389; Stevenson 1480:2; Tilley L506; Whiting *Drama* 222, 251 Blind Cupid, 288, 289, 296 The blinded God of Loue, *Scots* I 204; Madeleine Johnston *Comets Have Long Tails* (1938) 257; Ira Wolfert in P. Engle and H. Martin *Prize Stories 1955: The O. Henry Awards* (1956) 298 But Wes was as blind as any other lover.

7. Love laughs at locksmiths (43 Hall *Purchase* I 82; Haliburton *Nature* I 87–88; Durivage *Three* 38 you forget that "love laughs at locksmiths," 39). Apperson 385; NC 439; *Oxford* 390; Snapp 80:28; Stevenson 1468:8; Edmund Gilligan *Boundary Against Night* (1938) 87.

8. Love, they say, . . . is meat and drink, and a blanket to boot (35 Kennedy *Horse-Shoe* 37). Cf. NC 439 Love (7).

9. I have Hearn Folks Say That Love was Stronger Than Deth (59 Taliaferro *Fisher's* 225). Song of Solomon 8:6; Stevenson 1485–1486:13; Nancy Barr Mavity *The Other Bullet* (1930) 272 they say.

10. Their vocal exercise was love's labor lost (67 Richardson *Beyond* 468). Cf. Labor (1).

11. Come, sir, old love burns strong (20–22 Irving *Bracebridge* 141).

12. Truly saith the Italian proverb, "There are no ugly loves and no handsome prisons" (65 Richardson *Secret* 401). Apperson 449; *Oxford* 389; Tilley L545.

13. "The love of money is the root of all evil" (46 Cooper *Redskins* 139, 190; Melville *Typee* 168 Money . . . that "root of all evil," *Moby-Dick* I 6 we so earnestly believe money to be the root of all earthly ills; Lowell *Biglow* 129 Again, there is another ancient saw to the effect that money is the *root* of all evil; Shillaber *Mrs. Partington* 336; Smith *Arp* 73 for this here anno domini 1863 is powerful hard on the root of all evil; Richardson *Beyond* 510 The man in the play must have lived in a mining region before he learned the profound truth that "Honesty is the root of all evil, and money is the best policy"; Barnum *Struggles* 499 The inordinate love of money, no doubt, may be and is "the root of all evil"). 1 Tim. 6:10; Bradley 85; NC 446; Stevenson 1608:1, 2; Stoett 696; Tilley C746; Whiting *Drama* 122–123 Covetousness; R. M. Baker *Death Stops the Bells* (1938) 129 money is the root of all evil, the old adage; W. Y. Darling *The Bankrupt Bookseller* (Edinburgh 1947) 221 They who say that money is the root of all evil know little about the tree of life or its roots; A. E. Fielding, pseud. *The Mysterious Partner* (1929) 286 love of money; E. M. Rhodes *West Is West* (1917) 246 The love of unearned money is the root of all evil.

Love, vb. See Brother (3).

Lovely. See Day (12), May (1).

Loving. See Cat (13), Grapevine.

Low. See Bell (2), Memphis.

Lucifer (1), 1. Proud as Lucifer (25 Neal *Brother J* III 3; Haliburton *Attaché* I 217, III 187, *Nature* I 81–82,

Season-Ticket 9; Melville *Moby-Dick* II 190; Cary *Married* 102; Alcott *Little Women* 370). Apperson 514; NC 439; NED Lucifer 2; *Oxford* 521; Taylor *Comparisons* 64; Tilley L572; Whiting *Devil* 212–213:39; J. D. Carr *Poison in Jest* (1932) 156. Cf. Whiting *Scots* II 113.

2. We took a sip . . . and found it . . . strong as Lucifer (47 Melville *Omoo* 323).

Lucifer (2). Her eyes snapped like lucifers (66 Boucicault *Flying Scud* 195).

Luck, 1. With the consoling motto, "Better luck next time" (45 Mayo *Kaloolah* 122; Burke *Polly* 48 "Better luck next time," however, is my motto; Lincoln III 481). *Oxford* 41; Stevenson 1492–1493:11; R. S. Surtees *Mr. Sponge's Sporting Tour* (London [1853]) 86, *Plain or Ringlets?* (London [1860]) 350.

2. Luck Will Turn (73 Clemens *Gilded* II 310).

3. It is a true saying that no one knows the luck of a lousy calf (36 Crockett *Exploits* 13). Owen S. Adams "Traditional Proverbs and Sayings from California" *Western Folklore* VI (1947) 62:69; DA Calf 3 b (this quotation). Cf. *Oxford* 394 As good luck as the lousy calf, that lived all winter and died in the summer.

4. Thinks I, "There's luck in leisure," as I've hearn folks say (59 Taliaferro *Fisher's* 137). Apperson 388; *Oxford* 394; Stevenson 1583:11; John Esteven *While Murder Waits* (1937) 203.

5. To strike a breeze of luck. 34 DA Luck 2.

6. There is no telling which way luck or a half-broke steer will run (45 Hooper *Simon* 34).

Lucky, sb. Their debtor had "cut his lucky" and gone! (56 Kelly *Humors* 380). Farmer and Henley IV 245–246; NED Lucky, sb.²; Partridge 498.

Lucky, adj. It's better to be born lucky than rich (52 Cary *Clovernook* 248). Stevenson 1489:11. Cf. Apperson 283 Hap; *Oxford* 277; Tilley H135; Whiting *Scots* I 185.

Lucre. I can not be supposed to abound in the filthy lucre of this world (56 Whitcher *Widow* 183). Titus 1:11; Partridge 276; Stevenson 1494: 4.

Lumber. Ef you catch me a tradin' Fox Skins with *yeou* again, there ain't no lumber in the state o' Maine! (49 Dorson *Jonathan* 80). Cf. Snake (6, 7).

Lurch. I am not to be left in the lurch (53 Curtis *Potiphar* 197; Alcott *Little Women* 304). Apperson 358; Farmer and Henley IV 252; NED Lurch 3 e; *Oxford* 359; Stevenson 1494:6; Tilley L588.

Luxury. Give us the luxuries of life, and we will dispense with the necessaries (58 Holmes *Autocrat* 125).

Lying. It's as easy as lying (73 Clemens *Gilded* I 165). Apperson 175; *Oxford* 165; Partridge 253; Taylor *Comparisons* 37; J. B. Cabell *The Line of Love* (1926) 187.

Lynx, 1. Eyes like a lynx (50 Boker *World* 39). NED Lynx 1 b; Svartengren 169; Jonathan Stagge, pseud. *Murder by Prescription* (1938) 119 as lynx-eyed as a lynx.

2. Morgan eyed him like a lynx (67 Richardson *Beyond* 520). H. C. McNeile *Guardians of the Treasure* (1930) 198 watch.

ᓚ M ᓫ

Macdonald. Wherever Macdonald sits, there is the head of the table (37 Emerson *Works* I 105).

Mackerel. As dead as a mackerel (53 Hammett *Stray* 275; Clemens *Fairbanks* 171). Boshears 36:480; Taylor *Comparisons* 32–33; Whitman Chambers *Murder for a Wanton* (1934) 191.

Mad, 1. Staring at me as if he meant to swaller me hull, without vinegar or gravy sauce (44 Stephens *High Life* I 12, II 151 The feller looked mad enough tu eat me hull, without vinegar or sarse). Cf. Apperson 176; *Oxford* 166; Tilley S78.
   2. To get one's mad up. 67 DA Mad, sb.; NED Mad, sb., *Supplement* Mad, sb.; Partridge 503.
   3. See Bashan (1), Bear (12), Bedbug (2), Blaze (8), Bull (2), Dragon (1), Fire (4), Flugence (2), Hatter, Hen (4), Hornet (1), Loon (3), March 1 (1), Meat axe (1), Nature (1), Pea (4), Tucker, Wildcat (4).

Maelstrom. His appetite as unquenchable as the Maelstrom (56 Kelly *Humors* 120).

Maggot, 1. Froze two of the toes on my lame leg as stiff as maggots (54 Smith *Way* 57).
   2. The last maggot he has taken into his brain (23–24 Irving *Tales* 290; Smith *Downing* 237 But still a maggot in his head, Told Sam he was a ninny).

Apperson 390; Farmer and Henley IV 267; NC 439; Stevenson 1500–1501: 6; Tilley M6; H. M. Smith *Inspector Frost in Crevenna Cove* (1933) 184 had some maggot in his head.
   3. What maggot's bit you now? (43 Haliburton *Attaché* IV 4). Cf. Apperson 390; NED Maggot 2 c; *Oxford* 396; Tilley M5.

Magnet. Ez otherwise-minded indeed ez th'eends of a magnet (67 Lowell *Biglow* 319).

Magpie. They were chattering like magpies in Hindustani (49 Melville *Redburn* 219; Cary *Clovernook* 2d Ser. 104, *Married* 318; Chamberlain *Confession* 190; Alcott *Little Women* 101 party of magpies, 330 chattered like so many magpies). NC 439; Tilley P285; Whiting *Drama* 323:252. Cf. NED Magpie 2; Taylor *Comparisons* 56; Natalie S. Lincoln *The Secret of Mohawk Pond* (1928) 152.

Mahogany, 1. Arms as brown as a piece of old mahogany (39 Briggs *Harry* I 158; Haliburton *Attaché* IV 135 her skin is . . . as brown as mahogany).
   2. White dough gradually becoming mahogany brown (60 Whitehead *Wild Sports* 253).

Mahon. You're worse than a *Mahon soger* [i. e., no use on a ship]. (40 Dana *Two* 24).

Maid, 1. As blue as an old maid with tu much larnin (44 Stephens *High Life* II 168).

2. As dry as an old maid's lips (53 Hammett *Stray* 208).

3. Old maids fancy nobody knows how to bring up children but them (53 Haliburton *Sam* II 86). Apperson 21 Bachelor; *Oxford* 18; Stevenson 337:1; Tilley B10; William Faulkner *The Sound and the Fury* (1929) 311 a woman that couldn't even get a husband can always tell you how to raise a family. See Bachelor.

Main-brace. Come, let's splice the main-brace all round (49 Melville *Redburn* 398, *White Jacket* 208; Kelly *Humors* 423; Sedley *Marian* 417). Babcock 262; Farmer and Henley IV 271; NED Main-brace; *Oxford* 615.

Maine. See Dan.

Mainmast. You'll feel as strong as the mainmast (49 Melville *Redburn* 52). Whiting *Scots* II 97 mast.

Major. Nell stood it like a major for a while (76 Nash *Century* 152).

Make, sb. On the make. 69 DA Make, sb.; NED Make, sb. 8, *Supplement* Make.

Make, vb. Make or break, hit or miss (34 Crockett *Life* 34). Cf. *Oxford* 399; Tilley M48; A. E. Fielding, pseud. *The Cluny Problem* (1929) 35.

Man, 1. As drowning men seize at straws (23 Cooper *Pioneers* 40; Lewis *Odd* 168 with the tenacity of a drowning man clinging to a straw; Boker *World* 45 He catches at a straw; Willis *Fun* 39 a drowning vanity will catch at a straw; Smith *My Thirty* 455 That's a very small straw for a drownin' man to catch at; Taliaferro *Fisher's* 137 A drowndin' man will ketch at a straw; Browne *Artemus* 219 grasping the mane as drowning men seize hold of straws). Apperson 166; NC 440; NED Straw 8; *Oxford* 159; Stevenson 643:5; Stoett 2203; Tilley M92; NQ CXCIV (1949) 86 dying and desperate persons are apt to catch at every twig; *Catalogue of Political and Personal Satires . . . 1820–1827* (London 1952) X 582 No. 15120; Sir Walter Scott *The Fortunes of Nigel* (1822) II ch. 14 as a drowning man grasps to the willow-wand that comes readiest; James Aston *First Lesson* (1933) 89 cling; A. M. Chase *Murder of a Missing Man* (1934) 156 seized; E. S. Gardner *The Case of the Angry Mourner* (1951) 191 That, your Honor, is simply the desperate attempt of a drowning man to clutch at a straw.

2. As sure as I'm a living man (42 Irving *Attorney* 335; Hall *Purchase* I 172, 177, 178; Anon. *New Hope* 83). Cf. Alive (2).

3. Here we say, *A great man has not a great son.* But this proverb has marked exceptions; and, it is also observed that intellect runs in races (64 Emerson *Journals* X 42).

4. A man is known by the company he keeps (21 Loomis *Farmer's Almanac* 178; Cooper *Prairie* 240 They say a man can be known by the company he keeps; Emerson *Journals* II 300 A man is known by the books he reads, by the company he keeps, by the praise he gives, by his dress, by his tastes, by his distastes, by the stories he tells, by his gait, by the motion of his eye, by the look of his house, of his chamber; Melville *Omoo* 120 we were judged by the company we kept, 196 One Is Judged By The Company He Keeps [chapter title]). Cf. Emerson *Journals* I 340 A man is not known

by the company he keeps. See Apperson 394; Tilley M248. Cf. Bradley 66; *Oxford* 106; Stevenson 386–387:12; NQ 5 vii 445–446; 7 xi 208, 411; H. C. Bailey *A Clue for Mr. Fortune* (1936) 216 a man is judged by the company he keeps; Samuel Lover *Handy Andy* (1842, Everyman's Library) 213 The old adage hath it, Show me your company, and I'll tell you who you are; E. M. Rhodes *Beyond the Desert* (Boston 1934) 121; J. H. Wallis *The Politician* (1935) 71 the old saying.

5. The wholesome adage, "A man can disgrace only himself" (76 Nash *Century* 199).

6. In the maintaining of a principle which neither a man nor a mouse in all God's creation is opposing (58 Lincoln II 509; Clemens *Enterprise* 65 be a man or a mouse). Lean III 336; NED Man 7, Mouse 2 b; Whiting *Drama* 353:699.

7. The man who appeareth for himself . . . , saith my lord . . . [Neal's dots, indicating hesitation] Coke, hath a fool for his client (28 Neal *Rachel* 119; Haliburton *Nature* I 353 A man who pleads his own cause has a fool for a client; Jones *Batkins* 455 When a man is his own lawyer, he is apt to have a fool for his client. This is an old proverb). Apperson 353; *Oxford* 112; Stevenson 599:8 He who treats himself has a fool for a client, 1370:8; Woodard PADS VI (1946) 41; NQ CLXXXVI (1944) 206, 256, CLXXXVII (1945) 283, CXCIII (1948) 480, CXCIV (1949) 20.

8. In what census of living creatures, the dead of mankind are included; why is it that a universal proverb says of them, that they tell no tales (51 Melville *Moby-Dick* I 44; Smith *'Way* 124 dead folks tell no tales; Jones *Country* 287 Dead men tell no tales; Haliburton *Season-Ticket* 51 he was of the opinion dead men tell no tales; Clemens *Tom* 114). Apperson 138; NC 391; *Oxford* 132; Snapp 103:8; Stevenson 505:5; Tilley M511; Sir Walter Scott *Anne of Geierstein* (1829) ch. 14 Dead men have neither teeth nor tongue—they bite not, and they tell no tales; Herbert Adams *Oddways* (Philadelphia 1929) 265; W. Y. Darling *The Bankrupt Bookseller* (Edinburgh 1947) 255 Dead men don't keep bookshops or write diaries. Dead men tell no tales; William McFee *The Harbourmaster* (London 1932) 11 But stowaways are like dead men—they tell no tales.

9. It's no joke waiting for a dead man's shoes (36 Haliburton *Clockmaker* I 149; Kelly *Humors* 372 Waiting for dead men's shoes is a slow and not very sure business; Barnum *Struggles* 482 Waiting for dead men's shoes). Apperson 138; *Oxford* 132; Stevenson 2096:2; Tilley M619; Whiting *Drama* 221; John Donavan *The Case of the Rusted Room* (1937) 41.

10. "A marciful man is marciful to his beast" (53 Haliburton *Sam* I 270). Sir Walter Scott *Redgauntlet* (1824) II ch. 6.

11. Thar warn't a nigger lef in site afore a stutterin man cud whistil (67 Harris *Sut* 220).

12. A talking man is no better than a barking dog (27 Cooper *Prairie* 106).

13. A wilfu' man maun ha' his way (40 Cooper *Pathfinder* 339). Apperson 687; *Oxford* 709. Cf. Tilley W402.

14. Forward! Forward! every man for himself! [battle order]. (25 Neal *Brother J* III 90). Apperson 189; *Oxford* 178; Tilley M112; Whiting *Devil* 208; John Gay *Polly* (1729) II xii;

Herbert Asbury *The French Quarter* (1936) 156.

15. The seamen use another [proverb], "Every man for himself and God for us all," which has much true divinity (38 Emerson *Journals* V 56, 331 What just theology is in the popular proverb, "Every man for himself and the Lord for us all"; Taliaferro *Fisher's* 256 Ev'ry man for hisself, and God for all). Apperson 189; *Oxford* 178; Tilley M113.

16. Every man has his price (49 Haliburton *Old Judge* I 123; Jones *Batkins* 397 You told me everybody had a price). NC 441; *Oxford* 178; Stevenson 1878:3; NQ 5 ix 328, 371; 10 vii 367–368, 470–472, 492, viii 313, ix 378; 11 x 66; R. S. Surtees *Plain or Ringlets?* (London [1860]) 152 As we said before, he considers that every one has his price; E. D. Biggers *The Chinese Parrot* (Indianapolis 1926) 44.

17. Every man must learn once (40 Dana *Two* 319).

18. Every man to his taste (56 Whitcher *Widow* 80; Wallack *Rosedale* 18; Clemens *Sandwich* 145; Boucicault *Presumptive* 237). Apperson 191–192; NC 441; *Oxford* 178–179; Stevenson 2281:2; Tilley M101; M. McCarthy *The Groves of Academe* (1952) 115; Lee Thayer, pseud. *The Glass Knife* (1932) 233. Cf. Woman (15).

19. Every man to his own trade (55 Haliburton *Nature* I 187). Apperson 190; *Oxford* 179; Christopher Bush *The Death of Cosmo Revere* (1930) 74. See Trade (3).

20. Little men are sometimes very potent (46 Melville *Typee* 235). Cf. Apperson 372; Tilley M389; Whiting *Scots* II 95:6.

21. That are old sayin, "man made the town, but God made the country" (36 Haliburton *Clockmaker* I 251, *Attaché* I 235). Bradley 67; Lean II ii 709, III 473; *Oxford* 245; Whiting *Devil* 210; NQ 11 iii 126.

22. Men are willing to believe that which they most desire (c58 Stephens *Mary Derwent* 107).

23. Yes, said Aunt Polly, thoughtfully, men have their privileges (c58 Stephens *Mary Derwent* 195).

24. Man proposes and God disposes (c61 Chamberlain *Confession* 212 [cf. p. 18 l'homme propose, et Dieu dispose]; Richardson *Beyond* 42 The Missourians proposed, but the Kansans disposed; Barnum *Struggles* 307 you know, "man proposes but God disposes"). Apperson 397; NC 441; *Oxford* 403; Stevenson 981:6; Stoett 2578; Tilley M298; NQ 1 viii 411, 552, x 87, 202–203, 384; 4 ix 537–538, x 95, 323, 401, 480, xi 45; 5 x 306, 436, xi 206; 6 v 98, viii 7, 97, 254; 12 v 232; Van Wyck Mason *The Shanghai Bund Murders* (1933) 21 the old saying.

25. Many men, many minds, you know (46 Cooper *Redskins* 147; Melville *Confidence-Man* 6 Showing That Many Men Have Many Minds [chapter heading]). Apperson 586; NC 441; *Oxford* 406; Stevenson 1722:9; Tilley M583; Whiting *Drama* 128, 136, 245; Ellery Queen, pseud. *Halfway House* (1936) so many men, so many opinions.

26. "Do those words go together handsomely?" "Like the poor farmer's team, of an old man and a cow,—not handsomely, but to the purpose" (57 Melville *Confidence-Man* 269).

27. The Rothschilds have another maxim: "Never have anything to do with an unlucky man or place" (69 Barnum *Struggles* 479).

28. No man is going to die till his time comes (32 Kennedy *Swallow* 400). NC 395.

29. No one can tell what they are fit for till they are tried (35 Kennedy *Horse-Shoe* 392). Apperson 347; *Oxford* 344–345.

30. He went round the mounting, and the bullet arter him—so good a man, and so good a boy (59 Taliaferro *Fisher's* 67). DA Snake 7 (10).

31. It won't hurt me and it may amuse you, as the big man said when his little wife beat him (69 Alcott *Little Women* 444).

32. The great man makes the great thing (37 Emerson *Works* I 105).

33. But no matter, dear Pete, as the man said of the sausages—hope for the best, but be prepared for the worst (56 Kelly *Humors* 274). NC 370.

34. Shakespeare says: "The white man rules the day and the black man rules the night" (67 Richardson *Beyond* 539).

35. Verified the proverb that threatened men live long (67 Richardson *Beyond* 305). Apperson 628; *Oxford* 653; Stevenson 2310:7; Tilley F425; Whiting *Drama* 36; Agatha Christie *The Murder at the Vicarage* (1930) 18.

36. There are some proverbs or sayings which serve on many and opposite occasions. This one ought to be put up in every legislative hall and alderman's room throughout the republic: "Wise men change their minds; fools never do" (71 Jones *Batkins* 353). Apperson 696; *Oxford* 718; Stevenson 857:14; Tilley M420.

37. You may have heard the maxim, that "young men *may* die, but that old men *must*" (23 Cooper *Pioneers* 130; Wiley *Billy* 331 the old must die

and the young may die). Apperson 720; *Oxford* 739; Stevenson 524–525: 10; Tilley M609.

38. They were men before they were boys (54 Smith '*Way* 271).

39. You'll be a man before your marm (44 Stephens *High Life* II 143). Lean III 360; *Oxford* 400; Stevenson 1626:4; Tilley M179; J. T. Farrell *No Star Is Lost* (1938) 176 mother.

40. [He] maintains that "the harder a man works on a Coast-of-Maine farm, the worse he is off" (76 Nash *Century* 8).

41. Old fellers always *think* young ones fools; but young fellers sometimes *know* old ones is fools (40 Haliburton *Clockmaker* III 216, *Attaché* III 283 young folks *think* old fools is fools, but old folks *know* young folks is fools). Apperson 720; *Oxford* 739; Stevenson 43:5; Tilley M610.

42. See Dog (50).

Man in the Moon. I didn't know . . . any more than the man in the moon (33 Smith *Downing* 31, 213, '*Way* 184 that paper has no more to do with us, than it has with the man in the moon, *My Thirty* 306 the Whigs had no more business with him than they had with the man in the moon; Haliburton *Clockmaker* II 108 she don't know where it will take her to yet, no more than the man in the moon, *Old Judge* I 305 I know no more about that letter than the man in the moon, *Nature* I 350 every fellow says his ancestors were descended from the man in the moon; Hooper *Simon* 135 Andy didn't know a thing about it, no more 'n the man in the moon; Lowell *Biglow* 92 No more 'n the man in the moon, sez he; Melville *Mardi* I 345 Man has a more comprehensive view of the moon than the man in the moon himself. We know the moon is round; he only infers it; Langdon *Ida* 171 I know no more about the state of his negroes than the man in the moon; Hammett *Stray* 250 Had that very uncertain individual, the "Man in the Moon," with dog, and bush, and lantern—all his paraphernalia complete—made his appearance, and invited them to partake of the green cheese of which his kingdom is supposed to be formed, they certainly could not have been more astonished; Cary *Clovernook* 110, 178, 180; Shillaber *Mrs. Partington* 330 We do not know . . . no more 'n we do why mermaids were made, or the man in the moon; Lincoln VI 322 quite as likely to capture the man-in-the-moon, as any part of Lee's army; Kelly *Humors* 378 Don't know where he's gone to? growls the butcher. No more than the man in the moon; Barnum *Struggles* 571 the little fellow . . . was no more like the General than he was like the man in the moon). McAtee *Additional* 11; *Oxford* 401; Stevenson 1621:6; Svartengren 132–133; Tidwell PADS XI (1949) 14; Tilley M240; Whiting *Drama* 353:700, *Scots* II 96; Elsa Barker *The Redman Cave Murder* (1930) 28 know no more than.

Manners, 1. The canon was therefore issued that "after you" should be "manners" (37 Neal *Charcoal* 195; Stephens *High Life* I 16 Arter you is manners for me, 87, 90, II 30, 87). Apperson 3; Farmer and Henley IV 279; *Oxford* 5; Stevenson 1523:2; Tilley A61.

2. Manners before measures (49 Haliburton *Old Judge* I 222).

3. Manners is manners (c58 Stephens *Mary Derwent* 249).

Many. The saying that "many shall be called, but few chosen" (71 Jones *Batkins* 246). Matt. 20:16, 22:14; Bradley 65; Stoett 659; Yamamoto *Dickens* 252.

Map. I read it like a map (33 Neal *Down-Easters* I 12).

Marble, 1. The sky . . . looked as . . . cold as marble (50 Willis *Fun* 6; Bennett *Kate* 56). NC 442; Svartengren 314; L. W. Meynell *So Many Doors* (Philadelphia 1933) 265.

2. The sky . . . looked as hard . . . as marble (50 Willis *Life* 6). Svartengren 260. Cf. Stevenson 1075:9 stone.

3. Each savage remained motionless as marble (54 Bennett *Kate* 175).

4. She was pale as marble (56 Durivage *Three* 220; Stephens *Mary Derwent* 142 one other face, pale and stern as marble). Svartengren 235; Anthony Wynne, pseud. *The Red Scar* (Philadelphia 1928) 211.

5. The retreating sea, as smooth and hard as marble, and as broad, and apparently as level, as the plain of the Hermus (50 Willis *Life* 201). Svartengren 260.

6. And both horse and rider were still as if cut in marble (53 Willis *Fun* 265; Stephens *Mary Derwent* 248 She lay fainting and still as marble on her chamber floor). Anthony Gilbert, pseud. *The Murder of Mrs. Davenport* (1928) 97. Cf. Svartengren 261 firm.

7. Forehead as white as marble (40 Dana *Two* 344; Melville *Pierre* 458; Bennett *Kate* 112 her features had become white, almost as rigid, as marble; Stephens *Fashion* 301 face . . . white and still as the coldest marble, 405 Their faces [of the jury] white as marble, *Mary Derwent* 216 his lips grew white as marble; Langdon *Ida*

368 her face was whiter than marble). Svartengren 232; A. B. Caldwell *Turquoise Hazard* (1936) 9.

March (1), 1. She began to look as mad as a March hail storm (44 Stephens *High Life* II 123).

2. That was in the lion month of March (56 Melville *Piazza* 4). Cf. Apperson 401 March comes in like a lion and goes out like a lamb; Fife 119; Lean I 357; NC 442; *Oxford* 407; Stevenson 1526:2; Taylor *Index* 47; Tilley M641; NQ 7 xi 287, 393; Madeleine Johnson *Comets Have Long Tails* (1938) 129 fickle April, on the heels of a grumbling March lion, came in smiling.

3. "In March, many weathers," said the proverb (47 Emerson *Journals* VII 289). Apperson 401 (32); *Oxford* 407; Tilley M643.

March (2). Having previously made up her bundle, without which a lady never steals a march (33 Hall *Soldier's Bride* 174). NED March 3 b; Stevenson 1525:11.

Mare, 1. You can see with half an eye that the "grey mare is the better horse here" (36 Haliburton *Clockmaker* I 190, *Old Judge* II 130; Anon. *New Hope* 65). Apperson 274; Farmer 50; Farmer and Henley III 199–200; Green 168; *Oxford* 267; Stevenson 1527:2; Tilley M647; Whiting *Drama* 140, 237; NQ 6 ii 207, 279, iii 95, iv 138, 233, 256, 316, 456, v 96; 12 viii 430; E. W. Howe *Plain People* (1929) 2 I often heard father say his mother was 'the better horse' of his parents, as she ruled the family; Carolyn Wells *The Skeleton at the Feast* (1931) 125 his . . . wife fell gratefully into the rôle of gray mare.

2. You have found some mare's nest

(35 Kennedy *Horse-Shoe* 69; Haliburton *Clockmaker* I 122, II 285 [chapter heading], 288, *Sam* I 238, *Nature* I 20, II 398 it kinder amuses me to see a fellow find a mare's nest with a tee-hee's egg in it; Hammett *Stray* 43, 276, *Piney* 266 I shouldn't wonder if you'd nosed out a mare's nest). Apperson 402; Farmer and Henley IV 281; Green 231; NC 442; NED Mare's-nest; *Oxford* 408; Stevenson 1527:3; Tilley M658; C. B. Clason *The Purple Parrot* (1937) 284; Dorothy L. Sayers *Busman's Honeymoon* (1937) 215 full of cockatrice's eggs; NQ 3 ix 196; 4 viii 44; 7 iii 380, 480, v 173; 13 i 194.

3. See Door (2).

Marines. O hang your taboo . . . talk taboo to the marines (46 Melville *Typee* 301, *Mardi* I 69 but tell that to the marines, say the illiterate Jews and the jewellers, *Confidence-Man* 169 Your patrons, sir, seem your marines to whom you may say anything). Farmer and Henley IV 282; NED Marine 4 c; *Oxford* 646; Partridge 509; Stevenson 1528:5; NQ 3 xii 25, 78; 12 x 72; Andy Adams *The Ranch on the Beaver* (Boston 1927) 258; Cortland Fitzsimmons *No Witness!* (1932) 195.

Mark, 1. But this idea was shooting very wide of the mark (53 Hammett *Stray* 272; Jones *Winkles* 244 you came near the mark there, *Wild* 45 You are somewhat wide of the mark as respects my jeopardy). Apperson 566; NED Mark 7 e, Shoot 22 d(d); Stevenson 1528:7, 2099:11; Tilley M668.

2. Now a feller of rale ginuine grit would cum up to the mark tu once [i. e., not delay]. (44 Stephens *High Life* I 31).

3. Keep me up to the mark (71

Jones *Batkins* 198). NED Mark 12 c; Stevenson 1529:4.

4. Old jockeys who have never had a black mark against them (66 Boucicault *Flying Scud* 181). NED Black mark.

5. He could not throw well enough to make his mark in that famous western game of bull-pen (71 Eggleston *School-Master* 82). Bartlett 380–381; NED Mark 13 b; Stevenson 1529:3.

6. Wyoming expects every man of ye to stand up to the mark (c58 Stephens *Mary Derwent* 310).

7. I'll make you toe the mark (40 Dana *Two* 126, 295 [literal—a fist fight]; Stephens *High Life* II 64 [i. e., to match a bid in an auction], 68, 71; Stowe *Uncle* 379; Dorson *Jonathan* 57; Shillaber *Knitting-Work* 32; Nash *Century* 90). Bartlett 710; Farmer and Henley VII 145; Thornton III 404.

Market. He had brought his sorrows to an unpromising market (76 Clemens *Tom* 166). NED Market 1 b. Cf. Pig (14).

Marriage. Marriage, they say, halves one's rights and doubles one's duties (69 Alcott *Little Women* 487). Oxford 408. Cf. Stevenson 1533:1.

Marrow bones. Brung Jonathan Slick on his marrow bones (44 Stephens *High Life* I 110; Locke [Nasby] *Struggles* 220 South Carolina . . . wuz the first to get down on her marrow bones, and beg for peace like a dorg). Cf. Farmer and Henley IV 285.

Marsh. I wa'n't bawn in the mash to be fool' by trash! (c76 Clemens *Sketches* 241, 242, 246). For the spelling *mash,* see George P, Krapp, *The English Language in America* (1925) II 222–224. See Brush.

Master, 1. A good horse never loses anything by the eye of his master (35 Kennedy *Horse-Shoe* 228). Apperson 196; *Oxford* 412; Tilley M733. Cf. A. T. Sheppard *Here Comes an Old Sailor* (1928) 129 Nothing fats the horse like the King's eye.

2. He who would be master of his own, must not be bound to another (32 Loomis *Farmer's Almanac* 178).

3. One cannot serve two masters (38 Haliburton *Clockmaker* II 141). Matt. 6:24; Apperson 449; NC 443; *Oxford* 455; Stevenson 1546:1; Tilley M322; Whiting *Drama* 232; Henry Wade, pseud. *Constable, Guard Thyself!* (1935) 188. See Mistress (1).

4. The proverb, "like master, like man" had little application to this pair (46 Hall *Wilderness* 118). Apperson 366–367, 646 trim; Bradley 85; NC 443; *Oxford* 412, 671 trim; Stevenson 1547:4; Tilley M723.

5. When the master is away, the boys will play (20 Loomis *Farmer's Almanac* 177). Cf. NC 382 cat.

Match (1). [A dandy], fat as a match and quite as good looking (56 Kelly *Humors* 238). NC 443; Svartengren 186.

Match (2). That matches are made in heaven, may be (56 Melville "I and My Chimney" in *Works* XIII 288). Apperson 404; NC 443; *Oxford* 409; Stevenson 1533:10; Tilley M688; NQ i xi 106, xii 72–73, 195, 236, 295; 6 xi 353; Samuel Lover *Handy Andy* (1842, Everyman's Library) 329 Do you think . . . that *that* marriage was made in Heaven, where we are told that marriages *are* made?; A. M. Chase *Twenty Minutes to Kill* (1936) 129 Marriages are made in Heaven— that mush.

Matthew. What I've jist norated is true as the third of Mathy (59 Taliaferro *Fisher's* 58). Cf. Apostles.

Mattock. They knocked the leaf fat outen him, in wads as big as mattock handles (45 Hooper *Simon* 49).

May, 1. She was lovely as the month of May (59 Shillaber *Knitting-Work* 296). Cf. Tilley M763; Whiting *Scots* II 97; David Frome, pseud. *Mr. Pinkerton Finds a Body* (1934) 31 as lovely as a May morning; Marion N. Rawson *When Antiques Were Young* (1931) 207 looking fresh and sweet as a May morning.

2. An old proverb says, "To wed in May is to wed poverty" (20–22 Irving *Bracebridge* 360, 362 they are perfectly willing to marry in May and abide the consequences). Cf. Apperson 408; *Oxford* 411 Marry in May.

May-pole, 1. His arms was long as May-poles (59 Taliaferro *Fisher's* 205). Svartengren 283.

2. Tall as a may-pole (56 Kelly *Humors* 336). Apperson 619; Green 20; Svartengren 283; Tilley M778. Cf. Farmer and Henley III 350 hoppole; NC 460.

Me. Ye've heard the saying of "Love me, love my dog"; well, now, that means, read backwards, "Don't love me, don't love my dog" (40 Cooper *Pathfinder* 320; Melville *Pierre* 417 Love me, love my dog, is only an adage for the old country women who affectionately kiss their cows). Apperson 386–387; NC 439; NED Love, vb. 2 a; *Oxford* 391; Tilley D496; NQ 1 v 538; 11 ii 522–524, iii 51, 113–114, 173; R. S. Surtees *Mr. Sponge's Sporting Tour* (London [1853] 139; J. S. Fletcher *The Golden Spur* (1928) 169; M. P. Shiel *The Black Box* (London 1930) 32 love me, love my sheep; Cecil Roberts *Victoria Four-Thirty* (1937) 275; F. P. Keyes *The River Road* (1945) 272 This hasn't been a case of 'love me, love my dog'; J. P. Marquand *Melville Goodwin, USA* (Boston 1951) 343 I love you, Goodwin, Major Grundy said, but I don't love your dog.

Meadow. Wan't brung up in the medders to be kicked to death by grasshoppers (33 Neal *Down-Easters* I 124). See Brush.

Mealy. See Potato (3).

Mean. See Dirt (3), Dog-pie, Get-out, Indian (2), Jew, Job 1 (1), Nigger (3), Poison (2), Potato (4), Powder (1), Pusley, Sent, Sheep (9).

Means, 1. Yo no gib him by fair means you gib him by foul (40 Haliburton *Clockmaker* III 139). Stevenson 1552:3; NED Fair 15; T. L. Peacock *Melincourt* (1817 *Works* II [London 1924] II) 199; H. F. M. Prescott *The Man on a Donkey* (1952) 71 If fair won't serve, then must foul. Cf. Tilley M794.

2. See End (1).

Measles. [A story] is a spreddin faster nur meazils (67 Harris *Sut* 49).

Meat, 1. If it be true that a man loves the meat in his youth he cannot endure in his age (65 Sedley *Marian* 284).

2. To be one's meat [i. e., quarry, victim]. 72 DA Meat sb. 2.

3. To take meat [i. e., kill a man]. 46 DA Meat sb. 3 b (2).

Meat axe, 1. I feel as mad as a meat axe (55 Haliburton *Nature* I 85).

2. She looked at me as savage as a meat axe (34 Crockett *Life* 64; Davis

Downing 185 in Kentucky parlance, "is as savage as a meat-axe" [used of an axe]; Stephens *High Life* I 116, 198, 248, II 205; Burke *Polly* 149; Haliburton *Nature* II 192, *Season-Ticket* 363; Kelly *Humors* 99; Hammett *Piney* 43). Bartlett 552–553; DA Meat ax 2; Farmer 472; Farmer and Henley IV 297; Svartengren 414; Thornton II 764.

3. Sharp as a meat-ax. 56 DA Meat-ax 2.

4. She was . . . as wicked as a meat-axe (38 Haliburton *Clockmaker* II 127, III 67). DA Meat-ax 2.

Medicine, 1. To make medicine. 41 DA Medicine 3 c (1).

2. The leaders refused to take their own medicine (65 Richardson *Secret* 75). DA Medicine 3 c (2); Stevenson 1557:10 taste; E. D. Biggers *Behind That Curtain* (Indianapolis 1928) 175 the doctor must take his own medicine.

Mediterranean pass. To fit like a Mediterranean pass. 48 DA Mediterranean 2.

Meek. See Cat (14), Child (7), Dove (4), Lamb (7), Milk (1).

Meeting, 1. 'Twas as good as a meetin', now, really, to hear that critter pray (51 Stowe *Uncle* 2, 54).

2 .The third day he spoke "out in meeting" (55 Thomson *Doesticks* 54; Durivage *Three* 210 But a strict regard for truth compels us to "speak right out in meetin'"; Nash *Century* 70 I cum purty near speakin' right in meetin'). DA Meeting 3 b; Thornton II 836.

Meeting house, 1. I see thar was hell in him as big as er meetin' house (51 Burke *Polly* 149; Whitcher *Widow*

220; Hammett *Piney* 124). Cf. NC 429; Svartengren 289; Taylor *Comparisons* 16.

2. [Birds in flight] stuck up higher en a meetin' house (60 Whitehead *Wild Sports* 210). Cf. NC 429 House (3).

3. Everything was as still as a meeting house (54 Stephens *Fashion* 41).

Melancholy. See Cat (15), Drum (2), Mouse (1), Willow (2).

Mellow. See Grape (1), Horse-apple.

Melt. See Snow (11).

Memphis. A fillip . . . that would lay the "castled crag of Drachenfels" as low as Memphis (50 Willis *Life* 202).

Merit. It is an old saying that "Merit wins" (68 Clift *Bunker* 60).

Merry, 1. I am a great approver of the old maxim of "being merry and wise" (40 Haliburton *Letter* 307). Apperson 413; Lean IV 15; NED Merry 3 f; *Oxford* 420; Stevenson 1567:5; Tilley G324; Whiting *Drama* 144, 213, 231, 250.

2. See Bell (3), Cricket (5), Wedding (1).

Messmate. A messmate, before a shipmate; a shipmate, before a stranger; a stranger, before a dog—but a dog before a soldier (24 Cooper *Pilot* 259). *Oxford* 421.

Method. My madness . . . is not without method (44 Fairfield *Letters* 334; Baldwin *Flush* 193 He had method in his madness; Richardson *Secret* 247; Smith *Arp* 102 There was no method in this madness; Barnum *Struggles* 508). *Oxford* 422; Stevenson 1499:9; Bruce Norman *The Thousand Hands* (1927) 38.

Methuselah, 1. As . . . frosty as Mathusaler (44 Stephens *High Life* II 60).

2. As old as Methuselah (37 Neal *Charcoal* 65; Stephens *High Life* II 60 Mathusaler; Fairfield *Letters* 439 stories as old; Melville *Redburn* 44; Smith 'Way 65, 176; Taliaferro *Fisher's* 254 Mathuzlum; Paul *Courtship* 49; Locke [Nasby] *Struggles* 176 Methoozeler; Daly *Man* 50). Boshears 38:781; McAtee 46; NC 444; Taylor *Comparisons* 60; Tilley M908; J. D. Beresford *An Innocent Criminal* (1931) 5.

3. If they were to live as long as Merusalem (38 Haliburton *Clockmaker* II 309, *Attaché* I 130; Holmes *Elsie* 119 I've been workin' for that party longer'n Methuselah's lifetime).

Meum. And begin to see the just distinctions between *meum* and *tuum* (46 Cooper *Redskins* 397). NED Meum; *Oxford* 422; Stevenson 1853:5; Tilley M910; Whiting *Scots* II 99.

Mexican. The narrow streets of Taos . . . are usually crowded with "Mexican carriages." The burro or donkey . . . (67 Richardson *Beyond* 261). In 1954 tourists in Mexico were told that burros are "Mexican jeeps," clearly a favorite joke among the guides.

Michigander. They are with Dimokrasy ez the Michigander is with his itch —wood like to git rid uv it, but can't (64 Locke [Nasby] *Struggles* 113).

Middle, 1. There is a penance, as long as into the middle of next week (43 Haliburton *Attaché* II 265).

2. And nocked him about into the middle of next week (34 Davis *Downing* 105; Haliburton *Attaché* III 48; Stephens *High Life* I 89, II 130, 196,

239 that music had sent me into the middle of next week without my knowin it; Burke *Polly* 147; Porter *Major* 105 and the next moment he was knocked into the middle of the next three weeks). Sidney Williams *The Drury Lane Case* (1927) 153. Cf. Farmer and Henley IV 127.

Midnight, 1. Hair as . . . black as midnight (44 Stephens *High Life* II 245; Hawthorne "My Kinsman" in *House* 629). Fife 117; NC 444; Svartengren 246; Taylor *Comparisons* 18; Herbert Asbury *The Tick of the Clock* (1928) 44. Cf. Farmer and Henley IV 307.

2. The waters grew dark as midnight (28 Neal *Rachel* 37; Stephens *High Life* I 184 It was dark as midnight among the bushes, *Mary Derwent* 315). Boshears 36:472; NC 444; NED Midnight 4 b; Taylor *Comparisons* 32.

3. We must creep as still as midnight (39 Smith *Letters* 102).

4. Hair as thick . . . as midnight (44 Stephens *High Life* II 245).

Might, 1. Might often makes right here (23 Cooper *Pioneers* 8, 131 But might makes right; Judd *Richard* 106, 171, 398; Nash *Century* 161 Remember, Jack, that the doctrine 'might makes right' is not popular in this enlightened age). Apperson 416; Bradley 90; *Oxford* 423; Stevenson 1571:4; Tilley M922 Might overcomes right; Whiting *Drama* 254 Might masters right; NQ 4 viii 527, ix 81–82; H. H. Dunn *The Crimson Jester* (1933) 190; T. H. White *The Sword in the Stone* (1939) 62 Might is right. See Right, sb. (1).

2. We worked . . . with might and main (40 Dana *Two* 84; Alcott *Little Women* 140). Green 237; NED

Might 5; Stevenson 1571:8; Tilley M923.

Mild. See Infant (3), Lamb (8), Milk (2), Moonbeams, Potato (5).

Mile, 1. They's plenty not a thousand miles away as deserves it (71 Eggleston *School-Master* 159).

2. I'd walk forty miles to git old kit [his rifle] a wolf skelp (56 Kelly *Humors* 71; Porter *Major* 25 But I'll run a mile before I wait for a quarter race again). Andy Adams *The Outlet* (Boston 1905) 362 tell the old man . . . I'd ride a thousand miles for the chance; Thomas Middleton *A Trick to Catch the Old One* (1608) V i (*Works* ed. A. H. Bullen [London 1885] II 343) Ha! I'd walk ten mile a' foot to see that, i'faith.

Mile post. I passed him like a mile post (58 Hammett *Piney* 261).

Militia trainer, 1. As crank as a militia trainer with his regimentals on (44 Stephens *High Life* II 213). Cf. Svartengren 90 wrathy . . . militia officer.

2. As independent as a militia trainer (44 Stephens *High Life* II 119).

3. Butlers . . . like militia trainers jist tryin tu drill (44 Stephens *High Life* II 250).

Milk, 1. As meek as new milk (44 Stephens *High Life* II 96).

2. All is as mild as new milk again (35 Kennedy *Horse-Shoe* 209; Hammett *Piney* 34 he was . . . as mild as mother's milk). Svartengren 63; Caroline Gordon *The Garden of Adonis* (1937) 140 milk. Cf. Anthony Gilbert, pseud. *The Murder of Mrs. Davenport* (1928) 129 pure as mother's milk.

3. She's as sweet as milk (66 Boucicault *Flying Scud* 159). Svartengren 63 cream.

4., a. As white as skim milk in the face (44 Stephens *High Life* II 160, 162 as milk; Thomson *Doesticks* 214 as milk; Holmes *Professor* 179 as milk). NED Milk 1 b; Christopher Bush *The Death of Cosmo Revere* (1930) 7.

b. The milk-white seeds (46 Melville *Typee* 115, 128, *Mardi* I 182, 207, 293, *Redburn* 131, *White Jacket* 132, *Moby-Dick* I 176, 235, 237, 239, II 198 milky-white; Cary *Clovernook* 35 milk-white doves; Hawthorne *Mosses* 539; Cooke *Foresters* 398; Holmes *Professor* 234). Apperson 680–681; Boshears 41:1019; Taylor *Comparisons* 87; Tilley M931; Whiting *Drama* 320:225, *Scots* II 98; Lewis Robinson *The General Goes Too Far* (1936) 33.

5. Never cry for spilt milk (28 Neal *Rachel* 248; Smith *Downing* 47 No use to cry for spilt milk, 98, 189, 'Way 329, *My Thirty* 247; Haliburton *Clockmaker* I 294 over, 326, III 27, 50, *Season-Ticket* 61; Cary *Clovernook* 267 It's no use mourning over spilt milk; Burke *Polly* 96 over; Curtis *Potiphar* 67; Durivage *Three* 128; Whitcher *Widow* 50, 176; Kelly *Humors* 118, 392; Hammett *Piney* 101 for; Shillaber *Knitting-Work* 292; Taliaferro *Fisher's* 127 It warn't wuth while to grieve arter spilt milk). Apperson 126; Bartlett 636; Figh PADS XIII 12; NC 444; Oxford 122; Smith *Browning* 219; Stevenson 1573–1574: 9; Tilley M939; NQ CXCVI (1951) 239; Andy Adams *The Ranch on the Beaver* (Boston 1927) 88 There's no use crying; R. H. Fuller *Jubilee Jim* (1928) 90.

6. The milk in the coconut. 40 DA

Milk c (3); NED *Supplement* Milk 3 b; Partridge 167, 520; Gregory Baxter, pseud. *The Ainceworth Mystery* (1930) 101, 275.

7. Gin her some whiskey, an' she tuk it like milk (51 Burke *Polly* 69).

8. But when you cum to bring 'em down to thar milk, they'll turn out greener than Buffalo Bayou in September, and that's so powerful green that all the settlers on the banks skim off the top, and paint their cabins with it (58 Hammett *Piney* 45; Porter *Major* 20 I thought that would bring you to your milk). DA Milk (4).

9. Ugly enough to frighten children from crying, and turn the milk of a whole dairy (53 Haliburton *Sam* I 71; Smith *'Way* 244 She looked as if she'd turn milk sour quicker than a thunder-shower; Melville *Confidence-Man* 124 I hope I have the milk of kindness, but your thunder will soon turn it). Cf. Apperson 658.

10. Black or write . . . or half-and-half sometimes at the south, where they are called milk-and-molasses [i. e., mulattoes]. (33 Neal *Down-Easters* I 96). DA Milk c (2).

11. It is so full of milk and water it makes me fairly sick (59 Smith *My Thirty* 432; Nash *Century* 70 He's too milk-and-waterish). Stevenson 1573:8; Thornton II 580, III 245. Cf. Svartengren 393.

12. See Froth.

Milk-pail. But somehow a gal kicks over the milk-pail when she lets her ebenezer git up before a feller (44 Stephens *High Life* I 50).

Milk-weed-down. Fancy's cushin' . . . Makes the hard bench ez soft ez milk-weed-down (67 Lowell *Biglow* 335).

Mill (1), 1. He's been through the mill [i. e., has had toothache]. (56 Kelly *Humors* 90; Lincoln III 28 You know best, Judge, you have been through the mill; Holmes *Elsie* 177; Harris *Uncle Remus* 199 You look like you'd been through the mill). Bartlett 393, 703; Farmer and Henley IV 315, 316; NED Mill 1 b; Stevenson 1575: 3; Thornton II 581, III 246.

2. It is one thing in the mill, but another in the sack (52 Melville *Pierre* 418).

3. His tongue goes like a mill (32 Kennedy *Swallow* 370). Cf. *Oxford* 664; Whiting *Drama* 285, *Scots* II 98.

Mill (2). I say to the Genius, if he will pardon the proverb, In for a mill, in for a million (37–38 Emerson *Works* III 83–84). NED Mill, sb.[5] (with the remark that no quotation of "mill" in this sense was available).

Mill-pond, 1. The sloop . . . sailed on as quietly as if in a mill-pond (20–22 Irving *Bracebridge* 424).

2. It was as smooth as a mill-pond after the gale (40 Dana *Two* 254). NED Mill-pond; Svartengren 270; Daphne Du Maurier *The Du Mauriers* (1937) 168 the proverbial. Cf. Duck-pond.

Millstone, 1. Your heart is harder than the nether millstone (39 Briggs *Harry* II 134; Durivage *Three* 400). Job 41: 24; NED Nether 4 b; Svartengren 88; Gordon Gardiner *At the House of Dree* (1928) 288.

2. The burdens already hung like millstones about our necks (67 Richardson *Beyond* 315). Matt. 18:6; I Tim. 17:2; NED Millstone 3; W. E. Hayes *Black Chronicle* (1938) 103.

3. But they can't see through a mill-stone so fur as I can (33 Smith *Downing* 123, 225 you have that sharp knowing look, as though you could see right through a millstone; Haliburton *Clockmaker* I 126 I guess I can see as far into a millstone as the best on 'em, II 287 as them that picks the hole in-to it, III 167 I believe you could see a hole in a millstone if it was no bigger than the pint of a needle, providin' you picked it yourself, *Season-Ticket* 15, 331 I can see through a hole in a grindstone, as far as him that picks it; Stephens *High Life* II 8 Seeing as you can peak so consarned far into a mill-stun; Melville *Mardi* II 212 On Seeing into Mysteries through Millstones; Bennett *Kate* 50 I have no doubt he could see completely through a mill-stone, as we say in the East—provided, that is, there was a hole through it eight inches in diameter; Thomson *Plu-ri-bus-tah* 243 Liberty "saw through the mill-stone"; Riley *Puddleford* 34 he couldn't be expected to see a great way into a millstone; Whitcher *Widow* 232 I can see as fur into a millstone as anybody; Porter *Major* 15 one who can see as far into a millstone as the man who pecks it; Taliaferro *Fisher's* 53 Now I tried it [staring] good, just like I were trying to look through a mill-stone). Apperson 556; Farmer and Henley IV 318; NED Millstone 2 a; *Oxford* 425; Stevenson 2107:6; Tilley M965; Whiting *Drama* 354:712; H. S. Keeler *The Matilda Hunter Murder* (1931) 547 Mr. Ellwood . . . neither wishes to see the hole in a millstone nor the millstone either. See Grindstone (3).

Mill-stream. And ran on like a mill-stream, about a regatta (49 Haliburton *Old Judge* II 110).

Mince-meat. I'll chop you up as fine as mince meat (36 Haliburton *Clockmaker* I 179). Cf. Stevenson 2310:11.

Mind, 1. Mind was triumphing over matter (37 Neal *Charcoal* 187). Jean Potts *Death of a Stray Cat* (1955) 143 It was a triumph of mind over matter. Cf. Oscar Wilde *The Picture of Dorian Gray* (1891) ch. 4 women represent the triumph of matter over mind.
2. See Minute (2).

Mine, sb., 1. His hair was black as Lehigh's mines (39 Briggs *Harry* II 81).
2. A banker, who'd got as rich as a mine (68 Saxe *Poems* 95).

Mine, pron. Wut doos Secedin' mean, ef 't ain't . . . Thet wut is mine's my own, but wut's another man's ain't his'n? (67 Lowell *Biglow* 237). Apperson 677; NC 445; *Oxford* 425; Snapp 84:57; Stevenson 1834:8; Tilley M980.

Minister. As peart and perlite as a minister (43 Robb *Squatter* 98).

Mink, 1. Some white men has souls as black as a mink (55 Anon. *New Hope* 31).
2. As close [i. e., miserly] as a mink in winter (45 Judd *Margaret* I 116).
3. Pomp . . . ez quiet ez a mink (48 Lowell *Biglow* 146).

Minute, 1. 'Tis an old and vulgar maxim, Take care of the minutes, and the hours will take care of themselves; but like many vulgar things 'tis better than gold of Ophir, wisely used (27 Emerson *Journals* II 215). Cf. NC 456 pennies.
2. Like a gal's mind, no two minits alike (44 Stephens *High Life* II 27). Svartengren 22.
3. I'd a stood by her to the last minit (44 Stephens *High Life* I 51).

Mirror, 1. The steamer was booming on through a sea calm as a mirror (50 Willis *Life* 172).

2. A lake . . . clear and unbroken as a mirror (53 Willis *Fun* 140). NC 445.

3. His boots shone like a mirror (57 Riley *Puddleford* 138).

Misery, 1. "Misery," it is said, "brings us into strange company" (33 Hall *Soldier's Bride* 162; Judd *Margaret* II 100 Misery makes us unacquainted with strange bedfellows, Judge; *Harper's New Monthly Magazine* XXVIII [1864] 752 Misery makes strange bedfellows, says the old proverb). Apperson 418; NC 445; *Oxford* 426; Stevenson 1591:10.

2. You find it lonely, eh, . . . gulled yourself, you would have a companion (57 Melville *Confidence-Man* 145; Porter *Major* 194 and then they got friendly, for misery loves company, you know; Smith *Arp* 125 Misery loves company; Clemens *Roughing* II 147 misery loves company, *Tom* 145 but to have company in misery seemed something to be grateful for). Apperson 110 companion; Bradley 85; *Oxford* 106 company; Stevenson 1592:14; Tilley C571; J. B. Cabell *Figures of Earth* (1925) 173; J. M. Walsh *The Company of Shadows* (1931) 57 we had a companion in misfortune.

Misfortune, 1. And, as the song says, "Single misfortunes ne'er come alone" (36 Crockett *Exploits* 110). Ezek. 7:5; Apperson 419; NC 445; NED Misfortune 1 c; *Oxford* 426–427; Stevenson 1596–1597:6; Stoett 1676; Tilley M1012; Thomas Hood *Poems* (1826, ed. London 1911) 55 Miss-fortunes never come alone; R. S. Surtees *Mr. Sponge's Sporting Tour* (London [1853]) 168 misfortunes seldom come singly; Leslie Charteries *Wanted for Murder* (1931) 298 blessings, like misfortunes, never come singly.

2. What's one man's misfortune is another's good luck (45 Mayo *Kaloolah* 266). Cf. Loss (2).

Miss. A miss was as good as a mile (21 Cooper *Spy* 218, *Pathfinder* 170 If "a miss is as good as a mile," a hit ought to be better; Emerson *Journals* III 534 A ball passed through his cap and he cried, "A miss is as good as a mile" [reported to have been said at the battle of Lexington, April 19, 1775]; Dana *Two* 427 However, " a miss is as good as a mile," a saying which sailors very often have occasion to use; Haliburton *Sam* II 313; Wiley *Johnny* 206). Apperson 419; Lean II ii 666; NC 445; NED Miss 7; *Oxford* 427; Stevenson 1597–1598:8; NQ 7 iii 476, iv 77; Richard Hull, pseud. *Keep It Quiet* (1936) 150; P. B. Kyne *Tide of Empire* (1928) 9; Stark Young *So Red the Rose* (1934) 260.

Missionary. Now I have been thinking that these weaker brethren were living on "Missionary ground," as the saying is, and that the farmers who read the papers ought to come over and help them (68 Clift *Bunker* 44).

Mississippi. The old river men have a saying, that "the Mississippi never lets go of a man who has clothes on," and it is generally true (53 Hammett *Stray* 416).

Missouri. As riled as the old Missouri in a June rise (43 Robb *Squatter* 134).

Mistake, 1. One mistake . . . naturally leads to another (40 Haliburton *Clockmaker* III 194).

2. And when one of them made a

mistake on purpose, and drawed his curtains (58 Hammett *Piney* 123). Stevenson 1598:7.

3. Mistakes will happen (35 Crockett *Account* 227). Sidney Williams *The Murder of Miss Betty Sloan* (1935) 246. See Accidents (1).

Mistaken. See Shirt (1, 2).

Mistress, 1. A man can't serve two mistresses—his country and his wife (43 Haliburton *Attaché* IV 134). See Master (3).

2. She tried it on at first, saying your presence, sir, by going to bed missus and getting up master (60 Haliburton *Season-Ticket* 87).

3. The Mistress makes the morning, But the Lord makes the afternoon (42 Emerson *Journals* VI 202).

Mitten, 1. Dead as a mittin (59 Taliaferro *Fisher's* 75). Svartengren 142.

2. She has given Captain Tufthunt the mitten (43 Haliburton *Attaché* III 15, *Sam* II 43, 68 to save myself from gettin' the mitten, *Nature* I 190, *Season-Ticket* 227; Stephens *High Life* I 94, II 39, 74 afeard of gitting the mitten, 128 as solemncholy as a gal's that's got the mitten, *Mary Derwent* 193 They said . . . that he'd got the mitten straight out; Whitcher *Widow* 239; Holmes *Autocrat* 292–293 [he] "got the mitten" (pronounced mittin) two or three times; Barnum *Struggles* 57; Clemens *Love Letters* 51; Eggleston *School-Master* 86 Young men . . . were trembling in mortal fear of the "mitten"; Nash *Century* 68 Bessie Jones mittened me last evenin'). Bartlett 244, 398; Farmer 369; Farmer and Henley IV 323–324; Green 241; NED Mitten 3; Nixon PADS V (1946) 30; Schele de Vere 319; Stevenson 1600:5; Thornton II 585; Claudia

Cranston *Murder Maritime* (Philadelphia 1935) 178 hand; Mari Sandoz *Slogum House* (Boston 1937) 205 got. Cf. DA Mitten, vb.

3. If . . . I handle any folks without mittins (34 Davis *Downing* 4; Melville *Moby-Dick* I 336 However recklessly the whale may sometimes serve us . . . he can never be truly said to handle us without mittens). Apperson 281; Farmer and Henley IV 324; NED Mitten 1 b; *Oxford* 274; Stevenson 1600:3; Tilley M1028. Cf. Glove (4).

Mocking bird, 1. As easy as a mockin' bird whistles (43 Robb *Squatter* 145).

2. See Bird (3).

Mogul. I descended the stand big as Mogul (56 Kelly *Humors* 248).

Mohammed. Like the fabled coffin of Mohammed, he is always in a state of "betweenity" (37 Neal *Charcoal* 84; Richardson *Beyond* 484 where he hung, like Mohammed's coffin). *Oxford* 397; Stevenson 1500:2; Tilley M13.

Molasses, 1. Slick ez molasses (48 Lowell *Biglow* 81). Bradley 85; DA Slick 6 (2).

2. See Nougat.

Mole. A tongue . . . quiet as a mole (43 Robb *Squatter* 115).

Money, 1. When I'm shinin' away in Abram's bosom, like a piece uv new money (59 Taliaferro *Fisher's* 48, 76 His eyes shinin' away like new money). Boshears 33:250, 40:901; Halpert 841; NC 446.

2. You'll find that all the money you've made by Sunday work has burnt a hole in your pocket and dropped out (68 Clift *Bunker* 262). Apperson 421; McAtee PADS XV

(1951) 57; *Oxford* 428; Stevenson 1611:5; Tilley M1048; S. E. Morison *Builders of the Bay Colony* (1930) 308.

3. Like other speculators, he "looks for his money where he loses it" (69 Barnum *Struggles* 490). *Oxford* 383.

4. "Money is power," even in family circles (53 Willis *Fun* 102; Jones *Batkins* 387). G. B. Means and M. D. Thacker *The Strange Death of President Harding* (1930) 80.

5. Money is the sinew of war (71 Jones *Batkins* 370). Apperson 422; *Oxford* 429; Stevenson 2451:4; Tilley M1067.

6. Money makes the mare go (21 Loomis *Farmer's Almanac* 177; Hammett *Wonderful* 38 Colonel Jenkins proved the truth of an old law by its converse: Mares make the money go, 247 money, that in former times but "made the mare go," is now the only true patent of nobility). Apperson 422; Farmer and Henley IV 280; NC 446; *Oxford* 430; Partridge 509; Smith *Browning* 221; Tilley M1077; L. W. Meynell *Mystery at Newton Ferry* (Philadelphia 1930) 245.

7. If his wife didn't want to wear rings or artificials, it was money in his pocket (74 Eggleston *Circuit* 91).

8. Something pretty costs money; do you think it grows on bushes? (52 Cary *Clovernook* 110, 2d Ser. 118 Yes, but money doesn't grow on bushes). Lean III 466 gooseberry bushes, IV 49 Mince-pies don't grow on trees; F. Marryat *Peter Simple* (1834), ed. London 1929) 324 clothes don't grow on trees in ould Ireland; William McFee *The Harbourmaster* (London 1932) 371 Can I make money? Does it grow on trees out there?; Upton Sinclair *Between Two Worlds* (1941) 317 Money Grows on Trees [chapter heading]. See Blackberry (3), Bush (1).

9. The man had three or four daughters who, as the phrase goes, "gave you a good deal for your money" [i. e., were entertaining]. (53 Willis *Fun* 298).

10. Be careful, and not lose any money, for it's a hard thing to slip into a pus [purse], and it's easy to slip out (53 Cary *Clovernook* 2d Series 21).

11. As we sometimes say in America, "you pays your money and you takes your choice" (69 Barnum *Struggles* 503). DA Money 1 b; *Oxford* 491; Stevenson 348:11; Herbert Asbury *The French Quarter* (1936) 158 as the Louisiana darkies say.

12. See Love, sb. (13).

Monkey, 1. I think we can sleep as comfortably as twin monkeys in a menagerie (57 Bennett *Border* 116).

2. I kept grinning in the feller's face, like a monkey over a hot chestnut (44 Stephens *High Life* I 29, 175 young fellers . . . stood a grinning at me like so many hungry monkeys).

3. The prospect of another year after the Alert should sail was rather "too much of the monkey" (40 Dana *Two* 236).

Monkey shines. After cutting 'curlicues' and 'monkey shines' [figures in ice skating] till I was pretty tired (47 Dorson *Jonathan* 104; Thomson *Doesticks* 125 The right [hand] cut up a few monkey shines in the treble). Bartlett 401; DA Monkey (4); Farmer and Henley IV 336; Green 243; McAtee 43; Stevenson 478:3.

Month. They didn't see such a beautiful face once in a month of Sundays (36 Haliburton *Clockmaker* I 73, III

230 it would take a month of Sundays, *Attaché* III 108 it's a month of sundays a'most since I've seed you; Hammett *Wonderful* 17 that very indefinite space of time, a month of Sundays). Farmer and Henley IV 346, VII 311; McAtee 43; NC 446; NED Month 3 f; Randolph and Wilson 213; Stevenson 2245:9; E. B. Black *The Ravenelle Riddle* (1933) 166. See Week.

Moon, 1. Credit . . . 'most ez harnsome 'z a moon (67 Lowell *Biglow* 307).

2. His . . . hat shining and bright as a May moon (56 Kelly *Humors* 279).

3. Make 'em believe the moon is made of green cheese (38 Haliburton *Clockmaker* II 176, *Nature* I 219; Briggs *Harry* I 102 However if you are fond of argument, I will argue with you about the moon being made of green cheese, because that is a subject on which there may be doubts; Cooper *Redskins* 207 but folks an't obliged to believe the moon is all cheese, unless they've a mind to; Cary *Clovernook* 2d Ser. 272; Shillaber *Mrs. Partington* 210 don't you believe any of the gammoning stories about its being a green cheese; Holmes *Professor* 198–199 if a man should assert that the moon was in truth a green cheese, formed by the coagulable substance of the Milky Way, and challenge me to prove the contrary, I might be puzzled). Apperson 425; Farmer and Henley IV 347; NED Cheese 2 a, Moon 1 e; *Oxford* 431; Stevenson 1622:1, Stoett 1200; Whiting *Drama* 354:716; NQ 6 x 146; Gelett Burgess *Two O'Clock Courage* (Indianapolis 1934) 146 he could pretty nearly make you believe you was

made o' green cheese; Nancy Barr Mavity *The Case of the Missing Sandals* (1930) 159 I'd have believed that the moon was made of green cheese if she'd said so; Robb White *Run Masked* (1938) 268 there are some fools . . . who think that the moon is made of green cheese.

4. I could have jumped over the moon (33 Smith *Downing* 18; Haliburton *Clockmaker* III 109 ready to jump over the moon for delight). Iona and Peter Opie *The Oxford Dictionary of Nursery Rhymes* (Oxford 1951) 203.

Moonbeams. Captain Brown, who became suddenly as mild as moonbeams (56 Durivage *Three* 396). Svartengren 66.

Moonlight, 1. A smile as pure as moonlight (55 Stephens *Homestead* 24).

2. Her hair was . . . silvery as moonlight (c58 Stephens *Mary Derwent* 233).

3. All was as still as moonlight (38 Haliburton *Clockmaker* II 133).

Moonlight flitting. He resolved to cancel them [debts] by a moonlight flitting (53 Hammett *Stray* 47; Durivage *Three* 38 you have made a moonlight flitting). NED Moonlight 6 b; *Oxford* 432; Stevenson 834:4. Cf. NED Moon 3 e; Farmer and Henley IV 349.

Moonshine, 1. [A hunter] movin' as light and quick as moonshine from behind a cloud (55 Anon. *New Hope* 81).

2. That's all moonshine (51 Burke *Polly* 68; Hammett *Piney* 287 Now that Atashy story's nothin' but moonshine; Locke [Nasby] *Struggles* 202 I wuz prepared to bleeve the chivelry uv the South wuz a good part bottled

moonshine). Farmer and Henley IV 350; Green 26, 243; NED Moonshine; Stevenson 1623:3, 7. Cf. Tilley M1128.

3. You mustn't stand in other people's moonshine (37 Neal *Charcoal* 190). See Light, sb. (4).

4. See Mouthful.

Moose wood. As soople as moose wood (43 Haliburton *Attaché* III 46).

Mops. About daylight he was mops and brooms [i. e., drunk]. (43 Haliburton *Attaché* II 11, *Nature* I 48). Farmer and Henley IV 352; NED Mop 1 b.

More, 1. The more, the merrier (25 Neal *Brother J* I 271, III 156; Kennedy *Swallow* 29; Dana *Two* 237 is the sailor's maxim; Clemens *Enterprise* 167). Apperson 428; NC 446; *Oxford* 433; Stevenson 1566:12; Tilley M1153; NQ 11 v 429; Jane Allen, pseud. *I Lost My Girlish Laughter* (1938) 239; F. P. Keyes *The River Road* (1945) 110 I suppose it isn't just the thing to say 'The more the merrier' when you're going to a graveyard.

2. People might think there was more in it than met the ear (38 Haliburton *Clockmaker* II 128, *Attaché* II 64; Hammett *Stray* 308 there might be more in it than at first met the eye). Edwin Greenwood *The Deadly Dowager* (1935) 25 ear; Anthony Wynne, pseud. *The Case of the Gold Coins* (Philadelphia 1934) 74 eye.

3. "The more you drive a man, the less he will do," was as true with us as with any other people (40 Dana *Two* 121–122).

Morn. Clear as the rosy morn (73 Clemens *Gilded* II 308).

Morning. 1. Beautiful as morning (53 Curtis *Potiphar* 112). Cf. NC 446; Svartengren 222 fair.

2. Lookin' as bright as a spring mornin' (57 Riley *Puddleford* 256). Svartengren 226 dawn.

3. The Abolitionists . . . ez calm ez a summer mornin (66 Locke [Nasby] *Struggles* 251).

4. A wife . . . charming as the morning (50 Mitchell *Reveries* 37). Cf. Svartengren 222.

5. And the children . . . looked as fresh and rosy as the morning (32 Hall *Legends* 173). Svartengren 226 fresh . . . dawn.

6. A maiden lady of fifty . . . as gay as a May morning (33 Hall *Soldier's Bride* 190).

7. She's . . . as soft as a dooey morning (66 Boucicault *Flying Scud* 159). Cf. Svartengren 226.

8. We sor [saw] the bit of stuff comin' an' comin' out as sure and clear as the ye'rly mornin' and then we kept it darker (66 Boucicault *Flying Scud* 162).

9. Now, if you want to catch me asmugglin', rise considerably airly in the mornin', will you? (38 Haliburton *Clockmaker* II 231, *Attaché* III 170 a man must rise airly in the mornin to catch him asleep, *Old Judge* II 144 a man must rise up early in the morning to catch him napping; Smith *Letters* 97 if Sir John Harvey got hold of any of them logs, he would have to get up airlier in the morning than ever he did yet). Apperson 532; Farmer and Henley II 351. See Early (1).

Moses. Gave them partikilar Moses (55 Haliburton *Nature* II 409). DA Moses 3. Cf. Israel.

Mosquito. He'd a skinned a musketoe any day, for the hide and taller (44

Stephens *High Life* I 135). Cf. Flea (8).

Moth, 1. Others will return to Paris, as moths to the light (53 Curtis *Potiphar* 230). Cf. Hardie 470:132; *Oxford* 212 Fly; Tilley F394; Irving Brown *Deep Song* (1929) 203 flame; A. E. Fielding, pseud. *The Tall House Mystery* (1933) 136 he flutters around any casino like the proverbial moth.

2. A painted woodpecker passed by . . . as silently as a moth (60 Whitehead *Wild Sports* 90).

Mother, 1. I'm as tender as a mother to you (55 Hammett *Wonderful* 78).

2. A single mother's son of 'em (33 Smith *Downing* 70; Melville *Omoo* 61, *Typee* 44, *White Jacket* 135, 459, *Moby-Dick* I 111, 275, *Confidence-Man* 68; Hawthorne *Twice-Told* 179; Haliburton *Nature* I 193; Richardson *Secret* 87, 233; Saxe *Poems* 195 A health to our Mother, from each mother's son). Apperson 190–191; NED Mother's son; *Oxford* 435; Stevenson 2162: 8; Tilley M1202.

3. Does your mother know you're out? (40 Haliburton *Clockmaker* III 35, *Letter* 60; Thompson *Chronicles* 31 That's right, doctor, take him off before he gets hurt, for maybe his ma don't know he's out; Melville *Redburn* 50 But he only laughed at me, and said something about my mother not being aware of my being out; Smith *'Way* 299 your mother don't know you're out; Hammett *Piney* 43 I rayther reckon your anxious mother don't know ye'r out; Saxe *Poems* 191 *Alma Mater* rejoices, and knows you are out, 328 And did his mother know that he was out?; Holmes *Poet* 323 the saucy question, "Does your mother know you're out?" was the very same that Horace addressed to the bore

who attacked him in the *Via Sacra*). Farmer and Henley IV 360; NED Mother 1 g; Stevenson 1627:2; NQ 8 viii 4–5, 35, 153, 293, 356, xii 134, 197; H. C. Bailey *The Red Castle Mystery* (1932) 73; Edwin Greenwood *The Deadly Dowager* (1935) 45 grandmother . . . as they say.

4. Your mother don't know you [i. e., in bad shape]. (60 Haliburton *Season-Ticket* 17; Richardson *Beyond* 176 That would be a keen-eyed mother who could recognize her own son at a glance under the dirt and disguise of plains-travel). John S. Strange, pseud. *For the Hangman* (1934) 246. Cf. Stevenson 2310:9.

5. Not a few "rode their mother's colt" [i. e., walked]. (49 Eliason 159). See Shank's mare.

Mother Cary's chicken. As busy as a Mother Carey's chicken in a storm (23–24 Irving *Tales* 385).

Mother-tongue. It's my mother-tongue (25 Neal *Brother J* I 179, 380, 383, II 126, 173, III 151; Richardson *Beyond* 195 Talking in their mother tongue; Clemens *Innocents* I 238, II 95, *Tramp* I 172). NED Mother tongue; Whiting *Drama* 355:719, *Scots* II 101.

Mother-wit. Well, mother-wit kin beat book-larnin' at *any* game (45 Hooper *Simon* 41). Green 245; Gladys Mitchell *Mystery of a Butcher's Shop* (1930) 231. See Ounce (1).

Motionless. See Flounder (2), Marble (3), Statue (2).

Motions. Cuss you! I was only going through the motions (43 Lewis *Odd* 88; Lowell *Biglow* 293 go thru all the motions). Cf. NED Motion 3 b.

Moulds. They [trousers] sat to my legs like the tin moles [moulds] to a pair of tallow candles in freezing time (44 Stephens *High Life* I 67).

Mountain, 1. And if the mountain will not come to Mahomet, Mahomet must go to the mountain (45 Cooper *Satanstoe* 266; Hammett *Wonderful* 272 if Mahomet, forbidden by constitutional scruples and a *mens conscia recti,* can't go to the mountain, let the mountain come to Mahomet; Sedley *Marian* 313, 315, 333). Apperson 390–391; *Oxford* 436; Stevenson 1502:1; Stoett 207; Tilley M1213; G. O. Larson *The Western Humanities Review* VI (1952) 251 (an allusion made by Brigham Young); P. B. Kyne *Tide of Empire* (1928) 381; Anthony Wynne, pseud. *The Cotswold Case* (Philadelphia 1933) 183; Taylor *Investigations* 262.

2. He makes mountains of molehills (45 Cooper *Satanstoe* 126; Haliburton *Season-Ticket* 39 and magnify mole-hills into mountains, 176 and converted "moles into mountains" [a play on facial moles]; Alcott *Little Women* 269). Apperson 430, cf. 514; NC 447; NED Molehill 2; *Oxford* 436; Stevenson 1630:3; Margery Allingham *Dancers in Mourning* (1937) 267.

Mount Washington. A friend . . . frozen as stiff as Mount Washington (59 Shillaber *Knitting-Work* 364).

Mourner, 1. The chief mourner does not always attend the funeral (32 Emerson *Journals* II 530).

2. Well, I wouldn't crowd the mourners (65 Sedley *Marian* 287). DA Crowd 4 (2).

3. See Bench (2).

Mourning. I've a good mind to put your other eye in mournin' for ye (66 Boucicault *Flying Scud* 198). Farmer and Henley IV 364; NED Mourning 4 d.

Mouse, 1. As melancholy as mice in an empty mill (44 Stephens *High Life* I 97).

2. We are as poor as mice (66 Boucicault *Flying Scud* 161). David Frome, pseud. *In at the Death* (1930) 2. See Church-mouse.

3. I was quiet all like von mouse (37 Fairfield *Letters* 172; Robb *Squatter* 145 You must ve vair quiet as von leetel rat, vat dey call de mouse). Apperson 519; Boshears 39:844; NC 447; NED Mouse 2 a; Taylor *Comparisons* 67; Milward Kennedy, pseud. *Corpse Guard Parade* (1930) 296.

4. Snug as a mouse (c60 Paul *Courtship* 88). Tilley M1221.

5. As still as mice (33 Smith *Downing* 40, 186 a mouse, *Letters* 100; Stephens *High Life* I 41, 226 in a flour-bin, 244 a mouse, *Homestead* 95 a mouse; Thompson *Major* 155; Haliburton *Sam* II 15 a mouse; Whitcher *Widow* 349; Alcott *Little Women* 48, 215 mouse; Saxe *Poems* 416 a mouse). Apperson 519; Green 31; McAtee 62; NC 447; NED Mouse 2 a; Stoett 1574; Svartengren 384–385; Tilley M1224; Jesse Lilienthal *Gambler's Wife* (Boston 1933) 95. Cf. Svartengren 387 silent; Whiting *Drama* 321: 228 mute.

6. You are valiant as a mouse (35 Kennedy *Horse-Shoe* 532).

7. All were whist as mice (54 Smith *'Way* 40, 173 'll be as whist about it as a mouse; Riley *Puddleford* 249).

8. Hands . . . crept under the hankercher, like two mice in a pan of meal (44 Stephens *High Life* II 198).

Mouse-trap. The Gineral says he likes things simple as a mouse-trap (34 Davis *Downing* 56).

Mouth, 1. A fool's mouth hath no drought (52 Cary *Clovernook* 238).

2. Rather down in the mouth (33 Smith *Downing* 102; Stephens *High Life* I 94, II 43, *Mary Derwent* 280 don't get so down in the mouth; Burke *Polly* 19; Stowe *Uncle* 438 he was all down in the mouth; Bennett *Border* 169 quite down; Hammett *Piney* 81 He looked mighty like the gin-cocktail the barkeeper mixed up for him, and that war *down in the mouth*, in three shakes of a dog's tail, by the watch; Taliaferro *Fisher's* 151 mighty low down; Boucicault *Flying Scud* 217 [sick]; Bowman *Bear-Hunters* 389; Clift *Bunker* 156 She . . . had lost her calf, and was very much down). Farmer and Henley IV 366–367; Green 32; NED Mouth 4 b; Stevenson 1635:5; Wilson 567.

3. But arterwards . . . I made a larger mouth (65 Sedley *Marian* 468).

4. To make up one's mouth to it. 43 DA Mouth sb. 1 b (1); NED Mouth 2 c.

5. It makes my mouth water now to think what a beautiful row we had (58 Porter *Major* 88). Hardie 472:200; NED Mouth 2 c; Stevenson 1634–1635:16.

6. To put a bad mouth on. 35 DA Bad 2 b (2).

7. And, putting on a poor mouth, told the folks I had a touch of the small-pox (35 Kennedy *Horse-Shoe* 27). Bradley PADS XIV (1950) 53; Stevenson 1635:10; Thornton II 689; Wilson 578.

8. There are always enough that have their mouths open when it rains such rich porridge (33 Smith *Down-*ing 125). Cf. Apperson 522 (quot. 1895) If it should rain. See Dish (2).

9. See Hand (18).

Mouthful. It is only a mouthful of moonshine (53 Haliburton *Sam* I 40). Apperson 432; *Oxford* 437.

Move. See Removes.

Moveless. See Vise (3).

Much, 1. Too much of one thing is good for nothing (56 Cary *Married* 319). Apperson 640–641; *Oxford* 665; Tilley T158.

2. They seem much of a muchness (40 Cooper *Pathfinder* 415). Apperson 432; Farmer and Henley IV 370; NED Muchness 3; *Oxford* 438; Stevenson 1637:5; E. R. Punshon *Mystery of Mr. Jessop* (1937) 106.

3. I rather guess I must a took a little too much at Welch's grocery (71 Eggleston *School-Master* 131).

Muck. In addition to this, it was "as thick as muck," and the ice was all about us (40 Dana *Two* 385). Fife 119. Cf. Svartengren 398 common.

Mud, 1. It is as clear as mud (36 Haliburton *Clockmaker* I 227, II 302, III 115, 217, *Attaché* I 254, *Old Judge* I 311, *Sam* I 205, *Nature* I 207; Robb *Squatter* 173 this clear-as-mud evidence; Hammett *Piney* 13, 79; Whitehead *Wild Sports* 79; Lowell *Biglow* 289 clearer 'n mud). Boshears 35:406; Farmer and Henley IV 374; McAtee 18; NC 447; NED Mud 3; Taylor *Comparisons* 26; Wallace Irwin *The Julius Caesar Murder Case* (1935) 264.

2. He's as deep in the mud as we are in the mire, and he can't sink us without drowning himself (55 Anon. *New Hope* 367). Apperson 141; Stevenson 1638:5.

3. He's rich as mud (45 Hooper *Simon* 43; Whitcher *Widow* 87, 158). A. O. Friel *Mountains of Mystery* (1924) 13. Cf. Apperson 433 muck; *Oxford* 438; Tilley M1297.

4. Rotten as mud (59 Taliaferro *Fisher's* 192, *Carolina Humor* 16). Cf. Boshears 39:870 dirt.

Muddy. See Hog (4).

Mud fence. As ugly as a mud fence in a thunder storm. 39 DA Mud fence; NC 448; Taylor *Comparisons* 48–49 homely; J. D. Carr *The Mad Hatter Mystery* (1933) 283.

Mud turtle. See Turtle.

Mule, 1. A mule to drive and a fool to hold back, are two of the contrariest things I know (35 Kennedy *Horse-Shoe* 73).

2. Facs are contrary 'z mules, an' ez hard in the mouth (67 Lowell *Biglow* 310). NC 448. Cf. Taylor *Comparisons* 79 stubborn.

3. As headstrong as mules (36 Haliburton *Clockmaker* I 135).

4. Joe was obstinate as a mule (53 Hammett *Stray* 21). NC 448; Henry Holt *The Midnight Mail* (1931) 288.

5. Es quick an' vigrus es a muel (67 Harris *Sut* 283).

6. But the countryman was stubborn as a mule (56 Kelly *Humors* 132). NC 448; Taylor *Comparisons* 79; Lee Thayer, pseud. *Hell-Gate Tides* (1933) 31.

7. The mate was ugly as a mule (51 Melville *Moby-Dick* I 311).

8. I will go and see which way the mule kicks (55 Haliburton *Nature* II 14). See Cat (47).

Mullins. Merchant vessels which are neither liners nor regular traders, among sailors come under the general head of *transient ships,* which implies that they are here to-day, and somewhere else to-morrow, like Mullins's dog (49 Melville *Redburn* 135). Cf. Tilley T368. See Here (1).

Mum, 1. Mum is the word (36 Haliburton *Clockmaker* I 106, II 228, III 81, 90, *Attaché* IV 186, *Old Judge* II 157 Take mum for your text and watchword in future; Robb *Squatter* 113; Boker *Bankrupt* 87; Jones *Country* 320; Kelly *Humors* 76, 250; Porter *Major* 128 it's all "mum," you know—nothin to be said; Clemens *Gilded* I 13, 76). Farmer and Henley IV 385; NED Mum B; *Oxford* 439; Smith *Browning* 224; Stevenson 1640: 7; Tilley M1310; Whiting *Drama* 355:720; W. C. MacDonald *Destination Danger* (Philadelphia 1955) 142; E. C. Vivian *The Barking Dog Murder Case* (1937) 199. Cf. Apperson 571 Silence is wisdom.

2. See Quaker (1).

Murder, 1. I was as wrathy as murder (34 Davis *Downing* 22).

2. In new countries, murders breed murders (72 Clemens *Roughing* II 61). Anthony Boucher, pseud. *The Case of the Seven of Calvary* (1937) 129 Murder breeds murder.

3. Murder is catching (49 Melville *Mardi* I 133).

4. But though murder may out (37 Neal *Charcoal* 54; Hammett *Stray* 82–83 The man, of course, could not get out, but, according to the old saw, the murder and the secret did; Cary *Clovernook* 2d Series 73 Murder will out; Riley *Puddleford* 249 Murder will out). Apperson 433–434; NC 449; NED Murder 1 b; *Oxford* 439; Snapp 83:41; Stevenson 1641:10; Stoett 1551; Tilley M1315; Yamamoto *Dick-*

ens 328; Leo Bruce *Case for Three Detectives* (1937) 112.

Murray. He moight spake as grammathical as Lindley Murray himself, and nobody would be the better of it (74 Eggleston *Circuit* 101).

Mush. As for him, he looked like a feller who, when it rains mush, has got no spoon (53 Haliburton *Sam* II 288). Apperson 522 porridge; *Oxford* 531 pottage; Stevenson 1492:1; Tilley P510. See Dish (2).

Mushroom. Target companies spring up with the rapidity of mushrooms in an old pasture (55 Thomson *Doesticks* 77). E. C. Vivian *City of Wonder* (1923) 150. Cf. Stevenson 1642: 13; NED Mushroom 2 a; Tilley M1319.

Music. [You can't] face the music you blue bellys (63 Wiley *Johnny* 314). DA Music 3; Farmer and Henley II 364; NED Music 11; *Oxford* 184; Stevenson 1644:2; Patricia Wentworth *Danger Calling* (Philadelphia 1931) 23.

Muskmelon. Larfed sort of easy and nat'ral, as if she'd fed on nothing but ripe muskmellons for a hull fortnight (44 Stephens *High Life* II 151).

Muslin. He scouts at it [grog] as *thinner than muslin* (50 Melville *White Jacket* 218).

Musquash. As sound as a musquash (60 Holmes *Professor* 83).

Muss. She will come if she thinks ther's any chance for kickin' up a muss (56 Whitcher *Widow* 311; Lowell *Biglow* 350; Locke [Nasby] *Struggles* 261). Thornton II 599.

Must. Well, if it must be so, it must (57 Jones *Country* 52; Porter *Major* 77 Well, thinks I, if I must, I must). *Oxford* 440; Stevenson 1645:16; Tilley M1331.

Mustard, 1. The Indians all the time pouring it on us, as hot as fresh mustard to a sore shin (34 Crockett *Life* 99). Tilley M1332; P. G. Wodehouse *The Code of the Woosters* (1938) 261.

2. A number of chaps down there as warm as mustard about going to war (33 Smith *Downing* 146). Cf. Svartengren 32 keen, sharp.

Mute. See Codfish (3), Grave (5).

Mutton, 1. As dead as mutton [of sheep]. (38 Haliburton *Clockmaker* II 184; Kelly *Humors* 225). Apperson 137; NED Mutton 7; Svartengren 142; Charles Barry, pseud. *Death of a First Mate* (1935) 54.

2. The time had come for him to walk into one on 'em, . . . and fix his mutton for him right [i. e., kill him]. (58 Porter *Major* 190). DA Fix 3 b (3).

3. "To return to our muttons" (56 Durivage *Three* 119). Farmer and Henley IV 395; NED Mutton 7; Stevenson 1647:1; C. F. Gregg *I Have Killed a Man* (1931) 213.

Myself. Though I say it myself, who, perhaps, should be silent (27 Cooper *Prairie* 135; Smith *Letters* 38 though I say it myself, 45; Riley *Puddleford* 249 although she said it, who had not orter say it [indirect discourse]). *Oxford* 652; Tilley S114.

Nail, 1. They've floored him as dead as a nail (56 Jones *Wild* 27). See Doornail.

2. [Horse's] teeth as long as ten-penny nails (58 Porter *Major* 19).

3. Brought up on ten-penny nails, pynted at both eends [i. e., sharp in a trade]. (33 Neal *Down-Easters* I 18).

4. Demand three hundred thousand dollars . . . right down on the nail (59 Smith *My Thirty* 432–433; Lowell *Biglow* 306 he draws his Pay down on the nail). Apperson 435; Farmer and Henley V 8–9; NED Nail 8; *Oxford* 441; Stevenson 1649:9; Tilley N18; NQ 1 ix 196, 384; 7 ix 362, x 31, 214; 8 xii 83; 11 vi 47, 212; Edgar Wallace *The Northing Tramp* (1929) 13. See Cash (2).

5. Every speech the opposition makes is a nail in their coffin (38 Fairfield *Letters* 224). Apperson 435; *Oxford* 441.

6. I should have no objection to drive a nail in his track [i. e., to foil him]. (56 Lincoln II 348).

7. Just so did Bill Kemp, to a nail [i. e., exactly the same]. (35 Longstreet *Georgia* 16).

8. For want of a nail the shoe is lost, as Poor Richard says (45 Judd *Margaret* I 263–264). Apperson 666; *Oxford* 691; Tilley W29; Stevenson 1649:5; Johannes Bolte and Georg Polívka *Anmerkungen zu den Kinder- und Hausmärchen* III (Leipzig 1918) 335–337.

9. Looked cross enough . . . to bite a board nail off (33 Smith *Downing* 193, 216 looking as if he could bite, *Letters* 20 I don't know but she would have bit a board nail off, if she'd only had one in her mouth, '*Way* 62 look gritty enough to; Stephens *High Life* I 46 I could bit a ten penny nail right in two without feeling it a morsel; but it was no use quarrelling, II 42 a looking as parpendicular as if he'd eat tenpenny nails for breakfast, and topped off with a young crowbar, 65 At first I was mad enough to bite a tenpenny nail in tu without chawing; Taliaferro *Fisher's* 179 He looked like he could a made a meal out'n a kag uv tenpenny nails, fur all the world). Boshears 30:36; Halpert 50; McAtee 41; Thornton I 81; Phoebe A. Taylor *Octagon House* (1937) 200 you look mad enough to chew nails. Cf. Taylor *Comparisons* 51; Tilley N19.

10. I see you know how to hit the right nail on the head (33 Hall *Soldier's Bride* 20; Haliburton *Clockmaker* II 215 You've struck the right nail on the head this time, III 66, *Attaché* IV 88–89 Why don't they put the nail in the right place and strike it right strait on the head?, *Season-Ticket* 14 the nail; Stephens *High Life* I 219, II 193 the nail [arrived on time], *Homestead* 288 You always hit the nail on the head when you strike; Judd *Richard* 178 the nail; Browning

Forty-Four 45; Stowe *Uncle* 71 the nail; Cooper *Chainbearer* 176 t'e nail; Taliaferro *Fisher's* 144; Holmes *Professor* 146; Clift *Bunker* 289 the nail). Apperson 435; Farmer and Henley III 286, V 9; NC 449; NED Nail 7 a; *Oxford* 296; Stevenson 1649:10; Tilley N16; Whiting *Drama* 349:625, *Scots* II 102; J. M. Walsh *The Company of Shadows* (1931) 253.

Nail-rod. Red as a nail-rod (59 Taliaferro *Fisher's* 53).

Naked. See Apple (2), Born (1), Hog (5).

Name, 1. As sure as my name is Peter P. (28 Neal *Rachel* 238; Briggs *Harry* I 260; Mayo *Kaloolah* 60–61; Jones *Winkles* 4 as sure as my name is Griselda Guisset; Whitcher *Widow* 307 as sure as my name's Miss Samson Savage, 354 as true as my name's Joshuway Magwire; Holmes *Elsie* 132; Nash *Century* 135). See N. M. Penzer *The Ocean of Story* II (London 1924) 31–33, for a suggestion connecting the idea underlying the phrase with the Hindu "Act of Truth."
2. If . . . , my name's not Sam Townsend (43 Hall *Purchase* I 261, II 233; Irving *Attorney* 112; Burke *Polly* 31 If . . . , then my name ain't Peter Wilkins; Stephens *Mary Derwent* 249).
3. There is no truth in the proverb, that if you get up your name, you may safely play the rogue (36 Emerson *Journals* IV 97). Cf. Apperson 436; *Oxford* 442; Tilley N28. See Wit (3).
4. If I'm to have the name, I'll have the game (36 Haliburton *Clockmaker* I p. ix). *Oxford* 442; Stevenson 1653:9.
5. And it's an old saying—'To change the name, and not the letter,

You marry for worse, and not for better' (52 Cary *Clovernook* 72). Apperson 91; Stevenson 1544:1; NQ 1 viii 150.
6. When it comes down as if raining was no name for it (37 Neal *Charcoal* 215).

Nap, 1. To bring one's nap up. 45 DA Nap, sb. 2.
2. To get one's nap up. 49 DA Nap, sb. 2.

Naples. "See Naples and then die" (58 Holmes *Autocrat* 126; Clemens *Innocents* II, 21, 22 See Naples and die, *Gilded* I 135 Her sisters had gone to the city to show some country visitors Independence Hall, Girard College, and Fairmount Waterworks and Park, four objects which Americans cannot die peacefully, even in Naples, without having seen). *Oxford* 570; Stevenson 1658:7.

Napping. But I did not "catch him napping," as the phrase is (57 Bennett *Border* 240). Apperson 436–437; Farmer and Henley V 14; Green 250; NED Nap vb. 1 b; *Oxford* 85; Stevenson 1658:10; Tilley N36–37; W. S. Sykes *The Harness of Death* (1932) 3.

Natural. See Barn-owl, Get out, King (2), Life (4, 5), Picture (3), Pig-tracks (1).

Nature, 1. The Gineral got as hornety as all nature at this (34 Davis *Downing* 126, 239 as tuff as; Stephens *High Life* I 99 as mad as, 259 as mad as, II 70 as easy as; Lowell *Biglow* 77 ez sharp ez all nater; Haliburton *Old Judge* II 7 as jealous as). Thornton I 9.
2. Why! as true as natur he's druv up street (56 Whitcher *Widow* 87, 205 As true as nater, there she comes).
3. He hangs to it like all natur (34

Davis *Downing* 297; Stephens *High Life* I 8 shook my hand like, 38, 58 a larfin like, 112 shiny red velvet, figured off like; Lowell *Biglow* 43 with 2 fellers a drummin and fifin arter him like). Bartlett 807; DA Nature 1 b; Thornton I 9.

4. A head as full of emptiness as that horror which nature is said to entertain of a vacuum would permit (53 Hammett *Stray* 25). *Oxford* 443; Stevenson 1660:7; Tilley N42.

5. Natur' is natur' (27 Cooper *Prairie* 206, *Pathfinder* 35, 326, *Chainbearer* 428 Human natur'; Haliburton *Clockmaker* I 195 wherever you find it, III 116 that's a fact, 182, *Sam* I 94 human natur, II 98 all the world over; Hooper *Simon* 86 nater will be nater, all the world over; Riley *Puddleford* 96 human nature is always the same; Stephens *Mary Derwent* 195 human nature). E. C. R. Lorac, pseud. *Death of an Author* (London 1935) Human nature's the same all the world over.

6. But nater must have its course (45 Judd *Margaret* I 263).

7. There is natur' in all things (53 Haliburton *Sam* I 304).

8. Nature makes no leaps (60 Holmes *Professor* 167).

9. That beats all nater! (25 Neal *Brother J* I 158, II 93, III 145, *Down-Easters* I 123; Davis *Downing* 15, 104, 134, 218; Haliburton *Clockmaker* II 217, 229, *Old Judge* II 56, 97, *Nature* I 80, *Season-Ticket* 15, 220, 277; Smith *Letters* 131; Riley *Puddleford* 73; Paul *Courtship* 36). DA Nature 1 c; Thornton I 9, III 4.

10. Wherever *natur' does least, man does most*, said the Clockmaker (38 Haliburton *Clockmaker* II 226).

11. We cannot change our natures (56 Durivage *Three* 328). Tilley N50; L. H. Butterfield *Daedalus, Proceed-* ings of the American Academy of Arts and Sciences LXXXVI (1955) 77 but certain things do not change, and, you will forgive the truism, human nature is one of them.

Naught. See Nothing (5).

Neat. See Penny (1), Pin (1, 2), Waxwork (1).

Nebuchadnezzar, 1. As big as Nibuchadneezer (59 Taliaferro *Fisher's* 176). Cf. nebuchadnezzar, a very large wine bottle.

2. As for me, tell him to go to grass and eat bog hay till he's as fat as Nebuchadnezzar (44 Stephens *High Life* I 55).

Necessity, 1. Necessity, the mother of invention (40 Dana *Two* 190, 356 the economy and invention which necessity teaches a sailor; Whitcher *Widow* 375; Porter *Major* 31; Joseph Reynolds *Peter Gott, the Cape Ann Fisherman* (Boston 1856) 202; Richardson *Beyond* 363 In all new countries scarcity of money is the mother of invention; Alcott *Little Women* 20; Clemens *Roughing* II 4 Necessity is the mother of "taking chances"). Apperson 439; Bartlett *Familiar Quotations* 171, 200; NC 449; NED Necessity 5; *Oxford* 445–446; Stevenson 1664–1665:8; Tilley N61; NQ CLXXXVII (1944) 167, CXCIII (1948) 43; Louis Paul *A Horse in Arizona* (1936) 242.

2. The game was small, but necessity is not very particular (34 Crockett *Life* 118; Richardson *Beyond* 80 But necessity knows no scruples, and the famishing never criticise).

3. Necessity has no laws (40 Haliburton *Letter* 104; Jones *Winkles* 257 Oh, necessity knows no law, they say, 355; Melville *Confidence-Man* 25–26

necessity knows no law, and heeds no risk; Lincoln V 396 knows; Boucicault *Flying Scud* 158 knows; Clemens *Innocents* II 278). Apperson 438; NC 449 Need; NED Necessity 5; *Oxford* 445 Need; Stevenson 1677:9; Tilley N76; Whiting *Drama* 233, 274, *Scots* II 102–103 necessity, 103 need; NQ CLXXXV (1943) 55; Jim Tully *Beggars of Life* (1926) 280 of proverbs, rolling hackneyed down the ages, the truest of all is that necessity knows no law.

Neck, 1. I reckon I am the beatin'est man to ax questions in this neck of timber (74 Eggleston *Circuit* 147). Bartlett 421; NED Neck 11 b; Thornton II 604–605, III 258; R. J. Casey *Hot Ice* (Indianapolis 1933) 86 woods.

2. It looks mighty like you'd been turned out doors, neck and heels (54 Langdon *Ida* 349; Eggleston *School-Master* 37 They'd fetch you out of doors, sonny, neck and heels, afor Christmas). Apperson 439; NED Neck 6 b; Tilley N65. Cf. Farmer and Henley V 24–25 neck and crop.

3. As we came up into the current again, "neck and neck" (58 Porter *Major* 127; Eggleston *Circuit* 14 It was neck-and-neck twixt this ere and that air). Farmer and Henley V 25; NED Neck 9; Stevenson 1669:5.

4. It was neck or nothing (34 Crockett *Life* 198; Baldwin *Flush* 307; Hammett *Stray* 39; Irving *Wolfert* 236 clattering along the road in neck-or-nothing style; Smith *My Thirty* 428; Alcott *Little Women* 374). Apperson 439; Farmer and Henley V 25; NED Neck 8; *Oxford* 446; Stevenson 1670:4; Tilley N66; George Goodchild *The Monster of Grammont* (1930) 217.

5. See Shot (1).

Ned. Go to work raisin' permiscoous Ned (48 Lowell *Biglow* 94; Shillaber *Knitting-Work* 323 and so you are going to get married to raise Ned, are you?; Smith *My Thirty* 286 he'll be likely to raise Ned and turn up Jack; Wiley *Billy* 187 raise Ned). Berrey 140:11, 280:7, 293:3; Brewster *Am. Speech* XIV (1939) 268; DA Ned 2; Randolph and Wilson 97; Whiting *Devil* 246:8.

Need. Need makes the old wife trot (21 Loomis *Farmer's Almanac* 177). Apperson 439; NED Need 11; *Oxford* 446; Stevenson 1671:5; Tilley N79; Whiting *Drama* 131, 137. Cf. NC 449; Whiting *Scots* II 103.

Needle (1). Pathfinder's eye and hand are as true as the needle (40 Cooper *Pathfinder* 437; Hammett *Wonderful* 260 True as the needle, to the pole [fishing pole] The Captain clings amain; Saxe *Poems* 158 As true unto ye needle as Ye needle to ye pole). Stevenson 1672:4; Svartengren 10, 372.

Needle (2), 1. [A tailor] was always as sharp as a needle (33 Hall *Soldier's Bride* 176; Haliburton *Attaché* IV 39 It makes him as sharp as a needle, *Nature* I 245, 361; Stephens *High Life* I 174, II 101 eyes . . . as sharp as a hull paper of cambrick needles; Cooper *Chainbearer* 332; Smith *'Way* 23 It is as sharp as a needle with two pints; Hammett *Piney* 177; Taliaferro *Fisher's* 56; Bowman *Bear-Hunters* 393; Nash *Century* 89 sharper'n a cambric needle). Apperson 561; NC 450; Stevenson 2084:8; Svartengren 32–33, 255; Tilley N95; Augustus Muir *The Silent Partner* (Indianapolis 1930) 191.

2. I might make out to pick up a

single needle on this deck, old as I am, but I much doubt if I could pick one out of a haystack (40 Cooper *Pathfinder* 244; Hall *Purchase* II 65; Smith *'Way* 265 You might as well look for a needle in a hay-mow; Cary *Clovernook* 2d Series 22; Stephens *Fashion* 50 very much like searching for a needle in a hay-mow; Melville *Israel* 109 Don't know. Needle in a haystack; Kelly *Humors* 347 It was finding the needle in the hay stack—the pebble in the brook; Thomson *Elephant Club* 166; Taliaferro *Fisher's* 83 I mout as well a sarched for a needle in a haystack). Boshears 37: 645; Farmer and Henley IV 232; *Modern Language Forum* XXIV (1939) 79–80; NC 450; NED Needle 1 c; Taylor *Comparisons* 58; Whiting *Drama* 355:725; Marcus Magill, pseud. *Murder in Full Flight* (Philadelphia 1933) 60. Cf. Apperson 440 bottle; *Oxford* 446; Stevenson 1671:9; Tilley N97.

Needs. Needs must when the devil drives (49 Melville *Redburn* 332; Haliburton *Sam* I 267). Apperson 440; *Oxford* 447; Stevenson 563:6; Tilley D278; Whiting *Devil* 209, *Drama* 135, 180; NQ 5 xii 48, 134–135; R. H. Barham *Ingoldsby Legends* (1842, ed. London 1903) 300 the Elderly Gentleman drives; R. S. Surtees *Mr. Sponge's Sporting Tour* (London [1853]) 141 a certain gentleman drives; Dion Boucicault *Robert Emmet* in *Forbidden Fruit* (Princeton N. J. 1940) 298; J. B. Cabell *The Line of Love* (1926) 49.

Negro, 1. They begin to think there is a "negro in the fence" (58 Lincoln II 445). DA Negro 6 c; Farmer and Henley V 40. See Nigger (11).

2. It [liquor] made me feel so good that I concluded it was like the negro's rabbit, "good any way" (34 Crockett *Life* 42).

3. See African, Nigger.

Neptune. I thought myself to be looking as salt as Neptune himself (40 Dana *Two* 1).

Nervous. See Leaf 1 (1), Witch (1).

Nest, 1. The mouth [of a cave] is . . . covered up as close as a bird's nest (55 Anon. *New Hope* 342).

2. I have it here, all done up in tow, as snug as a bird's nest (36 Haliburton *Clockmaker* I 303).

3. He has only kept . . . your father . . . in ignorance in order to feather his own nest—quite a common affair (55 Anon. *New Hope* 307; Boucicault *Flying Scud* 207 And while you feather your own nest). Apperson 207; Farmer and Henley II 379; *Oxford* 197; Stevenson 792:10; Tilley N125–126.

4. If one land spekilation in ten turns out well, and is rael jam, it makes a man's nest (40 Haliburton *Clockmaker* III 180).

Nettles. Uncle Billy's a settin' on nettles [i. e., anxious to talk]. (58 Hammett *Piney* 110). Stevenson 1677:10; Madeleine Johnston *Comets Have Long Tails* (1930) 45 like a man on nettles.

Nevada. He . . . determined to do in Nevada as Nevada did (69 Clemens *Innocents* I 296). See Rome (2).

New, 1. Aunt Sonora said he looked "enymost as good as new" (57 Riley *Puddleford* 138; Alcott *Little Women* 27).

2. See Fire (5).

Newburyport. Newbury port's a rocky place, and Salom's very sandy,

Charleston is a pretty town, But Boston is the dandy (40 Haliburton *Clockmaker* III 208). For similar local rhymes, see Whiting *Harvard Studies and Notes in Philology and Literature* XIV (1932) 302–303.

[New Mexico], 1. According to a local proverb, the region is so healthy that its aged inhabitants never die, but dry up and are blown away (67 Richardson *Beyond* 253).

2. In that marvelously healthful climate there was some foundation for the current proverb that Yankees never died except from revolver shots, hard drinking, or a personal vice still more repulsive (67 Richardson *Beyond* 262).

News, 1. Bad news is soon tole [told]. (80 Harris *Uncle Remus* 59).

2. Ill news flies fast, they say (51 Hawthorne *Twice-Told* 129; Locke [Nasby] *Struggles* 548 Bad news travels fast). Apperson 325; NC 451; NED News 2 c; *Oxford* 316; Stevenson 1683:3; Tilley N148; Yamamoto *Dickens* 330; Wallace Irwin *The Julius Caesar Murder Case* (1935) 290.

New Zealander. Face was as greasy as that of a New Zealander (59 Shillaber *Knitting-Work* 219).

New Year. New year don't come but once in a twelvemonth (56 Durivage *Three* 405; Wiley *Billy* 175 once a year). See Christmas (1).

Niagara. You might jist as well try to swim up Niagara as to go for to stem it (38 Haliburton *Clockmaker* II 152).

Nice. See Pin (3), Toast, Wax (1).

Nick. Afore you can say Nick Biddle (43 Haliburton *Attaché* I 269). See Jack (3).

Nigger, 1. No matter ef his soul's black as a nigger (45 Hooper *Simon* 90; Harris *Sut* 76 Her har's es black es . . . a nigger haulin charcoal when he's had no brekfus'). Boshears 34: 358; NC 450; Taylor *Comparisons* 18.

2. I'm as humble as a dead nigger (66 Smith *Arp* 88).

3. It'd be mean as a nigger and meaner too for me to say a word about that document (55 Stephens *Homestead* 410).

4. Des [just] es proud ez a nigger widder cook 'possum (80 Harris *Uncle Remus* 53).

5. Keep yourself quiet as a nigger stealing corn (57 Bennett *Border* 288).

6. I am as Sassy as a big house Niggar (62 Wiley *Johnny* 172).

7. His boots as shiney as the face of an up-country nigger (58 Porter *Major* 148). Cf. NC 450:5.

8. Sooty as a nigger's eye lashes (44 Stephens *High Life* II 216).

9. It warn't two minits afore my teeth was as white as a nigger's (44 Stephens *High Life* I 69).

10. You look as *naiteral,* as the nigger said—don't know yer name though (33 Neal *Down-Easters* I 59, 47 Asked him what he thought of the war—"take it altogether—inside an' out, as the nigger said").

11. A nigger in the woodpile. 52 DA Nigger 6 d. See Farmer 237; NC 450; *Oxford* 452; Stevenson 1673:7; Thornton II 608, III 261; Helen Pearce "Folk Sayings in a Pioneer Family of Western Oregon" *California Folklore Quarterly* V (1946) 237: 119 He smells a nigger in the woodpile (*or* in the woodshed, *or* in the fence). Cf. African, Negro (1).

12. I have endured more already than a dead nigger in a doctor's shop

could stand (40 Haliburton *Clockmak-er* III 202).

13. A gone nigger. 40 DA Gone 1 (10). See Coon (7).

14. Has got a memory like a red nigger (57 Bennett *Border* 110).

15. They beat my back wusser nur a nigger beatin' hominy in a mortar (59 Taliaferro *Fisher's* 122).

16. New cow-hide boots, greased and blackballed 'till they looked like a nigger's face in cotton scrapin' time (58 Hammett *Piney* 117).

17. Working in short, not like a "nigger," but a galley-slave (43 Hall *Purchase* I 278; Burke *Polly* 117 We worked like a cornfield nigger ov a Christmas week; Haliburton *Sam* I 254 he works like a nigger; Clemens *Tramp* I 20). Boshears 34:306; DA Nigger 6 b; Randolph and Wilson 185; Stevenson 2621–2622:13; Svartengren 124 Negro; Neil Bell, pseud. *Crocus* (1937) 283 working almost six times as hard as the proverbial nigger.

18. See Negro.

Night, 1. Mr Doubleday . . . is about as black as a starless night (35 Fairfield *Letters* 32; Melville *Omoo* 264 night; Cary *Clovernook* 2d Series 30, 233, *Married* 33 eyes and hair as black as the night; Anon. *New Hope* 105, 268; Durivage *Three* 358 The brow of Rodrigo grew black as night; Clemens *Innocents* I 240). Boshears 34:360; NC 451; Taylor *Comparisons* 18; Whiting *Scots* II 104; Shirley and Adele Seifert *Death Stops at the Old Stone Inn* (1938) 50.

2. I have had dark feelings towards him, dark as night (45 Judd *Margaret* II 135). NC 451; Taylor *Comparisons* 32; Whiting *Drama* 321:234.

3. Her shawl was as sable as night (68 Saxe *Poems* 26).

Nighthawk. He was down upon me like a night-hawk upon a June bug (36 Crockett *Exploits* 154). See Duck (11).

Nightingale. [She] sang like a nightingale (32 Hall *Legends* 181; Irving *Wolfert* 349 a wakeful nightingale).

Nimble. See Cat (16).

Nineholes. To get put in the nineholes. 63 DA Nine 2 b.

Ninepence. I'll bet a leather ninepence against a Bungtown copper (58 Hammett *Piney* 257). Bartlett 83. Cf. Copper, sb. (3).

Ninepins. The panther knocked 'em over like nine-pins (60 Whitehead *Wild Sports* 339; Shillaber *Ike* 144 as if they'd been ninepins). F. W. Crofts *Found Floating* (1937) 288 go down like a ninepin.

Nines. A praisin a man's farm to the nines (36 Haliburton *Clockmaker* I 124, II 15, 98, 289 very nines, III 33 very nines, 45 very nines, 235, *Old Judge* II 144 very nine, *Season-Ticket* 222; Stephens *High Life* II 86 dressed off to the nines). Bartlett 192; Farmer and Henley V 45–46; NED Nine B 6 b; NQ 8 xii 469; 9 i 57, 211, 338, x 387, 456, xi 34, 90; Anthony Gilbert, pseud. *The Body on the Beam* (1932) all done up to.

Niobe. Weeping like Niobes (67 Richardson *Beyond* 80). Chaucer *Troilus and Cressida* i 699; Stevenson 2290:3.

Nip, 1. Nip and chuck (58 Porter *Major* 123).

2. Nip and tuck (53 Hammett *Stray* 193, *Piney* 63 for a while it was nip and tuck—*titus and pop-corn*—you'd best believe it; Locke [Nasby] *Struggles* 241; Smith *Arp* 32). Bart-

lett 426; DA Nip and tuck; Farmer 391; Farmer and Henley V 49; Green 403; McAtee 45; NED Nip 6; Schele de Vere 620; Stevenson 1689:1; Thornton II 610, III 262; Arthur Train *The Adventures of Ephraim Tutt* (1930) 673.

3. He craves a more vigorous *nip at the cable* [i. e., a stronger drink]. (50 Melville *White Jacket* 218). Babcock 263.

Nit. Dead as a nit (58 Field *Pokerville* 67; *Harper's New Monthly Magazine* XXXIV [1867] 405). Apperson 137; McAtee PADS XV (1951) 53; NC 452; Svartengren 352; Irvin S. Cobb *Murder Day by Day* (Indianapolis 1933) 33.

No. Won't take no for an answer (53 Haliburton *Sam* I 119, *Season-Ticket* 94; Paul *Courtship* 206). Stevenson 2576:9; *Boston Herald* Feb. 1, 1955, p. 32; Richard Hull, pseud. *Murder Isn't Easy* (1936) 6.

Noah. [The Sawins family] is . . . older than Noah's flood (67 Lowell *Biglow* 285). Cf. Taylor *Comparisons* 60.

Noble. All play and no work will soon fetch a noble to ninepence, and make bread timber short (43 Haliburton *Attaché* IV 279). Apperson 447; NED Noble 2 b; *Oxford* 65; Stevenson 2459:5; Tilley N194; Whiting *Drama* 355:731.

Nod (1). A nod is as good as a wink to a blind horse (36 Haliburton *Clockmaker* I 85, II 147, 322, III 41, 65, *Attaché* III 96–97, *Old Judge* II 86, *Sam* I 40, *Nature* I 320, II 6 a wink is no better nor a nod to a blind horse, *Season-Ticket* 342; Jones *Batkins* 470). Apperson 44; Farmer and Hen-

ley V 58; NED Nod 1, Wink 2; *Oxford* 459; Stevenson 1692:3; NQ 4 viii 44; Pierce Egan *Life in London* (1821, ed. London 1869) 371; C. F. Gregg *Murder of Estelle Cantor* (1936) 143 a nod is as good as a wink and I am no blind horse. See Wink (6).

Nod (2). See Land (2).

Noddy. No more than to murder the noddy that laid the golden eggs (49 Melville *Mardi* II 64). See Goose (6).

Noiselessly. See Fish (2).

Noonday, 1. It was as clear to me as noonday (69 Barnum *Struggles* 117). Apperson 101 day; Svartengren 363; Lytton Strachey *Elizabeth and Essex* (1928) 84.

2. Old Andries is as honest as noonday (45 Cooper *Chainbearer* 70). See Day (9), Light (1).

North Carolina. When I did git my *Norf Caroliner* up, the way I pitched it into him was a caution to mules (58 Porter *Major* 45). See Irish (3).

Nose, 1. It's as plain as the nose on your fa— (35 Longstreet *Georgia* 148; Briggs *Harry* I 112 he proves as plain as the nose on his face, which as you see is plain enough; Mayo *Kaloolah* 22; Smith *My Thirty* 432 as plain as the nose on a man's face). Apperson 452; Boshears 39:798; NC 452; *Oxford* 503; Taylor *Comparisons* 62; Anthony Abbot, pseud. *About the Murder of Geraldine Foster* (1930) 94.

2. A biting-the-nose-off operation, to manifest contempt for the face (59 Shillaber *Knitting-Work* 204; Cary *Married* 298; Smith *My Thirty* 308 I can't see any use there would be in biting my own nose off for the sake of

opposing his election). Apperson 131; McAtee 21; *Oxford* 126; Stevenson 1696–1697:11; Stoett 1631; NQ 4 ix 157; 7 viii 487; R. S. Surtees *Mr. Sponge's Sporting Tour* (London [1853]) 26; Ben Ames Williams *Hostile Valley* (1934) 134.

3. To break one's nose. 64 DA Break 12 b (4).

4. It is my 'biz'ness' to follow my nose—a pretty long one at that, you see (59 Taliaferro *Fisher's* 259). Apperson 222; Farmer and Henley V 69; NED Nose 8 a; *Oxford* 213; Stevenson 1697:7; Tilley N230; E. B. Black *The Crime of the Chromium Bowl* (1934) 212–213 follow a hunch as the old woman followed her nose.

5. At all events, he had his nose to the grindstone, an operation which should make men keen (37 Neal *Charcoal* 63; Barnum *Struggles* 460 keeps the noses of many worthy families to the grindstone). Apperson 452; NC 452; *Oxford* 462; Schele de Vere 620; Stevenson 1694:7; Tilley N218; Albert Halper *The Foundry* (1934) 114.

6. An' ef I've one pecooler feetur, It is a nose that wunt be led (48 Lowell *Biglow* 109; Jones *Winkles* 158 I hope she will lead him by the nose). Apperson 355–356; NC 452; *Oxford* 356; Stevenson 1695:3; Tilley N233; Jonathan Leonard *Back to Stay* (1929) 94.

7. Massachusetts republicans should have looked beyond their noses (59 Lincoln III 391; Clemens *Gilded* I 80 sees no further than the end of his nose). NC 452; Tilley N220; Leslie T. White *Homicide* (1937) 72 so could you if you'd look past your nose.

8. To use a hyperbolical phrase of Shorty's, "It was hot enough to melt the nose h'off a brass monkey" (47 Melville *Omoo* 246). Cf. Farmer 86;

Taylor *Comparisons* 28 Cold enough to freeze.

9. Some other fellow might knock my nose out of joint again (34 Crockett *Life* 65; Lowell *Biglow* 147 but there I put his nose some out o' jint, 263 It ain't *our* nose thet gits put out o' jint; Haliburton *Sam* II 270 he had put Captain Hooft Hoogstraten's nose out of joint; Langdon *Ida* 1 So, miss, your nose is out of joint [a brother had been born]; Smith *My Thirty* 386). Apperson 452; Farmer and Henley V 69; Hardie 472:202; Laughlin PADS II (1944) 25; McAtee 46; NED Nose 9 b; *Oxford* 461; PADS III (1945) 11; Stevenson 1697:3; Tilley N219; NQ 8 i 9, 524; Miles Burton *The Clue of the Fourteen Keys* (1937) 94.

10. They wur etarnally pokin' up their noses at us boys of the Bottom (43 Robb *Squatter* 59; Stephens *High Life* I 4 John would a turned up his nose at a long nine [a cigar], 96 they begin to turn up their noses at a rale true born American, 140 it's an etarnal shame for these chaps to curl up their noses at honest men; Alcott *Little Women* 148 I forgot that English people rather turn up their noses at governesses; Eggleston *School-Master* 72 she was so dog-on stuck up that she turned up her nose one night at a apple-peelin' bekase I tuck a sheet off the bed to splice out the table-cloth). *Oxford* 677; Stevenson 1698:2; Stoett 1625; Tilley N232.

11. I warn't likely to let him stick his nose into my bisness (44 Stephens *High Life* I 2; Lowell *Biglow* 95 wen crazy sarpents Stick their nose into our bizness). NED Nose 8 b; Stevenson 1696:10; Stoett 1627; Tilley N238.

Not care. See Beetle-ring, Bobee, Butter-nut, Button (3), Cent (1), Copper

(1), Curse (2), Dried-apple, Durn (1), Fig (2), Hair (8), Hog (7), Hooter, Horse (31), Pin (7), Rush (1), Shucks (1), Snap (1, 2), Snuff (3), Stiver (1), Straw (1), Tinker, Toad (9).

Not give. See Button (4), Durn (2), Fig (3).

Not value. See Pin (9), Straw (3).

Not weigh. See Feather (9), Pin (8).

Not worth. See Button (9), Cent (2), Copper (3, 4), Curse (4), Durn (3), Fig (5), Fillip, Hill (6), Powder (2), Rush (3), Salt (5), Shakes (5), Shoestring, Shucks (3), Stiver (2), Straw (4), Towstring.

Notch. Everything was cooked to the notch precisely (36 Crockett *Exploits* 54; Stephens *High Life* I 195 They'll [trousers] fit you to a notch). NED Notch 1 b; Thornton II 921.

Nothing, 1. Jest as easy as nothin (51 Burke *Polly* 33).

2. As short as nothin' (43 Haliburton *Attaché* I 230).

3. "Blessed be nothing," and "The worse things are, the better they are" are proverbs which express the transcendentalism of common life (c40 Emerson *Works* II 315). Cf. Lean III 433–434.

4. Expect nothin, and you shall not be disappointed (55 Haliburton *Nature* II 274). *Oxford* 49–50; Stevenson 721–722:14.

5. Naught will produce naught; nothing, nothing (45 Cooper *Chainbearer* 94; Melville *Pierre* 382 From nothing proceeds nothing). Apperson 454–455; NC 452; *Oxford* 462; Stevenson 1699:2; Tilley N285; Whiting *Scots* II 105; NQ 4 ix 217, 305, 416, 520, x 109–110, 198; Henry Fielding

Tom Jones (1749) VII ch. 2 for matters are so constituted that "nothing out of nothing" is not a truer maxim in physics than in politics; Edith R. Curtis *Lady Sarah Lennox* (1946) 60 Nothing comes of nothing.

6. Thank you for nothin' (53 Haliburton *Sam* II 84, *Nature* I 254). *Oxford* 648; Tilley N277.

7. There's nothing like trying, in this world (33 Smith *Downing* 141).

8. He must dance upon nothing, with a rope round his neck (33 Smith *Downing* 174). *Oxford* 128; Stevenson 1069:3.

9. I'm sartin I shouldn't a known her no more than nothing [i. e., not at all]. (44 Stephens *High Life* I 15).

10. The way she now broke for Springfield "is nothing to nobody" (35 Longstreet *Georgia* 116, 153 the way them women love punch is nothing to nobody). Bartlett 430; DA Nothing 2; Schele de Vere 620.

11. Remembering that "nothing risked, nothing gained" (64 Lincoln VIII 181; Eggleston *School-Master* 222 reminding himself that "if you resk nothin' you'll never git nothin'). Bradley 96; L. W. Meynell *On the Night of the 18th* (1936) 20 risk nothing, win nothing. Cf. Stevenson 2418:1.

12. Nothing that is violent is permanent (34 Loomis *Farmer's Almanac* 178).

13. Nothing venture, nothing have (c39 Emerson *Works* II 109). Apperson 454; NC 452; *Oxford* 465; Stevenson 2418:1; Stoett 2503; Tilley N320; Whiting *Drama* 271; NQ 4 v 316, 430 Nothing venture, nothing win; Charles Reade *Hard Cash* (1863, ed. London 1913) 545; E. M. Rhodes *Beyond the Desert* (Boston 1934) 49 Nothing venture, nothing gain.

Nougat. Talk as sweet as nugey or molasses candy (37 Neal *Charcoal* 190).

Now. Now or never (24 Cooper *Pilot* 282; Neal *Brother J* I 421; Melville *Typee* 336 I saw that now or never was the moment; Hawthorne "John Inglefield's Thanksgiving" in *House* 589; Lincoln IV 142 with such *"Now or never"* is the maxim, 278, 361; Clemens *Roughing* I 48). NED Now 8; *Oxford* 465–466; Stevenson 1702: 6; Tilley N351; Manning Coles, *Now or Never* (1951); Marquis James *Andrew Jackson, Portrait of a President* (Indianapolis 1937) 73.

Nowhere. To be nowhere [i. e., to be at a loss]. 59 DA Nowhere.

Number, 1. "I'm afeard, doctor, I'll soon be losing the number of my mess!" (a sea phrase, for departing this life). (47 Melville *Omoo* 156–157). Babcock 262; Stevenson 1702: 12.
2. See One (5).

Nurse. Nurses should not have pins about them (51 Judd *Margaret* II 277). Cf. Baby (7), Folks (2).

Nut, 1. Gottfried is brown as a nut (45 Judd *Margaret* II 276). NC 452; Svartengren 253; Geraint Goodwin *The White Farm* (1937) 218.
2. His skin was . . . a clear nut-brown (45 Mayo *Kaloolah* 156; Melville *Redburn* 214 His nut-brown beard, *White Jacket* 13, 22, 59). NED Nut-brown; Whiting *Drama* 321:236; Catherine Whitcomb *In the Fine Summer Weather* (1938) 162.
3. A Man-of-War Full as a Nut [chapter title]. (50 Melville *White Jacket* 94).
4. Ain't it ez good ez nuts, when salt is sellin' by the ounce For its own weight in Treash'ry-bons (67 Lowell *Biglow* 292).
5. She'll beat herself holler workin' for 'em, that woman will—holler as a bad nut (65 Elizabeth Stuart Phelps *Harper's New Monthly Magazine* XXX 325). Cf. Svartengren 296 worm-eaten nut.
6. Her teeth were as sound as a nut (57 Riley *Puddleford* 29; Smith *My Thirty* 447; Eggleston *School-Master* 207, 263). Kay C. Strahan *Death Traps* (1930) 152. Cf. Apperson 590 acorn; Stevenson 2174:9.
7. Bread . . . as sweet as a nut (56 Cooke *Foresters* 386). Stevenson 2259:1; Svartengren 307.
8. This was nuts to us [i. e., a pleasure]. (40 Dana *Two* 270; Judd *Richard* 125; Kelly *Humors* 310; Hammett *Piney* 163 Now all this was not exactly nuts to the old General; Boucicault *Flying Scud* 203 that would be nuts to crack [i. e., very easy to accomplish]. Apperson 460; Bartlett 432; Farmer and Henley V 79; NC 452; NED Nut 5 a; *Oxford* 466; Stevenson 1703:13; Tilley N363.
9. He's a pretty hard nut for Johnny Reb to crack (65 Richardson *Secret* 245; Eggleston *Circuit* 36 I'm a hard nut). NC 452; NED Nut 4 b; Stevenson 1704:1.
10. When nuts grow ripe, hogs grow fat (40 Haliburton *Clockmaker* III 72).

Nutcake, 1. Taste on't . . . it's good as nutcakes (45 Judd *Margaret* I 33).
2. Marm'll scold at me like nutcakes (45 Judd *Margaret* II 181).

Nutmeg. Cute as nutmeg [i. e., alert]. (33 Neal *Down-Easters* I 18).

Nutshell, 1. I'd take the hide from her as close as a nutshell (c60 Paul *Courtship* 118).

2. Empty, sir, and hollow as a nut shell (43 Hall *Purchase* I 158).

3. He said the whole business was in a nutshell, and he'd crack it (34 Davis *Downing* 80; Sedley *Marian* 320 The matter lies in a nutshell; Daly *Man* 14 Here it is in a nutshell; Clemens *Roughing* II 5). Farmer and Henley V 80; NED Nutshell 4; Stevenson 1704:11, 12; J. J. Connington, pseud. *Tragedy at Ravensthorpe* (1928) 109 our whole business.

O

Oak, 1. Tall oaks from little acorns grow (71 Jones *Batkins* 42). Apperson 461; Bradley 87; *Oxford* 466; Stevenson 1035–1036:15; Tilley S211 Of little seeds grow great trees; Burton E. Stevenson *The Gloved Hand* (1920) 337.

2. When the oaks are in the grey, Then, Farmers, plant away (42 Emerson *Journals* VI 202). Apperson 461 (8).

Oar, 1. I am once more on my oars [i. e., bankrupt]. (56 Kelly *Humors* 88).

2. Lay on your oars awhile . . . and we shall see (50 Melville *White Jacket* 281; Clemens *Letters* I 34). Farmer and Henley V 83 rest; NED Oar 5 b; Stevenson 1706:4; Edwin Balmer and Philip Wylie *When Worlds Collide* (1933) 14 rest.

3. I tho't I'd put in my oar (33 Smith *Downing* 137; Haliburton *Old Judge* II 144, *Sam* I 49, 60–61, 228; Lowell *Biglow* 44; Hammett *Piney* 50 shoved, 137 clapped; Clemens *Gilded* II 217; Nash *Century* 70 He put in his oar for Squire Gray). Apperson 461; Farmer and Henley V 83; NED Oar 5 a; *Oxford* 525; Stevenson 1706: 3; Tilley O4; Kathleen M. Knight *Seven Were Veiled* (1937) 206. Cf. Whiting *Drama* 356:738. See Shovel (1).

Oath, 1. Says the Spanish proverb, "Oaths are words, and words are wind" (67 Richardson *Beyond* 140). Stevenson 1707:2.

2. I'd a took my Bible oath cum straight off the Green Mountains (44 Stephens *High Life* I 407).

Oats, 1. You know that, and feel your oats (43 Haliburton *Attaché* II 157; Melville *Piazza* 25 as a rash, restive horse is said to feel his oats; Kelly *Humors* 385; Barnum *Struggles* 33; Clemens *Love Letters* 198). DA Oat 3; Farmer 396; Farmer and Henley V 84; Stevenson 1708:1; J. D. Carr *The Eight of Swords* (1934) 172.

2. My freak, which he termed "sowing my wild oats" (23–24 Irving *Tales* 202; Fairfield *Letters* 394 Poor old fellow [a sick horse], I fear he has "eat most of his wild oats"; Melville *Moby-Dick* I 70 sow his wild oats; Curtis *Potiphar* 64 an exhilarating case of sowing wild oats; Smith *'Way* 271 no wild oats; Haliburton *Season-Ticket* 170; Alcott *Little Women* 461; Clemens *Love Letters* 74, 110). Apperson 686–687; Farmer and Henley V 83–84, VII 353; Green 258; NED Oat 4; *Oxford* 709; Stevenson 1708:2; Tilley O6; Whiting *Drama* 364:865; David Hume *Bring 'Em Back Dead* (1936) 108.

Obstinate. See Devil (3), Mule (4), Pine-stump (2).

Ocean. A plain as broad and level as the ocean (46 Hall *Wilderness* 6). Svartengren 286 wide.

Odds, 1. I axes rot-gut no odds now (67 Harris *Sut* 85). DA Odds (beg); Thornton II 620, III 266.

2. He had all the odds (58 Porter *Major* 50; Eggleston *School-Master* 83 In the minds of all the company the odds were in his favor). NED Odds 4.

3. It raly don't make much odds what they call a chap (44 Stephens *High Life* II 119; Hooper *Simon* 96; Jones *Winkles* 387). NED Odds 2 c; Stevenson 1712:9.

Often. See Sun (3).

Oil, 1. Smooth as ile [of a man]. (33 Neal *Down-Easters* I 62; Lowell *Biglow* 376). Apperson 582; *Oxford* 600; Stevenson 2147:12; Svartengren 64; Tilley O25; B. H. Kendrick *The Whistling Hangman* (1937) 157. Cf. Whiting *Drama* 322:238.

2. They mix about as easy as ile and water (53 Haliburton *Sam* I 249, *Season-Ticket* 40 you may talk of ile and water not mixing, 370 It's a matter of what they call incompatibility— a long word that means when two naturs don't assimilate or mix pleasantly, like ile and water; Cary *Married* 299 they're just like ile and water . . . ; they won't mix). NC 453; Snapp 74: 22; Alice Campbell *Desire to Kill* (1934) 18; Mike Roscoe *Riddle Me This* (1952) 139.

3. This was only pouring oil upon flame (69 Barnum *Struggles* 147). Apperson 463; NC 453; NED Oil 3 c; *Oxford* 469; Stevenson 1715:8; Tilley O30; Whiting *Drama* 356:739, *Scots* II 106; Herbert Adams *The Damned Spot* (London 1938) 34 troubled flames.

4. His reproving frown would cast oil upon the waves (37 Neal *Charcoal* 21; Jones *Batkins* 346 I wish to pour oil over the troubled waters of discus-

sion). Apperson 463; NC 453; NED Oil 3 e; *Oxford* 469; Stevenson 1715–1716:10; NQ 6 iii 69, 252, 298, iv 174, vi 97, 377, x 307, 351, xi 38, 72; 7 iii 285, 482, x 386; 9 xi 520, xii 389; 10 x 200; 12 ii 87, 159; Edward Rathbone *The Brass Knocker* (1934) 99.

Oily. See Goose-grease (1), Lightning (5), Serpent (2).

Old. See Hill (3), Methusaleh (2), Noah, Sin (6).

Old Clooty. He is often in drink, and sich times he gits the Old Clooty in him as big as a yearlin' heifer (53 Cary *Clovernook* 2d Series 19). NED Clootie.

Old Harry, 1. And then I . . . hollows agin like the very ole Harry! (43 Hall *Purchase* I 176).

2. The others all foller hilter-skilter, as if the old Harry had kicked them on eend (44 Stephens *High Life* I 138, 150 fellers running up and down, hither and yon, as if old Nick had kicked them on eend). Cf. NED Old 9 b; Partridge 584.

3. A violent tornado . . . played the Old Harry with things generally (c61 Chamberlain *Confession* 67). Farmer and Henley V 97–98; Partridge 584; Whiting *Devil* 246:9.

4. Dirty-nosed nephews . . . who are forever . . . raising the Old Harry (50 Mitchell *Reveries* 23; Wiley *Billy* 187). Berrey 140:11, cf. 235:5, 284:4, 293:3; Whiting *Devil* 246:9.

Old Hickory. See Hickory.

Old maid. See Maid.

Old Man of the Sea. I'm sure Aunt March is a regular Old Man of the Sea to me (68 Alcott *Little Women* 39). *Oxford* 471; Stevenson 2048:8.

Old Nick, 1. As proud as old Nick (56 Cary *Married* 231).

2. Old Nick knows . . . and he won't tell (65 Sedley *Marian* 234).

3. See Old Harry (2). For comment on Old Nick see NED Old 9 b; Partridge 584; Ernest Weekley *Words and Names* (New York [1933]) 71–72.

Old Scratch, 1. If I mistake not, . . . you are he commonly called Old Scratch (23–24 Irving *Tales* 396, 400 Old Scratch must have had a tough time of it; P. H. Myers *Thrilling Adventures of the Prisoner of the Border* [1860] 50 Well, let him go then to the old scratch). NED Scratch sb.².

2. He's full of the Old Scratch (76 Clemens *Tom* 3).

3. It kicked so like old Scratch (49 Haliburton *Old Judge* I 317). *Oxford* 473.

4. My—my old woman (hic) would raise—rai—raise old scratch if I (hic), I went home to-to-night (56 Kelly *Humors* 191). NED Scratch sb.²

Olive. Minim received the olive branch (37 Neal *Charcoal* 150; Richardson *Beyond* 130 I have accepted the olive branch). NED Olive-branch.

Omnibus. You are a set as would laugh if you saw an omnibus run over your mother-in-law (66 Boucicault *Flying Scud* 158).

One, 1. Clear ez one an' one makes two (46 Lowell *Biglow* 47).

2. An' now it'll be as aisy to Moirton when he hears about it, as twice one is two (74 Eggleston *Circuit* 268). NC 453.

3. One darsen't and tother is afraid to fight (55 Haliburton *Nature* II 103, *Season-Ticket* 46, 243). Herbert As-

bury *The Gangs of New York* (1928) 97.

4. And ain't a No. 1 article (49 Haliburton *Old Judge* II 99). See A. 1.

5. It's a maxim of mine always to look out arter number one (43 Haliburton *Attaché* I 189, *Old Judge* I 216 for; Robb *Squatter* 98 I never told you afore why I *re*-mained in the state of number one; Lincoln I 365 to take care of "number one"; Dorson *Jonathan* 92; Lowell *Biglow* 135 though, fer ez number one's consarned, I don't make no objection, 268 When all is done, it's number one Thet's nearest to J. B.; Burke *Polly* 30 that attentive consideration for "No. One," for which Mr. P. Wilkins, Sr., was noted; Clemens *Letters* I 24; Shillaber *Mrs. Partington* 290 there's a thousand old things of more consekence to look arter . . . the first of which is number one; Durivage *Three* 300 Looked out for number one; Hammett *Piney* 33 and when any one tried to run a cross-cut saw on him, I guess they'd best look pretty sharp for number one; Derby *Squibob* 233 he has entirely lost the power of looking out for No. 1; Sedley *Marian* 119 He always looked out for number one, he did, but he didn't go in for no chizzlin'; Nash *Century* 27 God blesses the man as looks out for number one; and that's me). Farmer and Henley V 75; *Oxford* 466; Stevenson 1718:1, 2058:4; Nell Martin *The Mosaic Earring* (1927) 272.

Onion, 1. Thar were dad's bald hed fur all the yearth like a peeled inyin (67 Harris *Sut* 26). Boshears 33:213, 34:323; Halpert 818, 868; NC 453.

2. Off we went like a peeled ingun (43 Lewis *Odd* 49).

3. Her eyes sticking out like peeled

onions (44 Stephens *High Life* I 225; Bennett *Border* 435 you kin gamble on it, Freshwater, that our eyes kim rolling out like peeled inyuns).

4. We pull like inions all on one string (40 Haliburton *Clockmaker* III 308).

Open. See Day (13).

Open Sesame. They have only to pronounce the "open sesame" to have their wishes gratified (37 Neal *Charcoal* 170; Willis *Life* 318 His name had been so long to him an "open sesame"). NED Open sesame; *Oxford* 478; Stevenson 2079:6.

Opossum, 1. Her hare is grayer dan a 'possum's (43 Lewis *Odd* 144). NC 453.
2. Happy as a 'possum up a 'simmon-tree (59 Taliaferro *Fisher's* 240).
3. Ignorant of its virtue, as a 'possum is of corn cake (58 Porter *Major* 145).
4. Grinnin like a baked possum (44 Thompson *Major* 70). Boshears 32: 189 an opossum; DA Possum 3 c (4); Halpert 119; McAtee 31; NC 453.
5. To come the possum over. 62 DA Possum 3 c (3).
6. I'll play 'possum with you in the mornin', and be ready to start with you as early as you please (40 Haliburton *Clockmaker* III 164, *Attaché* II 254, *Nature* I 5; Hall *Purchase* II 201 he's not sick no how—it's all possum; Thompson *Chronicles* 93 he had no faith in "acting 'possum"; Burke *Polly* 187 So don't try to play possum on this child; Hammett *Stray* 96, 275, *Piney* 174 the boy, who wasn't much hurt arter all, but was smart enough to play possum; Kelly *Humors* 303 lying down in his frail vessel; either asleep or "playing possum"; Anon.

New Hope 16 a more vig'rous buck I never kotched playing 'possum afore, 240; Sedley *Marian* 358 I b'lieve he's some skunk of a lord playin' possum on the upper ten!). Bartlett 474, 485; Farmer 426, 434; Green 284; Schele de Vere 49; Stevenson 1837:7; Thornton II 675–676, III 293; Tidwell PADS XIII (1950) 18; F. J. Anderson *Book of Murder* (1930) 10.

Opulent. See Thunder (7).

Oracle. You're as good as a horicle (66 Boucicault *Flying Scud* 203). Cf. *Oxford* 610; Stevenson 1727:1; Tilley O74.

Orange. As yaller as an orange (36 Haliburton *Clockmaker* I 73, *Attaché* IV 135). Svartengren 251.

Orders. The old rule runs, "Obey orders, if you break owners" (24 Cooper *Pilot* 68; Neal *Rachel* 248 must obey orders if we break owners; Dana *Two* 151 said he,—"break *hearts,*" he might have said; Melville *Redburn* 36 the motto is, "*Obey orders, though you break owners*"; Stephens *Fashion* 189 and I always obey orders though I break owners). Babcock 260; Joanna C. Colcord *Sea Language Comes Ashore* (1945) 136–137.

Oriole. Lucy was as gay as an oriole [i. e., merry]. (55 Jones *Winkles* 4).

Ossa. Ossa upon Pelion becomes a tame and meaningless comparison (67 Richardson *Beyond* 426). *Oxford* 479; Tilley O81; Leighton Barret *Though Young* (1938) 245.

Ounce, 1. One ounce of the genuine horse sense is worth a pound of your book learning any day (36 Crockett

Exploits 14; Thompson *Chronicles* 99 larnin' isn't sense). Cf. Apperson 475; NED Ounce 1; *Oxford* 479; Tilley O87. See Book-learning; Mother-wit.

2. An ounce o' prevention is worth a pound o' cure (38 Haliburton *Clockmaker* II 244, *Sam* I 306, *Season-Ticket* 247; Cary *Clovernook* 197 preventive; Richardson *Beyond* 131 The ounce of prevention is cheap, the pound of cure costly). Apperson 511; Bradley 89; NC 454; *Oxford* 517; Stevenson 1877:4; Tilley P569; NQ 6 viii 517, ix 76–77, 217, 296, 373–374; 7 ii 492; Paul Thorne *Spiderweb Clues* (Philadelphia 1928) 39 the old copybook maxim.

3. They say that "an ounce of experience is worth a pound of theory" (45 Cooper *Chainbearer* 402). Cf. Apperson 475; *Oxford* 479–480; Tilley O85–87.

4. The last ounce broke the camel's back (36 Emerson *Works* I 33). See Camel (2), Feather (6), Grain 1 (1).

Out doors, 1. Big as all out o' doors (25 Neal *Brother J* I 111; Haliburton *Clockmaker* II 20 all out-doors, 42, 157, 170, III 78, *Season-Ticket* 105; Stephens *High Life* II 187 all out doors; Lowell *Biglow* 140 all ou' doors). Boshears 34:342; Brewster *Am. Speech* XVI (1941) 21; DA Outdoors 2 b; Hardie 466:18; McAtee 5; Taylor *Comparisons* 16; Thornton I 10; Wilson 514; Ellery Queen, pseud. *The Devil to Pay* (1938) 174.

2. As easy [i. e., unconcerned] as all out doors (44 Stephens *High Life* II 237).

3. A letter . . . as long as all out doors (33 Smith *Downing* 64). DA Outdoors 2 b.

4. A woman . . . as tall as all out-doors (44 Stephens *High Life* II 60).

Outside. But a rough outside often holds a smooth inside (21 Cooper *Spy* 129).

Oven, 1. The bottom of the pit was still as dry and comfortable as an oven (43 Hall *Purchase* II 206).

2. A place as hot as an oven (40 Dana *Two* 283; Cary *Clovernook* 70 bake oven; Paul *Courtship* 63; Clemens *Innocents* I 284, *Gilded* II 4). NC 454; Svartengren 311.

3. The muzzle of his pistol is as large as the mouth of a Dutch oven (43 Thompson *Chronicles* 149).

Owl, 1. An owl couldent have cotch a rat afore I was in site of Jo's with my gall [girl]. (58 Porter *Major* 84).

2. As blind as an owl [i. e., drunk]. (56 Kelly *Humors* 82). Berrey 106:8. Cf. NC 454; Svartengren 171 (blindness).

3. Iargo got Casheo drunk as a biled owl on corn whiskey (62 Browne *Artemus* 70, 78, 96). Apperson 166; DA Owl; NC 454; NED Owl 1 d; Randolph and Wilson 175; Taylor *Comparisons* 36; Louis Paul *A Horse in Arizona* (1936) 31 boiled; J. Frank Dobie *Coronado's Children* (Dallas 1930) 28 a covey of boiled owls.

4. They are as ignorant as owls (40 Haliburton *Clockmaker* III 55).

5. A man . . . as solemn as an owl in a storm (44 Stephens *High Life* I 174; Clemens *Sandwich* 130 as solemn as an owl). DA Owl; NC 454; Wyndham Lewis *The Apes of God* (1932) 281.

6. Still as the flight of an owl (45 Judd *Margaret* II 151).

7. As stupid as owls (53 Haliburton *Sam* I 13, *Nature* II 306). Svartengren 51; John Rhode, pseud. *Shot at Dawn* (1935) 28.

8. Lookin' as wise as an owl (43

Haliburton *Attaché* IV 30; Boker *World* 46 in the day time; Holmes *Poet* 118 old owl). Boshears 41:1035; NC 454; Taylor *Comparisons* 89.

9. Thee looks like an owl in an ivy-bush! (56 Kelly *Humors* 93). Apperson 479; NED Ivy-bush, Owl 1 d; *Oxford* 482; Stevenson 1732:9; Tilley O96; NQ 9 vii 16, 116, ix 157.

10. Stare like an owl in a thunder shower (33 Smith *Downing* 125; Haliburton *Season-Ticket* 11 they *did* stare, in a way that was a caution to owls, 38 to stare as hard as an owl, 220 stare like owls).

11. See Barn owl, Woods (2).

Owl bait. See Bait (2).

Ox, 1. As lazy as an ox (33 Smith *Downing* 36).

2. "Strong as an ox, and ignorant as strong" (40 Dana *Two* 178; Stephens *Fashion* 107 strong). Halpert 681; McAtee 62; NC 454; Taylor *Comparisons* 79; Margery Allingham *Police at the Funeral* (1931) 235.

3. Heart like an ox (56 Durivage *Three* 297).

4. "Strong enough to knock down an ox, and hearty enough to eat him" (40 Dana *Two* 377). Cf. C. J. Daly *Murder Won't Wait* (1933) 104 I'm hungry enough to eat the proverbial ox.

5. I'm an off ox at bein' druv (48 Lowell *Biglow* 110). Cf. Bartlett 435; DA Off 1 b (3); Stevenson 1734:6; Thornton II 620.

6. To drive the wrong ox. 37 DA Ox 1 d.

7. I didn't know hit from Beltashazur's off ox (67 Harris *Sut* 79). Cf. Stevenson 1734:6 Adam's off ox.

8. Where they don't know no more about the hire of a nigger than an ox knows the man who will tan his hide (66 Smith *Arp* 169).

9. He must plough with such oxen as he has (32 Kennedy *Swallow* 216). Apperson 504; *Oxford* 508; Stevenson 1817:7; Tilley O112.

10. I believe the black ox did tread on my toe that time (43 Haliburton *Attaché* I 89). Apperson 52; *Oxford* 48; Stevenson 1733:11; Taylor *Investigations* 262; Tilley O103; Whiting *Drama* 335:407, *Scots* II 107; Wyndham Lewis *The Apes of God* (1932) 593.

11. But this was his own ox which had been gored (67 Richardson *Beyond* 65). Stevenson 291:3; NQ CLXIII (1932) 427. See Bull (12).

12. "Licker" was at them all, and he loved it as a thirsty ox does pondwater (59 Taliaferro *Fisher's* 31, 231 And come runnin' to the spring, like thirsty oxen arter water). Cf. NC 481 steer.

13. Begun to rave like a mad ox (33 Smith *Downing* 180).

14. Sweating like an ox (56 Kelly *Humors* 423).

Ox yoke. As bow-backed as an ox yoke (44 Stephens *High Life* I 46).

Oyster, 1. They are as close as oysters [i. e., silent]. (69 Boucicault *Presumptive* 247). Robin Forsyth *The Pleasure Cruise Mystery* (1934) 210. Cf. NC 454; Svartengren 178 dumb.

2. As dumb as an oyster (63 Clemens *Enterprise* 80). DAE Clam 3 quot. 1889, Oyster 2; NC 454; Gregory Dean *The Case of the Fifth Key* (1934) 237.

3. He didn't believe he had as many brains as an 'ister (57 Riley *Puddleford* 34). Cf. Hardie 467:37.

P

P. To mind his own p's and q's (33 Smith *Downing* 188; Eliason 71 I must be on my P's and Q's; Haliburton *Attaché* IV 94, *Sam* II 300; Kelly *Humors* 189; Anon. *New Hope* 221 I'll try to mind my p's and q's better here after; Hammett *Wonderful* 68 he also requests Mr. P. in the future to mind his eye, as well as his P's and Q's). Apperson 481; Barrère and Leland II 55; Farmer and Henley V 121; Lean III 320–321; NED P (3); *Oxford* 484; Stevenson 1736:8; Taylor *Investigations* 262; Tilley P1; S. H. Adams *The Gorgeous Hussy* (Boston 1934) 486; T. H. White *The Sword in the Stone* (1939) 113.

Pace. Lob . . . soon discovered the truth of the well-known sporting maxim, that "It is the pace that kills (55 Hammett *Wonderful* 98). Lean IV 20; *Oxford* 484; Stevenson 1736–1737:9.

Paddy, 1. Well, the three cheers come as quick and as true as Paddy's echo [i. e., not as called for or expected]. (59 Smith *My Thirty* 313).

2. They do not tell how many [oil] wells yield lots at first, and, after a while, "kind o' gin out," like the Paddy's calf (68 Clift *Bunker* 266).

Pains. Great pains, small gains (51 Melville *Moby-Dick* II 190). Cf. Apperson 271 Great pain; *Oxford* 264; Stevenson 928:9; Tilley P16, 20.

Paint, sb., 1. You're . . . as pooty as paint (66 Boucicault *Flying Scud* 213). Apperson 511; Stevenson 1777: 2; A. E. Fielding, pseud. *The Wedding-Chest Mystery* (1932) 91.

2. Believing . . . that they were "putting too much paint in the brush" [i. e., exaggerating]. (59 Taliaferro *Fisher's* 43).

Paint, vb. 1. Sometimes we are granted a pass to visit the Citty [Richmond]. If not we run the Blockade, visit the Theaters maybe get on a big Whope [whoopee?] & Paint the thing red (64–65 Wiley *Johnny* 66). DA Paint; NED Paint vb.[1] 9; Partridge 691 red; Taylor *Index* 52; Molly Thynne *Murder in the Dentist Chair* (1932) 230. The examples, all later, specify "town."

2. See Doll.

Pair, 1. I can show as clean a pair of heels as any man (35 Kennedy *Horse-Shoe* 420; Joseph Reynolds *Peter Gott, The Cape Ann Fisherman* [Boston 1856] 134 But the Yanke [ship] showed a clean pair of heels). Apperson 568; NED Clean 3 d, Fair 8 d; *Oxford* 586; Stevenson 1122:8; Tilley P31; Gladys E. Locke *The Golden Lotus* (1927) 80.

2. As if he wouldn't touch some folks with a pair of tongs (38 Haliburton *Clockmaker* II 101, *Letter* 163, *Attaché* III 55, *Nature* II 339; Richardson *Secret* 300). Apperson 642;

Oxford 666; Stevenson 2354:7; Tilley P32; Thorne Smith *Turnabout* (1933) 256.

Pale, 1. To feel pale [i. e., sick]. 77 DA Feel 5.

2. See Ashes (2), Chalk (2), Clam (6), Death (9), Ghost (1), Girl (2), Lily (1), Marble (4), Potatocake, Rabbit (3), Sheet (1), Statue (3).

Pall. The shadow . . . lay black as a pall (72 Clemens *Roughing* II 229).

Pallid. See Death (10).

Palm. Except where money could carry the palm (54 Smith *'Way* 350). Stevenson 1741–1742:14 bear, gain; NED Palm 3.

Pan. So I jest shet pan [i. e., kept silent]. (58 Hammett *Piney* 67, 263; Sedley *Marian* 224 seems to me that if I had that [sum] I'd jest shet pan and slope for hum). Thornton II 795.

Pancake. He was squeezed as flat as a pancake (36 Haliburton *Clockmaker* I 37, III 25, *Attaché* II 122, *Old Judge* I 305, *Nature* I 112; Neal *Charcoal* 221; Hall *Purchase* I 158; Whitcher *Widow* 308 he's as green as grass and as flat as a pancake [of a preacher]). Apperson 218; Boshears 31:102, 36:563; Fife 118; McAtee 26; NC 454; NED Pancake 1; *Oxford* 209; Taylor *Comparisons* 41; George Dyer *The Catalyst Club* (1936) 60 proverbial. See Hoecake.

Pansy. Girlish fancies as innocent and fresh as the pansies in her belt (68 Alcott *Little Women* 132).

Pantaloons. Perhaps you do wear the pantaloons, said her husband, laughing (54 Langdon *Ida* 117). See Breeches.

Panther, 1. He was as active and as full of energy as a panther (53 Baldwin *Flush* 313).

2. Jerry was as brave as a panther with cubs (43 Lewis *Odd* 182).

3. Eight large dogs and as fierce as painters (34 Crockett *Life* 175; Haliburton *Attaché* II 173 as fierce as a painter).

4. Her step was as light as a panther's (43 Robb *Squatter* 133).

5. We didn't make quite as much noise as a panter and a pack of hounds (45 Hooper *Simon* 36; Porter *Major* 85 don't holler so! says the old 'oman, why you are worse nor a painter).

6. To grin like a panther. 49 DA Painter 2.

7. To run like a panther (painter). 45 DA Painter 2.

8. I screamed out like a young painter (34 Crockett *Life* 19; Taliaferro *Fisher's* 161 Screaming worse than a panther). Taylor *Comparisons* 61 wounded panther; Phoebe A. Taylor *The Mystery of the Cape Cod Players* (1933) 146 her screams would have put the proverbial panther to shame.

9. A-squallin' wusser nur a painter (59 Taliaferro *Fisher's* 163).

10. Sum ove the wimmen fotch a painter yell (67 Harris *Sut* 54).

Paper, 1. Your face is as white as paper (73 Clemens *Gilded* II 65). Christopher Bush *Dead Man Twice* (1930) 55.

2. Well, I wouldn't crowd the mourners no further than to say, it [marrying beneath herself] would be tight papers (65 Sedley *Marian* 287).

3. To play the papers [i. e., to gamble]. 59 DA Paper 2 b.

Par. And then all hands fired up, tell afore midnight they war all rayther above par [i. e., tipsy]. (58 Hammett *Piney* 81).

Part. See Business (3).

Partridge, 1. A girl . . . as plump as a partridge (44 Stephens *High Life* I 218; Haliburton *Old Judge* II 104, *Sam* I 296). Apperson 504; NC 455; Stevenson 766:9; Taylor *Comparisons* 63; Tilley P84.

2. She is as poor as a hen partridge that's hatchin' eggs (53 Haliburton *Sam* I 140).

3. You have kept as shy as young partridges (45 Judd *Margaret* II 181).

4. If my heart hasn't beat like a partridge on a dry log, sometimes, when I've catched her a looking at me (44 Stephens *High Life* I 47).

5. If you or Shelby wants to chase us, look where the partridge was last year (51 Stowe *Uncle* 77).

Pass. The town was coming to a pretty pass, indeed, that . . . (43 Thompson *Chronicles* 77; Locke [Nasby] *Struggles* 283 Captain McSlather thought things hed cum to a sweet old pass, when . . . ; Alcott *Little Women* 372 sad pass).

Passenger, 1. We sat down in the stern sheets, "as big as pay-passengers" (40 Dana *Two* 139).

2. Leaned over the rail, "as sick as a lady passenger" (40 Dana *Two* 448).

3. You has waked up de wrong passenger dis present time (55 Haliburton *Nature* II 300). Bartlett 736; Farmer 411; Schele de Vere 623.

Pat, 1. Andy and me will teach them . . . Pat's point of war—we will *surround* the ragamuffins (35 Kennedy *Horse-Shoe* 247; Smith *My Thirty* 339 unless we can get up a party that will

surround the whole of 'em, as the Irish corporal surrounded the half a dozen prisoners).

2. One glance satisfied me that there was no time to be lost, as Pat thought when falling from a church steeple, and exclaimed, "This would be mighty pleasant, now, if it would only last" (36 Crockett *Exploits* 153). Cf. Benjamin D'Israeli *Curiosities of Literature* (4 vols., 1862) III 463 As the fellow, that, drinking of St. Giles's bowl, as he went to Tyburn, said, That was good drink if a man might tarry by it. "St. Giles's bowl" was a drink given to a condemned man on his way to be hanged; see D. F. Bond "English Legal Proverbs" PMLA LI (1936) 929.

Patch. Until I had put everything in order,—"patch upon patch, like a sand-barge's mainsail" (40 Dana *Two* 202). Cf. Apperson 484–485 Patch by patch is yeomanly; but patch upon patch is beggerly; *Oxford* 488; Stevenson 1752:9; Tilley P94.

Patching, 1. Them crack oxen over at Clifty-ah ha'n't a patchin' to mine-ah (71 Eggleston *School-Master* 139; Nash *Century* 154 We ain't a patchin' to 'em). DA Patching 3; Green 268; Laughlin PADS II (1944) 25; McAtee 48. Cf. Farmer and Henley V 145 not a patch upon; NED Patch 10.

2. To smell the patching [i. e., to be threatened by danger]. 34 DA Patching 2.

Patience, 1. Patience is the greatest of virtues in a woodsman (40 Cooper *Pathfinder* 113). Apperson 485–486; Lean IV 80; *Oxford* 489; Stevenson 1754:2; Tilley P109; Whiting *Scots* II 108; C. J. Dutton *The Shadow on the*

Glass (1923) 227 a rare and great virtue.

2. Oh, how I long to see you all. But patience and red baize, you know, is the old proverb (46 Fairfield *Letters* 383). *Oxford* 489 Patience and flannel for the gout.

Paver. The other must have been a Samson then. "Strong as a pavior," is the proverb (57 Melville *Confidence-Man* 125).

Paw. He saw I was not to be made a cat's paw of (38 Fairfield *Letters* 186). NED Cat's paw 2; *Oxford* 84, cf. 90; Belden Duff *The Central Park Murder* (1929) 249. See Chestnut (3).

Pay, 1. Pay as you go up (51 Burke *Polly* 76; Clift *Bunker* 81 "Pay as you go" is the true principle for everything that isn't necessary, 274; Barnum *Struggles* 474 John Randolph, the eccentric Virginian, once exclaimed in Congress, "Mr. Speaker, I have discovered the philosopher's stone: pay as you go"). DA Pay 2; Stevenson 1761:7.

2. "He is well paid who is well satisfied" (67 Richardson *Beyond* 324). *Oxford* 485; J. B. Cabell *Jurgen* (1919, ed. 1922) 84.

Pea, 1. As brisk as a parched pea (36 Haliburton *Clockmaker* I 243). Cf. Taylor *Comparisons* 61.

2. Hair of a light pea-green tint (45 Mayo *Kaloolah* 494; Thomson *Plu-ri-bus-tah* 88 pea-green Mermaid).

3. The whiskers and the cap is as like as two peas (23 Cooper *Pioneers* 111, *Chainbearer* 63 as much alike as one pea is to another; Smith *Downing* 79 as much like it as two peas in a

pod, 88 as much alike as tu peas in a pod; Haliburton *Clockmaker* II 167, *Attaché* I 123, *Old Judge* I 160, *Sam* I 226, II 237, *Nature* I 348; Stephens *High Life* II 253 as much like . . . as two peas in a pod; Judd *Margaret* II 233; Hammett *Stray* 194 as much alike as peas from the same pod; Taliaferro *Carolina Humor* 83 Much alike as two black-eye peas; Sedley *Marian* 406, 442; Boucicault *Flying Scud* 211; Nash *Century* 28). Apperson 366; McAtee 40; NC 455; NED Pea 1 c; *Oxford* 680; Taylor *Comparisons* 54; Tilley P136; Anthony Berkeley, pseud. *The Piccadilly Murder* (1930) 17 two peas; Keith Preston *Pot Shots from Pegasus* (1929) 184 two peas in a pod.

4. To hop about as mad as a parched pea (40 Haliburton *Clockmaker* III 84, 286 hopped with rage like a ravin' distracted parched pea). Cf. Taylor *Comparisons* 61; Stevenson 1796:8.

5. As snug as a pea in its pod (42 Irving *Attorney* 130).

6. You are welcome, dear, welcome as green peas in June, or radishes in March (54 Stephens *Fashion* 132).

7. I nuver gins a thing up as long as there's a pea in the gourd (59 Taliaferro *Fisher's* 116).

8. And eout I beounced like a pea in a hot skillet (56 Kelly *Humors* 145; Porter *Major* 18 Popcorn jumped about like a pea on a griddle). Cf. DA Pea 3 d (like a parched pea on a shovel); *Oxford* 486; Mary N. Murfree (Charles Egbert Craddock, pseud.) *The Story of Keedon Bluffs* (Boston 1888) 85 a young child . . . ez could no mo' stan' still 'n a pea on a hot shovel.

Peaceable. See Lamb (9).

Peach, 1. Her cheeks bright as a ripe peach (55 Stephens *Homestead* 81).

2. As fair as a peach (40 Haliburton *Clockmaker* III 284). Cf. NC 455; Taylor *Comparisons* 64.

3. And to all but Indians juicy as a peach [i. e., friendly]. (57 Melville *Confidence-Man* 188).

4. And her chin is as round as a peach (50 Mitchell *Reveries* 109).

Peacock, 1. As conceited as peacocks (36 Haliburton *Clockmaker* I 135).

2. Struts about the room as proud as a peacock (43 Haliburton *Attaché* IV 178; Stephens *High Life* I 96, *Homestead* 319; Shillaber *Knitting-Work* 77). Apperson 514; Boshears 39:819; NC 455; *Oxford* 521; Taylor *Comparisons* 64–65; Tilley P157; Whiting *Drama* 322:245, *Scots* II 109. Cf. Randolph and Wilson 177.

3. He is as vain of his qualities as a peacock of his tail or a nightingale of his voice (35 Fairfield *Letters* 47; Boucicault *Flying Scud* 213; Clemens *Sandwich* 110 as vain as a peacock). NC 455; Svartengren 85; David Frome, pseud. *Mr. Pinkerton Has the Clue* (1936) 146.

4. Our friend collapsed into his original dimensions, in the folding of a peacock's tail (58 Porter *Major* 109).

Peanut. To sing peanuts to. 66 DA Peanut 1 c.

Pea-pod. Prim as a pea-pod (56 Whitcher *Widow* 258).

Pear. Pears and peaches aint often found on the same tree, I tell you (43 Haliburton *Attaché* IV 63–64). Cf. Stevenson 1228:10 To ask pears of the elm-tree.

Pearl, 1. Her "pearl-round" ear (50 Willis *Life* 259).

2. It would be "casting pearls before swine," and the good book said they mustn't do so (33 Smith *Downing* 116; Dana *Two* 175; Curtis *Potiphar* 186 To offer you a bouquet, madame, would be to throw pearls before swine). Matt. 7:6; Apperson 488; NC 455–456; NED Pearl 3 b; *Oxford* 493; Tilley P165; Whiting *Drama* 357:760, *Scots* II 109; P. G. Wodehouse *Sam in the Suburbs* (1925) 96 the proverb.

Pea-time. It war the last of pea-time with me sure, if I didn't rise fore the bar [bear] did (43 Lewis *Odd* 174; Sedley *Marian* 285 Why, he'll want ye to wait till ye look like the last of pea-time, and no one else'll have ye; Lowell *Biglow* 222 Ther's ollers chaps a-hangin' roun' thet can't see pea-time's past). Bartlett 345, 455; DA Last 2 a, Pea time 2; Farmer 413; Farmer and Henley V 155; NC 455; Schele de Vere 623; Stevenson 1769:1; Thornton II 651, III 282; Mary N. Murfree (Charles Egbert Craddock, pseud.) *The Despot of Broomsedge Cove* (Boston 1889) 174 Ye look like the las' o' pea-time.

Pebble. It was like finding the needle in the haystack—*the* pebble in the brook (56 Kelly *Humors* 347). Cf. G. K. Chesterton *The Innocence of Father Brown* (1911) 287 "Where does a wise man hide a pebble?" . . . "On the beach." "Where does a wise man hide a leaf?" . . . "In the forest"; R. Philmore *Short List* (London 1938) 246 You've heard the Chesterton tag—where do you hide a pebble? If you want to hide a corpse, arrange a battle.

Peccavi. In a few moments he usually . . . made him cry peccavi (43 Hall *Purchase* II 158). See Cavy.

Peck, 1. In a peck of trouble (33 Smith *Downing* 67; Thompson *Major* 106; Haliburton *Old Judge* II 110 troubles; Thomson *Doesticks* 224 troubles). Apperson 488; *Oxford* 493; Stevenson 2377:3; Tilley P172; C. B. Clason *The Death Angel* (1936) 155.

2. We must eat a peck of dirt before we die (45 Judd *Margaret* I 316). Apperson 178; NC 456; *Oxford* 165; Stevenson 581:5; Tilley M135.

Peckish. See Shark (2).

Peep, 1. As drunk as a peep. 55 DA Peep 2.

2. As tight as a peep. 64 DA Peep 2.

Peg, sb., 1. You must git a peg higher yit (44 Stephens *High Life* I 125, 137 ashamed of his acquaintance because he's got a peg above them in the way of money; Lowell *Biglow* 138 I could ha' pinted to a man thet wuz, I guess, a peg Higher than him, 288 rise a peg; Hammett *Piney* 170 Then come the string pieces—a peg above the sleepers [railroad ties]). Farmer and Henley V 161 hoist.

2. He is a peg too low now (40 Haliburton *Clockmaker* III 261). Cf. Tilley P181.

3. I'll take him down a peg (44 Thompson *Major* 192). Apperson 618; Farmer and Henley V 161; McAtee *Additional* 13; NC 456; NED Peg 3; *Oxford* 640; Schele de Vere 623; Stevenson 1770:5; Tilley P181; Woodard PADS VI (1946) 41.

4. Both they and the New Orleans volunteers refused to move a peg under any other commander than Gaines (58 Hammett *Piney* 183). NED Peg 4; Stevenson 1770:4.

Peg, vb. I shel pay wen one of my rich uncles pegs out (63 Locke [Nasby] *Struggles* 93, 164, 165; Harris *Sut* 86). Farmer and Henley V 162–163; NED Peg 13 f.

Pen-and-ink. She hit him a crack or two agin, that made him sing out pen-and-ink in real earnest (49 Haliburton *Old Judge* II 32, 109).

Pence. Take care of the pence, and the pounds will take care of themselves (20 Loomis *Farmer's Almanac* 177; Haliburton *Sam* I 63 There is an old sayin'). Apperson 490; NC 456; *Oxford* 640; Stevenson 1772:4; R. S. Surtees *Plain or Ringlets?* (London [1860]) 400–401; W. W. Jacobs *Snug Harbour* (London 1931) 448. Cf. Hardie 464:134 dimes, dollars; Tilley P213.

Pen-knife. A looking as sharp as a two-bladed pen-knife [i. e., neat, stylish]. (44 Stephens *High Life* II 173).

Penny, 1. The stable was neat as a penny (50 Judd *Richard* 224). Svartengren 218 ninepence.

2. A penny for your thoughts (57 Melville *Confidence-Man* 174). Apperson 489; NED Penny 9 a; *Oxford* 495; Stevenson 1773:2; Tilley P203; NQ 4 ii 460; Samuel Butler *Hudibras* (1664) Part II Canto iii v. 57 This was the penn'worth of his thought; R. M. Baker *Death Stops the Bells* (1938) 120; W. Y. Darling *The Bankrupt Bookseller* (Edinburgh 1947) 43 Pity made me give him a penny, but whose image and superscription will be on the penny which would buy my thoughts.

3. A penny saved is worth two arned (44 Stephens *High Life* I 33; Clift *Bunker* 39 a penny saved is two-pence earned). Apperson 490; NC 456; NED Penny 9 b; *Oxford* 495; Stevenson 1772:8; Tilley P206, 207;

NQ 10 vii 58, 97; J. T. Farrell *A World I Never Made* (1936) 301; M. Thompson *Not As a Stranger* (1954) 637.

4. In for a penny, in for a pound (46 Cooper *Redskins* 82; Bowman *Bear-Hunters* 191). Apperson 490; NC 456; NED Penny 9 f; *Oxford* 318–319; Stevenson 1773:6; Tilley P196; Yamamoto *Dickens* 326; W. McFee *The Harbourmaster* (London 1932) 212; John Metcalfe *Sally* (1936) 444.

5. There is a saying, "Penny wise, pound foolish," that is always a see-sawing up and down in some folks' mouths, that they call an old saw, as they do all such proverbs. I expect they call 'em so because of the teetering process which such sayings are always undergoing. There is a deal of pith in 'em, as a rule, though they are made to apologize for all sorts of shortcomings (58 Clift *Bunker* 35–36; Barnum *Struggles* 459 Penny wise and pound foolish). Apperson 490; Farmer and Henley V 167; NC 456; NED Penny-wise; *Oxford* 495; Stevenson 1771–1772:15; Stoett 1799; Tilley P218; John Dos Passos *The 42d Parallel* (1930) 31.

6. Squire Nokes always used to say that the bad penny will return (33 Smith *Downing* 77; Melville *Moby-Dick* I 206 Ha! boy, come back? bad pennies come not sooner). NC 456; *Oxford* 19; Stevenson 1773–1774:10 shilling; E. K. Gann *Soldier of Fortune* (1954) 309 I turned around and came back like a bad penny; P. B. Kyne *Tide of Empire* (1928) 391 Well, I'm back again, like a bad penny; John Rhode, pseud. *Peril at Cranbury Hall* (1930) 191 It's sure to turn up again, like the proverbial penny. See Shilling (1).

7. Turned a pretty penny (36 Crockett *Exploits* 21; Smith *Way* 216 attempted to turn a penny and get an honest living; Durivage *Three* 247 she is making an honest penny; Barnum *Struggles* 456 to turn an honest penny). Farmer and Henley V 167; NED Penny 9 e; *Oxford* 677; Stevenson 1773:3; Tilley P211.

8. If he had stolen the pennies from his grandmother's eyes (36 Crockett *Exploits* 125; Cary *Married* 131 mean enough to steal the coppers off the eyes of a dead man). Hardie 470:138; McAtee 42. Cf. Boshears 30:34; Halpert 28, 35; Marion N. Rawson *When Antiques Were Young* (1931) 249 he'd steal the pennies off a dead man's eyes.

Peony, 1. Cheeks . . . as red as a piney (44 Stephens *High Life* II 77; Alcott *Little Women* 373). Svartengren 249.

2. Blushing like a peony (56 Durivage *Three* 232, 294).

People, 1. It is an old proverb that "Every people has its prophet" (c54 Emerson *Works* VIII 112).

2. It takes a great many strange people . . . to make a world (55 Haliburton *Nature* II 15). Cf. Folks (3).

3. Some people are born lucky (52 Cary *Clovernook* 163). See Folks (4).

4. Young people *will* be young people, the world over (c60 Paul *Courtship* 74). Esther Forbes *Paradise* (1937) 294. See Boy (4).

Pepper. He is . . . as hot as pepper (55 Haliburton *Nature* I 81). NC 457; Taylor *Comparisons* 50. Cf. Boshears 38:684.

Pepper-box, 1. [They] were as evidently formed to be linked together, as ever were pepper-box and vinegar-cruet (20–22 Irving *Bracebridge* 467).

2. I felt as hot as a pepper-box (44 Thompson *Major* 180).

Pepper-corn. A testy old huntsman, as hot as a pepper-corn (20–22 Irving *Bracebridge* 22).

Pepperidge log. Whose captain is as tough as a pepperidge log (21 Cooper *Spy* 112; Davis *Downing* 145 it's tuffer than a pepperage log). Cf. NED Pepperidge 2; Thornton II 653.

Pepper pod. My face felt as red as a pepper pod (44 Thompson *Major* 83).

Perch. Her cheeks an' lips es rosey es a pearch's gills in dorgwood blossum time (67 Harris *Sut* 76).

Perfection. Perfection can't be expected in this world (66 Boucicault *Flying Scud* 189). Cf. Stevenson 1778:3.

Periagua. Tight as a Jersey oyster perryauger on a mud flat at low water [i. e., frozen tight]. (58 Porter *Major* 192).

Periwinkle. Her eyes as wet as periwinkles (55 Stephens *Homestead* 246).

Perpendicular. See Crowbar (1), Nail (9).

Perseverance. Sooner or later, perseverance achieves (65 Richardson *Secret* 406). Stevenson 434:12 Courage, perseverance conquer all before them. Cf. Apperson 491 Perseverance kills the game.

Persimmon, 1. If you didn't think all the peas in my corn field was er spillin in the floor, thar aint no simmons (51 Burke *Polly* 68).

2. Serena . . . smooth as a persimmon (58 Porter *Major* 53).

3. To bring down the persimmon. 57 DA Persimmon 3 c (4).

4. Cowollop, crosh, cochunk! we all cum down like 'simmons arter frost (43 Lewis *Odd* 50, 170 I fell off like 'simmons arter frost).

5. Puckered up her mouth as ef she had been eatin' unripe persimmons (43 Robb *Squatter* 138). Cf. Taylor *Comparisons* 61.

6. To rake (rake up, walk off with) the persimmons. 57 DA Persimmon 3 c (6).

7. See Bet, Huckleberry (2), Jump sb. (1), Pole (1).

Pert (peart). See Cricket (6), Minister, Pony, Puppy (1).

Pestle. My heart sot to beating in my bosom, like the pestle in an old fashioned samp mortar (44 Stephens *High Life* I 110).

Pet. Mrs. Perkins had been in a pet all afternoon (43 Thompson *Chronicles* 119). Farmer and Henley V 175–176; NED Pet; *Oxford* 641 Take pet; Stevenson 1713:9.

Peter. There's no harm in robbing Peter if you pay Paul with it (38 Haliburton *Clockmaker* III 34, *Old Judge* II 150 According to their creed, there is no harm in robbing Peter to pay Paul; Hall *Purchase* II 88; Saxe *Poems* 227 Without robbery of Peter, Paying thus his due to Paul). Apperson 534; Farmer and Henley V 177; Lean III 340–341; NC 457; NED Peter 2; *Oxford* 545; Stevenson 1783:8 borrow, 1783–1784:11 rob; Tilley P244; Kenneth Roberts *Northwest Passage* (1937) 429.

Peter Funk. A ringleted miss, who was put there to make Peter Funk bids against probable purchasers [i. e., a bogus bidder at auctions]. (55 Thomson *Doesticks* 135; Derby *Squibob* 107 Peter Funks; Saxe *Poems* 68 Of course 't was but a step, to sink From *Peter Funk* to politician, 156 Brown doesn't know "Peter" from Peter the great). Bartlett 461: Berrey 548:4; DA Peter Funk; Farmer 417; Schele de Vere 299–300; Thornton II 658–659, III 285.

Petticoat. Mind your own business, Bob Proffit, I've cooked for frolics afore you shed your petticotes (58 Porter *Major* 86).

Pew, 1. Getting into the 'Right Pew' (56 Kelly *Humors* 187).

2. You are in the wrong pew here (43 Haliburton *Attaché* I 228, *Old Judge* I 305, *Nature* II 41; Stephens *High Life* II 27 mebby the coot has led me into the wrong goose pen; Kelly *Humors* 382). Apperson 715 box; McAtee *Grant County* 3 church; *Oxford* 735–736; Tilley B575; Andy Adams *The Outlet* (Boston 1905) 138 Old sport, you're in the right church, but the wrong pew; Helen Reilly *McKee of Centre Street* (1934) 142 wrong pew.

Phantom. She glided by like a phantom (40 Dana *Two* 78). Cf. Svartengren 386.

Pharisee. Felt as proud as a Pharisee (55 Haliburton *Nature* II 172).

Philadelphia doctor (lawyer), 1. The premonitory symptoms [of love] are as evident to them [women] as are those of any other eruptive disease about to break out to a Philadelphia doctor (55 Anon. *New Hope* 283, 204 The Greenbrier doctors ain't as high

learnt as you are. . . . You got your sheepskin in Philadelphy, I guess).

2. I guess it would puzzle a Philadelphy lawyer to tell (33 Smith *Downing* 56, 88, 120, 'Way 63, *My Thirty* 305, 337; Crockett *Account* 19–20 which is the honest George Fox hat, I leave for Philadelphia lawyers and parsons to decide; Haliburton *Clockmaker* I 149, 250 it would take a Philadelphia lawyer to answer him; Cooper *Redskins* 10). Bartlett 462, 507; DA Philadelphia lawyer; Farmer 418; Farmer and Henley V 181; Schele de Vere 624; Stevenson 1373: 2; Taylor *Investigations* 261; Thornton II 659–660, III 286; Tidwell PADS XIII (1950) 21; Woodard PADS VI (1946) 42; NQ 2 vii 515; Kay C. Strahan *Death Traps* (1930) 290.

3. See Day (25).

Pickle. In a dreadful pickle (33 Smith *Downing* 42, 43 in the same pickle, 58, *My Thirty* 308 what sort of a pickle we're in, 345 in a pickle; Crockett *Life* 198 I was in a pretty pickle). NED Pickle 4; Stevenson 1789:6; Tilley P276; E. H. Ball *The Scarlet Fox* (1927) 203 as we vulgar Americans call it; Desmond Holdridge *Pindorama* (1933) 37 pretty.

Pickpocket. Miss Smith and Bibb were as thick as two pickpockets (35 Longstreet *Georgia* 93). Stevenson 48:12 agree like. See Thief (4).

Picture, 1. As beautiful as a picture (69 Clemens *Innocents* I 201).

2. As harnsome as a pictur (44 Stephens *High Life* II 181, *Homestead* 244, *Fashion* 133; Smith 'Way 345 Handsome as a pictur). Stevenson 776:10. Cf. Boshears 39:811; NC 457; Taylor *Comparisons* 64.

3. He done it like a wite man, tu, ez nat'ral ez a picter (48 Lowell *Biglow* 144).

4. Looking as "pretty as picters" (69 Alcott *Little Women* 316). NC 457; Svartengren 219; Taylor *Comparisons* 64.

5. They'd been at their high strikes, and was putty well up in the picters [i. e., nearly drunk]. (58 Hammett *Piney* 141).

6. He was gettin' too high up in the pictures enny how (51 Burke *Polly* 147 [was successful]). DA Picture 2 b; Stevenson 1789:13; Mary N. Murfree [Charles Egbert Craddock, pseud.] *The Mystery of Witch-Face Mountain* (Boston 1895) 235 Wat's 'way up in the pictur's!

7. The gal looked like a picter (44 Stephens *High Life* I 226, *Mary Derwent* 306).

8. He looked like the very picture of hard times (34 Crockett *Life* 177). Apperson 381 ill luck; *Oxford* 498; Tilley P278.

Pided. See Rattlesnake (1).

Pie, 1. As good as pie (44 Stephens *High Life* II 49; Haliburton *Nature* II 59). DA Pie 4 (3); NC 457; Taylor *Comparisons* 61; Thornton I 374.

2. Rich as a pie (66 Boucicault *Flying Scud* 218).

3. In the homely phrase of California, . . . it has "got enough pie" [i. e., used up]. (66 Clemens *Sandwich* 77). DA Pie 4 (4) this passage only.

Piece, 1. To fly all to pieces. 68 DA Fly 3.

2. Now that I've gin the minister a piece of my mind (44 Stephens *High Life* I 56, 174; Cary *Clovernook* 2d Series 162 I felt assured that she

would give Edward the "piece of her mind" with which she had first proposed to endow him; Whitcher *Widow* 84). Coombs PADS II (1944) 23; Hardie 472:197; McAtee *Grant County* 8; NED Piece 2 d.

3. If I could [answer], it wouldn't be talking but "speaking my piece" (60 Holmes *Professor* 18). DA Piece 2 b (1).

Piecrust, 1. Burnt up to a cinder! crisp as pie-crust, and twice as tough (49 Haliburton *Old Judge* II 276).

2. Biting off the words as short as pie crust (44 Stephens *High Life* II 26, 190; Shillaber *Knitting-Work* 301 breaking off in her subject shorter than pie-crust; Taliaferro *Fisher's* 117 My breath short as pie-crust, 123 and quit short off—short as pie-crust). DA Pie 4 (2); NC 457.

Pig, 1. As fat as a cobbet pig, as the boys here say (31 Eliason 103).

2. She is as fat as er pig (49 Eliason 63). Apperson 205; Boshears 36: 545; Hardie 467; NC 457; Taylor *Comparisons* 40, *Index* 32.

3. He's as sure gone as a stuck pig [i. e., dead]. (56 Jones *Wild* 108).

4. As good natured as a sucking pig (44 Stephens *High Life* II 70).

5. As happy as a pig in paradise (56 Eliason 103).

6. She would be as happy as a dead pig in the sunshine (c35 Eliason 72). NC 457. Cf. Apperson 607; *Oxford* 123; Taylor *Comparisons* 46; Tilley P297.

7. As pussy and pompous as a prize pig jest afore killing time (44 Stephens *High Life* II 92–93). Cf. Phoebe A. Taylor *The Tinkling Symbol* (1935) 284 as proud as a pig.

8. In a pig's eye (66 Locke [Nas-

by] *Struggles* 315). Octavus Roy Cohen *Star of Earth* (1932) 270; H. Wouk *The Caine Mutiny* (1951) 128; *The Saturday Evening Post Stories* (1954) 8.

9. Like a pig swimmin' agin stream, every time he struck out, he was a cuttin' of his own throat (43 Haliburton *Attaché* II 135). Green 24 hogs. See Current.

10. But it's "eat, pig, or die" (35 Crockett *Account* 90).

11. Root, little pig, or die (58 Porter *Major* 18 [a cry at a horse race]; Cary *Married* 305). See Hog (8).

12. The silent pig is the best feeder (55 Haliburton *Nature* I 201). Cf. Apperson 602; *Oxford* 620; Stevenson 2176:4; Tilley S681; Charles Reade *Jack of All Trades* (1858, ed. London 1932) 73 The silent hog eats the most acorns.

13. Well, I wish I may be turned ashore on a grating, with a pig for a coxswain (39 Briggs *Harry* I 178).

14. Bro't my pigs to a fine market (25 Neal *Brother J* II 224; Haliburton *Clockmaker* I 194 You've brought your pigs to a pretty market). Apperson 493–494; Farmer and Henley V 195; NED Pig 10 e; *Oxford* 297–298; Stevenson 1793:6; Tilley H503; C. G. Bowers *Jefferson in Power* (Boston 1936) 74 carry . . . good; Agatha Christie *The Mysterious Mr. Quin* (1930) 61 take . . . bitter; R. A. Freeman *Mr. Pottermack's Oversight* (1930) 157 brought . . . wrong. Cf. Market.

15. Do I look like buying a pig in a poke? (c58 Stephens *Mary Derwent* 216; Wallack *Rosedale* 52 Because neither of us would buy a pig in a poke). Apperson 494; NC 458; NED Pig 10 b; *Oxford* 72–73; Schele de Vere 521; Stevenson 1791–1792:10;

Stoett 1093; Tilley P304; NQ 1 x 187; 4 xi 198; Leslie Ford, pseud. *Ill Met by Moonlight* (1937) 25.

16. Frisking about like pigs in clover (54 Shillaber *Mrs. Partington* 164; Hammett *Piney* 133 they're wallerin' in the dimes jest like a pig in a clover-patch). DA Pig 2 b (1); Stevenson 370:10; Thornton II 664; Kay C. Strahan *The Meriwether Mystery* (1933) 291. Cf. Svartengren 349 pea-straw; Tilley P296.

17. They would get the wrong pig by the ear (33 Smith *Downing* 170; Curtis *Potiphar* 187; McCloskey *Across* 73; Nash *Century* 185 they'll find . . . they've ketched the wrong pigs by the ears). Apperson 715 sow; Bartlett 244–245; Farmer 419; Hardie 472:215; NED Pig 11; *Oxford* 607; Stevenson 1793:1; Tilley S685; Dorothy L. Sayers *Strong Poison* (1930) 75. See Sow (2).

18. They are now rooting arter it, like pigs arter groundnuts (54 Shillaber *Mrs. Partington* 336).

19. Screamin' like a stuck pig (43 Haliburton *Attaché* IV 29).

20. Squeak, squeak, went the fiddle . . . like a pig when he's being yoked (44 Stephens *High Life* I 36).

21. She squeals again like a stuck pig (40 Haliburton *Letter* 216; Kelly *Humors* 144 they'd pinch a fourpence till it'd squeal like; Paul *Courtship* 47). McAtee 61; NC 458; Taylor *Comparisons* 62.

22. Standin starin like a stuck pig (36 Haliburton *Clockmaker* I 95, *Season-Ticket* 294; Stephens *High Life* I 8, 179 with my mouth a leetle open, 204, II 71). Apperson 600; NED Stare 1 b; *Oxford* 618; Stevenson 2208:10; Tilley P307. See Calf (7, 8).

23. Stiffened out like a frozen pig (55 Thomson *Doesticks* 157).

Pigeon, 1. Serena . . . plump as a pigeon (58 Porter *Major* 53). Boshears 39:803; Taylor *Comparisons* 63.

2. The young gal . . . quiet as a pigeon (66 Bowman *Bear-Hunters* 389).

3. They begun to titter like two pigeons on a gutter (44 Stephens *High Life* II 150).

Pigsty. The Little Magician might as well go to a pig-sty for wool, as to beat around in that part for voters (36 Crockett *Exploits* 82–83). See Goat (1).

Pig's whistle. In less than a pig's whistle. 59 DA Pig 2 b (2).

Pig-tracks, 1. Jest as natural as pig-tracks (51 Burke *Polly* 161). Cf. Figh PADS XIII (1950) 14; Taylor *Comparisons* 29.

2. They are sending gentlemen there reg'lar as pig-tracks (53 Baldwin *Flush* 307).

Pike (1). I stand stiff as a pike (49 Melville *Mardi* II 189). Cf. Svartengren 274 straight.

Pike (2). As greedily as a pike (47 Dorson *Jonathan* 103).

Pikestaff, 1. It's as plain as a pikestaff (40 Haliburton *Clockmaker* III 115; Melville *Typee* 75). Apperson 499; Farmer and Henley V 222; NED Pikestaff, Plain 18; *Oxford* 503; Stevenson 1804:7; Svartengren 365–366; Tilley P322; NQ 8 ix 346, x 141, xi 32, CLIV (1928) 406, 444, 464, CLV (1928) 49; Eden Phillpotts *Mr. Digweed and Mr. Lumb* (1934) 205 the proverbial.

2. This gentleman stands stiff as a pikestaff (50 Melville *White Jacket* 361, *Moby-Dick* I 33). NED Pikestaff; J. C. Powys *Wolf Solent* (1929) 382.

3. I'll sit as straight as . . . a pikestaff (53 Haliburton *Sam* II 66).

Pillar, 1. I left the old fellow stiff as a pillar (53 Baldwin *Flush* 323).

2. Hunted about in this way, from pillar to post (33 Neal *Down-Easters* II 53; Crockett *Account* 113 driven from post to pillar; Kennedy *Horse-Shoe* 418 driven from post to pillar; Haliburton *Attaché* IV 135 dragged about from pillar to post; Smith '*Way* 297 Billy had been beaten about from post to pillar, and pillar to post; Barnum *Struggles* 521 Driven from pillar to post; Clemens *Love Letters* 61). Apperson 496; Farmer and Henley V 262–263; Lean III 286–287; NED Pillar 11; *Oxford* 500; Stevenson 1837–1838:8; Tilley P328; Whiting *Drama* 358:771; NQ 5 iv 169, 358; 6 vi 337, vii 38, 477; 10 iv 528, v 11; Herbert Asbury *The Barbary Coast* (1933) 143.

Pill pedlar. A tongue . . . civil as a pill pedlar (43 Robb *Squatter* 115).

Pin, 1. Dressed up as neat as a new pin (44 Stephens *High Life* I 162, 165, II 162, 193; Smith '*Way* 271; Paul *Courtship* 80; Barnum *Struggles* 550). Apperson 444; *Oxford* 445; Taylor *Comparisons* 58; Charlotte M. Russell *Murder at the Old Stone House* (1935) 83.

2. As neat as a pin (40 Dana *Two* 200; Taliaferro *Fisher's* 245; Paul *Courtship* 53). Boshears 38:762; McAtee 45; NC 458; Stevenson 1664:5; Taylor *Comparisons* 58; Adam Bliss *Murder Upstairs* (Philadelphia 1934) 195.

3. All fixed as nice as a new pin (33 Smith *Downing* 22).

4. As slick as a new pin (44 Stephens *High Life* I 219).

5. He was as "straight as a pin" (c60 Paul *Courtship* 265).

6. And are washed, until, in the language of old Aunt Barbara, they are "as sweet and clean as new pins" (c60 Paul *Courtship* 95). Nell Martin *The Mosaic Earring* (1927) 21 clean.

7. I shouldn't care a pin (39 Smith *Letters* 37; Riley *Puddleford* 252). Apperson 496; NED Pin 3 b; *Oxford* 78; Stevenson 1237:9; Tilley P333; Whiting *Drama* 358:772; G. A. Birmingham *Gold, Gore and Gehenna* (1927) 79.

8. Constitoounts . . . don't weigh the heft of a pin (48 Lowell *Biglow* 82).

9. I don't valy him . . . the matter of a pin's head (36 Haliburton *Clockmaker* I p. viii). NED Pin 3 c.

10. You might have heard a pin drop (33 Neal *Down-Easters* I 115; Haliburton *Sam* I 27; Derby *Phoenixiana* 189 dead silence—you might have heard a paper of pins fall). *Oxford* 287; Stevenson 1796:7; J. G. Brandon *The One-Minute Murder* (1935) 229 the dropping of the proverbial pin.

11. I rather guess it's a fact—stick a pin through it, for it's noticeable (60 Haliburton *Season-Ticket* 130). Bartlett 798; DA Stick 1 b (1); Thornton II 858, III 381–382.

12. I want to shine like a new pin (44 Stephens *High Life* I 63, II 83–84).

Pine, 1. She is as straight as a pine (56 Melville "I and My Chimney" in *Works* XIII 287). NC 458; Taylor *Comparisons* 78.

2. She looked as sweet as a pine (44 Stephens *High Life* II 150).

Pine knot. The Modoc . . . is as hard as a pine knot (74 Clemens *Letters* I 219). Boshears 37 (641); DA Pine knot 2; DAE Pine knot 2; NC 459.

Pine stump, 1. I was asleep in a minute as fast as a pine-stump (53 Haliburton *Sam* II 107).

2. As obstinate as a pine stump (43 Haliburton *Attaché* II 258).

3. Sat as silent as a pine stump (43 Haliburton *Attaché* III 99).

Pink, 1. Purty as a pink (44 Stephens *High Life* I 239). NC 459.

2. Smelling as sweet as a garden pink root in full blow (44 Stephens *High Life* II 80).

3. It [a house] shines like a pink (57 Riley *Puddleford* 256).

Pipe, 1. Put them into your pipe and smoke them (53 Haliburton *Sam* II 166, *Nature* II 11, 31; Melville "Cock-a-doodle-doo!" in *Works* XIII 159 Put that in your pipe and smoke it!). Allan PADS XV (1951) 67; Farmer and Henley V 212; McAtee 51; NC 459; NED Pipe 10 d; *Oxford* 527; Partridge 633; Snapp 108:156; Stevenson 1798:2; Stoett 1823; NQ 11 iv 207; John Fletcher *The Loyal Subject* (1618) II i (Beaumont and Fletcher *Works* [Cambridge, Eng. 1906] III 105) Fare ye well Sir, And buy a pipe with that; Lesley Frost *Murder at Large* (1932) 145; R. P. Warren *All the King's Men* (1946) 227. Cf. J. K. Bangs *A House-Boat on the Styx* (1895, ed. 1906) 19 Put that on your music rack and fiddle it, my little Emperor [Nero]; J. P. Marquand *Wickford Point* (Boston 1939) 113 Now butter that one on your dry toast, darling; M. McCarthy *The Groves of Academe* (1952) 34 Play *that* on your guitar.

2. He couldn't think of putting the Squire's pipe out arter that fashion (36 Haliburton *Clockmaker* I 305). NED Pipe 10 d.

Piper, 1. As drunk as a piper (c65 Clemens *Sketches* 48, *Sandwich* 184). Apperson 167; NED Piper ¹ 1 b; Partridge 634.
2. Them that danced should pay the piper (35 Crockett *Account* 202). See Fiddler (2).
3. Smokin Yankee segars, and cuss-in like pipers (44 Thompson *Major* 33). See Steamboat captain.

Pipe stem, 1. Plain as a pipe stem [i. e., clear]. (43 Robb *Squatter* 48; Judd *Margaret* II 119, *Richard* 144). Colver Harris *Going to St. Ives* (Philadelphia 1936) 106 as any pipestem.
2. Mr. Kendle came in and broke it [a conversation] right off short as a pipe stem (33 Smith *Downing* 229, *Letters* 122 [a leg]; Crockett *Life* 35 and broke the waggon tongue slap, short off, as a pipe-stem).

Pirate. But there ain't time for it jist now, as the pirate said to the hangman when he was a-tyin' of the knot (40 Haliburton *Clockmaker* III 145).

Pismire. As busy as pismires (35 Crockett *Account* 29). Svartengren 126.

Piss. The folks [here] is poorer than skim piss (64 Wiley *Billy* 187). Cf. Halpert 969 As poor as p— in a pumpkin.

Pistol. Pop! went something, eenamost as loud as a pistol (44 Stephens *High Life* I 22).

Pistol shot. Sudden as a pistol shot (59–60 Holmes *Elsie* 332).

Pit. But on looking around, the boys had cut the pit—*mizzled!* (56 Kelly *Humors* 366). Cf. Farmer and Henley V 217 fly (shoot) the pit; NED Pit 5; Partridge 636.

Pitch, sb. (1), 1. Black as pitch, and weather worse than ever (59 Boucicault *Dot* 126). Apperson 135; NC 459; NED Pitch 4; Taylor *Comparisons* 18; Tilley P357; Whiting *Scots* II 111; J. D. Carr *Hag's Nook* (1933) 124.
2. All else pitch black (51 Melville *Moby-Dick* I 219). NED Pitch-black; Dorothy Ogburn *Death on the Mountain* (Boston 1931) 72.
3. Nights as dark as pitch (32 Kennedy *Swallow* 220; Hall *Soldier's Bride* 228; Stephens *Fashion* 57, *Homestead* 329). Apperson 135; NC 459; NED Pitch 4; Taylor *Comparisons* 32; Tilley P357; David Frome, pseud. *Mr. Pinkerton Grows a Beard* (1935) 244.
4. Pitch dark (25 Neal *Brother* J III 390, *Rachel* 174; Irving *Attorney* 91 The night was pitchy dark; Dana *Two* 7; Durivage *Three* 368; Sedley *Marian* 174). NED Pitch-dark; E. Philips Oppenheim *The Man without Nerves* (1934) 110.
5. A hearty old blade that. Sound as pitch (23–24 Irving *Tales* 153).
6. The fire smoked as thick as pitch (50 Mitchell *Reveries* 28).
7. Black pitch sticks closer than white cream [i. e., a lie clings longer than "fair fame"]. (55 Melville *Israel* 120–121). Babcock 264.
8. My name is Pitch; I stick to what I say (57 Melville *Confidence-Man* 155, 168). Babcock 264.
9. Whoso toucheth pitch shall be defiled (65 Sedley *Marian* 416; Saxe *Poems* 347 Some of the pitch you handle, On your fingers will remain;

Clemens *Love Letters* 76). Sirach 13: 1 He that touches pitch shall be defiled; Apperson 498; Bradley 88; Hardie 465:166 You can't play with pitch without getting your fingers black; *Oxford* 667; Stevenson 1799–1800:12; Stoett 1794; Tilley P358; Whiting *Drama* 123, *Scots* I 111; NQ 5 iv 86; H. M. Smith *Inspector Frost in Crevenna Cove* (1933) 95.

Pitch, sb. (2), 1. To make one's pitch [i. e., to establish residence]. 23 DA Pitch 2 b.

2. To slink one's pitch [i. e., to become humble]. 53 DA Pitch 5 (1).

Pitch, vb. All hands "pitched in" (55 Thomson *Doesticks* 106; Hammett *Piney* 196 the Indians . . . incontinently "pitched in"—as the New York boys say). NED Pitch 23.

Pitcher, 1. Pitcher broke, at last—pitcher—well—ever see the well that Jacob dug (25 Neal *Brother J* II 224; Shillaber *Knitting-Work* 225 A pitcher that goes too often to the well may come back broken; Browning *Forty-four* 130 A pitcher which goes so often to the well will some day or other come back broken; Richardson *Beyond* 126 this pitcher which went so often to the well was at last broken). Apperson 498; NED Pitcher 1 b; *Oxford* 502; Stevenson 1801:1; Tidwell PADS XI (1949) 14–15; Tilley P501; Whiting *Drama* 20, 231; NQ 8 v 168, 255; Agatha Christie *The A. B. C. Murders* (1936) 47.

2. For there never was pitcher that wouldn't spill (58 Holmes *Autocrat* 301).

Pitchfork, 1. Looking pitchforks and hatchel teeth at the auctioneer (44 Stephens *High Life* II 70, 78 that old maid . . . began to look pitchforks and darning needles at me).

2. As soon as the rain should stop falling in pitch-forks (56 Cary *Married* 295; Wiley *Billy* 187 raining pitch-forks). George Dyer *The Long Death* (1937) 188 pitchforks and hammer-handles. See Plough-share.

Pitch-knot. She's tough as a pitch-knot (54 Smith *'Way* 238). Cf. NC 459 pine knot.

Pitch-pine. Don't know a pitch-pine hay-mow from a sugar maple-tree, says I, to let sich a spec (25 Neal *Brother J* I 156).

Pitiful. See Rabbit (4).

Place, 1. There was a place for everything, and everything was in its place (55 Haliburton *Nature* I 164, II 7; Emerson *Journals* IX 110; Riley *Puddleford* 223 a place for everything, and everything in its place; Sedley *Marian* 8 as my old grandmother used to tell; Smith *Arp* 66 Solomon says "there is a place for every thing, and a thing for every place"). Apperson 499; Bartlett *Familiar Quotations* 706 "There's a place for everything . . . ," Quoth Augustine, the saint; Fife 120; NC 459; *Oxford* 503; Stevenson 1803:6; Mary A. Hamilton *Murder in the House of Commons* (Boston 1932) 97; J. P. Marquand *Point of No Return* (Boston 1949) 498 there was a place for everything in Clyde and everything was in its place.

2. If you hadnt sat in that place, yourself, when you was young, I guess you wouldn't be so awful scared at it, you old goose you (55 Haliburton *Nature* I 152). Cf. Tilley W353.

3. It comes closer bein' the jumpin off place than any I ever hearn tell on (51 Burke *Polly* 67–68). Farmer 327–

328; McAtee 37; Stevenson 1282:9; Thornton I 504–505.

4. Jem and myself had been a year out of college and were passing through that "tight place" in life (53 Willis *Fun* 203; Kelly *Humors* 424 [He] has got you into a tight place; Locke [Nasby] *Struggles* 83 But we're in a tite place, 512). Bartlett 705; Thornton II 897.

5. See Colt (1).

Plain. See A. B. C. (4), Barking, Bear (14, 15), Book (1), Bootjack (5), Button (2), Day (14), Face (2), Floor-board, Hand (4), Nose (1), Pikestaff (1), Pipe stem (1), Poverty (1), Preaching (3), Print (2), Road (1), Shoe (2), Steeple, Sun (4), Wolf (10).

Plank, 1. They can swear through a nine-inch plank (60 Haliburton *Season-Ticket* 284). Apperson 613; *Oxford* 635.

2. Burning with ardour to "walk the plank" [i. e., to go on the stage]. (37 Neal *Charcoal* 114). Cf. NED Plank 6.

Plantain. And plantain thrives best when it is most trod upon, that I know (45 Judd *Margaret* II 253). Cf. Tilley C34 camomile.

Plastic. See Wax (2).

Plate. During a "hasty plate of soup" visit (51 Eliason 159).

Play, sb., 1. All play and no work will soon fetch a noble to ninepence, and make bread timber short (43 Haliburton *Attaché* IV 279; Alcott *Little Women* 121 all play and no work is as bad as all work and no play). Cf. Work, sb. 1; Apperson 8–9; *Oxford* 730; Tilley W842.

2. It is as good as a play (40 Hali-

burton *Letter* 47; Stephens *High Life* I 240 better than a play, II 106; Cary *Married* 291 it's as good as to go to the museum). NC 459; *Oxford* 250; Stevenson 1808:3; Svartengren 316; Tilley P392.

3. It was as grand as a play (40 Haliburton *Clockmaker* III 70).

4. Fair play's a jewel (23 Cooper *Pioneers* 193; Neal *Brother J* III 278, 392, *Down-Easters* I 81; Kennedy *Horse-Shoe* 206; Haliburton *Clockmaker* I p. x, II 320, III 55; Hooper *Simon* 32 but honesty beats it all to pieces; Jones *Country* 113; Lincoln IV 480). Apperson 199 Fair play, 499 Plain dealing; *Oxford* 503; Stevenson 1806:10; Tilley P381; NQ 3 viii 267, 317; Neil Bell, pseud. *Crocus* (1937) 324; W. Congreve *The Old Bachelor* (1693) IV vi plain dealing is a jewel, and he that useth it shall dye a beggar.

5. The more play the less dimes, a proverb never stale in thrifty minds (65 Sedley *Marian* 130). Cf. *Oxford* 505 The less play the better.

6. But Zeb had seen play [i. e., was experienced]. (33 Dorson *Jonathan* 116).

7. See Child (19).

Play, vb., 1. The common rule of the country, of "play and pay" (46 Cooper *Redskins* 399). Cf. Apperson 498 Pitch; *Oxford* 502; Tilley P360.

2. That thing was played out (62 Locke [Nasby] *Struggles* 59, 111). Farmer 426; NED Play, vb. 32; Thornton II 676, III 292–293. Cf. DA Played.

3. See Cat (56).

Playful. See Child (8), Kitten (7).

Pleased. See Couple.

Pleasures. But sweetest pleasures are the shortest, and a roast pig is no exception (58 Field *Pokerville* 54). Stevenson 1812:16.

Plentiful, Plenty. See Acorn (1), Blackberry (1), Dewdrop (2), Dust (1), Leaf 1 (3), Snowball (1).

Plough. His guiding motto through life had been—"He that by the plough would thrive, Himself must either hold or drive" (54 Smith *'Way* 30). Apperson 503; NC 459; *Oxford* 508; Stevenson 1816:7; Tilley P431.

Plough-share. It'll rain plough-shares and hoe-handles in five minutes (54 Langdon *Ida* 346). See Pitchfork (2).

Plucky. See Bull-terrier.

Plum, 1. As bright as a damson plum (44 Stephens *High Life* II 245).

2. It was kinder purply, like the damsons that grow in our corn lot (44 Stephens *High Life* I 104; Jones *Wild* 32 His nose was . . . as purple as a plum).

Plumb line. They are as true as a plum line (36 Haliburton *Clockmaker* I 309). Cf. Amber Dean *Collectors' Item* (1953) 31 as straight as a plumb line.

Plump. See Horse (9), Partridge (1), Pigeon (1), Strawberry (1).

Plymouth. See Pond (3).

Pocket, sb. It was as dark as a pocket (40 Dana *Two* 120; Hammett *Piney* 147 in a shirt). NC 460; Svartengren 238; Kathleen M. Knight *Seven Were Veiled* (1937) 205.

Pocket, vb. You can pocket it [i. e., swallow it]. (43 Thompson *Chronicles* 139). Apperson 504; Farmer and Hen-

ley V 236–237; NED Pocket 3; *Oxford* 509.

Poetry. Stocks are as flat as poetry (53 Boker *Bankrupt* 64).

Point, 1. Every livin thing hes hits pint, a pint ove sum sort (67 Harris *Sut* 87).

2. However I carried the point (56 Whitcher *Widow* 104). NED Carry 17 b, Point 28; Stevenson 1824:14.

3. Don't put too fine a point on it! (65 Sedley *Marian* 338).

4. When she does speak she always says something to the pint (56 Whitcher *Widow* 299). NED Point 27; Stevenson 1824:9.

Pointer. Jealous as a pet pinter (43 Robb *Squatter* 134).

Poison, 1. It makes the first bold, and pushin', and sassy as pison (58 Hammett *Piney* 99).

2. Well, Ben's wife was mean—meaner than pizen (56 Kelly *Humors* 365). NC 460.

3. Hate a sharper as I do pyz'n (33 Neal *Down-Easters* I 81; Haliburton *Clockmaker* II 260 he hates us like pyson, III 45–46, *Sam* II 103, 308, *Nature* I 147, II 22, 27, 290, *Season-Ticket* 220; Stephens *High Life* I 97; Hall *Purchase* I 261; Anon. *New Hope* 167; Whitcher *Widow* 239; Riley *Puddleford* 251; Hammett *Piney* 154 hated him worse'n pison). Farmer and Henley V 242; Svartengren 138; Tilley T361; Alice Campbell *Keep Away from Water!* (1935) 99.

Poker, 1. As stiff as a poker (38 Haliburton *Clockmaker* II 195, III 287, *Attaché* I 217, *Nature* I 197; Melville *Omoo* 163; Cary *Clovernook* 2d Series, 151; Durivage *Three* 117 as a cold poker [dead]; Whitcher *Widow*

258; Jones *Country* 154 She's as dead as a door-nail, and stiff as a poker; Alcott *Little Women* 8). Apperson 602; Boshears 40:964; McAtee 62; NC 460; Taylor *Comparisons* 78; O. F. Jerome *The Murder at Avalon Arms* (1931) 179.

2. As straight as a poker (38 Haliburton *Clockmaker* II 195, III 236). Boshears 40:970; Halpert 677; Hardie 468:75; L. W. Meynell *On the Night of the 18th* (1936) 289 poker-straight.

Pole, 1. The longest pole gets the persimmon. 63 DA Persimmon 3 c (5). Cf. DA Simmon 1 b; NED Persimmon 3.

2. A common chap couldn't a touched him with a ten foot pole (44 Stephens *High Life* I 39; Anon. *New Hope* 149 Please God, he shouldn't tech 'em with a forty-foot pole; Lowell *Biglow* 226 we'll fix ye so's 't a bar Would n' tech ye with a ten-foot pole). DA Forty 2 b.

Policy. In short, sir, as the Irishman said—in short, sir—there is policy in war (25 Neal *Brother J* II 97, III 278 [not credited to an Irishman]). Tilley P462.

Polished. See Razor (3), Steel (3).

Polite. See Basket (1).

Politics. Politics "made us acquainted with strange bedfellows" (71 Jones *Batkins* 188). Stevenson 1829:7; H. L. Ickes *Diary* (1954) II 51 Politics may make strange bedfellows, but this event proves that it also makes strange co-workers. Cf. Misery, Poverty (2), William McFee *The Harbourmaster* (London 1932) 125 war.

Pompous. See Pig (7).

Pond, 1. The beach was as smooth as a pond (40 Dana *Two* 87). Svartengren 270 mill-pond.

2. Little ponds never hold big fish (38 Haliburton *Clockmaker* II 268).

3. Their proverb is that there is a pond in Plymouth for every day in the year (43 Emerson *Journals* VI 428).

Pony. Lookin' ez peart ez a circus pony (80 Harris *Uncle Remus* 37).

Poor, sb. The poor aids the poor (43 Robb *Squatter* 11).

Poor, adj., 1. It's no disgrace to be poor, but it's often confoundedly unhandy! (56 Kelly *Humors* 400).

2. They were poor and proud (55 Haliburton *Nature* II 283; Riley *Puddleford* 20 proud, and poor; Smith *Arp* 135; Alcott *Little Women* 380 Poor and proud, as usual). Apperson 506; *Oxford* 510; Tilley P474; Bertram Atkey *Smiler Bunn* (1927) 76. Cf. Whiting *Drama* 28.

3. See Cheese (2), Church-mouse, Job (2, 3, 4), Mouse (2), Partridge (2), Piss, Rat (4), Shadow (1).

Poor box. Now I'm as hungry as a poor box (37 Neal *Charcoal* 191).

Poplar. Miss Scruggs . . . "as tall and as straight as a poplar tree" (37 Neal *Charcoal* 107; Stephens *Mary Derwent* 205 You are straight and proud as a poplar).

Poppy. Her face got as red as a poppy (44 Thompson *Major* 92; Alcott *Little Women* 227).

Popular. See Hen (5).

Porcupine. Why, the hold feller's has tough has ha porkerpine with ha chill (50 Boker *World* 34).

Pork, 1. And then I sot down agin as streaked as lean pork [i. e., embarrassed]. (44 Stephens *High Life* I 187, 224 I began to feel streaked as lean pork in the bottom of a barrel).

2. I ain't so 'fond o' pork as to eat hogyokes (56 Whitcher *Widow* 99). Cf. *Oxford* 392 Loved mutton; Tilley B23, M1339.

3. It's too much pork for a shilling (42 Irving *Attorney* 101).

Porpoise, 1. She is as fat as a porpus (68 Clift *Bunker* 61). Svartengren 184–185.

2. He commonly goes it like a porpus [i. e., snores]. (54 Smith *'Way* 23, 27).

3. Puffing and blowing like a porpoise (37 Neal *Charcoal* 43; Shillaber *Ike* 42).

4. The boat stopped all tu once, and begun tu snort and roll on the water like a sick porpoise (44 Stephens *High Life* II 146).

Port. You wouldn't refuse us a port in a storm [also literal]. (38 Haliburton *Clockmaker* II 163; Saxe *Poems* 90 By the nautical rule of "Any port—" You may add the rest at leisure). Apperson 12; NC 460; *Oxford* 11; Stevenson 1831:8; Bill Adams *Ships and Women* (Boston 1937) 222; Colver Harris *Murder in Amber* (1938) 109.

Possessed. Fellers a yelling and a kicking up their heels like all possessed (44 Stephens *High Life* I 37; Kelly *Humors* 104 [Indians] coming after me like all possessed; Riley *Puddleford* 137 lording it all over the house like all possess'd, 161 two boys were shakin' like all possess't). Bartlett 8, 807; DA All 3; Taylor *Comparisons* 63; Thornton I 11.

Possession. And possession is nine points out of ten (32 Kennedy *Swal-*

low 217; Cooper *Redskins* 253 Possession's good in law; Melville *Moby-Dick* II 146 Is it not a saying in everyone's mouth, Possession is half of the law: that is, regardless of how the thing came into possession? But often possession is the whole of the law; Riley *Puddleford* 208 Possession is *more'n* nine p'ints of the la' in Puddleford; it's ninety-nine—it's most as good as a patent; Richardson *Beyond* 185 observing that the nine points of the law were in our favor, 304 Possession being nine points of the law). Apperson 507; NC 460; NED Point 12, Possession 1 d; *Oxford* 512; Stevenson 1831–1832:12; Tilley P487; P. B. Kyne *Tide of Empire* (1928) 371; Phoebe A. Taylor *Figure Away* (1937) 101 a coarse, crass old adage; Juanita Brooks *The Pacific Spectator* III (1949) 297 and in this country possession was all ten points of the law.

Possum. See Opossum.

Post, sb., 1. As def as a post (36 Haliburton *Clockmaker* I 273, *Letter* 41, *Season-Ticket* 149; Jones *Winkles* 8, *Country* 156; Alcott *Little Women* 432 as unmoved as the post which is popularly believed to be deaf; Barnum *Struggles* 122). Apperson 139; Boshears 36:483; McAtee 22; NC 460; Taylor *Comparisons* 33; Tilley P490; Edwin Greenwood *The Fair Devil* (1935) 115. Cf. Whiting *Drama* 323: 264.

2. Stiff as a post (68 Saxe *Poems* 89, 129 as any post). Svartengren 262; Lesley Frost *Murder at Large* (1932) 94. Cf. Apperson 602 stake.

3. Still as a post (51 Burke *Polly* 53). Svartengren 384; William Faulkner *The Sound and the Fury* (1929) 258.

4. As thin as a whippin post (36 Haliburton *Clockmaker* I 328).

5. Between you an' me an' the post (33 Neal *Down-Easters* I 23, 126; Haliburton *Attaché* IV 98; Stephens *High Life* II 173). Apperson 47; *Oxford* 43; J. S. Fletcher *The Kang-Ho Vase* (1926) 281. See Bedpost.

Post, vb. And I reckon I'll jest keep on to Frisky and git posted on the new dodges (65 Sedley *Marian* 162–163). NED Post vb ¹ 9.

Pot, sb., 1. His face wur as black as a pot (67 Harris *Sut* 155). Fife 117.

2. The doctor was a "little pot, and soon hot" (20–22 Irving *Bracebridge* 390; Emerson *Journals* IV Small pot, soon hot). Apperson 372; NC 461; NED Pot 13 d; *Oxford* 374; Stevenson 1840:2; Tilley P497.

3. Pot always calls kettle an ugly name (55 Haliburton *Nature* II 81; Shillaber *Knitting-Work* 191; Clemens *Gilded* II 336 An old version of what the Pot said to the Kettle). Apperson 507; NC 461; NED Pot 13b; *Oxford* 512–513; Stevenson 1840:14; Stoett 1870; Tilley K21; Theodore Roscoe *Murder on the Way!* (1935) 141; E. K. Gann *Soldier of Fortune* (1954) Isn't the pot calling the kettle black?

4. Among our ministers he is actilly at the top of the pot (40 Haliburton *Clockmaker* III 112). DA Pot 3 b (2).

5. All gone to pot (36 Haliburton *Clockmaker* I 317; Smith *Letters* 100 he said the beans might go to pot for what he keered; Melville "Cock-a-doodle-doo!" in *Works* XIII 160; Let the world and all aboard of it go to pot; Hammett *Wonderful* 104). Apperson 507; Farmer and Henley V 268–269; NED Pot 13 f; *Oxford* 242; Stevenson 1840:3; Tilley P504; NQ 4 iii 33, 70,

10 vii 106; David Frome, pseud. *The Black Envelope* (1937) 192. Cf. Whiting *Scots* II 112.

Pot, vb. A fact you can "pot and pickle" [i. e., note for future use]. (57 Willis *Paul* 79).

Potato, 1. Our system's sech, the thing'll root ez easy ez a tater (68 Lowell *Biglow* 284).

2. Some of these York cheps are green as young potatoes (44 Stephens *High Life* II 27).

3. As mealy as a pink eyed potater jest out o' the pot (44 Stephens *High Life* II 212).

4. As mean as a frozen potater [i. e., ill-tempered]. (44 Stephens *High Life* II 16, 96).

5. The people took skinnin' ez mild ez a tater (67 Lowell *Biglow* 322).

6. Quicker than you could peel a pratie (43 Robb *Squatter* 103).

7. As soft as a mealy potatoe with the skin off (44 Stephens *High Life* II 62, 197 she looked up as soft as a mealy potater, 245 His voice was as soft as a mealy potater). NC 461.

8. There warn't no fight in ye more'n in a mashed potater (67 Lowell *Biglow* 287).

9. Only remember that, if a bushel of potatoes is shaken in a market-cart without springs to it, the small potatoes always get to the bottom (58 Holmes *Autocrat* 291).

10. The potatoes and point of an Irish peasant (25 Neal *Brother J* I 75). Apperson 508; *Oxford* 513. Cf. Green 75 Butter-and-point.

11. That's the tatur [i. e., that's the fact]. 35 DA Potato 1 b (2).

12. Tell that to the potatoes. 56 DA Potato 1 b (3).

13. Old Col. Johnson answered him, but it was rather "small potatoes"

(35 Fairfield *Letters* 34; Robb *Squatter* 23 Van Buren was small potatoes; Hall *Purchase* II 84 Ay! certain small-potato patriots; Stephens *High Life* II 110; Thompson *Major* 10 I give 'em joy with their small potaters; Cooper *Redskins* 506 the brains of your "small-potato" legislature; Willis *Fun* 49 all Shinford would agree . . . that he was . . . a "small potato"; Smith *'Way* 42 get away with them small potatoes; Whitcher *Widow* 188 the Presbyterian minister here is such small potaters; Browne *Artemus* 22, 130; Locke [Nasby] *Struggles* 74). Bartlett 612; DA Small potato; Farmer 495; Farmer and Henley V 270; Green 284; NED Potato 5 a; Schele de Vere 400–401; Stevenson 1842:1; Thornton II 816, III 360; C. G. Booth *The Cat and the Clock* (1935) 76.

14. This is what I call small potatoes and few of a hill (36 Crockett *Exploits* 25; Haliburton *Clockmaker* II 199 in a hill, III 304, *Attaché* I 93; Smith *My Thirty* 395 It makes me feel so much like digging small potatoes and few in a hill; Clift *Bunker* 118 rather small potatoes and few in the hill). Bartlett 612; DA Small potato 1; Farmer 496; Figh PADS XIII (1950) 14; McAtee PADS XV (1951) 60; Randolph and Wilson 192; Schele de Vere 401; Stevenson 1842:1; Thornton II 816; Woodard PADS VI (1946) 41; R. P. Tristram Coffin *Lost Paradise* (1934) 143.

15. You had better drop that as you would a hot potato (40 Dana *Two* 244–245; Stephens *High Life* I 75 I sot there . . . a fingering it [a hat] over as if it had been a hot potato, II 58, 98, 198; Sedley *Marian* 422 the wind's dropping us like a hot potato). Boshears 32:163; DA Hot 5 b (2); NC 461; Taylor *Comparisons* 64; E.

S. Gardner *Murder Up My Sleeve* (1937) 163.

Potato cake. You are as pale as a potato cake (59 Boucicault *Dot* 119).

Potato hill. His belly pintin up like a big tater hill (67 Harris *Sut* 254).

Pot-luck. To take pot-luck with me (33 Smith *Downing* 48, *'Way* 170; Haliburton *Clockmaker* III 66; Melville *Moby-Dick* I 70 dip into the Potluck of both worlds, 80 try potluck at the Try Pots). Farmer and Henley V 273–274; Green 285; NC 461; NED Pot-luck; Stevenson 580:2; Tidwell PADS XI (1949) 9; J. G. Brandon *The One-Minute Murder* (1935) 78.

Poverty, 1. As plain as poverty (55 Haliburton *Nature* I 351; Paul *Courtship* 33 [obvious]).

2. Poverty makes us acquainted with strange bedfellows sometimes (38 Haliburton *Clockmaker* II 257, *Letter* 120 Poverty brings you acquaintance with strange company). Apperson 508–509; Stevenson 1845:5; Herman Landon *Three Brass Elephants* (1930) 35. See Misery (1), Politics.

Powder, 1. I call this hull hunt about as mean an affair as damp powder (58 Porter *Major* 143).

2. He ain't worth the powder that would kill him (35 Crockett *Account* 25; Haliburton *Clockmaker* III 49 He ain't worth powder and shot, *Nature* II 15; Kelly *Humors* 397 not worth the powder that would blow it up). McAtee 46; Stevenson 2644:4; George Dyer *The Catalyst Club* (1936) 204 enough powder to shoot you with; Caroline Gordon *The Garden of Adonis* (1937) 232 the powder and ball it'd take to blow 'em up with. Cf. Whiting *Devil* 225:13.

3. Pooh! they [wolves] are not worth the powder and shot, unless you can shoot two at a time (45 Mayo *Kaloolah* 42). NED Powder 3 b.

4. Whether the fun pays for the powder is a matter of debate (53 "Editor's Drawer" *Harper's New Monthly Magazine* VII 709).

Powder horn. I was as dry as a powder horn (34 Crockett *Life* 142; Kelly *Humors* 364; Thomson *Elephant Club* 137; Hammett *Piney* 110; Chamberlain *Confession* 101). McAtee 24; Svartengren 190.

Powder-house. His pockets were "as dry as a powder-house" (57 Riley *Puddleford* 85). Boshears 36:509; Halpert 347.

Powder-monkey. Dry as powder-monkeys (56 Kelly *Humors* 423).

Powerful. See Samson (1).

Practice. Practice makes perfect, and that's a fact (43 Haliburton *Attaché* III 61; Anon. *New Hope* 89; Riley *Puddleford* 168). Apperson 509; NC 462; *Oxford* 684; Stevenson 1859–1860:11; Tilley U24; Charles Reade *Hard Cash* (1863, ed. London 1913) 485.

Practise. We preach America, but practise Europe (54 Emerson *Letters* IV 441; Clemens *Letters* I 86 We preached our doctrine and practised it too; Saxe *Poems* 22 I wish that practising was not So different from preaching, 134 His preaching wasn't sanctioned by his practice, 189 When parsons practise what they preach; Alcott *Little Women* 295 he practised what he preached, 331 one who had learned the difference between preaching and practising). Apperson 509; NC 462; *Oxford* 514–515; Ste-

venson 1870:10; Tilley P537a; T. L. Peacock *Melincourt* (1817), *Works* II London [1924] 262 I should not much mind what you say, if you had not such a strange habit of practising what you preach; E. R. Punshon *Genius in Murder* (Boston 1933) 139; Vincent Starrett *The Blue Door* (1930) 48 a man who preached one thing and practised another.

Prairie. We war jest outside of Galveston, the water as smooth as a perara (58 Hammett *Piney* 66).

Praise. Praise to the face is open disgrace (40 Haliburton *Clockmaker* III 222, *Old Judge* I 211, *Sam* II 271). *Oxford* 515; Stevenson 1860:4.

Pray. See Angel (9).

Preach. Certain wits . . . , reversing the Indian's remark, say "Poor preach —poor pay" (43 Hall *Purchase* I 70).

Preacher. Enough to make a preacher swear (61 Wiley *Billy* 28).

Preaching, 1. As sartin as preachin' [said to be a Yankee phrase in contrast to the Southron's "as sure as shooting"]. (53 Hammett *Stray* 118, *Piney* 59). S. L. Bradbury *Hiram Harding of Hardscrabble* (Rutland, Vt. 1936) 141.

2. That's as clear as preaching (35 Kennedy *Horse-Shoe* 165; Haliburton *Attaché* IV 184; Smith *My Thirty* 405, 415).

3. That's as plain as preachin' (40 Haliburton *Clockmaker* III 205, *Sam* I 207).

4. Maybe it's all right ez preachin' (46 Lowell *Biglow* 45).

5. It's as true as preaching (32 Kennedy *Swallow* 317; Crockett *Life* 82; Burke *Polly* 19; Smith *'Way* 334 as Major Buck's preachin', *My Thirty*

441; Haliburton *Nature* I 57, 351, II 156; Anon. *New Hope* 341; Taliaferro *Fisher's* 72; Clift *Bunker* 84, 181; Eggleston *Circuit* 101). Cf. Kathleen M. Knight *The Wheel That Turned* (1936) 158 sure.

Pretty, 1. Pretty is as pretty does (53 Haliburton *Sam* I 136). McAtee *Grant County* 8; NC 462; Stevenson 539:2; Tiffany Thayer *The Cluck Abroad* (1935) 24. See Handsome (1).

2. See Angel (4), Canary (2), Paint (1), Picture (4), Pink (1), Sunflower (3).

Prevention. Only, if I was the gal's father . . . , I'd think prevention was better than cure (65 Sedley *Marian* 144). See Ounce (2).

Price. See Man (16).

Pricks. But it is hard to "kick against the pricks" (46 Cooper *Redskins* 312). Acts 9:5; Apperson 339; NC 462; NED Kick 1 c, Prick 13; *Oxford* 333; Stevenson 1293–1294:10; Tilley B680, F433; Whiting *Drama* 134, 351:659, *Scots* II 113; Katharina von Dombrowski *Land of Women* (Boston 1935) 203.

Pride, 1. Pride will have a fall, some day, that's the Lord's truth (35 Kennedy *Horse-Shoe* 145; Haliburton *Clockmaker* I 5 Pride must have a fall, 151; Melville *Piazza* 271 And so pride went before the fall; Riley *Puddleford* 249 Pride must have its fall; Alcott *Little Women* 75 But, alas, alas! pride goes before a fall; Saxe *Poems* 40 the Summer of pride should have its Fall; Jones *Batkins* 436 Pride will have a fall; Clemens *Letters* I 295). Prov. 16:18; Apperson 512; Bradley 89 goes before; NED Pride 1 e; *Oxford* 518; Stevenson 1882:5–7;

Stoett 955; Tilley P581; Whiting *Drama* 158, *Scots* II 113; J. D. Carr *Death Whispers* (1943) 255 goeth before; Jackson Gregory *Ru the Conqueror* (1933) 101 has a fall; *Catalogue of Political and Personal Satires . . . 1820–1827* (London 1952) X 449 No. 14709.

2. She put her pride in her pocket (69 Alcott *Little Women* 310). Harold E. Stearns *The Street I Know* (1935) 198.

Prim. See China aster (2), Peapod.

Prince. We live here like princes (38 Fairfield *Letters* 214; Clemens *Letters* I 92 I fare like a prince, 107 He lives like a prince). NC 463.

Print, 1. I'll tell you all about 'em right off as easy as big print (43 Haliburton *Attaché* IV 176). Svartengren 347.

2. As plain as print (44 Stephens *High Life* II 22; Cooke *Foresters* 297). NC 463; NED Plain 18 b; Svartengren 364–365; Mrs. Wilson Woodrow *The Moonhill Mystery* (1930) 235.

3. That's as true as print (56 Jones *Wild* 187).

Printing. This beats printing [i. e., is very good indeed]. (57 Melville *Confidence-Man* 328).

Prison. Ez safe ez in a prison (67 Lowell *Biglow* 293).

Procrastination. The great rule of his life was, that procrastination was the thief of time (64 Clemens *Washoe* 107, *Innocents* II 144, *Sketches* 189 [ascribed to Franklin]; Saxe *Poems* 124 To Procrastination be deaf,—(A homily sent from above,)—The scoundrel's not only "the thief Of time," but of beauty and love!). Apperson 513;

Oxford 519; Stevenson 1890:16; Vincent McHugh *Caleb Catlum's America* (1936) 290.

Prodigal. See Hydrant.

Profound. See Death (11).

Proof, 1. The proof of the pudding's chawin' the bag, as the fellow said (35 Longstreet *Georgia* 162; Stephens *High Life* II 38 The proof of the pudding is in eating the bag).
2. The proof of the pudding is in the eating thereof (55 Derby *Phoenixiana* 43; Jones *Country* 165; Clift *Bunker* 195 There's a good deal of truth in the old adage). Apperson 514; Bradley 89; *Oxford* 520; Stevenson 1898:6; Tilley P608; Herbert Best *The Mystery of the Flaming Hut* (1932) 284 the old adage; R. E. Fitch *The Pacific Spectator* V (1951) 368 With regard to this assertion . . . the proof is in the pudding; Stark Young *So Red the Rose* (1934) 225.
3. He had got a little above proof [i. e., tipsy]. (55 Hammett *Wonderful* 70).

Prophet. And you know there ain't any country but what a prophet's an honor to, as the proverb says (73 Clemens *Gilded* I 45). Matthew xiii: 57; *Oxford* 520–521; A. Fredericks, pseud. *The Mark of the Rat* (1929) 35.

Proud. See Boy (2), Devil (4), Dollar (4), Hen (6), King (3), Lizard (2), Lucifer (1), Nigger (4), Old Nick (1), Peacock (2), Pharisee, Poplar, Turk (2), Turkey 2 (4).

Providence. Providence favored the strongest battalions (67 Richardson *Beyond* 103). *Oxford* 522; Stevenson 983:1.

Prudence. It occurred to me that "prudence was the better part of valor" (c56 Cartwright *Autobiography* 329). Malcolm Burr *A Fossicker in Angola* (London 1933) 59 prudence is the better course. See Discretion.

Psalms. He mought just as well have sung psalms to a dead horse, for my mind was made up (36 Crockett *Exploits* 81). Bartlett 809; DA Horse 8 (1). Cf. *Oxford* 705 To whistle.

Psyche. A creature as slight as Psyche (53 Willis *Fun* 260).

Pucker. Don't put yourself in a pucker (25 Neal *Brother J* II 366; Smith *Downing* 143 I felt in such a pucker to know what I was going to get, 189, 207, 227; Stephens *High Life* I 148, 171, 195, II 44; Paul *Courtship* 274). Bartlett 501; Farmer and Henley V 309–310; Green 290; NED Pucker 2; Thornton II 707.

Pudding, 1. Travels without anecdotes is like a puddin' without plums —all dough (38 Haliburton *Clockmaker* II 85).
2. Don't stop stirrin' till the pudden's done (34 Davis *Downing* 19).

Pull. It required a long pull and a strong pull (43 Thompson *Chronicles* 29; Derby *Squibob* 199 A long pull, a strong pull, and a pull altogether; Alcott *Little Women* 474). *Oxford* 381; Stevenson 1915:9; *Catalogue of Political and Personal Satires . . . 1820–1827* (London 1952) X 71 No. 13770 A long pull and a Strong pull and a pull alltogether.

Pullet, 1. Polly's got a heart as soft as a pullet's egg (c60 Paul *Courtship* 50).
2. I felt my neck a floundering

about, like a pullet with its neck twisted (44 Stephens *High Life* I 88).

3. They huddled together like pullets under an old cart (44 Stephens *High Life* II 185).

Pump, 1. They are as stupid as a pump (43 Haliburton *Attaché* I 266).

2. She was as tall as a pump (53 Willis *Fun* 304). Cf. Svartengren 275.

3. Betwixt you and me and the pump (56 Durivage *Three* 113). See Gatepost (2).

Pump bolt. I am as steady as a pump bolt, now (36 Haliburton *Clockmaker* I 178, 259).

Pumpkin, 1. [A slaughtered hog] bare as a punkin (56 Kelly *Humors* 360).

2. Your head is swelled as big as a pumkin (43 Robb *Squatter* 82). DA Pumpkin 5 c.

3. Green as a punkin [i. e., unsophisticated]. (58 Hammett *Piney* 172). Cf. DA Pumpkin 5 c (pumpkin vine).

4. If this here world was round like a big punkin (43 Hall *Purchase* I 157; Riley *Puddleford* 297 Their faces as round as pumpkins, and as red, too).

5. His skin was tanned yellow as a pumpkin (59 Taliaferro *Fisher's* 125). Boshears 41:1045; NC 463; Taylor *Comparisons* 89.

6. Flufkins was . . . anxious . . . , to use his own words, be "some pumpkins" (51 Dorson *Jonathan* 72, 85 I remarked that he was certainly "some pumpkins," 131 you are indeed *pumpkins to the core!* I have heard about being 'pumpkins'; Hammett *Wonderful* 334 Your Lieutenant is some punkins, *Piney* 63; Thomson *Plu-ri-bus-tah* 105, 158, 222; Kelly *Humors* 139 A man of "some pumpkins" and "persimmons" at home, 187 New Year's Day is some considerable "pumpkins" in many parts of the United States; Willis *Paul* 360; Porter *Major* 118; Cary *Married* 189; Wiley *Johnny* 166; Browne *Artemus* 196 Alexander the Grate was punkins . . . but Napoleon was punkinser; Lowell *Biglow* 259; Clift *Bunker* 111). Bartlett 626–627; DA Pumpkin 2 b; Farmer 443; Farmer and Henley V 322; McAtee 60; NED Pumpkin 2 b; Schele de Vere 525; Stevenson 1915:13; Thornton II 829–830, III 366; Stanley Johnson *Professor* (1925) 243.

7. Grew like a pumpkin [a boy]. (54 Smith '*Way* 149).

Punctual. See Clock (3).

Pup, 1. He was as blind as a pup [i. e., drunk]. (35 Crockett *Account* 66).

2. Es quick es yu cud kiver a sick pup wif a saddil blanket (67 Harris *Sut* 24).

Puppy, 1. Just as piert as a puppy (58 Hammett *Piney* 40, 302).

2. As tickled as a puppy dog (44 Stephens *High Life* I 193).

3. Pete . . . crawled away like a whipped puppy (71 Eggleston *SchoolMaster* 168).

Pure. See Angel (5), Dew (2), Moonlight (1), Snow (4), Violet (2), Water (3).

Purple, 1. They may talk Freedom's airy Tell they're pupple in the face (48 Lowell *Biglow* 46). See Black (3).

2. See Plum (2).

Purse, 1. The vulgar proverb, "I will get it from his purse or get it from his skin," is sound philosophy (c39 Emerson *Works* II 111).

2. They cannot make a "silk purse

out of a sow's ear" (46 Cooper *Red-skins* 128; Judd *Margaret* II 51; Cary *Married* 299). Apperson 571–572; NC 463; *Oxford* 589; Stevenson 2176–2177:7; Tilley P666; NQ 4 i 519; 8 vi 451–452 Well, there's no making a whistle of a pig's tail; Hulbert Footner *A Self-Made Thief* (1929) 143; E. K. Gann *Soldier of Fortune* (1954) 193 A girl who tried to make; R. P. Warren *All the King's Men* (1946) 105 You haven't got a sow's ear to make a silk purse of.

3. He ain't no more like he was dan a silk pus is like a sow's ear (55 Anon. *New Hope* 145).

Purser, 1. *"Purser rigged and parish damned"* is the sailor saying in the American Navy, when the tyro first mounts the lined frock and blue jacket, aptly manufactured for him in a state prison ashore (50 Melville *White Jacket* 475–476). Babcock 260.

2. The ideas that sailors entertain of pursers is expressed in a rather inelegant but expressive saying of theirs: "The purser is a conjurer; he can make a dead man chew tobacco"—insinuating that the accounts of a dead man are sometimes subjected to post-mortem change (50 Melville *White Jacket* 256).

Pusley. Meaner than pusley. 58 DA Pusley 1 b.

Puss. The trade of "puss in the corner," or of shoving a man out of his property, in order to place one's self in (45 Cooper *Chainbearer* 182).

Pussy. See Pig (7), Turkey 2 (5).

Pussy cat. As affectionate as a pussy cat (44 Stephens *High Life* I 154).

Putty. Soft as putty (67 Richardson *Beyond* 503). NC 463; Svartengren 266.

֍ Q ֍

Quaker, 1. They were all as mum as a Quaker meetin (34 Davis *Downing* 34).

2. It's enough to make a Quaker kick his grandmother (56 Durivage *Three* 343). Cf. Boshears 30:41 I'm so mad I could slap my granny. See Grandmother (5), Stone (13).

Quarrel. See Cat (58), Two (9).

Queen, 1. Happy as a queen (Alcott *Little Women* 311). NC 464; A. T. Sheppard *Here Comes an Old Sailor* (1928) 293.

2. She used to dress up like a queen (44 Stephens *High Life* I 236).

Queen of Sheba. I worn't so wise ez thet air queen o' Sheby (48 Lowell *Biglow* 58). Svartengren 26. Cf. NC 479 Solomon.

Queer. See Folks (1).

Question, 1. He had made up his mind to pop the question that very day (51 Burke *Polly* 26; Boucicault *Flying Scud* 204 Well, hang me, if the old lady ain't been and popped the question. I wonder what sort of a Leap Year this comes in; Barnum *Struggles* 591). NED Pop, vb.[1] 6; Stevenson 1926:4.

2. The Squire there asked me a civil question, and that desarves a civil answer,—at least that's manners where I come from (58 Hammett *Piney* 285; Haliburton *Season-Ticket* 155). Cf. Answer (1); Stevenson 1926:8; Tilley Q9.

3. Ask no questions that may lead to deceitful answers (27 Cooper *Prairie* 417; Haliburton *Clockmaker* II 228 ax me no questions, and I'll tell you no lies, *Attaché* IV 62, *Nature* I 273; Sedley *Marian* 407 Ask no questions, and get no lies, will be his motto at election time). McAtee *Additional* 11, PADS XV (1951) 52; NC 464; *Oxford* 15; Stevenson 1394:2; NQ 9 iii 47, 157 stories; F. L. Packard *The Big Shot* (1929) 282; W. C. MacDonald *Destination Danger* (Philadelphia 1955) 140, 321.

Quick. See Ball-hornet, Cat (17), Cat's cradle, Death (12), Flash (1), Fox (6), Foxtrap (1), Grasshopper (4), Gunpowder, Hat (3), Hell (4), Light (2), Lightning (2), Look, sb. (1), Mule (5), Paddy (1), Potato (6), Pup (2), Quicksilver, Rat (5), Rifleball (1), Scat, Shooting (2), Steeltrap (1), Thought (2), Thunder (8), Toad (2), Turtle (4), Wink (1), Winking (1).

Quicksilver. They seem'd tu go thru . . . her as quick es quick silver wud git thru a sifter (67 Harris *Sut* 40).

Quiet. See Baby (2), Cat (18), Grave (6), Kitten (8), Lamb (11), Mink (3), Mole, Mouse (3), Nigger (5), Pigeon (2), Statue (4), Wagon (1).

Quietly. See Mill-pond (2).

Quiver. See Aspen leaf, Leaf (6).

✥ R ✥

Rabbit, 1. What is it that makes me humble as a rabbit . . . ? (54 Stephens *Fashion* 109).

2. As innocent as a rabbit in a box-trap (44 Stephens *High Life* I 222).

3. Face as pale as a rabbit's belly (43 Lewis *Odd* 51).

4. Looked at me as pitiful as a rabbit in a trap (44 Stephens *High Life* II 261).

5. I swanny if my heart didn't jump like a rabbit at the sight of a piece of sweet apple in snow time! (44 Stephens *High Life* I 28). NC 464. Cf. J. D. Carr *The Burning Court* (1937) 173 as jumpy as a rabbit.

6. Keep a civil tongue in your head; or you'll buy the rabbits (25 Neal *Brother J* II 51, 156 if that air invoice aint ready soon, thee'll buy the rabbit, I guess; Smith *'Way* 13 he must look out, or he'll buy the rabbit).

7. They run like rabbits (45 Hooper *Simon* 53). NC 464; Nancy Barr Mavity *The Fate of Jane McKenzie* (1933) 11.

Raccoon, 1. It's as dead . . . as a skin'd racoon (34 Davis *Downing* 145).

2. See Coon.

Race, 1. The battle is not always to the strong, neither is the race to the swift (24 Cooper *Pilot* 153; Kennedy *Horse-Shoe* 99 "The battle is not always to the strong . . . nor is the craft of soldiership without its

chances." "If we had listened . . . to musty proverbs, Charleston would have this day been in the secure and peaceful possession of the enemy"; Crockett *Exploits* 150 The proverb says, "The race is not always to the swift, nor the battle to the strong"; Fairfield *Letters* 437 Truly the race is not always to the swift or the battle to the strong; Hammett *Piney* 239 the race is not always to the swift, nor the battle to the slow; Haliburton *Season-Ticket* 28 The race). Eccl. 9:11; Bradley 90; *Oxford* 530; Stevenson 1930:2; P. B. Kyne *Tide of Empire* (1928) 115 swiftest; Stark Young *So Red the Rose* (1934) 185 swif's' [swiftest].

2. And then the itinerant system will be very much like a man riding a race with the reins of his horse's bridle tied to a stump (c56 Cartwright *Autobiography* 505).

Race-horse. She'll walk up to Cape Horn like a race-horse (40 Dana *Two* 352, 456 passed us like a race-horse; Smith *'Way* 326–327 the Susquehanna has got her head up, and is running like a race-horse).

Racer. As hard as a racer [horse]. (60 Haliburton *Season-Ticket* 24).

Rack, 1. But you will find me standing up to my rack (34 Crockett *Life* 211, *Account* 189, 214; Thompson *Major* 54 make him stand up to his rack;

Baldwin *Flush* 60; Hammett *Stray* 215 They can't get Horseley to come up to the rack; Riley *Puddleford* 103–104 all you've got to do is to stand up to the rack, vote for true men, 157). Bartlett 654; DA Rack 4 b; Thornton II 853. See Lick-log.

2. I was determined to stand up to my rack, fodder or no fodder (34 Crockett *Life* 61, *Account* 137). Green 31; Thornton II 853. See Lick-log.

Radiant. See Angel (6), Summer-squash.

Radish, 1. As easy as you'd pull up a spring raddish (51 Burke *Polly* 118).
2. See Pea (6).

Rag, 1. If he ain't as limber as a rag (25 Neal *Brother J* II 67; Kelly *Humors* 83; Smith *Arp* 97 Her neck became as limber as a greasy rag). Boshears 38:719; Halpert 482. Cf. Taylor *Comparisons* 54.
2. Wilted down as limpsey as a rag (33 Smith *Downing* 224). Thornton I 543. Cf. NC 464.
3. A well-directed blow sent him [a dog] . . . as senseless as a rag, into his master's arms (60 Whitehead *Wild Sports* 48).
4. All of them, rag-tag, an' bobtail (25 Neal *Brother J* II 292, 302 rag, tag, and bob-tail; Baldwin *Flush* 87 Rags, Tag and Bobtail; Kelly *Humors* 168 The "private conveyance" . . . waiting to carry them, band-box and bundle, rag-tag and bobtail, 232 suppers and parties to the rag-tag and bobtail; Cary *Married* 291 you look like rag-shag-and-bobtail; Clemens *Roughing* I 9). Apperson 616; Farmer and Henley VII 56–57; NED Rag-tag; *Oxford* 638; Stevenson 2268:

3; Tilley T10; Whiting *Drama* 366: 382; NQ 2 xii 110; 3 v 518; 7 xii 5, 93, 194; William Faulkner *The Sound and the Fury* (1929) 258 ragtag and bobtail. Cf. Tag; NED Tag 10 (tag and rag).
5. I've got to stay here, till the old man drops the rag and gives the word (79 Clemens *Tramp* I 174).
6. Folks actilly *do* say I take the rag off quite (40 Haliburton *Clockmaker* III 202, 294, *Attaché* II 128, 135, 250, III 169, *Sam* I 83; Hammett *Piney* 115 I swan to man ef it didn't take the rag off of any picter in creation I ever see; Sedley *Marian* 103 I guess Sacramenty and Frisky'll have to take the rag off the Bar). Bartlett 511, 689.
7. Why it's rather takin' the rag off the bush, ain't it? (43 Haliburton *Attaché* I 226, II 131, *Sam* I 116, *Nature* II 122, 278, *Season-Ticket* 362; Stephens *High Life* I 49, 56, 118; Taliaferro *Fisher's* 86, *Carolina Humor* 77). DA Bush 5 (1); Farmer 107; Figh PADS XIII (1950) 15; Randolph and Wilson 291; Stevenson 258–259:10; Thornton II 884, III 394.
8. What a red rag is to a bull, Turner's "Slave Ship" was to me (79 Clemens *Tramp* I 218). NED Red rag 3; *Oxford* 536; Taylor *Comparisons* 67; Tilley R59; Nancy B. Mavity *The Other Bullet* (1930) 123.

Rag baby. He looks as helpless as a rag baby (73 Clemens *Gilded* II 60).

Ragged. See Colt (2).

Rail, 1. As thin as a rail (72 Clemens *Roughing* I 108). Boshears 40:986; NC 464; Taylor *Comparisons* 82; John S. Strange, pseud. *For the Hangman* (1934) 183.
2. He looked just's if he'd swaller'd

a rail, and shrunk to it (58 Hammett *Piney* 80).

3. See Devil (10).

Railroad. Every stitch was as long as a railroad (55 Thomson *Doesticks* 138).

Rain, 1. It never rains, but it pours (36 Emerson *Journals* IV 76; Cooper *Satanstoe* 242 With them, it did not rain often; but when it did rain, it was pretty certain to pour; Paul *Courtship* 141). Apperson 522; Green 26; Lean IV 20; NC 465; *Oxford* 531–532; Stevenson 1930–1931:10; R. S. Surtees *Mr. Sponge's Sporting Tour* (London [1853]) 109, 201; J. B. Priestley *Angel Pavement* (1930) 451; Dorothy Ogburn *Ra-ta plun!* (Boston 1930) 18; T. H. White *The Sword in the Stone* (1939) 94 It never hails but it pours.

2. See Cat (60), Dish (2), Know (2), Pitchfork (2), Plough-share, Spikes.

Rainbow, 1. A bird . . . all feathered off as bright as a rainbow (44 Stephens *High Life* I 156). Cf. Svartengren 222 splendid.

2. Her face would make a halo, rich as a rainbow (50 Mitchell *Reveries* 32).

Ram, 1. Headstrong as a ram (50 Boker *World* 8).

2. Butt like rams (59 Taliaferro *Fisher's* 198). NC 465.

Ramrod, 1. He walked out of the room as stiff as a ramrod (55 Haliburton *Nature* I 145). NC 465; Svartengren 60; Michael Keyes *The Dead Parrot* (1933) 252.

2. Stood as straight as two ramrods (49 Haliburton *Old Judge* I 303; Hammett *Piney* 142 haven't your friends been enjien' themselves too much to carry this thing out straight as a ramrod?). McAtee 62; NC 465; Taylor *Comparisons* 78; Stanley H. Page *The Resurrection Murder Case* (1932) 18.

3. A young docter, wif ramrod laigs (67 Harris *Sut* 54).

Ram's horn, 1. As crooked as a ram's horn (34 Davis *Downing* 324; Haliburton *Clockmaker* III 49 he is more crookeder in his ways nor a . . . ram's horn; Hammett *Stray* 54 his inclination, which, without being what may be technically described as "crooked," nevertheless had as many twists and ramifications as the horn of a veteran of the flock and fold; Clift *Bunker* 137). Apperson 122; Green 18; McAtee *Grant County* 4; Svartengren 278–279; A. C. and C. B. Edington *The Monk's-hood Murders* (1931) 120.

2. I guess it all come straight's a ram's-horn in the eend, though (58 Hammett *Piney* 34). Apperson 122, quot. 1658, 531 Right; *Oxford* 543; Svartengren 370; Tilley R28; Whiting *Scots* II 115.

3. His disposition is twisted like a ram's horn (37 Neal *Charcoal* 196).

Rapid. See Telegraph.

Rash. See Whirlwind (1).

Raspberries. Lips . . . looked like two red rosberries jest a going to drop off from their bushes (44 Stephens *High Life* II 150).

Rat, 1. Brave es a trap't rat (67 Harris *Sut* 278). Cf. Herbert Adams *The Empty Bed* (Philadelphia 1928) 231 a cornered rat will fight.

2. As dead as a drownded rat (33 Smith *Downing* 25). Svartengren 145 rat.

3. She's as gray as a rat (56

Whitcher *Widow* 38, 82; Saxe *Poems* 169 His locks are as gray as a rat; Clemens *Roughing* II 158). NC 465.

4. Poor as any rat (55 Melville "Jimmy Rose" in *Works* XIII 263). Apperson 505; NED Rat 2 c; *Oxford* 510; Svartengren 343; A. E. W. Mason *The Prisoner in the Opal* (1928) 299 a rat.

5. As quick as a rat runs through a kitchen (35 Kennedy *Horse-Shoe* 248).

6. I was as wet as a drowned rat (34 Crockett *Life* 41, *Exploits* 117 as a thrice drowned rat; Haliburton *Attaché* IV 112–113). Boshears 41: 1013; McAtee 70; NC 466; NED Rat 2 b; Taylor *Comparisons* 86; Tilley M1237.

7. Oh, goodness! we are nothing but poor rats in the trap, now! (56 Jones *Wild* 72). Cf. NC 466:8; W. S. Masterman *The Bay Bloodhounds* (1936) 262 caught like a rat in a trap.

8. It is like giving advice to a rat when his leg is in the trap (44 Stephens *High Life* I 94).

9. To give one rats [i. e., to berate]. 62 DA Rat 6 b.

10. I smell a rat (25 Neal *Brother J* II 291, 292; Smith *Downing* 136; Haliburton *Clockmaker* III 69, 173; Hall *Purchase* II 43; Cooper *Satanstoe* 168; Anon. *New Hope* 40; Lowell *Biglow* 109; Riley *Puddleford* 141; Boucicault *Dot* 124 You smelt a rat in the wedding cake?; Paul *Courtship* 166 to "smell the rat"; Barnum *Struggles* 703; Harris *Uncle Remus* 45). Apperson 580; Farmer and Henley V 377; Green 344; NC 466; NED Rat 2 a; *Oxford* 598; Stevenson 1937:1; Tilley R31; Whiting *Drama* 364:855; *Catalogue of Political and Personal Satires . . . 1811–1819* (London 1949) IX 833 No. 13040; Jane Allen,

pseud. *I Lost My Girlish Laughter* (1938) 142.

11. Where are you going with that tear in your eye, like a travelling rat? (50 Melville *White Jacket* 164).

Rates, 1. Sure as rates (33 Smith *Downing* 56; Haliburton *Clockmaker* I 250, II 45, III 185, *Attaché* I 146, II 173, III 48, IV 156, *Nature* II 122). DA Rate 1 b (1).

2. True as rates (49 Haliburton *Old Judge* II 266, *Sam* I 13, 197).

Rat hole. I felt shrunk to nothing, and could have crept into a rat-hole (23–24 Irving *Tales* 197). Cf. Knot-hole (2).

Rat traps. My eyelids . . . have been snapping like rat traps [i. e., sleepy]. (35 Kennedy *Horse-Shoe* 400).

Rather. Pass 'em by—ruther o' the rutherest, as a body may say [i. e., excessively—here—ugly]. (25 Neal *Brother J* II 438).

Rattle. See Gourd (2).

Rattlesnake, 1. The old feller looked as pided as a rattle-snaik (45 Hooper *Simon* 103).

2. But we'll fix him, as sure as you ever kilt a rattle snake (55 Anon. *New Hope* 340).

Raven, 1. Hat—blacker than the wet plumage of the raven (25 Neal *Brother J* III 8, *Down-Easters* I 170 hair blacker than the wing of a raven; Saxe *Poems* 345 "Raven-white" was once the saying, Till an accident, alack! Spoiled the meaning, and thereafter It was changed to "Raven-black"). Apperson 51; Fife 117; NC 466; NED Raven 4 (raven-black), Taylor *Comparisons* 18; Whitman Chambers *Murder for a Wanton* (1934) 21 raven black.

2. Boots dark and glossy as the raven's wing (55 Hammett *Wonderful* 241; Anon. *New Hope* 70). Svartengren 244.

Razor, 1. [He] was tearin' about last night as blue as a razor! [i. e., in high feather]. (65 Sedley *Marian* 195). DA Razor 2 c (intoxicated).

2. As cute as a razor (44 Stephens *High Life* II 38, 72). Cf. Val Gielgud *The Ruse of the Vanished Women* (1934) 186 keen.

3. As polished and shiney as a new razor (43 Hall *Purchase* II 29).

4. Sharp's a razor [i. e., clever, shrewd]. (25 Neal *Brother J* III 386; Stephens *High Life* I 212; Judd *Richard* 229; Taliaferro *Fisher's* 161). Apperson 561; Boshears 40:897; McAtee 55; NC 466; Randolph and Wilson 175; Taylor *Comparisons* 71; Tilley R36; Whiting *Drama* 324:272, *Scots* II 116.

5. This norwester cuts like a razor (54 Smith '*Way* 57).

6. Yankees, who, as I have heard them say, would rather be shaved with a sharp razor than a dull one (51 Hawthorne *Twice-Told* 127).

Read. See Book (1), Fox (9), Map.

Ready. See Cat (19).

Reason, 1. There's reason in all things (59 Smith *My Thirty* 251). Cf. Apperson 525; *Oxford* 534; Stevenson 1940: 4; Ralph Rodd *The Secret of the Flames* (1929) 81.

2. There is reason even in roastin' an egg (38 Haliburton *Clockmaker* III 173). Apperson 525; *Oxford* 534; Stevenson 1940:11; Tilley R49.

Reckoning. Short reckonings make long friends, as the sayin' is (38 Haliburton *Clockmaker* III 38–39). Ap-

person 568; *Oxford* 585; Stevenson 1943:11; Tilley R54.

Red. See Apple (3), Ball (1), Beef, Blaze (1, 2, 9), Blood (1), Bull (3), Carnation, Carnelian, Cherry (1, 2), Cock (1), Currant wine, Fire (6, 7), Flannel, Geranium, Goose's foot, Lightning (4), Lip (2), Lobster, Nailrod, Peony (1), Pepper pod, Poppy, Pumpkin (4), Rooster (2), Rose (5, 6), Ruby, Strawberry (2), Turkey 2 (6).

Red-handed. So he isn't taken redhanded, after-claps may go to the devil (45 Hooper *Simon* 37). NED Redhanded; Whiting *Scots* II 116; D. Q. Burleigh *The Kristiana Killers* (1937) 179.

Reefer. In the Navy it has become a proverb that a useless fellow is "*as much in the way as a reefer*" [i. e., midshipman]. (50 Melville *White Jacket* 30). Babcock 259.

Reel, 1. Right off the reel [i. e., quickly]. (33 Neal *Down-Easters* I 14, 79, 106; Stephens *High Life* I 45, 51; Haliburton *Old Judge* I 27, *Season-Ticket* 286; Hammett *Piney* 102). DA Right 6 b (3); NC 466; NED Reel 2 c; Thornton II 621; W. B. M. Ferguson *The Black Company* (1924) 81.

2. Sharp off the reel [i. e., at once]. (25 Neal *Brother J* I 156).

Refreshing. See Water (4).

Regular. See Book (2), Chronometer, Clock (4), Clockwork (2), Pig-tracks (2), Sun (5).

Relations. In this country, a feller aint to blame for his relations, that's one comfort (44 Stephens *High Life* II 81). Bartlett *Familiar Quotations*

1056; Stevenson 1296:2 God gave us our relations, but thank God we can choose our friends.

Remember. Well, well, 'tisn't best to remember everything (59 Shillaber *Knitting-Work* 162).

Removes. Franklin thought a few moves was as bad as a fire (56 Kelly *Humors* 277; Barnum *Struggles* 472 The old proverb says, "Three removes are as bad as a fire," but when a man is in the fire, it matters but little how soon or how often he removes). Apperson 629; NED Remove 5; *Oxford* 654; Stevenson 314:2; Thomas Hood *Comic Annual* (London 1832) 17 but as people say, two Lincolnshire removes are as bad as a fire of London.

Republics. Republics are ungrateful (43 Robb *Squatter* 20; Holmes *Autocrat* 26 Are Republics still ungrateful, as of old?; Locke [Nasby] *Struggles* 552 Republics hev alluz bin ungrateful).

Resolute. See Lion (6), Tiger (2).

Restless. See Cockroach.

Revenge. Revenge is sweet (33 Neal *Down-Easters* II 56; Boucicault *Flying Scud* 207; Clemens *Love Letters* 132 Revenge is wicked . . . But it is powerful sweet). Apperson 528; NC 466; *Oxford* 539; Stevenson 1973:4; Tilley R90; Sir Walter Scott *A Legend of Montrose* (1819) Ch. 13 and every thorough-bred soldier will confess that revenge is a sweet morsel; H. L. Ickes *Diary* II (1954) 170 it must be true that revenge is sweeter than most other feelings; J. S. Strange, pseud. *Silent Witnesses* (1938) 224.

Reward. He . . . long since went to his reward (c56 Cartwright *Autobiography* 62).

Rhinoceros, 1. Strong as a rhinoceros (50 Willis *Life* 368).

2. A glance . . . would have made a hole in the hide of a rhinoceros (53 Willis *Fun* 320).

Rhyme. Without rhyme or reason (49 Melville *Mardi* I 132; Saxe *Poems* 124 There's not the least reason nor rhyme; Barnum *Struggles* 57 without destroying both rhyme and reason; Clemens *Innocents* II 124). Apperson 529; NC 467; NED Rhyme 3 b; *Oxford* 540; Stevenson 1976:14; Taylor *Investigations* 263; Tilley R98; Whiting *Drama* 360:799, *Scots* II 117; Lewis Carroll *Rhyme and Reason* (London 1883), a title; Desmond Holdridge *Pindorama* (1933) 154.

Ribbon. To a ribbon [i. e., precisely]. 41 DA Ribbon 4 d.

Ribbongrass. I should feel as streaked as a piece of ribbongrass [i. e., embarrassed]. (44 Stephens *High Life* I 194).

Rich. See Bank (2), Cream (2), Croesus, Festus, Jew (2), King (4), Mine, sb. (2), Mud (3), Pie (2), Rainbow (2), Sin (6).

Ride. I'm dog-on ef they wouldn't rout out and give your Uncle Billy a dry ride [i. e., a ride on a rail]. (58 Hammett *Piney* 153).

Riffle. To make the riffle [i. e., to be successful]. 57 DA Riffle 1 b.

Rifle. The rail-fence appeered strate as a rifle [i. e., ran so fast that]. (43 Lewis *Odd* 51; Hall *Purchase* I 157 and I kin prove it straight as a rifle).

Rifle-ball, 1. An idea quick and penetrating as a rifle-ball (45 Hooper *Simon* 22).

2. The road is as straight as the

track of a rifle-ball (67 Richardson *Beyond* 566).

Rifle-barrel. I've hearn that he'd got religion and come out straight as a rifle-barrel (58 Hammett *Piney* 169).

Rifle gun. Goin' fast as the report of a rifle gun (59 Taliaferro *Fisher's* 150).

Right, sb. (1). On the supposition that right is stronger than might (45 Cooper *Chainbearer* 326). Cf. Might (1); Tilley M922; Whiting *Scots* II 117.

2. Right is right, and wrong is wrong (76 Nash *Century* 46).

Right, adj., 1. I leave this rule for others when I'm dead, Be always sure you're right—then go ahead (34 Crockett *Life* Title-page, 13 according to my own maxim, just "go ahead," *Exploits* 77 so go ahead, Crockett; Durivage *Three* 79 Colonel Crockett's golden maxim, *"Be always sure you're right, then go ahead"*; Kelly *Humors* 214 Had the old Colonel [Davy Crockett] never uttered a better idea than that everlasting good motto—"Be sure you're right, then go ahead!"; Clift *Bunker* 125 "Be sure you're right then go ahead." Davy Crockett got out considerable truth when he started that proverb; Barnum *Struggles* 474–475 Davy Crockett said: "This thing remember, when I am dead, Be sure you are right, then go ahead"). Bradley 90; DA Ahead 2 (1); Stevenson 1989:10.

2. See Hair (7), Leg (3), Preaching (4), Trivet (1).

Right, adv., 1. I'm sure you daubed it onto Lidy Ann right and left (56 Whitcher *Widow* 279; Hammett *Piney* 159 The bank made loans right and left). NED Right and left 1 b.

2. See Reel (1).

Rigid. See Tombstone (2).

Riled. See Missouri.

Riley. See Thunder (10).

Ringbolt. That points to the ringbolt, I tell *you* [i. e., to the essential matter]. (50 Judd *Richard* 301).

Rinse. For a clean rinse is better than a dirty wipe, any time (43 Haliburton *Attaché* II 215).

Riot Act. And propriety the magistrate who reads the riot-act (60 Holmes *Professor* 72). Stevenson 1993:9; Taylor *Index* 56.

Rip. To let her rip. 46 DA Rip 1 b.

Ripe, 1. Old age is ripeness, and I once heard say, "Better ripe than raw" (57 Melville *Confidence-Man* 232).

2. A nation might "get so very ripe as to become a little rotten" (57 Riley *Puddleford* 196). Cf. NC 467 Soon ripe; Stevenson 1994:6; Whiting *Drama* 121, 165, 286, 290, *Scots* II 117.

Rise. Up! b'ys; up! rise and shine; time to get at it agin! (47 Melville *Omoo* 247).

River, 1. A heart . . . strong as a tempest, wild as a rushing river (50 Mitchell *Reveries* 81).

2. The threat that terrifies more than whipping or torture of any kind is the threat of being sent down river (51 Stowe *Uncle* 107). Stevenson 2070:8 sold down. Cf. DA River 3 (5).

3. I don't believe that are chap'll ever set the north-river afire (33 Neal *Down-Easters* I 101; Whitcher *Widow* 236 he's a very nice young man, tho' I guess he won't never set the river afire; Clemens *Innocents* I 12; Jones *Batkins* 496 the torch of my genius, to use a common phrase, would "nev-

er set the river on fire"). Apperson 622–623 Thames; *Oxford* 576; Stevenson 2293:7; Sir Basil Thomson *Who Killed Stella Pomeroy?* (1936) 48 my writings have not yet set any river on fire.

Roach. Sound as a roach (25 Neal *Brother J* III 297; Cary *Clovernook* 2d Series 124 I . . . slep as sound as a roach). Apperson 590; Farmer and Henley VI 299; NED Roach 1 b; Stevenson 2174:6; Svartengren 154; Tilley R143.

Road, 1. It seems to me that the road out is jest as plain as the road to mill (59 Smith *My Thirty* 346, 362; Barnum *Struggles* 457 The road to wealth is, as Dr. Franklin truly says, "as plain as the road to mill"). Svartengren 362 clear, 366–367 highway.

2. But the longest road must have an end (54 Shillaber *Mrs. Partington* 292).

3. The road to the head lies through the heart (38 Haliburton *Clockmaker* II 16).

4. There is no royal road to learning (24 Emerson *Journals* I 393; Barnum *Struggles* 482 says the proverb). *Oxford* 550; Stevenson 1379:4; L. P. Smith *Words and Idioms* (Boston 1929) 239.

5. You haven't seen enough of the world yet to know which is the best road to mill (39 Smith *Letters* 23).

Roar. See Bull (9).

Roast. If the newly-married couple were to dance together on their wedding-day, the wife would thenceforth rule the roast (20–22 Irving *Bracebridge* 361, 364; Smith *Downing* 57, 'Way 131; Hammett *Wonderful* 44 She ruled the roast—and the boiled; Whitcher *Widow* 364 The cook actu-

ally "ruled the roast" at Colonel P.'s in more than one sense; Saxe *Poems* 89). Apperson 540; Farmer and Henley VI 39; Lean III 310; NED Roast 1 b; *Oxford* 551; Stevenson 1013:9; Tilley R144; Whiting *Drama* 361:810, *Scots* II 117–118; NQ 2 iv 152; 4 viii 64; 6 iii 127, 169, 277, 396, 432, 477, 495, 512; Phoebe F. Gaye *Good Sir John* (1930) 84. See Roost.

Robin, 1. As good-natered and kind as a robin red breast in the spring time (44 Stephens *High Life* II 149). Cf. Tilley R146.

2. By this time her hand and mine had got about as intimate as tew young robins in a nest (44 Stephens *High Life* II 222).

3. Trying to look like a love-sick robin on an apple-tree limb (44 Stephens *High Life* II 97).

Robin Hood. The way some folks have of going round "Robin Hood's barn" to come at a thing (56 Kelly *Humors* 220; Smith *My Thirty* 362 We seem to be going all round Robin Hood's barn). Apperson 536; NC 467; Stevenson 2001:4; NQ 5 ix 486, x 15; R. M. Gay *The Pacific Spectator* I (1947) 179 Life begins to look like a detour round Robin Hood's barn; Sinclair Lewis *The Man Who Knew Coolidge* (1928) 17 but when it came to *talking*, why say he wandered all round Robin Hood's barn; M. McCarthy *The Groves of Academe* (1952) 148; E. M. Rhodes *Beyond the Desert* (Boston 1934) 201–202 Road goes all around Robin Hood's barn to get to my place; Phoebe A. Taylor *Figure Away* (1937) 130.

Rock, 1. Cold as a rock (25 Neal *Brother J* I 167).

2. As firm as rocks (69 Barnum *Struggles* 205). Apperson 671 weak

(2); Boshears 36:555; NC 467; Stevenson 2001:7; Svartengren 261; Tilley R151; Wyndham Lewis *The Apes of God* (1932) 127. Cf. NED Rock 8 c (rock-firm).

3. I'm as hard as a rock (c60 Paul *Courtship* 31). McAtee 32; NC 467; Taylor *Comparisons* 46; Tilley S878; Addison Simmons *Death on the Campus* (1935) 173.

4. Immovable as a rock (43 Hall *Purchase* I 171). Svartengren 386 unmoved.

5. A concern [business enterprise], now, that will put the sixpences to sleep as sound as rocks (56 Kelly *Humors* 227). Svartengren 169; A. S. McLeon *The Case of Matthew Crake* (1933) 137 a rock; Adam Bliss *Murder Upstairs* (Philadelphia 1934) 169 sleep like a rock.

6. His forehead—like a rock—steadfast (25 Neal *Brother J* III 25).

7. The locks of canals are strong as rocks (68 Saxe *Poems* 93). Svartengren 392 shore of rock.

8. And that was the rock he split on (59 Smith *My Thirty* 421; Lincoln VI 308).

9. George stood up like a rock (51 Stowe *Uncle* 128). Jackson Gregory *The Emerald Murder Trap* (1934) 326.

Rocket, 1. It sends up the sperits ez lively ez rockets (67 Lowell *Biglow* 318).

2. We sent her through the water like a rocket (40 Dana *Two* 262). Cf. Augustus Muir *The Silent Partner* (Indianapolis 1930) 223 he'll be off like a rocket.

3. See Sky-rocket.

Rocking chair. [A] pony, whose motion was as easy as a rocking-chair (20–22 Irving *Bracebridge* 118).

Rod, 1. And kiss the rod that beat you (21 Cooper *Spy* 220). NED Kiss 6; *Oxford* 340; Stevenson 1314:2; Tilley R156.

2. Solomon recommends a liberal use of it. Spare it, says he, and you spoil the child (49 Haliburton *Old Judge* I 235; Judd *Margaret* I 262; Shillaber *Mrs. Partington* 53 if she spared the rod she would spile that 'ere child; Clemens *Tom* 3). Prov. 13: 24; Apperson 592–593; Lean IV 252; NC 468; NED Spare 6; *Oxford* 609; Stevenson 344:8; Tilley R155; Whiting *Drama* 88, 195–196, 197; NQ 6 iii 66; J. T. Farrell *No Star Is Lost* (1938) 253, 553.

Rogue. The good old maxim of "setting a rogue to catch a rogue" (23–24 Irving *Tales* 385; Melville *White Jacket* 235 Believed in the old saying, *Set a rogue to catch a rogue*). Apperson 624 thief; *Oxford* 649; Stevenson 2003:10; Tilley T110. See Thief (6).

Roguery. There is roguery in all trades but our own (55 Haliburton *Nature* II 12). Cf. Apperson 345 Knavery; *Oxford* 342; Tilley K152. See Trade (2).

Roguish. See Squirrel (2).

Roland. A Rowland for an Oliver (40 Haliburton *Letter* 104; Hammett *Stray* 170 he gave . . . rather more than a Roland for his Oliver; Boucicault *Flying Scud* 213 Talk about diamond cut diamond, or a Roland for an Allover; Barnum *Struggles* 502 received a prompt Roland for his Oliver). Apperson 536–537; Farmer and Henley VI 45–46; NED Roland 2; *Oxford* 547; Stevenson 2003:3; Tilley R195; NQ 1 i 234, ii, 132, ix 457; R. A. J. Walling *Marooned with Murder* (1937) 244; Cecil M. Wells *Death in the Dark*

(London 1955) 13 Roger thought he might return a Rowland for an Oliver. Cf. P. Aebischer "Les trois mentions plus anciennes du couple 'Roland et Olivier,'" *Revue belge de philologie et d'histoire* XXX (1952) 657–675.

Roll. The fishermen have this saying, "A penny roll would choke him"; his swallow is so very small [of the right whale]. (51 Melville *Moby-Dick* II 105).

Rome, 1. Rome wasn't built in a day (23 Cooper *Pioneers* 229; Neal *Down-Easters* I 51; Crockett *Exploits* 57; Judd *Margaret* II 302). Apperson 537; NC 468; *Oxford* 547–548; Stevenson 2004:10; Tilley R163; NQ 9 iv 327; M. E. Corne *Death at the Manor* (1938) 134; T. H. White *The Sword in the Stone* (1939) 58.

2. When at Rome do as the Romans do, I held to be so good a proverb, that being in Typee, I made a point of doing as the Typees did (46 Melville *Typee* 282; Sedley *Marian* 109 Being in Rome, you must do as Romans do, 416; Clemens *Tramp* II 54 they . . . learn to do in Rome as Rome does). Apperson 537; NC 468; NED Rome 1 b; *Oxford* 547; Stevenson 2005:1–2006:5; Tilley R165; NQ 4 vi 74, 178; P. B. Kyne *Tide of Empire* (1928) 311; Willard Price *Pacific Adventure* (1936) 68. See Frisco, Nevada, Turkey (1).

Roof, 1. She undertook with all her veight to sit upon my knee. Fourteen stun six, I thought the roof had fell in (66 Boucicault *Flying Scud* 172).

2. They yellered and hollered enough to split the ruff off the house (44 Stephens *High Life* I 36). Cf. DA Roof 2 raise the roof.

Room, 1. You stand starin' and a gapin' there, as vacant as a spare room (49 Haliburton *Old Judge* I 208).

2. George! a Yankee pedlar's soul wud hev more room in a turnip-seed tu fly roun in, than a leather-wing bat hes in a meetin-hous (67 Harris *Sut* 79).

3. His room would be the better part of his company (34 Crockett *Life* 61; Kennedy *Horse-Shoe* 146 old granny's room is more wanted than her company; Haliburton *Clockmaker* II 279 I liksh your place more better as your company; Hall *Purchase* II 210 some, whose "room was better than their company"; Stephens *High Life* I 99 but I s'pose my room's as good as my company, II 78, *Mary Derwent* 249 gals that like his room better'n his company; Melville *Redburn* 320 crabbed old men . . . who would much rather have your room than your music, *White Jacket* 77 some fellows never knew when their room was better than their company; Cartwright *Autobiography* 401 your room will be better than your company). Apperson 538; NED Company 1 d, Room 11 b; *Oxford* 548; Stevenson 386:3; Tilley R168; Whiting *Drama* 360:807, *Scots* II 118–119; Caroline Gordon *The Garden of Adonis* (1937) 71.

Roost. They allers rule the roost (57 Riley *Puddleford* 251). DA Roost 2; Stevenson 2013:9; R. W. Winston *It's a Far Cry* (1937) 165. See Roast.

Rooster, 1. You are as crazy as a mad rooster (34 Davis *Downing* 104).

2. He looked as red as a rooster (39 Smith *Letters* 23).

3. It made my neck look as slim and shiney as our big red rooster's

used to when he stretched his head out in the sun to see how many old hens and spring pullets he'd got about him (44 Stephens *High Life* I 68).

4. As spunky as er Dominicker rooster (51 Burke *Polly* 151).

5. Breeches . . . as wet as a young rooster in a spring rain (51 Burke *Polly* 118).

Root, sb., 1. Then we abjure the proceeding, root and branch (42 Irving *Attorney* 250, 319). Malachi 4:1; NED Branch 6 b, Root 12.

2. To come the roots over [i. e., to trick]. 56 DA Root 1 b (1).

3. Grab a root [i. e., do one's part] (c63 Wiley *Billy* 187). DA Root 1 b (2).

Root, vb. See Hog (8).

Rope, 1. He has magnetized a rope of sand, and bound me with it (53 Hammett *Stray* 210). Apperson 538; NC 468; NED Rope 5 b; *Oxford* 548; Stevenson 2007:2; Tilley R174.

2. Give 'em rope (34 Davis *Downing* 225; Crockett *Account* 106 give a fellow rope enough to hang himself, 214; Cartwright *Autobiography* 342 I gave him rope, as the sailors say; Haliburton *Season-Ticket* 299 give 'em rope enough and they will hang themselves; Henry Morford *The Days of Shoddy* [Philadelphia 1863] 447 this woman would hang herself directly, if I should give her rope enough). Apperson 538; Hardie 469:101; *Oxford* 548; Stevenson 2008:1; Tilley T104; Lilian Bamburg *Beads of Silence* (1927) 189.

3. The captain, who had been on the coast before, and "knew the ropes" (40 Dana *Two* 73, 261, 361 [2]; Mayo *Kaloolah* 94 he'll know the ropes yet; Burke *Polly* 59 an' I

wouldn't a cared much then, ef it had been in a place whar I knowed the ropes; Haliburton *Sam* I 70 To handle a ship, you must know all the ropes; Kelly *Humors* 76; Thomson *Plu-ri-bus-tah* 186 But the old man "Knew the ropes"; Melville *Confidence-Man* 159 You are like a landsman at sea; don't know the ropes; Stephens *Fashion* 293 So you're not a chicken after all, know the ropes; Nash *Century* 192 He knows the ropes). Babcock 262; NED Rope 4 c; *Oxford* 344; Stevenson 2007:7; Thornton II 750, III 331; E. S. Gardner *The Case of the Substitute Face* (1938) 260.

4. I worked on a farm six weeks once, when I was a boy, and learnt to pull every rope in the ship (54 Smith *'Way* 187).

5. I cum purty near . . . tellin' 'em Elton [a village] wouldn't pull a rope for him, if he got the nominashun (76 Nash *Century* 70).

6. They pull together like one rope reeved through two blocks (36 Haliburton *Clockmaker* I 35).

7. Show me the ropes (60 Haliburton *Season-Ticket* 226). James O'Hanlon *Murder at Malibu* (1937) 157.

8. Or, as the French say, "to talk of a rope in a house where the squatter has been hanged" (55 Haliburton *Nature* I 81). Apperson 280 Halter (3); Green 22; *Oxford* 548; Tilley H59.

Rope-walk. A face as long as a rope-walk (50 Melville *White Jacket* 388).

Rose, 1. As bloomin' as a rose (38 Haliburton *Clockmaker* II 125; Shillaber *Mrs. Partington* 318 Jemima, my dear, you look as blooming as the rose in June, and twice as sweet). Cf. Svartengren 221 fair.

2. We remained as centless as the

last rose of summer. That is a poor joke, but it is in pathetic harmony with the circumstances, since we were so poor ourselves (72 Clemens *Roughing* II 162–163). Cf. NC 469; Taylor *Comparisons* 69.

3. Gals . . . as fresh and sweet as full-blown roses (44 Stephens *High Life* I 156, II 246 her cheeks looked as fresh as a full blown rosy; Riley *Puddleford* 122 you look as fresh as a new-blown rose; Alcott *Little Women* 154 as fresh and sweet as a rose). Apperson 235; Fife 118 NC 468; Svartengren 155–156; Tilley R176; Whiting *Drama* 324:276.

4. You look as harnsome as a full-blown rose this morning (44 Stephens *High Life* I 104).

5. With cheeks as red as a rosy (44 Stephens *High Life* I 218; Hawthorne *Twice-Told* 215 Blushing as red as any rose; Shillaber *Mrs. Partington* 71 Her cheek was red as the rose). Apperson 526; Boshears 39:859; NC 468; *Oxford* 535; Taylor *Comparisons* 68; Tilley R177; Whiting *Scots* II 119; Paul Haggard *Death Talks Shop* (1938) 245.

6. Brunettes, some with rose-red colors (59–60 Holmes *Elsie* 50).

7. As ruddy and bright as a full-blown rose (56 Kelly *Humors* 244).

8. Gals . . . as . . . sweet as full-blown roses (44 Stephens *High Life* I 156, *Fashion* 288 tears . . . sweet as a rose, 299; Lowell *Biglow* 326 A Scriptur' name makes it ez sweet ez a rose). NC 468; Taylor *Comparisons* 80; Tilley R178; Whiting *Drama* 324:376.

9. You must be the responsible captain, he will be the actual one, under the rose (53 Haliburton *Sam* I 106; Richardson *Secret* 417 stealing a portion under the rose; Saxe *Poems* 345

And was wont to meet him slyly, Underneath the blushing rose). Apperson 658; Farmer and Henley VI 53–54, VII 254; NED Rose 7; *Oxford* 682; Stevenson 2008:6; Tilley R185; Bruce Norman *The Thousand Hands* (1927) 114.

Rosy, sb. As he "tossed the rosy" [i. e., drank wine]. (53 Cary *Clovernook* 2d Series 318).

Rosy, adj. See Morning (5), Perch.

Rotten, 1. I am afeerd we shall be rotten afore we are ripe (38 Haliburton *Clockmaker* II 200). Randolph and Wilson 206. Cf. Tilley R133; Whiting *Chaucer* 86, *Drama* 165. See Ripe (2).

2. See Mud (4).

Rough. See Bear (16), Corncob (2).

Round, adj. See Apple (4), Appletree, Billiard-ball (2), Bull (3), Peach (4), Pearl (1), Pumpkin (4), Sugar kettle.

Round, adv. Guess we shall hev to come round [i. e., fall into accord]. (48 Lowell *Biglow* 66; Eggleston *Circuit* 83 How did you fetch the Captain round? [i. e., make him agreeable]). Cf. NED Come 44, Get 42 a.

Row, 1. I knew it was a hard row to hoe (35 Crockett *Account* 69, *Exploits* 28 I have a new row to hoe, a long and a rough one; Robb *Squatter* 122; Stephens *Homestead* 342; Lowell *Biglow* 48 You've a darned long row to hoe, 269, 392; Smith *'Way* 127; Eggleston *Circuit* 114). Bartlett 277, 539; DA Row 1; Farmer 289, 465; Farmer and Henley VI 64; NED Row 6 b; *Oxford* 550; Schele de Vere 608; Stevenson 2011:1; Thornton I 421, II

753, III 183; Van Wyck Mason *The Washington Legation Murders* (1935) 91 hard; Christopher Bush *The Perfect Murder Case* (1929) 119 long; A. E. Apple *Mr. Chang's Crime Ray* (1928) 66 rough.

2. We had to hoe our own row up, and found it a purty tough one [i. e., make our own way in the world]. (44 Stephens *High Life* II 107, 201 I . . . couldn't hoe my row a bit; Riley *Puddleford* 248 the Birds can hoe their own row; Haliburton *Season-Ticket* 304 who ever hoes his own row, gets the most corn). Bartlett 288; DA Row 3; Farmer 289; NC 469; NED Row 6 c; Schele de Vere 608; Stevenson 2011:1.

3. Joe's bellicose—so's Mose—Mose hoes Joe's rows [i. e., in a fist fight]. (55 Thomson *Doesticks* 47). Stevenson 1872:7.

4. He . . . could weed his own row, and keep it clean too (59 Taliaferro *Fisher's* 28, 257 You look like you mout be a man what can weed yer own row, clean at that). NC 469.

5. If the Confederacy has no better soldiers than those we are in A bad roe for stumps (63 Wiley *Johnny* 346).

6. S'posin' Jack should get ugly, father, he'd have us in a short row? (76 Nash *Century* 132).

Rub. There's the rub (59 Lincoln III 432, IV 160; Lowell *Biglow* 341; Daly *Man* 48). NED Rub 3 c; *Oxford* 550; Stevenson 2011:3; Stoett 1195; Tilley R196.

Rubicon. He Crosses the Rubicon [chapter heading]. (52 Melville *Pierre* 254; Smith *Arp* 101 my friends inside had passed the Rubicon; Richardson *Secret* 254 you can cross this Rubicon). NED Rubicon 1; *Oxford* 551; Stevenson 2011:6; Tilley R197; H. K. Webster *The Quartz Eye* (1928) 11.

Ruby. Shining red like a ruby (20–22 Irving *Bracebridge* 189).

Rudder. He who will not be ruled by the rudder must be ruled by the rock (67 Richardson *Beyond* 476). Apperson 540; *Oxford* 552; Stevenson 2012: 1.

Ruddy. See Rose (7).

Rule, 1. It was one of the good rules that won't work both ways (37 Neal *Charcoal* 67; Haliburton *Clockmaker* III 54 It's a bad rule that won't work both ways, *Attaché* I 247; Cooper *Redskins* 220, 471; Anon. *New Hope* 375 Well, my friends, it's a bad rule that won't work both ways). Bradley 91 bad rule; Snapp 88:36; Stevenson 2013:12; W. N. McCartney *Fifty Years a Country Doctor* (1938) 93 poor rule.

2. All general rules have their exceptions (40 Cooper *Pathfinder* 148, *Satanstoe* 13 but this, though true as a whole, was a rule that had its exceptions, *Chainbearer* 219 He belonged to the rule, and not to its exception; Hooper *Simon* 9 there is no rule without an exception, 55 an exception; Haliburton *Old Judge* II 64 there is no rule without an exception). Apperson 540; *Oxford* 552; Stevenson 2014:1; Tilley R205; R. S. Surtees *Mr. Sponge's Sporting Tour* (London [1853]) 67 there is no rule without exception; Raymond Robins *Murder at Bayside* (1933) 8 Thomas Evans was the proverbial exception to the rule. See Exception (2).

3. [He] had the honour to prove the rule by being an instance to the contrary (37 Neal *Charcoal* 115). Cf. Exception (1).

Ruler. Blows straight as rulers (59–60 Holmes *Elsie* 33).

Rum. They'd oughter Combine jest ez kindly ez new rum an' water (67 Lowell *Biglow* 319).

Rumpus. [They] . . . kicked up sich a darned rumpus that I raly begun to be afear'd (44 Stephens *High Life* II 1; Porter *Major* 51 A terrible rumpus was kicked up about the race). NED Rumpus (make a).

Run, sb., 1. To get the run upon [i. e., to make a butt of]. 48 DA Run 11 a.
2. To keep the run of [i. e., to maintain touch with]. 62 DA Run 11 b.

Run, vb., 1. It always made Silly mad to have any body else run the deacon down, though she used to give it tew him herself, like the dragon sometimes (56 Whitcher *Widow* 353). NED Run 73 j.
2. I would not advise any man to try to run over me (58 Porter *Major* 23).
3. See Deer (5), Dog (49), Greyhound (4), Rabbit (7), Race-horse, Turtle (12), Wheel (3), Wheelbarrow, Wildfire.

Rush, sb., 1. I don't care a rush (45 Fairfield *Letters* 355; Melville *Moby-Dick* I 92; Stephens *Mary Derwent* 309; Clift *Bunker* 277). NED Rush 2 a; Tilley S917; Whiting *Drama* 361: 812.
2. I should not have regarded the matter a rush (32 Kennedy *Swallow* 329). Farmer and Henley VI 86.
3. Not one of them is worth a rush (58 Lincoln III 93). Apperson 458; NED Rush 2 a; Stevenson 2642:12.

Rush, vb. See Bull (10).

Russet. I suppose I am like a Roxbury russet,—a great deal the better the longer I can be kept (51 Hawthorne *House* 376).

Rusties. But it won't do for us to be cutting rusties here at this time of night (37 Neal *Charcoal* 111; Hammett *Piney* 64 The old coon never cuts any of his rusties about me). Brewster *Am. Speech* XVI (1941) 22; DA Rusty 2 b; Randolph and Wilson 238; Schele de Vere 537; Wilson PADS II (1944) 48. Cf. Green 313.

S

Sabbath, 1. In the State of Maine, we have understood, some distance up the Kennebec river, near the lumbering region, is a place where it is commonly reported the Sabbath stops (50 Judd *Richard* 322). Cf. Sunday (3).

2. To travel beyond the Sabbath [i. e., to cross the Mississippi River]. 26 DA Sabbath 1 b.

Sable. See Night (3).

Sack, 1. I gin Judy White the sack right off the reel (44 Stephens *High Life* I 51; Eggleston *School-Master* 254). Apperson 23; Farmer and Henley VI 90; Green 313; NED Sack 4; *Oxford* 19–20; Randolph and Wilson 280; Stevenson 2021:5; *Catalogue of Political and Personal Satires . . . 1811–1819* (London 1949) IX 271 No. 12082; Milward Kennedy, pseud. *Death in a Deck-Chair* (London 1930) 111.

2. They wouldn't have got whipped like a sack (36 Haliburton *Clockmaker* I 85, II 21 lick you like a sack, III 113 lick; Smith *My Thirty* 328 licked).

Saddle, 1. As brown and smooth as an old saddle (72 Holmes *Poet* 6).

2. Puttin' the saddle on the right horse (40 Haliburton *Clockmaker* III 303). Apperson 542; Farmer and Henley VI 92; NED Saddle 2 d; *Oxford* 554; Stevenson 2022:2; Tilley S16.

3. She see that I looked sort of puzzled, and I s'pose she begun to think that I shouldn't buy the saddle (44 Stephens *High Life* I 222).

4. It would be a great thing, when this trick is attempted upon us, to have the saddle come up on the other horse (58 Lincoln III 330).

5. At last the knight was in the saddle [i. e., a knightly mood prevailed]. (74 Eggleston *Circuit* 166). NED Saddle 2 a; Stevenson 2022:4.

Safe, 1. Safe and sound (44 Stephens *High Life* I 52, II 192). McAtee 54; NED Safe 1 b; Stevenson 2022:7.

2. See Bear (18), Dead, sb. (1), Thief (3), Toad (1).

Saffron. Her neck . . . was as yaller as a saffron bag (44 Stephens *High Life* I 115; Barnum *Struggles* 533 as yellow as saffron). NC 469; Svartengren 251; Whiting *Scots* II 120.

Sahara, 1. Found it as dry as Sahara (67 Richardson *Beyond* 318). Edwin Greenwood *Pins and Needles* (London c1935) 97 She had waked from her Sunday nap dry as the Great Sahara; J. W. Vandercook *Murder in Fiji* (1936) 287.

2. See Desert.

Sail, 1. My way is, to make sail when the wind's fair (66 Bowman *Bear-Hunters* 393).

2. You may then take in a little sail, if you please (36 Fairfield *Letters* 81). NC 470.

315

Sailor, 1. He was a true sailor, every finger a fish-hook (40 Dana *Two* 274). *Oxford* 555.

2. Nowhere, perhaps, are the proverbial characteristics of sailors shown under wilder aspects than in the South Seas (47 Melville *Omoo* p. vii).

3. The common saying that "the better you try to serve sailors the worse they try to serve you" (45 Mayo *Kaloolah* 106).

4. These two men both perished from the proverbial indiscretions of seamen (47 Melville *Omoo* 55). Cf. Halpert 99; NC 470 As drunk as a sailor.

5. Perhaps it is prejudice though, for I believe we sailors are proverbial for that (55 Haliburton *Nature* I 56).

6. The proverbial restlessness of sailors (47 Melville *Omoo* 188).

7. A strange story, rife among them [man-of-war's men], curiously tinctured with their proverbial superstitions (50 Melville *White Jacket* 111).

8. Swars like a Salor (61 Wiley *Billy* 185). NC 479; Taylor *Comparisons* 70; Charles G. Givens *The Rose Petal Murders* (Indianapolis 1935) 28.

9. See Fish (15).

Saint. He was stiff as a saint in the temple of Isis (59 Shillaber *Knitting-Work* 276).

Saint Peter. Dead as Saint Peter (50 Boker *World* 39).

Salamander. I lay still as a salamander (59 Taliaferro *Fisher's* 136).

Salt, 1. We must take the liberty, for the moment, of "putting them below the salt" (53 Willis *Fun* 348). NED Salt 7 b; *Oxford* 559–560; Stevenson 2029:2.

2. Your yeomen are the salt of the earth (46 Cooper *Redskins* 180; Clemens *Love Letters* 38; Jones *Batkins* 197 You, Aunt Dolly, are one of the salts of the earth). Matt. 5:13; NED Salt 3 a; Stevenson 2029–2030:8; Yamamoto *Dickens* 253; E. S. Gardner *The Case of the Angry Mourner* (1951) 35 And we both know that daughter of yours is the salt of the earth.

3. I was determined to give him salt and vinegar [i. e., a beating]. (34 Crockett *Life* 29).

4. You don't earn your salt (40 Dana *Two* 24; Stephens *High Life* I 1 He don't arn salt to his parrage, nor never did; Cary *Clovernook* 2d Ser. 64 earn; Nash *Century* 124 Squire Shaw don't make enough out o' the office to buy salt for his porridge). C. G. Givens *The Jigg-Time Murders* (Indianapolis 1936) 186 earned. Cf. Stevenson 2028:5.

5. Not worth his salt. (51 Stowe *Uncle* 134). Apperson 549; NC 470; NED Salt 2 g; *Oxford* 734; Stevenson 2642:2; Kathleen M. Knight *Acts of Black Night* (1938) 235.

6. Take him [a dog] off, Jinks, or he'll eat me without salt! (37 Neal *Charcoal* 147; Haliburton *Clockmaker* II 287 They'd fairly eat the minister up without salt; Hooper *Simon* 56 I'll eat Satan raw and unsalted, ef any of you ever git a foot of that land!). Stevenson 662:9, 2029:1; Tilley S78.

7. A great big fish he cum up and lick him down like salt (59 Taliaferro *Fisher's* 190–191).

8. They could lick him up like salt [i. e., defeat him readily]. (58 Hammett *Piney* 155).

9. I wish we could find out the way of sprinkling salt on their tails, and make 'em [ideas] wait till we want to use 'em (37 Neal *Charcoal* 12). Stevenson 2029:5; Lynn Brock, pseud. *The Stoke Silver Case* (1929)

20 putting salt on the young man's tail. Cf. Bird (23).

Saltpeter. Don't forgit to gin the town below particular saltpetre (43 Robb *Squatter* 31). DA Particular (this example).

Salt River. He rowed the Tories up and down Salt River [i. e., in a speech]. (35 Crockett *Account* 46; Hall *Purchase* I 261 If I don't row you up salt creek in less nor no time, II 180 I hope I may be rowed up Salt River if; Lowell *Biglow* 56 Saltillo's Mexican, I b'lieve, fer wut we call Saltriver; Haliburton *Nature* I 27–28 We rowed him up to the very head waters of Salt River in no time [with an explanatory note obviously taken from Bartlett], *Season-Ticket* 362; Smith *My Thirty* 315 ff. [a lengthy discussion of Salt River as political limbo], 341 I'll go into retiracy, and settle on the banks of Salt River for life). Bartlett 540, 547; DA Salt River 3; Farmer 469; Farmer and Henley VI 98; McAtee 30 Salt Creek; Schele de Vere 346; Thornton II 760–761, III 337.

Sam, 1. To see Sam [i. e., to be impressed by the merits of the Know-Nothing party]. 55 DA Sam 1 b.

2. It's like Sam's hat-band which goes nineteen times round and won't tie at last (55 Haliburton *Nature* II 415). Cf. NC 394 Dick; Taylor *Comparisons* 47.

Sam Hill [i. e., Hell]. 39 DA Sam 2.

Samson, 1. Powerful as Samson (55 Melville *Israel* 3). Cf. NC 470; Svartengren 391 strong; Taylor *Comparisons* 79; Whiting *Drama* 325:280, *Scots* II 120–121.

2. I shall feel about as stout as Samson (53 Melville "Cock-a-doodle-doo!" in *Works* XIII 150).

Samuel (**Sam**) **Patch,** 1. Afore yeou could say Sam Patch (56 Kelly *Humors* 360). Cf. Jack 1 (3, 4).

2. If he had been Samuel Patch, he could not have made a better dive (55 Hammett *Wonderful* 102). Thornton II 762, III 337. See a long verse account in Smith *Downing* 235–239.

3. "Alas, poor Yorick," as Sam Patch said (66 Smith *Arp* 95).

Sancho. Had a lively time in my seminary, this morning, for the children acted like Sancho (69 Alcott *Little Women* 366).

Sand, 1. The rattlesnake's son [a man] was exceedingly thirsty—the sands of Africa were not more so (51 Burke *Polly* 62). Cf. Sahara; Svartengren 190 desert.

2. This petty election is, in fact, the grain of sand that is to turn the presidential scale (53 Willis *Fun* 322).

3. For want of sand in [h]is craw (62 Wiley *Johnny* 238, 314 you have got no sand in your craw; Harris *Sut* 102 I tell yu he hes lots ove san' in his gizzard). DA Sand 2 f (3); Farmer and Henley VI 99 craw; McAtee 54; Stevenson 2033:4 craw. Cf. Randolph and Wilson 209; Farmer 470.

4. To knock the sand from under [i. e., to upset his calculations]. 47 DA Sand 2 f (1).

5. To throw sand in the wheels. 77 DA Sand 2 f (4); Stevenson 1497:3.

Sandbur. To stick like a sandbur. 70 DA Sand 2 f (2).

Sap, 1. Sap-green Mermaid (c56 Thomson *Plu-ri-bus-tah* 88).

2. Sap runs best after a sharp frost (45 Judd *Margaret* II 97).

3. I felt the blood a biling up into my face like hot sap in a sugar kettle (44 Stephens *High Life* II 25).

Sapling. So poor an' thin that they had to lean up agin er saplin' to cuss (51 Burke *Polly* 147). See Backbone (3), Dog (2). Cf. Apperson 355 Lazy as Ludlam's dog; *Oxford* 355; Tilley L587.

Sarcophagus. He is as silent as a sarcophagus (55 Jones *Winkles* 12).

Sardine. It packs as closely as sardines in a box (66 Clemens *Sandwich* 15; Alcott *Little Women* 143 Eleven other knights packed together without their heads, like sardines). NC 470; Partridge 727; Taylor *Comparisons* 60–61, 83; J. S. Fletcher *The Eleventh Hour* (1935) 6.

Sassafras root, 1. As homely as a sassfras root (44 Stephens *High Life* II 69).

2. A name as long and crooked as a sassfras root (44 Stephens *High Life* I 101).

Satan, 1. Satan found plenty of mischief for idle hands to do (68 Alcott *Little Women* 122 [Isaac Watts *Divine Songs* no. 20], 460 Satan is proverbially fond of providing employment for full and idle hands). Apperson 144 If the devil catch a man idle, he'll set him at work, 321; *Oxford* 139, 312 An idle brain is the devil's shop; Tilley B594.

2. They run orf as tho Satan his self was arter them with a red hot ten pronged pitchfork (62 Browne *Artemus* 159).

3. The hackmen . . . came clattering on behind as if Satan had kicked 'em on eend (58 Porter *Major* 50). See Old Harry (2).

4. Patty Sprig . . . pulls away like a little satan (54 Shillaber *Mrs. Partington* 315).

5. This is something like Satan reviling sin (36 Crockett *Exploits* 177; Haliburton *Nature* I 237–238 "How good we are, ain't we," as sin said when the devil was rebukin' of him). Apperson 147–148; *Oxford* 561; Tilley D262.

Satin, 1. The nap of his hat lay shining and smooth as satin (55 Stephens *Homestead* 59). Svartengren 59.

2. Ay! but you'll come out like satin in the sunshine (66 Boucicault *Flying Scud* 213). Cf. Boshears 40: 927; NC 470.

Sauce. Sass for the goose ought to be sass for the gander too (34 Davis *Downing* 211; Haliburton *Attaché* II 103 What's sarce for the goose, is sarce for the gander, *Nature* II 181, 396; Smith *My Thirty* 336; Lowell *Biglow* 267 I guess . . . Thet sauce for goose ain't *jest* the juice for ganders with J. B.). Apperson 266; Farmer and Henley VI 103; NC 470; NED Sauce 1 b; *Oxford* 561; Stevenson 2035:4; Tilley S102; NQ 6 vi 408, ix 329, 395, 478; Tom Burnham *The Western Humanities Review* VIII (1954) 160 *and what is sauce for the anser femina is not necessarily sauce for the gander;* Wallace Irwin *The Julius Caesar Murder Case* (1935) 136 gander . . . goose; Arthur Train *The Adventures of Ephraim Tutt* (1930) 336; Upton Sinclair *Between Two Worlds* (1941) 79 What is sauce for one goose is sauce for every other.

Saucer. His eyes were as big as saucers (36 Haliburton *Clockmaker* I 37, *Nature* II 76; Willis *Life* 4 And immense black eyes? Saucers!; Judd *Mar-*

garet I 178; Taliaferro *Fisher's* 56 Head big as a sasser; Harris *Uncle Remus* 51 his eyes look big ez Miss Sally's chany sassers). Boshears 34: 344; Farmer and Henley VI 104; Halpert 75; NC 470; NED Saucer 4, Saucer eye; Svartengren 288; Taylor *Comparisons* 16.

Saucy. See Blaze (10), Horse (9), Jay-bird (2), Nigger (6), Poison (1).

Saugh. The saugh [sallow, willow] kens the basketmaker's thumb.—Scottish Proverb (40 Emerson *Journals* V 472).

Sausage, 1. Kill you dead as chopped sassudge (43 Hall *Purchase* II 155).

2. But no matter, dear Pete, as the man said of the sausages—hope for the best, but be prepared for the worst (56 Kelly *Humors* 274).

Sausage meat. I'll larrup you tell your mammy won't know you from a pile of sassage meat (51 Burke *Polly* 151). See Mother (4).

Savage, sb. [A savage's] inconstancy and treachery are proverbial (46 Melville *Typee* 101).

Savage, adj. See Bear (19), Cat (20), Charon, Dog (18), Earthquake (1), Meat axe (2), Steel trap (2), Tigress.

Saw. Thar were a chap that I tried to run a saw on here in Texas, a while ago (58 Hammett *Piney* 43; Porter *Major* 68 "Running a Saw" on a French Gentleman [title]). DA Run 20 (2); Farmer and Henley VI 105.

Say, 1. However, I said nothing, though I thought the more (49 Melville *Redburn* 20). Apperson 551 little; *Oxford* 563; Stevenson 2307:8; Tilley L367; Whiting *Drama* 201, *Scots* II 139 Think, 161 Word (11).

2. That . . . was a thing easier said than done (21 Cooper *Spy* 97, *Pilot* 166, *Prairie* 96, *Pathfinder* 81 That is easily said, but not so easily done; Haliburton *Clockmaker* I 326, *Old Judge* II 35; Nash *Century* 201). Apperson 543; NC 469; *Oxford* 165; Tilley S116; E. D. Biggers *The Chinese Parrot* (Indianapolis 1926) 78.

3. No sooner said than done (33 Neal *Down-Easters* II 124; Haliburton *Attaché* II 15, IV 246, *Sam* II 200, 245, 288; Melville *Omoo* 20; Smith *My Thirty* 335). NED Say 2 k; *Oxford* 458–459; Stevenson 2307:5; Tilley S117; Kenneth Livingston *The Dodd Cases* (1934) 221.

4. Soonest said, soonest over (50 Boker *World* 35). Cf. Apperson 588 Soonest begun.

5. What's said can't be onsaid (56 Whitcher *Widow* 241). See Do (7).

6. See Least, Less.

Say-so. Dog on my cat, ef they ain't a hull team, and a big dog under the waggin, ef you'd only take thar saysoo for it (58 Hammett *Piney* 45). Green 317; Partridge 729; Thornton II 767, III 339.

Scarce. See Hen (7).

Scary. See Colt (3).

Scat. Quicker'n scat (c54 Dorson *Jonathan* 87). DA Scat.

Scent. Some of the other party got scent of this (58 Hammett *Piney* 155; Boucicault *Flying Scud* 179). NED Scent 2 d.

Scew-horn. Doubtless a small force of the enemy is flourishing about in the Northern part of Virginia, on the "*scew-horn*" principle, on purpose to divert us in another quarter (63 Lincoln VI 189).

School. I . . . drank freely . . . until I did not care whether school kept or not (c61 Chamberlain *Confession* 138; Clemens *Letters* I 64, *Enterprise* 74, *Roughing* I 274). DA Keep 2 (2); Mike Teagle *Murders in Silk* (1938) 165 tight enough not to care.

Schoolmaster. They've got a cant phrase here, "the schoolmaster is abroad," and every feller tells you that fifty times a day (36 Haliburton *Clockmaker* I 121–122). NED Schoolmaster 1 b; *Oxford* 565; Stevenson 2041:4.

Scissors, 1. The gale was now at its height, "blowing like scissors and thumb-screws" (40 Dana *Two* 276).

2. You must gin him scissors [i. e., scold violently]. (43 Robb *Squatter* 31, 64 gin him scissors, 169; Clemens *Fairbanks* 98 We have all given you scissors for not stopping here). DA Scissors 2; Farmer and Henley VI 115. Cf. NED Scissors 2.

Scores. And now they were going to pay off old scores (58 Porter *Major* 120; Boucicault *Flying Scud* 227 It's clearing off old scores). Cf. NC 471; NED Score 11 b; Tilley S148.

Scotch. See Devil (5).

Scratch, sb. (1). They'll have to come to the scratch for it (39 Smith *Letters* 62, *My Thirty* 354 the British didn't come up to the scratch, 420; Stephens *High Life* II 44 up to; Derby *Phoenixiana* 111 up to; Haliburton *Season-Ticket* 326 it was hard work to fetch her up to the scratch at last; Saxe *Poems* 153 When it came to the scratch). Farmer and Henley VI 124; NED Scratch 5; *Oxford* 567; Schele de Vere 318; Stevenson 2045:4; Molly Thynne *The Draycott Murder Mystery* (1928) 300.

Scratch, sb. (2). See Old Scratch.

Scratch, vb. To scratch for oneself. 50 DA Scratch 3 (1).

Scream. See Panther (8), Pig (19), Wildcat (6).

Screw, 1. I must admit there is a screw loose somewhere [i. e., something wrong]. (36 Haliburton *Clockmaker* I 260, *Attaché* II 24 No screw loose there, IV 266 I seed . . . where the screw was loose, *Sam* I 94 If there is only one screw loose, it is all day with it, II 60 there's a screw loose between you two; Irving *Attorney* 146; Cooper *Redskins* 15; Hammett *Stray* 280; Anon. *New Hope* 268; Holmes *Autocrat* 52–53 no doubt she thought there was a screw loose in my intellects; Smith *My Thirty* 440; Clemens *Sketches* 51; Lowell *Biglow* 264 A screw's gut loose in everythin' there is; Barnum *Struggles* 669; Jones *Batkins* 95; Holmes *Poet* 90). Bartlett 561; Farmer and Henley VI 128–129; Green 33; NC 471; NED Screw 3 b; *Oxford* 568; Partridge 738; Stevenson 2046:4; Christopher Bush *The Crank in the Corner* (1933) 212.

2. They would put on the screws (50 Judd *Richard* 58, *Margaret* II 101; Boucicault *Flying Scud* 165 Put the screw on while Goodge is in feather). Bartlett 561; NED Screw 2 b; Stevenson 2046:2.

3. Albeit she did certainly put the screws to the managers (58 Field *Pokerville* 89).

Screw-auger. Gouge like screw-augers (59) Taliaferro *Fisher's* 198).

Scriptures. That's as true as the Scriptures (56 Whitcher *Widow* 27, 29). See Apostles.

Scylla. And flying from Scylla you were liable to encounter Charybdis

(21 Cooper *Spy* 302; Hammett *Stray*
57 A modern version of Scylla and
Charybdis; Riley *Puddleford* 131 the
old 'oman was between Scyller and
Charabides; Richardson *Beyond* 444
Parsimony is the Charybdis which
they shun with so much terror that a
good many go to pieces upon the Scyl-
la of Extravagance). NED Scylla;
Oxford 568; Stevenson 2046–2047:7;
Tilley S169; Whiting *Scots* I 148; E.
C. Vivian *The Barking Dog Murder
Case* (1937) 17.

Sea, 1. The beach . . . is like a gray
mirror, bright as the bosom of the sea
(50 Willis *Life* 206).
   2. Calm as the summer sea (69 Alcott *Little Women* 317). Cf. Svartengren 270.
   3. That's a blue-water philosophy:
as deep as the sea (24 Cooper *Pilot*
208; Melville *Mardi* II 391 She is
deeper than the sea). NC 471; Taylor
Comparisons 33.
   4. His sea-green eyes (24 Cooper
Pilot 126; Thomson *Plu-ri-bus-tah* 88
Though she was a sea-green Mermaid;
Sedley *Marian* 335). NED Sea-green.
   5. Life . . . spreads out as level as
the sea (50 Mitchell *Reveries* 180).
Cf. NC 444 millpond; Svartengren
272 pond.
   6. I'll fight them thieves till the sea
goes dry (71 Eggleston *School-Master*
132). Robert Burns "A Red, Red
Rose" (1796) in *Complete Poetical
Works* (Boston 1897) 250 Till a' the
seas gang dry.
   7. You are all at sea now (28 Neal
Rachel 108, *Down-Easters* II 145 My
lawyer and myself were all at sea).
Farmer and Henley VI 136; NED Sea
10 b; Stevenson 2047:9; N. A. Tem-
ple-Ellis, pseud. *The Inconsistent Vil-
lains* (1929) 218.

Sea-gull. Now [a bark] white as the
sea-gull (58 Holmes *Autocrat* 41).

Seal, 1. As fat as a seal (43 Haliburton *Attaché* II 219, *Sam* I 270). Whiting *Scots* II 122.
   2. I have got him seal fat as high
as the knees (60 Lincoln IV 13). DA
Seal 3.

Sea-lawyer. They don't fancy sea-
lawyers (50 Melville *White Jacket*
485). Babcock 258; NED Sea-lawyer;
Thornton III 348 ship's lawyer.

Sea legs. I had not got my "sea legs
on," was dreadfully sea-sick (40 Dana
Two 7, 10; Clemens *Innocents* I 14).
NED Sea legs.

Seat. Come forward, then, and sit
upon the anxious seat, and have your
soul prayed for (39 Briggs *Harry* II
135). Bartlett 15; DA Anxious 2 (4);
Farmer 18; Thornton I 17, III 8; Tidwell PADS XI (1949) 3. See Bench
(1).

Sebastopol. It's worse than Sebastopol
to get into (66 Boucicault *Flying Scud*
206).

Secret. See Grave (7).

See, 1. I should a good deal rather
see the money than hear about it (54
Smith *'Way* 176). Apperson 43 Better
have it. Cf. Seeing (3).
   2. Well, we shall see what we shall,
to-morrow (52 Cary *Clovernook* 264).

Seed. "Gone to seed" may be consid-
ered a slang expression; and, as a conscientious writer, far be it from me to
use slang (74 Eggleston *Circuit* 87).
Tidwell PADS XI (1949) 10. Cf. Farmer and Henley VI 139; NED Run
69 e.

Seeing, 1. But seeing is believing (32
Kennedy *Swallow* 32; Smith *Downing*

226; P. H. Myers *The King of the Hurons* [1850] 79; Burke *Polly* 38; Haliburton *Sam* I 41, II 180; Irving *Wolfert* 323; Sedley *Marian* 414; Clemens *Roughing* I 84; Nash *Century* 303). Apperson 556; NC 471; *Oxford* 571; Stevenson 2105:12; Tilley S212; NQ 5 x 229, 318; Frank Hamel *Lady Hester Stanhope* (London 1913) 191; F. P. Keyes *The River Road* (1945) 307 it's the sort [of secret] where seeing is believing; J. P. Marquand *B. F.'s Daughter* (Boston 1946) 386 Seeing is believing, isn't it?

2. The homely adage that *seeing's believing, but feeling's the truth* (Anon. *New Hope* 194). NQ 5 xi 157 Seeing is believing, but touching is the truth.

3. Seein' um's better'n hearin' tell un um (80 Harris *Uncle Remus* 39). Cf. See (1).

Self-preservation. Self-preservation is a law that will justi—ah; we are overheard (25 Neal *Brother J* III 18; Smith *My Thirty* 431 Self preservation is the first law of nature with States as well as with individuals, 448 self-preservation, you know, is the first law of nature; F. Copcutt *The Knickerbocker* XXV [1845] 62 The first law of nature, Sir, self-preservation). Apperson 557; Lean IV 92; NED Self-preservation; *Oxford* 573; Stevenson 2068–2069:1; Tilley S219; NQ 8 ii 246; P. B. Kyne *Tide of Empire* (1928) 90 first law of human nature; E. S. Gardner *Top of the Heap* (1952) 206 Loyalty is a fine thing, but self-preservation is the first law of nature.

Senseless. See Rag (3).

Sensitive. See Eel (5).

Sent. Lookin' as mean as a critter that was sent for, and couldn't come (43 Haliburton *Attaché* II 258, *Season-Ticket* 220 You look like a fellow that's sent for and can't come [i. e., weary]; Thompson *Major* 129 Why he looks like he was sent for and didn't want to go). Boshears 32:170; NC 472.

Seraph. A voice, sweet as a seraph's (54 Melville *Confidence-Man* 174).

Serene. See Violet (2).

Serious. See Barn (1), Judge (1).

Sermon. A nine [cigar] . . . as long as a sarmon and as crooked as a corkscrew (44 Stephens *High Life* II 176). Bartlett 807.

Serpent, 1. As hateful as the serpent (32 Hall *Legends* 5).

2. A tongue "iley as a sarpent" (43 Robb *Squatter* 115). Cf. NED Serpent 1 d.

Set, sb. Any how she seems to be making a dead set at him (56 Whitcher *Widow* 153; Jones *Country* 377 if you would make a dead set at Sally Weighton; Sedley *Marian* 101 If she were resolved to make a dead set against you, you'd have left your bones among the Pawnees, 325). NED Set 10 c; Partridge 211, 746. Cf. NED Set 7.

Set, adj. See Bayonet, Button (7), Flint (6).

Sewed. So, then ye'r fairly sewed up, ain't ye [i. e., entangled in a confusion]. (51 Stowe *Uncle* 72). NED Sew 4 c (b).

Shad, 1. You are as deff as a shad (36 Haliburton *Clockmaker* I 258, *Sam* I 157). Svartengren 175.

2. Flat enough; "like a shad in a platter" (25 Neal *Brother J* I 272).

3. The old mare looked as lank as a shad (44 Stephens *High Life* II 140).

4. You look as thin as a shad in summer (44 Stephens *High Life* II 7, *Mary Derwent* 372; Francis Wayland *A Memoir of the Life and Labors of the Rev. Adoniram Judson, D. D.* (2 vols., Boston 1853) II 293 She has . . . become "as thin as the shad that went up the Niagara"; Nash *Century* 65 his wallet don't look like the last run o' shad). Cf. Bartlett 807; Svartengren 189.

5. "Not strong enough to haul a shad off a gridiron" (40 Dana *Two* 377).

Shade. A series of vaultings and tumblings, which "laid in the shade" all previous performances of the sort (45 Hooper *Simon* 87; Cartwright *Autobiography* 77 religion . . . throws these idols into eternal shade).

Shadow, 1. As poor as the shadder of a bean pole (62 Browne *Artemus* 212).

2. And Mr. F. sombre as a shadow (53 Curtis *Potiphar* 217).

3. He was thin as a shadow (49 Melville *Redburn* 74; Alcott *Little Women* 535). Cf. NC 472.

4. I must stick to her, like her shadow (50 Willis *Life* 365; Taliaferro *Fisher's* 264 And cling to me like one's shadow; Clemens *Love Letters* 47 After following you like your shadow for weeks). Cf. NC 472; Stevenson 2081:5 follow; Tilley S263; Whiting *Drama* 325:285.

5. Mere phantoms which flit along a page, like shadows along a wall (57 Melville *Confidence-Man* 90). Whiting *Chaucer* 171, cf. *Scots* II 123.

6. He had worn himself to a shadow (43 Robb *Squatter* 36). NED Shadow 6 f.

Shady. Keep shady, was the parting word of the stranger knight (54 Shillaber *Mrs. Partington* 333; Hammett *Piney* 84 Keep shady, says he [i. e., keep quiet and observe], 154 but mind, you're bound to keep shady [i. e., not to disclose secrets]). DA Shady; Farmer and Henley VI 149.

Shake, sb., 1. In hafe a shake Bingham broke through 'em (58 Hammett *Piney* 283). Partridge 748; V. L. Whitechurch *Murder at the Pageant* (1931) 34.

2. I guess I'll be after [them] in a double brace of shakes (56 Kelly *Humors* 410). Partridge 87 brace; NQ 3 i 91, 334.

3. In a couple of shakes of a sheep's tail (58 Hammett *Piney* 260; Taliaferro *Fisher's* 75 in three shakes of a sheep's tail, 127 Afore three strokes ov a mutton's tail; Harris *Sut* 113 in the shake of a lamb's tail; Shillaber *Ike* 50 two shakes of a sheep's tail). Brewster *Am. Speech* XIV (1939) 264 dead lamb's tail; Farmer and Henley I 315; Green 328; McAtee 65; NC 431 jerks, 472 shakes; NED Shake 2 h; Partridge 1029 donkey's, monkey's tail; Stevenson 1081:4 three; R. P. Tristram Coffin *Lost Paradise* (1934) 71 three. See Sheep (5), Wag.

4. In two shakes of a marlinspike (55 Hammett *Wonderful* 103).

5. You are no great shakes (28 Neal *Rachel* 80; Neal *Charcoal* 199 Anyhow, his legs are no great shakes, 215; Stephens *High Life* I 121 It kinder strikes me that she aint no great shakes herself, II 110, 175; Mayo *Kaloolah* 60 they're [Indians] no great shakes; Kelly *Humors* 302; Lowell *Biglow* 122 you're some gret shakes; Whitcher *Widow* 33; Thomson *Elephant Club* 158; Riley *Puddle-*

ford 313; Derby *Squibob* 44 he ain't worth shakes; Locke [Nasby] *Struggles* 283 wuz no grate shakes). Bartlett 575; DA Shake 6 a; Farmer and Henley VI 151; Green 328; NED Shake 7; Schele de Vere 631; Thornton II 780–781; NQ 1 v 443; 3 ii 52; 5 viii 184, xii 369, 473; 9 iii 169, 277, 352, 493; 11 iii 129, 173, 257, 338; Sloane Callaway *The Crime at the Conquistador* (1938) 141.

6. To give him the cold shake. 75 DA Shake 6 b.

7. He determined to have one "fair shake" at the birds, even if he had to go on Sunday (43 Thompson *Chronicles* 88). Bartlett 205; Green 135; Schele de Vere 601, 631; Thornton II 778, III 345.

Shake, vb. See Aspen leaf, Dog (51), Leaf (6).

Shank's mare. So Dick and Jule had to ride "Shanks' mare" (58 Porter *Major* 90). Bartlett 576; Bey PADS II (1944) 60; Farmer and Henley VI 157; Green 329; NED Shank 1 b; *Oxford* 579; Tidwell PADS XIII (1950) 19; NQ 2 iv 86, 115, 338; 10 i 345, 415; A. O. Friel *Mountains of Mystery* (1924) 80. See Mother (5).

Shark, 1. As hungry as a shark (49 Haliburton *Old Judge* I 34). Cf. Svartengren 182 ravenous; Eric Linklater *Ben Jonson and King James* (London 1931) 45 ravenous.

2. I'm as peckish as a shark (56 Kelly *Humors* 123).

Sharp, 1. Sharp's the word (53 Boker *Bankrupt* 91). Apperson 561; Farmer and Henley VI 162; NED Sharp 4 g (b); *Oxford* 579; Stevenson 2084:12.

2. See Arrow (1), Bamboo briar, Darning needle, Hawk (7), Meat axe (3), Nature (1), Needle 2 (1), Pen-knife, Razor (4), Steel (6), Steel trap (3), Vinegar (1).

Sheep, 1. He was as woolly as a sheep [i. e., fuzzy-minded]. (57 Riley *Puddleford* 266). Boshears 41:1041; Halpert 749. Cf. Svartengren 40 mazed.

2. Ma says she's a sheep in lamb's clothing (49 Haliburton *Old Judge* I 146). Cf. Apperson 466 Old (D 1); *Oxford* 470; Partridge 259, 467, 546, 583.

3. I may as well die for an old sheep as a lamb (44 Stephens *High Life* I 197). Apperson 562; Bradley 67 hanged for a cow as a calf; *Oxford* 276; Stevenson 1067:4; Tiffany Thayer *The Cluck Abroad* (1935) 119 die for an old sheep as a lamb; Gretchen Finletter *Harper's Magazine* CCIX (July 1954) 38.

4. One scabby sheep will infect a whole flock (36 Haliburton *Clockmaker* I 250). Apperson 563; NC 472; *Oxford* 564; Stevenson 2086:7; Tilley S308; Whiting *Scots* II 123.

5. Afore a right smart, active sheep could flop his tail ary time (45 Hooper *Simon* 41). Cf. Shake (3).

6. As awk'ard as a flock of sheep jest arter shearing time (44 Stephens *High Life* II 69).

7. Mr. Walter soon had 'em as gentle as sheep (55 Jones *Winkles* 85, *Country* 342 He's as g-gentle now as a s-sh-sheep). Cf. NC 472; *Oxford* 234; Taylor *Comparisons* 43.

8. We're innersent as a hull flock of sheep (76 Nash *Century* 185, 198 He said his father was "innersent as a sheep"). Svartengren 317 harmless.

9. Looking about as mean as a new-sheared sheep (49 Haliburton *Old Judge* I 297). Cf. NC 472; Tilley S295, S299; Whiting *Drama* 325:286.

10. As perfectly submissive as a

sheep in the hands of the shearer (56 Jones *Wild* 80).

11. I'm allers right up an down like a sheep's tail goin' over a wall (33 Neal *Down-Easters* I 79).

12. Cast many a sheep's eye (33 Smith *Downing* 99; Haliburton *Letter* 64; Melville *Mardi* I 132; Wallack *Rosedale* 7 She's been casting sheep's eyes in a certain direction; Eggleston *School-Master* 57 She cast at him what are commonly called sheep's-eyes). Apperson 563; NED Sheep's eye; *Oxford* 580; Stevenson 735:11; Tilley S323; Whiting *Drama* 362:833; Diplomat [John F. Carter] *Death in the Senate* (1933) 89.

13. They went at it like a flock of sheep in salting time (44 Stephens *High Life* II 61).

14. Looking arter me as if I'd been stealing a sheep (44 Stephens *High Life* II 53).

15. He shut his eyes with all his might, and tried to think of sheep jumping over a wall (54 Smith *'Way* 273). Frederica De Laguna *The Arrow Points to Murder* (1937) 238 he saw not the proverbial sheep jumping one by one a shadowy fence.

16. But to work a farm where the rocks are so near together, that the sheep's noses have to be sharpened before they can graze between them, is not a very profitable business (56 Durivage *Three* 58). Henry H. Cochrane, *History of Monmouth and Wales* (East Winthrop, Maine, 1894) I 34 Whether the statement that the old gentleman made a practice of filing the noses of his sheep, that they might reach the scanty verdure that grew in the close crevices of that rockbound hill had any foundation in fact, the historian of that town must determine. (Of Zadoc Bishop, said to have moved from Monmouth, Maine, to a hill farm in Leeds in 1783).

Sheep-shears. You're as snappish as a par o' sheep-shears (59 Taliaferro *Fisher's* 259).

Sheep-skin, 1. A face like a dry sheep-skin (67 Harris *Sut* 131).

2. His face wer pucker'd like a wet sheep-skin afore a hot fire (67 Harris *Sut* 44).

Sheet, 1. Pale as a sheet (43 Thompson *Chronicles* 142, *Major* 155; Irving *Wolfert* 181; Hammett *Piney* 249). Boshears 39:789; Svartengren 235; H. R. Mayes *Alger* (1928) 196.

2. She turned as white as a sheet (44 Stephens *High Life* I 183, 250; Thompson *Major* 174; Haliburton *Sam* I 107, *Season-Ticket* 361; Judd *Richard* 413; Hammett *Piney* 137; Holmes *Elsie* 193; Browne *Artemus* 153; Locke [Nasby] *Struggles* 262; Clemens *Roughing* I 270, *Gilded* I 9, *Tom* 266, *Sketches* 87). Apperson 680; Boshears 41:1021; McAtee 71; NC 472; Taylor *Comparisons* 87; Cornelia Penfield *After the Deacon Was Murdered* (1933) 87.

3. Sheet-white (55 Melville "Tartarus" in *Works* XIII 248). Rufus King *The Lesser Antilles Case* (1934) 209.

4. The Captain 3 sheets to the wind (21–22 Eliason 300; Dana *Two* 200 Seldom went up to the town without coming down "three sheets in the wind"; Haliburton *Nature* I 176 two sheets in the wind; Taliaferro *Fisher's* 33). Farmer and Henley VI 170; Green 330; NED Sheet 2; *Oxford* 654; Stevenson 639:14; Wilson 589; A. B. Caldwell *Turquoise Hazard* (1936) 234.

Sheeting. Ez cheap ez onbleached sheetin' (67 Lowell *Biglow* 280).

Sheet-iron. The sail, which was about as stiff as sheet-iron (40 Dana *Two* 377).

Shelf. They [French girls] are virtually put on the shelf as soon as the wedding excitement is over (69 Alcott *Little Women* 423). NED Shelf 1 d.

Shell, 1. The rough shell may have a good kernel (43 Robb *Squatter* 120).

2. Many of the improvements . . . were then "in the shell" (Burke *Polly* 28). NED Shell 6 b.

Sherry. Asa was as cool as a sherry cobbler (c60 Paul *Courtship* 261).

Shilling, 1. The Bad Shilling (40 Haliburton *Clockmaker* III 142 [chapter heading], 144 Did you never mind, squire, how hard it is to get rid of "a bad shillin'," how everlastin'ly it keeps a-comin' back to you, 156 Cuss them bad shillin's, they are always a-comin' back to you, 159 They are like a bad shillin' . . . you can't get rid of them). NED Shilling 5; Stevenson 1773:10, 2090:11 ill shilling; H. G. Wells *Experiment in Autobiography* (1934) 123 the bad shilling back again. See Penny (6).

2. I'll cut you off with a shilling (76 Nash *Century* 34). *Oxford* 126; Stevenson 2090:8; Terry Shannon *The Catspaw* (1929) 237 without even the proverbial.

3. We haven't a shilling to bless ourselves with (c60 Paul *Courtship* 136). Cf. Apperson 123 Cross; *Oxford* 119; Tilley C836; Whiting *Drama* 339:481.

4. He can last, but won't give thirty shillings in change for a sovering (66 Boucicault *Flying Scud* 217).

Shine, sb., 1. They couldn't come any of them thar shines over him (43 Robb *Squatter* 151). DA Shine 5 (4).

2. So I'd thank 'em not to be *cutting their shines* about me (33 Hall *Soldier's Bride* 224; Stephens *High Life* I 180 the post-office feller cut up his shines, and ordered the folks about; Stowe *Uncle* 73 my gals don't cut up no such shines, 82; Hammett *Piney* 180, 290 You never ketch Sam tellin' the old Judge any of them dreadful shines he used to cut; Shillaber *Ike* 218). Bartlett 166–167, 581; DA Shine 5 (1); Farmer and Henley VI 177; Green 331; Partridge 757; Schele de Vere 324; Thornton II 785–786.

3. To make a shine with. 47 DA Shine 5 (5).

4. Somehow, it kinder seemed to me the New York Express took the shine off the papers thet I'd seen (44 Stephens *High Life* I 26, 74, 86; Hammett *Piney* 28 if any man can take the shine out of *you*, uncle Billy, 'taint me; Porter *Major* 13 anything could take the shine out of her that had the audacity to try it). Bartlett 582; DA Shine 5 (2); Farmer and Henley VI 177; Green 331; NED Shine 4 d; Partridge 756; Schele de Vere 632.

5. Somehow I'd taken a shine to the Express (44 Stephens *High Life* I 25, 110 a gal that he's a beginning tu take a shine arter, II 95, 175; Hammett *Piney* 101 I've took a considerable wonderful shine to you; Eggleston *School-Master* 155 I never tuck no shine that air way; Nash *Century* 34 I wonder if Parson Green's church, that you take such a shine to, will tide you over then!). Bartlett 582; DA Shine 5 (3); Farmer and Henley VI 177; Green 331; NED Shine 4 (2); Partridge 756; Thornton II 785.

Shine, vb. See Bottle (5, 6), Button (6), Dollar (7), Drummond light (2), Flicker, Mirror (3), Money (1), Moon (2), Pin (12), Pink (3), Satin (1), Silver (2).

Shingle, 1. Now he [a fish] comes as easily as a shingle (55 Anon. *New Hope* 247).

2. As straight as a shingle in all his dealins (36 Haliburton *Clockmaker* I 299, III 37 she is as straight as a shingle in her talk, right up and down, and no pretence, *Season-Ticket* 228 I like a man that's right up and down, as straight as a shingle; Hall *Purchase* II 268; Thompson *Major* 110 things is gone on jest as strate as a shingle; Anon. *New Hope* 368 and if he don't walk as straight as a shingle; Hammett *Piney* 37 there was the bill straight as a shingle). Boshears 40: 971; Halpert 678; NC 473.

3. To hoist (hang out) one's shingle. 42 DA Shingle 1. Cf. NED Shingle 1 d.

4. The tragedians in the Bowery and Chatam street of to-day don't start the shingles on the roof (62 Browne *Artemus* 207).

Shingle-maker. Lazy es a shingle-maker (67 Harris *Sut* 198). Randolph and Wilson 178.

Shiny. See Nigger (7), Razor (3), Rooster (3), Wintergreen.

Ship, 1. And if necessity compels, with our dying breath cry to all around, "Don't give up the ship!" (c56 Cartwright *Autobiography* 438). Stevenson 2091:6; NQ CLVI (1929) 453; J. T. Farrell *Studs Lonigan: The Young Manhood of Studs Lonigan* (1935) 402 as Napoleon said.

2. As has often been said, a ship is like a lady's watch, always out of repair (40 Dana *Two* 16, 423 She is, as sailors say, like a lady's watch, always out of repair). Apperson 564 A ship and a woman; *Oxford* 581; Tilley S350, W658; A. T. Sheppard *Here Comes an Old Sailor* (1928) 116 a woman and a ship ever want mending.

3. Ah! 't will be a golden day, When my ship comes o'er the sea (68 Saxe *Poems* 28; Jones *Batkins* 55 She was always talking about when her ship came home she would pay her bill). NED Ship 3; *Oxford* 581 comes home; Stevenson 2091:5; G. D. H. Cole and M. Cole *Death in the Quarry* (1934) 230 comes in; John Goodwin, pseud. *When Dead Men Tell Tales* (1928) 287 it is proverbially a pleasant sight to see one's ship come home.

4. Having, as usual, cleared the ship for action, he commenced (58 Hammett *Piney* 49). See Deck.

5. The proverb says "You must have a ship at sea in order to burn two candles at once" (69 Barnum *Struggles* 458–459).

Ship-shape, 1. Arter I'd examined the consarn to be certain all was shipshape (44 Stephens *High Life* II 52, 116). Farmer and Henley VI 180; NED Ship-shape.

2. It was ship-shape, and Brister (Bristol) fashion (23 Cooper *Pioneers* 74; Dana *Two* 120, 204; Melville *White Jacket* 15). Apperson 564; NED Bristol 3; *Oxford* 581; Stevenson 2091:10; Russell Thorndike *The Slype* (1928) 98.

Shirt, 1. You are as much mistaken, as if you had burnt your shirt (54 Smith *'Way* 190; Taliaferro *Fisher's* 190 And he gits in a ship—a big un, too—and tinks dat is de place fur him;

but he miss him fur as ef he'd aburnt he shirt).

2. And if I ain't as much mistaken as the man who lost his shirt, fortin' awaits us (65 Sedley *Marian* 117). Stevenson 2092:12.

3. I say, you durn'd ash cats, jis' keep yer shuts on (67 Harris *Sut* 19). McAtee 37; NC 473; Stevenson 2094: 2; Woodard PADS VI (1946) 39; R. P. Warren *All the King's Men* (1946) 51; M. Thompson *Not As a Stranger* (1954) 251; Mark W. Clark *Calculated Risk* (1950) 85 And he had a fine way of helping to smooth ruffled tempers. "Now just keep your shirt on, Wayne," he said frequently when I would become particularly discouraged by delays, or on other occasions when I wanted to get some project under way in a hurry. "Just keep your shirt on!"

4. Whew! said the stranger, don't tear your shirt (55 Dorson *Jonathan* 57). DA Shirt 2 b (4).

Shirt bosom. Anyone with sense enough to tell his shirt bosom from the main royal (45 Mayo *Kaloolah* 108).

Shirttail. If he didn't make a straight shirttail for the door, may I never make another pass (58 Field *Pokerville* 132). DA Shirt 2 b (1); Farmer 484; Randolph and Wilson 207–208. Cf. Coat-tail.

Shoat. I'm afeard he's a gone shote (44 Stephens *High Life* II 155). See Coon (7).

Shock. A feeling of relief flashed over me as quick as an electric shock (c56 Cartwright *Autobiography* 35, 192 I felt a flash of indignation run all over me like an electric shock).

Shoe, 1. I'm as easy as an old glove, but a glove aint an old shoe to be trod on (36 Haliburton *Clockmaker* I p. xi; Emerson *Works* II 240 These old shoes are easy to the feet; Hammett *Piney* 256–257 I'd been down here so long, where tradin' was as easy as an old shoe; Lowell *Biglow* 324 easy'z an ole pair o' shoes). Apperson 175; McAtee 24; NC 473; NED Shoe 2 m; Stevenson 204:6; Taylor *Comparisons* 38. Cf. D. L. Teilhet *Journey to the West* (1938) 124 as domestic and comfortable as an old shoe.

2. She used to be jest as plain as an old shoe (44 Thompson *Major* 11; Taliaferro *Fisher's* 258). Boshears 39: 799; NC 473; Taylor *Comparisons* 62.

3. A clouted shoe hath oft-times craft in it, as Deacon Ramsdill says (45 Judd *Margaret* I 318).

4. If so I wouldn't be in the shoes of eyther (25 Neal *Brother J* III 237). Green 332; NC 473; NED Shoe 2 k; Stevenson 2094:5; Roger Garnett *Death in Piccadilly* (London n.d. [c1935]) 179 I'd hate to be in your shoes. Cf. Boot (4); Tilley C473.

5. If the shoe fits you, you can wear it a little wile, Jack (76 Nash *Century* 125). Cf. Cap (1).

6. They know where the shoe pinches (46 Emerson *Journals* VII 221; Lowell *Biglow* 139 This, at the on'y spot thet pinched, the shoe directly eases; Haliburton *Sam* I 263 That's one o' the places where the shoe pinches, 266 there is another place the shoe pinches, *Nature* II 393; Derby *Phoenixiana* 160 that's exactly "where the shoe pinches"; Lincoln II 358 They know where the shoe pinches, 374, VII 413 As the proverb goes, no man knows so well where the shoe pinches as he who wears it; Clemens *Innocents* II 149 The shoe not only

pinched our party, but it pinched hard). Apperson 565; NC 473; NED Shoe 2 f; *Oxford* 583; Stevenson 2096: 3; Stoett 2003; Tilley M129; Whiting *Drama* 39, *Scots* II 124; Margery Allingham *Kingdom of Death* (1933) 100; Halldor Laxness *Salka Valka* (transl. F. H. Lyon, Boston 1936) 219 but he who wears the shoe knows best when it pinches.

7. A place where he told me afterwards he threw up his shoes and stockings, a jacket lined with tripe (I give his own language) and his commission (33 Neal *Down-Easters* I 74; Taliaferro *Fisher's* 260–261 He may puke up his stockin's afore I'll go a-near him). Cf. McAtee 65 toe nails.

8. I wouldn't wipe my old shoes on him (56 Whitcher *Widow* 237, 243).

Shoe-leather. You saw as pretty a fellow hanged as ever trod shoe-leather (23–24 Irving *Tales* 436; Neal *Brother J* II 35 quite a spunky chap . . . as ever trod shoe leather, 446 as brave a man as; Smith *Downing* 147 a keener set of fellows never . . . trod shoe-leather; Longstreet *Georgia* 24 a leetle of the best man at a horse-swap that ever; Haliburton *Clockmaker* II 289 a smarter set o' men than they be never stept into shoe-leather, *Season-Ticket* 38 that ever trod, 222 as ever trod; Stephens *High Life* I 133 the harnsomest gal that ever, 233, II 237; Burke *Polly* 83 that ever; Smith *'Way* 319 she would not have the best man that ever trod shoe-leather; Whitcher *Widow* 345 he was about as contemptible a specimen of a man as ever walked shoe-leather; Nash *Century* 236 one of the best wimmen that was ever crowded into shoe leather). Apperson 306 Honest; Green 332; NED Shoe 2 m, Shoe-leather; Stevenson 994:11, 2096:1; Svartengren 401; Tilley M66; Whiting *Drama* 368:909. Cf. Sole leather (3).

Shoemaker. A shoemaker must not go beyond his last (21 Loomis *Farmer's Almanac* 178; Nash *Century* 11 His theory is, that a shoemaker should stick to his last). Apperson 104 Cobbler; *Oxford* 99–100; Tilley C480. See Cobbler.

Shoe-string, 1. To tie one's own shoestring. 54 DA Shoestring 5 b (1).

2. A poor beggar, not worth a shoestring (57 Melville *Confidence-Man* 95). Apperson 458:40 shoe-buckles; NED Shoe 6 c (not worthy to tie her majesty's shoe-strings); *Oxford* 583.

Shoot, sb., 1. To take the shoot [i. e., set forth boldly]. 37 DA Shoot 6 (1).

2. To take a shoot after [i. e., take a liking to]. 47 DA Shoot 6 (2).

3. To make a straight shoot. 53 DA Shoot 6 (4).

Shoot, vb. See Dog (53).

Shooting, 1. I done it jist as easy as shootin' (45 Hooper *Simon* 23). NC 473.

2. I'd let him go quicker'n shootin' (76 Nash *Century* 325).

3. As sure as shutin' (43 Robb *Squatter* 68, 75 shootin'; Burke *Polly* 148 shooting; Hammett *Stray* 116 [said to be a "Southron's phrase" in contrast to the Yankee's "as sartin as preachin"]; Field *Pokerville* 12, 85; Hammett *Piney* 59, 61). DA Shooting 2 b; McAtee 63; NC 473; Stevenson 2249:11; Taylor *Comparisons* 80; Thorne Smith *Skin and Bones* (1933) 223.

Shop, 1. To give the best one has in the shop. 70 DA Shop 1 b.

2. In the first place, the wind got

tired of doing bisnis in the same line, and shut up shop (58 Hammett *Piney* 135, 140 there's a quarter; now travel; and just shut up shop about this; Lowell *Biglow* 323 We'd better take maysures for shettin' up shop). Farmer and Henley VI 190; NED Shop 8 b; *Oxford* 587; Stevenson 2100:12. Cf. Apperson 569; Tilley S394.

Short, sb. It comes from the devil, that's the short of it (51 Stowe *Uncle* 246, *id.* the short of the matter is; Bennett *Kate* 235). NED Short B 2.

Short, adv. Short and Sweet just like a rosted maget (63 Wiley *Billy* 187; Lowell *Biglow* 226 To cut it short, I wun't say sweet, they gi' me a good dip). Apperson 567; NED Short 8 c; *Oxford* 584; Stevenson 2101:2; Tilley S396; Terry Shannon *The Catspaw* (1929) 227.

Shot, 1. A shot in the neck [i. e., intoxicated]. 30 DA Shot 3 b (1).

2. By a long shot (37 Neal *Charcoal* 189; Kelly *Humors* 211 Not by a long shot; Riley *Puddleford* 278; Hammett *Piney* 60 suthin' that . . . didn't consarn me by a long shot; Stephens *Mary Derwent* 250; Eggleston *School-Master* 157; Nash *Century* 18). DA Shot 3 b (2); Farmer and Henley VI 195; NED Shot 9 d; Partridge 492; Elizabeth S. Holding *The Death Wish* (1934) 108.

3. Off like a shot (25 Neal *Brother J* I 107, III 287; Smith *Downing* 87 off he goes like, 189; Haliburton *Clockmaker* II 57 to up Hudson like, *Old Judge* I 300, II 291, *Sam* I 261, II 109; Chamberlain *Confession* 162 I passed them like a shot; Harris *Sut* 132 I . . . cross'd hit like; Clemens *Innocents* I 44). R. C. Ashby *He Arrived at Dusk* (1933) 192. Cf. Farmer

and Henley IV 198, VI 195; NC 473; NED Shot 7 d; Taylor *Comparisons* 72.

4. I'm off, like shot off a shovel (44 Stephens *High Life* II 47; Anon. *New Hope* 83 like a shot from a shovel; Kelly *Humors* 287 the excited landlord's eyes danced like shot on a hot shovel; Derby *Phoenixiana* 329).

5. It is quite immaterial what shot brings down the pigeon, so that we get him (32 Kennedy *Swallow* 201).

6. The first shot is worth a dozen afterward (34 Davis *Downing* 93). Cf. Apperson 214 First blow; *Oxford* 204.

7. It makes somewhat of a hole in their lockers (40 Dana *Two* 142, 175 the shot was getting low in the locker at the oven, 296 Never say die, while there's a shot in the locker; Smith *'Way* 170 The last shot I had in the locker went to pay for my breakfast; Melville *Piazza* 213 Peru found itself . . . with few shot in the locker. In other words, Peru had not the wherewithal to pay off its troops). Babcock 259; Hardie 470:146; NED Locker 5 b.

8. The one who "caves" first shall pay the shot (55 Hammett *Wonderful* 64). Apperson 487; Farmer and Henley VI 195; NED Shot 23; Stevenson 1764:1; Tilley S398.

9. Away went their mill, shot, lock, and barrel (34 Crockett *Life* 21). See Lock, Stock (4).

Shote. See Shoat.

Shot-gun. Likened him unto a kickin shot-gun—dangerous only to them ez held it (64 Locke [Nasby] *Struggles* 114).

Shoulder, 1. To come from the shoulder. 73 DA Shoulder 1 b (2).

2. To overleap one's shoulder [i. e., to overextend one's self]. 34 DA Shoulder 1 b (1).

3. Put my shoulder to the wheel (33 Smith *Downing* 221, *My Thirty* 247, 277, 442; Riley *Puddleford* 84 always put his shoulder to the public wheel). NED Shoulder 3 e; *Oxford* 586; Stevenson 2101:7; Tilley S403; Leslie Ford, pseud. *By the Watchman's Clock* (1932) 133 have.

4. Sofy tarned her "cold shoulder" at me so orful pinted (43 Robb *Squatter* 99; Haliburton *Old Judge* I 311 he had got a cold shoulder from Minna Vroom, II 18 gave them a cold shoulder, *Season-Ticket* 373; Hammett *Wonderful* 39 His friends and relations treated him to the cold shoulder; Melville "I and My Chimney" in *Works* XIII 290; Eggleston *School-Master* 221; Clemens *Gilded* I 198). Farmer and Henley II 152; NED Cold shoulder; *Oxford* 102; Stevenson 2101: 11; NQ 3 xi 498; 7 ix 228; 9 xii 128; Will Scott *The Mask* (Philadelphia 1929) 106.

Shovel, 1. There is no necessity of your putting in your shovel here (63 Clemens *Enterprise* 105, *Washoe* 98). DA Shovel 2 b (2). See Oar (3).

2. He went at it shovel and tongs (44 Stephens *High Life* I 40, II 255). DA Shovel 2 b (1). See Hammer (3).

Show, 1. This New Year's day here in New York is sartinly as good as a show (44 Stephens *High Life* I 167). NC 474; E. D. Biggers *The Chinese Parrot* (Indianapolis 1926) 79. Cf. Play (2).

2. To go on with the show. 67 DA Show 3 b (2).

3. To have no show. 68 DA Show 3 b (3); NED Show 3 c.

Shroud. The sea white as a shroud (40 Melville *Mardi* I 142).

Shucks, 1. It's curus . . . that what some folks want so much, other folks don't kear shucks for (65 Sedley *Marian* 256).

2. Will fight . . . until their hides cannot hold shucks for the bullet holes (51 Burke *Polly* 176; Eggleston *School-Master* 155 I'd lick you till yer hide wouldn't hold shucks, *Circuit* 39 the picture of Christian thrashing Apollyon till his hide wouldn't hold shucks). Randolph and Wilson 216.

3. He ain't wuth shucks (43 Robb *Squatter* 135; Burke *Polly* 51; Hammett *Stray* 98; Riley *Puddleford* 267; Chamberlain *Confession* 261 Ye ain't worth shucks). Bartlett 588–589; DA Shuck 3 b; Farmer and Henley VI 201; Green 334; NED Shuck 2 b; Stevenson 2644:2; Thornton II 794–795.

Shuffle. And I knowed, too, that I wa'n't able to shuffle and cut with him [i. e., to equal him]. (34 Crockett *Life* 140). Cf. NED Shuffle 2 b.

Shun. See Small pox (1).

Shy. See Fawn (3), Loon (4), Partridge (3), Turkey 2 (7).

Siamese. Now, you two hook on to one another like two Siameses (37 Neal *Charcoal* 77). Cf. NC 474; *Oxford* 587. The Siamese twins were first exhibited in Boston and elsewhere in 1829.

Sick. See Death (13).

Side, 1. Great pussy fellers, as big as the side of the house (44 Stephens *High Life* I 124, 177, II 5; Hammett *Piney* 286 a dollar [was] as big as the side of a house). Cf. Boshears 34:331; NC 474; Taylor *Comparisons* 21.

2. His back wus as black as a side ove upper lether (67 Harris *Sut* 154).

3. Didn't know him from a side of sole-leather (45 Hooper *Simon* 113; Porter *Major* 23; Kelly *Humors* 276). Thornton I 522, III 223.

4. There are two sides to every question (32 Kennedy *Swallow* 13; Cooper *Pathfinder* 151 It would be an indifferent question . . . that hadn't two sides to it; and I've known many that had three; Holmes *Professor* 60 There are two sides to everything, *Poet* 81 two sides to everybody, as there are to that piece of money, 280 So there are two sides to the question; Clift *Bunker* 103 There is tew sides to all questions; Jones *Batkins* 318 there are two sides to the question, 349, 382 There are two sides to it, *ib.* there generally are just two sides to everything, when there are not more than two). Bradley 89; Lean IV 145; NC 474; NED Side 17 d; *Oxford* 680; Stevenson 1926:3; Benjamin Disraeli *Henrietta Temple* (1836) ch. 20 (London [1927]) 424 There are always two sides to a case; Charles Reade *Hard Cash* (1863) ch. 9 (London 1913) 138 but most human events, even calamities, have two sides; R. C. Woodthorpe *The Shadow on the Downs* (1935) 15.

5. I could get on the blind side of her [i. e., dupe her]. (66 Boucicault *Flying Scud* 178). Apperson 54; Green 33; Stevenson 197:5; Tilley S429.

6. Not while I'm on the green side of the turf (66 Boucicault *Flying Scud* 190).

7. And though he was yet on the green side of thirty (43 Thompson *Chronicles* 162). Cf. Hulbert Footner *Dangerous Cargo* (1934) 22 sunny side.

8. On the wrong side of forty (54 Smith *'Way* 50). Means Davis *Murder without Weapons* (1934) 125 thirty. Cf. NED Shady 2 b.

9. Hintin' that he is of gentle blood, only the wrong side of the blanket (43 Haliburton *Attaché* II 113). Apperson 715; *Oxford* 736; Randolph and Wilson 115; Wilson PADS II (1944) 40; Brian Flynn *The Case of the Black Twenty-two* (Philadelphia 1929) 228 born.

10. Then, tew, ther was a careful set . . . that wanted to be "right side up"; and not bein' able to determine for sartin which would turn out to be the popular party (56 Whitcher *Widow* 332).

11. Knows which side o' his bread *his* butter is on (25 Neal *Brother J* II 300, III 392; Smith *Downing* 51 I know which side my bread is buttered better than all that, 82 Jack knows which side his bread is buttered, 126, 160, 252, *My Thirty* 398; Stephens *High Life* I 233 She . . . had a sort of notion which side her bread was buttered on, II 199; Burke *Polly* 82 Mr. Stubbleworth "knew which side of his bread the butter was on," 147 ef that feller Arch Coony don't mind which side of his bread's buttered, I'll git hold of him one of these days; Stowe *Uncle* 49 a particular species of wisdom . . . vulgarly denominated "knowing which side his bread is buttered"; Eliason 140 I So [show] him wich sid of his bered is buterd [the writer anticipates a fight]; Clift *Bunker* 71 Josiah . . . knows on which side his bread is buttered). Apperson 64; NC 375; *Oxford* 346; Stevenson 232–233:8; Tilley S425; NQ 4 ix 263, 328; Anthony Armstrong, pseud. *The Trail of the Black King* (Philadelphia 1931) 317.

12. To teach 'em larf on tother side of de mouth (36 Haliburton *Clockmaker* I 98, 216 The larf is on the other side of his mouth, *Sam* II 180; Stephens *High Life* I 33; Stowe *Uncle* 68; Taliaferro *Fisher's* 32, 150). McAtee 39; NC 474; NED Laugh 1 b; *Oxford* 352; Stevenson 1355:11; Tidwell PADS XIII (1950) 20; Tilley S430; Woodard PADS VI (1946) 39; Charles Barry, pseud. *Murder on Monday?* (1932) 58.

13. He . . . was thus caused to laugh on the wrong side of his mouth (56 Kelly *Humors* 426; Porter *Major* 39 Sort o' laughin' out o' the wrong side o' my mouth; Barnum *Struggles* 268). Apperson 352; NC 474; NED Laugh 1 b; Tilley S430; Max Saltmarsh *The Clouded Moon* (1938) 80.

14. Shinny on your own side. 66 DA Shinny, vb.; Stevenson 1541–1542:9.

15. When you've hearn me thro' you'll talk t'other side of your mouth (51 Burke *Polly* 50).

16. You're like the hootin' owl, Misther Goodwin; it's the black side ye're after lookin at all the toime (74 Eggleston *Circuit* 112).

17. We put the best side out (44 Stephens *High Life* II 74). Tilley S431.

18. I raly thought the critter would a split her sides (44 Stephens *High Life* I 225). NED Split 3 c.

Sideways. If he dared look sideways at his [i. e., another's] wife or sister (44 Stephens *High Life* I 217). NED Sideways 3 b.

Sieve, 1. It leaked like a sieve (60 Haliburton *Season-Ticket* 287). McAtee 39; NC 474; *Oxford* 356; Taylor *Comparisons* 72.

2. He's been out for some exercise, he wants a lot of flesh taken off him; in fact he wants regularly pulling through a sieve (66 Boucicault *Flying Scud* 168).

Sigh, sb. In the same breath—soft as a sigh (50 Mitchell *Reveries* 38).

Sigh, vb. See Grampus.

Sight, 1. Out of sight, out of mind (32 Kennedy *Swallow* 7; Stowe *Uncle* 8 you know). Apperson 476; McAtee 47; NC 476; NED Sight 10 b; *Oxford* 480; Stevenson 2106:14; Stoett 1691; Tilley S438; Whiting *Drama* 33, 84, 128, 140, 273; NQ 3 viii 474, 546; E. R. Punshon *The Cottage Murder* (Boston 1932) 10.

2. Not by a darned (long) sight. 34 DA Sight 5 b (2).

3. I'll make him see sites! (51 Burke *Polly* 147; Porter *Major* 24 he'll see sights before he gets his money). Green 336.

Sign. All signs fail in a dry time (68 Clemens *Fairbanks* 40). Bradley 99; NC 475; Taylor *Index* 29.

Signed. What's signed, is signed; and what's to be, will be (51 Melville *Moby-Dick* I 117).

Silence. The old principle, that silence gives consent (23 Cooper *Pioneers* 391; Crockett *Exploits* 93 all the world over; Derby *Phoenixiana* 273 Silence gives a cent; Whitcher *Widow* 355; Melville *Confidence-Man* 111 silence is at least not denial, and may be consent). Apperson 571; NC 475; NED Consent 1 c; *Oxford* 589; Stevenson 2112:3; Stoett 2688; Tilley S446; Whiting *Drama* 20, *Scots* II 125; Anthony Gray *Dead Nigger* (London 1929) 143.

Silent. See Cat (21, 22), Church (2), Death (14), Grave (8), Pine-stump (3), Sarcophagus, Sphinx.

Silently. See Moth (2).

Silk, 1. Coats [of horses] bright as silk (58 Holmes *Autocrat* 95).

2. Fine as silk . . . and leetle finer (36 Crockett *Exploits* 64; Briggs *Harry* I 72 "Are you well?" "Fine as silk," said Mr. Lummucks; Stowe *Uncle* 3 His black hair, fine as floss silk; Derby *Phoenixiana* 248 replied to my inquiries concerning his health, that he was "as fine as silk, but not half so well beliked by the ladies"; Hammett *Piney* 65 Getting along as fine as silk, 260 and in a couple of shakes of a sheep's tail we was a doin' our three minutes jest as fine as silk; Porter *Major* 84 girls at a dance . . . "as fine as silk"; Boucicault *Flying Scud* 159 She's . . . as fine as silk). Boshears 36:551; Farmer 240; McAtee 26; NC 475; Taylor *Comparisons* 40; Thornton I 316; David Frome, pseud. *The Strange Death of Martin Green* (1931) 67.

3. The river and bay are smooth as a sheet of beryl-green silk (58 Holmes *Autocrat* 170).

Silk weed. Shoes . . . felt as soft as a silk weed pod (44 Stephens *High Life* I 198). Cf. Boshears 40:952 silk; NC 475; NED Silk 1 c; Svartengren 266; Taylor *Comparisons* 76; Whiting *Drama* 325:290, *Scots* II 125.

Silver, 1. Sound as silver (60–63 Taliaferro *Carolina Humor* 16).

2. Shoe-boots a-shinin' like silver (45 Hooper *Simon* 20; Durivage *Three* 193 His sides shone like silver; Richardson *Beyond* 213 In a stream bright and shining as silver). Whiting *Scots*

II 125. Cf. Boshears 40:904; Tilley S453; Whiting *Drama* 325:291.

Silver mine, 1. "Once a silver mine, always a silver mine," is the favorite theory (67 Richardson *Beyond* 374).

2. The Mexican proverb that only three classes of men work silver mines: those who have other people's money to spend, those who have more money than they know what to do with, and fools (67 Richardson *Beyond* 254.

3. The Spanish proverb says it requires a gold-mine to "run" a silver one, and it is true (72 Clemens *Roughing* II 93).

Silvery. See Moonlight (2).

Simon pure. The real Simon Pures (33 Smith *Downing* 211; Haliburton *Sam* II 173; Durivage *Three* 117; Taliaferro *Carolina Humor* 23; Richardson *Beyond* 545 the original simon-pure prohibitory law; Clift *Bunker* 117 A Simon Pure country wedding; Barnum *Struggles* 214 the "Simon pure"; Clemens *Roughing* I 171). DA Simon 3; Farmer and Henley VI 211; NC 475; NED Simon Pure; Randolph and Wilson 190; Stevenson 1910:8; D. L. and Hildegarde Teilhet *The Crimson Hair Murders* (1936) 100.

Simple. See Loon (5), Mousetrap.

Simple-hearted. See Child (3).

Sin, 1. A sin to Crocket (44 Stephens *High Life* I 190; Eliason 294 City Election will be a sin to crocket). Randolph and Wilson 198; Thornton II 798.

2. And the way we makes the wool and the petticoats fly, is a sin to snakes (43 Dorson *Jonathan* 95).

3. Bitter as sin (43 Robb *Squatter* 33).

4. He's [a lobster] cross as sin! (56 Kelly *Humors* 240).

5. [Pigs] greasy and sassy as sin (56 Kelly *Humors* 359).

6. The family is older than sin, and as rich too (43 Haliburton *Attaché* IV 165–166).

7. Jest ez sure ez sin (67 Lowell *Biglow* 264).

8. As ugly as sin (36 Haliburton *Clockmaker* I 97, *Nature* II 87, *Season-Ticket* 194; Baldwin *Flush* 172 if she had been as ugly as original sin). Apperson 658; Boshears 40:995; McAtee 69; NC 475; NED Sin 2 c; *Oxford* 682; Taylor *Comparisons* 84; Tilley S465; Helen Burnham *The Telltale Telegram* (1932) 40.

9. An he kin fight like sin (65 Sedley *Marian* 94).

10. I got to hate it like sin (40 Haliburton *Clockmaker* III 102). Will Scott *The Mask* (Philadelphia 1929) 16.

11. An' to plunder ye like sin (48 Lowell *Biglow* 47).

12. Don't chew none, but smokes like sin (65 Sedley *Marian* 358).

13. They *will* stick like sin (67 Lowell *Biglow* 326). Partridge 770.

14. An' kep' me pris'ner 'bout six months, an' worked me, tu, like sin (48 Lowell *Biglow* 147; Kelly *Humors* 361 Daown in another place they were saltin' and packin' away, like sin).

Sing. See Lark (12).

Sink, 1. Sink or swim,—hit or miss, he [William Ellery Channing] writes on, & is never responsible (42 Emerson *Letters* III 102; Cartwright *Autobiography* 338 Take a firm hold of the gig, and sink or swim, never let go; Smith *Arp* 151; Barnum *Struggles* 118). Apperson 574; NC 475; NED Sink 1 c; *Oxford* 592; Stevenson 2262:4; Tilley

S485; Whiting *Drama* 363:840; Anthony Pryde, pseud. *The Secret Room* (1929) 43.

2. See Lead (2).

Sinner, 1. It was harder than a sinner's heart (50 Melville *White Jacket* 76). Cf. Taylor *Comparisons* 46 Pharoah's, whore's.

2. As I am a livin' sinner (60 Whitehead *Wild Sports* 334–335).

3. It's as true as you and I are mortal sinners (55 Anon. *New Hope* 340).

4. The greater sinner the greater the saint (43 Haliburton *Attaché* IV 265, *Old Judge* II 15, *Sam* I 170, II 265). Apperson 272; Stevenson 2026:9.

Sister. As much interested . . . as if she'd been my own sister (44 Stephens *High Life* II 240).

Sit, 1. Sho ez youer settin' dar (80 Harris *Uncle Remus* 85).

2. As true as I set here (56 Whitcher *Widow* 90).

3. In hope of the blissful time when somebody should "set up" with her of evenings [i. e., to pay court to]. (71 Eggleston *School-Master* 74).

4. It was as cheap to sit as to stand, and every bit and grain as easy too (40 Haliburton *Clockmaker* III 63, *Attaché* III 7 sittin' is just as cheap as standin' in a general way, *Old Judge* I 208 Sitting is as cheap as standing, when you don't pay for it, and twice as easy, II 158 sitting is as cheap as walking, if you don't pay for it, *Sam* I 116, *Season-Ticket* 220; Hammett *Stray* 266 Guess I'll set down; cheap settin's standing). Apperson 92; NC 475–476; *Oxford* 89; Stevenson 327:9; Tilley S495; J. J. Connington, pseud. *The Sweepstake Murders* (Boston 1932) 148 sitting.

Six, 1. Near about six of one, and half a dozen of tother (36 Haliburton *Clockmaker* I 86, III 22, 123, 150, *Attaché* II 142, *Old Judge* II 34, *Sam* I 82, *Nature* I 168, 348, *Season-Ticket* 40, 243; Hall *Purchase* II 138 six of one and so forth; Stephens *High Life* I 107; Durivage *Three* 272; Cary *Married* 185; Sedley *Marian* 143; *Puck* II [1877] No. 42 p. 7). Apperson 575; Brewster *Am. Speech* XIV (1939) 266; McAtee 57; NC 476; NED Six 2 f; *Oxford* 594; Stevenson 2123:6; Lesley Frost *Murder at Large* (1932) 73.

2. I knew a chap 'twould whip the whool boodle of 'em an' give 'em six (33 Neal *Down-Easters* I 61; Neal *Charcoal* 97 If it wasn't for grief, I'd give both of you six, and beat you too the best day you ever saw, goin' the rale gum and hickory). See Two (3).

3. To come to short sixes [i. e., to a fight]. 34 DA Short 4 f (1).

4. And as he spent all his time in attending to the affairs of the nation, of course his affairs all went to sixes and sevens (39 Briggs *Harry* I 101; Cooper *Chainbearer* 326 all would be at sixes and sevens; Shillaber *Mrs. Partington* 323 Old Mrs. Twist . . . left all her work hanging, as she said, by "sixes and sevens," to go and help bring the man to; Stephens *Mary Derwent* 291 but you al'ezs make me fling everything to sixes and sevens when you come). Apperson 575; Farmer and Henley VI 219–220; Lean III 306; NC 476; NED Six 5; *Oxford* 594; Stevenson 2123:7; Stoett 2393; Tilley A208; Whiting *Drama* 364:850, *Scots* II 126; Yamamoto *Dickens* 128; NQ 1 iii 118, 425; 9 x 55–56, xi 266; 11 viii 190; Samuel Butler *Hudibras* (1678) III i 588 Or wager laid at six and seven; Helen Ashton *Doctor Serocold* (1930) 273.

Sixpence, 1. Looking as tickled as if he'd found a sixpence (44 Stephens *High Life* I 241).

2. So you see he is the same old sixpence he used to be (33 Smith *Downing* 185; Haliburton *Nature* I 177 you are the old sixpence, and nothin' will change you). NED Sixpence 2 c.

3. See Thrip.

Sixty, 1. Cold as sixty (49 Dorson *Jonathan* 79).

2. Though like sixty all along I fumed an' fussed an' sorrered (48 Lowell *Biglow* 135; Dorson *Jonathan* 87 the crowd yelled and hurra-ed like sixty; Kelly *Humors* 104 I took to my heels like sixty; Riley *Puddleford* 248 abuses . . . Elvira . . . like sixty). Bartlett 796; DA Sixty 1; Farmer and Henley VI 220; McAtee *Additional* 2; NED Sixty B 1 b; Partridge 773; Kay C. Strahan *The Desert Lake Mystery* (Indianapolis 1936) 174 doubt it.

Skeleton, 1. I'll soon be as thin as the living skeleton who was being shown for a penny at the shop in High Street (66 Boucicault *Flying Scud* 158). NC 476; Taylor *Comparisons* 82.

2. It [an Indian on the warpath] was the skeleton at the feast (60 Whitehead *Wild Sports* 269). NED Skeleton 1 c; *Oxford* 594; Stevenson 2123:8; A. J. Rees *Aldringham's Last Chance* (1933) 17.

3. Perhaps he keeps his 'skeleton in the closet' (76 Nash *Century* 312). NED Skeleton 1 b; *Oxford* 594; Stevenson 2123–2124:9; Yamamoto *Dickens* 338–339; NQ 1 ii 231; 3 viii 109; 7 viii 413; Edith R. Curtis *Lady Sarah Lennox* (1946) 232 Caroline had now ceased to treat her sister like the family skeleton; William McFee *The Harbourmaster* (London 1932) 23 But

Frank, as he put it, 'had a skeleton in the cupboard.'

Skewer. A look so soft and killing, it went right straight through his heart, like a pine skewer through a chunk of butcher's meat (44 Stephens *High Life* I 240).

Skim-milk. It's no skim-milk story . . . but upper crust, real jam (38 Haliburton *Clockmaker* II 99).

Skin, 1. His britches are dressed buckskin, tight as the skin (59 Taliaferro *Fisher's* 153). NC 476; Svartengren 324 near.

2. Deacon Bedott was as tight as the skin on his back [i. e., miserly]. (56 Whitcher *Widow* 30, 127 tew his back). Cf. Fletcher Pratt *Double Jeopardy* (1952) 201 she started out being just as tight as the skin on an apple [i. e., uncommunicative].

3. Skin o' my teeth, I guess (25 Neal *Brother J* I 109, II 103, 307, *Down-Easters* I 81 I love to git away jist by the skin o' my teeth, 106 Whatever you git out o' them, you git by the skin o' their teeth; Clemens *Roughing* I 49 he only missed it by the skin of his teeth, *Gilded* I 243). Job 19:20; NC 476; NED Skin 5 g; *Oxford* 595; Stevenson 709:4; Tilley S510; NQ 7 iii 225, 372, iv 213; 12 i 167, 291; L. J. Blochmann *Bombay Mail* (Boston 1934) 39; Thornton Wilder *The Skin of Our Teeth* (1942), a title. See Johannes Hoops *Englische Studien* LXIV (1940–1941) 392.

4. Seeing that the skin is nearer than the shirt (49 Haliburton *Old Judge* II 64, *Sam* II 145). Apperson 437–438; *Oxford* 444; Stevenson 2057:7; Tilley S356.

5. O, heavens! grant me patience! I shall fly out of my skin (36 Crockett *Exploits* 116). Tilley S507; Whiting *Drama* 345:563.

6. I raly thought the critter would a jumped out of her skin, she was so awful mad (44 Stephens *High Life* I 48, 242 I shall be so happy, I shall want to jump out of my skin; Smith '*Way* 61 I jumped as if I were going out of my skin; Daly *Man* 13 I'm ready to jump out of my skin for joy). Farmer and Henley VI 228–229; NED Skin 5 f; Stevenson 1273:13; Stoett 2345; Nicholas Trott *Monkey Boat* (1932) 26. See Hide (3).

7. "Joe" was scared and wanted to save his skin (64 Lincoln VII 520). Farmer and Henley VI 228–229; NED Skin 5 h; Stevenson 2125:8; Lilian Bamburg *Beads of Silence* (1927) 255.

8. He shouts, so shrilly, that your "skin creeps" (45 Hooper *Simon* 53). NED Creep 6.

9. They [corsets] set to the shape like the skin to a bird (44 Stephens *High Life* I 221). Cf. Halpert 113.

10. I sometimes wonder they don't clear out to a new country, where every skin hangs by its own tail (35 Crockett *Account* 50). Cf. Ernst Jünger *The Storm of Steel* (transl. B. Creighton, London 1929) 194 I have always made it a rule to let any one carry his own skin to market where he pleases.

Skipper. As chirk and lively as a skipper (34 Davis *Downing* 20). NED Skipper 1 d; Mitchell B. Garrett *Horse and Buggy Days on Hatchet Creek* (University, Alabama, 1957) 59 frisky white worms.

Skirts. I clear my skirts (54 Smith '*Way* 27). DA Skirt; W. B. Foster *From Six to Six* (1927) 77, 84.

Skunk, 1. They jist cut him as dead as a skunk (43 Haliburton *Attaché* I 139, IV 119).

2. To kill another skunk [i. e., to create a new scandal]. 63 DA Skunk 3 d (2).

3. I had enough liquor plump in me to swim a skunk (58 Porter *Major* 87).

4. Let ev'ry man "skin his own skunks" (34 Davis *Downing* 101; Sedley *Marian* 243 I don't bet nuthin' on the Britisher, and he kin skin his own skunks, he kin; Jones *Batkins* 450 "You and Mr. Bean must skin your own skunks." She said she had no skunks to skin, and did not understand my allusion. I thought she seemed offended, and I told her I was only using a rhetorical figure of speech, natural enough in the mouth of a farmer. I did not suppose, literally, she had any skunks to skin, and I supposed a fisherman might, under the same circumstances, be justified in saying let every one skin their own eels; and if she had no objection, I would withdraw the word skunks and substitute eels. She said eels were less offensive in idea than skunks, but as she had none, either of the quadrupeds or the finny tribes, to flay, she would prefer plain English, which she supposed simply meant that Mr. Batkins had no interest in any affair between herself and Mr. Bean). Bartlett 599; DA Skunk 3 d (1); Farmer 490; Schele de Vere 55; Stevenson 1236:7; Herbert Corey *Crime at Cobb's House* (1934) 62 I'm through. He can skin his own snakes. See Axe (3).

Sky. His best coat, of sky-blue (55 Irving *Wolfert* 196; Alcott *Little Women* 101). NED Sky-blue; Taylor *Comparisons* 20 blue as the sky.

Sky-high. Not blown up sky high (34 Crockett *Life* 144; Hall *Soldier's Bride* 226; Dana *Two* 168 knocked to pieces or thrown sky-high; Hooper *Simon* 45 blown him sky high; Stowe *Uncle* 257 blown sky-high; Anon. *New Hope* 40 Blown sky-high, by jiminy!; Cartwright *Autobiography* 134 blow the Methodists skyhigh; Whitcher *Widow* 241 yer aunt blowed me up sky high; Riley *Puddleford* 206 blow the case sky-high, 276; Eggleston *School-Master* 147 blow us all sky-high, *Circuit* 328). Boshears 37:663; Green 339; McAtee 58; NC 476; NED Sky-high; Taylor *Comparisons* 48.

Sky-rocket. He shot over across like a sky-racket (58 Hammett *Piney* 114, 148 up we all went like so many sky-rackets). See Rocket.

Slab. A face . . . as wide as a slab (44 Stephens *High Life* II 90).

Slate, 1. His wig was gone, and, bald as a slate (59 Shillaber *Knitting-Work* 312).

2. To break the slate. 65 DA Slate 2 b (1).

Slave. I was content to toil like a slave (53 Boker *Bankrupt* 69; Cary *Married* 39 worked like a bought slave).

Sled. Don't stop your sled for jumpers (44 Stephens *High Life* II 205).

Sleep. See Baby (11), Dutchman (4), Hog (14), Image (2), Infant (5), Log (7), Monkey (1), Statue (7), Top 2 (2), Trojan.

Sleepy. See Hops (2).

Sleeve. I laugh in my sleeve (36 Haliburton *Clockmaker* I 71, 99, II 235, III 176, *Sam* I 186 sniggered, *Nature* I 244; Stephens *High Life* I 30; Cooper *Redskins* 166 he would be very apt to laugh at it, in his sleeve; Hawthorne *Mosses* 455; Clemens *Letters* I 231 smiling). Farmer and Henley VI 247; NED Laugh 1 b, Sleeve 2 d; *Oxford* 352; Stevenson 1351–1352:14; Tilley S535; Whiting *Drama* 364:856, *Scots* II 126; Hulbert Footner *The Mystery of the Folded Paper* (1930) 160.

Slick. See Bear (20), Biscuit (2), Bottle (2), Chalk (3), Goose-grease (2), Grease (1), Hat (4), Molasses (1), Pin (4), Smoothing iron, Whistle, sb. (3).

Slight. See Psyche.

Slim. See Rooster (3).

Slimpsey. See Eel (7).

Slip, 1. Well, well, young man, it was only a slip of the tongue (54 Shillaber *Mrs. Partington* 343). NED Slip 10 d; Stevenson 2342:4; Tilley S538 (the "slip" reveals the truth).
2. There is many a slip 'twixt the cup and the lip (32 Kennedy *Swallow* 320, *Horse-Shoe* 301 the adage; Crockett *Exploits* 92 says the proverb; Hall *Purchase* II 98; Fairfield *Letters* 357; Jones *Winkles* 343; Shillaber *Knitting-Work* 359). Apperson 129; Farmer and Henley VI 251; Figh PADS XIII (1950) 14; NC 477; NED Slip 9 b; *Oxford* 123; Stevenson 2139–2140:5; Taylor *Index* 25; Tilley T191; NQ 8 viii 345; Dane Coolidge *War Paint* (1929) 211; Arthur Train *The Adventures of Ephraim Tutt* (1930) 647. See Whiskey.

Slippery. See Eel (6), Glass (2).

Slow, 1. But slow is sure (27 Cooper *Prairie* 66, *Satanstoe* 34 slow but sure, *Chainbearer* 86 slow but sure; Hawthorne *Twice-Told* 387 Slow and sure!). Apperson 579; Bradley 93; *Oxford* 597; Stevenson 2142:7; Tilley S544; Anita Boutell *Death Brings a Storke* (1938) 81 Slow and sure; William Gore, pseud. *The Mystery of the Painted Nude* (1938) 85.
2. See Cat (22), Lightning (6), Woman (11).

Sly. See Fox (7), Weasel (6), Wild cat (2).

Small, adj. See Auger hole (1), End (7).

Small, adv. You had better sing mighty small (37 Neal *Charcoal* 111; Thompson *Chronicles* 139 If he don't sing small; Stephens *High Life* II 59 I guess it would have made that chap sing small if she had; Clemens *Enterprise* 187). Bartlett 796; Farmer and Henley VI 213; NED Small 4 b; Stevenson 2165:5; Winifred Greenleaves *The Trout Inn Mystery* (1929) 109.

Smallpox, 1. People shunned 'em like the small-pox (45 Hooper *Simon* 103).
2. It took like the small pox, and was carried tumultuously (66 Smith *Arp* 155).

Smart, vb. It is better once to smart than always to ache (54 Smith *'Way* 139). Cf. Apperson 46 Better tooth out; *Oxford* 39 Better eye out; Tilley E226, T419.

Smart, adj. See Foxtrap (2), Lightning (7, 8), Steeltrap (5).

Smartest. Cause the smartest on us gets tripped up sometimes (51 Stowe *Uncle* 54).

Smelt. As dead as a smelt (57 Riley *Puddleford* 103; Clemens *Enterprise* 77). Svartengren 146; Richard Peckham, pseud. *Murder in Strange Houses* (1929) 285.

Smile. See Sun (12).

Smiling. See Basket (2).

Smoke, sb., 1. If you see smoke, there must be fire (c38 Emerson *Works* II 102; Sedley *Marian* 411 Fire there must be where so much smoke had been). Apperson 582; NC 477; *Oxford* 454, 458; Stevenson 812:1; Tilley F282, S569; Whiting *Scots* II 116; Andrew Lang *Cock Lane and Common Sense* (1894) 13 Even people of open mind can, at present, say no more than this is a great deal of smoke, a puzzling quantity, if there be no fire, 356 The undesigned coincidences of testimony represent a good deal of smoke and proverbial wisdom suggests a presumption in favor of a few sparks of fire; William McFee *The Harbourmaster* (London 1932) 375; E. S. Gardner *The Case of the Drowning Duck* (1942) 148 Where there's so much smoke, there *must* have been a little fire.

2. If we didn't gallop 'um like smoke (25 Neal *Brother J* II 94; Smith *Downing* 73 go at it tie and tie like, 87 took it away like, 107 went to work like, 113 fighting like, *Letters* 25, 59, *My Thirty* 382; Davis *Downing* 18 pull'd away like; Crockett *Exploits* 21 circulated like; Haliburton *Old Judge* I 297 work like; Durivage *Three* 41 firin' like; Porter *Major* 61 hated Sam "like smoke"; Clemens *Fairbanks* 55 lectures me like). Farmer and Henley VI 271; Green 344; NED Smoke 4 h.

3. [Bank shares], which were to vanish like smoke in the hands of the holders (55 Irving *Wolfert* 173).

4. There's more smoke than fire there (33 Smith *Downing* 136; Hall *Purchase* I 41 it is not "all smoke" you now see—there is some fire here too). Cf. Tilley S568.

5. And have more smoke than powder (40 Haliburton *Letter* 198).

6. Now, to use a fighting phrase, there is nothing like boarding an enemy in the smoke [i. e., a verbal attack to soften resistance]. (49 Melville *Mardi* I 104, II 162 Tiffin over, and the blue-sealed calabash all but hid in the great cloud raised by our pipes, Media proposed to board it in the smoke. So goblet in hand, we all gallantly charged, and came off victorious from the fray).

Smoke, vb. See Volcano.

Smoker. They carry on so like the old smoker [Devil?]. (33 Smith *Downing* 135).

Smooth. See Billiard-ball (2), Cheek, Duck-pond, Egg (4), Eggshell (1), Floor (3), Glass (3), Grease (2), Hone, Ivory, Key, Marble (5), Mill pond (2), Oil (1), Persimmon (2), Prairie, Saddle (1), Satin (1), Silk (3).

Smoothing iron. Shaved my face as slick as a smoothin iron (44 Thompson *Major* 94).

Snag. But one day the old miser ran foul of a snag (56 Kelly *Humors* 131; Riley *Puddleford* 248 If she don't run agin a snag some day). McAtee 53; NED Snag 1 c. Cf. DA Snag 2 b (to catch on [hit] a snag).

Snail, 1. We ought . . . not to be creeping along like a snail (51 Burke *Polly* 11). Cf. Boshears 40:936; NC 477; Taylor *Comparisons* 74; Whiting *Drama* 326:295, *Scots* II 126.

2. Suffering them to lag on at a snail's pace (23–24 Irving *Tales* 302; Riley *Puddleford* 192). Apperson 582–583; Farmer and Henley VI 275; Green 345; NED Snail 2 b; *Oxford*

600; Stevenson 2148:6; Tilley S583; M. McCarthy *The Groves of Academe* (1952) 115.

Snake, 1. Latet anguis in herba (32 Kennedy *Swallow* 171; Saxe *Poems* 176 You've heard of the snake in the grass, my lad; Of the viper concealed in the grass; Clemens *Tom* 39 a guileful snake in the grass). Apperson 583; Boshears 38:731; Farmer and Henley VI 275; McAtee *Grant County* 9; NC 478; NED Snake 2 b; *Oxford* 601; Stevenson 2149:7; Tilley S585; Whiting *Scots* II 122 serpent; Herbert Crooker *The Hollywood Murder Mystery* (1930) 152.

2. Cold as a coiling water-snake (60 Holmes *Professor* 226).

3. Soople as a great snek (25 Neal *Brother J* I 268). Cf. NC 478:10.

4. As sure as there are snakes in Virginny (36 Crockett *Exploits* 18; Haliburton *Clockmaker* III 122, *Attaché* II 5–6, *Sam* II 121 If it warnt bitter, then there are no snakes in Virginny, *Nature* I 341, *Season-Ticket* 293).

5. To be above snakes. 51 DA Above 2.

6. If he don't, there's no sneks (33 Neal *Down-Easters* I 118; Crockett *Account* 88, *Exploits* 53; Stephens *High Life* II 202). DA Snake 7 (2); Randolph and Wilson 216. See Catfish, Lumber.

7. If I didn't, there no sneks in our part o' the country (33 Neal *Down-Easters* I 47; Stephens *High Life* I 52 then there's no snakes on the green mountain, that's all; Smith *'Way* 327 there's no snakes in Oquago, 331, 333).

8. Hate 'em . . . like snakes (55 Melville *Israel* 121, *Confidence-Man* 187; Eggleston *Circuit* 92 They do say

he *does* hate the Methodis' worse nor copperhead snakes). Cf. Whiting *Drama* 326:296.

9. That man down there has got the snakes (70–73 McCloskey *Across* 72). Cf. Berrey 130:9 (delirium tremens); DA Snake 4; NED Snake 2 d.

10. To have snakes in one's boots [i. e., to be drunk]. 77 DA Snake 7 (13).

11. There's them down our way that case-hardened they don't see snakes under a week [of steady drinking]! (65 Sedley *Marian* 225). DA Snake 7 (15).

12. Oh, wake snakes, and walk your chalks! (35 Longstreet *Georgia* 10; Haliburton *Clockmaker* III 182 I'd make him wake snakes, and walk his chalks, as the western folks say, *Attaché* I 118–119, 268, IV 217, *Nature* I 224–225 Come, rouse up, wake snakes and walk chalks, 371 and push off with the Captain, II 141–142, *Season-Ticket* 295; Hooper *Simon* 23 Wake snakes! day's a breakin'; Taliaferro *Fisher's* 36 Wake snakes, the winter's broke; Whitehead *Wild Sports* 40 Wake, snakes, day's a breaking). Bartlett 735; DA Snake 7 (5); Farmer 498–499; Farmer and Henley VII 284; Schele de Vere 212–213; Thornton II 929; Bon Gaultier [Theodore Martin and W. E. Aytoun] *The Book of Ballads* (1855, 11th ed. Edinburgh 1870) 47.

13. See Sin (2).

Snap, sb., 1. I don't keer a snap for the fattest of 'em (33 Smith *Downing* 140, 158, *My Thirty* 392; Shillaber *Knitting-Work* 291 For all of her violence cared not a snap; Kelly *Humors* 384). NED Snap 15 b; R. L. Goldman *Judge Robinson Murdered!* (1936) 89.

2. And don't care a snap of my finger for either (36 Haliburton *Clockmaker* I 162, III 189, *Attaché* IV 162, *Nature* I 16, *Season-Ticket* 306; Wiley *Billy* 290). R. T. M. Scott *Murder Stalks the Mayor* (1936) 41.

Snap, vb. See Rat traps.

Snappish. See Sheep-shears.

Sneaking. See Turkey 2 (8).

Sneezed. I tell you what it is, the feller warn't to be sneezed at on a rainy day, if he did cum from the country (44 Stephens *High Life* I 14, 55–56 in a fog, II 106, 191; Whitcher *Widow* 114 Sniffles ain't to be sneezed at, ye know). Bartlett 619; Farmer and Henley VI 279–280; NED Sneeze 2; *Oxford* 601; S. F. Bartlett *Beyond the Sowdyhunk* (Portland, Me. 1937) 110.

Snore. See Bear (33).

Snow, 1. Rightly is this soft March snow, falling just before seed-time, rightly is it called "Poor Man's Manure" (54 Melville "Poor Man's Pudding" in *Works* XIII 192, 193). NC 478. Cf. Apperson 15 April (22).
2. As cool and soft as snow (69 Alcott *Little Women* 444).
3. The biscuits were as light and white as new fallen snow (53 Cary *Clovernook* 2d Ser. 106).
4. You are as pure as snow (69 Clemens *Love Letters* 76, *Gilded* II 221 pure-minded). NC 478.
5. Mr. Wallop's vest was as spotless as snow (39 Briggs *Harry* I 242; Stephens *Fashion* 114 spotless as crusted snow).
6. White as snow (33 Hall *Soldier's Bride* 109 teeth, 113 counterpane; Dana *Two* 204; Stephens *High Life* I 111, 161, 164 as the cleanest handful

of snow you ever see, II 260, *Mary Derwent* 222 lips, 233 hair, 282 face; Cooper *Satanstoe* 59; Melville *White Jacket* 55; Hawthorne *Twice-Told* 36, 255; Cary *Clovernook* 18 thin locks white as snow, 2d Ser. 133; Haliburton *Nature* II 30; Mayo *Kaloolah* 149; Browning *Forty-Four* 242; Chamberlain *Confession* 118 belts; Paul *Courtship* 52; Clemens *Sandwich* 53, *Innocents* I 262, *Fairbanks* 160, *Tramp* II 66 that girl turned as white as the snows of Mont Blanc; Saxe *Poems* 213). Apperson 681; Boshears 41: 1022; McAtee 71; NC 478; Taylor *Comparisons* 87–88; Tilley S591; Whiting *Drama* 326:297, *Scots* II 126–127; Marjorie K. Rawlings *The Yearling* (1938) 120.
7. A loaf of cake as white as drifted snow (44 Stephens *High Life* I 165).
8. The village church, as white as the driven snow (33 Hall *Soldier's Bride* 15; Neal *Down-Easters* I 133; Fairfield *Letters* 280 shirts). Apperson 681; Hardie 468:81; Taylor *Comparisons* 88; Tilley S591.
9. Corn, parched till it be whiter than the upland snow (27 Cooper *Prairie* 111).
10. Snow-white (49 Melville *Mardi* I 145, 158, II 373, *Redburn* 294, 294–295, *White Jacket* 107, 430, 454, *Moby-Dick* I 234, 235, 251, 256, 296, 315, II 243, 326, *Pierre* 2, 53, 154, 255, 264, 321, "Paradise" in *Works* XIII 234, "Tartarus" in *Works* XIII 242, *Piazza* 197, *Confidence-Man* 320; Hawthorne *Twice-Told* 237, *Mosses* 539, "Ethan Brand" in *House* 498; Stephens *Homestead* 183; Clemens *Tramp* I 171). NED Snow-white.
11. I melt like snow in a June shower (c60 Paul *Courtship* 31). Valentine Williams and D. R. Sims *Fog*

(Boston 1933) 193 melted like snow in the sun.

Snowball, 1. Fips and levies ain't as plenty as snowballs in this 'ere yearthly spear (37 Neal *Charcoal* 182).

2. Hand, as soft and white as a snowball (44 Stephens *High Life* II 220).

3. It gathered weight and power like a snow-ball (57 Riley *Puddleford* 252). Taylor *Comparisons* 75; Tilley S595.

Snow bank. Cool as a snow bank (69 Alcott *Little Women* 317).

Snow-bird. Jumping about like a mountain snow-bird (59 Taliaferro *Fisher's* 95).

Snowdrop, 1. The youngest was a fair and gentle creature of ten, delicate as a snowdrop (59 Shillaber *Knitting-Work* 230). Cf. NED Snowdrop 1 b.

2. White feet ez snowdrops innercent (68 Lowell *Biglow* 373).

Snow-flake, 1. This fair hand, now white as a snow-flake (54 Shillaber *Mrs. Partington* 244).

2. The umbrella . . . descended gently as a snow-flake (54 Shillaber *Mrs. Partington* 130).

Snow flea. The applicants for his place are as thick as snow fleas (38 Fairfield *Letters* 216). Cf. Taylor *Comparisons* 81 fleas.

Snow storm. She jest sidled up as softly as a snow storm (44 Stephens *High Life* II 61).

Snuff, 1. He's up to snuff (36 Haliburton *Clockmaker* I 224, II 79 ain't up to, III 162 not jist exactly up to, *Attaché* II 53, 144, IV 136, *Sam* II 303; Neal *Charcoal* 123; Saxe *Poems* 37; Barnum *Struggles* 234; Nash *Cen-*

tury 147). Apperson 660; Bartlett 730; Farmer and Henley VI 288; NED Snuff 3 a; *Oxford* 601–602; Stevenson 2152:5; Leighton Barret *Though Young* (1938) 112.

2. The Sandwich Islanders rode down, and were in "high snuff" [i. e., exhilarated, perhaps drunk]. (40 Dana *Two* 148). DA Snuff 2 b (2); NED Snuff 3 c (this passage with the definition "elated").

3. Why nobody cared a pinch of snuff (43 Haliburton *Attaché* IV 246). Cf. NED Snuff [3] 2 b.

4. He oughtn't to mind it a snuff (43 Thompson *Chronicles* 79). Cf. NED Snuff 1 or Snuff 2.

Snug. See Bug (2, 3), Flea (4), Mouse (4), Nest (2), Pea (5).

Soak, 1. In soak [i. e., ready]. 33 DA Soak 1 a.

2. In soak [i. e., in pawn]. 45 DA Soak 1 b.

3. In soak [i. e., in jail]. 69 DA Soak 1 c.

Soap, 1. Lifts up the latch of his door as soft as soap (36 Haliburton *Clockmaker* I 37). Svartengren 266; Mary Mitchell *A Warning to Wantons* (1934) 23.

2. Just like soap. The longer you keep it, the better it grows (45 Judd *Margaret* II 247).

3. Pretty near out of soap [i. e., without money]. (48 Eliason 286). DA Soap 1.

4. Tom Lane's soft-soaping letter (42 Fairfield *Letters* 299; Stephens *High Life* II 99 Give me a warm, honest welcome, but less soft soap; Hammett *Wonderful* 240 Mons. Hypolite Sault-sault, "High Polite Soft-Soap"; Whitcher *Widow* 279; Barnum *Struggles* 211 plenty of "soft soap" . . . I

explained, as best I could, how the literal meaning of the words had come to convey the idea of getting into the good graces of people and pleasing those with whom we are brought in contact). Bartlett 624–625; Farmer and Henley VI 290; NED Soft soap 2; Stevenson 829:5; Louis Pendleton *Down East* (1937) 213.

Soap suds, 1. And down I went, like soap suds into a sink (47 Dorson *Jonathan* 104).

2. See Suds.

Sober. See Clam (7), Clock (5), Damned, Deacon (2), Judge (2), Vicar, Walrus.

Sociable. See Chicken (2), Kitten (9).

Socks. To knock the socks off [i. e., to defeat decisively]. 64 DA Knock 4 b.

Sodder (Sawder, Solder). I came a little of Samuel's soft sodder over the old man (44 Stephens *High Life* I 51, 62, 124; Eliason 296 I . . . can by a little soft sodda get them make the dust fly; Cartwright *Autobiography* 342 and he laid on the soft sodder thick and fast). Bartlett 624; Farmer 503; Farmer and Henley VI 105, 293; Green 317; NED Sawder, Soft Sawder; Schele de Vere 635–636; Stevenson 829:5; Wilson 592.

Sodom, 1. There's Squire Longbow, as desolate as Sodom (57 Riley *Puddleford* 140).

2. It now began to storm like Sodom (52 Dorson *Jonathan* 135).

Soft. See Bear (21), Brook, Butter (2), Cat (23, 32), Dough (2), Dove (5), Feather (2), Heart (1), Milkweed-down, Morning (7), Potato (7), Pullet (1), Putty, Sigh, sb., Silk weed,

Snow (2), Snowball (2), Soap (1), Sponge (1), Spruce, Velvet, Warbling.

Soldier, 1. A hull regiment of chimnies, all a sending out smoke like a company of Florida sogers (44 Stephens *High Life* I 234).

2. The bottle went the rounds of our mess, until it was pronounced a dead soldier (c61 Chamberlain *Confession* 117). Partridge 211. Cf. NED Marine B 4 d.

3. In trying to *come* the old soldier over another man [i. e., deceive, cheat]. (53 Baldwin *Flush* 275). Apperson 466; NED Come 28 c, Soldier 2 b; *Oxford* 473; Stevenson 2158:4.

Sole-leather, 1. The liver got as hard as sole-leather (57 Riley *Puddleford* 164; Harris *Sut* 85 my hole swaller an' paunch am tann'd hard es sole leather).

2. His moral compunctions were as tough as sole-leather (56 Kelly *Humors* 210). Cf. Whitleather.

3. A better citizen . . . never . . . trod sole leather in that State (56 Kelly *Humors* 184). Cf. Shoe leather.

4. See Side (3).

Solemn. See Coffin (1), Death (15), Graveyard (1), Hat cover, Jackass (1), Judge (3), Owl (5), Tombstone (3).

Solid. See Church (3).

Solomon, 1. As wise as Solomon (72 Holmes *Poet* 207). NC 479; Taylor *Comparisons* 89; Tilley S609.

2. A clever feller but no kin to Solomon (49 Eliason 103).

Somber. See Shadow (2).

Something, 1. When people expect to get "something for nothing" they are sure to be cheated (69 Barnum *Strug-*

gles 132). Cf. Stevenson 2161:7; Fletcher Pratt *Double Jeopardy* (1952) 9 You don't get something for nothing.

2. Something is better than nothing—nothing is better than starving (42 Irving *Attorney* 188). Apperson 587; NC 479; *Oxford* 603; Tilley S623; B. A. Botkin, ed. *Folk-Say* I (1930) 130 as everybody knows.

Son, 1. A lying old son of a sea-cook (46 Melville *Typee* 45). Babcock 258; Farmer and Henley VI 296.

2. Seventh son of a seventh son [i. e., one possessing natural medical skill]. (33 Neal *Down-Easters* I 15; Crockett *Life* 16 I was the fifth son. What a pity I hadn't been the seventh! For then I might have been, by *common consent,* called *doctor*).

Song, 1. I got it for half nothin', a mere song (40 Haliburton *Clockmaker* III 167; Melville *Omoo* 176 to be sold for a song, *Redburn* 135, 252 to pawn them for a song, *White Jacket* 224 to be bought up for a song; Hammett *Stray* 283 sold him . . . for a song, *Piney* 281; Smith *'Way* 247 Stone has got tricked out of his farm for a mere song, *My Thirty* 297 to the tune of half of Mexico for a song; Clemens *Letters* I 67, *Sandwich* 39, *Gilded* I 47, II 187; Clift *Bunker* 174 I sold that piece of land for a song). Apperson 587; NED Song 5; Stevenson 2164:11; Tilley S636; Anthony Gilbert, pseud. *The Body on the Beam* (1932) 251 sold for proverbial song.

2. Bime by, . . . ye'll sing another song (65 Sedley *Marian* 276).

3. He may yet be taught to sing a different song (37 Lincoln I 104). Farmer and Henley VI 213; NED Sing 10 a; *Oxford* 592; Stevenson 2163:9; Tilley S637; Whiting *Scots*

II 127; Thorne Smith *The Night Life of the Gods* (1932) 179. Cf. NC 490.

Soon. Better too soon than too late (71 Jones *Batkins* 477).

Sooner. The sooner the better (24 Cooper *Pilot* 86; Fairfield *Letters* p. xxxii; Stowe *Uncle* 389; Durivage *Three* 402 the sooner this fellow's out of the way the better; Jones *Country* 51, 317; Alcott *Little Women* 394; Jones *Batkins* 273). Stevenson 2167: 1; Tilley S641; Whiting *Drama* 364: 859; Oscar Gray *The Bagshot Mystery* (1929) 161; F. P. Keyes *The River Road* (1945) 162 she would marry him after all, and the sooner the better. Cf. Early (2).

Soot. Black like soot (51 Melville *Moby-Dick* I 338). Apperson 51; Boshears 34:361; NC 479; NED Soot 4 b (soot-black); Taylor *Comparisons* 18; Tilley S642; Whiting *Scots* II 127; Eden Phillpotts *The Captain's Curio* (1933) 58.

Sooty. See Nigger (8).

Sore. See Boil.

Sorrow. Holding with Sancho Panza that a fat sorrow is better than a lean (67 Richardson *Beyond* 228). Apperson 205; *Oxford* 193–194; Stevenson 2168:3; Tilley S650.

Soul, 1. A soul above soap and candles (37 Neal *Charcoal* 54). Cf. *Oxford* 606 above buttons; Stevenson 2171:2.

2. For a while I was afraid to say my soul was my own (34 Crockett *Life* 36; Haliburton *Clockmaker* I 237 he's afeerd to call his soul his own, III 70 as if they darsn't call; Stephens *High Life* I 258 without daring to say her soul was her own). NED Soul 4;

Stevenson 2172:6; Tilley S667; Whiting *Scots* II 128; R. M. Baker *Death Stops the Bells* (1938) 118.

Sound. See Baby (3), Curse (1), Musquash, Nut (6), Pitch (5), Roach, Rock (5), Silver (1), Whistle, sb. (4), Woodchuck (3).

Soup, 1. As thin as the homeopathic soup that was made by boiling the shadow of a pigeon that had starved to death (58 Lincoln III 279). Cf. NC 479.

2. You swallowed your soup without singin out scaldins, and you're near about a pint and a half nearer cryin than larfin (36 Haliburton *Clockmaker* I 175).

Sour. See Apple (1), Buttermilk, Greek (1), Vengeance, Vinegar (2).

Sow, 1. Sows over-littered eat their own pigs (45 Judd *Margaret* II 97).

2. You got the wrong sow by the ear this time (40 Haliburton *Clockmaker* III 65, *Letter* 64). Apperson 715; Bartlett 244; Farmer and Henley VI 300–301; Figh PADS XIII (1950) 15; Green 33; NED Sow 3; *Oxford* 607; Stevenson 2175–2176:13; Tilley S685; NQ 3 i 232, 338; A. M. Chase *Murder of a Missing Man* (1934) 126. See Cow (7), Pig (17).

Spade. He called things by their right names; and when he wanted a spade, he did not ask for a hoe (45 Cooper *Chainbearer* 145, *Redskins* p. viii calling a "spade a spade"). Apperson 592; Farmer and Henley VI 301–302; NC 479; NED Spade 2; *Oxford* 75; Stevenson 2194:1; Tilley S699; Whiting *Drama* 364:866, *Scots* II 129; NQ 1 iv 274, 456, 2 ii 26, 120, iii 474, v 246, x 58; 6 ii 310, iii 16, 476, ix 260; 7 i 366, 496; 10 iii 169, 214; Maurice Chideckel *Strictly Private* (1928) 115.

Span. It was span clean this morning! (50 Judd *Richard* 133).

Spaniel. As cow'd as a whipt spaniel (57 Riley *Puddleford* 86).

Spanish. Which means to take a feller up jest by the slack o' 's trowsis An' walk him Spanish clean right out o' all his homes an' houses (48 Lowell *Biglow* 58). Berrey 67:6; DA Walk 2 (5); NED Spanish C; Stevenson 2441:10.

Sparrow-hawk. He went ofen that pallet an' outen that camp jis' like a sparrer-hawk starts tu fly frum the soun ove a shot-gun (67 Harris *Sut* 111).

Spatter. They [old men] used to be thick as spatter when I was a boy (45 Judd *Margaret* II 63). DA Spatter.

Spear, 1. Straight as a spear (25 Neal *Brother J* III 398).

2. See Grass (7).

Speck. Not a speck in a puddle to a Pork-haouse—a Cincinnatty Pork-haouse (56 Kelly *Humors* 357). Cf. DA Pork 2 (11), Speck n.[2]

Speech. The German proverb, that "speech is silver, while silence is golden" (65 Richardson *Secret* 34). Apperson 594; Bradley 92; NC 480; *Oxford* 612; Stevenson 2113:14; NQ 3 i 452; 7 i 75; Stoett 2141; Brian Flynn *The Ladder of Death* (Philadelphia 1935) 214. See Richard Jente "German Proverbs from the Orient" PMLA XLVIII (1933) 33–37.

Spermaceti. Transparent as sparmacity (43 Robb *Squatter* 157).

Sphinx. As silent as a sphinx (69 Alcott *Little Women* 317). Gertrude Beasley *My First Thirty Years* (Paris 1925) the Sphinx. Cf. Svartengren 177 dumb.

Spick. Spic-and-span new temple (54 Melville "Two Temples" in *Works* XIII 174; Bowman *Bear-Hunters* 448 [his] fancy to keep all spick and spander for his wife). Apperson 595; Faden 267; Farmer and Henley VI 309; Green 353; NED Span-new, Spick and span new; *Oxford* 613; Tilley S748; NQ 1 iii 330, 480, v 521–522; 4 iv 512; 9 vi 307; 10 v 160; R. S. Surtees *Plain or Ringlets?* (London [1860]) 151 a spic and span new scarlet coat. See Span.

Spider. He sucks em all out es dry es a spider dus a hoss-fly (67 Harris *Sut* 174).

Spigot. While we are saving and scrimping at the spigot, the government is drawing off at the bung (48 Lowell *Biglow* 131; Barnum *Struggles* 459 This is an illustration of Dr. Franklin's "saving at the spigot and wasting at the bung-hole"). Apperson 550; Bradley 96; Hardie 464:125; NED Spigot 3 a; *Oxford* 609; Stevenson 2182:1; Tilley S750; Woodard PADS VI (1946) 42. See Bung.

Spikes. He . . . swore he'd be thar, ef hit rain'd red hot railroad spikes an' bilin' tar (67 Harris *Sut* 261).

Spin. See Top 2 (3).

Spinning wheel. As black as an Irish spinning wheel. 37 DA Irish 2 b.

Spirit-rapper. He was as crazy as a spirit-rapper, all the rest of the day (59 Shillaber *Knitting-Work* 211).

Spirits (1). I sing to keep up my spirits (51 Melville *Moby-Dick* II 277).

Spirits (2). Up again they hopped, light as spirits and twice as natural (43 Robb *Squatter* 90).

Spit and image. See Image (3).

Spiteful. See Hen (8).

Split. Driving like split down that street (33 Smith *Downing* 95; Stephens *High Life* I 200 off we driv full split up town, II 161, *Mary Derwent* 336 a-riding like split). Bartlett 638; Farmer and Henley VI 317; NED Split 4 a.

Splurge. She tries to cut a spludge and made folks think she's a lady (56 Whitcher *Widow* 89, 206; Thomson *Elephant Club* 310 Cut as big a splurge in your borrowed clothes as possible). Bartlett 165, 638–639; DA Splurge 1 b; Farmer 508; Farmer and Henley VI 317; NED Splurge 1; Schele de Vere 550. Cf. Thornton II 837.

Spoke. To put a spoke in the wheel for our folks [i. e., give assistance]. (38 Haliburton *Clockmaker* II 220; Thompson *Major* 67 Won't you be a spoke in my wheel?). Apperson 597; Farmer and Henley VI 318, VII 326; Green 33; McAtee *Grant County* 8; NED Spoke 3, 4 a; *Oxford* 615; Stevenson 2200:10; Tilley S769. [Many of the examples mean to hinder rather than to aid].

Sponge, 1. As soft as sponge (c60 Paul *Courtship* 33). Svartengren 64.

2. I . . . threw down the sponge, surrendered at discretion (c61 Chamberlain *Confession* 241; Clemens *Enterprise* 187 Ruel threw up the sponge, *Sketches* 19, *Roughing* II 47 throwed up the sponge [i. e., died]; Browne *Artemus* 117 Other primy donnys may as well throw up the sponge first as last). Bartlett 797; Farmer and Henley VI 319–320; NED Sponge 1 c; *Oxford* 656; Stevenson 2201:6; George Goodchild *The Monster of Grammont* (1930) 223.

Spoon, 1. Born with silver spoons in their mouths (36 Haliburton *Clockmaker* I 203, *Attaché* II 110 with the eend of the silver spoon he was born with, a peepin' out o' the corner of his mouth, *Sam* I 64 you was born with a silver spoon in one hand, and a silver fork in the other; Robb *Squatter* 176; Lowell *Biglow* 81 Fer the silver spoon born in Dermoc'acy's mouth; Melville *White Jacket* 41 *Mad Jack* must have entered the world . . . not with a silver spoon, but with a speaking trumpet in his mouth; Barnum *Struggles* 483 You were born with a golden spoon in your mouth; Jones *Batkins* 11 I was not born . . . "with a silver spoon in my mouth," 280 somebody being "born with a silver spoon," according to the old saying). Apperson 572; Babcock 263; Farmer and Henley VI 210; NC 475; NED Spoon 3 c; *Oxford* 57; Stevenson 187:1; Tilley S772; NQ CLXVII (1934) 371, 412; Christopher Reeve *The Ginger Cat* (1929) 183.

2. Wat Adair is a fool . . . who is never content but when he has other people thrusting their spoons into his mess (35 Kennedy *Horse-Shoe* 143). Stevenson 2201:10 broth.

Spoony. See Girl (2).

Sportive. See Lamb (12).

Spot, 1. Feelin all over in spots about goin off so [i. e., embarrassed]. (44 Stephens *High Life* II 10). Farmer 509.

2. In spots [i. e., at intervals]. 52 DA Spot 4 b (1).

3. He'd make more [dimes] than thar wer spots ontu forty fawns in July (67 Harris *Sut* 62).

4. To go to the spot [i. e., to satisfy]. 68 DA Spot 4 b (3).

5. To knock the spots off. 56 DA Spot 4 b (2).

6. It was touching the young man upon a sore spot (54 Shillaber *Mrs. Partington* 141). Cf. *Oxford* 666.

7. This last divilment touched him in a soft spot [i. e., vexed him greatly]. (58 Hammett *Piney* 284).

Spotless. See Snow (5).

Spout. She had even taken the shoes off my feet, and shoved them up the spout along with my new hat (39 Briggs *Harry* II 76; Thomson *Plu-ri-bus-tah* p. xx This is how this naughty poem Once was 'up a spout' in Broome Street; Wiley *Johnny* 131 we are done gon up the Spout the Confederacy is done whiped; Smith *Arp* 23 Where is Fremont? I hear he has gone up a spout, 108 It went up a spout). Bartlett 258; Farmer and Henley VI 323; McAtee 30; NED Spout 4 b; Schele de Vere 201, 309; Stevenson 966:10; Vernon Loder *Death of an Editor* (1931) 21.

Sprat. If they throw a sprat it's to catch a mackerel (38 Haliburton *Clockmaker* II 287). Apperson 597–598; NED Sprat 2 c; *Oxford* 616; Stevenson 818:10; D. V. Duff *The Horned Crescent* (London 1936) 107 the old proverb about a sprat to catch a mackerel.

Spread. See Measles, Wildfire.

Spring. A locket that you can see your face in, as clear as in a spring of water (55 Irving *Wolfert* 272).

Spring water. Everything on the [vegetable] stand fresh as spring water (54 Stephens *Fashion* 299).

Springy. See Steel trap (6).

Sprouts. He . . . told the rest to put me through the sprouts (55 Thomson *Doesticks* 244; Kelly *Humors* 252 threatened "the Western member" with a course of legal sprouts; Barnum *Struggles* 409 putting Barnum through a course of sprouts). Bartlett 643; DA Course, Sprout 2; NED Sprout 4.

Spruce, sb. Ez soft ez spruce (67 Lowell *Biglow* 280).

Spruce, adj. See Bluejay, Fiddle (2).

Sprung. He's the broth of a boy . . . when he's a leetle sprung [i. e., tipsy]. (55 Anon. *New Hope* 180). Partridge 817.

Spry. See Bird (5), Cat (24), Catamount (3), Cricket (7), Fox (8), Kitten (10), Lightning (5), Weasel (7), Wildcat (3).

Spunk. To get one's spunk up. 34 DA Spunk 1.

Spunky. See Bull-dog (2), Rooster (4), Thunder (11).

Spur, 1. So let us pad our saddles according to the old recipe, "A spur in the head is worth two on the heel" (32 Kennedy *Swallow* 294). Apperson 598; *Oxford* 616; Stevenson 2203:11; Tilley S791. Cf. NED Spur 3 b.
2. The spur won't hurt where the hide is thick (53 Haliburton *Sam* I 243). Stevenson 2203:9.
3. He won his spurs (71 Jones *Batkins* 190, 259 I had no spurs to win, 298, 344, 347). Apperson 688; NED Spur 3; *Oxford* 711; Stevenson 2203: 7; Tilley S792; Whiting *Drama* 370: 950.
4. I invariably regret the things I do on the spur of the moment (71 Clemens *Letters* I 182). NED Spur

sb.[1] 2 d; *Oxford* 616; Anthony Berkeley, pseud. *The Second Shot* (1930) 265.

Square, adj., adv., 1. There's fifty dollars, you and I are square (56 Kelly *Humors* 89).
2. If you're a mind we'll call the matter square (56 Kelly *Humors* 419; Clemens *Enterprise* 169; Lowell *Biglow* 238 we'll up an' call it square).
3. I'll be out bright and early to make all square (56 Kelly *Humors* 82, 119 that made us about square; Conant *Earnest Man* 169 we settle up our secular accounts, and make all square with the world). NED Square 10 e.
4. Suppose we sell off all the horses, and sell one of your farms, and pay up square (51 Stowe *Uncle* 282; Lowell *Biglow* 279 Ther' warn't nut one on them thet come jes' square with my idees). Cf. Tilley S796; Whiting *Drama* 365:870.

Squash. I blushed as blue as a Ginny squash (44 Thompson *Major* 14).

Squeal. See Pig (21).

Squirm. See Bobworm, Eel (12).

Squirrel, 1. As chipper as a squirrel in the fall time (44 Stephens *High Life* II 161). Cf. Svartengren 159; Tilley S797.
2. As roguish as a chip squirrel (44 Stephens *High Life* II 233).
3. You can't find a striped squirrel in every hollow fence pole, but that's the place to look for them (76 Nash *Century* 18).
4. He clumb, like a squirl (25 Neal *Brother J* II 7). NC 480.
5. Makin a nise like squirrils a-climbin a shell-bark hickory (67 Harris *Sut* 53).

6. Squirrel's jump [i. e., a short distance]. 38 DA Squirrel 3 b.

Stack. I hath theen many outrages, but thith Famus business caps the stack and saves the grain (59 Taliaferro *Fisher's* 23, *Carolina Humor* 77). Apperson 81.

Staddle. Lonesome ez steddles on a mash without no hayricks on (48 Lowell *Biglow* 141). Schele de Vere 552.

Staff. As straight as a staff (57 Riley *Puddleford* 225).

Stake, 1. As stiff as a stake (54 Smith *'Way* 58). Apperson 602; Stevenson 2115:4; Tilley S809; Whiting *Drama* 327:307, PADS XI (1954) 28 n. 5.
2. To make a stake. 73 DA Stake 4 e.
3. He "pulled up stakes," and proceeded farther west (23 Cooper *Pioneers* 467; Stephens *High Life* II 40 I can up stakes, and go hum agin, 256 it's time for us to haul up stakes and go hum; Burke *Polly* 176; Judd *Margaret* II 161 When our Jessie died we thought we should have to pull up stakes; Smith *'Way* 367, *My Thirty* 440 So we up stakes and sot sail agin; Kelly *Humors* 265 and so he up stakes and made a fresh *dive*, Taliaferro *Fisher's* 134; Sedley *Marian* 13, 129). Bartlett 503; DA Stake 4 a; NED Stake¹ 1 e; Schele de Vere 184–185; Thornton II 708, 850, III 307.

Stalactite. A man . . . calm and unmovable as a stalactite (53 Willis *Fun* 290.

Stale. See Ale.

Stand, 1. As sure as I stand here (43 Thompson *Chronicles* 159). Svartengren 358. Cf. Randolph and Wilson 180.

2. As true as I stand here (42 Irving *Attorney* 150). Tilley S818.
3. I want a husband (as they say when they advertise for a doctor's horse) "warranted to stand without hitching" (57 Willis *Paul* 361).

Standing. People may get tireder by standing still than by going on (35 Kennedy *Horse-Shoe* 521).

Star, 1. As bright as the stars (44 Stephens *High Life* I 102, 181 eyes, as bright as the brightest star in the gill-dipper). Boshears 35:377; NC 480; NED Star 1 b; Svartengren 227; Taylor *Comparisons* 21; Whiting *Scots* II 131.
2. Faster nur a shootin' star (59 Taliaferro *Fisher's* 64).
3. The mare made her appearance, looking . . . fine as a star (58 Porter *Major* 117).
4. Jest as true's de stairs is a shinin' up in de sky dis yer minute (54 Langdon *Ida* 121; Cooke *Foresters* 130 False! she's as true as the stars!).
5. Thanking his stars that nobody "seen him do it" (56 Kelly *Humors* 281; Stephens *Mary Derwent* 221 she hasn't the power, thank my stars). NED Star 3 b.
6. Such are born under a lucky star (69 Alcott *Little Women* 281).
7. And makes your eyes twinkle like stars in a frosty night (55 Haliburton *Nature* I 135). Boshears 34:298; Halpert 185; Whiting *Chaucer* 174. Cf. NC 480; Whiting *Scots* II 131.
8. When the stars fall agin maybe the women will be harmonized [i. e., never]. (66 Smith *Arp* 141).

Starch, 1. So there they sot, still as starch (58 Porter *Major* 194).
2. Even Mr. Bargin seemed to have the starch taken out of him (39 Briggs

Harry II 184; Burke *Polly* 148; Locke [Nasby] *Struggles* 314 the starch wuz out uv him, and he wuz worsted; Eggleston *School-Master* 41). DA Take 2 b (3); Farmer 515; Farmer and Henley VI 350.

Stare, 1. It tante them that stare the most, that sees the best always (36 Haliburton *Clockmaker* I 87, *Sam* I 41). Bartlett 801.
2. See Calf (7, 8), Owl (10), Pig (22).

Start, 1. A good start wins the race (55 Haliburton *Nature* I 338). Stevenson 2209:2 timely start.
2. An airly start makes easy stages (36 Haliburton *Clockmaker* I 100). Cf. Stevenson 1930:7.
3. Nearly made a false start (50 Boker *World* 39). Stevenson 2209:2.

Statue, 1. Cool, calm as a statue (45 Mayo *Kaloolah* 363; Clemens *Gilded* II 260 Laura calm and firm as a statue).
2. They stood as motionless as so many statues (20–22 Irving *Bracebridge* 421; Hall *Soldier's Bride* 35 Militia, standing motionless as statues; Hammett *Stray* 174 statue). Cf. NC 481; Svartengren 383; Holmes *Autocrat* 100 motionless as the arm of a terra-cotta caryatid.
3. The judge . . . pale and still as a statue of marble (54 Stephens *Fashion* 403; Cary *Married* 414 pale and cold).
4. Then he would stand up in the darkness quiet as a statue (54 Stephens *Fashion* 75).
5. The paddler is as still as a statue (60 Whitehead *Wild Sports* 354). NC 481; Svartengren 382.
6. Sat like a statue (57 Riley *Pud-*

dleford 192; Barnum *Struggles* 97). Cf. Boshears 33:277.
7. Slept like a statue (63 Clemens *Enterprise* 74).
8. Stood like a statue (56 Cooke *Foresters* 54).

Steadfast. See Rock (6).

Steady. See Bishop (3), Death (16), Horse (10), Judge (4), Pump bolt.

Steam, 1. Breath as warm and sweet as the steam from an apple-sarse cag when the sarse is sot off to cool (44 Stephens *High Life* II 248).
2. But I'd got the steam up [i. e., was excited]. (44 Stephens *High Life* II 68). NED Get 72 g, Steam 7 q.
3. Wise has been letting off the steam again (35 Fairfield *Letters* 38; Stephens *High Life* I 253, II 94 like a junk bottle of cider letting off steam; Whitcher *Widow* 258 he was ripe for fun, and determined to let off the steam some way or other; Holmes *Professor* 221 A'n't it fun to hear him blow off steam?). Leslie Ford, pseud. *The Simple Way of Poison* (1937) 197 "It would seem to be letting off a bit of old steam." Old steam is the idiom, I believe. Cf. NED Steam 7 d (blow off).

Steamboat captain. Cussin' wus nor a steamboat cap'n (51 Burke *Polly* 51). See Piper (3).

Steam boiler. The mother-in-law is a queer invention, as full of flaws and dangers as a second-hand steam boiler (70 Daly *Man* 47).

Steam-engine. He goes ahead so much like a steam-engine (39 Smith *Letters* 49; Hammett *Stray* 270 we went through the woods like, *Piney* 173 I treated to segars, and we was a puffin' away like steam-ingins; Riley *Puddle-*

ford 86 It'll run rite off like; Paul *Courtship* 90 snores like). NC 481; NED Steam-engine (c).

Steel, 1. It was a clear steel-blue day (51 Melville *Moby-Dick* II 326; Cary *Clovernook* 35 The steel-blue swallows). NED Steel 15; Vincent Starrett *The Blue Door* (1930) 298.

2. Brave as steel (56 Durivage *Three* 64, 252). Svartengren 113.

3. A hard stone, polished and bright as steel (66 Bowman *Bear-Hunters* 131).

4. Hair, steel-gray (49 Melville *Mardi* II 248). NED Steel 15; C. J. Dutton *Poison Unknown* (1932) 130.

5. I tell you that old man is honest, honest as steel (54 Stephens *Fashion* 308).

6. My wife is . . . sharp as steel (c58 Stephens *Mary Derwent* 215).

7. He's true as ter steel (23 Cooper *Pioneers* 457, *Satanstoe* 43 as true as steel; Irving *Attorney* 30; Haliburton *Old Judge* II 277; Stowe *Uncle* 259 trusty and true as steel; Holmes *Professor* 71; Durivage *Three* 17 true as the steel of his Toledo blade; Jones *Country* 29, 211, 213, 215; Anon. *New Hope* 84 old Ruler [a dog] is true as steel; Lincoln II 475; Browne *Artemus* 60). Apperson 647; NC 481; NED Steel 2 b; *Oxford* 672; Stevenson 2380:5; Svartengren 10–11; Tilley S840; Whiting *Drama* 327:309, PADS XI (1949) 28 n. 5, *Scots* II 131; Anthony Pryde, pseud. *The Secret Room* (1929) 179.

Steel trap, 1. Quick as a steel trap for a trade (33 Smith *Downing* 46). Svartengren 375.

2. He look't savidge es a sot steel trap, baited with asnick (67 Harris *Sut* 69).

3. A fellow . . . as sharp as a steel trap (36 Crockett *Exploits* 20; Sedley *Marian* 168 That air Pangburn . . . is sharper'n a steel trap, he is).

4. She pressed me so close, and then sprang up as short as a steel-trap (55 Haliburton *Sam* II 272).

5. As smart as a steel-trap [i. e., active and healthy]. (33 Smith *Downing* 224, *Letters* 93, 'Way 271; Stephens *High Life* I 223, *Homestead* 273; Nash *Century* 236). DA Smart (b); Hardie 467:22; Svartengren 375; Taylor *Comparisons* 74; Thornton II 817; Woodard PADS VI (1946) 42; A. M. Chase *Twenty Minutes to Kill* (1936) 104.

6. Here I am down tu York agin, as large as life and as springy as a steel trap (44 Stephens *High Life* II 12).

7. He sprung like a steel-trap (33 Smith *Downing* 197).

Steelyards. Ye've got to set . . . as stiff as stillyards, or the picter'll be spiled (56 Whitcher *Widow* 214–215).

Steeple. The odds 'twixt her an' us is plain 's a steeple (67 Lowell *Biglow* 259).

Steer, 1. I . . . am as limber and frisky as a two-year old steer (62 Browne *Artemus* 139).

2. They pulled agin each uther like ontu two wile steers in a yaller-jackids nes' (67 Harris *Sut* 268).

Stem, 1. They were moored, stem and stern, in a grog-shop (40 Dana *Two* 294, 453).

2. Not but wut *I* hate Slavery . . . , stem to starn (48 Lowell *Biglow* 144). NED Stem 2 b; Stevenson 154:5.

Step, 1. The old saying, There is only a step between me and death (69 Barnum *Struggles* 328). NED Step 7 b.

2. There is but a slight step from the privateersman to the pirate (23–24 Irving *Tales* 383).

3. Napoleon has said, there is but a step between the sublime and the ridiculous (33 Hall *Soldier's Bride* 102, *Wilderness* 57 proving that men and brutes are separated by a step as brief as that which divides the sublime from the ridiculous). Stevenson 1987:9; NQ 1 v 100–101, 187; 2 iv 86; 3 vii 280, 366, xii 379, 491; 5 iii 406.

Stepped. I ruther guess I stepped high [i. e., was elated]. (44 Stephens *High Life* I 29).

Stern. See Marble (4).

Steven. To exchange . . . money . . . "even steven" (66 Smith *Arp* 64). DA Even 2; Thornton I 293; Ray Bradbury *The October Country* (1955) 72 It's a fifty-fifty fight. Even-Stephen; C. C. Munz *Land without Moses* (1938) 203 But hit would be even Stephen.

Stew. A thousand petty disquietudes of civilized life, that once kept you . . . in—"a stew" (43 Hall *Purchase* I 99; Jones *Winkles* 135 She's in a mighty stew about it). Farmer and Henley VI 360; NED Stew 6; Stevenson 69:7.

Stick, sb., 1. Baker's bread dry as a stick (56 Whitcher *Widow* 337). NC 481; Svartengren 300; Taylor *Comparisons* 36.

2. More spots . . . than you could . . . shake a stick at between now an' everlastin' (33 Neal *Down-Easters* I 18, 135 made more poetry 'an you could shake a stick at; Smith *Downing* 51 more carrots and potatoes than you can throw a stick at, 203 more fine pictures than you could shake a stick

at in a week, 'Way 286, *My Thirty* 337; Hall *Purchase* I 85–86 more of her subjects than we could shake a stick at; Eliason 103; Stowe *Uncle* 196 laziness . . . ruins more souls than you can shake a stick at; Whitehead *Wild Sports* 113). Bartlett 574–575; Boshears 31:111; DA Stick 4 b; McAtee *Additional* 12; NC 481; Schele de Vere 631; Stevenson 2213:12; Thornton II 779, III 345; R. P. Tristram Coffin *Lost Paradise* (1934) 148.

3. There was nothing to treat a friend to that was worth shaking a stick at (35 Crockett *Account* 87; Shillaber *Ike* 33 No one to him can shake a stick). Cf. DA Stick 4 c.

4. And off to Rhode Island, and marries her quick stick (60 Haliburton *Season-Ticket* 222, 223 he scrabbles out quick stick). Farmer and Henley VI 363–364 quick sticks.

5. I did not want to be tarred with the same stick (35 Crockett *Account* 86; Haliburton *Clockmaker* I 255, II 143, *Attaché* III 288, *Old Judge* II 147, *Sam* II 166). Hardie 471:186; NED Tar (c); *Oxford* 644; Morrison Dupree *A Tap on the Shoulder* (1929) 166.

6. And he ought to have beat me like breaking sticks [i. e., readily]. (58 Porter *Major* 50).

7. He cut . . . stick [i. e., departed]. (36 Haliburton *Clockmaker* I 63 his stick, II 140, 151, *Attaché* I 270, II 196, 263, IV 70, *Sam* II 92, *Season-Ticket* 292; Neal *Charcoal* 190 Marry or cut stick; Stephens *High Life* I 140, 209, II 215, 241; Stowe *Uncle* 48; Hammett *Wonderful* 40 When the Colonel's ready money began—in Job's vernacular—to cut stick, *Piney* 55; Thomson *Elephant Club* 170; Jones *Wild* 156, 199; Shillaber *Knitting-Work* 308; Clemens *Sketches* 362 cut

your stick—vamose the ranch). Bartlett 166; Farmer and Henley VI 363; NED Cut 43; Partridge 829; Randolph and Wilson 238; Stevenson 2214:2; NQ 2 viii 413, 478, ix 53, 207; 3 xi 397, xii 137; 5 i 386, 493; 9 ii 326, 414, iii 272, 434; 10 viii 348, ix 132; J. J. Connington, pseud. *Tragedy at Ravensthorpe* (1928) 98 cut my stick to the door.

8. I have an idea that gall will either die a sour old maid, or have to take a crooked stick for a husband at last (53 Haliburton *Sam* II 134, *Season-Ticket* 327 I always told you you carried too stiff an upper lip, and that you would have to take a crooked stick at last). Farmer 517; Green 32; NED Stick 12; Schele de Vere, 212; Stevenson 453:11; Caroline Gordon *The Garden of Adonis* (1937) 92 you are the kind'll go through the woods and pick up a crooked stick, 93–94. Cf. Woodard PADS VI (1946) 7.

Stick, vb., 1. But we are in, and stick or go through, must be the word (60 Lincoln IV 55).

2. See Bark 1 (2, 4), Bee (12), Bloodhound, Bur (3), Candle (5), Death (25), Dog (55), Fun (3), Lamprey-eel, Leech (3), Shadow (4), Sin (13), Tick (2), Wax (6).

Stick-in-the-mud. Old stick-in-the-mud is made a magistrate (49 Haliburton *Old Judge* II 263, *Sam* I 289). Bartlett 662; Bradley PADS XIV (1950) 64; Farmer and Henley VI 364; Green 363; NED Stick-in-the-mud; Stevenson 2213:14; Woodard PADS VI (1946) 22; Bruce Graeme, pseud. *The Imperfect Crime* (Philadelphia 1933) 54.

Stiff. See Board (1), Bristle, Bull beef, Crowbar (2), Fire stick, Flag-

staff (1), Grenadier (1), Iron (3), Leg (4), Maggot (1), Mount Washington, Pike, sb. (1), Pikestaff (2), Pillar (1), Poker (1), Post (2), Ramrod (1), Saint, Stake (1), Steelyards, Tent-pole, Wedge (3), Zero.

Still. See Cat (25), Death (17), Grave (9), Graveyard (2), Kitten (11), Marble (6, 7), Midnight (3), Moonlight (3), Mouse (5), Owl (6), Post (3), Salamander, Starch (1), Statue (3, 5), Stock (1), Stone (11), Stump (2), Turtle (5).

Stitch. A stitch in time saves nine (25 Neal *Brother J* II 220; Haliburton *Clockmaker* II 220; Melville *Mardi* I 53 [chapter heading]). Apperson 603; NC 481; NED Stitch 5; *Oxford* 622; Vincent McHugh *Caleb Catlum's America* (1936) 76.

Stiver, 1. There wasn't nobody left that I cared a stiver for (54 Smith *'Way* 171). Farmer and Henley VI 370; Green 365; NED Stiver 2.

2. The country wont be worth a stiver (33 Smith *Downing* 168). Farmer and Henley VI 370.

Stock, 1. Our hero stood stock still (25 Neal *Brother J* II 161, 308; Kennedy *Swallow* 230; Melville *Omoo* 71, *Redburn* 77, "Poor Man's Pudding" in *Works* XIII 197, *Israel* 100, 104, "Apple-Tree Table" in *Works* XIII 326). Green 365; NED Stock still; Ethel Loban *The Calloused Eye* (1931) 218.

2. He did not take quite so much stock in Dr. Small as his wife did (71 Eggleston *School-Master* 200). Bartlett 663; DA Stock 5 c.

3. Ve have been taking stock of the place (66 Boucicault *Flying Scud* 164). Farmer and Henley VI 371.

4. It will sartinly be the making of the Slick family, stock, lock, and bar-

rcl (43 Haliburton *Attaché* IV 58–59, *Nature* I 197, II 340). NED Lock 5, Stock 28 b; *Oxford* 622, Stevenson 1446:9. Cf. Lock; Shot (8); Farmer and Henley VI 371 stock and block; NED Stock 1 c (stock and block).

5. Sell you out, stock and fluke (35 Crockett *Account* 89; Durivage *Three* 176 I have been ruined, stock and fluke). Bartlett 663; Farmer and Henley VI 371.

Stocking, 1. She will stretch the stockin' a little [i. e., exaggerate]. (39 Smith *Letters* 44). See Blanket (3), Gallows (2).

2. See Shoe (7).

Stomach, 1. Enough to turn the stomach of a horse (25 Neal *Brother J* II 299; Stephens *High Life* I 3 It was enough to turn one's stomach to look at the spit box). NED Turn 12, 12 b.

2. His stomach begins to turn agin the chickens (44 Stephens *High Life* I 216).

3. Some how er nuther it don't set well on thar stomachs to see the Jack take the ace (58 Hammett *Piney* 83). Cf. Stevenson 2218:3.

4. Don't his vittles set well on his stummick? (62 Browne *Artemus* 163). Cf. Tilley S874.

5. "Unless your stomach be strong do not eat cockroaches." Disregarding this wise African proverb I tried a morsel of the fiery dish (67 Richardson *Beyond* 248).

Stone, 1. In literature, as in trade, the old proverb holds good, "a rolling stone gathers no moss" (23–24 Irving *Tales* 150; Emerson *Works* I 33, *Letters* II 26 But let me hope that my rotations are ended & that now I shall sit still & gather moss; Haliburton *Letter* 114 They say; Derby *Squibob*

110; Sedley *Marian* 112 is just the one which *does* gather moss in gold countries). Apperson 537; NC 481; NED Moss 3 b, Rolling stone 1; *Oxford* 547; Stevenson 2218–2219:6; Tilley S885; Whiting *Drama* 145; Yamamoto *Dickens* 326–327; NQ 4 i 396; 6 xi 246, 418–419; Robert Carson *The Revels Are Ended* (1936) 208.

2. Stone blind (35 Crockett *Account* 83; Longstreet *Georgia* 28; Melville *Mardi* II 8, *Redburn* 243–244; Stowe *Uncle* 73; Alcott *Little Women* 510; Clemens *Gilded* I 281). NED Stone-blind; Svartengren 173; Whiting *Drama* 327:313; Oliver Martyn *The Man They Couldn't Hang* (1933) 56. Cf. Lowell *Biglow* 79 folks's stone-blindness.

3. Cold . . . as a stone (45 Mayo *Kaloolah* 305; Whitcher *Widow* 229 ther is times when I feel as cold as a stun; Cary *Married* 57 anything [food] will be as cold as a stone). Apperson 106; McAtee 19; NC 481; Svartengren 314; Tilley S876; Phoebe Hunt, pseud. *Murder at Scandal House* (1933) 134.

4. Stun cold (44 Stephens *High Life* II 111, *Mary Derwent* 294, 300). Green 366; NED Stone 19; Stevenson 377–378:11; Taylor *Comparisons* 28; Whiting *Drama* 327:313; J. M. Walsh *The Company of Shadows* (1931) 162.

5. Dead as a stone (45 Mayo *Kaloolah* 305). Green 366; NC 482; NED Stone 3 c; Taylor *Comparisons* 33; Whiting *Chaucer* 174, *Drama* 327: 313, *Scots* II 132; *Catalogue of Political and Personal Satires . . . 1820–1827* (London 1952) X 485 No. 14798.

6. Stone dead (25 Neal *Brother J* II 207; Irving *Attorney* 363; Hall *Purchase* I 197; Judd *Margaret* II 52; Hawthorne *Twice-Told* 253, *House*

310; Anon. *New Hope* 112, 292; Kelly *Humors* 94, 149, 175 Jake Hinkle was . . . stone dead—*pegged out!;* Harris *Uncle Remus* 145). Green 366; NC 482; NED Stone 19; Schele de Vere 554; Taylor *Comparisons* 33; Whiting *Drama* 327:313; Alice Campbell *Keep Away from Water!* (1935) 141. Cf. Tilley S898.

7. Jo stood dumb as a stone (68 Alcott *Little Women* 85). Svartengren 178. Cf. Whiting *Drama* 328:313 See thou bee a stone . . . I ment thou shouldest nothing saye; Dorothy Ogburn *Death on the Mountain* (Boston 1931) 199 mum.

8. Yes; in the midst of it all she stood . . . firm as stone (c58 Stephens *Mary Derwent* 222). Job 41:24; Svartengren 261; Mary Plum *The Killing of Judge MacFarlane* (1930) 200.

9. Ralph's countenance was . . . hard as stone (71 Eggleston *School-Master* 144, 150). Apperson 284; NC 482; Taylor *Comparisons* 46 rock; Svartengren 260–261; Tilley S878; Whiting *Drama* 327:313. Cf. NED Stone 19 stone-hard.

10. But Pete was as immovable and unconscious of the lash as would have been a stone (56 Jones *Wild* 11).

11. He sat as still as a stone (76 Clemens *Tom* 121). Apperson 602; Stevenson 2215; Taylor *Comparisons* 78; Tilley S879; Whiting *Drama* 328, *Scots* II 133; Lee Thayer, pseud. *The Glass Knife* (1932) 137.

12. Ther' 's times when I'm unsoshle ez a stone (67 Lowell *Biglow* 334).

13. They was charmin enuff to make a man throw stuns at his grandmother, if they axed him to (62 Browne *Artemus* 17). See Quaker (2).

14. I don't want to leave any stone unturned (33 Smith *Downing* 234; Riley *Puddleford* 39). Apperson 358; Farmer and Henley VI 375; NC 482; NED Stone 16 c; *Oxford* 359; Stevenson 2219:1; Tilley S890; Agatha Christie *Man in the Brown Suit* (1924) 218.

15. An unfortunate wretch, whose day of birth must surely have been marked with a black stone (53 Hammett *Stray* 251).

16. [If the ladies left quickly], it would be a white stone . . . in the fortunes of the beau! (56 Kelly *Humors* 283 [he was hiding in great discomfort]; Melville *Confidence-Man* 188 A day in my boyhood is marked with a white stone). Apperson 681; *Oxford* 408; Stevenson 2218:5; Tilley S891.

Stone fence. She was as ugly as a stone fence (34 Crockett *Life* 57). Cf. Boshears 37:668, 40:992; Taylor *Comparisons* 84.

Stool. The unphilosophic attempt to sit upon two stools (37 Neal *Charcoal* 83; Haliburton *Clockmaker* III 67 Whap you come to the ground, like a feller atween two stools). Apperson 656; Farmer and Henley VI 377; Green 32; NED Stool 3 a; *Oxford* 43; Stevenson 2221:4; Tilley S900; NQ 2 xi 27; 4 v 13, x 181; Jack Lindsay *1649* (London 1938) 386 a man must beware the proverb of falling between two stools.

Story (1). And a feeling purty considerably rily in the upper story (44 Stephens *High Life* I 123, 175 You must be soft in the upper story; Lowell *Biglow* 350). Farmer and Henley VII 262–263; NED Story 1 c; Stoett 337.

Story (2), 1. A good story is never spiled in the tellin', except by a crittur that don't know how to tell it (43 Haliburton *Attaché* IV 91). Apperson 618 Tale (1); *Oxford* 643; Stevenson 2272:5.

2. But after a spell, the minister gits to be an old story (56 Whitcher *Widow* 246).

3. Well, to make a long story short (56 Whitcher *Widow* 328). Stevenson 2223:4.

Stout. See Samson (2).

Straight. See Arrow (2), Bean-pole, Bee line (1), Bird (13), Board (1), Bootjack (6), Broomstick (1), Bulrush, Candle (1), Cannon ball, Chalk-line (1), Crow (4), Die, sb. (1), Drill-sergeant (1), Fish-hook (2), Flagstaff (2), Gun (1), Gun-barrel, Hair (2), Line (1), Loon (6, 7), Pikestaff (3), Pin (5), Pine (1), Poker (2), Poplar tree, Ram's horn (2), Ramrod (2), Rifle, Rifleball (2), Rifle-barrel, Ruler, Shingle (2), Spear (1), Staff, String (2), Sunday, Tent-pole, Topmast (2), Way (3).

Straightforward. See Line (2).

Stranger, 1. To fight the stranger [i. e., to drink deep and often]. c45 DA Fight 3 (2).

2. Soon after our arrival I was introduced with marked ceremony to the "stranger" [i.e., given a drink]. (51 Burke *Polly* 131). Cf. DA Stranger (2).

Stratagem. All stratagems fair in war, you know (53 Cary *Clovernook* 2d Series 271).

Straw, 1. They don't care a straw how the world jogs (38 Haliburton *Clockmaker* II 212, *Season-Ticket* 341; Irving *Attorney* 204; Thompson *Major* 132 three straws; Cooper *Satanstoe*

246, *Redskins* 318, 463; Whitcher *Widow* 260; Clemens *Enterprise* 128, *Sandwich* 84, *Tramp* I 277). Apperson 458; Farmer and Henley VII 7; NED Straw 7; *Oxford* 78; Stevenson 2225:7; Tilley S917; Whiting *Drama* 365:876, *Scots* II 134.

2. I'll never give up—no—not so much as a straw, to nobody (25 Neal *Brother J* I 201). Whiting *Drama* 365:876.

3. And, as I don't value office a straw (65 Sedley *Marian* 321).

4. No harpooner is worth a straw (51 Melville *Moby-Dick* I 113; Hammett *Stray* 225; Porter *Major* 51; Clemens *Roughing* II 17). Apperson 458; Farmer and Henley VII 6–7; Green 368; NC 482; *Oxford* 624–625; Tilley S918; Whiting *Drama* 365:876, *Scots* II 134.

5. Straws show how the wind drives (35 Crockett *Account* 214; Haliburton *Clockmaker* II 38 Them little matters are like throwin' up straws, they show which way the wind is; Cary *Clovernook* 2d Series 234; Riley *Puddleford* 107 straws thrown out to determine which way the wind blew; Alcott *Little Women* 243). Apperson 605; Bradley 93; NED Straw 8; *Oxford* 625; Stevenson 2225:3; Tilley S924; Andy Adams *The Ranch on the Beaver* (Boston 1927) 99 As straws tell which way the wind blows; Anthony Abbot, pseud. *About the Murder of Geraldine Foster* (1930) 75; Edith R. Mirrielees *The Pacific Spectator* VIII (1954) 3 They [reports to the editor] are, of course, no more than straws in the wind. See Wind (18).

6. S— had begun, by this time, to see "straw for his bricks," in the course matters were taking (50 Willis *Life* 323). Exod. 5; NC 375 *Oxford* 64; Stevenson 243:2; Tilley B660.

357

7. I would n't lay a straw in the girl's way if I could (53 Cary *Clovernook* 2d Series 225).

Strawberry, 1. Still there was but a single bud [on a rosebush], a noble one, plump as a strawberry (54 Stephens *Fashion* 309).
2. With lips smiling and red as strawberries (c58 Stephens *Mary Derwent* 246).
3. Her mouth . . . jest like a bunch of ripe strawberries, jest ready tu drop from the stems (44 Stephens *High Life* II 246).

Streak, sb., 1. I had a streak of fat and a streak of lean over it—got lost several times (66 Clemens *Letters* I 107).
2. I went down to the Express office like a streak of chalk (44 Stephens *High Life* I 43, II 126; Hammett *Stray* 270 he went off like a greased streak, *Piney* 259 went by it like a streak; Smith *'Way* 242 starting off like a streak). DA Streak 2 (1); Green 369; NED Streak 3 c; Christopher Bush *The Death of Cosmo Revere* (1930) 136 shot off.
3. To make a streak for. 75 DA Streak 2 (2).

Streaked, i. e., embarrassed. See Bartlett 670–671; DA Streaked 2; Farmer and Henley VII 8–9; NED Streaked 2; Schele de Vere 637–638; Thornton II 865, III 384. See Apple (5), Pork (1), Ribbongrass, Tiger (3), Trousers.

String, 1. The snake hanging as limber as a string (59 Browning *Forty-Four* 381; Harris *Sut* 144 wet string).
2. She wer stretched out strait as a string (67 Harris *Sut* 42; Clemens *Gilded* I 270). Allan PADS XV (1951) 67; NC 482; Taylor *Comparisons* 78;

The Aresbys, pseud. *Murder at Red Pass* (1931) 230.
3. It might be well enough to have two or three strings to my bow (33 Smith *Downing* 134; Haliburton *Sam* II 274 So you like two strings to your bow; Jones *Country* 376 And now I've got only one string to my bow; Anon. *New Hope* 95 They [women] like to have two strings to their bow; Daly *Man* 51 I've got twa strings, as they say, to ma' bow; Clemens *Letters* I 350 three). Apperson 656; Farmer and Henley I 309–310; NED String 4 b; *Oxford* 681; E. S. Sheldon *Romanic Review* XIII (1922) 77–80; Stevenson 2730:4; Stoett 297; Tilley S937; Whiting *Drama* 221; Hugh Baker *Cartwright Is Dead, Sir!* (Boston 1934) 238.

Strong, 1. Bull Dogge . . . says I have piled it up to strong (55 Thomson *Doesticks* 91). Partridge 841.
2. See Bear (22), Bull (4), Bullmoose, Horse (11), Lion (7), Lucifer 1 (2), Mainmast, Paver, Rhinoceros (1), Rock (7), Tempest (1).

Stubborn. See Mule (6).

Stuck up. See Fire stick.

Study, sb. Relapse into a brown study (25 Neal *Brother J* I 94, *Down-Easters* I 173; Kennedy *Swallow* 199; Irving *Attorney* 377; Hooper *Simon* 24; Melville *Redburn* 137, *Moby-Dick* I 20, *Confidence-Man* 122; Burke *Polly* 102, 175; Durivage *Three* 82; Clemens *Innocents* II 260–261; Eggleston *Circuit* 42 And so he fell into the brownest of studies). Apperson 70; Green 70; NED Brown study; *Oxford* 67; Stevenson 2231:9; Tilley S945; Whiting *Drama* 336:422; NQ 1 i 352, 418; 3 i 190; 6 ii 408, iii 54, v 53–54.

Study, vb. See Trojan.

Stuff. Kate is made of the right sort of stuff (57 Jones *Country* 211). Cf. Stevenson 2232:5.

Stump, 1. As dead as two old stumps (59 Smith *My Thirty* 345).

2. It's no use a-sittin' here as still as two rotten stumps in a fog (40 Haliburton *Clockmaker* III 153; Browning *Forty-four* 150 and there I had to remain as still as a stump).

3. Fortunately, she requires but little more than a good listener, otherwise I should have found myself pretty often against a stump (40 Fairfield *Letters* 287). DA Stump 5 c (5).

4. To fool around the stump [i. e., to beat around the bush]. 80 DA Fool 3.

5. Nothing on arth puts a feller to his stumps like pulling in the same team with a purty gal (44 Stephens *High Life* I 46). DA Stump 5 c (9).

6. Stir your stumps (25 Neal *Brother J* II 313; Haliburton *Clockmaker* II 324; Stephens *High Life* II 201; Bennett *Border* 96; Riley *Puddleford* 146; Clemens *Gilded* I 29). McAtee 62; NED Stump 1 c; *Oxford* 621; Stevenson 2233:8; Tilley S946; D. Q. Burleigh *The Kristiana Killers* (1937) 45.

7. You're up a stump (76 Clemens *Tom* 16, *Tramp* II 80 find himself "up a stump" . . . as Joseph Addison would say). DA Stump 5 c (3); NED *Supplement* Stump 2 c; Partridge 843; Elsa Barker *The Cobra Candlestick* (1928) 63.

Stump fence. She was . . . homely as a stump fence (62 Browne *Artemus* 15). Cf. Cox *Southern Folklore Quarterly* XI (1947) 264; NC 406; Taylor *Comparisons* 48–49.

Stupid. See Coot, Owl (7), Pump (1).

Submissive. See Sheep (10).

Subtle. See Eel (7).

Success, 1. Nothing succeeds like success (67 Richardson *Beyond* 418). Apperson 454; Lean IV 67; NC 483; *Oxford* 464; Stevenson 2236:5; NQ 5 x 88; 6 v 189; Kenneth Conibear *Northland Footprints* (London 1936) 113.

2. Success is its own reward, sir, to them as loves their art (69 Boucicault *Presumptive* 251).

Sucker, 1. I'm thirsty as a sucker in a salt bail (60–63 Taliaferro *Carolina Humor* 79).

2. I'm a gone sucker (43 Haliburton *Attaché* III 179; Robb *Squatter* 170 I'm a saved sucker, 174; Stephens *High Life* II 166; Durivage *Three* 143; Taliaferro *Fisher's* 163). Bartlett 677; DA Gone 1 (11); Stevenson 2237:1; Thornton I 373. See Coon (7).

Sudden. See Pistol shot, Texas norther, Thought (3).

Suds, 1. And that threw 'em all into the suds, head and ears (33 Smith *Downing* 68, 198 we shall be likely to catch you all in the suds [i. e., unprepared]; Hall *Purchase* I 42 to catch the inamorata "in the suds," 250 Josey's wife now appeared *en deshabille* [the footnote explains, "French, for being caught 'in the suds' "]). Apperson 358 Leave (8); Bartlett 798; Farmer and Henley VII 24; NED Suds 5 a; *Oxford* 629; Stevenson 2238:2; Tilley S953.

2. See Soap suds.

Sugar, 1. She looked sweeter than sugar (34 Crockett *Life* 63; Paul

Courtship 184 a voice as sweet as sugar). Boshears 31:117, 40:979; NC 483; Taylor *Comparisons* 80; Whiting *Drama* 328:315; Mrs. Baillie Reynolds *Very Private Secretary* (1933) 23. Cf. NED Sugar 4 c (sugarsweet).

2. I know he is neither sugar nor salt [i. e., can go out in the rain]. (32 Kennedy *Swallow* 294). Apperson 441; NC 483; NED Sugar 2 b; *Oxford* 630; Stevenson 1931–1932:5; Roger Torrey *42 Days for Murder* (1938) 239 He ain't made of sugar or salt. Don't make a baby of him.

3. As far excells . . . as "Sugar does Saltpeter" (38 Eliason 103).

Sugar candy. As short and sweet as sugar candy (36 Haliburton *Clockmaker* I 309, *Attaché* II 223 The Elder smiled as sweet as sugar candy, III 66, IV 248). Svartengren 306.

Sugar kettle. As round as a sugar kettle (43 Hall *Purchase* II 214).

Sugar-planter. Boys, the way me and Stag-Horn set up to that thar fire, was like to courting a sugar-planter's daughter (57 Bennett *Border* 295).

Sugar-snow. Lay motionless, as some sugar-snow in March (57 Melville *Confidence-Man* 5).

Suit, sb. He found his suit ready made and fitted afore he thought he was half measured [i. e., received a beating]. (36 Haliburton *Clockmaker* I 175).

Suit, vb. See T.

Sulky. See Bear (23).

Summer's day. That fellow was about as superfluous a piece of wicked flesh as I say—as a man would meet on a summer's day journey (35 Kennedy *Horse-Shoe* 151). Apperson 256

Good; Farmer and Henley VII 26; Tilley S967.

Summer-squash. She came to dinner as radiant as a summer-squash (53 Willis *Fun* 215).

Sun, 1. Bright as the sun (26 Conant *Earnest Man* 335; Porter *Major* 53 Bright as the sun, the merry minx talked on). Boshears 35:378; NC 483; Taylor *Comparisons* 21; Whiting *Drama* 328:316, *Scots* II 135.

2. It's ez clear ez the sun is at noon (48 Lowell *Biglow* 93; Boker *World* 31 This sad matter is as clear to me . . . as the sun at noonday; Conant *Earnest Man* 28 clear to his own mind as the sun in heaven; Clemens *Sketches* 337 as clear as the sun). Apperson 101; Stevenson 363:2; Svartengren 363; Tilley S969; Whiting *Drama* 329:316, *Scots* II 135; George Goodchild *The Monster of Grammont* (1930) 243 sun-clear.

3. Jis' es ofen es the sun sets, an' fifteen times ofener ef thar's half a chance (67 Harris *Sut* 81).

4. The matter is about as plain as the sun in the heavens (68 Clift *Bunker* 153). Cf. Whiting *Scots* II 135 patent.

5. Father is as regular as the sun (68 Alcott *Little Women* 174). Cf. NC 483.

6. As sure as the sun rises (45 Hooper *Simon* 68). Cf. NC 483 sets.

7. Meredith's horse will win as sure as the sun shines (66 Boucicault *Flying Scud* 205). NC 483.

8. As true as the sun will rise tomorrow (33 Smith *Downing* 129, *Letters* 63).

9. But come let's liquor, the sun is gettin' over the foreyard, as we sailors say (53 Haliburton *Sam* I 158, *Nature* I 36 When the sun is over the fore-

yard, they know the time of day as well as the captain, and call for their grog). Cf. NED Foreyard[2], quot. 1844.

10. Leaving old Cumberland between two suns (59 Taliaferro *Fisher's* 156). See Day (18).

11. He's going home to Down East . . . so far eastward . . . that they have to pry up the sun with a handspike (50 Melville *White Jacket* 164). Babcock 260.

12. A smilin on me like a June sun (44 Stephens *High Life* II 247).

Sunday, 1. His list of songs seemed to be as long as a rainy Sunday (36 Crockett *Exploits* 120).

2. I go now to Dr. Spring's meeting always as straight as Sunday comes round (44 Stephens *High Life* I 169).

3. Spite of (the) merchant seamen's maxim, that *there are no Sundays off soundings. No Sundays off soundings,* indeed! No Sundays on shipboard! (50 Melville *White Jacket* 193). Babcock 260. Cf. Sabbath (1).

4. See Month, Way (15), Week.

Sunday-go-to-meeting. Sunday-go-to-meeting hat (43 Dorson *Jonathan* 96; Sedley *Marian* 341 St. Lawrence, and the rest o' them old-fashioned back counties, where they put on their Sunday-go-to-meetins to vote in). See Clothes (4).

Sun-down. He'd foller the case to the back side of sun-down (57 Riley *Puddleford* 266).

Sunflower, 1. And the daughter as frenchified as a sunflower (32 Kennedy *Swallow* 283).

2. As gaudy as a sunflower (59 Browning *Forty-four* 203).

3. A woman . . . purty es a sunflower (67 Harris *Sut* 36).

4. She shows among wimen like a sunflower amung dorg fennel (67 Harris *Sut* 75). Cf. NED Sunflower 2 c.

Sunshine, 1. As clear as sunshine (54 Smith '*Way* 25). Svartengren 363; Frank H. Shaw *Atlantic Murder* (1933) 250.

2. Round they come like a streak uv sunshine (59 Taliaferro *Fisher's* 67).

Superstitious. See Indian (3).

Supple. See Eel (8), Moose wood, Snake (3), Walnut gad.

Sure. See Ace (5), Alive (4), Apostles, Born (2), Breath (1), Day (15), Death (18), Devil (6, 16), Die, sb. (2), Egg (5, 6), Fate (3), Father (2), God (1), Gun (2, 3), Income-tax, Lightning (9), Live (2), Log (3), Lord 1 (1), Morning (8), Name (1), Rates (1), Rattlesnake (2), Shooting (3), Sin (7), Sit (1), Snake (4), Stand (1), Sun (6, 7), Woman (12), World (2).

Surgeon. The French prejudice which embodies itself in the maxim "young surgeon, old physician." (72 Holmes *Poet* 119). Le Roux de Lincy *Le Livre des Proverbes Français* (Paris 1842) I 178.

Surly-looking. See Thundercloud (3).

Swallow, sb., 1. I am as free as air, and independent as a swallow (57 Jones *Country* 52).

2. As swift as the swallows (54 Shillaber *Mrs. Partington* 71). Svartengren 378; Taylor *Comparisons* 81; Tilley S1023; Whiting *Scots* II 136.

3. And before a swallow could flap his wings, my knife was in his throat (56 Cooke *Foresters* 18).

4. The little boat going like a swallow (40 Dana *Two* 169).

5. One ripple does not make a wind, any more than one swallow a summer (56 Melville *Piazza* 132; Locke [Nasby] *Struggles* 416 One swaller don't make a spring). Apperson 612; NC 483–484; NED Swallow 1 c; *Oxford* 634; Stevenson 2253:5; Stoett 1265; Tilley S1025; NQ 3 v 53, 83; 4 vii 292; Francis Beeding, pseud. *Death Walks in Eastrepps* (1931) 67.

Swallow, vb. See Crane.

Swamp. I . . . felt eenamost as much alone as if I'd been in a Connecticut cranberry swamp (44 Stephens *High Life* I 57).

Swamp girl. [A dog] jumped—like a swamp gal into a jar of pickles (43 Lewis *Odd* 132).

Swan, 1. No *rara avis* was honest John, (That's the Latin for "sable swan") (68 Saxe *Poems* 35). NED Swan 2 d; *Oxford* 49; Tilley S1027; Alice Campbell *Keep Away from Water!* (1935) 18 a black swan. Cf. Whiting *Drama* 113.

2. When it expires like a dying swan, it sings its own funeral hymn (55 Haliburton *Nature* II 276). Apperson 612–613; NED Swan 2 b; *Oxford* 634; Stevenson 2254–2255:5; Stoett 2681; Tilley S1028; Whiting *Drama* 366:880, *Scots* II 136; R. C. Woodthorpe *Death Wears a Purple Shirt* (1934) 97 the melodious charm of a dying swan.

Sward. Old sward wants turning under once in a while (45 Judd *Margaret* II 161).

Swarm. See Bee (14, 15), Butterfly (2).

Swath. Didn't he cut a swarth! (44 Stephens *High Life* I 136; Kelly *Humors* 91, 101, 245). Bartlett 165; DA Cut 17 (2); NED Swath 3 c; Stevenson 478:8; Thornton I 232, III 392.

Swear. See Preacher, Sailor (8), Trooper.

Sweat. See Coal-kiln, Ice-pitcher, Tiger (11).

Sweet, 1. It is an old proverb that "after the sweet comes the bitter" (59 Browning *Forty-four* 342). *Oxford* 635; Cf. Stevenson 2259:4.

2. Sweets to the sweet (69 Alcott *Little Women* 509). Bradley 93; *Oxford* 636; Stevenson 2259:2; Patricia Wentworth *Danger Calling* (Philadelphia 1931) 227.

3. See Breath (3), Candy (1), Cat (26), Catnip (2), Flower (3), Hay (1), Honey (3), Jujube, Milk (3), Nut (7), Pin (6), Pink (2), Rose (3, 8), Seraph, Steam (1), Sugar (1), Sugar candy.

Swell, sb. Miss Billins . . . would say I was tryin' to cut a swell, and couldent make it out (56 Whitcher *Widow* 225).

Swell, vb. See Baking, Bear (34), Bird (25), Bullfrog, Horse (37), Toad (7).

Swift. See Arrow (3), Deer (2), Flash (2), Goat (2), Lightning (10), Swallow, sb. (2), Thought (4), Wink (5).

Swig. To take a "swig at the halyards," as they called it (49 Melville *Redburn* 60, *White Jacket* 218 a more vigorous *nip at the cable*, a more sturdy *swig at the halyards* [i. e., to take a drink]). Babcock 263.

Swim, sb. No, he won't in the swim along with me (69 Boucicault *Pre-*

sumptive 253). Farmer and Henley VII 47; NED Swim 7; Stevenson 2203:3; Thornton III 392.

Swim, vb. See Fish (14), Frog (3).

Swine. Swine that run at large in the woods make the sweetest pork (45 Judd *Margaret I* 263).

Swing. See Top 2 (4).

Swingletree. When Ham Rachel . . . begins a thing, he carries it through, ur breaks the swingle-tree (59 Taliaferro *Fisher's* 258).

Swoop. Should I let selfish desire, with one fell swoop, bear down every principle of right (57 Bennett *Border* 51; Locke [Nasby] *Struggles* 406 at one fell swoop). NED Swoop 3 b; *Oxford* 637; Stevenson 2264:1.

Sword, 1. Teeth long as a sword (59 Taliaferro *Fisher's* 161).

2. They were at swords' points at once (40 Dana *Two* 121). Clifford Knight *The Affair of the Heavenly Voice* (1937) 126.

3. Every . . . event was like a two-edged sword, and cut both ways (40 Dana *Two* 113; Sedley *Marian* 216 Likewise he is a two-edged sword, cuttin' both friend and foe). See Glaive, Way (4).

4. All they that take the sword shall perish by the sword (33 Neal *Down-Easters* I 41; Saxe *Poems* 21 But "they who take," thus saith the Lord, "Shall also perish by the sword"). Matt. 26:52; Bradley 94; Stevenson 2265:3; Whiting *Drama* 7, 10, 28; Abraham Merritt *Creep, Shadow, Creep* (1934) 148 Those who live by the sword must die by the sword.

5. Over his devoted head daily and nightly hung the sword of Damocles (67 Richardson *Beyond* 305). *Oxford* 637; Stevenson 2264:7; Brian Flynn *Five Red Fingers* (1938) 170.

T

T. To a T (38 Haliburton *Clockmaker* II 111 suit you, III 213 You've got it to a T.—To a T! said he (the old soft horn,) how is that? I really don't onderstand how you have a T. in it at all.—Oh dear! said I, no more we have; it's nothin' but a sayin' of ourn, a kind of provarb; it's a cant phrase, 298 suit, *Letter* 21 fit you exacaly, *Sam* I 25 that's my idea; Dana *Two* 222 the yards were squared "to a *t*," 428 with sails cut to a *t*; Lowell *Biglow* 67 his view o' the thing, 124 suit me, 139 both air sooted, 338 the wind's opinions; Durivage *Three* 192 suit you, 332 fit you; Whitcher *Widow* 334 it's her, 348 suited him; Jones *Country* 168 that's his character; Stephens *Mary Derwent* 255 that noose in it'll fit that feller's neck; Boucicault *Dot* 139 fit it; Saxe *Poems* 162 suit). Farmer and Henley VII 54; McAtee 63; NC 484; NED T 1 c; Schele de Vere 639; Stevenson 2267:1; Tidwell PADS XIII (1950) 20; Woodard PADS VI (1946) 29; Leighton Barret *Though Young* (1938) 53.

Table, 1. Flat as a table (55 Melville *Israel* 2).
2. We might have turned the tables on the Yankees (21 Cooper *Spy* 160; Kennedy *Horse-Shoe* 517; Haliburton *Attaché* I 118, II 173, *Old Judge* I 234, II 67, *Season-Ticket* 330; Melville *Mardi* I 201, *Redburn* 157; Thomson *Plu-ri-bus-tah* 251; Richardson *Secret* 144, 506; Alcott *Little Women* 75, 333). Farmer and Henley VII 55; NED Table 4 c; *Oxford* 677; Stevenson 2267:2; Tilley T4; Henry Holt *The Midnight Mail* (1931) 261.

Tack. I have turned right about, I am tother tack now, and the long leg, too (36 Haliburton *Clockmaker* I 178; Dana *Two* 9 you must begin on a new tack). NED Tack 7.

Tackle, 1. I rather think we shall hitch tackle like anything [i. e., agree, get along together]. (44 Stephens *High Life* I 26, II 46).
2. A feller come by and kinder slacked tackle [i. e., slowed down]. (44 Stephens *High Life* I 11, II 142).

Tag. A tag-rag and bob-tailed follower (43 Hall *Purchase* II 24; Melville *White Jacket* 9 the tag-rag and bobtail of the crew; Haliburton *Sam* II 298 tag-rag and bobtail, *Nature* I 15). Apperson 616; Farmer and Henley VII 56–57; NED Tag 10 b (tag and rag); *Oxford* 638; Stevenson 2268:3; Tilley T10; Whiting *Drama* 366:882; *Catalogue of Political and Personal Satires . . . 1820–1827* (London 1952) X 17 No. 13578 The tag rag and bobtail, and sans-culottes fellows; Lawrence Kirk *Whispering Tongues* (1934) 252 all this tag, rag and bobtail. See Rag (4).

Tail, 1. To use a very expressive Westernism, "*Dave's tail was up*," and every possible preparation was made to preclude a failure [i. e., his spirit was aroused]. (53 Hammett *Stray* 97). Farmer 526–527; H. C. Bailey *The Twittering Bird Mystery* (1937) 188 keep. See Head (6).

2. He jus' turn'd tail tu the battil groun (67 Harris *Sut* 103). Farmer and Henley VII 235; NED Tail 11 d; Stevenson 2268:9.

3. I arter him like the tail to a kite (44 Stephens *High Life* II 24).

4. We . . . marvelled off with our tails atween our legs (58 Hammett *Piney* 43, 279 is that you, Jimmy! with your tail atween yer legs, a runnin' like a whipped hound from them Mexican cowards?). NED Tail 11 b; Stevenson 2269:1; Taylor *Comparisons* 35; Dorothy L. Sayers *The Unpleasantness at the Bellona Club* (1928) 120. See Dog (38).

5. See Cow's tail (1), Lizard (2).

Tailor, 1. He belonged to that numerous class, that it is perfectly safe to trust as far as a tailor can sling a bull by the tail—but no farther (36 Crockett *Exploits* 90). Boshears 31:95; DA Bull 9 e (this example). Cf. Apperson 649; Tilley T556. See Bullock, Cat (34).

2. He [a tailor] worked like a man —or, more properly speaking, like the ninth part of a man (33 Hall *Sailor's Bride* 176; Haliburton *Attaché* I 100 Whether it takes nine tailors to make a man, I can't jist exactly say, *Nature* I 63 Gallop and 8 More Taylors Make a Man, 246 that is a covered joke at a tailor being only the ninth part of one [a man]; Saxe *Poems* 36 She perfectly scorned the best of his clan, And reckoned the ninth of any man An exceedingly Vulgar Fraction). Apperson 446; Farmer and Henley VII 61–62;

NED Tailor 1 b; *Oxford* 453; Stevenson 2269:7; Tilley T23; Dorothy L. Sayers *The Nine Tailors* (1934) 65, 99.

Take, 1. Your father's fortune was ample. He couldn't take it with him (55 Jones *Winkles* 165). Stevenson 1984–1985:15; E. S. Gardner *The Case of the Rolling Bones* (1939) ch. 7 He can't take it with him, ch. 15 After all, you know, you can't take it with you.

2. See Smallpox (2), Wildfire.

Tales. We must not tell tales out of school (32 Kennedy *Swallow* 267; Kelly *Humors* 76 let's drink—no tales out of school, ha, ha!; Jones *Batkins* 357 and did not "tell tales out of school"). Apperson 619; Farmer and Henley VII 67–68; NC 484; NED School 1 e; *Oxford* 643; Stevenson 2272–2273:1; Tilley T54; Florence Yeager and Eli Colter *Jungle Woman* (1935) 297.

Talk, sb., 1. All talk and no cider, as the sayin' is (40 Haliburton *Clockmaker* III 276). Bartlett 121; DA Cider 2; Farmer 146; Schele de Vere 591; NQ 2 v 233.

2. Talk don't hurt (76 Clemens *Tom* 13).

3. Talk is cheap, it don't cost nothin' but breath (43 Haliburton *Attaché* I 59, *Season-Ticket* 73 It's chape talkin'). NC 484; Snapp 109:164; Stevenson 2279:12; Andy Adams *The Outlet* (Boston 1905) 63 Talk's cheap but it takes money to buy whiskey; Stephen Chalmers *The Affair of the Gallows Tree* (1930) 26; *Puck* II (1877) No. 29 p. 13; E. M. Rhodes *West Is West* (1917) 288.

4. That's the talk [expression of approval]. 57 DA Talk 3 b.

Talk, vb. See Book (8), Uncle.

Talker. Your militia are great talkers, and little doers (40 Cooper *Pathfinder* 195). Apperson 273; NC 484 Big talk and little deeds; *Oxford* 644; Stevenson 229:5 braggers, 2038:2; Tilley T64.

Talking. Talking will never build a stone wall or pay our taxes (33 Smith *Downing* 61). Cf. NC 484.

Tall, 1. To walk tall [i. e., proudly]. c45 DA Tall 1 b; NED Tall (B).
2. See Grenadier (2), Maypole (2), Outdoors (4), Poplar tree, Pump (2).

Tame. See Lamb (13).

Tan-bark. The circus-rider prayed fur me, like he was beatin' tan-bark off uv trees in dade uv winter (59 Taliaferro *Fisher's* 122). See Devil (8), Hell (13); Taylor *Comparisons* 34; DA Tanbark 1.

Tangent. Madame, you shouldn't let your tongue fly off in a tangent this way (c56 Thomson *Elephant Club* 270). NED Tangent A 2, B 1 c.

Tan-yard. I've clared the tan-yard [i. e., frightened the congregation out of church]. (59 Taliaferro *Fisher's* 39, 44).

Taos lightning. Converted into whiskey, known throughout the far West as "Taos lightning" (67 Richardson *Beyond* 260). DA Taos 2.

Tap. Thinks says I there's a tap lost about this wagon [i. e., something is wrong]. (66 Smith *Arp* 154).

Tapis. Poor Jenks, now on the *tapis* for more ill news, approached the person in waiting (56 Kelly *Humors* 47).

NED Tapis (b); Partridge 865. Cf. NED Carpet 1 b; Tilley C97.

Tar, 1. As black as tar (62 Wiley *Billy* 113). Green 383; NC 484; Taylor *Comparisons* 19.
2. A tar-black line (c60 Paul *Courtship* 30).
3. The things there does look like they was painted with tar [i. e., were bad, corrupt]. (51 Burke *Polly* 141).

Tar barrel. To have one's hand in a tar barrel [i. e., to be in a fix]. 34 DA Tar (b) 1.

Tar brush. She has a touch of the tar brush (40 Haliburton *Letter* 64). Farmer and Henley VII 76; NED Tar 1 c (a touch of tar), Tar-brush; Stevenson 2280:4; Agatha Christie *Murder in Mesopotamia* (1936) 30.

Tartar. But for once they [pickpockets] caught a tartar (20–22 Irving *Bracebridge* 60; Hall *Soldier's Bride* 227 and do you think . . . the ungrateful wretch didn't march off; swearing he had caught a tartar, *Purchase* I 131 otherwise two tartars of a very unpleasant character may be caught; Melville *Omoo* 360 He not only caught a queen, but a Tartar, when he married her; Jones *Winkles* 221, *Country* 53; Thomson *Plu-ri-bus-tah* 209 He had caught a female Tartar; Browne *Artemus* 38 But he caught a Tomarter when he got hold of me; Lowell *Biglow* 309, 327; Eggleston *School-Master* 238). Apperson 89–90; Farmer and Henley II 53, VII 83; NED Tartar 4; *Oxford* 85; Stevenson 2280–2281:7; Tilley T73; NQ 1 vi 317, viii 73; Vernon Loder *Red Stain* (1932) 126. Cf. Green 383.

Taunton. They are as weak as Taunton water (38 Haliburton *Clockmaker*

II 213, *Attaché* II 73). See Water (5).

Tavern. But a tavern is a tavern (c58 Stephens *Mary Derwent* 293).

Taxes. Taxes is taxes (76 Nash *Century* 65).

Tea kettle. In your old age, when your voice is cracked like an old tea kettle (62 Browne *Artemus* 113).

Team, 1. Tired as a prairie team (43 Robb *Squatter* 42).
2. Birdsall says his wife is a whole team at it [chess]. (37 Fairfield *Letters* 167; Haliburton *Clockmaker* III 284 She was a whole team and a horse to spare, *Attaché* III 8, 162, *Sam* I 24, 47, *Season-Ticket* 286; Hammett *Piney* 45 Dog on my cat, ef they ain't a hull team and a big dog under the waggin; Sedley *Marian* 176 I'm a hull team, I am. Likewise, . . . with a little yaller dog under the wagon, 177 It bein' the fashion . . . for Pikes and hull teams, let alone little yaller dogs under the wagon, to keep their eyes skun). Bartlett 756, 810; DA Team 1; Farmer 256; Schele de Vere 221–222; Thornton II 888–889, III 397.
3. To drive too much team. 42 DA Team 5 b.
4. The old sloop a scooting down the sound like a four-horse team (44 Stephens *High Life* II 139).

Teapot. But if I didn't see natoral h-ll,—in August at that,—I *am* a teapot (58 Porter *Major* 122).

Tecumseh. D-d-dead as Tecumseh (51 Burke *Polly* 177). See Caesar (3).

Teetotum. Twirlin' like a tee-to-tum on the watters (c60 Paul *Courtship* 27). Cf. NED Teetotum 1, 3.

Telegram. Flew by the admiring company like a telegram (66 Clemens *Sandwich* 50, *Roughing* I 170 the horse darted away like a telegram).

Telegraph. By signs, as rapid as the telegraph (53 Boker *Bankrupt* 75).

Tell. You can't never tell (71 Eggleston *School-Master* 124; Shillaber *Ike* 177 We can't sometimes most allers tell how anything's going to turn out before it happens). Miles Burton *The Clue of the Fourteen Keys* (1937) 111; E. M. Rhodes *Beyond the Desert* (Boston 1934) 112 You never can sometimes most always tell; M. Thompson *Not As a Stranger* (1954) 321; R. P. Warren *All the King's Men* (1946) 47.

Telling. Oh marm, that's telling (44 Stephens *High Life* I 208). Farmer and Henley VII 93 tellings.

Temperate. See Watercress.

Tempest, 1. [A heart] strong as a tempest (50 Mitchell *Reveries* 81).
2. Getting up another tempest in a teapot (36 Crockett *Exploits* 49, 195; Fairfield *Letters* 80; Judd *Richard* 362; Whitcher *Widow* 330). Apperson 604; Farmer and Henley VII 88–89; NC 485; NED Tea-pot; *Oxford* 624; Stevenson 2221:10; Stoett 2191; NQ 10 xi 388, 456; 11 ii 86, 131, 173–174, 255; CXCIV (1949) 18, 86; W. Y. Darling *The Bankrupt Bookseller* (Edinburgh 1947) 137 This is no heat about nothing—no storm in a tea-cup; H. L. Ickes *Diary* (1953) I 691 The whole thing was a very silly tempest in a very small teapot; Kathleen M. Knight *Death Blew Out the Match* (1935) 30; E. M. Rhodes *West Is West* (Boston 1917) 167.

Tempus. See Time (10).

Tender. See Cat (27), Lamb (14), Mother (1).

Tender-hearted. See Baby (4).

Ten-pins. The men would drop like so many ten-pins (58 Clemens *Letters* I 36–37).

Tent-pole. As straight and stiff as a tent-pole (69 Clemens *Innocents* II 202).

Tether. You see the end of your tether now (28 Neal *Rachel* 224). NED Tether 4; R. J. Casey *Hot Ice* (Indianapolis 1933) 243.

Texas. Gone to Texas. 30 DA Texas 3 d.

Texas fever. The "Texas fever" is raging (54 Eliason 91). See California fever (2).

Texas norther. An excitement, sudden and fierce as a Texas norther (67 Richardson *Beyond* 149). Farmer 393. Cf. DA Texas 3 b (13).

Thick, sb. Through thick and thin (33 Smith *Downing* 68, 131, 134, 176, 193, 195, 230, *Letters* 103, *My Thirty* 369; Davis *Downing* 21, 88, 93, 264; Melville *Mardi* I 20, *Redburn* 203; Baldwin *Flush* 265, 310; Lincoln III 416; Taliaferro *Fisher's* 23, 212; Paul *Courtship* 277; Lowell *Biglow* 386; Alcott *Little Women* 144; Clemens *Letters* I 157, *Fairbanks* 154). Apperson 623; Farmer and Henley VII 99; Green 387; *Oxford* 648; Stevenson 2295:4; Tilley T101; Whiting *Drama* 367:892; J. J. Brandon *The One-Minute Murder* (1935) 97.

Thick, adj. 1. To spread it on thick. 65 DA Spread 3 (a).

2. See Acorn (2), Bee (7), Bird (15), Blackberry (2), Blackbird (4), Cat (28), Cocklebur, Cowpea (1), Flea (5), Fly, sb. (3), Fool (13), Frog (2), Hail (3), Hailstones (1), Hair (3), Hops (1), Huckleberry (1), Leaf (4), Midnight (4), Pickpocket, Pitch, sb. 1 (6), Spatter, Thief (4), Three, Toad (3), Tree (1).

Thief, 1. Some people have bad names, but all are not thieves that dogs bark at (32 Kennedy *Swallow* 216). Apperson 624; *Oxford* 649; Stevenson 2297:3; Tilley A117.

2. There we see 'em as busy at work as a thief in a mill (39 Smith *Letters* 100).

3. As safe as a thief in a mill (40 Haliburton *Letter* 193, *Sam* I 148). Apperson 543; Farmer and Henley VII 104; *Oxford* 554; Svartengren 351–352; Tilley T102.

4. Him and me got as thick as two thieves (38 Haliburton *Clockmaker* II 92, III 223, *Attaché* III 19, *Sam* II 90; Clemens *Letters* I 122 I am thick as thieves with the Rev. Stebbings). Apperson 624; Farmer and Henley VII 99; McAtee 65; NC 485; NED Thick 10; Taylor *Comparisons* 81; W. W. Jacobs *Snug Harbour* (1931) 484.

5. Save a thief from hanging and he will cut your throat (45 Judd *Margaret* I 53). Apperson 550; *Oxford* 562; Stevenson 2299:9; Tilley T109.

6. Besides the thief would be sure to be caught: "Set a"—member of a certain class—you know *that* proverb, too (53 Baldwin *Flush* 296). Apperson 624; Bradley 94; Hardie 463:95; NED Thief 1 c; *Oxford* 649; Stevenson 2300:3; Tilley T110; L. W. Meynell *Mystery at Newton Ferry* (Philadelphia 1930) 143.

Thin. See Crane (1), Crow (5), Flagstaff (3), Gossamer, Lath, Locust, Muslin, Post (4), Rail (1), Shad (4), Shadow (3), Skeleton (1).

Thing, 1. All things are double, one against another (c38 Emerson *Works* II 109).

2. All things in moderation are good (49 Melville *Mardi* II 340). Stevenson 1602:3.

3. All things must have an end (57 Riley *Puddleford* 305; Clemens *Tom* 232 But all things have an end). Apperson 8; *Oxford* 180; Stevenson 677: 5; Tilley E120; Whiting *Drama* 223; H. Ashton-Wolfe *Outlaws of Modern Days* (1937) 161.

4. The proverb says, that if all lost things went to the moon, how full of good advice it would be (39 Smith *Letters* 14–15).

5. Dr. Franklin's adage, "if you wish a thing done; *go;* if you do not, *send*" (53 Hammet *Stray* 343). *Oxford* 690; Stevenson 2063–2064:11.

6. Judge not things by their names. This, the maxim illustrated respecting the isle toward which we were sailing (49 Melville *Mardi* I 313).

7. Strang things do sometims turn up, as Tummus said when Betty housemaid was found floating on the river (40 Haliburton *Letter* 239).

8. I'm tryin my best . . . to take things jest as I find 'em (66 Smith *Arp* 164). *Oxford* 642; Stevenson 415: 4; Tilley T29, 196; Whiting *Scots* II 138.

9. Very often, as the old maxim goes, the simplest things are the most startling, and that, too, from their very simplicity (49 Melville *Mardi* I 22).

10. "Blessed be nothing" and "The worse things are, the better they are" are proverbs which express the tran-scendentalism of common life (c40 Emerson *Works* II 315).

11. Is there any thing new under the sun? (67 Richardson *Beyond* 325). Eccl. 1:9; Hardie 470:149; *Oxford* 464; Stevenson 1680–1681:8; Tilley T147; William Morton, pseud. *The Mystery of the Human Bookcase* (1931) 20.

12. I think old George Wolf knows a thing or two (35 Crockett *Account* 122; Irving *Attorney* 101; Anon. *New Hope* 63 In the phraseology of Ben, he "was gittin' to know a thing or two"; Lowell *Biglow* 337). Farmer and Henley IV 130–131; Partridge 463; Stevenson 1326:13. Cf. McAtee PADS XV (1951) 61.

13. I'll show you a thing or two (37 Neal *Charcoal* 137).

14. There's many a true thing said in jest (23–24 Irving *Tales* 65). Apperson 647–648; *Oxford* 672; Stevenson 1267:5; Tilley W772.

15. Too much of any thing . . . is not good . . . but too much rum is jist enough (36 Haliburton *Clockmaker* I 63, *Nature* II 141 too much of a good thing is good for nothing). Apperson 640–641; Bradley 77; *Oxford* 665; Stevenson 1637:6; Tilley T158; Whiting *Drama* 92.

Think. See Hear.

Thinking. Thinking's one thing and knowing's another, as the fellow said (35 Longstreet *Georgia* 162). Cf. Apperson 625; *Oxford* 651; D. Q. Burleigh *The Kristiana Killers* (1937) 178 to think is one thing, to prove another.

Thirsty. See Cartload, Desert (3), Sucker (1).

Thistledown. I blow it to the wind like the thistledown (57 Jones *Country*

114). Cf. George Granby *The Secret of Musterton House* (1929) 149 as light as.

Thorn, 1. A thorn in the flesh (55 Haliburton *Nature* II 325). II Cor. 12:7; Hardie 466:16; NED Thorn 2; Stoett 468; Gordon Gardiner *At the House of Dree* (1928) 27.

2. And ever since he has continued to be a thorn in the side of those who are unlucky enough to come into contact with him (37 Neal *Charcoal* 197; Hammett *Piney* 192 The fleet . . . was the very thorniest of all thorns in the Mexican sides; Richardson *Secret* 164 Mr. Prentice was a thorn in the side of the enemy). Numb. 23:55; NED Thorn 2; R. S. Surtees *Mr. Sponge's Sporting Tour* (London [1853]) 133 a terrible thorn in my side; Roger Delancey *Murder Below Wall Street* (1934) 94.

3. What sorrows are before the poor old man with such thorns in his pillow! [i. e., to have a worthless son]. (68 Clift *Bunker* 95).

4. I say, Rodney, my best friend, I know I've always been a thorn in your skirts (66 Bowman *Bear-Hunters* 42).

Thorny. See Honey-locust.

Thought, sb. 1. A country where speech is as free as thought (32 Hall *Legends* 43). Cf. Apperson 627; *Oxford* 652; Tilley T244.

2. As quick as thought (21 Cooper *Spy* 117, 291, *Pilot* 51, 166; Neal *Brother J* I 273; Melville *Omoo* 84; Cartwright *Autobiography* 218; Browning *Forty-four* 189; Clemens *Enterprise* 79, *Innocents* I 50, 215). Apperson 518–519; NC 485; NED Thought 3; Svartengren 374; Taylor *Investigations* 264; Ian Greig *Tragedy of the Chinese Mine* (1931) 70.

3. Sudden as thought (43 Robb *Squatter* 131).

4. Swift as thought (49 Melville *Mardi* I 181). NED Thought 3; Tilley T240; Whiting *Scots* II 139. Cf. Svartengren 374.

5. Dark thoughts lead to dark deeds (55 Haliburton *Nature* I 226).

Thought, vb. No sooner thought than done (54 Smith *'Way* 115). See Say (3).

Thrasher. As lively as a thrasher (49 Haliburton *Old Judge* I 34). Green 389; NED Thrasher [2].

Thread, 1. A sailor knows too well that his life hangs upon a thread, to wish to be often reminded of it (40 Dana *Two* 427; Boker *World* 3 Her honor hangs by a thread). NED Thread 12; Stevenson 2264:7; Tilley T250. Cf. Stoett 481.

2. Ther' wuz n't no occasion To lose the thread (67 Lowell *Biglow* 283).

Three. As thick as three in a bed [i. e., intimate]. (44 Stephens *High Life* II 165, 210). Apperson 624; Boshears 40:983; Figh PADS XIII (1950) 15 four; Halpert 698 four; McAtee PADS XV (1951) 61 four; NC 485; NED Thick 10; Svartengren 294, 328; Woodard PADS VI (1946) 43. See Two (2).

Thrip. I'm jest as good for old Miss Stallinses consent as a thrip is for a ginger cake (44 Thompson *Major* 87, 189 he's jest as good for President next fall as; Eliason 103 McDugald is as good for beating you as a sixpence is for a Ginger cake). Cf. NED *Supplement* Ginger-cake; Thornton II 895, III 400.

Thumb, 1. He had risen against his master . . . And beneath his thumb had got him (c56 Thomson *Plu-ri-bus-tah* 251; Sedley *Marian* 372 As to Gollop, he's . . . highly useful to Ingott, and completely under his thumb; Boucicault *Presumptive* 240 You have got both father and son under your thumb; Jones *Batkins* 385 I was under your thumb, as the saying is). Farmer and Henley VII 115; *Oxford* 656–657; Stevenson 2315:6; Stoett 507; Francis Beeding, pseud. *The House of Dr. Edwards* (1928) 124.

2. And the unforgiving Cuffee . . . Kept his cruel thumb upon him (c56 Thomson *Plu-ri-bus-tah* 254).

3. And them that's left to suck their fingers will always be biting their thumbs at you (59 Smith *My Thirty* 402). Farmer and Henley I 206; NED Bite 16, Thumb 5 e; *Oxford* 46; Stevenson 2315:4; Tilley T273; Whiting *Scots* II 140.

Thunder, 1. Big as thunder (43 Hall *Purchase* I 53; Judd *Richard* 185; Porter *Major* 189 Polar bears, you know —big as thunder).

2. A look as black as thunder (34 Davis *Downing* 274; Hall *Purchase* I 177; Kennedy *Horse-Shoe* 393; Anon. *New Hope* 181; Haliburton *Season-Ticket* 368; Lowell *Biglow* 305 I own Things look blacker'n thunder). Apperson 52; NC 486; Stevenson 193:1; Svartengren 58, 246; W. S. Masterman *The Rose of Death* (1936) 104.

3. As cross as thunder (37 Neal *Charcoal* 55; Smith *My Thirty* 393).

4. Irresistible as thunder (54 Smith *'Way* 25).

5. Voice . . . loud as thunder (51 Hawthorne *House* 324; Sedley *Marian* 94 hollerin' . . . louder than thunder, and sharper than a steam-en-

gine!). NC 486; Taylor *Comparisons* 54).

6. Mad as thunder (58 Field *Pokerville* 131).

7. Ez opperlunt ez thunder (48 Lowell *Biglow* 120).

8. Quick as thunder (59 Taliaferro *Fisher's* 201).

9. Spittin' would spile a trade there as quick as thunder does milk (40 Haliburton *Clockmaker* III 154). Green 32. See Milk (9).

10. As riley as thunder [i. e., angry]. (53 Hammett *Stray* 229).

11. He was as spunky as thunder (34 Davis *Downing* 75).

12. True as thunder (49 Haliburton *Old Judge* II 264).

13. He was as wrathy as thunder (34 Davis *Downing* 34, 111).

14. Here we commenced going not *like* thunder, but certainly *in* thunder and earthquake (43 Hall *Purchase* I 21; Thompson *Major* 40 I run like thunder, 57 we went hummin along jest like iled thunder; Jones *Wild* 137 He boxed my ears like, *Country* 191 snoring like; Hammett *Piney* 289 the apprisers marked 'em up like thunder; Taliaferro *Carolina Humor* 62 It stunk like). McAtee *Additional* 10; Thornton II 895.

15. Beat 'em all to thunder, er bust a biler (74 Eggleston *Circuit* 17).

16. The summons of the 'squire came upon them like a clap of thunder out of a clear sky (43 Thompson *Chronicles* 129; Locke [Nasby] *Struggles* 412 It cum to us onexpected, like a clap uv thunder from a clear sky).

17. Oh, I gin him thunder and lightnin' stewed down to a strong pison, I tell you (45 Hooper *Simon* 36). Cf. DA Thunder 2 b (to give particular thunder).

18. It's my own nose, and I'll pick

thunder out of it (65 Derby *Squibob* 31).

19. [Lawyers] play thunder with lives and property trusted to 'em (58 Hammett *Piney* 171).

20. You folks air raisin thunder with this grate country (62 Browne *Artemus* 63). Whiting *Devil* 247:13.

Thunderbolt. Jist streaked it off like a greased thunderbolt (40 Haliburton *Clockmaker* III 240). Cf. Lightning (14, 15).

Thunder cloud, 1. An' you may look as black as a thunder-cloud, if you please (28 Neal *Rachel* 210; Fairfield *Letters* 93; Haliburton *Clockmaker* I 188; Melville *Israel* 145; Stephens *Mary Derwent* 292). A. M. Chase *Twenty Minutes to Kill* (1936) 5.

2. He looked as cross as a thunder cloud (33 Smith *Downing* 209).

3. Surly-looking as a thunder-cloud (57 Melville *Confidence-Man* 164–165).

4. Gloom about like a thunder-cloud (53 Curtis *Potiphar* 102). Svartengren 58.

Thunder-gust. Away they went like a thunder-gust (34 Crockett *Life* 177; Anon. *New Hope* 226 He come at me like a thunder-gust through the bushes).

Thunder-squall. The cook, who, seein's turnin' blue wasn't in his line, no how, looked blacker than a thunder-squall off Hatteras (58 Hammett *Piney* 136). Cf. Svartengren 58.

Thunder-storm. Mr. Potiphar looked like a thunder-storm (53 Curtis *Potiphar* 198). Svartengren 58. Cf. Diplomat [J. F. Carter] *Death in the Senate* (1933) 126 as black as.

Tick, 1. As full as a tick. 22 DA Tick 2 b; Apperson 241; NC 486; Taylor *Comparisons* 42–43; Tilley T281.

2. Simon Suggs will allers be found sticking thar, like a tick onder a cow's belly (45 Hooper *Simon* 65). Cf. Bartlett 809; Figh PADS XIII (1950) 14; NC 486.

Ticket. Thet's the ticket (48 Lowell *Biglow* 79, 383; Kelly *Humors* 81 Champagne and turtle, that's the ticket; Hammett *Piney* 134; Bowman *Bear-Hunters* 383). Farmer and Henley VII 119; Stevenson 2317:1; NQ 2 iii 407; 7 i 409, 494; R. S. Surtees *Mr. Sponge's Sporting Tour* (London [1853]) 8 only to a young gemman, you know, it's well to have 'em [horses] smart, and the ticket, in short; W. M. Thackeray *The Newcomes* (1853–1855, ed. London 1926) 76 only she's not—she's not the ticket, you see; E. M. Rhodes *West Is West* (1917) 193 You're the ticket, gov'nor; P. B. Kyne *Tide of Empire* (1928) 121, 291; Barnaby Ross, pseud. *The Tragedy of Y* (1932) 40; J. P. Marquand *So Little Time* (Boston 1943) 156.

Tickle, 1. Tickle me, Davy, tickle me true, And in my turn, I'll tickle you too (35 Crockett *Account* 166; Curtis *Potiphar* 145 "You tickle me and I'll tickle you; but, at all events, you tickle me," is the motto of the crowd, 153 You tickle, and I'll tickle, and we'll all tickle, and here we go round—round-roundy!). Cf. Apperson 100 Claw, 337 Ka', 554 Scratch; Bradley 95; Oxford 96, 329, 567; Stevenson 2317:3; Tilley C405, K1.

2. They stopped as if they were tickled to death to see her (44 Stephens *High Life* I 106, 141, II 1, 6; Kelly *Humors* 82). NED Death 12 b;

Stevenson 2317:4; Mary N. Murfree [Charles Egbert Craddock, pseud.] *The Mystery of Witch-Face Mountain* (Boston 1895) 206.

3. See Puppy (2), Sixpence (1), Trout (1).

Tide, 1. I think the tide is turning (59 Smith *My Thirty* 311). Cf. Stevenson 126:10.

2. Finding the tide all against him (59 Smith *My Thirty* 309).

Tidings. Good tidings, like bad, seldom come alone (65 Richardson *Secret* 376).

Tie. See Hog (15).

Tiger, 1. He looks as fierce as a tiger (36 Haliburton *Clockmaker* I 136, *Attaché* IV 30; Smith *Letters* 93, *'Way* 261 barking as fierce as a tiger; Stephens *Mary Derwent* 348). NC 486; Svartengren 92.

2. As resolute as a tiger (34 Crockett *Life* 38).

3. Feeling as streaked as a tiger in the show [i. e., embarrassed]. (44 Stephens *High Life* II 232).

4. As wild and fierce as a tiger (42 Irving *Attorney* 139). Cf. Svartengren 92 furious.

5. To buck the tiger [i. e., to gamble]. 59 DA Buck 1 b; NED Tiger 9 a; Stevenson 250:5.

6. Hev you never fit the tiger? [i. e., gambled for high stakes]. (65 Sedley *Marian* 180). DA Tiger 2 c.

7. He . . . will fight like a tiger (36 Fairfield *Letters* 74; Haliburton *Attaché* I 160 and fit like a tiger; Melville *Omoo* 355 fought, *White Jacket* 476; Smith *My Thirty* 275; Richardson *Beyond* 67). Boshears 32:176; Halpert 108; NC 486; Arthur Gask *Murder in the Night* (1932) 38.

8. He leaped upon his prey like a tiger among sheep (54 Smith *'Way* 49).

9. His face spotted like a he-tiger (55 Thomson *Doesticks* 52).

10. My son John sprung like a young tiger (39 Smith *Letters* 70).

11. I've sweat like a tiger (59 Smith *My Thirty* 376).

Tight. See Bark 1 (3), Bladder, Bottle (3), Devil (7), Drum (3), Drumhead, Peep (2), Periagua, Skin (1, 2), Wax (3).

Tigress. Looking as savage as a Bengal tigress (45 Hooper *Simon* 109).

Timber, 1. After this outbreak he must "break for tall timber" (43 Robb *Squatter* 36; Hall *Purchase* I 193 make tracks for the tall timber; Bennett *Border* 435 we put out for tall timber). Bartlett 777; DA Timber 3; Schele de Vere 185.

2. He's made out on straight-grained timber (55 Anon. *New Hope* 343).

Timber-head. Dead as a timber-head (49 Melville *Redburn* 316). Babcock 263.

Time, 1. Any time is no time (71 Jones *Batkins* 399). See Anything.

2. In less than no time (44 Stephens *High Life* I 139, 163; Hooper *Simon* 88; Stowe *Uncle* 25; Porter *Major* 58).

3. No time so good as the present (23 Cooper *Pioneers* 329). Apperson 455; *Oxford* 659–660; Stevenson 1874:11; Tilley T310; Charles Barry, pseud. *Death of a First Mate* (1935) 195.

4. No time to swap knives [i. e., no time to change plans]. 71 DA Swap 2 (3). See Horse (18).

5. Time and tide wait for no man (23 Cooper *Pioneers* 293; Neal *Broth-*

er J II 36; Clemens *Innocents* II 116 And time will wait for none). Apperson 634; NC 486; *Oxford* 658; Stevenson 2322:12; Tilley T323 tarry; Sir Walter Scott *Rob Roy* (1818) II c. 5 wait; Andy Adams *The Ranch on the Beaver* (Boston 1927) 199 waited; Phoebe A. Taylor *The Mystery of the Cape Cod Tavern* (1934) 261.

6. The third time the score shall be cleared (27 Cooper *Prairie* 160; Dana *Two* 400 and the third time, he said, never failed; Saxe *Poems* 65 "Once more, my gallant boys!" he cried; "*Three times!*—you know the fable"). Apperson 626; *Oxford* 651; Stevenson 1484:2, 2312:2; Tilley T319; Whiting *Scots* II 142; R. S. Surtees *Plain or Ringlets?* (London [1860]) 288 Third time's catching [in a foxhunt], 345; Colver Harris *Murder in Amber* (1938) 65 the third time never fails; J. R. R. Tolkien *The Hobbit* (Boston 1938) 218 the third time pays for all; Mary Lee Settle *Harper's Magazine* CCXI (Sept. 1955) 77, 78.

7. There is a time for all things (60 Haliburton *Season-Ticket* 12, 61 for all things in natur'; Barnum *Struggles* 485 having a time and place for every thing). Apperson 192, 634; NC 486; *Oxford* 659; Stevenson 2329:1 a time and place for everything; Tilley T314; J. P. Marquand *Melville Goodwin, USA* (Boston 1951) 147 a time and place for everything.

8. But . . . to everything there is a time and a judgment (50 Judd *Richard* 350).

9. But time and chance happen to all men (59 Smith *My Thirty* 401). Apperson 634.

10. "Tempus fugit"—and we fly with it (45 Fairfield *Letters* 358; Haliburton *Old Judge* II 98 Time flies, *Season-Ticket* 104 Time flies, but mon-

ey makes wings to itself, and flies faster; Sedley *Marian* 171, 362). Apperson 634; NC 487; *Oxford* 659; Smith *Browning* 224; Stevenson 2323:2; Tilley T327; Gilbert Collins *Death Meets the King's Messenger* (1934) 260.

11. Time hath tales to tell (49 Melville *Mardi* II 260; Haliburton *Season-Ticket* 326 Time will tell tales). Cf. NC 487 Time will tell; Tilley T333 Time discloseth all things; Whiting *Drama* 237 Time the thinge shall trye; Charles Reade *Hard Cash* (1863, London 1913) 90 Time will show, *A Simpleton* (1878, London 1907) 214 show; E. M. Rhodes *West Is West* (1917) 87 show.

12. You must remember that time is money (23 Cooper *Pioneers* 156; Haliburton *Attaché* I 136, *Sam* I 167, II 146; Hammett *Stray* 214; Shillaber *Mrs. Partington* 136; Durivage *Three* 297 Time precious—money [old saw]; Melville "I and My Chimney" in *Works* XIII 308 with a business man; Bowman *Bear-Hunters* 149; Augustin Daly *The Big Bonanza* 200; Saxe *Poems* 398 That "Time is Money" prudent Franklin shows; Clemens *Gilded* II 112). Apperson 634; Bradley 94; Lean IV 163; *Oxford* 659; Stevenson 2318:8; Stoett 647; NQ 4 ii 37, 115, iii 162; R. A. J. Walling *The Corpse with the Dirty Face* (1936) 28; E. S. Gardner (A. A. Fair, pseud.) *Top of the Heap* (1952) 63.

13. Time is precious (35 Kennedy *Horse-Shoe* 306; Durivage *Three* 297 Time precious—money—[old saw]). Tilley N302; Whiting *Scots* II 142; Brian Flynn *The Case of the Black Twenty-two* (Philadelphia 1929) 158.

14. Time, which at last makes all things even (65 Richardson *Secret* 209, *Beyond* 28 But time at last makes all things even).

15. We'll leaf time to show t'e trut (45 Cooper *Chainbearer* 375; Susan Sedgwick *Walter Thornley* [1859] 423 Well, well, time will show). Tilley T324. Cf. Apperson 635; *Oxford* 659; Whiting *Drama* 40, 113.

16. Time truly works wonders (49 Melville *Mardi* I 314; Kelly *Humors* 87; Jones *Batkins* 321 Time and patience work wonders). *Oxford* 660; Stevenson 2329:4.

17. That beats my time all holler! (71 Eggleston *School-Master* 85; Harris *Uncle Remus* 73 Well, ef dis don't bang my times). DA Beat 3 (2); McAtee *Additional* 6.

18. When I desire to speak of the various beauties of this feathered pledge of friendship, language can't come to time (55 Thomson *Doesticks* 248). Schele de Vere 592.

19. Ware propaty growed up like time [i. e., rapidly]. (48 Lowell *Biglow* 120). Cf. DAE Time 10.

20. If you want to know the time of day, here's the boy that can tell ye [i. e., to know what's what]. (54 Smith *'Way* 56). Farmer and Henley VII 128.

21. Yes, you see, Andy, Missis wants to make time [i. e., delay]. (51 Stowe *Uncle* 51). Cf. DA Make 9 (3) to make time (to cover a distance rapidly).

22. And fell to eating rapidly, as if he wished to make up for lost time (58 Porter *Major* 176).

23. To have l'arnt to take time by the forelock (45 Cooper *Chainbearer* 366, 430 It's always pest to "take time py t'e forelock," t'ey say; Hawthorne *Mosses* 549 Father Time, together with the old gentleman's gray forelock; Shillaber *Mrs. Partington* 183 I'll take Time by the foretop, as Solomon says; Jones *Wild* 209; Alcott *Lit-*

tle Women 114 I will try to take time by the fetlock, 117 Now, as there's nothing like "taking time by the fetlock," as Winkle characteristically observes, 484; Barnum *Struggles* 521). Apperson 635; NED Forehead 1 c, Forelock 2; *Oxford* 658–659; Stevenson 2324:3; Taylor *Investigations* 264; Tilley T311; Whiting *Drama* 166, cf. *Scots* II 142; S. L. Bradbury *Hiram Harding of Hardscrabble* (Rutland, Vt. 1936) 206.

Timid. See Fawn (4).

Tin-horn. Clear an' loud es a tin-ho'n (67 Harris *Sut* 250). Cf. NC 426.

Tinker. I didn't care a tinker's cus (44 Thompson *Major* 78; Riley *Puddleford* 101 Not that I care any thing about the office itself, for I don't, a tinker's ladle). Apperson 456:6, 458; NC 487; NED Tinker 1 d; NQ 8 xi 345, 452, 496; Anthony Gilbert, pseud. *The Murder of Mrs. Davenport* (1928) 232. Cf. Stevenson 2332:5 tinker's dam.

Tired. See Death (19), Dog (19), Team (1).

Tit, 1. Tit for tat (38 Haliburton *Clockmaker* II 227, *Letter* 104, *Attaché* II 103; Emerson *Works* II 109; Hall *Purchase* II 290; Melville *Redburn* 61; Jones *Wild* 241). Apperson 635; Farmer and Henley VII 138; NC 497; NED Tit 1; *Oxford* 661; Stevenson 2332–2333:7; Tilley T336; NQ 2 v 247; Arthur Train *The Adventures of Ephraim Tutt* (1930) 585.

2. Hit or miss, right or wrong, tit or no tit, that's the tatur (40 Haliburton *Clockmaker* III 248, 298 Tit or no tit, that's the tatur).

Toad, 1. I can hide you where you will be as safe as a toad in a rock (57

P. H. Myers *Thrilling Adventures of the Prisoner of the Border* [1860] 169).

2. Mrs. Perkins . . . saluted the "calfskin" as a toad catches flies—so quick that few saw the operation (43 Thompson *Chronicles* 119).

3. They were as thick as toads arter a rain (36 Haliburton *Clockmaker* I 207, III 91–92 arter a rain storm; Stephens *High Life* I 216 arter a rain storm).

4. You will be one of the "biggest toads in the puddle" (71 Jones *Batkins* 150). Bartlett 42; Farmer 53; Hardie 466:2 frog; McAtee *Grant County* 10; Thornton I 62, III 26; E. S. Gardner *The D. A. Calls It Murder* (1937) 228 a big toad in a small puddle.

5. No more of a branch, I wow, than a toad wants a tail, as the nigger said (25 Neal *Brother J* II 26, 37 "Man is born to trouble, as the sparks fly upward."—"As a toad wants a tail," quoth Jotty, *Down-Easters* II 40 no more 'n a toad wants a tail, ebbery bit an' grain; Smith *Downing* 23 he was as different from father as a toad wants a tail, 110 buying what they didn't want, more than a toad wants two tails, *My Thirty* 405 the Union isn't the organ of the Government, any more than a toad wants a tail, every bit and grain). Cf. Bartlett 809; Svartengren 337 toad with a side pocket; NQ 4 xii 385, 435; 5 i 18. See Cat (53).

6. A prententious hotel, "squat like a toad" (50 Willis *Life* 200).

7. Without swellin like a toad to outshine the British (44 Stephens *High Life* II 83). Apperson 614; *Oxford* 636; Tilley T362. Cf. Taylor *Comparisons* 65; Whiting *Scots* II 142.

8. Always "under the harrow" (69 Barnum *Struggles* 485; Jones *Batkins* 369 You have heard of the toad under the harrow). Apperson 636; Bartlett 809; NED Toad 1 c; *Oxford* 661; Randolph and Wilson 178; Stevenson 2324:3; Tilley F764; J. J. Connington, pseud. *The Boathouse Riddle* (Boston 1931) 251 another poor devil under the harrow; Talbot Mundy *Tros of Samothrace* (1934) 297 he felt himself a toad beneath the harrow of misfortune; NQ 4 xii 126, 339, 437; 5 i 16; 7 xii 260; 8 xi 367.

9. I don't care a toad's blessing (c60 Paul *Courtship* 195).

10. See Hop-toads, Knee-high.

Toadstool. That made things rise in value, like a toad stool in a hot night (44 Stephens *High Life* I 139).

Toast. Every thing nice and warm as toast (55 Stephens *Homestead* 16). Apperson 315; NC 487; Taylor *Comparisons* 84; Tilley T363.

Tobacco, 1. And somehow my teeth looked as yaller as if I'd been chawing tobacco a hull week (44 Stephens *High Life* I 68).

2. And besides I've got a sorter notion that it's allers best for every man to chaw his own tobakker (58 Hammett *Piney* 59, 63 ef he didn't make the passengers on his flat chaw their own tobakker, hit's no matter, 71). Figh PADS XIII (1950) 12.

Toe, 1. The toe that's tramped on feels most (35 Crockett *Account* 89).

2. Trod on the toes of the Brokers (34 Davis *Downing* 101, 181 if I have trod on any one's toes; Haliburton *Season-Ticket* 9 they don't see other folks' toes they are for ever a-treadin' on; Clift *Bunker* 128 felt his toes trodden upon a little). Farmer and Hen-

ley VII 197; NED Toe 5 i, Tread 4 b. Cf. Tilley T373.

Toe-nails. She wer gal all over, from the pint ove her toe-nails tu the aind ove the longes' har on the highis knob on her head (67 Harris *Sut* 78). Cf. Tilley C864, T436. See Top 1 (1).

Toil, sb. It has been an apothegm these five thousand years, that toil sweetens the bread it earns (54 Hawthorne *Mosses* 22).

Toil, vb. See Slave.

Tom. Loaned out to Tom, Dick, or Harry (35 Crockett *Account* 171; Nash *Charcoal* 116 an emacerated, every-day, threadbare cognomen—a Tom, Dick, and Harry denomination; Stowe *Uncle* 8 sold to Tom, Dick, and the Lord knows who; Melville *Pierre* 355 with Tom, Dick, and Harry; Haliburton *Sam* II 104 and Harry, *Season-Ticket* 226 or Harry; Whitcher *Widow* 92 and Harry; Clemens *Letters* I 90, 372 and Harry; Alcott *Little Women* 529 overrun with Toms, Dicks, and Harrys!). Apperson 637; Farmer and Henley VII 151; NED Tom 1 a; Stevenson 2338:1; Tilley T376; NQ 6 xi 487; 8 vi 244; CLI (1926) 460; W. M. Thackeray *The Newcomes* (1853–1855, London 1926) 429 He took an interest in the affairs of Jack, Tom, and Harry around him; Helen Ashton *Doctor Serocold* (1930) 103; Margery Allingham *Death of a Ghost* (1934) 16 or Harry; John Dos Passos *The Big Money* (1936) 111; H. R. Patch *On Rereading Chaucer* (Cambridge, Mass. 1939) 257 Chaucer . . . loves the individual Tom and Dick and Harry.

Tom Cox. Every man who has been three months at sea knows how to "work Tom Cox's traverse,"—"three turns round the long-boat, and a pull at the scuttled butt" (40 Dana *Two* 90; Melville *White Jacket* 388 Can't a feller be workin' here, without being 'spected of Tom Coxe's traverse, up one ladder and down t'other). Babcock 263; Joanna C. Colcord *Sea Language Comes Ashore* (1945) 194.

Tom Haynes. That's sufficient, as Tom Haynes said when he saw the elephant (35 Longstreet *Georgia* 10). See Elephant (2).

Tom Walker. They always would have their way in spite of every body and Tom Walker besides (33 Smith *Downing* 139). Cf. Boshears 36:503.

Tomahawk. [He] buried the tomahawk (28 Neal *Rachel* 152). NED Tomahawk 2.

Tomb. It's as dull as tombs here (68 Alcott *Little Women* 54).

Tombstone, 1. As cold as a tomb stone (44 Stephens *High Life* II 187). Cf. NC 487.
2. His face all the while as rigid as a tomb-stone (57 Riley *Puddleford* 148).
3. She is not . . . as solemn as a tombstone (36 Fairfield *Letters* 70).
4. The critter was as white as a tomb stun (44 Stephens *High Life* II 218).

To-morrow. Leave nothing for tomorrow which can be done to-day (c50 Lincoln II 81; Boucicault *Flying Scud* 220 Yes, it's a hold saying, and a true one . . . "Never put off till today, what you can do tomorrow"). Apperson 517; NC 487–488; *Oxford* 526; Stevenson 2340:6; Tilley T378; Julian Duguid *Green Hell* (1931) 256 Allard put off to-day what he could do to-morrow; Georgette Heyer *They Found Him Dead* (1937) 144.

Tongs. See Pair (2).

Tongue, 1. Your'n [tongue] is hung in the middle and runs at both ends (56 Cary *Married* 293; Clemens *Roughing* I 241 A tongue hung in the middle). NC 488; Sidney Williams *The Aconite Murders* (1936) 139; Blanche C. Clough *Grandma Spins Down-East Yarns* (Portland, Me., 1953) 50 Jane's tongue was hung in the middle and moved both ways, 118.

2. But a still tongue is a wise one (39 Briggs *Harry* II 137). *Oxford* 621; Stevenson 2345:1; Tilley T401; C. F. Gregg *Inspector Higgins Sees It Through* (1934) 103 a still tongue shows a wise head.

Tony, 1. And showed him whar Tony hid the wadge [i. e., worsted him]. (59 Taliaferro *Fisher's* 118).

2. I can lick the whole possercommertatus of yer afore you can say Toney Lumpkins three times (59 Taliaferro *Fisher's* 36). Cf. Jack (3).

Tool, 1. Edged tools ain't the safest things in the world to play with (60 Haliburton *Season-Ticket* 342). Apperson 179; NED Edge-tool 2; *Oxford* 325; Stevenson 2350:5; Tilley J45; Whiting *Drama* 122, cf. 118, 119; Mrs. Baillie Reynolds *Very Private Secretary* (1933) 300.

2. Edged tools never wound thee when thee is used to them (55 Haliburton *Nature* I 226).

Tooth, 1. But if he is too late, or too soon, it is like drawing teeth (40 Dana *Two* 232; Jones *Batkins* 66 It was like pulling out my teeth to take as much from my stock of money). Cf. McAtee *Grant County* 8; Taylor *Comparisons* 81; Tilley M1097.

2. It's a little hard to have one's misfortunes cast in his teeth (35 Kennedy *Horse-Shoe* 56). NED Cast 65; *Oxford* 81; Stevenson 2353:1; Tilley T429.

3. In spite of my teeth (25 Neal *Brother J* II 181; Haliburton *Clockmaker* II 221 your, III 225 his; Melville *Typee* 239 and eat them in spite of its teeth). Apperson 597; NED Tooth 5; Stevenson 2353:2; Tilley S764; Whiting *Drama* 367:904, *Scots* II 144.

4. That leetle squalling youngen of hern, that was so cross it's teeth couldn't cut straight, but stuck out, catecornering, all round its gums (44 Stephens *High Life* I 46).

5. We've got a sweet tooth (38 Haliburton *Clockmaker* II 320; Shillaber *Mrs. Partington* 213 I have heard of people's having a sweet tooth, but I verily believe the whole of my boy's— he has but four—are all sweet). Bartlett 686; Bradley PADS XIV (1950) 66; Green 377; NED Sweet C 1, Tooth 2 a; *Oxford* 636; Stevenson 2352:4; Tilley T420.

6. That cut their wisdom teeth as soon as they were born (35 Crockett *Account* 67). NC 488.

7. I have a tooth agin the fellow [i. e., a grudge]. (69 Boucicault *Presumptive* 251–252.

8. I've told him, to his teeth (25 Neal *Brother J* II 220, *Down-Easters* I 108, 161). NED Tooth 6 b; Whiting *Drama* 367:904.

9. Tooth and nail (33 Smith *Downing* 95 follow him up, 117 fighting against it, *Letters* 46 flies right in her face, *My Thirty* 370 fight agin him, 386 oppose the nomination, 448 fit agin us; Crockett *Exploits* 91 hang on; Haliburton *Clockmaker* I 229 a drivin away at each other, the whole blessed

time, tooth and nail, hip and thigh, hammer and tongs, 233, II 96; Stephens *High Life* I 69 went at my hair, II 100 made up my mind, 110 went to storming a hull regiment; Melville *Redburn* 146 hung on with; Thomson *Plu-ri-bus-tah* 188 Tooth and nail, was fighting, scratching, For some property she claimed there; Lincoln II 16 go to work). Apperson 641; Farmer and Henley VII 160–161; NED Tooth 7; *Oxford* 200 Fight; Stevenson 2252–2253:11; Stoett 790; Tilley T422; Whiting *Drama* 367:905, *Scots* II 144; E. D. Biggers *Keeper of the Keys* (Indianapolis 1932) 119 battle.

10. Go agin King Alkohol tooth and toe nail (44 Thompson *Major* 59, 189 I go for Mr. Clay, tooth and toe nail [i. e., support]; Hammett *Piney* 116 father went agin it). McAtee 67; NED Tooth 7; M. J. Freeman *The Murder of a Midget* (1931) 63. Cf. McAtee *Grant County* 6.

11. See Hen (7).

Toothache. He hangs on like a toothache (34 Davis *Downing* 280).

Top (1), 1. From top to toe (44 Stephens *High Life* II 192; Hooper *Simon* 77 from the top of your head to the end of your big toe nail; Cartwright *Autobiography* 48). Lean II ii 936; NED Top 25; Smith *Browning* 221; Stevenson 1096:2; Tilley T436. See Toe-nails.

2. I should always get to the top of the ladder (33 Smith *Downing* 27, 219; Stephens *High Life* I 124 if Cherry street aint at the top of the mark afore many weeks, it'll be because I move my office out on it, 241 It'll be the top of the notch). Cf. DA Top 2 b (top of the heap); Stevenson 1689:7 up to the last notch.

Top (2), 1. Her head danc'd round like a top (57 Riley *Puddleford* 306).

2. Sleeps, like a top (25 Neal *Brother J* II 341; Hammett *Stray* 153; Durivage *Three* 187, 189). Apperson 577; Hardie 471:168; NED Sleep B 1 e, Top² 1 b; Svartengren 168; Tilley T440; NQ 3 xii 345, 421; J. J. Farjeon *Sinister Inn* (1934) 134 the proverbial.

3. With his head spinning like a top (32 Kennedy *Swallow* 241; Taliaferro *Fisher's* 117 My heart was a spinnin' round like a top). Boshears 33:273; Halpert 160; NC 488.

4. The yards swing round like a top (40 Dana *Two* 232).

5. My head began to whirl round like a top [i. e., drunk]. (44 Stephens *High Life* II 111).

Tophet. Jake feels as cross as Tophet (68 Clift *Bunker* 104). Cf. Taylor *Comparisons* 50 hot.

Topmast, 1. As long as a spare topmast (40 Dana *Two* 377).

2. The tail stood straight as a topmast (54 Shillaber *Mrs. Partington* 258).

Tortoise. They are as contented as tortoises, *ici-bas* (53 Willis *Fun* 289).

Touch. 'Twas just touch and go whether any on us came out alive (65 Sedley *Marian* 94). Farmer and Henley VII 179; NED Touch and go.

Touchy. See Horse (12).

Tough. See Buffalo (1), Catamount (4), Gristle, Halter, Hickory (1), Laushong, Nature (1), Pepperidge log, Porcupine, Sole leather (2), Whitleather, Wire (1).

Tow, 1. But the early Westerners were as inflammable as tow (74 Eggleston *Circuit* 104).

2. Does his hair grow and is it as white as tow? (44 Fairfield *Letters* 317).

Tower. A "tower of strength" in almost every law case (43 Thompson *Chronicles* 134). Stevenson 2355:7. Cf. Whiting *Scots* II 144.

Tow string. It [law] ain't worth a tow string (c58 Stephens *Mary Derwent* 298).

Town, 1. An' when . . . Jeff . . . comes to pick his nobles out, *wun't* this child be in town [i. e., in a favored situation]! (62 Lowell *Biglow* 284).

2. See Paint vb. (1).

Traces. Sich fellers may kick in the traces when you goad 'em a leetle with the truth (44 Stephens *High Life* II 174; Boucicault *Flying Scud* 179 kicking over the traces, 184 kick over the traces). Farmer and Henley IV 98; NED Kick 1 c; *Oxford* 334; Stevenson 1293:7. Cf. DA Trace, n.[3]

Track, 1. I suppose you got off the track in your dream (57 Jones *Country* 19; Shillaber *Knitting-Work* 191 You are off o' the track—miles out of the way; Locke [Nasby] *Struggles* 314 His Highness wuz completely turned off the track). Schele de Vere 360; Stevenson 2356:9. Cf. DA Track 2 d (5).

2. I'll die in my tracks fust! (45 Hooper *Simon* 129; Porter *Major* 201; Eggleston *School-Master* 144, 162). DA Track 2 b (3); Stevenson 2356:7; Thornton III 408.

3. That derned fool flew the track after I had got a good hand (51 Burke *Polly* 47). DA Track 2 c (4).

4. To have the inside track. 57 DA Inside track.

5. Make tracks for the sloop agin (44 Stephens *High Life* I 26, 49–50, 141; Willis *Life* 372–373 we . . . "made tracks," as the hunters say, for our destination; Stowe *Uncle* 49; Jones *Wild* 133; Hammett *Piney* 215 dog on ef I ain't fer makin' tracks outer the tall timber right piert; Porter *Major* 45). Bartlett 381; NED Track 9; Schele de Vere 360; Stevenson 2356: 7; Thornton II 570; Tidwell PADS XI (1949) 15; Wilson 602.

6. He had entirely yielded the track to his formidable rival (58 Field *Pokerville* 41).

7. See Bear (15), Wolf (10).

Trade, 1. A trade's a trade, ye know (58 Hammett *Piney* 262, 264, 265). See Bet.

2. We all think, all trades have tricks but our own (43 Haliburton *Attaché* III 288; Bennett *Border* 120 Thar's tricks to all trades 'cept ourn). Bradley 95; Tilley M1345 There is a mystery in the meanest trade; C. B. Clason *The Fifth Tumbler* (1936) 180 tricks to all trades; F. P. Keyes *Dinner at Antoine's* (1948) 330 But there's tricks to all trades; Andy Adams *A Texas Matchmaker* (Boston 1904) 226 Then reminding us that there were "tricks in all trades but ours," *The Ranch on the Beaver* (Boston 1927) 107 Remember there are tricks in all trades but ours, 293. See Roguery.

3. Every man at his trade (66 Bowman *Bear-Hunters* 348). See Man (19).

4. Free trade and sailors' rights is our maxim (38 Haliburton *Clockmaker* II 227; Jones *Batkins* 20 The war, "for sailor's rights and free trade" [i. e., of 1812]).

5. Trade's the spirit of life (45 Cooper *Chainbearer* 250). Cf. Tilley T463.

Trail, 1. Off the trail. 34 DA Trail 4 b (2). Cf. Track (1).

2. On the wrong trail. 33 DA Trail 4 b (1).

Training. True as training (49 Haliburton *Old Judge* II 283).

Transparent. See Crystal (3), Glass (4), Spermaceti.

Trap, 1. I wonder how you'll like being caught in your own trap (66 Boucicault *Flying Scud* 211; Barnum *Struggles* 672 The editor was fairly caught in his own trap). NC 488–489.

2. He "saw through the trap" that was set for him (45 Hooper *Simon* 80).

3. See Mouse trap, Rat trap, Steel trap, Wolf trap.

Traveller, 1. It is as well to remember that a lazy traveller makes a long journey (27 Cooper *Prairie* 96).

2. But stay-at-homes say travellers lie. Yet a voyage to Ethiopia would cure them of that; for few sceptics are travellers; fewer travellers liars, though the proverb respecting them lies (49 Melville *Mardi* I 346). Apperson 643–644; *Oxford* 668–669; Stevenson 2364:1–4; Tilley M567, T476; H. C. Kittredge *Mooncussers of Cape Cod* (Boston 1937) 75 travellers never do lie, though fools at home condemn them.

Tray. You love the old dog Tray (50 Mitchell *Reveries* 164; Richardson *Beyond* 67 a weak young man, who like poor dog Tray had fallen into bad company). Stevenson 605:11. Cf. Taylor *Comparisons* 39.

Treasure. His treasure is there, and his heart also (53 Baldwin *Flush* 73). Matt. 6:21; Stevenson 2367:11; Tilley T485.

Treat. See Dog (56), King (7), Lord 2 (5).

Tree, 1. He had seen the Indians as thick as trees in the wood (34 Crockett *Life* 104).

2. I know of no way but to judge a tree by its fruit (38 Fairfield *Letters* 229; Lincoln I 347 By the fruit the tree is known). Matt. 12:33; Apperson 645; NC 489; *Oxford* 670; Smith *Browning* 226; Stevenson 2370:7; Tilley T497; Whiting *Drama* 109, *Scots* II 144; T. L. Peacock *Crotchet Castle* (1831, *Works* IV [London 1924]) 114 shall be known by its fruit; D. H. Lawrence *Lady Chatterley's Lover* (n. p. 1928) 40.

3. Durable trees make roots first (34 Emerson *Journals* III 247, *Works* I 33 Long-lived trees).

4. I'm up a tree (25 Neal *Brother* J I 112, 177, 318, II 103; Smith *Downing* 57, 237; Haliburton *Clockmaker* I 151, II 16, 295, III 103, 278, *Attaché* III 179, *Season-Ticket* 300). DA Tree 1 d (2); Farmer and Henley VII 198; McAtee 69; NED Tree 7; *Oxford* 669; Schele de Vere 49; Stevenson 2369:5; Thornton II 921; W. C. Brown *Laughing Death* (Philadelphia 1932) 140.

5. But when he was "up the tree," a little sprung or *tight*, as you may say, he was . . . chock full of wolf and brimstone (56 Kelly *Humors* 184). Berrey 106:7.

6. Barking up the wrong tree (32 Hall *Legends* 46, 65; Crockett *Life* 61, 164, *Account* 205 sapling, *Exploits* 20, 89; Davis *Downing* 266; Haliburton *Clockmaker* III 58, 297, *Attaché* III 11–12, IV 244, *Nature* I 273; Anon. *New Hope* 64 Why, Pomp, you ar barking up the wrong tree, or this is no possum; Hammett *Stray* 96, 137, *Piney* 43, 45, 82, 152–153; Shillaber

Mrs. Partington 135). Bartlett 30–31; DA Bark 1; Farmer 39; NC 489; Schele de Vere 49, 186; Stevenson 122:12; Thornton I 43; Woodard PADS VI (1946) 34; Henri Weiner *Crime on the Cuff* (1936) 273.

7. Never clamb a tree, for nothin– arter owls [i. e., go on a wild-goose chase]. (25 Neal *Brother J* I 164).

Tremble. See Aspen (2), Aspen-leaf, Leaf 1 (7).

Trick, 1. And I do not know that it would be a "trick worth an egg" to make any mystery of these two persons (53 Willis *Fun* 116).

2. Every trick is good in war (35 Kennedy *Horse-Shoe* 29).

3. You know a trick worth two of that (40 Haliburton *Letter* 217, *Old Judge* I 36; Durivage *Three* 156). Apperson 645; Farmer and Henley VII 201; NED Trick 12; *Oxford* 670; Stevenson 2373:2; Tilley T518; E. B. Black *The Ravenelle Riddle* (1933) 219. See Two (4).

Trigger, 1. Es easy'z pull a trigger (67 Lowell *Biglow* 280).

2. Your valet there . . . seems as quick on the trigger as his master (53 Willis *Fun* 291; Hammett *Stray* 121 I'm mighty easy on the trigger; Porter *Major* 65). DA Trigger 2; McAtee 51; NED Trigger 3; M. J. Freeman *The Murder of a Midget* (1931) 93.

Trim. See Greyhound (3).

Triumph. See Mind.

Trivet, 1. It'll put you as right as a trivet (66 Boucicault *Flying Scud* 201; Shillaber *Ike* 137). Apperson 531; Farmer and Henley VII 208; Green 30 tribet, 305; NED Trivet 3; *Oxford* 543; Stevenson 1990:8; Svartengren

369–370; Stuart Palmer *The Puzzle of the Red Stallion* (1936) 73.

2. True as a trivet (43 Haliburton *Attaché* II 10).

Trojan. Sleep . . . like a Trojan (35 Kennedy *Horse-Shoe* 344; Mitchell *Reveries* 169 study like a Trojan; Kelly *Humors* 89 I'll off coat and go work like; Clemens *Enterprise* 85 worked like). Farmer and Henley VII 208; NC 489; NED Trojan 2 b; Stevenson 2379:3; Svartengren 123; Taylor *Investigations* 264. Cf. Green 402.

Trooper. "Does he swear?" "Yes–like a trooper" (25 Neal *Brother J* III 276; Kennedy *Swallow* 223 added to his trooper-like accomplishment of swearing till he made people's hair stand on end; Haliburton *Attaché* III 27; Melville *Omoo* 89; Jones *Country* 129; Kelly *Humors* 134 cursing aloud in his grief–like a trooper, 311; Stephens *Mary Derwent* 194; Paul *Courtship* 186; Wiley *Billy* 102; Browne *Artemus* 183 like an infooriated trooper; Barnum *Struggles* 221). Apperson 613; McAtee 63; NC 489; NED Trooper 1 b; *Oxford* 635; Stevenson 2255–2256: 13; Svartengren 109; Lilian Bamburg *Beads of Silence* (1927) 93.

Trooper's horse. To turn in like a trooper's horse is to go to bed all standing, ready for a sudden call–parade order–winter uniform–full dress (37 Neal *Charcoal* 205–206). Cf. NED Trooper 1 b You will die the death of a trooper's horse, that is "with your shoes on" [i. e., be hanged].

Trouble. You're allers bor'ring trouble (57 Riley *Puddleford* 119; Clemens *Washoe* 39). NC 489; Wilson 522; J. H. Wallis *Murder Mansion* (1934) 138.

Trough. Walk up to the trough, fodder or no fodder, as the man said to his donkey (71 Eggleston *School-Master* 76). DA Trough 1. See Fodder (2, 3), Rack (1, 2).

Trousers. As streaked as a pair of old cotton trousers in washing time [i. e., embarrassed]. (44 Stephens *High Life* II 169).

Trout, 1. As tickled as so many trout round a bait (44 Stephens *High Life* II 170).
2. [Courtesy] like a speckled trout diving in a brook, jest enough to give a curve to the water and no more (44 Stephens *High Life* II 29).
3. Off she was a going like a trout with a fish-hook in his mouth (44 Stephens *High Life* II 66).
4. Easy, jest like a trout sailin along the bottom of a brook (44 Stephens *High Life* II 246).
5. I . . . feel as the fellah did when he missed catchin' the trout (60 Holmes *Professor* 170).

True. See Alive (5), Blue (3), Book (3), Bud (1), Creature, Death (20), Earth, Fate (4), Genesis, Gospel (2), Gun (4), Hair (4), Holy Writ, Live (3), Matthew, Nature (2), Needle (1), Paddy (1), Plumb line, Preaching (5), Print (3), Rates (2), Scriptures, Sinner (3), Sit (2), Stand (2), Star (4), Steel (7), Sun (8), Thunder (12), Training, Trivet (2), Woman (13), World (3).

Trumps, 1. When sense is trumps, why I can lead off with an ace, if I like (60 Haliburton *Season-Ticket* 61).
2. Brown is often put to his trumps (c56 Thomson *Elephant Club* 307; Barnum *Struggles* 576 often "put me to my trumps" for an excuse). Ap-

person 648; Farmer and Henley VII 216; Green 32; NED Trump 2 c; *Oxford* 526; Stevenson 2381:9; Tilley T545.

Trust, 1. Put not your trust in money, but put your money in trust (58 Holmes *Autocrat* 49).
2. There is an old sayin', "Put not your trust in Princes" (43 Haliburton *Attaché* IV 7). Ps. 146:3; *Oxford* 525; Stevenson 1886:6.

Truth, 1. As the saying is, you understand, there is "more truth than poetry" in the principle (71 Jones *Batkins* 256). Hardie 470:141; Louis Paul *A Horse in Arizona* (1936) 3.
2. Tell the truth and . . . shame the devil (25 Neal *Brother J* II 294; Haliburton *Season-Ticket* 237 speak truth and shame the devil; Emerson Bennett *Viola; or, Adventures in the South-West* [Philadelphia (1862)] 182 Speak the truth and shame the Father of Lies). Apperson 649; Bradley 95; NED Shame 4 d; *Oxford* 646; Smith *Browning* 222; Stevenson 2389–2390:15; Tilley T566; Whiting *Devil* 209–210; Anthony Abbot, pseud. *About the Murder of the Night Club Lady* (1931) 255; F. P. Keyes *Dinner at Antoine's* (1948) 332 Tell de troof an' shame de debbil, lak de preacher say.
3. The truth is not to be spoken at all times (36 Crockett *Exploits* 114; Haliburton *Old Judge* II 98 It don't do to tell the truth at all times, that's a fact). Apperson 650; *Oxford* 9; Stevenson 2393:8; Tilley T594; Whiting *Drama* 84, 212.
4. Truth is a jewel (35 Crockett *Account* 232). Cf. *Astounding Science Fiction* (June 1948) 17 "Truth is a jewel with many facets," defined Prince Gautama.

5. The old adage, that "truth is strange, stranger than fiction" (45 Mayo *Kaloolah* 67; Shillaber *Knitting-Work* 279 Truth is stranger than fiction; Jones *Batkins* 416 the old adage). Apperson 650; Bradley 74 fact; NC 490; *Oxford* 185; Stevenson 2393: 7; Lord Acton "Inaugural Lecture on the Study of History" in *Essays on Freedom and Power* (Meridian Book 1955) 38 But the neglected truth, stranger than fiction, is that this [repudiation of history] was not the ruin but the renovation of history; Ralph Rodd *The Secret of the Flames* (1929) 301; J. P. Marquand *Melville Goodwin, USA* (Boston 1951) 13 You mean, Gilbert, . . . that truth is stranger than fiction.

6. It is said that truth is to be found in . . . the depths of a well (49 Haliburton *Old Judge* I 102). Apperson 650; *Oxford* 674; Stevenson 2393–2394:10; Tilley T582; W. N. Macartney *Fifty Years a Country Doctor* (1938) 100 there may have been a little truth at the bottom of the well.

7. It is said that truth is to be found in the wine-butt (49 Haliburton *Old Judge* I 102). Apperson 693; *Oxford* 714; Stevenson 2524–2525:3; Tilley W465; Robert Graves *Claudius the God* (1935) 158 the man who made the proverb 'There's truth in wine' must have been pretty well soaked when he made it.

8. The truth will out (33 Neal *Down-Easters* I 150; Emerson *Journals* IV 304; Stephens *High Life* II 242 some time or other; Melville *Confidence-Man* 109). Stevenson 2391:11; Tilley T591; Christopher Bush *The Case of the Chinese Gong* (1935) 34.

9. He quotes the old Persian maxim, and says, they have been taught "to ride, to shoot, and to speak the truth" (20–22 Irving *Bracebridge* 107).

Tub, 1. Well, let every tub stand on its own bottom, I say (54 Shillaber *Mrs. Partington* 78, *Knitting-Work* 301 It used to be the remark of Elder Stick that every tub should stand; Haliburton *Nature* II 119 must stand; Riley *Puddleford* 87 "Every tub orter stand on its own bottom," as the Apostle Paul, Shakspeare, John Bunyan or some other person said; Taliaferro *Carolina Humor* 36 I am very thankful for that consolatory, incomparable and brilliant Scripture which says, "Every tub must stand"; Clift *Bunker* 78 Let every tub stand upon it's own bottom, and when it has none, let it cave in). Apperson 193; Bradley 96; Farmer and Henley VII 220; McAtee 25; NC 490; *Oxford* 675; Stevenson 2397: 4; Tilley T596; NQ CLXXI (1936) 321; Andy Adams *The Ranch on the Beaver* (Boston 1927) 90 Let every tub rest on its own bottom; Herbert Adams *The Golf House Murder* (Philadelphia 1933) 78.

2. Tubs for the whale (49 Haliburton *Old Judge* I 124). Apperson 651; NQ 1 viii 220, 304, 328; *Oxford* 675; Tilley T597.

Tuck. To take the tuck out of. 78 DA Tuck 2.

Tucker. Old Bill got mad as "tucker" (51 Burke *Polly* 164). DA Tucker 1.

Tumble. To take a tumble to. 77 DA Tumble (b).

Tune, 1. To the tune the "Old Cow died of" (53 Haliburton *Sam* I 89, *Season-Ticket* 61 What the plague is the sense of harping for ever on old grievances—it's the tune the Old Cow died of). Apperson 119; Coombs

PADS II (1944) 22; Farmer and Henley VII 227; McAtee 68; NED Tune 2 e; *Oxford* 675; Stevenson 2398:6; NQ 11 xi 248, 309, 443, 501–502; CXCVII (1952) 130, 219, 281.

2. They all on 'em know the old toon, sez he (48 Lowell *Biglow* 94). Stevenson 2398:6.

3. It's a very different tune they sing (38 Haliburton *Clockmaker* II 159). Cf. Farmer and Henley VI 212–213 another song; *Oxford* 592; Stevenson 2398:4; Tilley S637; Rufus King *The Fatal Kiss Mystery* (1928) 162.

4. They began to whistle another tune (25 Neal *Brother J* III 137; Judd *Richard* 198 You will perhaps sing another tune, by and by). NC 490. Cf. Farmer and Henley II 72; NED Tune 4 b.

Turk, 1. He walked out of the room . . . as grand as a Turk (55 Haliburton *Nature* I 145).

2. Prouder 'n the Gran' Turk (67 Lowell *Biglow* 235). Cf. NED Turk 2 c.

3. Fight like a Turk (59 Smith *My Thirty* 264, 298). Green 404. Cf. NC 490; Svartengren 123.

Turkey (1). On the principle, that when a feller is in Turkey, he must do as the Turkeys do; or when they go from Canady to Buffalo, do as the Buffaloes do (43 Haliburton *Attaché* IV 247; Curtis *Potiphar* 141 When you are in Turkey—why, gobble; Willis *Fun* 113 possibly she might be inclined to "do in Turkey as the Turkeys do"). See Frisco, Rome (2).

Turkey (2), 1. Neck and bosom crimson as a strutting gobler's snout (45 Hooper *Simon* 62).

2. Fierce as a turkey gobbler at a red blanket (44 Stephens *High Life* II 203). Cf. Lewis Robinson *The General Goes Too Far* (1936) 106 turkeycock.

3. As hungry as the chap that said a turkey was too much for one 'n' not enough for two (60 Holmes *Professor* 169). Cf. Apperson 265 Goose; *Oxford* 665 Too much.

4. As proud as a lame turkey. 38 DA Turkey 9 (2).

5. As . . . pussy as a turkey-gobbler (44 Stephens *High Life* II 89). Cf. Svartengren 83 proud; Tilley T612.

6. The Frenchman turned as red as a turkey's topping (44 Stephens *High Life* I 40, 98–99 blushed as red as a turkey's comb, II 89 as red . . . as a turkey-gobbler; Willis *Life* 327 Red as a turkey-cock grew the old baronet; Haliburton *Sam* II 91 as red as a turkey-cock). Apperson 526; Boshears 39:860; NC 490; Stoett 752; Svartengren 247.

7. [Girls] as shy as wild turkies (43 Hall *Purchase* II 11).

8. As sneaking as a turkey gobbler ketch'd out in a rain storm (44 Stephens *High Life* II 93).

9. Brimming over with soft sodder, like a darn'd turkey gobbler, stuffed out with Injun meal (44 Stephens *High Life* I 239). Cf. NC 490.

10. Others, who carried lesser sized "turkies" [i. e., were less drunk]. (51 Burke *Polly* 177; Hammett *Piney* 151 got a considerable turkey on, 152 ye don't know what "gittin' a turkey on" means, nor whar it come from, nor how it got there; I'm dog-on ef ye do [a story in explanation follows, pp. 152–158]). Bartlett 724; DA Turkey 9 (3) to catch a turkey; Farmer and Henley VII 229.

11. He . . . won't get a chance to

say turkey to a good-lookin gal to-day
(45 Hooper *Simon* 86). Cf. Bartlett
691; DA Turkey 9 (4 a); Farmer 543;
Farmer and Henley VII 68; NED
Turkey 2 d; Schele de Vere 203;
Thornton II 912, III 412–413.

12. To talk turkey. 30 DA Turkey
9 (1 a). The story is scarcely appo-
site).

13. You "Turkey with a surname!"
Why have you not written to me? (55
Eliason 159).

Turkey-cock. Fierce as a turkey-cock
(55 Langdon *Ida* 145).

Turkey dream. All the while a body
would suppose him to be asleep, or in
a "turkey dream" at least (45 Hooper
Simon 40).

Turn, sb. He did me a good turn
once, and one good turn deserves another (39 Briggs *Harry* I 158; Thompson *Chronicles* 105; Haliburton *Old
Judge* II 41, *Sam* II 2, *Season-Ticket*
359; Baldwin *Flush* 21; Jones *Winkles*
51; Clift *Bunker* 61; Daly *Man* 20;
Nash *Century* 324). Apperson 470–
471; NC 490; NED Turn 23; *Oxford*
257; Stevenson 1401:1; Tilley T616;
Whiting *Scots* II 146; K. S. Cole *I'm
Afraid I'll Live* (Boston 1936) 167.

Turn, vb., 1. And turn and turn about
was fair play (34 Davis *Downing*
275; Stephens *High Life* II 80 it is no
more than the fair thing if we take
turn about; Lincoln I 350 Turn about
is fair play, 352, 353, 359, 361, 365
you then thought a little more favor-
ably of "turn about" than you seem
to now; Haliburton *Sam* I 58 I'll tell
you what is fair, and that is turn and
turn about, *Nature* I 246). Apperson
652; McAtee 68; NC 490; NED Turn
28 d; *Oxford* 676; Stevenson 1806:10,
2399:7; Sir Walter Scott *The Heart*

of Midlothian (1818) ch. 16 time
about's fair play; Harriette Ashbrook
Murder of Sigurd Sharon (1933) 56.

2. See Dog (57).

Turnip. An old silver watch, thick as a
turnip (23–24 Irving *Tales* 291). Cf.
NED Turnip 3 b.

Turnpike. His sermon was as long as
a turnpike (44 Fairfield *Letters* 341).

Turtle, 1. The preachin' didn't do me
much good that day, sartin as a turkle
fallin' off uv a log into a mill-pond (59
Taliaferro *Fisher's* 118–119).

2. As easy and comfortable as a
mud-turtle astraddle of a sawyer (66
Clemens *Washoe* 112).

3. He is as lazy as a land-turtle (35
Kennedy *Horse-Shoe* 168). Cf. NC
490.

4. They nabbed me quick as a
snappin' turkle (59 Taliaferro *Fisher's*
126).

5. Still as a turkle (59 Taliaferro
Fisher's 156).

6. Bite like loggerhead turtles (59
Taliaferro *Fisher's* 198).

7. He made that dodge jis' like a
mud-turkil draps ofen a log when a
big steamboat cums tarin a-pas' (67
Harris *Sut* 83).

8. His anger would hang on to him
like a turkle does to a fisherman's toe
(34 Crockett *Life* 33).

9. Hangs on like a snappin turtle
(34 Davis *Downing* 147; Haliburton
Attaché II 26 by hanging on to it like
a snappin' turtle).

10. Hold on like a snappin turtle
(34 Davis *Downing* 75).

11. Lazying about here like a mud
turtle, nine days after it's killed (45
Judd *Margaret* I 42).

12. I run like a mud turkel (66
Smith *Arp* 129).

13. He . . . knew a snappin' turtle from a snag, without larnin' (43 Robb *Squatter* 64).

14. Jase stuck up his head like a mud turtle in the sun (44 Stephens *High Life* I 162).

Turtle-dove. "Skylarking" . . . as happily together as turtle-doves in a clover-patch (56 Kelly *Humors* 423–424). Magdalen King-Hall *Gay Crusader* (1934) 262 happy as two turtle-doves; Geraint Goodwin *The White Farm* (London 1937) 83 billing and cooing like a turtle dove; Carolyn Wells *The Skeleton at the Feast* (1931) 208 those two turtle-doves.

Tweedledum. It is strange such a difference should be made "between Tweedledum and Tweedledee" (55 Anon. *New Hope* 97; Browne *Artemus* 214 Who said there was no difference 'tween tweedledum and tweedledee?). Farmer and Henley VII 240; NED Tweedledum; *Oxford* 678; Stevenson 2401:5, 6. Cf. Judd *Margaret* II 281–282 Is it not, after all, only a circular race between Tippee and Twaddle? Tippee is now ahead, Twaddle soon overtakes her, Tippee falls behind; so round and round they go; which leads, or which is beaten, who can tell?

Twenty. Like twenty. 39 DA Twenty.

Twig, 1. Jest as the twig is bent the tree's inclined (44 Stephens *High Life* I 54; Melville *Confidence-Man* 195; Locke [Nasby] *Struggles* 74 "Jest ez the twig is bent," et settry; Jones *Batkins* 23, 42 Just as the twig is bent). A. Pope *Moral Essays* (c1730) i, line 150; Bradley 95; Thomas Hood *Poems* (1840, London 1911) 575; Sinclair Lewis *The Man Who Knew Cool-*

idge (1927) 94 as the Good Book says, The tree is inclined as the twig is bent; Robert Carson *The Revels Are Ended* (1936) 33; H. L. Ickes *Diary* (1954) II 253 I told him that at that time [i. e., 1957] the bough would be inclined as the twig had been bent in 1940. Cf. Apperson 38; Stevenson 2371:4–8.

2. If All the Twigs was Pens And the Rivers was ink And I Had the Fingers To use them I Codent Moore Than Describe The Love That I Have for You (59 Taliaferro *Fisher's* 224). Cf. Iona and Peter Opie *The Oxford Dictionary of Nursery Rhymes* (Oxford [1951]) 436–438; Irving Linn "If All the Sky Were Parchment" PMLA LIII (1938) 951–970.

3. Whether that there Rawley had hopped the twig [i. e., die]. (42 Irving *Attorney* 376; Haliburton *Attaché* IV 160 You may get well, or hop the twig, or do what you like). Farmer and Henley III 347; NED Hop 6 a; *Oxford* 303; Partridge 404; Stevenson 507:2.

4. But come, hop the twig [i. e., depart, leave]. (37 Neal *Charcoal* 14). *Oxford* 303; Partridge 404.

Twinkle, sb. I'll be back in a twinkle (c60 Paul *Courtship* 262). NED Twinkle 2.

Twinkle, vb. See Star (7).

Twinkling, 1. Settle this matter in a twinkling (32 Kennedy *Swallow* 243; Melville *Omoo* 116, *Israel* 137, *Confidence-Man* 148; Hawthorne *Twice-Told* 437; Cary *Married* 64; Clemens *Roughing* I 212). NED Twinkling 3 c; Stevenson 2402:5; Tilley T635; Barnaby Ross, pseud. *Drury Lane's Last Case* (1933) 94.

2. In the twinkling of a case-knife

(54 Smith *'Way* 35). Cf. *Oxford* 678 bedpost; Tilley T634; NED Twinkling 3 d.

3. In the twinkling of an eye (21 Cooper *Spy* 94, 113, 131, 217, 260, 273, *Satanstoe* 403, *Chainbearer* 297, *Redskins* 299; Neal *Brother J* I 23; Haliburton *Clockmaker* II 44, *Nature* II 291; Dana *Two* 177, 227; Melville *Typee* 196, *Omoo* 274; *White Jacket* 128; Hawthorne *Mosses* 87, "Main Street" in *House* 473; Richardson *Secret* 156 in something less than the, 282, *Beyond* 128; Smith *Arp* 61 tinkling, 87; Clemens *Roughing* I 52–53, 81). I Cor. 15:52; Apperson 653; NED Twinkling 3 b; *Oxford* 678; Smith *Browning* 222; Stevenson 2402: 3; Tilley T635; Whiting *Drama* 368: 919, *Scots* II 146; Neil Gordon *The Shakespeare Murders* (1933) 239.

Twist. The whole twist and tucking. 35 DA Tucking 3.

Two, 1. I'll fit the handle on to them in tu tu's (36 Haliburton *Clockmaker* I 153, II 120, 150, III 169, 202, *Sam* I 216). NED Two II 2 g; NQ 2 vi 437 The Americans say in 'two two's'; Beatrice Grimshaw *Victorian Family Robinson* (1935) 127.

2. And a thousand dollars of my own with it to keep it company, like two in a bed (53 Haliburton *Sam* II 289). See Three.

3. Tom B. Devill could *shykeen* and bullyrag Ned Boller's shirt off, and give him two in the game (53 Baldwin *Flush* 279; Taliaferro *Fisher's* 70–71 Ef he didn't slap down his tail and outrun creation, and give it two in the game). See Six (2).

4. I know a story, worth two o' that (25 Neal *Brother J* II 18, III 277 joke; Smith *Downing* 118 dose; Haliburton *Clockmaker* II 14 thing, 317 trick). See Trick (3).

5. An' lookin' round, ef two an' two make four (67 Lowell *Biglow* 337). NC 491 As sure as; *Oxford* 678; Stevenson 2402:8 As clear as; Tilley T641; NQ 10 xii 109, 231; T. L. Peacock *Melincourt* (1817, *Works* [London 1924]) II 78 We are in no danger of forgetting that two and two make four; Sir Walter Scott *Rob Roy* (1819) II ch. 5 as certainly . . . as that; Benjamin Disraeli *Sybil* IV ch. 4 (1845, London [1927]) 252 Why I've been thinking of it ever since I knew that; R. S. Surtees *Mr. Sponge's Sporting Tour* (London [1853]) 184 but then we go [i. e., amount to] a large party ourselves—two and two's four—to say nothing of the servants.

6. Two can play at that game (43 Haliburton *Attaché* III 48, *Season-Ticket* 277 before you try that game, recollect two can play at it; Irving *Attorney* 241; Jones *Winkles* 324 Oh, it is a game at which two can play; Cartwright *Autobiography* 192 if he should undertake to chastise me, as Paddy said, "There is two as can play at that game"). NED Two 2; *Oxford* 232; Stevenson 993:3; Sir Walter Scott *Woodstock* (1826) I ch. 15 I'll show you that two can play at the game of wrestling; Anthony Trollope *Is He Popenjoy?* (1878) ch. 30 (World's Classics ed. I 290) Because you know it requires two to play at that game; Sydney Horler *The Evil Château* (1931) 244; E. S. Gardner *The Case of the Drowning Duck* (1942) 182 When it comes to being nasty, two can play at that game very nicely.

7. That game is fair, for two can play at it (32 Hall *Legends* 25–26).

8. Three are poor company (33

Hall *Soldier's Bride* 154; Haliburton *Season-Ticket* 213 Three is a very inconvenient limitation, constituting, according to an old adage, "no company"; Sedley *Marian* 143 Two's company and more isn't, eh?). Apperson 655; Farmer and Henley VII 109; Hardie 465:157; Lean II ii 736; NC 491; NED Company 1 d; *Oxford* 680; Stevenson 386:1; Tilley O56; NQ 8 xii 268; 9 ii 136; Christopher Bush *Dead Man Twice* (1930) 25 two's company and so on; Anna G. Hatcher *Modern Language Notes* LIX (1944) 517 This "two's company, three's a crowd" attitude; J. P. Marquand *So Little Time* (Boston 1943) 205 Two made company, and three made a crowd.

9. It takes two to make a quarrel (45 Judd *Margaret* II 95). Apperson 655; Bradley 89; NC 464; *Oxford* 681; Stevenson 1924:1.

Types. To put the types on [i. e., to send a constable with a warrant]. 49 DA Type 3 b.

U

Ugly. See Cuscaroarus (1), Fly (6), Hornet (2), Horse (13), Milk (9), Mud fence, Mule (7), Sin (8), Stone fence, Witch (2), Wolf (17).

Unbroken. See Mirror (2).

Uncle. My Viking talked to me like my uncle (49 Melville *Mardi* I 20). Cf. NC 401 Dutch uncle; NED Uncle 1 e; Taylor *Investigations* 264.

Uncompromised. See Babe (6).

Unconscious. See Stone (10).

Uneasy. See Fish (3).

Union. That "union is strength" is a truth that has been known, illustrated and declared in various ways and forms in all ages of the world (43 Lincoln I 315). Bradley 96; *Oxford* 683; NQ 2 x 190; Herbert Adams *The Strange Murder of Hatton, K. C.* (Philadelphia 1933) 279. Cf. Stevenson 2407:6; Tilley U11.

Unknown. The proverb says, "The unknown is always great" (69 Clemens *Innocents* II 84).

Unlike. See Cabbage (2).

Unmovable. See Stalactite, Wax-work (2).

Unsocial. See Stone (12).

Up, 1. I won't have the door opened, and that is the up and down of the matter (54 Langdon *Ida* 359). Cf. NED Up and down.

2. On the (dead) up and up [i. e., honestly]. 63 DA Up and up.

Upright. See Bolt.

Use, 1. Use is everything (40 Cooper *Pathfinder* 104). Apperson 660; Tilley U23; Jeffrey Farnol *The Crooked Furrow* (1938) 171. Cf. Whiting *Drama* 53.

2. But use makes perfect (45 Cooper *Chainbearer* 366). Stevenson 2411:10. Cf. Apperson 509 Practice; *Oxford* 684; Tilley U24; Whiting *Scots* II 147.

V

Vacant. See Room (1).

Vain, adj. See Peacock (3).

Vain, adv. He never chose to labor in vain (68 Saxe *Poems* 152). Tilley V5. Cf. Apperson 348; NED Vain 5.

Valiant. See Mouse (6).

Valley. It was owned by another pet of ours, who, years ago, went down the dark valley and left us (59 Shillaber *Knitting-Work* 39; Locke [Nasby] *Struggles* 243 and in fourteen days he slept in the valley [i. e., died]). Cf. NED Shadow 1 b (the valley of the shadow of death).

Variety. Dat right, Bill,—take all de wives you can get,—bariety am de spite of life (54 Langdon *Ida* 111). Bradley 96; Stevenson 2416:1. Cf. *Oxford* 685 Variety is charming; Stoett 2126; Tilley C229; Whiting *Scots* I 148 Changeis ar sueit [sweet].

Velvet. Piles of mosses, soft as velvet (57 Riley *Puddleford* 13).

Vengeance. Plum-sass as sour as vengeance (56 Whitcher *Widow* 338).

Venison. As fresh as venison without salt (40 Cooper *Pathfinder* 46).

Vessel. Empty vessels being the very ones of all the world to make a noise, when tossing to and fro in the turbulent sea of politics (53 Hammett *Stray* 348). Apperson 182; Bradley 72; Hardie 464:128; *Oxford* 171; Stevenson 676–677:17; Tilley V36; William McFee *The Harbourmaster* (London 1932) 9 It is the empty vessel that makes the most noise; Kurt Steel, pseud. *Murder Goes to College* (Indianapolis 1936) 283 The more hollow the vessel, the louder the sound.

Vicar. Sober as a vicar (68 Saxe *Poems* 58).

Vigilance. Eternal vigilance is the price of travel (67 Richardson *Beyond* 79; Jones *Batkins* 198 "eternal vigilance was the price of liberty"). Cf. J. Bartlett *Familiar Quotations* (13th ed. 1955) 380 b; Stevenson 1388:3.

Vigorous. See Mule (5).

Vinegar, 1. She answered him "No!" as sharp as vinegar (54 Shillaber *Mrs. Partington* 337). Apperson 561; *Oxford* 579; Tilley V63. Cf. Svartengren 97 sour [i. e., ill-tempered].

2. As sour as vinegar (38 Haliburton *Clockmaker* II 57; Stephens *High Life* I 103 The Count looked as sour as a vinegar barrel, 227; Taliaferro *Carolina Humor* 62 As sour as apple vinegar). Boshears 40:959; NC 491; Svartengren 304; Taylor *Comparisons* 77. Cf. Tilley T63.

3. Vinegar is the son of wine (36 Emerson *Works* I 33).

Violet, 1. An eye as blue as a violet in spring (54 Shillaber *Mrs. Partington* 267).

2. They [eyes] were as pure and serene as violets that have caught their hue by looking up to heaven (c58 Stephens *Mary Derwent* 267).

Virginia (1). Four ancient spinsters, virtuous as Virginia (55 Irving *Wolfert* 120).

Virginia (2). Like old Virginia, he never tires (67 Richardson *Beyond* 441).

Virginia fence. To make a Virginia fence [i. e., to walk drunkenly]. 67 DA Virginia fence 2.

Virtue, 1. I made a merit of necessity (53 Hammett *Stray* 21–22; Cary *Clovernook* 2d Series 264 virtue; Lincoln III 282 virtue; Richardson *Secret* 364 virtue). Apperson 663; NC 491; NED Necessity 5, Virtue 4; *Oxford* 688; Stevenson 1668–1669:4; Tilley V73; Oscar Gray *The Bagshot Mystery* (1929) 208; William Roughead *Malice Domestic* (Edinburgh 1928) 202 merit.
2. Virtue is its own reward, as the parson says (32 Kennedy *Swallow* 216; Hall *Purchase* II 23; Willis *Fun* 121 But virtue, if nothing more and no sooner, is its own reward; Holmes *Elsie* 70; Browne *Artemus* 41, 157; Alcott *Little Women* 332 feeling that virtue was not always its own reward; Locke [Nasby] *Struggles* 373; Clemens *Sketches* 189 [ascribed to Franklin]). Apperson 663; NC 491; *Oxford* 687; Stevenson 2434–2435:7; Tilley V81; Yamamoto *Dickens* 329–330; NQ 2 ix 499–500; 6 viii 427; ix 54, 295; William Gore, pseud. *The Mystery of the Painted Nude* (1938) 194

a case where virtue isn't its own reward.

Virtuous. See Virginia (1).

Vise, 1. A crusty old fellow, as close as a vice [i. e., stingy]. (51 Hawthorne *Twice-Told* 130).
2. Close as a *vice*, eh! [i. e., uncommunicative]. (33 Hall *Soldier's Bride* 19).
3. As moveless as if screwed in a vice (43 Hall *Purchase* I 128).

Visit. Acting it would appear on the principle that short visits make long friends (45 Judd *Margaret* I 292). Apperson 568; Stevenson 2436:3.

Voice. Vox populi, vox dei (46 Cooper *Redskins* 277; Melville *Confidence-Man* 219 "For the voice of the people is the voice of truth. Don't you think so?" "Of course I do. If Truth don't speak through the people, it never speaks at all; so I heard one say." "A true saying"; Haliburton *Season-Ticket* 233 their favorite maxim, "Vox populi, vox Dei"; Judd *Margaret* I 261). Apperson 664; NED Vox 1; *Oxford* 688; Stevenson 1776–1777:8; Tilley V95.

Volcano. And John smoked on like a volcano (51 Stowe *Uncle* 139).

Volume. They said little, but they looked volumes (57 Bennett *Border* 61). NED Volume 3 b (speak, tell).

Voyage. Sailors who had just come from a plum-pudding voyage, as they called it (that is, a short whaling voyage in a schooner or brig, confined to the north of the Line, in the Atlantic Ocean only). (51 Melville *Moby-Dick* I 106). Cf. DA Plum 2 (6).

W

Wafer. The partition is as thin as a wafer (55 Derby *Phoenixiana* 320). NC 491; NED Wafer 1; Svartengren 292.

Wag. In the wag of a dead lamb's tail (56 Kelly *Humors* 137). See Shake, sb. (3).

Wagon, 1. Quiet es a greased waggin, runnin in sand (67 Harris *Sut* 243).
2. Wait for the wagin, gentlemen [i. e., hold your horses, go slow]. (45 Hooper *Simon* 45).

Wagon-tire. And here's the Speckled Snake [an Indian] as cold as a wagon tire (32 Hall *Legends* 37, 88, 213; Porter *Major* 17 You'll lay him out cold as). DA Cold 2 (1); Thornton I 190.

Wait. He who can wait hath what he desires (45 Judd *Margaret* I 278). *Oxford* 179–180, quot. 1642.

Walking papers, 1. Gave him his walking papers (43 Lewis *Odd* 71; Nash *Century* 326). DA Walking 2 (10) take, give; Partridge 936; Schele de Vere 647.
2. If it hadn't been for Ben, I should have got my walking papers from this world (55 Anon. *New Hope* 231).

Walking ticket. She had given Henry a walking ticket (29 Eliason 124, 303; Haliburton *Clockmaker* III 73 These asses of travellers will get a walkin' ticket; Whitcher *Widow* 84 He's got his *walkin' ticket* now, 307). Bartlett 736–737; DA Walking 2 (13); Farmer 550; Farmer and Henley VII 288; Partridge 936; Stevenson 2441:2; Woodard PADS VI (1946) 32.

Wall, 1. Bushes have ears, as well as walls (32 Hall *Legends* 231; Kennedy *Horse-Shoe* 222 Trees and walls have ears at this time, 336 as cautiously as if the walls of his mill had ears; Haliburton *Clockmaker* III 168 walls have ears, *Old Judge* I 143, *Sam* I 219 for partitions have ears, *Nature* II 76 and who knows but trees have; Cary *Clovernook* 2d Series 164 saying that walls have; Durivage *Three* 250 Walls have sometimes ears). Apperson 665–666; NC 492; *Oxford* 690; Smith *Browning* 222; Stevenson 654–655:8; Stoett 1581; Tilley W19; Leo Bruce *Case for Three Detectives* (1937) 217; E. K. Gann *Soldier of Fortune* (1954) 54 The plates have ears in this place.
2. I shall go to the wall for bread and meat (59 Lincoln III 400). NED Wall 13; Tilley W15.

Wallflower. As they [two young men] stood "playing wallflower" for the moment, at a military ball (56 Durivage *Three* 93). Bartlett 737; Farmer and Henley VII 290; NED Wallflower 3.

Walnut. As big as a shag-bark walnut (44 Stephens *High Life* II 27).

Walnut gad. Hurra! but don't it make a feller feel as suple as a green walnut gad (44 Stephens *High Life* II 12, 142).

Walrus. I'll make him sober as a walrus (45 Judd *Margaret* II 89).

War, 1. It would be a war to the knife (71 Jones *Batkins* 327). NED Knife 1 b; *Oxford* 692; Stevenson 2448:6.

2. But the way to be redressed . . . is to carry the war into Africa (55 Jones *Winkles* 202). Helen McCloy *Dance of Death* (1938) 237.

Warbling. Soft as the warbling of a he-dove before he pitches into a pea-hatch (43 Lewis *Odd* 73).

Wares. He had brought his wares to the wrong market (53 Baldwin *Flush* 154). See Pig (14). Cf. F. W. Crofts *The Cheyne Mystery* (1926) 124 sell one's wares in the best market.

Warm. See Blaze (11), Bug (4), Mustard (2), Steam (1), Toast.

Waste. Wilful waste makes woeful want (43 Haliburton *Attaché* IV 279). Apperson 687; Bradley 96 Waste makes want; NC 492; *Oxford* 694; Stevenson 2457–2458:9; Tilley W81; Woodard PADS VI (1946) 43.

Watch. See Cat (52, 57).

Water, 1. Being brought up where wine is as common as water (69 Alcott *Little Women* 276).

2. He seemed to read it off as easy as water (44 Stephens *High Life* II 36).

3. Pure as spring water (44 Stephens *High Life* II 109).

4. As refreshing to his weary mind as a drink of cold water to a fever-patient (74 Eggleston *Circuit* 198).

5. Waiter, more cocktail, that last was as weak as water (43 Haliburton *Attaché* I 136). Apperson 670–671; Boshears 41:1006; NC 492; Taylor *Comparisons* 85; Tilley W88; W. D. Steele *The Man Who Saw Through Heaven* (1927) 213. See Taunton.

6. You will be as welcome to it as the water that runs (45 Hooper *Simon* 120). Cf. Randolph and Wilson 179.

7. Dirty water will quench fire (21 Loomis *Farmer's Almanac* 178).

8. To back water. 44 DA Back 3 (11).

9. That argument won't hold water (55 Haliburton *Nature* II 118). Farmer and Henley VII 301; NED Hold 32, Water 1 f (bear); NC 493; E. O'Duffy *The Bird Cage* (1933) 95.

10. This province is stagnant; it tante deep, like still water, neither (36 Haliburton *Clockmaker* I 92). Cf. Apperson 602–603; NC 493; *Oxford* 621; Stevenson 2464:4, 9; Stoett 2531; Tilley W123; NQ 4 iv 133, v 420 Still waters run deep, and the devil lies at the bottom, vi 185, 257, 424; William McFee *The Harbourmaster* (London 1932) 138.

11. We were allowed a tin pot full of hot tea (or, as the sailors significantly call it, "water bewitched") sweetened with molasses (40 Dana *Two* 36, 386 our common beverage—"water bewitched and tea begrudged," as it was; Hawthorne *House* 120 like an old lady's cup of tea, it is water bewitched). Farmer and Henley VII 302; NED Water 2 c; *Oxford* 694; Stevenson 2462:1; Tilley W118; William Johnston *The Affair in Duplex 9B* (1927) 261. Cf. Boshears 41:1007.

12. The proverbial evanescence of a thing writ in water (51 Melville *Moby-Dick* II 344). Tilley W114; "Here lies one whose name was writ in water" (John Keats' epitaph).

13. This poor fellow was always getting into hot water (40 Dana *Two* 105; Hall *Purchase* II 293 this placed our learned men in what is called hot water; Clemens *Enterprise* 106; Locke [Nasby] *Struggles* 314; Richardson *Beyond* 222 getting into hot water oftener than cold; Barnum *Struggles* 485). Farmer and Henley III 365, VII 301–302; NC 492.

14. That leaves politics to them as like dabblin' in troubled waters (38 Haliburton *Clockmaker* II 52). Cf. Apperson 217 fish; *Oxford* 206, 207–208; Stevenson 821:6; Tilley F334; Whiting *Scots* II 151.

15. Lor [law] jis' rolls ofen his back like draps ove warter ofen a duck or mallard (67 Harris *Sut* 174). Apperson 169; McAtee *Additional* 12; PADS XV (1951) 62; NC 492; NED Duck 2; *Oxford* 695; Taylor *Comparisons* 84–85; Tidwell PADS XI (1949) 13–14; Jane Allen, pseud. *I Lost My Girlish Laughter* (1938) 170 like the proverbial water off a duck. Cf. Holmes *Professor* 130 a mental shake, . . . which throws off your particular grief as a duck sheds a raindrop from his oily feathers.

16. The least shake of a truth would suit a downright politic feller as well as water would a mad dog, and no better (44 Stephens *High Life* I 41).

17. Squandering money like water (72 Clemens *Roughing* II 137). NED Water 1 f; Stuart Martin *The Trial of Scotland Yard* (1930) 230 pour out.

18. "I believe *I will take water*" (a common expression, signifying that the person using it would take a nonsuit) (53 Baldwin *Flush* 275; Clemens *Innocents* I 220). Bartlett 690; DA Water 3 (1); NED Water 8 c; Stevenson 2459:3; Thornton II 884.

19. I'm sorry to throw cold water on the subject (51 Melville *Moby-Dick* I 216; Hammett *Piney* 190 and then threw a bucket of cold water on it; Alcott *Little Women* 270; Locke [Nasby] *Struggles* 416). Farmer and Henley VII 113; Green 33; McAtee 50; Stevenson 2461:4.

20. Water never rises above its level (57 Riley *Puddleford* 202). Cf. Bradley 96 seeks its level; NC 493.

21. Whilst water runs and grass grows we'll see no nicer place (65 Sedley *Marian* 441).

Watercress. A teetotaller to the backbone, as temperate as a watercress (44 Stephens *High Life* II 197).

Water haul. It having been understood up town, that as to sport to-day the races would prove a water-haul (58 Porter *Major* 13; Taliaferro *Fisher's* 74 fur [for] I'd made a water haul that time, fur sure and sartin [i. e., an unsuccessful hunt]). NED Water 29; Thornton II 933, III 423; Joseph Kirkland *Zury* (Boston 1887) 50.

Wave. You cavaliers, who roam the seas, are unsteady as the waves (55 Irving *Wolfert* 357).

Wax, 1. Nice as wax (56 Kelly *Humors* 285).

2. [An arm] as plastic as softened wax (60 Holmes *Professor* 237).

3. Let two of us . . . get H— and J— tight as wax [i. e., drunk]. (56 Kelly *Humors* 80). Cf. NC 493; Svartengren 263.

4. They hold us together like wax (59 Smith *My Thirty* 362).

5. He manipulated men like wax (67 Richardson *Beyond* 45). F. H. Shaw *Atlantic Murder* (1933) 114.

6. I am sticking to Portland like wax (33 Smith *Downing* 74, 129, *My*

Thirty 379; Crockett *Life* 135; Neal *Charcoal* 133; Lincoln II 252). Stevenson 2466:1.

7. Well, I guess I warmed the wax in the ears of that fellow with the narrow brimmed white hat (58 Porter *Major* 18).

Wax-end. The words stuck like wax-eends in my throat (44 Stephens *High Life* II 136).

Wax figure. She . . . fainted away as dead as a wax figger (64 Clemens *Washoe* 79).

Wax-work, 1. Neat as wax-work (33 Smith *Downing* 60). DA Wax 4 b. Cf. Svartengren 219 wax.

2. You've got to set as onmovable as a wax-work (56 Whitcher *Widow* 214).

3. There warn't a thing that didn't fit exactly into its place like wax-work (44 Stephens *High Life* I 164). DA Wax 4 b.

Way, 1. Every which way (44 Stephens *High Life* I 243, II 4; Shillaber *Mrs. Partington* 125 looked every witch way). Bartlett 203; Farmer 228; Green 133; NED *Supplement* Every 1 f.

2. As familiar with every one of them as with the way to his own corn-crib (45 Hooper *Simon* 28).

3. Straight as the way to the grave (73 Clemens *Gilded* I 269).

4. That cuts both ways (76 Nash *Century* 79).

5. Well, have your own way and live the longer (53 Cary *Clovernook* 2d Ser. 39).

6. Everybody has their ways (56 Cary *Married* 101).

7. Never let him know what you desire. Look one way, and row another (25 Neal *Brother J* II 310; Smith *My Thirty* 287 We must look one way all the time, and row t'other). Apperson 380; *Oxford* 384–385; Tilley W143.

8. The round-about way is often the nearest home (32 Kennedy *Swallow* 211; Melville *Omoo* 297 In short, the longest way round was the nearest way to Taloo). Apperson 379; Bradley 97; *Oxford* 192; Stevenson 2468:12; Tilley W158; J. C. Addams *The Secret Deed* (1926) 136. Cf. 51 Melville *Moby-Dick* II 278 Round the Cape of Good Hope is the shortest way to Nantucket. Babcock 264.

9. The shortest way is commonly the best way (45 Cooper *Satanstoe* 123).

10. Went the way of all flesh (43 Haliburton *Attaché* IV 100). Apperson 670; NED Way 6 c; *Oxford* 696; Stevenson 2467:9; Tilley W166; Whiting *Drama* 369:934; Francis Beeding, pseud. *The Little White Hag* (1926) 190.

11. That's jest the way with the world (44 Thompson *Major* 90; Haliburton *Old Judge* II 157 It's the way of the world; Wiley *Billy* 331; Alcott *Little Women* 324 it's the way of the world; Saxe *Poems* 23 of). Stevenson 2466:5 world, 2467:9 all earth; Norman Forrest *Death Took a Publisher* (1938) 107.

12. There's more ways to kill a cat than one (39 Smith *Letters* 91, 'Way 166 As it is said, "there are more ways than one to skin a cat"; Eggleston *School-Master* 147 I don't know how, but they's lots of ways of killing a cat besides chokin' her with butter). Apperson 88; Bradley 64; McAtee 58; NC 382; *Oxford* 696; Stevenson 297: 5; Woodard PADS VI (1946) 35; Mrs. Wilson Woodrow *The Moonhill Mystery* (1930) 251; Stuart Palmer

The *Puzzle of the Silver Persian*
(1934) 50 than choking it with butter;
Robert Graves *Claudius the God*
(1935) 147; F. P. Keyes *The River
Road* (1945) 387 choking it to death
with cream cheese.

13. There's more ways to kill a dog
besides choking him with butter, you
know (43 Thompson *Chronicles* 35).
Apperson 494; NC 398–399; Stevenson 1790:16 pigs; Tilley W156 than
hanging; R. W. Winston *It's a Far
Cry* (1937) 134 melted butter; W.
C. MacDonald *Destination Danger*
(Philadelphia 1955) 120 But you can
kill a dog without choking him with
butter).

14. But there's more ways of getting into a lot than by taking down the
bars (55 Stephens *Homestead* 370).

15. With their hair looking a thousand ways for Sunday (36 Haliburton
Clockmaker I 67, III 185 his hair
looked a hundred ways for Sunday,
Season-Ticket 300 his eyes starein six
ways for Sunday; Porter *Major* 21 My
friend that looked so many ways for
Sunday [i. e., was crosseyed]).
Coombs PADS II (1944) 22; Green
374; NC 493; NED Way 9 c (nine
ways, two ways for Sunday).

16. There's no *two ways* about it
(32 Hall *Legends* 51, 88; Stephens
High Life I 137). Bartlett 431, 742;
Green 257; NED Way 14 j; Partridge
942; Stevenson 2466:15; Thornton II
612–613, III 264.

17. See Heart (20).

Weak. See Baby (5), Cat (29), Child
(9), Infant (4), Kitten (12), Taunton,
Water (5).

Wealth. He who would bring home
the wealth of the Indias, must carry
out the wealth of the Indias (37 Emerson *Journals* IV 254). *Oxford* 65.

Wear. A somewhat false and dangerous maxim: "better wear out than rust
out (43 Hall *Purchase* II 48; Barnum
Struggles 520 It is better to wear out
than rust out). Apperson 46; Lean III
432; NC 493; *Oxford* 42; Stevenson
2020:3; Tilley W209; NQ 6 vi 328,
495, vii 77, viii 158, 254–255.

Weasel, 1. As active as a weasel (36
Haliburton *Clockmaker* I 231).

2. Eyes as black and keen as a
weazle's (44 Stephens *High Life* II
93).

3. Cute as a weasel (36 Haliburton
Clockmaker I 136).

4. I grew as lank as a weasel (23
Cooper *Pioneers* 236). Cf. Green 418.

5. They look'd at this, jis' 'bout es
long es a weazel looks at a cumin
rock (67 Harris *Sut* 120).

6. As sly as a weasel (34 Davis
Downing 22). Carlton Talbott *Droll
Parade* (1930) 19.

7. The youngest on 'em's 'mos'
growed up, rugged and spry ez weazles (67 Lowell *Biglow* 234).

8. Catch a weasel asleep! (25 Neal
Brother J III 269, *Down-Easters* I 3;
Smith *Downing* 27; Haliburton *Clockmaker* I 117 You might as well catch
a weasel asleep as catch him, II 149,
231 if you want to catch a weasel, you
must catch him asleep, *Sam* I 146
Yankees and weasels aint often caught
nappin', *Season-Ticket* 101 You might
as well try to catch a weasel asleep as
to find them napping; Stephens *High
Life* I 122; Durivage *Three* 349; Kelly *Humors* 317; Nash *Century* 132).
Apperson 672; Bartlett 105; *Oxford*
85; NQ 5 xii 146, 258; Charles Lever
Charles O'Malley (1841, Boston 1910)
I 11; J. J. Connington, pseud. *The Tau
Cross Mystery* (Boston 1935) 117. See
Duck (5).

Weather, 1. Get under the weather (57 Melville *Confidence-Man* 173). Apperson 658–659; Babcock 261; Green 408; NC 494; Thornton II 917; NQ 2 v 216; 8 xi 246, 338, xii 34; Mary N. Murfree (Charles Egbert Craddock, pseud.) *The Mystery of Witch-Face Mountain* (Boston 1895) 154 He 'pears sorter under the weather now.

2. I took care to make fair weather with her daughter [i. e., get on the right side of]. (35 Kennedy *Horse-Shoe* 20). NED Weather 2 b; Tilley W221.

Weather-eye. Cock your weather-eye up aloft (50 Melville *White Jacket* 295, *Moby-Dick* I 197 Keep your weather-eye open). Babcock 261; NC 404; *Oxford* 332; John Dos Passos *The 42d Parallel* (1930) 20.

Web. As fine as a spider's web (44 Stephens *High Life* II 22). See Cobweb (1).

Wedding, 1. We'll make it as merry as a wedding (c58 Stephens *Mary Derwent* 254).

2. There is a well-known old proverb, which says "one wedding makes many" (20–22 Irving *Bracebridge* 453). Apperson 474; *Oxford* 698; Stevenson 1536:4; Tilley W231.

Wedge, 1. Lay out the poor soul as cold as a wedge (57 Riley *Puddleford* 130). McAtee *Additional* 7; Taylor *Comparisons* 28; Irvin S. Cobb *Murder Day by Day* (Indianapolis 1933) 19 iron wedge.

2. As dead as a wedge (76 Clemens *Tom* 87). NC 494; Paul Green *Wide Fields* (1928) 99.

3. Poor old Jake laid out, stiff and cold as a wedge (56 Kelly *Humors* 175). Svartengren 142 dead.

Weed, sb. Girls . . . grow like weeds (67 Richardson *Beyond* 144). Boshears 32:191; McAtee *Additional* 9; NC 494; Taylor *Comparisons* 85; Vincent McHugh *Caleb Catlum's America* (1936) 40.

Weed, vb. He that neglects to weed will surely come to need (31 Loomis *Farmer's Almanac* 178).

Week. You couldn't guess for a week a Sundays (33 Smith *Downing* 49; Stephens *High Life* II 62 But it would take a week of Sundays to tell you all). Farmer and Henley VII 311; McAtee *Grant County* 11; NED Week 6 c; Cornelia Penfield *After the Deacon Was Murdered* (1933) 177. See Month.

Weep. See Niobe.

Weight, 1. The animal is worth his weight in gold (21 Cooper *Spy* 288; Neal *Brother J* I 100 her; Kennedy *Horse-Shoe* 251 his; Dana *Two* 104; Stephens *High Life* II 160 she's worth her weight in silver dollars; Hawthorne *House* 124 its; Judd *Margaret* I 78; Stowe *Uncle* 5 her; Curtis *Potiphar* 139 its; Haliburton *Nature* I 71 your, II 20; Barnum *Struggles* 579 her). Apperson 714; NED Weight 9; *Oxford* 734; Stevenson 2478:6; Tilley W253; Whiting *Scots* II 153; A. J. Small *The Death Maker* (1925) 238.

2. He would . . . swear that he . . . could whip his weight in wild cats! (33 Hall *Soldier's Bride* 239; Haliburton *Clockmaker* II 160 We can whip our weight of wild cats, 192, *Attaché* III 203). DA Whip 4; Farmer and Henley II 393; Figh PADS XIII (1950) 13; McAtee 40; Randolph and Wilson 214; Stevenson 1512:6; Thornton II 940, III 427; Bon Gaultier [i. e., Theodore Martin and

W. E. Aytoun] *The Book of Ballads* (1845, 11th ed. Edinburgh 1870) 47 But I will in wildcats whip my weight; Charles Kelly and H. Birney *Holy Murder* (1934) 190.

Welcome. See Pea (6), Water (6).

Well, sb. A mystery that is as deep as a well (24 Cooper *Pilot* 164). Boshears 36:488; NC 494; NED Well 4; Taylor *Comparisons* 33; Mary N. Murfree (Charles Egbert Craddock, pseud.) *The Despot of Broomsedge Cove* (Boston 1889) 486.

Well, adv., 1. Leave well enough alone (36 Crockett *Exploits* 61, 81; Haliburton *Clockmaker* II 193 there's nothin' like leavin' all's well alone; Cooper *Redskins* 444 Why 'ey won't let well alone; Riley *Puddleford* 315 let). Apperson 361; Hardie 463:100; NC 494; NED Well, adj. 7 c; *Oxford* 360; Stevenson 2479–2480:12; Tilley W260; Marcus Magill, pseud. *Death in the Box* (Philadelphia 1931) 66 Let well alone; Leighton Barrett *Though Young* (1938) 15. Cf. Tilley W260.

2. "If you can't speak well of a man, hold your tongue" is his motto (76 Nash *Century* 12). Cf. Apperson 551–552; *Oxford* 563; Tilley S112.

Wet. See Periwinkle, Rat (6), Rooster (5).

Whale, 1. The South Seaman's slogan in lowering away: "A dead whale, or a stove boat!" (47 Melville *Omoo* 83, *Moby-Dick* I 200 And what tune is it ye pull to, men?). Babcock 256; Joanna C. Colcord *Sea Language Comes Ashore* (1945) 64.

2. That sagacious saying in the fishery,—the more whales the less fish (51 Melville *Moby-Dick* II 138). Babcock 256.

3. The young males . . . are by far the most pugnacious of all leviathans, and proverbially the most dangerous to encounter (51 Melville *Moby-Dick* II 142).

4. His eyes closed like a whale in a calm (58 Field *Pokerville* 119).

What. Cute feller, too!—knows what's what (25 Neal *Brother J* II 81; Whitcher *Widow* 213 I know'd what was what; Riley *Puddleford* 247; Taliaferro *Fisher's* 170; Sedley *Marian* 131 This 'ere yaller stuff [gold] teaches folks what's what). Apperson 677–678; Farmer and Henley VII 323; McAtee 38; NC 494; NED What 8 a; Partridge 948; Stevenson 1327:7; Tilley K178; Whiting *Drama* 140; J. J. Connington, pseud. *Grim Vengeance* (Boston 1929) 210.

Wheat, 1. As good as wheat (45 Hooper *Simon* 56; Burke *Polly* 23, 108, 150, 152 ole wheat; Hammett *Piney* 302; Taliaferro *Fisher's* 176 in the mill-hopper; Clemens *Tom* 271). Bartlett 254; DA Wheat d (1); NC 494; Svartengren 316; Taylor *Comparisons* 44.

2. It's all wheat. 65 DA Wheat d (2).

3. I would sift the wheat from the chaff (23 Cooper *Pioneers* 330). NED Wheat 1 b; Leslie Charteris *Wanted for Murder* (1931) 4 sort.

4. Happily, there is always more wheat than there is chaff (69 Barnum *Struggles* 397).

Wheatbin. Her eyes were as dry as wheatbins (c60 Paul *Courtship* 51).

Wheel, 1. He has as much use for it . . . as my old waggon here has for a fifth wheel (56 Haliburton *Clockmaker* I 268, III 162; Melville *Moby-Dick* I 115 A soul's a sort of fifth wheel to a

wagon; Shillaber *Mrs. Partington* 236
The wheel she spins on would be harder to find, a great deal, than the fifth
wheel of a coach, *Knitting-Work* 401
she . . . didn't care any more about
the virtoo of the thing than the fifth
wheel of a coach; Smith *My Thirty*
429 it's no more use to you than the
fifth wheel to the coach; Wiley *Billy*
267 even say that a chaplain was a
sort of fifth wheel). Apperson 210;
Lean III 358; NC 495; NED Fifth 1 c;
Oxford 200; Stoett 1910; Tilley W286;
Whiting *Scots* II 153; A. B. Caldwell
Turquoise Hazard (1936) 251. Cf.
Stevenson 2482:9.

2. It would require a little money to
grease the wheels (71 Jones *Batkins*
186). Bartlett 261; NED Grease 4.

3. My head run round like a spinnin' wheel (40 Haliburton *Clockmaker*
III 23).

4. I talked to him about the "wheels
within wheels" which moved this great
musical enterprise (69 Barnum *Struggles* 335). Ezek. 1:16; Apperson 678;
Farmer and Henley VII 326; Lean IV
145; NED Wheel 13 b; *Oxford* 703;
Stevenson 2483:2; Tilley W289; Mil-
ton Propper *The Boudoir Murder*
(1931) 311.

Wheelbarrow. She went on [talking]
like a jolly old wheelbarrow (54 Shillaber *Mrs. Partington* 354, *Knitting-
Work* 189 This, continued she, running on like a wheelbarrow).

Whippoorwill. We begun to grin like
two whip-por-wills in a black alder
bush (44 Stephens *High Life* II 179).

Whirl. See Top 2 (5).

Whirlwind, 1. A temper as rash and
unreasonable as the whirlwind (37
Neal *Charcoal* 198).

2. We sprung up the rise like a
whirlwind (66 Boucicault *Flying Scud*
170). NC 495. Cf. NED Whirlwind 4
whirlwind-like; Svartengren 381.

Whisky. Thar's a heap ove whisky
spilt twixt the counter an' the mouf,
ef hit ain't got but two foot tu travil
(67 Harris *Sut* 24). See Slip (2).

Whist. See Fish (4), Mouse (7).

Whistle, sb., 1. He smacks him thro'
the ribs—clean as a whistle (25 Neal
Brother J II 41, *Rachel* 160; Davis
Downing 67 rich and clean as a whistle; Mayo *Kaloolah* 41; Kelly *Humors*
168–169; Paul *Courtship* 25 I'm "dead
flat broke"—busted as clean as a whistle). Apperson 101; Boshears 35:403;
McAtee 18; NC 495; NED Whistle 1
b; Randolph and Wilson 178; Taylor
Comparisons 26; Harriette Ashbrook *A
Most Immoral Murder* (1935) 48.

2. I am as clear now as a whistle
[i. e., after taking Saratoga water].
(34 Davis *Downing* 36, 42 [plain, evi-
dent], 48, 250; Haliburton *Sam* II 272
shouted out as clear as a whistle;
Anon. *New Hope* 365). NC 495;
NED Whistle 1 b; Svartengren 361;
H. L. Davis *Honey in the Horn* (1935)
232.

3. Slick as a whistle (33 Neal
Down-Easters I 7, 104; Smith *Down-
ing* 36, *Way* 243; Crockett *Life* 19;
Davis *Downing* 14, 78, 202; Halibur-
ton *Clockmaker* I 126, *Attaché* IV
281; Stephens *High Life* I 198; Kelly
Humors 86). Allan PADS XV (1951)
67; Bartlett 607; Boshears 40:928;
DA Slick 6 (3); Farmer and Henley
VI 248; McAtee 58; NC 495; Taylor
Comparisons 74; Thornton II 810; W.
E. Hayes *Black Chronicle* (1938) 173.

4. Alive and safe, and sound as a
whistle (39 Smith *Letters* 78–79). Cf.

J. T. Farrell *No Star Is Lost* (1938) 606 healthy.

5. To wet our whistles (34 Crockett *Life* 142; Kennedy *Horse-Shoe* 199; Neal *Charcoal* 47, 140; Hawthorne *Twice-Told* 171; Riley *Puddleford* 30). Apperson 677; Farmer and Henley VII 340; NED Whistle 2; *Oxford* 703; Stevenson 2485:12; Tilley W312; Whiting *Drama* 369:940; Wilson 606; H. W. Freeman *Hester and Her Family* (1935) 199.

6. Dr. Franklin's famous whistle (34 Hawthorne *Mosses* 548; Dorson *Jonathan* 75 the thought flashed through the mind of the Yankee that he was paying 'too dear for the whistle'; Browning *Forty-four* 276 The old panther might make him, as Dr. Franklin says, "pay too dear for his whistle"; Clift *Bunker* 138 the city folks were paying pretty dear for their whistle). DA Whistle (b); Farmer and Henley VII 340; NC 495; NED Whistle 1 b; *Oxford* 491; Stevenson 2486:5.

Whistle, vb. Biddle may whistle for 'em (34 Davis *Downing* 206; Neal *Charcoal* 213 the real owners, like me, may go whistle; Clemens *Tramp* II 70). Hardie 470:125; NED Whistle 9; Stevenson 2486:8; Tilley W313; Whiting *Drama* 370:944; C. St. John Sprigg *The Corpse with the Sunburned Face* (1935) 135 for my money.

White, 1. My aunt blessed me shortly before she was called to "walk in white" [i. e., to die]. (50 Willis *Life* 145).

2. See Alabaster, Almond, Angel (7), Ashes (3), Belly (1), Cambric, Candle (2), Chalk (4), Cloth (2), Corpse (1), Curd (1, 2), Death (21), Diamond (5), Egg (8), Flax, Foam, Frogstool, Frost (1), Froth, Ghost (2), Goods (1), Ice (4), Ivory (2), Lily (2, 3), Lotus, Marble (7), Milk (4), Nigger (9), Paper (1), Sea-gull, Sheet (2, 3), Shroud, Snow (3, 6, 7, 8, 9, 10), Snowball (2), Snowflake, Tombstone (4), Tow (2), Wool (1).

Whitehead, 1. To clear out (study) like a whitehead. 30 DA White 3 (5).

2. You'd better paddle up the street like a white-head (37 Neal *Charcoal* 201). Cf. Taylor *Comparisons* 88; Dorson *Jonathan* 112 I ran like a white-head.

White man, 1. As crank as a white man (44 Stephens *High Life* I 148).

2. Off slid Mister *bar*, laffin' out *loud*, as I'm a white man (43 Robb *Squatter* 110).

Whitleather. Tough as whitleather (40 Haliburton *Letter* 196; Taliaferro *Fisher's* 184). Apperson 642; Boshears 40:990; NC 496; NED Whitleather 1 b; Stevenson 2355:2; Tilley L166. Cf. Green 423; McAtee 70–71; Taylor *Comparisons* 83; Tidwell PADS XI (1949) 15; Wilson 607, 614.

Whoa. There was no "whoa" to him (44 Stephens *High Life* I 252).

Whole. To go the whole. 21 DA Whole 2 (1). See Animal.

Why. There is always a why for every wherefore in this world (40 Haliburton *Clockmaker* III 106; Cary *Clovernook* 2d Series 18 She talked a long chapter of whys and wherefores). Apperson 683; Farmer and Henley VII 349; NC 496; *Oxford* 707; Stevenson 2490:10; Tilley W331.

Wicked. See Bear (24), Cain (1), Meat axe (4).

Wide. See Slab, Wolf trap.

Wide awake. See Hawk (8).

Widow. Widders will be widders (56 Whitcher *Widow* 298). See Boy (4).

Wife, 1. I'de as leaf travel as stay home with a scoldin' wife, cryin' children, and a smoky chimney (53 Haliburton *Sam* I 11). Apperson 582; *Oxford* 655; Taylor *Investigations* 261; Tilley H781.
2. Old wives' fables (56 Melville "Apple-Tree Table" in *Works* XIII 318). Apperson 465; NED Old wife 1, Tale 5 b, Wife 1 b; *Oxford* 473; Tilley W388; Whiting *Scots* II 154; G. K. Chesterton *Collected Poems* (London 1927) 116.

Wild, 1. But then she [a gun] play'd de very wild wid de ducks (55 Anon. *New Hope* 156; Jones *Wild* 10 But love can play the "wild" with any young man). DA Wild 4 (1); Stevenson 2507:1.
2. See Bear (25), Colt (4), Hawk (9), Indian (4), Kitten (13), Loon (8), River (1), Tiger (4).

Wildcat, 1. As fierce as a wild-cat (34 Crockett *Life* 62; Haliburton *Clockmaker* III 154). Cf. Taylor *Comparisons* 57 mean.
2. Sly as a wild-cat (59 Taliaferro *Fisher's* 78).
3. Bingham was . . . spry as a wild-cat (58 Hammett *Piney* 283). Cf. Svartengren 158 agile.
4. I would have agreed to fight a whole regiment of wild cats (34 Crockett *Life* 50; Haliburton *Clockmaker* II 246 he looked as mad as if he could a swallered a wild cat alive; Hall *Purchase* II 158; Taliaferro *Fisher's* 127 I felt I could a whipped a

string o' wildcats long as Tar River). Stevenson 1512:26. See Weight (2).
5. How like a wildcat she jumped! (51 Stowe *Uncle* 68).
6. Screamed like a wildcat (59 Taliaferro *Fisher's* 54).

Wildfire. Had run through the woods like wild fire (25 Neal *Brother J* I 147; Smith *Downing* 170 run, 'Way 339 flew, *My Thirty* 411 take; Haliburton *Clockmaker* II 282 ran all over Boston; Hammett *Stray* 395 spread; Cartwright *Autobiography* 264 gaining and spreading; Richardson *Beyond* 386 spread; Barnum *Struggles* 40 sold). NC 496; NED Wild-fire 5 c; Jane Allen, pseud. *I Lost My Girlish Laughter* (1936) 218–219 spread; Desmond Holdridge *Witch in the Wilderness* (1937) 302 ran.

Will, sb. (1), 1. You must take the will for the deed (38 Haliburton *Clockmaker* II 23; Anon. *New Hope* 93; Smith *My Thirty* 334). Apperson 687; NED Will 22; *Oxford* 709; Stevenson 2509–2510:11; Tilley W393; Whiting *Drama* 76; John Rhode, pseud. *The Murders in Praed Street* (1928) 35 as the saying is.
2. Burmah is now shut against us . . . ; and where there is a will there is a way (38 Conant *Earnest Man* 443–444; Irving *Attorney* 148 With a will, Jack, there is always a way; Cooper *Satanstoe* 148 Vere dere ist a vill, dere ist a vay; Haliburton *Nature* II 187; Jones *Winkles* 181 the old proverb, wherever; Lincoln II 409; Clift *Bunker* 39; Saxe *Poems* 122 [title]. Apperson 687; McAtee 70; NC 497; NED Way 13, Will 22; *Oxford* 710; Stevenson 2510:12; Tilley W157; E. S. Gardner *The Case of the Sulky Girl* (1933) 7 the old saying.
3. See Good will.

Will, sb. (2). A will is a will (58 Holmes *Autocrat* 301).

Will, vb. Nolens volens (40 Dana *Two* 112; Cooper *Chainbearer* 43 intends to marry me, will ye, nill ye; Melville *Moby-Dick* I 211 Will I, nill I; Irving *Wolfert* 241 will-ye, nill-ye). Apperson 688; Stevenson 2511:8; Tilley W401; Whiting *Drama* 370:948, *Scots* II 154–155; Jeffrey Farnol *Winds of Chance* (Boston 1934) 227 Will I, nill I.

Willamilla. Throughout the Archipelago this saying was a proverb—"You are lodged like the king in Willamilla" (49 Melville *Mardi* I 270). A manufactured proverb, but see King (6), Prince.

Willow, 1. You are as grave as a weeping willow (57 Jones *Country* 173). Cf. NED Willow 1 d.
2. She is not as melancholy as a weeping willow (36 Fairfield *Letters* 70).

Wilt. See Cabbage (3).

Wind, 1. As free as the wind of the desert (28 Neal *Rachel* 239; Clemens *Sandwich* 21). Apperson 234–235 wind; NC 497 wind; NED Wind 7; Svartengren 340; C. G. Givens *All Cats Are Gray* (Indianapolis 1937) 28 wind.
2. As idle as the wind (59 Lincoln III 355).
3. Its an ill wind . . . that blows nobody any good (23 Cooper *Pioneers* 232, *Pilot* 13 that blows luck to nobody; Haliburton *Clockmaker* II 287, *Attaché* III 173; Fairfield *Letters* 395; Mayo *Kaloolah* 283; Derby *Phoenixiana* 69; Cary *Married* 396; Clemens *Innocents* I 263). Apperson 326; NC 497; NED Wind 15; *Oxford* 317–318; Stevenson 2514:4; Tilley W421;

Whiting *Drama* 143, 152, 233; Yamamoto *Dickens* 329; Andy Adams *The Ranch on the Beaver* (Boston 1927) 90 It's an ill wind that don't blow some one home; Herbert Adams *Mystery and Minette* (Boston 1934) 208; E. K. Rand *Founders of the Middle Ages* (Cambridge, Mass. 1928) 157 that blows nobody good luck.
4. It's an ill wind that blows nowhere (34 Davis *Downing* 87; Stowe *Uncle* 48 dat ar a fact; Shillaber *Ike* 49 that don't blow anywhere).
5. There's some mischief in the wind (35 Kennedy *Horse-Shoe* 136, 228 harm; Haliburton *Clockmaker* I 179 and look if there was nothin partikilar in the wind, *Season-Ticket* 11 something; Irving *Attorney* 196 trouble; Mayo *Kaloolah* 85 something; Thompson *Chronicles* 66 something; Melville *Moby-Dick* I 163 something special; Jones *Winkles* 193 foul play). Babcock 260; Farmer and Henley VII 355; NED Wind 20; Tilley S621; Whiting *Drama* 370:954; Christopher Bush *The Perfect Murder Case* (1924) 288 something.
6. What's in the wind now? (35 Kennedy *Horse-Shoe* 372; Irving *Attorney* 61; Haliburton *Attaché* II 89; Melville *Moby-Dick* II 278; Stowe *Uncle* 446; Willis *Fun* 320 He had become aware during this process what was "in the wind"; Lincoln II 356; Clemens *Gilded* I 56; Nash *Century* 129 She'll think somethin's in the wind if we send her away). NED Wind 20; Stevenson 2514:9; John Cournos *Grandmother Martin Is Murdered* (1930) 74 What was in the wind?
7. In the expressive language of the sailor, "eating into the wind" (49 Mayo *Kaloolah* 24). Cf. NED Eat 13.
8. I've got wind of the whole af-

fair (56 Kelly *Humors* 425). NED Wind 16 b.

9. I shall go, of course, "wind and weather" permitting, as the sailors say (37 Fairfield *Letters* 174, 320 Tomorrow, wind and weather permitting, I am to make a short speech). NED Wind 5.

10. He went like the wind, full split (36 Haliburton *Clockmaker* I 253; Smith '*Way* 190 one that will sail like the wind; Clemens *Sandwich* 53 sweeping by like). NC 497. Cf. Taylor *Comparisons* 88 drive; Philip MacDonald *The Polferry Riddle* (1931) 85, 90.

11. So the wind's in that quarter! (32 Kennedy *Swallow* 94). Apperson 690; Farmer and Henley VII 355 door; NED Corner 8, Door 6 c; *Oxford* 712; Stevenson 2515:7; Tilley W419; Whiting *Drama* 370:954. Cf. Augustus Muir *The Silent Partner* (Indianapolis 1930) 124 So that's the way the wind blows.

12. Then the wind blows from another quarter to-day (32 Kennedy *Swallow* 266).

13. But the winds themselves are not more changeable than public opinion (43 Thompson *Chronicles* 76). Cf. NC 497; Whiting *Drama* 332: 366, *Scots* II 155 Wind 3, 6.

14. This text: "They that sow the wind shall reap the whirlwind" (53 Curtis *Potiphar* 64). Hosea 8:7; Apperson 592; NED Whirlwind 2; *Oxford* 608; Stevenson 2179:1; Tilley W437; Nellise Child *The Diamond Ransom Murders* (1935) 131 sowing the wind and reaping the whirlwind.

15. And he so young that you'd hardly think the wind had ever blown on him! (45 Cooper *Chainbearer* 263).

16. What wind has blown you up here? (35 Kennedy *Horse-Shoe* 148).

Apperson 690; NED Wind 15; *Oxford* 711–712; Tilley W441; Whiting *Drama* 370:952.

17. She was struck, just between wind and water, with Hafen's rigmarole (32 Kennedy *Swallow* 326; Haliburton *Clockmaker* I 183 That shot was a settler, it struck poor Sall right atwixt wind and water). Farmer and Henley VI 188, VII 355; NED Shot 7 d, Wind 8 b; *Oxford* 711; Stevenson 2512:5; Tilley W436; R. C. Woodthorpe *The Shadow on the Downs* (1935) 263 hit.

18. That is what I call knowing which way the wind blows! (27 Cooper *Prairie* 203; Crockett *Life* 61 I knowed she would then show some signs, from which I could understand which way the wind blowed; Thompson *Major* 69 I see how the wind blows; Lincoln I 477 in showing which way the wind blows; Stowe *Uncle* 54 Didn't I see which way the wind blew dis yer mornin'?; Clemens *Tom* 4 Tom knew where the wind lay now; Harris *Uncle Remus* 96 he know w'ich way de win' 'uz blowin'). Apperson 690; NED Wind 15 b; *Oxford* 345; Stevenson 2515:1; David Frome, pseud. *The Black Envelope* (1937) 226 might blow. See Straw (5).

19. It raised the wind! It brought the rhino! (43 Hall *Purchase* II 175; Hooper *Simon* 48–49 but Mr. James Peyton was determined that he would "raise the wind" for his uncle; Fairfield *Letters* 437 Mrs. C. is . . . without the means of raising the wind I presume except to a very limited extent say a few dollars; Lowell *Biglow* 130 even to this day, *raising the wind* is proverbial for raising money; Riley *Puddleford* 293; Clemens *Enterprise* 186, *Sandwich* 6; Locke [Nasby] *Struggles* 376). Farmer and Henley

VII 355–356; Green 296; NED Raise 7; *Oxford* 532; Stevenson 2514:6; Louis Tracy *A Mysterious Disappearance* (1927) 70.

20. He went so fast, he did, that he split the wind (59 Taliaferro *Fisher's* 73). DA Wind (b) 2; McAtee 61; NC 497.

21. He had to sail pretty close to the wind (53 Haliburton *Sam* I 26; Clemens *Sandwich* 12 a-sailin' too close to the wind). NED Wind 22; *Oxford* 555 Sail near; F. W. Crofts *The Cheyne Mystery* (1926) 199 sailing rather close.

22. Sabe dere wind to cool dere soup wid (40 Haliburton *Letter* 20). *Oxford* 331; Tilley W422. Cf. Apperson 65–66. See Breath (2).

23. It was like spitting against the wind—rather like raising sail in a hurricane (50 Judd *Richard* 183). Apperson 596; *Oxford* 615; Stevenson 2199:8; Tilley H356; Whiting *Scots* II 155; NQ CLXVII (1939) 280.

24. The notice of a lord will at any time take the wind out of your sails when a lady is in the case (53 Willis *Fun* 350; Cartwright *Autobiography* 513 By this time I had well-nigh taken the wind out of the doctor's sails; Jones *Country* 336; Hammett *Piney* 54 ner had the wind took out of his sails in his life; Locke [Nasby] *Struggles* 406 At one fell swoop the wind is knockt out uv the sales uv the Northern Dimocrisy; Clift *Bunker* 61). NED Wind 3 b; *Oxford* 641; Partridge 722; Stevenson 2513:7; Richard Blaker *The Jefferson Secret* (1929) 27 knock'd; Stuart Palmer *The Puzzle of the Silver Persian* (1934) 242 take.

25. We've throwed to the winds all regard for wut's lawfle (67 Lowell *Biglow* 310). NED Wind 25 b.

26. The sailors whistled and whistled for a wind (49 Melville *Redburn* 384, *White Jacket* 127 and "whistle for a wind," the usual practice of seamen in a calm). Babcock 263; *Oxford* 705; Tilley W440.

27. Tom had . . . tried to "whistle her down the wind" [i. e., forget her] (76 Clemens *Tom* 104). NED Whistle, vb., 7 b.

28. I rode like the wind (c58 Stephens *Mary Derwent* 229).

Windmill. His arms flying like a windmill (57 Riley *Puddleford* 104).

Window. If-so-be that a man wants to walk the quarter-deck with credit . . . he mustn't think to do it by getting in at the cabin-windows (23 Cooper *Pioneers* 73; Dana *Two* 424 I didn't come through the cabin windows! If I'm not mate, I can be man). Cf. Apperson 692; NED Window 4 b; *Oxford* 103; Tilley W456; Whiting *Scots* II 156. See Hawse-holes.

Windward, 1. Up to San Francisco, or, as it is called, "chock up to windward" (40 Dana *Two* 158).

2. The Pilgrim's crew envied me . . . and seemed to think I had got a little to the windward of them, especially in the matter of going home first (40 Dana *Two* 236; Willis *Fun* 350–351 Let who will get to the windward of us by superior sailing; Nash *Century* 306). Joanna C. Colcord *Sea Language Comes Ashore* (1945) 209; NED Wind 3 b; Windward A 1 b.

Wine, 1. A good book, like good wine, needs no bush (43 Haliburton *Attaché* II 26). Apperson 264; Bradley 97; *Oxford* 257–258; Stevenson 2518:2; Stoett 2572; Tilley W462; Taylor *Investigations* 264; Vincent McHugh *Caleb Catlum's America* (1936) 25.

2. If *In vino veritas* be a true saying (57 Melville *Confidence-Man* 87; Richardson *Beyond* 418 In wine is friendliness if not truth). Apperson 693; *Oxford* 714; Tilley W465. See Truth (7).

3. The wine being in and the wit being out (37 Neal *Charcoal* 175; Haliburton *Attaché* I 35 When the wine is in, the wit is out, *Nature* II 86; Thompson *Chronicles* 151). Apperson 164; Green 35 drink; NC 498; NED Wine 1 f (b); *Oxford* 6; Stevenson 2523:7; Tilley W471; Whiting *Drama* 134; Vaughan Williams *And So—Victoria* (1937) 51 with wine in, wits go out.

Wing, 1. I'd like to try my wings (69 Alcott *Little Women* 360).

2. See Crow (2).

Wink, 1. As quick as wink (25 Neal *Brother J* I 111; Haliburton *Clockmaker* I 85, 140, 164, 232, 315, II 139, 159, 194, 255, 306, III 68, 185, *Letter* 163, *Attaché* II 185, III 239, 277, IV 32, *Old Judge* I 305, II 88, 112, 284, *Sam* I 102, 120, 146, 173, II 15, 25, 34, 76, 170, *Nature* I 243, *Season-Ticket* 375; Smith *Letters* 98 a wink; Stephens *High Life* II 72; Sedley *Marian* 131, 418; Lowell *Biglow* 146 quicker 'an you could wink; Clemens *Enterprise* 153, *Sketches* 20). Boshears 39:837; NC 498; Taylor *Comparisons* 66; Vernon Patterson *All Giants Wear Yellow Breeches* (1935) 83 a wink; Mignon G. Eberhart *While the Patient Slept* (1930) 197 before one could wink; Leighton Barret *Though Young* (1938) 100 in the wink of an eye.

2. Would have had me stirring in a wink (35 Kennedy *Horse-Shoe* 232). NED Wink 3.

3. In two winks of a hum-bird's eye (39 Smith *Letters* 101).

4. You see, I seed in three winks . . . that that feller didn't own the horse (74 Eggleston *Circuit* 147).

5. Blows . . . swift as winks (60 Holmes *Elsie* 33).

6. A wink to a blind horse is as good as a nod (60 Whitehead *Wild Sports* 67). See Nod (1).

7. Ride over you like wink (38 Haliburton *Clockmaker* II 73, 283, III 15, 232, *Attaché* I 111, 136, 222, III 65, *Old Judge* II 41, *Sam* I 119, 149, 155, II 271, 285, *Nature* I 33, 104, 116, 193, 194, II 238, 271, *Season-Ticket* 45, 297, 303, 320).

8. The moon . . . evidently unsatisfied . . . just then gave the wink to that myth, the clerk of the weather, and down came the rain by buckets full (55 Hammett *Wonderful* 102; Jones *Winkles* 387 Your uncle says he will give him the wink, *Country* 168 Sam . . . was to give me the wink when to stop). NED Wink 2. Cf. Stevenson 2528:2.

9. He recognized me at once, tipped me an impudent wink (23–24 Irving *Tales* 157; Irving *Attorney* 222).

10. And so enjoy his forty morning winks (68 Saxe *Poems* 134). Farmer and Henley III 61; NED Wink 1 c; Stevenson 2527:11; Keith Trask *Murder Incidental* (1931) 129.

Winking, 1. Ez quick ez winkin' (48 Lowell *Biglow* 49; Porter *Major* 84 quicker nor winkin). W. B. M. Ferguson *The Black Company* (1924) 299.

2. Jumped up like winkin' (49 Haliburton *Old Judge* I 317). Farmer and Henley VII 358; NED Winking 4.

Winky. Tosses it off like winky (60 Haliburton *Season-Ticket* 112).

Winter. No, if you want to know the inns and the outs of the Yankees—I've wintered them and summered them; I know all their points (36 Haliburton *Clockmaker* I 87; Smith *'Way* 177 I've summered and wintered Mr. Rider, and know just what he is). NC 442; Tilley W516; Whiting *Journal of Celtic Studies* I (1949) 127.

Wintergreen. Lips . . . shiny as a harnful [handful] of wintergreen berries (44 Stephens *High Life* II 195).

Wire, 1. Virgins uv forty-five . . . tough ez wire (65 Locke [Nasby] *Struggles* 179). Cf. Svartengren 260; Whiting *Drama* 333:369.
2. Tha seem to be on wires about the alarm (60 Eliason 138, 286). NED Wire 8 b; Agatha Christie *The Seven Dials Mystery* (1929) 198 I was all, as you say, on wires, the cat on the hot bricks.
3. It all came about from their pulling the wrong wires (55 Hammett *Wonderful* 84; Lowell *Biglow* 319 I forgut thet *we're* all o' the sort thet pull wires). Bartlett 762; DA Wire 4 b (1); NED Wire 8; Schele de Vere 261.

Wisdom. See Justice.

Wise. See Donkey (1), Owl (8), Queen of Sheba, Solomon.

Wish. Their wish was father to the thought (55 Richardson *Secret* 460). Apperson 699; Bradley 97; *Oxford* 32 Believe; Stevenson 2542:16; Vernon Loder *Between Twelve and One* (1929) 14.

Wit, 1. What says the proverb? Wit's in the wane when the moon's at full

(35 Kennedy *Horse-Shoe* 66). Apperson 425; *Oxford* 431. Cf. Tilley W555.
2. Boughten wit is always the best (40 Haliburton *Clockmaker* III 39, *Attaché* II 211 is the best in a general way). Apperson 699–700; *Oxford* 58; Stevenson 2546:3; Tilley W545; Whiting *Drama* 78, 272.
3. Thence [see Name (3)] the balancing proverb, that in every wit is a grain of fool (36 Emerson *Journals* IV 97).
4. See Wine (3).

Witch, 1. He was as nervous as a witch (68 Alcott *Little Women* 75). NED Witch 1 d; A. M. Chase *Twenty Minutes to Kill* (1936) 135.
2. Ugly as the witch of Endor (33 Neal *Down-Easters* I 146). Apperson 658 a witch; Boshears 40:997 a witch. Cf. Halpert 722; *Oxford* 720.
3. She could sail like a witch (56 Durivage *Three* 339).

Withe. All as limber as a with (34 Davis *Downing* 20).

Withy. See Hickory (1).

Wive. But then you know a man can't wive and thrive the same year (55 Haliburton *Nature* II 270). Apperson 701; NC 498; *Oxford* 721; Stevenson 1536:7; Tilley Y12; Whiting *Drama* 17.

Wolf, 1. A wolf in sheep's clothing (33 Smith *Downing* 112; Kennedy *Horse-Shoe* 174 is no uncommon sight in the world; Cooper *Satanstoe* 252, *Chainbearer* 323; Haliburton *Sam* II 301 Scriptur' don't warn us agin wolves, except when they have sheep's-clothin' on, *Season-Ticket* 346 I have heard tell of wolves in sheep's clothing afore now; Jones *Batkins* 484 During the war, though in sheep's

clothing, he became a wolfish and san-
guinary parson). Apperson 701; Mc-
Atee *Grant County* 11; NC 498; *Oxford* 723; Stevenson 2555:2; Tilley
W614; Whiting *Drama* 246, 333:370,
371:957, *Scots* II 157; Robert Hare,
pseud. *The Hand of the Chimpanzee*
(1934) 126.

2. Death, to be sure, has a mouth
as black as a wolf's (49 Melville *Mardi*
I 36). Apperson 135 Dark; John
Rhode, pseud. *Dead Men at the Folly* (1932) 1 as black as a wolf's throat,
as the French say.

3. As bloodthirsty and as cowardly
as a wolf (53 Hammett *Stray* 147).

4. More cunning than this proverbially cunning animal [a wolf] was
gifted with (35 Kennedy *Horse-Shoe*
171).

5. It's dark as a wolf's mouth (51
Stowe *Uncle* 78). Apperson 135; Svartengren 239.

6. A "scared wolf" warn't nothing
to him. He run faster'n six scared
wolves and a yearlin' deer (45 Hooper *Simon* 145; Taliaferro *Fisher's* 72
Faster nur you uver seen a scared wolf
run).

7. As hungry as a wolf, two-thirds
famished (33 Neal *Down-Easters* I
88; Crockett *Life* 89 we were all as
hungry as wolves, 152; Kennedy
Horse-Shoe 148 as hungry as wolves
in winter). Apperson 319; Boshears
38:691; NC 498; Tilley W601; Van
Wyck Mason *Seeds of Murder* (1930).
89. Cf. Taylor *Comparisons* 51.

8. He was as impudent as a wolf
(c56 Cartwright *Autobiography* 134).

9. As irreconcilable as the wolf (32
Hall *Legends* 5).

10. She seed it all as plain as a
wolf's track around a sheep-pen (55
Anon. *New Hope* 72).

11. Does the wolf destroy the wolf,
or the rattler strike his brother? (27
Cooper *Prairie* 397). Apperson 703;
Stevenson 2553–2554:5; Tilley W606;
Paul McGuire *Murder at High Noon*
(1935) 147 Wolf should not eat wolf.
See Dog (25).

12. A year ago we were struggling
to keep the wolf from our door (76
Nash *Century* 281). Apperson 702;
Oxford 331, 722; Stevenson 2553:4;
Tilley W605.

13. Money must be made, or we
should soon have the wolf at the door
(55 Irving *Wolfert* 283; Saxe *Poems*
241 The wolf is ever howling at my
door). Hardie 471:193; NED Wolf 5;
Means Davis *The Chess Murders*
(1937) 236.

14. A-grinnin there . . . like a
wolf in a bear-trap (25 Neal *Brother
J* I 159).

15. Howled like a pack of wolves
(45 Hooper *Simon* 73). McAtee 35.

16. The pack of juveniles . . .
pounced upon it like hungry wolves
(57 Jones *Country* 17).

17. Ugly enough to tree a wolf. 30
DA Wolf (b).

18. It wakened my wolf wide awake
[i. e., got my dander up]. (58 Porter
Major 89).

Wolf trap. A mouth as wide as a wolf-
trap (55 Anon. *New Hope* 252).

Woman, 1. Grandfather Slick was
raised all along the coast of Kent in
old England, and he used to say there
was an old sayin there, which, I expect, is not far off the mark: A woman, a dog, and a walnut tree, The more
you lick 'em the better they be (36
Haliburton *Clockmaker* I 245). Apperson 703; Bradley 98; Lean I 455;
Oxford 609; Stevenson 2558:5; Tilley
W644; NQ 3 ix 153; 10 ix 170, 198,

x 15, 152; Newton Gayle *The Sentry-Box Murder* (1935) 152.

2. A woman always will have her way (71 Jones *Batkins* 400). Cf. Apperson 707; *Oxford* 726; Stevenson 2582:10 her will; Tilley W723; Whiting *Drama* 32, 238, 267, *Scots* II 158; Elsa Barker *The Cobra Candlestick* (1928) [Dedication].

3. Nor [a woman] insist on the ultimate word (68 Saxe *Poems* 9, 169 "Nay, my dear," interrupted my wife, Who began to be casting about To get the last word in the strife). Apperson 707; NC 499; *Oxford* 726; Stevenson 2581:6; Tilley W722; H. M. Smith *Inspector Frost in the City* (1930) 122.

4. Well, I can't say it's a woman lost or a man thrown away; it's much of a muchness [i. e., of a marriage]. (60 Haliburton *Season-Ticket* 87).

5. A woman can never keep a secret (45 Cooper *Chainbearer* 176). Cf. Apperson 706; *Oxford* 723; Stevenson 2054:6; Tilley S196, W649; Whiting *Scots* II 159; John Rhode, pseud. *Murder at the Motor Show* (1936) 178 Betty knew, and she is almost certain to have given Mrs. Marble a hint. You know what women are.

6. The woman who "calc'lates" is lost (58 Holmes *Autocrat* 49; Chamberlain *Confession* 162 I held up and like a woman who hesitates was lost). *Oxford* 724 deliberates; Louis Tracy *The Woman in the Case* (1928) 32 the woman who hesitates is lost; the man who hesitates seldom or never does what he ought to do.

7. A significant proverb, that a woman could throw out with a spoon faster than a man could throw in with a shovel (31 Emerson *Journals* II 442). Apperson 631; Bradley 98; Brewster *Am. Speech* XIV (1939)

265; *Oxford* 451; Stevenson 2564:8; Tilley W370. Cf. Apperson 21 The back door robs the house; Lean III 399; NC 364 back door, 496 wife, 498 woman; *Oxford* 18; Tilley D48; Wilson 572.

8. Men's fortunes, as the Chinese proverb avers of women's hearts, stand a great deal of breaking (67 Richardson *Beyond* 60).

9. A woman's place is in her home (44 Stephens *High Life* II 121). Stevenson 2585:10–2586:4; R. A. J. Walling *The Corpse with the Dirty Face* (1936) 100.

10. He is as gentle as a woman when he has no rival near him (53 Willis *Fun* 287). Cf. Hans Duffy, pseud. *Seven by Seven* (1933) 183 his knotty hands were as gentle as the traditional woman's.

11. Confound this powder—it's as slow as a woman (33 Dorson *Jonathan* 116).

12. As sure as I'm a live woman (56 Whitcher *Widow* 379).

13. As true as I'm a live woman (56 Whitcher *Widow* 317; Sedley *Marian* 25 As I am a woman it is true).

14. Didn't I tell ye so, as the old woman said, when the hog eet the grinstone (33 Neal *Down-Easters* I 118).

15. However, everyone to his liking, as the old woman said (35 Kennedy *Horse-Shoe* 77). Cf. Man (19).

16. There now! its all gut to be strained over agin! as the old woman said, when the dog p—d in her milk-pan (33 Neal *Down-Easters* I 135).

17. What next as the woman said to the man who kissed her in the tunnel (55 Haliburton *Nature* II 62).

18. It's like the old woman's soap—if it don't go ahead, it goes back (59 Smith *My Thirty* 284).

19. In classic authors we are often warned, There's naught so savage as a "woman scorned" (68 Saxe *Poems* 291). W. Congreve *The Mourning Bride* (1697) iii.8.43 Nor Hell a Fury, like a Woman scorn'd; Stevenson 2566–2567:6; Whiting *Devil* 220–221; E. M. Rhodes *West Is West* (1917) 233 Hell hath no fury—question marks; William McFee *The Harbourmaster* (London 1932) 323 And she, hell having no fury like a drunken flapper scorned, told a tale, 353 They say Hell hath no fury like a woman scorned; Damon Runyon *Money from Home* (1935) 106 You know the saying.

20. I am different from other women; my mind changes oftener (71 Clemens *Letters* I 190). *Oxford* 347–348; William N. Macartney *Fifty Years a Country Doctor* (1938) 146 We are told that it is a woman's privilege to change her mind. Cf. NC 499:8; *Oxford* 724, 725; Tilley W674, W698.

21. I've allays thort sence then, boys, that wimmin wur a good deal like *licker,* ef you love 'em too hard thar sure to throw you some way (43 Robb *Squatter* 100).

Wonder, 1. Every nine days must have its wonder (23–24 Irving *Tales* 165; Haliburton *Nature* II 335 A nine days' wonder; Clemens *Roughing* II 140 it . . . made toothsome gossip for nine days; Jones *Batkins* 167 less than a nine days' wonder, 376). Apperson 446; NED Nine 4 b; *Oxford* 726; Stevenson 2588:3; Tilley W728; Whiting *Scots* II 159; NQ 1 iv 192; 2 xi 249, 297, 478–479; 4 iv 133; 5 vii 128; 7 i 520, ii 55, 154; R. C. Ashby *He Arrived at Dusk* (1933) 286; T. H. White *The Sword in the Stone* (1939) 44.

2. Wonders will never cease (36 Haliburton *Clockmaker* I 100; Briggs *Harry* I 126 Wonders will not soon cease, I do believe; Boucicault *Flying Scud* 200). Apperson 708; NC 499; *Oxford* 726; Stevenson 2587:9; R. S. Surtees *Mr. Sponge's Sporting Tour* (London [1853]) 117, *Plain or Ringlets?* (London [1860]) 373 Well, wonders will never cease!; Addison Mizner *The Many Mizners* (1932) 130.

Wood, 1. I was 'tarmined to give a deal on the dead wood [i. e., to venture on an unpromising chance]. (43 Lewis *Odd* 172).

2. I've dead wood on him (62 Locke [Nasby] *Struggles* 176; Richardson *Beyond* 134 "I have the dead wood on him" was used familiarly meaning "I have him in my power" [from the game of ten-pins]). Thornton I 242, III 108.

Woodbine. To go where the woodbine twineth. 70 DA Wood 5 (2).

Woodchuck, 1. As crank as a woodchuck [i. e., conceited]. (44 Stephens *High Life* II 57–58).

2. [She] was as cunning as a red fox or a gray woodchuck (60 Holmes *Elsie* 201).

3. As sound as a woodchuck (60 Holmes *Professor* 83). DA Woodchuck (b).

4. Find out, by your larnin', squire; never seed a wood chuck in a toadhole, I guess (25 Neal *Brother J* I 108).

5. I'd like to show him how to tell a wood-chuck from a skunk (40 Haliburton *Clockmaker* III 73).

6. This is like a woodchuck in clover (45 Judd *Margaret* I 65).

7. To sleep like a woodchuck. 35 DA Woodchuck (b).

Woodcock. He called his friends together and put them through on woodcock (56 Kelly *Humors* 293). Is this connected with "Woodcock" (simpleton, dupe), for which see NED Woodcock 2?

Wooden nutmeg. 25 DA Wooden nutmeg.

Woodpecker. And away went the bar like a whirlygust uv woodpecks were arter it (59 Taliaferro *Fisher's* 138, 177 And at it we went like a whirlygust uv woodpeckers). NC 495 Whirlwind.

Woods, 1. I didn't want the captin to think I'd ben brought up in the woods (44 Stephens *High Life* II 188, 247 looked at me, as if a man that didn't like cards must a been brought up in the woods).
2. I warn't born in the woods to be scared by an owl (36 Haliburton *Clockmaker* I 174–175, *Attaché* II 127, *Old Judge* I 307 I warn't brought up in, *Sam* I 325, II 25 You are a stupid booby too, to be scared by an owl, seein' you was raised in the woods, *Season-Ticket* 105, 361; Stephens *High Life* I 84 I guess I'll let 'em see that I warn't brought up in the woods to be scared of owls, II 248; Judd *Margaret* I 70). Apperson 60; *Oxford* 377; Stevenson 2591:3. See Brush, Meadow.
3. Never hourra, till you're out o' the wood (25 Neal *Brother J* III 269, *Down-Easters* I 119 I never hourray till I'm out of the woods; Burke *Polly* 151 Don't holler till you're out'n the woods; Hammett *Stray* 105 I gave Joe a piece of my mind about "hallooing before he was out of the woods"). Bartlett 290–291; Bradley 97; Green

22; NC 499; *Oxford* 272. Cf. Stoett 879.
4. I can see into the woods as far as them that have gold specs (56 Cary *Married* 393).
5. That body [i. e., person] may as well see us also "out of the woods" (43 Hall *Purchase* I 98; Fairfield *Letters* 415 The Baron certainly cannot marry anybody until he "gets out of the woods." He is now buried up in hair; Lincoln II 447 We are not yet clear out of the woods by a great deal; Richardson *Secret* 485 you are out of the woods for the present; Smith *Arp* 48 I know we ain't out of the woods). Apperson 708; *Oxford* 727; Stevenson 2591:1; Thornton III 434; Herbert Adams *Caroline Ormesby's Crime* (Philadelphia 1929) 102.

Wood-saw. See Leg (1).

Wood-sawyer. But if you live in the forecastle, you are "as independent as a wood-sawyer's clerk" (nauticé), and are a *sailor* (40 Dana *Two* 62, 137 all as independent and easy as so many "woodsawyer's clerks"; Stephens *High Life* I 219; Clemens *Letters* I 24; Taliaferro *Fisher's* 267 wood-sawyer). DA Wood sawyer 2.

Wool, 1. Our sins of scarlet might be washed white as wool (52 Cary *Clovernook* 51; Langdon *Ida* 333 The hair which showed itself under her scanty turban was literally "white as wool"). Svartengren 231; Taylor *Comparisons* 88; Whiting *Scots* II 160.
2. A brute dyed in the wool (39 Briggs *Harry* I 60, 90 his virtues were all his own, and they were dyed in the wool; Stephens *High Life* II 40 ginuine American, dyed in the wool; Haliburton *Nature* II 409, *Season-Ticket* 282 double-dyed). Bartlett 197;

DA Dyed-in-the-wool, Wool-dyed; Farmer 561; Green 128; NED Wool 1 g; Schele de Vere 267–268; Stevenson 2596:4; Thornton I 277–278, III 125; David Fox, pseud. *The Doom Dealer* (1923) 215 Yank.

3. And she'll be in yer wool (51 Stowe *Uncle* 48).

4. To draw the wool over my eyes (38 Haliburton *Clockmaker* II 11, III 42, 187, *Letter* 199, *Season-Ticket* 101; Whitcher *Widow* 153 he ain't so big a fool as to have the wool drawed over his eyes in that way; Lowell *Biglow* 308 Manassas done sumthin' to-w'rds drawin' the wool O'er the green, antislavery eyes o' John Bull). Bartlett 765; DA Wool (b) spread; Farmer 561; John S. Strange, pseud. *The Clue of the Second Murder* (1929) 244 drawn.

5. To pull the wool over your eyes (43 Haliburton *Attaché* I 54, 128, 142; Judd *Richard* 260; Hammett *Stray* 96 they can't pull the wool over this child's eyes; he's got 'em both skinned, *Piney* 290 The wool was pulled over the eyes a leetle the slickest, and no mistake; Sedley *Marian* 100). Bartlett 503; Brewster *Am. Speech* XVI (1941) 24; DA Wool 1 (6); Farmer and Henley VII 363; NC 500; NED Wool 1 g (b); Schele de Vere 625; Stevenson 2596:5; Thornton II 708, III 307; D. P. Hobart *Hunchback House* (Racine, Wis. 1928) 178.

6. Going out for wool and coming back shorn (55 Haliburton *Nature* II 402; Hammett *Piney* 253 there's a proverb about going out after wool, and coming home shorn; Richardson *Beyond* 291 In June an Arapahoe war party went out for wool and came back shorn). Apperson 709; NC 499; NED Wool 1 g (f); *Oxford* 728; Stevenson 2595:5; Tilley W754.

7. I shouldn't be astonished if the new Vice President's head should get wool gathering (35 Crockett *Exploits* 84; Haliburton *Clockmaker* II 293 If it's your wit . . . you are alookin' for, it's gone a wool-gathering more nor half an hour ago, III 121 my mind goes a wool-gathering sometimes, *Nature* I 281 your head is always a wool-gathering). Apperson 709; Green 428; NED Wool-gathering 2; *Oxford* 721; Stevenson 2595:12; Tilley W582; R. G. Anderson *The Tavern Rogue* (1934) 61.

Wooly. See Sheep (1).

Word, 1. A kind word is never lost (52 Cary *Clovernook* 61).

2. A word and a blow with Watty, boy (25 Neal *Brother J* I 106; Kennedy *Horse-Shoe* 261 I can make a blow go further than a word upon occasion; Haliburton *Old Judge* I 235 Let it be a word and a blow; Melville *Mardi* II 175 rather choleric—a word and a blow; Smith *My Thirty* 279 a word and a blow, and the blow always first). Apperson 710; Farmer and Henley VII 363; NC 500; NED Word 16; *Oxford* 728; Stevenson 2605:5; Tilley W763; Whiting *Drama* 371:960; Beldon Duff *The Central Park Murder* (1929) 159–160.

3. A word to the wise—will always suffice (40 Haliburton *Clockmaker* III 302, *Attaché* I 256). Apperson 209; Bradley 98; NC 500; *Oxford* 728; Stevenson 2611:7; Tilley W781; Whiting *Drama* 121, *Scots* II 160; Rosamond Lehmann *The Weather in the Streets* (1936) 384.

4. The President was as good as his word (33 Smith *Downing* 218; Stephens *High Life* I 45; Thompson *Major* 195; Durivage *Three* 406; Riley *Puddleford* 258; Paul *Courtship* 197;

Clemens *Tramp* II 166). Stevenson
993:5; Caryl Brahms, pseud. and S. J.
Simon *A Bullet in the Ballet* (1938)
107.

5. Few words is best, among friends
of long standing (45 Cooper *Chainbearer* 237). Apperson 209; *Oxford*
199; Tilley W796; Whiting *Drama*
129.

6. But soft words butter no par-
snips (40 Haliburton *Letter* 65, *Attaché* I 89 as the sayin' is). Apperson
200 Fair words; NC 500 Fine (soft)
words; *Oxford* 187; Stevenson 2608:
1; Tilley W791; NQ 6 xi 228–229,
358; 8 v 174; Roger Scarlett *Cat's Paw*
(1931) 59 fine words.

7. The word of a gentleman is as
good as his bond (46 Cooper *Redskins* 361; Hammett *Stray* 207 your
word is as good as your bond, and
neither of them worth a copper; Anon.
New Hope 193; Melville *Confidence-
Man* 136 Mr. Truman's word is his
bond; Haliburton *Season-Ticket* 284
the word of a Quaker; Lowell *Biglow*
286 men whose word wuz full ez
good's their note; Clemens *Enterprise*
55). Apperson 710; McAtee 71; NC
500; *Oxford* 300; Stevenson 2613:3;
Tilley M458; E. D. Biggers *The Chinese Parrot* (Indianapolis 1926) 90.

8. There's many a true word said
in joke (38 Haliburton *Clockmaker*
II 320, *Sam* II 219 in jest; Smith *My
Thirty* 393 There's many a word spoke
in jest that's turned into arnest before
it's done with). Apperson 647–648;
Oxford 672; Stevenson 1267:5; Tilley
W772; Leslie Ford, pseud. *The Simple Way of Poison* (1937) 149.

9. He's a man that never eats his
own words (60 Haliburton *Season-
Ticket* 361–362, 363 He has had to
eat so many of his own words . . .
that his swallow was affected, and

sore throat supervened). Apperson
177; *Oxford* 166; Stevenson 2600:4;
Tilley W825; Dermot Morrah *The
Mummy Case Mystery* (1933) 146.

10. I could hardly get to slip in a
word edgeways (34 Crockett *Life* 61;
Smith *Letters* 132 if there's room
enough for me to get in a word edgeways; Robb *Squatter* 107 Couldn't git
in a show of talk, edgeways; Stephens
High Life I 106 there wasn't much
chance for me to get in another word
edgeways, 153 afore I could get a
chance to stick in a word edgeways;
Thompson *Major* 69; Whitcher *Widow* 309; Paul *Courtship* 56 before I
could get a word out edgeways).
Green 130; NED Edgeways 2 b;
Roger Delancey *Murder Below Wall
Street* (1934) 231 edgewise.

11. Words cost but little, and sometimes lead to friendships (27 Cooper
Prairie 11, *Chainbearer* 23 Fine words
cost but little). Tilley W808 Good
words cost nought. Cf. Tilley W804,
W805.

Work, sb., 1. It was all work and no
play with him (38 Haliburton *Clockmaker* II 84; Daly *Man* 49 You vants
it all work and no play?; Cary *Clovernook* 2d Series [ed. 1884] 129 "All
work and no play" was still the order
of her life). Bradley 98; Helen Burnham *The Telltale Telegram* (1932)
169. Cf. Apperson 8–9; NC 500; *Oxford* 730; Stevenson 1258:7; Tilley
W842; Yamamoto *Dickens* 326; J. K.
Bangs *A House-Boat on the Styx*
(1895, New York 1906) 17; John Dos
Passos *The Big Money* (1936) 500 All
work and no play—you know the adage. Cf. Play, sb. (1).

2. Bad work follers ye ez long's ye
live (67 Lowell *Biglow* 263).

3. Their maxim is . . . "no work

no honey" (36 Haliburton *Clockmaker* I 22). Cf. NC 500.

4. Cus the luck—what a pity I didn't wake up—thar'd been old works down thar in the lane if I'd jest happen'd to come to 'bout that time (43 Thompson *Chronicles* 48).

5. Very hard work & very small cry (43 Emerson *Letters* III 116). Cf. Cry.

Work, vb., 1. The old saying, "them that don't work should not eat" (35 Crockett *Account* 99; Emerson *Works* II 109 Who doth not work shall not eat; Smith '*Way* 137 the Bible says, "He that will not work, neither shall he eat"). II Thess. 3:10; *Oxford* 730; Stevenson 2623:6; Whiting *Drama* 96, 195.

2. They say, "God won't be too hard upon the poor fellow," and seldom get beyond the common phrase which seems to imply that their sufferings and hard treatment here will be passed to their credit in the books of the Great Captain hereafter,—"*To work hard, live hard, die hard, and go to hell after all, would be hard indeed!*" (40 Dana Two 44). *Oxford* 730.

3. See Beaver (6), Beer barrel, Charm (1), Dog (58), Horse (39, 40), Indian (14), Nigger (17).

World, 1. He's got a heart as big as the world (25 Neal *Brother J* I 144).

2. As sure as the world (40 Haliburton *Letter* 311, *Sam* I 121, *Nature* II 49, 95, *Season-Ticket* 202). McAtee *Additional* 13; NC 501; William March *Company K* (1933) 77.

3. As true as the world (44 Stephens *High Life* I 247; Whitcher *Widow* 55).

4. You see Mr. Hartsook, my ole man's purty well along in the world [i. e., well-to-do]. (71 Eggleston *School-Master* 59).

5. Among the rest, was the world and all of eggs (49 Haliburton *Old Judge* II 169).

6. Queen was there then; and where she is, of course all the world and its wife is too (43 Haliburton *Attaché* II 34). Apperson 711; NC 501; NED Wife 2 b (c); *Oxford* 731; Stevenson 2631:5; C. F. Gregg *Murder of Estelle Cantor* (1936) 1.

7. Half the world, it is said, knows not how the other half lives (c36 Emerson *Works* III 119). Stevenson 2629:3.

8. For, say they [the English whalers], when cruising in an empty ship, if you can get nothing better out of the world, get a good dinner out of it, at least (51 Melville *Moby-Dick* II 210).

9. In a gineral way, if you want the world to be with you, you must be with the world (53 Haliburton *Sam* II 146). Cf. Whiting *Drama* 79, 160.

10. So the world wags! (46 Cooper *Redskins* 248). Apperson 360–361; NC 501; NED Wag 7 c; *Oxford* 732; Stevenson 2633:3; Tilley W879; Whiting *Drama* 371:963, *Scots* II 161; J. B. Cabell *The Line of Love* (1926) 132, 150.

11. The world wasn't made in a day—took six, I think (59 Taliaferro *Fisher's* 268). Stevenson 2628:5. See Rome (1).

12. This is a wicked world (35 Kennedy *Horse-Shoe* 206). Apperson 683; *Oxford* 707; Lynn Brock, pseud. *Murder at the Inn* (1929) 149.

Worm, 1. He's es dead as a still wum (67 Harris *Sut* 20).

2. Even the worm turns when he is trodden upon (54 Langdon *Ida* 242;

Jones *Batkins* 347 There is a point that makes even a worm turn; that is, when the booted heel of man is ready to crush him). Apperson 712; NC 501; *Oxford* 669; Stevenson 2634:1, 9; NQ 4 iv 135–136; Tilley W909; Arthur Gask *Murder in the Night* (1932) 39; H. F. M. Prescott *The Man on a Donkey* (1954) 138; R. P. Warren *All the King's Men* (1946) 142 It looks like he is a long worm with no turning. [This is mingled with "It's a long lane that has no turning"].

Worm fence. My poetry looked as zigzag as a worm fence (36 Crockett *Exploits* 31).

Wormwood. My life is bitter as wormwood (51 Stowe *Uncle* 17). Svartengren 303.

Worse. Not much the "worse for wear" (45 Hooper *Simon* 40). Cf. Apperson 192–193; *Oxford* 180; Stevenson 2635:14; Tilley W207.

Worst. "All's for the worst" is a very common motto (37 Neal *Charcoal* 207).

Wound. Wounds, by a sharp knife, are easily cured (25 Neal *Brother J* II 284).

Wrath. A little woman streaking it along through the woods like all wrath (34 Crockett *Life* 63; Porter *Major* 88 she fell to kickin *an* a hollerin, *an* a screetchin like all rath). Bartlett 766;

Farmer 562; Schele de Vere 649; Thornton I 9, III 4.

Wrathy. See Murder (1), Thunder (13).

Wrinkle, 1. I'm d–d apt to get what he knows, and in a ginral way gives *him* a wrinkle into the bargain (45 Hooper *Simon* 41; Porter *Major* 14 and thinking I might get a wrinkle by prying into the mystery of quarterracing). NED Wrinkle 8.

2. I'll give you . . . a new w[r]inkle on your horn [i. e., teach you a lesson]. (36 Haliburton *Clockmaker* I 106, II 29, 103, 291, III 30, 303, *Letter* 311, 312, *Attaché* IV 252 it has enabled me to see the world, has given me some new wrinkles on my horn, *Sam* I 1, 147, 193). Farmer and Henley VII 365; Randolph and Wilson 102; Stevenson 1172:7.

Wrong, 1. Old men say that one wrong brings another (65 Sedley *Marian* 60). Cf. Apperson 470 One extreme.

2. Truly it is much better to suffer wrong than to do wrong! (59 Stephens *Fashion* 412). Stevenson 2656: 13.

3. Can two wrongs make a right (40 Haliburton *Clockmaker* III 22; Lowell *Biglow* 258 two wrongs don't never make a right). Apperson 657; NC 501; *Oxford* 681; Stevenson 1991: 4.

✎ Y ✎

Yankee, 1. The remark became trite among the troops, "All a Yankee is worth is his shoes" (62 Wiley *Johnny* 115).

2. To come Yankee over. 34 DA Yankee 5 (2).

3. To play Yankee with. 41 DA Yankee 5 (3).

Yards. Pay up old scores, or "square the yards with the bloody quill-driver" (40 *Dana* Two 285, 319 You'd better square the yards with her, and make the best of it; Kelly *Humors* 252 [He] threatened "the Western member" . . . unless he . . . came up and squared the yards). Joanna C. Colcord *Sea Language Comes Ashore* (1945) 175.

Yarn, 1. To leave the poor, talkative old brigadier without . . . a single bit of yarn to run out, as the sailors have it [i. e., without a story to tell]. (25 Neal *Brother J* I 8).

2. He only put that out for a kinder wheel, to spin a yarn on (58 Hammett *Piney* 153). NED Yarn 2.

3. And it was only because they're weaker than we be, that we haven't licked 'em into spun yarn (56 Durivage *Three* 341).

Year, 1. It will be all the same a hundred years hence (50 P. H. Myers *The King of the Hurons* 278; Haliburton *Nature* II 272 You will find it "all the same a year hence"). Apperson 7 All will be one at the latter day

[i. e., Judgment Day]; Lean IV 21; NC 501; *Oxford* 8; Stevenson 69:2 all one, 2658:12; Tilley Y22; Stella Gibbons *Miss Linsey and Pa* (1936) 272; John Rhode, pseud. *The Harvest Murder* (1937) 163 thousand years.

2. Would scare them out of a year's growth (36 Haliburton *Clockmaker* I 164, III 168 frightened out of, *Season-Ticket* 44 frightened out of, 85 startled out of, 321 frightened out of; Stephens *High Life* I 14, 43 frightened . . . out of, 112). McAtee 55, PADS XV (1951) 60; Vernon Loder *Between Twelve and One* (1929) 182 frighten; William Morton, pseud. *The Mystery of the Human Bookcase* (1931) 173 scared.

3. Seven years (56 Melville "I and My Chimney" in *Works* XIII 311; Clemens *Sandwich* 91, *Roughing* I 56, 142, II 303, *Tramp* I 18). Apperson 559; Stevenson 2659:5; Tilley Y25; Whiting *Drama* 362:827, *Scots* II 163; F. H. Shaw *Atlantic Murder* (1933) 212.

Yell, 1. It ain't them that yell the loudest that feel the most (60 Haliburton *Season-Ticket* 56).

2. See Cuscaroarus (2), Hyena (3), Indian (12).

Yellow, 1. It seems as if Beelzebub had stamped him [a tale-bearer] with his private signal, and every thing he looks at appears to turn yaller (54 Shillaber *Mrs. Partington* 344). Cf.

NED Yellow 2; *Oxford* 325 Jaundiced eye; Tilley A160; Stevenson 731:4.

2. Yellow behind the gills. 78 DA Yellow 2 b.

3. See Blanket (1), Buttercup (2), Codex Vaticanus, Cornsilk, Dog (20), Gamboge, Gold (6), Kite (1), Orange, Pumpkin (5), Saffron, Tobacco (1).

Yellow-hammer. Like a love-sick yaller-hammer hankering arter a mate (44 Stephens *High Life* II 66).

Yellow jacket. We've all been as bisy as yaller jackets in cotton blossom (44 Thompson *Major* 65).

Yesterday. I guess I warn't born yesterday (36 Haliburton *Clockmaker* I 126, 319, II 288, *Attaché* III 283, *Old Judge* II 42, *Sam* I 53, 77, 147, 226, 266, II 301, *Nature* I 273, II 13, 90, 404, *Season-Ticket* 14, 27, 101, 240). NED Yesterday 2; *Oxford* 57; Stevenson 185:2; Dennis Wheatley *They Found Atlantis* (Philadelphia 1936) 149.

Yoke, 1. They draw in the same yoke [i. e., are married]. 50 DA Draw 6 (2).

2. There wasn't a gal in all Weathersfield could pull an even yoke with her a stringing onions (44 Stephens *High Life* I 46, 102, 156, II 58 pulled about an even yoke). Cf. NED Yoke 8 equal yoke.

Z

Zacchy. I haven't seen a queerer fellow since the times of 'Zacchy in the mealbag' (37 Neal *Charcoal* 112).

Zephyr. A step as light as the zephyr (32 Hall *Legends* 124).

Zero. He sat there stiff as Zero (59 Shillaber *Knitting-Work* 312).

Zig-zag. See Worm-fence.